OF REVELATION AND REVOLUTION

Of

REVELATION

and

REVOLUTION

VOLUME TWO

*The Dialectics of Modernity
on a South African Frontier*

John L. Comaroff and Jean Comaroff

THE UNIVERSITY OF CHICAGO PRESS
Chicago and London

Jean Comaroff is the Bernard E. and Ellen C. Sunny Distinguished Service Professor of Anthropology and the chair of the Department of Anthropology at the University of Chicago. She is the author of *Body of Power, Spirit of Resistance*. John L. Comaroff is the Harold H. Swift Distinguished Service Professor of Anthropology at the University of Chicago, and also a Senior Research Fellow at the American Bar Foundation. He is a co-author of *Rules and Processes*, and the editor of *The Meaning of Marriage Payments* and *The Boer War Diary of Sol T. Plaatje*. They have co-edited *Modernity and Its Malcontents* and co-authored *Ethnography and the Historical Imagination*.

The University of Chicago Press, Chicago
The University of Chicago Press, Ltd., London

© 1997 by The University of Chicago
All rights reserved. Published 1997
Printed in the United States of America
06 05 04 03 02 01 00 99 98 97   1 2 3 4 5

ISBN: 0-226-11443-0 (cloth)
ISBN: 0-226-11444-9 (paper)

Library of Congress Cataloging-in-Publication Data

The Library of Congress catalogued the first volume as follows:
Comaroff, Jean.
    Of revelation and revolution: Christianity, colonialism, and
    consciousness in South Africa / Jean Comaroff and John L. Comaroff.
        p.   cm.
    Includes bibliographical references (p.) and index.
    ISBN 0–226–11441–4 (cloth).—ISBN 0–226–11442–2 (paperback)
        1. Tswana (African people)—History.   2. Tswana (African people)—
    Missions.   3. Tswana (African people)—Social conditions.
    4. London Missionary Society—Missions—South Africa.   5. Wesleyan
    Methodist Missionary Society—Missions—South Africa.   6. Great
    Britain—Colonies—Africa.   South Africa—History.   I. Comaroff,
    John L., 1945- .   II. Title.
    DT1058.T78C66   1991
    303.48'241'00899639775—dc20   90–46753
                                                                        CIP
The ISBNs for the second volume (subtitled *The Dialectics of Modernity on a South African Frontier*) are 0–226–11443–0 (cloth) and 0–226–11444–9 (paper).

∞ The paper used in this publication meets the minimum requirements of the American National Standard for Information Sciences—Permanence of Paper for Printed Library Materials, ANSI Z39.48-1984.

for Isaac Schapera
with affection, respect, gratitude

He has nothing to lose, he tells himself and so he reaches for the stars. For where do we go when it falls apart in our hands and we are left with less than we started with? Begin again? And with what? Where are the dreams to fill the souls of the wandering exiles? What revolution can they subscribe to? The days of Muhammed Ali and Napoleon, the Post-Colonialists and Pan-Africanists, of Communists and Socialists and all the other "-ists," all of them are gone. And yet the past has come back with a vengeance, and we must think our way out. Where are the damn poets when we need them?

Jamal Mahjoub
Letter from Sudan, 30.xi.95

CONTENTS

ix

ILLUSTRATIONS

PREFACE

March 1994
Mafikeng, Bophuthatswana, South Africa

> *People out in Mafikeng. Small groups block the streets with cement and*
> *burning tyres. . . . An armed contingent of Bophuthatswana police oc-*
> *cupy the town square, occasionally sending out patrols to clear the barri-*
> *cades. . . . Then five military vehicles appear. They are packed with*
> *uniformed Bophuthatswana soldiers. Driving past, the soldiers raise their*
> *fists and point a single finger at the sky. Suddenly the street is alive as the*
> *crowd cheers them on. The police look on. At that precise moment I knew*
> *the regime had lost the battle.*
>
> Derek Forbes, University of Bophuthatswana (1995:4)

And so it had. Apartheid had been given the finger. Bophuthatswana, the
Tswana ethnic "homeland," was liberated. Mafikeng had been, so to speak, relieved. Finally.

A last-ditch effort was made to defend this ragged remnant of the *ancien
régime* by Afrikaner patriots in pickup trucks. The tragi-farcical raid of these
counter-revolutionaries wasted a few precious lives, won a few celebrated sec-
onds on the news screens of the world, flickered, and died ignominiously at a
dusty roadside. Soon, in all likelihood, it will be forgotten by everyone but the
bereaved. What *is* likely to remain in the memory of local people, however, is
that defiant finger in the air. In a single, spontaneous gesture of dismissal it
appeared to bring to an end the long conversation between Southern Tswana
and white "settlers," European colonizers *en effet*. One of the darker chapters in
the chronicle of these peoples had unraveled in a piece of street theater.

In reality, of course, neither endings nor beginnings are ever that neat. And
yet, in many respects, the narrative of Tswana colonization *had* completed itself,
finally running its course from Revelation to Revolution. We resume our account here in the postcolonial moment, both in South Africa and the world at
large. Interestingly, the concluding scenes of this last imperial drama had a distinctly anachronistic feel to them. Those who took to its stage used the robust
rhetoric of resistance to confront the unambiguous forces of evil and inequality
that faced them. In language that sounded more of the 1960s than the 1990s,

they mouthed, without the slightest hint of irony, enlightenment ideals of free-dom. In fact, the epic transition from apartheid to democracy touched the imagination of people everywhere largely *because* it recalled an age of lost inno-cence; an age before new global flows and alignments, new world-historical real-ities and uncertainties, had melted away the firm outlines and limitless opti-misms of Eurocentric modernity.

How useful is it, in these circumstances, to continue to explore colonialism in its classic mode? Is there anything but illustrative detail to add to an old story, a tale whose long overdue conclusion makes its significance all too obvious? Is its study of any real use to us in understanding the world of the postcolony—and the mechanisms at work in making and masking the elusive, expansive reali-ties of the here-and-now? Has the time not come for us to follow the lead of Subaltern scholars in casting off, once and for all, the lingering hold of empire on both our histories and our grasp of the present? For some, the answers are quite clear-cut. Many postcolonial literary and political figures, for example, are eager to close the book on the Eurocentric past; for good reason, they seek to measure their distance from imperial hegemonies, and to remake their worlds, by refusing, as Simon During (1987:33) says, "to turn the Other into the Same." Within the Western academy, too, there are those who believe that colonialism is old business. On the particular subject of colonial evangelism, for instance, Etherington (n.d.:3) has decided that "the verdict is in." Does this mean that we have enough evidence to determine motive, cause, and responsibility? If so, should the court of history now move on to more challenging, unsolved prob-lems? Some have said as much of Western imperialism at large; that the fall of the Soviet empire—and apartheid in its wake—finally ushered out this epoch, marking also the demise of the forms of industrial economy that had un-derpinned European domination. The naive certainties that once sustained the modernist masterbuilders, and that reached their apotheosis in socialisms of various stripes, have decomposed before our eyes. The past has truly become another country. As a result, its crude conceptual tools, like the cast-iron ma-chines that cranked out its stock-in-trade, are now *passé,* no match for the flexi-bilities and the virtual realities of the new millennium.

It all sounds compelling enough. But our own view is different. While, at least in one obvious sense, the making of the modern world *has* run its course, its grand narrative has been rendered all the more enigmatic by the sheer unex-pectedness of its closing scenes. Some rather surprising antiheroes seem to have got the last laugh on history. To be sure, the events of the late twentieth century have forced us to revise many well-worn assumptions. As "tradition" and "trib-alism" enjoy a renewed salience and face down the confident universalisms of modernity, as religion thrives and the nation-state sickens, the jury is still very much out on some of the enduring issues of social theory. Can we really claim to comprehend the connections among ideology, economy, and society? Or the relationship of culture to power, and the purchase of both on human subjects, individual and collective? We are not persuaded that such questions can ever be settled once and for all. Nor that the difficult challenges posed by them will be laid to rest as soon as the "facts are in."

Readers who believe otherwise—that we can solve the great conundrums of the long run purely by recourse to the empirical—will not see the point in what we do. Of course we seek to adduce new evidence, to re-evaluate old evidence, even to ponder what might count as evidence in the first place; we are not the sort of "postmodernists" that some of our critics claim. But that is not our main purpose. The object of the exercise, as we see it, is to rethink the ways in which history has been made and marked, its realities contested, re-presented, and authorized. In the specific case of South Africa, it prompts us to consider how many features of the present have emerged out of the paradoxes and contradictions of the past; out of the tensions, endemic to the colonial outreach, between "universal truths" and "parochial cultures," between a society founded on individual rights and one characterized by racial (dis)enfranchisement, between the world of the free citizen and that of the colonial subject. These tensions suffused the encounter between Africans and Europeans, animating histories that eluded easy control by their dramatis personae, histories carved out of the dialectics of exchange, appropriation, accommodation, struggle.

As all this implies, there is still much to learn from the late colonial world, much still to glean in the passage from then to now. We distrust the (*fin-de-siècle?*) tendency to cast the current moment—postcolonial, post-cold war, post-Fordist, postmodern, or whatever—in terms of transcendence or negation, as part of a telos of cutoffs and contrasts. While there may be understandable reasons for a politics which effaces the past, it is important not to confuse its tactics with the way in which history is made. Our own material suggests some surprising and complex continuities between the time of the great imperial outreach and the late twentieth-century era of global expansion. The kinds of shifts occasioned by the Age of Revolution, 1789–1848—in production, the speed and scale of exchange, the experience of space, the nature of personhood—have uncanny parallels in the New World Order. Writing in post-Thatcherite Britain, we are struck repeatedly by the rising ghost of Adam Smith, his hidden hand as visible in the commodified culture of the contemporary world as it was in our story of long ago. Alongside these parallels, patently, are the equally significant discontinuities, detours, and dead ends on the high road between those days and these. All of which demands that we think ever more searchingly about the many faces and ages of colonialism and capitalism. Or rather, in respect of the latter, the "market system." The word capitalism, which rattles the chains of old ideologies, is, Kenneth Galbraith recently observed, also out of fashion.

What we have here, then, is an account of a colonial past that reaches into the present—each chapter carries forward into this century—and contemplates the fashioning of the future. As in the previous volume, we seek to explore how very broad processes were made manifest in a specific case; namely the encounter, in the South African interior, between Southern Tswana and the colonial evangelists of the British Nonconformist missionary societies, themselves harbingers of a more invasive European presence. In this regard, note our title, which some literal-minded readers have deemed too sweeping, too ambitious. It is less the product of hubris than of a commitment to the founding method of anthropology, which assumes that particular facts are also always instances of general social forces. And that generalities, in turn, have no real life apart from the ethnographic particulars that produce them.

In volume 1, we set down the broad outlines and opening gestures of the encounter. More a spiraling, many-layered conversation than a straightforward process of conversion or colonial domination, this exchange of signs and objects spanned more than a century, and served as a point of intersection between ever more entangled worlds. In volume 2, we follow the continuing history of the Word in this part of Africa where, despite its relative failure to draw large numbers of orthodox followers, it inspired some unexpected interpretations of the sacred text—and gave rise to a range of homegrown Christianities. Meanwhile, resigned to a more entrenched battle for souls, the evangelists devoted themselves increasingly to the civilizing mission; to the methodical effort, that is, to reform the everyday life of Southern Tswana. We examine their painstaking attempts to recast African personhood and production, African habits and homes, African notions of value and virtue. And we document how their initiative ran up against indigenous orientations and intentions. From the protracted dialectic that ensued, there emerged novel hybrids, fresh forms of cultural practice, on both sides: new ways of perceiving subjects and consuming objects, new senses of style and beauty, new classes and ethnicities, new discourses of human rights and social wrongs. It also prepared the ground for the differentiation of rural black society in the hinterland, for its fragmentation along deepening lines of social and cultural distinction. One product of this process, as is well known, was the rise of an articulate, educated elite, many of whom were to figure on the national stage—and to whose history we shall return in volume 3, on colonial pedagogy.

But the civilizing mission was no mere exporter of finished products and final truths. The frontier was also integral to the making of the European metropole, to the rise of modernity at home, to the forging of new translocal horizons picked out by the "twin forces" of Christianity and commerce. We show how the passage of old ideas and new goods wove the threads of an imperial fabric, reshaping both its consumers and its producers; how the African interior served as a seam against which emerging British bourgeois identities took shape—both in the immediate experience of the evangelists and in the consciousness of the wide popular readership that followed their adventures and consumed their images. As we shall see, too, the experiments of the godly pioneers at the margins of empire came to color perceptions and policies back in England, foreshadowing "missions" to other "Africas," not least to the *terra incognita* of the Victorian industrial city. Thus did "center" and "periphery," the "modern" and the "traditional," "orthodoxy" and "apostasy," "colonizer" and "colonized"—all enclosed more in quotes than they ever were enclosed by history—construct and constrain each other. And eachs' others. Plural, on both sides. Thus, too, was a history at once dialogical and dialectical made by the actions of Africans and Europeans on one another. It is the playing out of this history, especially on the terrain of everyday life, that lies at the core of the present volume.

This study has by now acquired a history of its own, having incurred many debts and generated a sheaf of spirited commentaries. "Sheaf" is the appropriate term here; it denotes a pile of papers, some corn, and a bundle of arrows. We acknowledge the care, generosity, and thoughtfulness with which many, if not all, of our colleagues and critics have engaged our work. We have learned enormously from these interventions, and respond to a number of them in the Introduction.

Scholarship is even more of an interactive process than we often allow, of course, and the present volume is the fruit of many conversations, both long and short. It has also been molded by a host of influences, some more explicit than others. Among the most protracted and constructive of our exchanges have been those with Isaac Schapera, once and still our teacher. Now over ninety years old, he remains the most unnervingly acute of critics, with a forthright intolerance of authorial self-indulgence. Having read every word of this text with his incomparable thoroughness and expertise, he has left his imprint on it in more places than we are able to mention. We dedicate the book to him with great affection, and in appreciation of his lifelong commitment to the infinite richness of Tswana history and ethnography.

We owe much to continuing discussions with colleagues and students in the African Studies Workshop and the Department of Anthropology at the University of Chicago, an enduringly vital, irreverent, creative place. Indeed, ours is a truly interdisciplinary community, and faculty of departments ranging from music to medical ethics have addressed themselves, at one or another time, to the issues with which we deal here. Arjun Appadurai and Marshall Sahlins, in particular, have been important interlocutors, as well as close friends. Both think about the human predicament in strikingly original ways, refusing to divorce anthropology from an engagement with the world at large; each, in his own inimical manner, is a source of constant stimulation to us. Maureen Anderson, Benjamin Miller, Jan-Lodewijk Grootaers, Hylton White, Jesse Shipley, and Anne-Maria Makhulu have been fastidious, imaginative research assistants; they have helped in countless ways in the preparation of this volume. Brad Weiss offered a most enlightening reading of chapter 5, and Ellen Schattschneider and Mark Auslander have been remarkably adept at pointing us in the direction of scholarly exchanges that we might otherwise have missed. Our deepest gratitude goes to them all. Also to Jamal Mahjoub for permission to quote from his extraordinarily beautiful, disturbing "Letter from Sudan," which he read on BBC Radio 4, in the program *Continent Adrift*, on 30 November 1995.

Various parts of the study have been presented to audiences in North America and elsewhere; we have tried our best to do justice to the wealth of insightful comment received. In Paris, Catherine Benoit, of the Centre d'études africaines, École des hautes études en sciences sociales, helped us navigate the Bibliotheque Nationale, where we worked on the Paris Evangelical Mission Society archives. And Francis Zimmerman was a genial guide to the French academy, a mystifying world to callow Anglo-Saxons. In June 1966, we were privileged to have the manuscript discussed, chapter by chapter, by an unusually fine group of scholars at the Research Centre Religion and Society, University of Amsterdam. For their critical acuity and kind welcome, we thank Gerd Baumann, Peter Geschiere, Birgit Meyer, Prabhu Mohapatra, Peter Pels, Rafael Sánchez, Wim van Binsbergen, Peter van Rooden, and, especially, Patricia Spyer.

We visited Mmabatho/Mafikeng, South Africa—once the center of a large Southern Tswana chiefdom, then capital of the "independent" homeland of Bophuthatswana, now the administrative hub of the Province of North West—in the summers of 1991, 1995, and 1996. There a number of friends, colleagues, and students engaged us and our work with great generosity and interest. While at the University of the North West in 1996 we were warmly hosted by the History Department, which gave us a formal affiliation and made various facilities available to us. James Drummond read chapter 3 with rare insight and expertise; he also reacquainted us with parts of the region we had not seen for some time. In addition to all their other kindnesses, Neil Roos and Jen Seif accompanied us, and took the photographs, when we visited the nearby Lotlamoreng Cultural Park, where our account opens.

In England, where we wrote much of this book, various kin, colleagues, and friends offered us unstinting support. Shula Marks is a kindred spirit whose own work is a perpetual inspiration to us; her thoughts on ours have always compelled us to think harder, to dig deeper. Her comments on both this and the previous volume have added much to the final product. So, also, has our longstanding dialogue with Terence Ranger, who graciously read an all but complete version of the manuscript and offered us his characteristically astute reactions, especially to chapter 2. Another African historian, Brian Willan, has long been an unselfish source of information on early twentieth-century Tswana literati and political figures, several of whom are critical to our narrative. In a different vein but as important, the International Centre for Contemporary Cultural Research at the University of Manchester gave us an academic affiliation. While we were there, Richard and Pnina Werbner provided intellectual stimulation, mirth, and much practical assistance; and Hector Blackhurst kindly eased our forays into the John Rylands Library. David and Shirley Levy, and Max and Pat Hodgson of the Red Lion Inn at Litton, fed and watered our endeavors.

The research for this and the following volume was supported by generous grants from the National Science Foundation, the Spencer Foundation, the Lichtstern Fund of the Department of Anthropology at the University of Chicago, and the American Bar Foundation. In respect of the last, the ABF, our special thanks go to Bryant Garth, the director, and to the other faculty fellows. Not only have they been exceptionally tolerant in putting up with the prolonged absences necessitated by our research and writing; they have also responded sagely to our often unformed scholarly enthusiasms. Anne Ch'ien and Katherine Barnes of the Department of Anthropology have been unusually caring, patient, and efficient in administering the affairs, and answering to the needs, of the most long distance of their commuters. It is hard to find adequate words to express our appreciation to them.

Our children, Josh and Jane, have grown along with this project, which must often have seemed to them like a life sentence. Now impressive young scholars in their own right, they have twice accompanied us back to our research site in the North West province of South Africa, and have—despite themselves—become more than a little engaged with the issues that have obsessed us for so long. They continue to be the most loving, scathing, bemused, creative of critics. We thank them for having given us and our discipline the benefit of the doubt.

Ravensdale, Derbyshire
November, 1995

CHRONOLOGY

1698	Society for Promoting Christian Knowledge (SPCK) founded.
1701	Society for Propagating the Gospel (SPG) founded.
1780	Barolong polity splits into four chiefdoms (Ratlou, Ratshidi, Rapulana, and Seleka) after civil war.
1795	First British administration of the Cape.
	London Missionary Society (LMS) founded.
1799	LMS begins work in South Africa.
	Religious Tract Society founded.
1802	Abortive effort to establish LMS station among the Tlhaping at Dithakong.
1803	Administration of the Cape passes to the Batavian Republic by the Treaty of Amiens.
1806	Second British occupation of the Cape.
1807	Abolition of the slave trade.
1813	Wesleyan Methodist Missionary Society (WMMS) formed.
1816–17	First sustained LMS outreach to the Tlhaping.
	First WMMS station in the South African interior.
1816–28	Rise of the Zulu kingdom under Shaka; period of migration and upheaval throughout southern Africa (*difaqane*).
1818	John Philip sent to the Cape Colony by the LMS.
1821	Moffat founds permanent LMS station among the Tlhaping at Kuruman.
	Kay travels to Tswana territory to set up first WMMS station there.
1822	Broadbent and Hodgson of the WMMS make sustained contact with the Seleka-Rolong.
1822–23	Southern Tswana polities attacked by Tlokwa and Fokeng.
1823	Griqua and Tlhaping force, under Robert Moffat, defeat Tlokwa.
1832	The Matabele under Mzilikazi settle in Tswana territory; attack surrounding communities.
1833	Thaba 'Nchu founded; WMMS station established there.
1834–38	Emancipation of the slaves at the Cape.
1835–40	Voortrekkers leave the Cape Colony.
1838	Zulu army defeated by Boers at Blood River.
1839	Period of fragmentation and realignment of Tlhaping polities.
1841	Opening of Lovedale Missionary Institution.

1851	WMMS mission established among the Tshidi by Ludorf.
1852	Sand River Convention; Transvaal gains independence.
	Boers attack Kwena and destroy Livingstone's station; also attack Tshidi, forcing Montshiwa into exile at Moshaneng.
1854	Bloemfontein Convention; Britain abandons the Orange River Sovereignty.
1862	Mackenzie founds LMS station among the Ngwato.
1865	Mafikeng established by Molema.
1867	Diamond discovered near Hopetown; diggers pour into Griqualand; disputes break out among Southern Tswana, Griqua, and white settlers over diamondiferous territory.
1870	Robert Moffat retires from the Tlhaping mission.
1870–71	Further diamond discoveries; Kimberley founded; Bloemhof hearing under Lieut.-Governor Keate of Natal.
1871	Britain annexes Griqualand West.
1872	Cape Colony acquires "responsible government."
	Moffat Institution established at Shoshong, later moved to Kuruman.
1877	Shepstone annexes the Transvaal, making it a British colony.
	Montshiwa returns to Tshidi territory, settling at Sehuba.
1878	Griqua Rebellion.
	Outbursts of resistance against state intervention and the mission presence among Southern Tswana; LMS stations attacked.
1880	Transvaal rebels successfully against Britain; "First Anglo-Boer War" breaks out.
1881	Pretoria Convention; retrocession of Transvaal.
1881–84	Sustained hostilities among Southern Tswana chiefdoms and the white settlers of the Transvaal borderland.
1882	Boers proclaim Stellaland and Goshen independent republics on Rolong and Tlhaping land; Montshiwa forced into subjection by the Transvaal.
1882–86	Economic depression in southern Africa.
1884	London Convention amends Pretoria Convention.
	Whitehall agrees to establish a protectorate over the Southern Tswana: British Bechuanaland formally comes into existence, and Mackenzie is appointed its first Deputy Commissioner.
	Transvaal annexes Goshen.
	Battles between white freebooters and Rolong intensify; Montshiwa made to surrender most of his land.
1885	Warren Expedition sent to Bechuanaland.
	British Bechuanaland made into a Crown Colony; Bechuanaland Protectorate proclaimed over northern chiefdoms.

1886	Witwatersrand proclaimed a gold mining area.
	Land Commission established by British administration to settle territorial disputes in Bechuanaland. Hut tax introduced in British Bechuanaland.
1889	Charter over (northern) Bechuanaland granted to British South Africa Company (BSAC).
1893	Ndebele (Matabele) War.
1894	Annexation of Pondoland largely completes formal incorporation of blacks into the colonies of the Cape and Natal and into the South African Republic and Orange Free State.
1895	British Bechuanaland incorporated into the Cape Colony.
	Chiefs protest planned transfer of Bechuanaland Protectorate to BSAC governance.
1895–96	Jameson Raid ends BSAC presence in the Protectorate; British government takes administrative control.
1896	Rinderpest cattle pandemic among the Tswana.
1896–97	Construction of Mafeking-Bulawayo railway.
	Tlhaping rebellion in the Langeberg; resistance against the colonial regime spreads to other parts of Southern Tswana territory.
1899– 1902	Anglo-Boer War (Siege of Mafeking, 1899–1900).
1900	Founding of first Setswana newspaper in Mafikeng.
1903–5	South African Native Affairs Commission.
1904	Tiger Kloof established.
1910	Union of South Africa established.
1912	South African Native National Congress (later the African National Congress) formed.
1913	Natives Land Act no. 27 passed; limits African holdings to "scheduled native areas."

ONE

INTRODUCTION

Historical reality has many ways of concealing itself. A most effective way consists in displaying itself in the full view of all.

Octavio Paz (1976:xi)

I N THE EARLY 1990s, with apartheid well into its eleventh hour, the "homeland" government of Bopthuthatswana committed anthropology, at least of a sort. It built the curious Lotlamoreng Cultural Park some eight miles south of its capital, Mmabatho.[1] In the arid scrubland, a series of small adobe "villages" was erected, each representing the lifeways of one of South Africa's "traditional" peoples. Interspersed among them was a scattering of new age stone circles and towering clay figures. The most notable of these, a twenty-foot-tall female of unidentifiable race, had fig leaves in her lap and a leg that tapered into a cloven hoof. Notwithstanding the frequent assertion that postmodern pastiche is "subversive of the signature," these effigies actually sported one: the initials of Credo Mutwa, nationally known sculptor, author, and self-appointed "Custodian of . . . Tribal Relics."[2] Some would say ethnokitsch. The park might have been an authored fantasy in concrete, but it was also a clutch of old clichés struggling to be reborn into a world where ethnic essentialism was rapidly being revised as identity politics. As Tom Nairn[3] once observed, the true content of the postmodern often turns out to be the prehistoric.

Prominent in this history-as-pastiche was a faithfully reproduced Victorian

1

PLATE 1.1 *Mission Church, Lotlamoreng Cultural Park [N. Roos, August 1995]*

mission complex, its gnarled gateway bearing the legend *Lesedi la Rona* (Our Light) and "Mission School." The dove of the London Missionary Society hovered above the portal of an austere, whitewashed chapel. But in the counterfeit churchyard a less restrained array of images had been put in play. Here sacral realism met Disneyland. And it spawned a series of spectacular scriptural scenes; a wry contrast, this, to the Puritan aesthetic of nineteenth-century Nonconformism, with its long-standing distrust of the seduction of the eye (chapter 2). A cast of huge biblical characters stood side by side: a black Eve entwined in a Day-Glo serpent, a pale Christ crucified before a lank-haired Mary Magdalene (plates 1.1 and 1.2). Their prematurely peeling paint underscored the fact that even contemporary celebrations of timeless truths may quickly become monuments to passing moments—and regimes.

For events had rapidly overtaken the construction of the cultural park, rendering its mute, mutant images stillborn. Apartheid met its end soon after the site was opened to the public. Bereft of its founding impetus, it was an instant anachronism, outmoded even as it was introduced to its intended market.[4] But history had refigured it in a yet more salutary manner. When we visited the apparently abandoned site in August 1995, we found its "ruins" inhabited. The "traditional Tswana village" had metamorphosed into a thoroughly modern pri-

PLATE 1.2 *Crucifixion, Lotlamoreng Cultural Park [N. Roos, August 1995]*

vate space: a neatly swept courtyard, plastic buckets, clotheslines, and a large transistor radio announced the presence of residents more real than authentic. Likewise the model Zulu, Ndebele, Xhosa, and Southern Sotho compounds, each of which was distinguished from the next by a casual sprinkling of symbols. These, too, had been occupied—by ethnically *un*marked members of the local poor. In a truly surreal moment, a woman recognized our confusion and, taking on the role of tour guide, began to offer utterly fanciful exegeses of the riot of ethnic images before us: of clay cattle and lions, stone barbecue pits, Polynesian gods, and North American eagles bleached by the winter sun. The other inmates, females all, simply went about their domestic chores, hanging out faded wash-and-wear dresses and shirts above "primordial" walls.

History might have hidden itself here in a fulsome display of the past. But it also kept bursting through the cracking *cultural* facade of the park. On the surface of it, this was the past re-presented as farce, time flattened into spatial bites just large enough to be taken in at a glance. Yet, for all its postmodern opportunism, the fantasy was composed of more than a random smattering of simulacra. On the contrary, its coordinates were surprisingly predictable. They were animated by one *ur*-theme, indeed, the very one that organizes our own narrative: the encounter of ever more ethnically stereotyped peoples with the colonial missions. Strikingly, this encounter was made out to be a confrontation between everyday African life—its "villages" turned out to be a series of *domestic* compounds—and European civil society as embodied in the Protestant church and school. A recuperation of local history-in-the-making, it was a whimsical reprise of precisely the processes that concern us in this study.

The display in the park was designed with a very different intent, of course. It froze—friezed?—the evangelical enclave and the ethnicized "natives" of southern Africa into discrete positions along an eternal frontier, each cast in a respectful attitude toward the other, all of them set off forever from the political and material forces that had put them in contact in the first place. But history has a habit of intruding upon, of unfreezing, the most timeless of myths. As a living archaeology, the site revealed the ways in which Europeans and Africans had actually become inseparably intertwined, alike profoundly altered in the process. This fact was made plain by the squatters who had repossessed the ersatz recreations of their own "tribal" past: their domestic debris, lying amidst the artlessly painted symbols that adorned the adobe yards, recalled how the colonial mission had tied Southern Tswana into a global order of goods and signs. Like graffiti scrawled across a formal text, the presence of these unscripted actors bespoke the political economy of empire, the era of apartheid, and the (markedly feminized) rural poverty that had come along with them. Even the giants in the churchyard revealed a suppressed history, a fertile congress of proper Protestant representation with a less restrained sense of the divine image. This union would give rise to diverse local Christianities—to the separatist churches and revitalized rites, the preachers, prophets, and pythons that we explore in some detail below.

Lotlamoreng Park, then, underscored the enduring salience, not to mention the ambiguities and contradictions, of the story we recount in *Of Revelation and Revolution*. Colonial evangelism seemed, at least there and then, to retain a continuing hold on popular re-visions of the past. To be sure, the prominent place accorded the whitewashed mission station in this relic of apartheid endorsed the Nonconformists' own image of their heroic role. And yet the recommissioned monument, as a *lived* landscape, told a different tale. Its unauthorized inhabitants—human flotsam of poverty, migration, forced repatriation—proclaimed that history has many modalities, that its authorized narratives never say it all. Their spare, unruly possessions interrupted the visual pageantry of the park, demonstrating how established accounts can be destabilized by counterpositioned realities; by other stories in other media. The official exhibit might have foregrounded the grand confrontation of Christianity and Civilization with primal ethnicity. But its reclaimed ruins opened up another historical terrain: that of the everyday and, above all, the domestic. This, significantly, was the terrain on which the "Bechuana" missions had anchored their work of salvation: here that they had sought to remake persons by means of ordinary things like clothes and cupboards and soap; here that the merchants and labor recruiters who followed them strove to make their inroads; here that the large, often long-distance forces of History came to rest on "local" ground. And here that people of all sorts had put available resources to the task of producing and reproducing their world.

OUTLINES: THINGS SAID, THINGS TO BE SAID

In the study of which the present volume is a piece, we seek to explore how these various historical processes played themselves out in the long encounter between the Nonconformist missions, the peoples who became known as "the Tswana," and significant others in nineteenth-century South Africa. From its opening moments, described in volume 1, this encounter occurred at several levels and in multiple registers: in the intimacies of physical contact and everyday conversations; in routine exchanges and interpersonal dramas; in ritual speech, religious argument, and symbolic gesture; in the spiraling flow and counterflow of signs and objects, means and ends, that drew indigenous communities into an expansive imperial economy; in the countless interactions and transactions that shaped the formal institutions of colonial society and its governance.

As we have insisted all along, this was a *dialectical* encounter in that it altered everyone and everything involved, if not all in the same manner or measure. And it had close parallels elsewhere in the contemporary world, a world deeply affected by Eurocentric forces—mercantilism, Christianity, civiliza-tion—whose very existence rested on their universalist claims and horizons. Wherever they reached, these forces became embroiled in local histories, in lo-cal appropriations and transpositions, and were deflected in the process—often in surprising, sometimes in subversive, always in culturally meaningful ways. Macrocosmic modernities, in sum, were at once singular and plural, specific and general, parochial and global in their manifestations. Notwithstanding the homogenizing thrust of Market Capitalism, Protestantism, and the other "isms" of the age, there grew up, all around the so-called peripheries of empire, multi-ple market systems and modes of production, differently domesticated churches and creeds and currencies, homegrown nationalisms and hybrid rationalisms. These call for understanding not as tokens of a generic type or as mere vernacu-lar facsimiles of one another. They are to be accounted for in terms of what it was that made them particular: the precise concatenations and transactions of power, economy, and culture unleashed in various places and times by that ep-ochal historical process which we gloss as "colonialism."

Although it focuses primarily on the years between 1820 and 1920, our narrative of that epochal process spans the time between two revolutions: the great transformation of circa 1789–1848 that laid the ground for modernity as we know it, and the late twentieth-century revolution (circa 1989–?) presently reconstructing the parameters and polarities of the mature capitalist world (J. L. Comaroff 1996). In volume 1 we examined the Nonconformist missions to the Tswana in light of the role of "benevolent" imperialism—and of the histori-cal conditions that gave rise to it—in the making of postenlightenment Europe. While they served as outriders of empire, we argued, colonial evangelists did not carry a ready-made, fully realized social formation to the frontier. Rather, it was in the confrontation with non-Western societies that bourgeois Britons honed a sense of themselves as gendered, national citizens, as Godly, right-bearing individuals, and as agents of Western reason (cf. Dirks 1992:6). It was in the course of this confrontation, too, that Southern Tswana, products of a very different cultural and political universe, came to redefine themselves in relation to centers elsewhere; to others who saw them as anachronistic, mar-ginal, and ethnically marked—but also as potential Christians, consumers, and colonial subjects.

The encounter between the Nonconformists and the peoples of the South African interior, then, joined populations with divergent cultural perspectives, dissimilar intentions, dissonant notions of value—and distinctly unequal ca-pacities to control the terms of their unfolding relations. Not surprisingly, their early exchanges initiated a protracted dialogue based in part on misrecognition, in part on shared interests, in part on alliances across the very lines that divided them. These parties acted as mirrors to and for each other, refracting and reify-ing new orders of social distinction and identity—and struggling to master the hybrid language, the swirl of signs and objects, that circulated among them. From this long conversation came the stark imaginative dualisms—white/black, Christian/heathen, *sekgoa/setswana* (European ways/Tswana ways)—that developed on both sides of the frontier; also, the syncretisms and transgressions—the pious conversions, the cultural appropriations, the "magical" arrogation of the "medicine of God's word" (*RRI*:228f.)—that simultaneously undermined those very dualisms, dichotomies, and distinctions. Indeed, irony undid most efforts to reduce the encounter to a stereotypic confrontation between two "sides," much as it was typically represented as such, much as some of the *dramatis personae* tried to make it just that.

For one thing, the Southern Tswana world was hardly homogeneous, unchanging, or "simple," a consideration which the evangelists underestimated, often at great cost, in their eagerness to colonize African consciousness. They also misperceived the divisions *inside* European colonial ranks, within which they were relatively powerless actors. For their part, Southern Tswana learned quickly that all colonizers were not alike, that differences among them had material consequences; this notwithstanding the discovery that, despite promises to the contrary, even those blacks who identified closely with the church and with Western life-ways remained noncitizens in white society. What is more, Tswana who took what the Protestants had to offer found *themselves* changed as a result—and irrevocably drawn into dialogue on terms not always of their choosing.

In volume 2 we move on to explore how these processes worked themselves out over the much longer run: how "margin" and "metropole" recast each other as Africans and Europeans, plural both, came to mark their similarities and dissimilarities, to inhabit and inhibit one anothers' fantasies—and taken-for-granted practices. As we shall see, the missionaries were to be caught in the old modernist tension between universal truth and local (for which read racialized, cultural) difference. In order to convert "natives" into "civilized" Christians they had to make other into same, to erase the distinctions on which colonialism was founded; this being something which few colonizers have ever been quick to do. On the other hand, they had no choice but to recognize the reality of a creolized African Christianity whose very vitality—often ascribed to the peculiarities of African "nature"—spoke to the Europeans of apostasy, even paganism. Nonconformists in Britain, it turns out, were conformists abroad. Hence their distress at the fact that, when most Tswana finally entered the church, they either became "nominal" Christians or remade Protestantism in their own image. Image*s*, actually, since a multiplicity of Christianities was to emerge. As this implies, the London Missionary Society and Wesleyan Methodist Missionary Society were to have limited success in instilling their own orthodoxies. But they did rather well in conveying the less quiescent qualities of the Protestant spirit: the tradition of dissent, with its trust in the practical power of revealed truth. Products of the Revival, their gospel was often passionate and always pragmatic. It fired the new forms of consciousness that took shape among Southern Tswana, both in the chapel and beyond, in the wake of colonization. To wit, the humanist impulses of the missionaries, if not necessarily their doctrinal teachings, struck a chord with indigenous ideas of action in the world, of healing and the making of history, of moral infraction and entitlement, of community and civility.

The widespread indifference that met their theological disquisitions only strengthened the resolve of the colonial evangelists, persuading them that the revitalization of the African soul required a "revolution in habits." Like the bourgeois revolution of which the mission itself was a part, this one began at home. The unrestrained, unclothed heathen body was, to European Protestant sensibilities, no fit abode for a vigilant Christian conscience; neither was the heathen hut a place to nurture industry in the divine cause. Moral degeneracy had to be reversed by material self-improvement.

Here, in Charles Taylor's (1989:233) apt phrase, was a "theology of ordinary life," one in which honest personal ambition helped build the common good; one which saw the promotion of wealth and truth as mutually enhancing activities, both being modes of producing virtue. Christian political economy, whether as explicit philosophy or implicit disposition, was more than a clutch of market metaphors, more even than a sacred endorsement of this-worldly enterprise. It was, above all, an optimistic theory of value that put capitalist business to the pursuit of salvation and the construction of God's kingdom on earth. Pious labor yielded worth, which was vastly amplified if mortals could be induced to maximize their providentially given potential—and to build, through their own rational exertions, a self-regulating, moral society. This, in Africa, was to be realized through enlightened agriculture, and by the kinds of exchange among "corporate nations" that increased riches and put paid to the "sullen isolations" of savagery (*RRI*:122; see below). In the liberal humanist worldview of the missionaries, such pursuits involved the conversion of value from lower to higher species, requiring universal, standardized, fungible currencies—like money and the word—all of which were ultimately redeemable in the form of grace and eternal life. Viewed thus, conversion and civilization were two sides of the same coin, two related means of "trading up," of accumulating merit and honoring the Glory of God.

This vision was not without its contradictions. Apart from all else, it flirted openly with Mammon. Which, for the Nonconformists, posed an obvious problem: while their faith in human improvement might have been thoroughly modern, they were also latter-day Puritans, with a lingering distrust of money and material things. Any effort to hitch spiritual conversion to the redemptive powers of the market, therefore, was bound to be ambivalently regarded, seen, in part, as opening the way to corrupting influences. Still, Africans were taught the "benefits" of cash cropping, of selling their labor, of making a civilized, "comfortable" living. In fact, the colonial evangelists tried hard to persuade them to use intensive farming techniques—techniques that bore within them an unspoken agrarian aesthetic, a gendered sociology of production, and a set of practical dispositions all attuned to the promise of profit.

Industriousness, so-called, was also spurred by the cultivation of desire; by the stimulation of "wants" in place of "wantonness." This the LMS and WMMS did by resort to objects. Not just any objects, of course—the acquisition of trifles for their own sake was unGodly—but those seen as requisites of the refined self. Thus was the commodity deployed in the service of civility, and the shopwindow, that *locus classicus* of consecrated seduction, dressed to display its enchantments. Thus did the missionaries, with the worthiest of intentions, sponsor "careful" consumption, even recycling old clothes from England to promote it. Thus did they strive to impress upon Africans the meaning of money. Honest toil, patently, was not enough to reform would-be converts. Also needed was a judicious exposure to those goods integral to the construction of proper personhood, decent domesticity, and social distinction.

The civilizing mission in the South African interior, then, was a quest to refurnish the mundane: to focus human endeavor on the humble scapes of the everyday, of the "here-and-now" in which the narrative of Protestant redemption took on its contemporary form. Here, à la Foucault, salvation became healing; enlightenment, education; God's calling, provident enterprise. Here also law was envisaged as an ensemble of rules and regulations, entitlements and sanctions. Hence right became rights, and a man's estate was taken to be the measure of his accumulated worth and status. What is more, in their eagerness to root this vision of human possibility on African soil, the LMS and WMMS invited other whites, mostly men of trade, to join them—which further opened the door to the liberal forces of Euro-modernism and industrial capitalism. These, as it turned out, were forces of which the evangelists had limited understanding. And over which they had even less control.

Inevitably, the Nonconformists ran up against Southern Tswana modes of production and consumption, concepts of value, and being-in-the-world; as we have said and shall show, this was to transform *them* and their world in profound, unexpected ways. Often in spite of themselves, moreover, they also became imbricated in colonial economy, society, and governmentality—which is why, in this volume, we enter ever more deeply into the encompassing colonial world and the diffuse, complicated processes involved in its construction. Like the civilizing mission itself, these processes were contested, appropriated, joined, turned aside, acquiesced in by (few, many, all) Africans at different times and in different places; such things depending on emerging lines of social and cultural distinction, on patterns of relationship and conflict, on economic and political considerations both ephemeral and enduring. The colonial encounter also had the effect of reinforcing some features of indigenous lifeways, altering or effacing others, and leaving yet others unengaged. Along the way, too, new hybrids came into being: new aesthetic styles and material arrangements, new divisions of wealth and senses of identity, new notions of peoplehood, politics, and history.

This fitful dialectic of the long run carried right into the present—where, in each of the chapters, we follow it. Its traces, so many shards of a fractious, fragmented past, litter the cultural and social landscape of the "new" South Africa. Like the Lotlamoreng Cultural Park.

POST THE PAST AND PAST THE POST

It has been our claim that the story of the Nonconformist missions in South Africa casts new light on the nature of nineteenth-century British colonialism. That story also reveals much about modernity itself. Indeed, it calls into question a number of received assumptions—some of them perpetuated by poststructuralism, post-Marxism, and other postmodern isms—about the telos and temporalities, the periodization and motivation of modern European history.

For a start, the rise of these missions gives clear evidence that the "Age of Modernity" did not constitute a sharp, radical break from what came before; that the social and cultural practices of the epoch were themselves a complex product of things old and new, things continuous and discontinuous. Although the ideological offspring of the industrial revolution, the great Protestant evangelical societies were born of, and bore within them, a series of connections with the preindustrial era. Many of their emissaries to South Africa, for example, were descended from British peasant families displaced by the effects of the agricultural revolution of the early eighteenth century (*RRI*:75, 82f.). As such, they were living links to an agrarian past—one already enmeshed in colonial relations with Ireland and the New World—that retained a strong hold on their moral sensibilities. It also provided the pre-text and the model for the kind of yeoman-capitalism they tried to cultivate among Tswana. This mélange of the feudal and the progressive might have taken its particular shape in Bechuanaland from the conjuncture between mission social biography and African cultural ecology. But it was not merely to be found at colonial peripheries. Wiener (1981), among others, has shown that, far from being killed off by an ever more rational, rationalized political economy, some "premodern" values enjoyed ongoing hegemony in industrializing Britain; all the more so where segments of the aristocracy made common cause with a rising bourgeoisie that was increasingly ill at ease with the spirit of progress it had sold to much of the world.

Continuities of this sort, and countless examples come easily to mind, cast a telling light on the interconnections among colonialism, capitalism, and the culture of modernity. Above all, they call into question, if not for the first time, the neat, sequential stages of those ideal-typical, ideal-teleological models—shared by many Marxists and modernization theorists—according to which the West first develops a mature capitalist order, itself both an economic "system" and a "civilization," and then exports[5] it to the precapitalist, "underdeveloped" world (see, e.g., Jameson 1984, after Mandel 1978).[6] As Nederveen Pieterse (1989:xi) says, this view of the past, as tenacious as it is crass, is wholly insensitive to the premodern dimensions of contemporary Europe, its construction and expansion—save as atavistic survivals. And it neglects a long history of imperialism that predated late nineteenth-century monopoly capitalism (cf. Cain and Hopkins 1993). But, even more, it masks the importance of the encounter with nonindustrial, non-Western peoples and practices in the making of modernity itself.

This, however, is not to downplay the salience of the rise of capitalism either for colonialism or for cultural modernism. Nor for our story. Quite the opposite: we also agree with Mandel (Jameson 1984:78) that, far from making Marx's classic analysis redundant, the ascendance of the global post-cold war economy, being the "purest form of capital yet to have emerged," confirms many of his insights about its origins and evolution; hence the uncanny resemblance, noted below, between the fervent monetarism of our "new world order" and the language of Puritan political economy of the late 1700s. But we also insist that the social and cultural constitution of this economy was more complex than is often suggested: that European capitalism was always less rationalized and homogeneous than its own dominant ideology allowed; always more internally diverse, more localized in its forms, more influenced by moral and material considerations beyond its control—and, finally, wrought more by its confrontation with the rest of the world than by purely endogenous forces. Despite its own self-image and its affinity for rationalization, it was shot through with the features it projected on colonial others: parochialism, syncretism, unreason, enchantment.

Our narrative also raises questions about the other end of the history of modernity, about its relation to "postmodernity," "postcoloniality," or "post-Fordism." Such terms, of course, refer to different dimensions of the same late twentieth-century moment (Adam and Tiffin 1991). Each turns on a displacement from, a putative end to, the recognizable forms of "Western society as we know it." Some have insisted on the continuities that underlie these moves back to the future—post the past and past the posts, so to speak—whether they be seen in terms of *neo*-imperialism (B. Parry 1987),[7] *late* capitalism (Mandel 1978; D. Harvey 1989), or the "contradictions of a modernism which has gone on too long" (Frow 1991:141); a modernism, says Hebdige (1988:195), "without the hopes . . . which made modernity bearable." But there has also been a widespread tendency to read the present as a point of rupture; in particular, with the grand imperial narratives, and the totalizing world-historical forces, of the

European enlightenment. For some, this rupture promises a liberating disengagement, a freedom from the constraint of coherence, a positive politics of polyphony and fractured identity. For others, it spells descent into a dismal, historyless hyper-reality (Baudrillard 1988:166f.), into a refractory universe where authority is democratized into disarray, into a postcolonial state-of-being characterized not by established modes of governance but by the "banality of power" (Mbembe 1992).

What might the civilizing mission in nineteenth-century South Africa have to say about any of this? Quite a lot, as it happens. Most notably, it reveals the subtle mix of continuities, ruptures, and elisions that link the early imperial epoch to the present; all of which should caution us against seeing, in the passage from past to future, brute contrasts and radical breaks—themselves evocative of the stark dualisms of the modernist *Weltbild*—instead of more nuanced, dialectical histories. Many things commonly taken to be typical of postcoloniality, metonymic even of postmodernity, were present in colonial contexts— hence, in the fabric of modernity itself. The overseas missions, for example, were nodes in a global order, their stations pegging out a virtual Empire of God no less ether-real than is cyberspace today. On the ground, displaced Europeans tried to resituate "native" peoples on maps centered elsewhere, maps that marginalized the local; they also set in motion processes that animated a great deal of physical and imaginative movement. For both sides this involved dislocation, the kind of breach between spatiality and social being often associated with postmodernity (Frow 1991:146; cf. Appadurai 1990; Bhabha 1994:5). It, too, was accompanied by talk of epochal change.

Indeed, from early on, colonial evangelists in South Africa wrote repeatedly of the great transformations running through African life, transformations of which Southern Tswana were equally aware: massive migrations, social disruptions, cultural hybridizations. These they either welcomed as a liberation from received forms of authority, territoriality, and the stifling closures of custom, or lamented as a descent into disarray, a symptom of the gathering incoherence of everyday life. For good or ill, the age of tradition was always just before yesterday's dawn, no more than a generation back. In this context, missionary efforts to anchor indigenous populations into the emerging colonial order relied not merely on the control of labor flows, but also on the circulation of goods. African subjects were reoriented and reoriented themselves, in large part, through recommissioned European objects; more accurately, through *regimes* of such objects. Already in the first half of the nineteenth century they lived in a translocal world, one in which sites of consumption and production were frequently a continent apart. Moreover, attempts to cultivate their tastes, to civilize them through style, involved an "aestheticization of everyday life," yet another tendency often labeled postmodern or post-Fordist (Frow 1991:148).

There were other parallels as well, arising out of dialogical exchanges; from colonialism, that is, viewed as a "discursive formation." The colonial evangelists hoped, by means of their texts and talk, to implant a universal creed in Tswana hearts and minds, to render their Good News in the vernacular without leaving any cultural residue. As we have seen, their exertions added syncretic complexity to an already complex, fluid field of local signs and practices. And they induced profound perceptions of difference and of fractured selfhood (*RRI*:218, 243). In colonized contexts like this, double consciousness was endemic. "Referential slippage" routinely undermined efforts to pin down the "real" (Slemon 1991:7; Hutcheon 1991:76). People born of such worlds were very much at home with hybridity, mimesis, and cultural fusion (Bhabha 1984). They rode the contradictions of modernity long before those contradictions were forced on the awareness of an increasingly alienated West; before the cold war ended and the anomic bomb fell on so many troubled ethnoscapes, so many inner cities and rural wastelands, nations and states-in-crisis across the globe.

We are *not* suggesting that these features of colonial societies were identical in nature or in origin to those often taken to typify the postcolonial or postmodern condition. The latter, however it may be characterized, is the outcome of real differences in the capacities of technology and the workings of global capital; in the form and distribution of patterns of production; in the media-mediated circulation of signs and styles; in the part played by consumption in constructing persons and relations. But we *are* saying that, despite these differences, important continuities emerge from histories like the one we recount here—and from such fragments, such congealings of historical consciousness and practice, as the simultaneously pre-and postmodern Lotlamoreng Cultural Park. Continuities of this kind make us skeptical of "news of the arrival and inauguration of a whole new type of society" (Jameson 1984:55); also—and here is the point—of calls for wholly different modes of knowing and interpreting it.

We may, as we have said (p. 6), be in the midst of an Age of Revolution not unlike that of 1789–1849 (J. L. Comaroff 1996). Hence all the discussion, both in Western academia and in public spheres across the planet, of a rising transnational economy based on virtual currencies and electronic transactions, cyber-capital and flexible accumulation, mobile manufacture and labile resource deployment; of the crisis and reconstitution of nation-states; of the deterritorialization of culture; of the emergence of new diasporas, new forms and flows of labor; of the re-formation of relations of production and reproduction as they configure "*the* family"; of the end-of-almost-everything as we know it. But, like all revolutions, this one is compounded of elements past, present, and futuristic. What is more, colonialism is still very much with us, be it in the urban "jungles" of the Americas, Europe, or Asia, in Rwanda or, as Saro-Wiwa (1995; see below, n. 19) reminds us from his victim's grave, in Ogoniland. In such contexts, indeed wherever difference is most fetishized, the "benefits of universal modernity [continue to] seem most worth fighting for" (During 1991:27).

13

The implication is plain enough: to conclude that the colonial age is over, or that modernity ended with it, is premature. It is crucial not to move on too quickly, not to close the page once and for all on a historical movement whose effects still impinge on the lives of millions of people (cf. Dirks 1992:5). Forgetting the more egregious aspects of the colonial past, which some self-identifying "postcolonials" would have us do, may be part of healing—as well, understandably, of a certain species of tactical politics. It was also, as Renan ([1882] 1990:11) famously remarked, part of the making of nationalism and other sorts of modernist identity. But it is bad for the writing of history, not least in its anthropological mode. And write it surely we must—in as multivocal, dialectical a manner as we know how. Otherwise we simply cede all grasp of contemporary global realities, and of their construction, to the masters of the market. Or, worse yet, to the ideologues of a new age political economy that looks ever more suspiciously like its eighteenth-century precursor.

*****

The impact of colonialism may continue to make itself felt in the everyday lives of many postcolonial societies. And the jury may still be out on its place in the history of modernity—whose end postmodernity, whatever it may actually turn out to have been, appears less to herald than to post-pone, to complicate rather than to kill off. But this leaves us with some conceptual work to do. Most obviously, we are yet to say what exactly we mean by colonialism, modernity, and the everyday, the three terms on which our account—and much of the ongoing work of anthropology, historical and contemporary—rests most heavily.

CONCEPTUAL THEMES, THE SEQUEL

In volume 1 we laid out the conceptual scaffolding of the study as a whole, seeking to interrogate and to specify its key terms: culture, hegemony, and ideology, power and agency, representation, consciousness, and their cognates. Here, following our opening comments, we turn, in a rather different vein, to the epistemic issues that lie at the core of this volume: How exactly are we to conceive of colonialism? And, since it is crucial to the kind of historical anthropology we seek to do, how are we to apprehend "the everyday"? What are the connections between the two? Between both and the rise of "modernity"? Did "Europe's colonization of the world," as Herbert Lüthy (1964:36) once said, really mark "the painful birth" of the modern? With some notable exceptions, all three terms—colonialism, the everyday, and modernity—tend to be treated, in the orthodox social sciences at least, as if they were self-evident, as if we all shared an understanding of their denotations and connotations. We may argue over cause and effect, over historical determinations or periodizations, over a host of other matters; but, more often than not, it is assumed that the concepts themselves may be taken as read.[8] This is unfounded and unfortunate. It stands in the way of thinking afresh about the kinds of colonialism that continue to pervade our own everyday world. Or about the kind of hold exercised by modernity on the history of the present and future.

Colonialism: Or, *"when time presses and history suppresses"*[9]

A great deal has been written recently about colonialism, albeit more about its character and implications than about the concept itself. Much of this has been in the revisionist mode. It has become commonplace, for example, to observe that the term covers a range of historical phenomena far broader, and older, than is often allowed (cf. Delavignette 1964:7f.); also that, over the past decade or so, there has been a sea-change in approaches to its analysis, partly at the insistence of those once colonized. Gone, or in retreat, are received forms of modernization theory, with their confident narratives of progress and their utopian liberal humanism; similarly the Marxist alternatives, which treated colonialism as a reflex of the rise of capitalism and, hence, of the articulation of modes of production, of unequal exchange between center and periphery, of underdevelopment and dependency.

In their place has arisen a growing concern with the contingent, constructed, cultural dimensions of "othering" (e.g., Dirks 1992; Thomas 1994); with the invention of tradition and, in the tradition of the inventive Foucault, the making of imperial subjects through dispersed disciplinary regimes (e.g., T. Mitchell 1991; Stoler 1995); with the agency of the colonized and its impact on Europe and Europeans (cf. Trotter 1990:5f.). At its most extreme, an almost Althusserian overdetermination has been replaced by a Derridean indeterminacy, which treats the phenomenon as diffuse, protean, necessarily incoherent. Even among the less post-marked, dialectics have given way to dialogics, political economy to poetics, class conflict to consumption, the violence of the gun to the violation of the text, world-historical material processes to local struggles over signs and styles, European domination to post-Hegelian hybridity.

We exaggerate, of course. There remain many, including ourselves, who argue for a range of positions between the extremes, between the past and the post, as it were. Indeed, it is our view that neither image of colonialism is right or wrong; that each refers to different moments in, different perspectives on, different aspects of its workings over the long run. Still, the effect of this pendulum swing has been liberating. While much may have been left out in the lurch, it has had the salutary effect of freeing our thinking from a series of old paradigmatic constraints—and of pointing very clearly to those questions that remain less than fully answered.

The most fundamental, patently, is what *is* colonialism? Or, to be more precise, what is distinctive about it?

Once upon a time, the answers seemed self-evident. True, as Etherington (1984:2–3) has said of imperialism, the term itself has always been difficult to pin down, having had a history of "shifty, changing meaning."[10] Nonetheless, at least until recently, both scholarly and popular imaginings clustered around one basic axiom: that colonialism, in its modern guise, had to do, above all, with the extension of political, economic, social, and other forms of control by metropolitan European powers over so-called "third world" peoples. For many, this boiled down to three things: the "exploitation of indigenous peoples";[11] the imposition of sovereign authority;[12] and the establishment of a permanent settler population, usually marked off as racially distinct from "the natives" (this last often being taken as the feature that distinguished it from imperialism).[13] Indeed, even standard dictionary definitions, those arbiters of congealed wisdom, suggest that colonialism described the "acquisition and exploitation of colonies [themselves "underdeveloped distant" lands] for the benefit of the mother-country."[14]

The nature and extent of that exploitation has been debated—among both colonizers and colonized, by European scholars as well as subalterns—since the very beginning; so, too, has the question of who gained from it, how, and in what measure (cf. Phillips 1989:1f.; Semmel 1993:1f.). But, stereotypically, colonization has long been associated, more or less, (i) with spatial distance and racial difference, re-presented typically in the argot of center-and-periphery, civilization-and-barbarism; (ii) with the extension of overrule by a well-developed imperial state, usually through the offices of a local colonial administration; (iii) with the active presence of expatriate colonists, among them settlers, missionaries, plantation and mine managers, the staff of chartered companies, and government personnel; (iv) with the imperatives of political economy.[15] Its moral dimensions might have been a matter of argument across the ideological spectrum. Yet even those who disagreed violently on this issue were likely to concur on its mechanics. It is striking, for instance, that nineteenth-century men of business in South Africa—men who referred to themselves, proudly, as "capitalists" and "colonialists"—shared with neo-Marxists of almost a hundred years later a very similar understanding of the workings of colonialism; especially of colonial capitalism.

None of these certainties seem quite so assured nowadays. For a start, there is a burgeoning literature dedicated to demonstrating that colonization was everywhere more than merely a process in political economy—or one vested primarily in the colonial state (see, e.g., Fields 1985; Dirks 1992; Thomas 1994; Cooper and Stoler 1989, 1997).[16] Both in volume 1 and again here, we ourselves argue that it was as much a cultural as a political or economic encounter: as much about, say, cartography or counting as about the practical logic of capitalism; as much about bodily regimes as about the brute extraction of labor power or the underdevelopment of local economies;[17] as much as anything else about "inscribing in the social world a new conception of space, new forms of personhood, and a new means of manufacturing the real" (Mitchell 1991:ix). We argue also that, of all colonizers, it was evangelists who made the most thoroughgoing efforts to revolutionize African being-in-the-world (cf. Bohannan 1964:22). In Bechuanaland, to be sure, they did so, with complex and substantial consequences, for more than sixty years *before* the arrival of a British administration.

But this is not all.

Few would insist anymore that colonization necessarily involves spatial distance between centers and peripheries, rulers and ruled. Some time ago, Hechter (1975) used the term "internal colonialism"[18] to underline the similarities between the Celtic fringe of the United Kingdom and Britain's overseas "possessions"; recently it has been evoked to describe power relations *within* a postcolony.[19] Nor was he alone in making the point which, as practical politics, goes back a very long way in the British imagination; *vide* Edmund Spenser's thoughts on Ireland, circa 1595 (see chapter 3). Even closer to home, as we (1992) and others have noted, the inner cities of nineteenth-century England, like those of twentieth-century Europe and America, were regarded little differently from the most "backward" of colonies abroad; chapter 6 elucidates the extraordinarily close parallels between Africa and "outcast" London drawn in both literary and scientific texts of the period. These inner city "jungles" (Hebdige 1988:20) were also sites from which value, primarily in the form of labor, was extracted for the enrichment of a rising bourgeoisie—and into which the cultural outreach of the civilizing mission stretched in an effort to remake their rude inhabitants. Today they are the ground on which the spatial and temporal coordinates of colonialism meet, on which the metropole and the margins of empire fold into each other, on which "time presses and history suppresses." For it is here that most colonial subjects-turned-immigrants live, often at the edges of an economy which offers them limited prospect of formal employment, often well beyond the social and aesthetic sight lines of polite society.

The conflation of inner city with imperial fringe suggests, in turn, that the association of colonialism with race, strong though it was and still is, was neither inevitable nor uncomplicated.[20] What made the uncivil of a nineteenth-century Manchester or Liverpool "slum" into a colony of savages, and demanded that they be "taken in hand," was not the color of their skins or other *innate* bodily characteristics. It was their social class. Destitution—itself the product of a lack of material and cultural capital, of self-possession and self-discipline—made them radically, unmistakably different; "unthinkable" said E. M. Forster's fictional imperialist, Henry Wilcox (1992:58; see chapter 6). Admittedly, this difference was typically seen to have physical and dispositional effects. And there *were* times when whites were converted into racial others. The Irish are a celebrated case in point, but the same applied to Boers in South Africa; the latter, a hybrid population of non-British "Europeans," were likened at times to black Africans by the English,[21] who ruled over them intermittently. Nonetheless, the elision of race, physicality, social inferiority, and political subordination was far from universal. The historical relations among them, in fact, were exquisitely complicated.

In sum, while political domination and economic exploitation, spatial distance and racial difference might have been features of most colonial situations, they cannot be taken, a priori, to separate colonialism from other forms of structured inequality, other forms of dominion and overrule. Nor, of course, can "cultural imperialism" (cf. Tomlinson 1991). There are also those who have argued, usually by implication, that they cannot be taken as defining features at all, being merely the crude motifs of an imperial European narrative retold from the vantage of its own protagonists. This, at least, is a corollary of some postcolonial moves to reconstruct its historiography—sometimes as literary criticism, sometimes as fiction, sometimes as anthropology, sometimes as all of them at once—in order to assert the agency of colonial subjects above all else. In the most radical cases, any hint that culture and consciousness might have been colonized, or that "others" might ever have been victims, is eschewed. On occasion, even, those who were once the white heroes or antiheroes of empire are refigured as the dupes of those whom they sought to rule, and whom they periodically interned, dispossessed, killed. A far cry, this, from Frantz Fanon or Albert Memmi, Ken Saro-Wiwa or Steve Biko, or, in South Africa of an earlier day, Sol Plaatje and S. M. Molema, articulate "native" voices who spoke about the contradictory experience of being colonized—consciousness, culture, and all—in very different terms; often much darker, more concretely political, more concerned with what it meant to be acted upon. It would be ironic if these voices were to be stifled and distorted by the voice-over of a postcolonial discourse that has so much to say about the agency of the colonized.

For the time being, we beg the question that lurks here; we shall come back to it. More immediately, what is important about all these revisionist accounts of colonialism, and they are many and varied, is *not* whether they are correct or incorrect, factual or fanciful. It is that, taken together and placed alongside older ones, they chart the diverse perspectives it is possible to hold on the same beast. Recall the parable, now reduced to a cliché, told by a medieval Sufi teacher about blind men who try to make out an elephant by feel alone: each depicts it as something quite different—a rope, a fan, a tree—depending on where they touch it. Ernst Haas (1986:707) has used the analogy in respect of nationalism, Tomlinson (1991:8) of cultural imperialism. It applies equally to colonialism, which clearly feels different depending on where—or, since histories and elephants are not the same kind of thing, when—people happen to touch it. Or are touched by it. For some of those who were its subjects and objects, it *was* about domination and violence, invasion and exploitation, even genocide; for others, an ongoing struggle in which they sometimes gained and sometimes lost; for yet others, an ambiguous process of making themselves and their worlds anew—and, in varying degree, on their own terms. For some, it appeared to be primarily about the material conditions of existence, about the sale of their labor, the seizure of their lands, the alienation of their products; for others, it was equally an encounter with European knowledge and techniques and modes of representation. For some it was all of these things, for others it was few of them. But for everyone it involved a distinctive experience: the experience, offered Sartre (1955:215; see Zahar 1974:19), of coming to feel, and to *re-cognize* one's self as, a "native."

Colonialism, then, has always been, simultaneously, *both* a monothetic and a polythetic business, everywhere the same yet different, obviously singular yet palpably plural (cf. Memmi 1965:xff.).[22] This is why it is so difficult to define or to pin down conceptually; why, also, it resists being reduced easily to abstract theoretical statement; why there is no sense in reviewing, or trying to bring to order, the enormous literature written in pursuit of a general theory.[23] From the very first, colonialism was at once a constantly unfolding, mutating, unruly *process* and an infinitely intricate order of evanescent, often enigmatic, *relations;* indeed, the practical effort to define and control its terms was often part of that process, those relations.[24] Nevertheless, things may be said in a propositional voice about it; propositions that do not themselves amount to a "Theory of Colonialism," but sketch out a theoretical orientation toward its study.

Let us offer seven. None of them is entirely original in its own right; as we are the first to acknowledge, they owe much to recent work in the historical anthropology of colonialism. While they do not address the question of historical origins or first causes, and are confined exclusively to the modern period,[25] these propositions do, we believe, point the way to some fresh comparative insights into the whole beast. They also frame our excursion into the South African past in general, and colonial evangelism among Southern Tswana in particular.

We begin with the most familiar, the most straightforward, if not perhaps the least contentious.

The First: Colonialism was simultaneously, equally, and inseparably a process in political economy and culture. This is *not* to say that it had political, economic, and cultural dimensions which played themselves out in parallel, and in some proportion to each other. That would imply that these dimensions were separable in the first place. To the contrary: they were indissoluble aspects of the same reality, whose fragmentation into discrete spheres hides their ontological unity.

The general point is to be underscored since, in treating colonialism as a "cultural formation" (Dirks 1992:3), a discursive field (Seed 1991), or a Foucauldian regime of power/knowledge (Mitchell 1991), it is easy enough to lose sight of material production: to pay it lip service as we focus on problems of consciousness, representation, subjectivity, textuality (see chapter 9)—or worse, to relegate it to the background rumble of realist history. Which is not, if we listen to "natives" almost anywhere, how colonization was experienced. Neither may the problem be rectified merely by addition, by appending to our present cultural concerns more by way of material context.

Conversely, to explain colonialism purely in terms of the historical logic of European capitalist expansion—once the basic axiom of a whole species of theory of imperialism[26]—is also to miss the point, even if the conception of capitalism is broadened to include its cultural facia. Empire was always also a corollary of the global production and consumption of a particular postenlightenment worldview (e.g., Nederveen Pieterse 1989:20). For example, the campaign of colonial evangelists in South Africa to transform Tswana agriculture was, simultaneously, about aesthetics *and* modes of production, about the inscription on the landscape of imaginative, tactile geometries, *and* about crops, labor, and machines (below, chapter 3). Reciprocally, many Southern Tswana responded to the European outreach by refusing to allow a wedge to be forced between the material and symbolic planes of their own world, let alone between its spiritual and temporal dimensions.

To put the matter plainly, then, it may be that efforts to account for colonialism in terms of the "laws" of capitalist development, or the material imperatives of modernization, have been widely discredited; that the problems of the dependency paradigm have been well and truly revealed; that "world systems" theories, Marxist and Marxoid alike, have been shown to be seriously flawed; that their Weberian alternatives, grounded in liberal political economy, have proven no more persuasive. But this is *not* to say that colonization had nothing to do with the growth of industrial capitalism, that underdevelopment did not occur, or that transnational political and economic forces had no effect on the lives of "local" people everywhere (cf. Dirks 1992:19). Any such claim would be absurd. On the other hand, so would the presumption that a "cultural" or "discursive" or "dialogical" approach could explain all. The point, as we have said, is to demonstrate how, in particular places and periods, colonialism, capitalism, and modernity constituted and played off each other, manifesting themselves simultaneously as *both* political economy and culture.

The next proposition is a negative one and hence is hard to formulate directly. It refers to long-standing concerns, across the social sciences, about the character of the colonial state (see above, n. 16). The term itself conflates two institutional planes: imperial governance, centered at the metropole, and the administration of "overseas possessions." Historically speaking, their articulation varied a great deal. In fact, the various levels of government subsumed in "the colonial state" were, at times, remarkably disordered, inchoate, internally conflicted. At times, too, authority abroad was very weak—just as, "at home," the political will to rule the world fluctuated widely throughout the nineteenth century (*RRI*:78). Again, we do not intend to go over old ground here; each major theoretical tradition had or has its own take on the colonial state—from Marxism, according to which it was simply the political armature of capital, to modernization theory, which saw it as a vehicle of enlightened development and the rule of law. For our own part, we find it difficult to speak in the abstract of "*the* colonial state" at all. Across the temporal and spatial axes of the imperial epoch, differences in regimes of rule and technologies of command were enormous. So, too, were the kinds and degrees of intrusiveness, coercion, and terror perpetrated in the name of civilization. But one thing *can* be said. It picks up on the *double entendre* alluded to in volume 1; namely, that "state" refers at once to a modality of political order and to a condition of mind-and-being. And so,

> *The Second:* To the extent that colonization effected a change in the state-of-being of "native" populations, it typically depended less on the formal apparatus of colonial states—historically plural now—than on other agents of empire; among them missionaries, men of business, settlers, soldiers of fortune. Even when these states were at their most elaborate, from the late nineteenth to the early-mid twentieth centuries, their political control—both their instrumental capacity and their capillary power to mold the everyday lives of indigenous peoples—was always incomplete, sometimes quite limited; which is why they relied so much on techniques of representation, often highly ritualized, to assert and amplify their presence. Frequently, moreover, they depended heavily on other European expatriates, including those with whom they intermittently came into conflict, to achieve their ends.[27]

In many contexts, for a variety of reasons, government was a fairly late arrival on the scene: a state of colonialism—effected by what we may call, after Gluckman et al. (1949), "non-commissioned officers" of the Crown[28]—often preceded the colonial state by decades. This, by turn, conduced further to the secondary role of the latter in colonization, a point that resonates oddly with Gallagher and Robinson's once controversial notion of the "informal empire."[29] In Bechuanaland, as we have said, overrule occurred almost a century after the presence of Europeans was first felt by Southern Tswana. Here, in fact, is evidence that colonizers unattached to the state might play historical roles usually associated with it; also, following our first proposition, that their interventions were indissolubly cultural and material. With the discovery of diamonds in South Africa in the 1860s, waves of Tswana migrants moved, apparently at their own volition, to the diggings in search of employment. And they did so *before* Her Majesty's Government annexed the territory, *before* a British administration began to organize the flow of labor.[30] As we show in chapter 4, Nonconformist evangelists, who themselves had ambivalent relations with officialdom (*RRI*:chap. 7), were instrumental in this: they set in motion processes which, over the long run, reoriented indigenous perceptions of money and goods, work and wants. It did not take the presence of the state, in other words, to create the conditions for an industrial labor supply (cf. Cooper and Stoler 1997). It took a state of mind, and that was a product of forces much greater, much more embracing, than those enclosed in the political domain.

A footnote here, to gesture toward the topic we treat in the next section.

The refusal to presume the primacy of the state is integral to a view of colonialism that begins—but does *not* end—by emphasizing its quotidian qualities rather than its portentous aspects. This we hold, accords with the way in which it was apprehended by peoples like Southern Tswana, especially in the nineteenth century. For most colonial subjects, the European embrace, whether or not it was orchestrated from centers elsewhere, presented itself less in the form of methodical stately action than in the everyday practices of the frontiersmen of empire. This is not to deny that global economics or regional politics, or indeed the state, had a major impact on black South Africans. They clearly did. But it was from the bottom up, through a myriad of mundane exchanges, that the forms of European modernity first found their way onto the African landscape, there to become the object of the protracted process—that curious mix of consent and contestation, desire and disgust, appropriation and accommodation, refusal and refiguration, ethnicization and hybridization—subsumed in the term "the colonial encounter." Consequently, in the account below we strive for a historical anthropology of multiple perspectives: one told not from any single "side," or in any single register, but situated, as it were, in the eye of the dialectic.

This leads us toward the following proposition, which we state in a series of steps, moving from the general to the specific, the more to the less familiar.

The Third: Colonialism was as much involved in making the metropole, and the identities and ideologies of colonizers, as it was in (re)making peripheries and colonial subjects. In spite of the self-representation of Europeans at home and abroad—or the much invoked trope of the civilizing mission—it had little to do with the export, by a mature imperial society to benighted savages overseas, of highly cultivated practices and institutions. To the contrary, colonies were typically locales in which the ways and means of modernity—themselves often insecure, precarious, and contested—were subjected to experimentation and then reimported for domestic use.

Much has been made of this lately[31]—if usually in rather general terms, and often illustrated with purely literary examples. Neither is the point exactly novel. Said Delavignette (1964:8–9), more than thirty years ago:

[C]olonization has had a transforming effect on metropoles at all levels. . . . [T]he countries colonized have had just as much influence on the colonizing powers as these prided themselves on spreading overseas. Colonization has never been a one-way affair.

It was the act of colonization that actually created the "metropolis," he went on to say, not vice versa. Similarly Sartre (1965:xxv–xxvi, after Memmi 1965), "The colonial situation manufactures colonizers as it manufactures colonies. . . . [I]t is the movement of things," a matter with which we shall be closely concerned throughout this volume, "that designates colonizer and colonized alike."

So far so good. But still too general. In our own view, there are three quite separate senses in which, and sites at which, colonialism constructed colonizers and their "centers."

(i) At the frontiers of empire, expatriate "colonial societies," and those who made up their various cadres, tended—sometimes despite themselves[32]—to be profoundly affected by the encounter with "native" peoples and cultures.

It has been said, by George Orwell ([1937] 1962:108f.) among others,[33] that expatriates regularly reconfigured themselves and their social standing away from Britain. But we also intend something else here: that the encounter with colonized peoples altered the very foundations of European worlds abroad. It yielded new, localized cultural forms, reaching into everything from the aesthetics of architecture and attire, through such domesticities as diet and daily ablutions, to relations of production. Ironically, these often shared a great deal with (changing) indigenous signs and practices—many of which were condemned by colonizers as "primitive."

(ii) "At home," in Europe, the refinement of bourgeois "civilization," of modernity and its ideological underpinnings, was achieved in major part with reference to the colonies: through the imaginative resources they provided for self-discovery and the production of potentially powerful knowledge; through the kinds of cultural and physical trial-and-error which they permitted; through the forms of governmentality, legality, and material production which they fostered.

We shall encounter many examples as we proceed though our narrative. Others have provided yet different ones. All of them add up to one conclusion: that the colonies were crucial to the formation of modern European nation-states, to the imagined communities that composed them, and to the triumph of the bourgeoisie that lay at the core of their historical self-fashioning. This entailed an applied sociology, an exercise in social control and class (re)formation:

(iii) Also at the metropole, colonies became models of and for the "improvement" of the underclasses—imaginative vehicles, that is, for representing their "condition" and for rendering them tractable and ruly—especially in the fast growing industrial cities.

For the rising bourgeoisies of Europe, the greatest threat to civilization, and to their own ascendancy, was a population living in dire, disorderly poverty. Hence the felt need to instill in the underclasses a "proper" sense of morality, decency, and hygiene, a respect for property and prosperity, a measure of self-control and modest ambition. Without these things there was little assurance of social order, let alone of a compliant, well-regulated labor force. In Britain, the "savage peoples" of South Africa were held up as an ethnological template for the classification and reconstruction of the poor and lowly at home; the "elevation" of the former served both as an example to the latter and as the justification for a civilizing mission into the *terra incognita* of the inner city (chapter 5).

Thus far we have spoken of colonizer and colonized in the singular, as if each were an abstract form, a historical "type." It is now time for refinement.

The Fourth: Despite their existence as powerful discursive tropes, and their strategic deployment in the politics of decolonization, neither "*the* colonizer" nor "*the* colonized" represented an undifferentiated sociological or political reality, save in exceptional circumstances. Nor, in any uncomplicated sense, did the opposition between them—for all its reification in the name of imperial overrule and in struggles against it. Both the categories and the contrast were repeatedly ruptured and compromised, their boundaries blurred and their content re-invented.

"*The* colonizer" typically consisted of cadres divided, to a greater or lesser degree, by social status, ideological disposition, and various kinds of interest. Nor did they always share a language and a culture, not to mention a gender. And, over time, they frequently came into open conflict with one another (*RRI*:chap. 7).[34] Likewise "*the* colonized," who, apart from their own prior cultural and linguistic diversities, were also differentiated by status and gender; also, as the European presence made itself felt, by processes of class formation and social distinction.

What is more, an intricate web of ties came to transect the imaginative—and, later, political and legal—cleavages between colonizers and colonized. This did more than merely create creolized identities. It also yielded counterstereotypic affinities and alliances. In South Africa, some British missionaries confessed themselves much closer to black Christian elites, whom they likened to "respectable" whites, than to Boer settlers, whom they were wont to portray in pejorative, racial terms. For their part, the Africans sometimes spoke patronizingly of their "non-civilized" compatriots,[35] and entered easily into the society of liberal English expatriates, especially under the aegis of the church and its schools.[36] This sociology of sameness and difference, which had analogues everywhere, will prove important in laying bare the effects of colonial evangelism on Southern Tswana. Here, though, it is the more general point that is salient. While it has become almost statutory to note that complicated connections existed among colonizers and colonized, the analytic implications that follow are not so well-recognized. As we shall see, an understanding of these connections is crucial if we are to make sense of the pluralities and polyphonies of any colonial society, its dialectics and determinations; crucial, that is, in establishing what kinds of difference differences in kind really made as worlds apart were conjoined.

And yet, for all the tangled composition of colonial worlds, their own historical dynamics conduced to imaginative simplification, to the objectification of stark, irreducible contrasts.

The Fifth: Despite the internal complexity of colonial societies, they tended to be *perceived* and *re-presented*, from within, in highly dualist, oppositional terms; terms that solidified the singularity of, and distance between, ruler and ruled, white and black, modernity and tradition, law and custom, European and *non*-European, capitalism and its antitheses, and so on. The objectification of this order of differences was intrinsic to the gesture of colonization itself. To the extent that European colonial hegemonies took root, it underlay a grammar of distinctions that insinuated itself into the world of the colonized, entering into their own self-construction and affecting the ways in which they inhabited their identities.[37]

It is, of course, against just these processes that much postcolonial writing has been directed[38]—and against which much anticolonial resistance in the postwar period pitted itself.

Colonial societies rarely consisted, for any length of time, of two discrete worlds, each whole unto itself, caught up together in the interdependencies of a Hegelian master-slave relationship. (This *pace* Elbourne n.d., who suggests that we argue the opposite; see chapter 9.) Neither were they founded, objectively speaking, on "dual" economies. They were increasingly integrated totalities, their various parts bound together ever more indivisibly. In industrial-revolution Britain, the country and the city were figuratively set apart in rough proportion to the degree that they became structurally fused (*RRI*:73). So it was with the worlds of colonizer and colonized "overseas": the more tightly they were interwoven, the deeper the conceptual contrast drawn between them. And, as "at home," each came to stand, iconically, for a clutch of signs and practices, of aesthetic and ideological values. Interestingly, in light of the comparison with Britain, the country-city distinction was also exported to South Africa: "native" life was designated rural, while English expatriate society cast itself as urban—even though, in the nineteenth century, some African "villages" were much larger and more elaborate than were the major colonial towns (*RRI*:127). Southern Tswana, in fact, would hear the colonial missionaries refer to their densely settled world repeatedly as the "countryside."

It is easy to offer a functionalist explanation for all this. Something like: the more the "natives" became an indispensable part of colonial society, the more that black elites arose and syncretic identities were fashioned, the more that social barriers were ruptured, the more it became necessary for Europeans to legitimize their dominance—which they could only do by disclaiming the capacity of colonized peoples to rule themselves or even to determine their own destiny. Nor is such an explanation entirely wrong. After all, those who hold the reins of power often *do* behave like good functionalists. And, to be sure, the exercise of colonial authority has long grounded inequality in this kind of logic, forcing black-and-white contrasts in the face of sociologies that point in other directions. But it is incomplete. The construction of a binary, racialized world, at least in South Africa, had a cultural archaeology: it was traceable back to the way in which postenlightenment Europeans had come to represent Africa, congealing fluid local identities into stereotypic, named forms of otherness (see *RRI*:chap. 2).

The poetics of contrast also manifested themselves, within colonial societies, in more parochial, prosaic contexts. In volume 1, we showed how the encounter between the missions and Southern Tswana led to the objectification, in counterpoint, of two cultural repertoires, *sekgoa* and *setswana*. Like the porous line (or, more accurately, middle ground) between them, these repertoires, both of them colonial hybrids, altered markedly over time; all the more so as the universe that embraced them drew everyone in it ever closer together. Far from being frozen in eternal opposition, they were profoundly historical, their substance constantly being reworked as social conditions shifted. Given the challenge from Europeans who set out to transform their lives in the name of civilization, it is not surprising that the Africans should have erected their own alterities, their own tropes of otherness. Or that these would be enfolded under the banner of *setswana*. The latter provided a means of asserting some control, imaginative as well as material, over a world increasingly out of it. In short, the symbolic politics of dualism and difference here were a refraction of the general tendency of colonial encounters to force ever deeper conceptual wedges into ever more articulated, indivisible orders of relations. If we labor the point, it is because we have been repeatedly misrepresented on this issue.[39]

The next proposition ought to be self-evident to anthropologists. The need to state it at all arises from the fact that, in much Western writing, academic and lay alike, "non-Western" societies are still portrayed in simplifying, stereotypic terms. Even in colonial historiography, these societies are sometimes reduced to banal, ahistorical generalities, the kinds of thing that echo early nineteenth-century European imaginings: they are said to be patriarchal and gerontocratic, kinship-based, communal, pervaded by ritual and magicality, and so on. Such generalities make for bad history, bad anthropology, bad everything. And so:

> *The Sixth:* Contrary to the way in which "non-Western" societies have been described in the scholarly and popular literatures of the West, these societies were never "closed," "traditional," or unchanging. Nor were they founded simply on kinship, communalism, ascriptive status, patriarchy, or any other such "principles." They tended, rather, to be complex, fluid social worlds, caught up in their own intricate dynamics and internal dialectics, the workings of which had a direct effect on the terms of the colonial encounter.

As we showed in volume 1, Southern Tswana polities were liable to large-scale changes of form and content long before the arrival of Europeans. They continued to be afterwards as well. These fluidities were partly a product of their endogenous features, partly a function of external relations. And they expressed themselves in a wide range of social and cultural practices. Because of them, for example, some lived in large centralized chiefdoms, others in scattered peasant hamlets, and yet others under a variety of arrangements in between. Such variations determined whether and how Southern Tswana communities were missionized; when and on what terms they entered into the colonial economy; the extent to which they were subjected to land expropriation and violence; how, reciprocally, they dealt with the intrusion of whites, about which many of them took fairly aggressive positions, seeking to seize the economic, political, military, and cultural initiative. None of these dynamics and determinations are remotely understandable—not here nor anywhere else—as long as colonial historiography or historical anthropology satisfies itself with two-dimensional, abstract descriptions of the worlds of colonized peoples.[40]

> *The Seventh:* Colonialism was founded on a series of discontinuities and contradictions. Having arisen in dialectic relationship with industrial capitalism[41]—itself the product, in part, of an earlier global expansion—its culture reinscribed world history in its own Eurocentric terms. Colonizers everywhere purported to export modernity, designating all others as "premodern." They espoused an enlightened legal system but invented and enforced "customary law"; offered that their civilizing mission would convert "natives" into sovereign citizens of empire, autonomous individuals one and all, but abetted their becoming ethnic subjects in a racially divided world; held out the prospect of prosperity but left a legacy of poverty; undertook to save colonized people from the prison-house of tradition but reified and concocted traditions in which to enclose them; spoke of removing difference but engraved it ever more deeply onto the social and physical landscape.

Many have commented on the contradictions of colonialism, of course. Marxist *dependistas*, postcolonial *literati*, social historians, cultural critics, political activists: almost everyone who has engaged the topic from a critical perspective has had something to say about them. So shall we. For, as we suggest elsewhere (1992:211), those contradictions—which, arguably, motivated the colonial process from the first—reveal the ideological scaffolding upon which rested the European will to expand itself and to dominate others. They also lay bare the material, moral, and social physics that underpinned technologies of imperial overrule. But, even more importantly, it was in the fissures and interstices of the European outreach, in the seams made visible by its paradoxes and inconsistencies, that the initiatives and counter-actions of colonized peoples took root; here that their readings of the encounter yielded legible signs on which to muse. And act.

These seven propositions come together in the central argument of this study, which was set out in volume 1 and is taken further here. It is that, far from being a simple exercise in domination and resistance—though both occurred in more or less explicit, more or less intentional forms—colonial encounters everywhere consisted in a complex dialectic: a dialectic, mediated by social differences and cultural distinctions, that transformed everyone and everything caught up in it, if not in the same way; a dialectic that yielded new identities, new frontiers, new signs and styles—and reproduced some older ones as well; a dialectic animated less often by coercive acts of conquest, even if violence was always immanent in it, than by attempts to alter existing modes of production and reproduction, to recast the taken-for-granted surfaces of everyday life, to re-make consciousness; a dialectic, therefore, founded on an intricate mix of visible and invisible agency, of word and gesture, of subtle persuasion and brute force on the part of all concerned. This, again, is why colonialism escapes easy definition. Or reduction to bland generalities. Nineteenth-century colonizers, it is true, typically tried to gain control over the practices through which their would-be subjects constructed themselves and their worlds. But the very act of so doing set in motion processes much too complicated and ambiguous of outcome to be rendered as a grand Eurocentric narrative of modernity-in-the-making; or, inversely, as an African romance.

Two qualifications here. The first is that "dialectic" is not meant to connote a formal, abstract, or strictly teleological movement through time and space (see chapter 9). It is intended, rather, to imply a process of reciprocal determinations; a process of material, social, and cultural articulation—involving sentient human beings rather than abstract forces or structures—whose interdependent destinies cannot be assumed to follow a straightforward, linear path. And whose outcome cannot, as a result, be stipulated a priori. The point of the present study, we stress, is not just to rehearse a script whose denouement was known before we began. It is to pose several problems, the answers to which are neither self-evident nor prefigured: (i) How, and to what extent, did the encounter be-tween "the Bechuana" and British colonizers (primarily colonial evangelists) make *both* the Africans and Europeans into what they became, i.e. particular kinds of (patently hybridized) historical subjects? (ii) What equations of materi-ality and meaning, power and practice, were activated in the course of their interaction? (iii) How did it happen that a bewilderingly tangled field of cross-cutting social and cultural ties sedimented, imaginatively, into an engagement between two "sides"? (iv) How, along the way, were the worlds of both, and the world that encompassed them both, reshaped?

This introduces the other qualification: that, in no colonial theater was *ev-ery*thing—on any "side"—pulled into the intercourse between colonizers and colonized, there to be worked over as the dialectic unfolded. Some signs and practices eluded direct involvement, seeming to remain encapsulated and be-yond assail. It is these things that appeared to persist relatively unmarked by, and outside of, history; which is not to say, obviously, that their meaning-in-context or their social value was unaltered. What is more, those that were drawn in were not all implicated to the same degree. In Bechuanaland, for instance, spiritual life and agrarian practice, clothing and architecture, labor and bodily dispositions, among other quotidian things, became central and were often con-tested; much more so than, say, patterns of public decision making or rituals of office.

If, then, we are to enlarge our grasp of colonialism in general, and of colo-nial evangelism in particular, it is necessary to focus our gaze on the dialectics of everyday life at the imperial frontier. These, in turn, are to be "read" in rela-tion to two things, each working itself out in its own times and spaces, even as they began to intersect with and infuse each other: the rise of modernity, of capitalism and its "civilization," in Europe (*RRI*:chap. 2); and the parallel his-tory of the South African interior, where new polities, cultural practices, and social arrangements were equally under construction (*RRI*:chap. 4). But this, as we said earlier, raises a fundamental question: What is to be understood by "the everyday"? And how is it connected to the making of "the modern"?

The Everyday as Epiphany

[O]ne can not form a correct idea of missionary work except by examina-tion of the minutiae.

David Livingstone (1857:205)

Let us approach these issues by situating them within the purview of the present study. And within their own broader historical context.

Colonial missionaries might have conceived of their crusade, and repre-sented it, in heroic terms (*RRI*:172f.). But, as we have said, theirs was no ordi-nary epic. It was an epic of the ordinary. There were good reasons why this was so, why so much of the evangelical encounter took place on the plane of the quotidian. The Nonconformists, creatures of a remarkable historical epoch, fetishized the mundane because, according to their democratizing creed, humans immortalized themselves through humble, humdrum acts of virtue. Heathens, they assumed, lacked the opportunity to do so since they lived, day-in and day-out, in rank, unroutinized disorder. It followed that a crucial goal of the Protestant outreach was to implant the methodical habits that produced civil, self-disciplined Christian subjects. Teaching Africa to "cultivate herself" demanded that the missions nurture the kind of everyday existence which would put the keys to the kingdom within the grasp of everyone.

Nonconformism, in sum, had at its core an every *deus-ex-machina*. Treasures were laid up on earth, as they were in heaven, by the steady accumulation of modest practical achievements. Little by little. This obsession with particulars and practicalities, with David Livingstone's "minutiae," long anticipated the preoccupations of Elias (1982), Goffman (1959), de Certeau (1984:ix), and others, who have located the logic of whole ways of life, past and present, in their mannered details. We shall have many opportunities to note the parallel between nineteenth-century Nonconformist mission methods and the concerns of twentieth-century theorists of practice. Both evince a distrust of contemplative truths, opting instead for a vision of *homo faber*, of human life as the product of instrumental action. Both display what Hannah Arendt (1958:52) termed the "modern enchantment with 'small things.'"

Neither, significantly, are unique in stressing the quotidian as *the* preeminent site of human activity. To the contrary: while seldom defined, "the everyday" appears ubiquitously across the entire range of modernist social thought. It is usually taken to be the natural habitat of the ordinary, average person—however s/he may be conceived—doing ordinary, conventional things. At the same time, though, it is invariably typified by what it is *not*, which is the first of its paradoxical qualities: the everyday is not the extraordinary or the mythic; it is not the macrocosmic or the transcendent, the philosophical or the heroic; it is not the formal and certainly not the global. For early Nonconformists, the everyday was not the eternal or the divine, although its spaces were in many ways consecrated ground. Even those late twentieth-century thinkers who see nothing much in life beyond the banal—out of existential *angst* or analytic predilection—generally use the term in relation to an absent referent: a paradise or paradigm or politics lost.

The everyday, in other words, is seen at once as integral and residual to modernity-as-lived. Like the water in which fish swim, it is the amorphous, largely unremarked medium of life itself; much like "culture" in the received anthropological sense of the term. Everywhere, it is nowhere in particular. Even those who try to give it positive shape usually situate it, by analogy to history-as-theater, in the shadows of the dramatic action, where the "extras" of the piece (*kleine Leute;* Lüdtke 1995:3) go about their unscripted tasks: in the home, on the street, at anonymous sites of labor and leisure.[42] Sometimes these players are treated as "active accomplices of history," be they barefoot protagonists or "fascism's everyday face" (Lüdtke 1995:4–5; cf. Lüdtke 1982; L. Auslander 1996). But much of their activity occurs beyond the arc lights, in the private or domestic realms, or in the netherworld of the inarticulate underclasses.[43] The quotidian is also frequently situated beneath the level of philosophical reflection or historical self-consciousness (Baudrillard 1970; cf. Brecht 1980). Lefebvre (1971:24f.; see Lave n.d.), oddly, goes as far as to oppose it (the humble, recurrent, undated) to the "modern" (brilliant, novel, transitory).

Those who seek to move the everyday to center stage, then, find themselves having to reverse figure and ground, to arrive at means for mapping the unmarked and justifying the trivial. Hence the call of the South African humanist, Njabulo Ndebele (1991:47), to "rediscover the ordinary" as an antidote to the spectacular heroics of colonial power. Or the feminist insistence that "the personal is political" (cf. L. Auslander 1996). Or de Certeau's poetic preamble to *The Practice of Everyday Life* (1984:v), which ponders the irony of freighting "the ordinary man" with a salience once reserved for gods and muses. Our own, more modest objective is less to invert the status of the everyday than to treat it as a properly proportioned part of the workings of society and history. For us, the very significance of the quotidian lies in its paradoxes, in its absent presence. It is, to repeat, the "naturalized habitat" of the modern subject. In our earlier discussion of hegemony (*RRI*:19f.), we noted that it was precisely by means of the residual, naturalized quality of habit that power takes up residence in culture, insinuating itself, apparently without agency, in the texture of a life-world. This, we believe, is why recasting mundane, routine practices has been so vital to all manner of social reformers, colonial missionaries among them.

This last point, the extraordinary place of the ordinary in colonial evangelism, is crucial here. The everyday was the privileged terrain of the missionary movement because it brought the Protestant ethic in line with the spirit of capitalism; because, as Taylor (1989:211) reminds us, it was the defining feature of the culture of modernity; because, therefore, it was the taken-for-granted medium of both European civilization and salvation. In this regard the Nonconformists were right: the quotidian, as they apprehended it, had no exact counterpart in contemporary Africa. Tswana might have put much emphasis on human agency (*RRI*:142f.). But they made no thoroughgoing distinction between the sacred and the temporal, Sabbath days and workdays, the awesome and the ordinary; ancestral spirits, who lingered around home and hearth, intervened directly in the affairs of their descendants, making social being a co-production of the living and the dead. This, perhaps, is why African existence seemed to the Christians to be an ill-defined succession of events, bereft of any rational order, predictability, or seriality. Such cultural differences underscore the danger of assuming that "the everyday" (like "the domestic"; see chapter 6) means the same in all times and places. As our account will show, it played a highly specific role in the shaping, and the export, of European modernity; "modernity," itself always historically constructed, being understood here as an ideological formation in terms of which societies valorize their own practices by contrast to the specter of barbarism and other marks of negation (Comaroff and Comaroff 1993:xiif.).

Integral to the very idea of modernity, and underlying the centrality of the everyday within it, was a historically reconfigured image of, a model for, the human subject. As Taylor (1989:213f.) notes, this subject, to whom the Protestant mission was addressed, was born of a shift of moral values initiated by the Reformation: "goodness" now lay less in contemplating the Divine Order, or in questing after sacral honors, than in the fullness of "life itself." Virtue became vested in ordinary, rather than epic, words and deeds and intentions—in disciplined labor and domestic existence, in small acts of good work and service to others. The "higher" heroic pursuits, by contrast, took on the taint of presumption and vanity. This leveling was linked, Taylor (215f.) goes on, to the Protestant rejection of salvation as mediated by the church; to the triumph of a faith in redemption through personal commitment and in a calling fulfilled within the modest limits of daily existence. Nowhere was the gospel of the ordinary more piously affirmed than in the Puritan fold, which renounced ecclesiastical authority in favor of simple, accessible truths: those to be found, by anyone, in the Scriptures—or by the direct apprehension of the Lord's creation.

Out of this vision evolved the fully fledged bourgeois subject; that biologically framed, legally constituted, morally accountable, right-bearing citizen subsumed in modern European selfhood. In volume 1 we discussed the rise of this Promethean everyman (gender and irony, alike, intended). Here we pursue its production in the everyday, both at home and abroad. But we concentrate primarily on the colonial frontier, that potent space of cultural fabrication and transformation, of symbolic struggle, accommodation, fusion, and transgression; this, as we have said, was the site at which most explicit attention was paid to the process by all concerned—and it is here, therefore, that the everyman discloses himself most vividly.

We also stress, amidst all its attributes, one characteristic of the postenlightenment self that was especially vital to its place in Protestant theology, practice theory, and the history of modernity: its double life as subject and object (cf. Lüdtke 1995:6). This being was, at once, unique and faceless, a selfconscious individual and an impersonal noun defined by gender, generation, race, class, and creed; at once "somebody," a named mortal, and "anybody," the generic "man in the street." This double persona has prompted a wealth of philosophical reflection and artistic exploration. It has also had many paradoxical consequences, among them that "daily life" has come to be perceived in many Western contexts both as a fugue of distinctive biographies *and* as an affair of statistically average, aggregated human ciphers. The reconciliation of this tension, of the need for the sentient self to come to terms with its generic humanity, lay at the core of most existential discourses on the modern condition, be they spiritual or materialist, romantic or emancipatory. Thus the Protestant sense of salvation required that believers first acknowledge the inherent sinfulness of mankind, then seek personal redemption through faith and patient works. And the Puritan idea of a calling involved the pursuit of grace by subserviating selfishness to the service of the "common good" (cf. Taylor 1989:225). In a not unsimilar vein, as Heller (1984:19–20) observes, Marx thought that individuals could "transcend [their] particularity" by formulating a conscious relationship with the human species. This relationship, he held, forged an inner synthesis of what was both "singular and genetically general" about the person, a synthesis that also gave proper, "perfectly intelligible" order to "the [practices] of every-day life" (Marx 1967,1:79). Alienation was fed by particularity, by the pursuit of private wealth or self-preservation at the cost of values essential to the development of *homo sapiens* as a whole.[44]

As in the Puritan case, the Marxian drama was one of pragmatic self-construction, a process that presumed, for its context, the steady continuity of the everyday. Here, too, the latter was taken to be the time and space of ordinary things and passions, of the humdrum acts of fabrication and consumption that simultaneously produced sentient subjects and objective worlds. Note also the parallel with the Protestant idea of conversion. Anonymous heathens were reborn as named Christians when, having transcended the mortal sins of selfish, superstitious savagery, they found personal salvation in membership of a worldwide congregation of believers; thus did they become citizens of, and enter into principled relations with, a universal moral community. Like other instances of everyday epiphany, this one implied a specific attitude to the mundane material environment. It existed as the providential means for human ends that were at once substantial and transcendent, individual and collective—and were achieved by dint of good habit and the self-disciplined conduct of daily life.

As all this implies, European pragmatism had, by the early nineteenth century, been cast in the idiom of industrial capitalism, with its specific forms of wealth and value, fabrication and exchange, labor and leisure, space and time. Long before the advent of mining and manufacture in South Africa, for example, evangelists strove to instill the routines and dispositions of wage work, the pleasures of consumption, the enclosed proprieties of the domestic estate, the cleavage between the public and the private. In this respect, the world of rational production presumed two conditions: (i) a predictable context of operation, in the here-and-now, in which as much as possible was quantifiable, routinized, and susceptible to control; and (ii) human subjects who could objectify their own essence, know their "nature," sell their labor and its fruits, and buy back their humanity—with value added. Consumption as a medium of self-creation would become ever more prominent an ethical concern, in the church and beyond, as the commodity economy expanded. For commodities were personal possessions, quotidian "belongings." Commodification, wrote Marx (1967,3:830), "the personification of things and conversion of production relations into entities," was the "religion of everyday life" (cf. Godelier 1977:163). Goods, whose ownership and transaction became an elaborate moral and communicative art, an aesthetic of the ordinary, also had the capacity to make fine distinctions among persons. But, like those whom they distinguished, these objects shared certain properties. For one thing, they were bought and sold by means of currencies that enabled diverse qualities to be equated, represented, and transacted; currencies that allowed generalized standards of worth to be applied, in principle, to anything and everything. Each and every day.

The chapters below document processes of commodification in the nineteenth-century South African interior. They seek, among other things, to show how changing patterns of production, exchange, and consumption—wrought in part by the civilizing mission, in part by an expanding market in labor and goods—recast existing regimes of value and property; how they altered the construction and representation of personhood, status, and identity; how work contracts and schedules had the effect of standardizing space and time, of bureaucratizing biographies; how peoples became "populations" of "labor units," the stuff of universal measures, statistical norms, and other rationalizing frames upon which were stretched the tight-knit mesh of modernity. These were all means of colonization, of course, and *could* be taken as evidence for Foucault's post-Weberian vision of the everyday as a banal inversion of Protestant pragmatics; of the quotidian as the context in which anonymous, totalizing power pressed most potently on human persons. From this perspective, the intimate subjections of the daily round were not only an implacable instrument of global uniformity. They ensured, paradoxically, that modernity had no truly self-conscious subjects, no cognizing individuals.

But the story we tell here is *not* a narrative of remorseless subjection. It suggests that neither processes of commodification nor technologies of rationalization ever advance in so totalizing, mechanical a fashion as to make human consciousness a mere cipher of "power" or "profit."[45] To repeat what we have said before, with emphasis added: when looked at up close, the modalities of the modern turn out to be multiple, fragmentary, and cross-bred. This is the case, also, with "the" everyday. The civilizing mission to Bechuanaland—and the imperial offensive that followed—had to take hold of local ground, to displace the regimes of value and meaning established there. As it sought to do so, the mundane became an arena of complex exchanges rarely reducible to the zero-sum of domination or resistance. The landscape of the lived world was slowly reshaped in the image of colonial capitalism, it is true. However, that image was constantly ruptured and refigured, yielding half-caste currencies, playful synthetic styles, and mixed modes of production. There were indeed converts, both to the church and to the ethos of the market. Yet they were never mere mimics of their mentors.

The Tswana case gives ample evidence of de Certeau's (1984:xii) claim that the consumption of mass-produced goods and signs does not preclude their creative redeployment. At the same time, along the frontiers opened up by the colonial presence, some very ordinary actors tried to hold the line against the erosion of certain indigenous values. Battles were waged on the home front against things and habits seen to bear unwanted influences. Christian dress codes, architectural aesthetics, and domestic forms were flouted, for example, and new folk styles were crafted; despite European urgings, cows were sold only *in extremis*, the enchantments of money were ambivalently received, and syncretic currencies were devised. All of which spoke unequivocally of efforts to sustain "local authority" (de Certeau 1984:106) in the wake of the rationalizing thrust of imperial overrule. Such assertions—like the struggles surrounding the impact, late in the century, of land and labor legislation—could escalate beyond the everyday. At times they coalesced into more explicit forms of protest, and drew comment from audible national voices, such as the emerging black press and new "native" political organizations.

Which takes us back to where we started. The colonial encounter—whatever its higher motives, wherever lay its politics of grandeur—was first and foremost an epic of the ordinary. This was not just because of its radically reformist ambitions, which made it necessary to implant new hegemonies, and therefore to cultivate the quotidian. It was also because of its cultural origins in enlightenment humanism and market capitalism, which made the everyday the profane portal to self-fulfillment, even to eternity. The Nonconformists would confront African peoples committed in a very different way to life's pragmatic details, to the unending play of divinity and death in human experience. The effects of the rich ensuing dialogue on daily existence are our primary concern here. Whatever its determinations, this is a history whose grand sweeps must be sought, in the most profound of senses, through the pattern of its minutiae.

Before we begin to tell it, though, we must make one detour.

CRITICAL QUESTIONS, METHODOLOGICAL MATTERS

We knew that we were taking a risk by publishing volume 1 well in advance of this one: that we would be criticized for failing to discuss things we intended to treat later. All the more so since our narrative is not chronological or linear, but thematic; not an event history but the historical anthropology of an expansive epochal process. Despite efforts to anticipate the problem, some of our concerns proved justified. While the book was positively reviewed—with a few exceptions, to which we shall return—most of the reservations expressed stemmed from having to pronounce on a study of large scale from the vantage of its early phases. We hope that volumes 2 and 3 will serve as an adequate answer to them.

On the other hand, there are advantages to a project so extended over, and distended by, time. For one thing, it affords an opportunity to receive constructive comments and to absorb their lessons; also to rebut hostile arguments. Most of all, though, it permits us to engage questions of broader interest provoked by this study—and to ponder how our work has been tossed about by the larger intellectual and political waves buffeting the academy at the present time.

This, then, is our moment to answer back.

In responding to our interlocutors we do not seek to reply to every small quibble of fact or interpretation that has arisen. Our objective is to make (or, in a few instances, to reiterate) more general points of concept and method. Where we have been convinced by criticisms, they are assimilated, with appropriate acknowledgment, into the account to follow; it would be petty to pursue the others here.[46] Nor do we justify our theoretical position yet again in the hope of converting skeptics. It is fully laid out in the introduction to the previous volume, and is supplemented in *Ethnography and the Historical Imagination*. We can only hope that the present work will make a yet more persuasive case for it. In the Introduction to volume 1 we advised anyone uninterested in abstract conceptual argument to skip forward twenty-six pages. Likewise here: those lacking the stomach for scholarly disputation may wish to turn, still clearheaded, to the next section.

*****

Since all historical accounts are themselves situated, let us begin by restating, in a few sentences, whence we set out on this one. It was conceived, in the mid-1980s, from within sociocultural anthropology, a discipline then straining to relate its concepts and concerns to world-historical processes, both past and present; straining, also, to rethink the old antinomy between "self" and "other"—not merely by reversing its terms, but by examining how, and to what effect, modernist forms of difference came to be constructed, imaginatively and materially, in various times and places. In this, our analytic horizons were not the same as those of most social historians. Some of the latter, in fact, have seen our effort to position a detailed "local" case on such a large-scale global canvas—and to rely on unconventional (often non-narrative) methods of historical ethnography—as pure hubris; worse yet, either as a laborious statement of the obvious or as a specious pursuit of the uninterpretable. For us, and for many of those who have engaged with our work, none of this is the case. Historical ethnography at once global and local *is* worth doing, out of humility rather than hubris, precisely because it *does* call forth fresh insights, because it raises demanding questions of interpretation, determination, and possibility. It is a misapprehension of the terms of this self-imposed challenge, we believe, that lies behind some of the reactions we have received from outside sociocultural anthropology. Underneath others lurks a perception that we have transgressed territorial boundaries best left intact. Of which more in due course.

Much the same might be said of our decision to do an ethnographic history of the colonial mission itself. Again, we write from a discipline long lambasted for ignoring the impact of colonialism on "peoples without history" and vice versa; for assuming that tradition, ritual, magic are the preserve of non-Europeans; for treating Western social and cultural conventions, if they are paid any heed at all, as matters of self-evident practical reason. In this work we scrutinize the European evangelists (whites, that is, whom anthropologists are regularly accused of not studying)—their worlds, their lives, their enchantments, their everyday practices—in the same way as we scrutinize the Africans whom they set out to convert: as human beings constrained by, and seeking to navigate, the social universe in which they found themselves.[47] It is true that, in telling our story, we concentrated first on their outreach; they, after all, established the colonial mission, just as Europe colonized Africa, rather than the other way around. But we did not (*pace* Sanneh 1993:91, n. 31; see below, chapter 2, n. 132) ever imply that their project succeeded in any straightforward sense. Or that it simply determined the way in which the encounter played itself out. Or that it had the effect of robbing Africans of their "agency," that abstraction greatly underspecified, often misused, much fetishized these days by social scientists (see below).

Quite the converse: we argued, as we do in our earlier work, that the colonial evangelists were constantly diverted from their religious, cultural, political, and social objectives by African interventions of one kind or another; that European ways and means were repeatedly appropriated, refashioned, and put to their own ends by Southern Tswana. Not that the latter always *said* as much, or narrated their side of the story in reported speech. Words, as all social scientists ought to know—even if some deny the fact—make up only a small proportion of the expressive actions and interactions that fill the space of social existence. It is precisely because these actions and interactions had as palpable an impact as they did on European colonizers of all stripes that we insist on a dialectical history, a history of reciprocal determinations. Nonetheless, we do not hesitate to argue, as well, that the presence of the colonial mission (and others who came in its wake) had considerable consequences for everyday Southern Tswana life. That much is attested to by the social realities of twentieth-century southern Africa, and by the recollections of many black South Africans.

In short, history was made here—the verb is as imprecise as it is fashionable—by a wide range of parties caught up in an ongoing, evanescent flow of (often unequal) exchanges. Each defined itself and its significant others in the process; each was composed of people situated in a variety of social predicaments and possessed of their own forms of agency; each had its own intentions, constraints, and preferred expressive styles; each mobilized its own resources and modes of empowerment in seeking to act effectively in and upon a changing world. And each term in this great historical equation changed over time. We reiterate the general point because some scholars, such as Elbourne (n.d.) and du Bruyn (1994), have taken issue with us, to useful effect, over the dialectics and determinations of the processes in question; we return to consider such arguments in the Conclusion (chapter 9), where it is most appropriate to evaluate these things. Also because a historian of the new generation, Paul Landau (1995:xxii), has accused us of failing to allow the Tswana to "generate their own conflicts, and so their own history." His recent study of Christianity among Ngwato in the Bechuanaland Protectorate to the north, *The Realm of the Word*, is an interesting, imaginative work, enriched by field research.[48] It claims, by contrast to earlier work, to give voice to Tswana themselves, in particular by demonstrating how they made Christianity their own.

While we admire this study, we find in it a large measure of irony. Here, to wit, is an obviously gifted young scholar trying hard to seize the ethnographic high ground.[49] It seems that just as anthropologists retreat, chastened, from seeking to "speak for," to "give voice" to others, their colleagues from cognate disciplines come forward to assume the role. Of course, we are delighted that creative historians find our disciplinary perspectives appealing, although it would be better accompanied by a constructive dialogue about the limitations of our contrasting methods. As to whether we do justice to the fact that Tswana brought their own agendas to the colonial encounter, to the fact that they domesticated significant features of Western religion and culture, we leave it to readers of our past and present work to judge.

Just one remark, however, since it has implications for things to come. Landau (1995:215) stresses, correctly, that his study describes "a special case." The story of Ngwato Christianity, indeed of the Ngwato political past, *is* quite unique. Even more striking is the contrast between the colonization of the Bechuanaland Protectorate and that of the Southern Tswana. The former involved a light British presence, *very* indirect rule, and greater de facto autonomy for local authorities than obtained in most British "possessions"; the habitat of the latter, near the diamond fields in South Africa, assured them of much more intrusive, conflict-laden relations with Europeans, many of whom coveted their land and labor from early on. The corollary will be self-evident. The use of "a special case" from the Protectorate to generalize about "the" Tswana experience of colonialism in any of its aspects, or about their "agency," does violence to historical specificity: to the historical specificity of the reactions of *different*

Tswana to empire, depending on their social and physical situation in southern Africa; of their varied reactions to the religion, culture, and everyday practices of its bearers (see below, chapter 3). This is a point that Landau (1995:211) himself tacitly acknowledges at the end of his book, but of which he makes nothing. In taking on ethnographic perspectives, and in disputing the analyses of others, historians have to be careful to avoid the very criticism with which they have vexed anthropologists: that of not locating their work adequately in time and space. And of condemning "their" peoples to islands beyond history. Landau's sensitive account of the role of the church in the development of a culture of self-rule among the Ngwato, for example, echoes classic Africanist monographs in relegating historical processes of the long run, and of subcontinental scale, to a brief epilogue. It is here that we are told, somewhat precipitously, of the "sudden demise" of the Ngwato Kingdom. As if the process had not been gathering momentum—within *and* beyond the local scene, local politics, local agency, local interactions—for decades.[50] It is the effort to anticipate just such events, and to trace them back to the dialectics of the colonial encounter, that underlies our study—which, we are the first to concede, has its own limitations. None of us can have it all ways or say everything at once.

Or, indeed, satisfy everyone's expectation of what writing history, let alone historical anthropology, ought to be about.

That is why we do not intend to comment at length on our role in the ongoing debate over the future of African historiography, a matter which has been much discussed in South Africa.[51] There, it seems, our work is taken to be a harbinger of the dread threat of postmodernism.[52] Ironic this, as in much of American cultural anthropology—and, heaven knows, among postmodernists—it is seen as nothing of the sort. Shortly before his death, E. P. Thompson (1993:262) observed that there "are still a few ineducable positivists . . . who do not so much disagree with the findings of social historians as they wish to disallow their questions." There are not so few, apparently, who are discomforted by those which historical anthropologists insist on asking. Perhaps—for all our own desire for a positive, if not a positivist, interdisciplinarity—we are all the more of a threat *because* we come from outside; in particular, from the end of our discipline that combines interpretivism with political economy, and evinces a critical, often unorthodox view of evidence, explanation, and the object of interrogating the past. And which, all of a sudden, is being taken seriously by those who used to look to history, in its more conventional forms, for solutions to the problems of the present.

Whether or not this is so, the reaction in more orthodox South African academic circles has been predictable. It has been to discredit the challenge by suggesting that none of us damned by the "p" word have respect for "the facts." We use archives "selectively." (Is it possible, or better, to use them *un*selectively?) And we pay attention to our writing—by trying to relate the form, content, and intent of what we say—which is dismissed as the privileging of style over substance. No matter that we have gone to great lengths to situate ourselves, synthetically, amidst the crosscurrents of contemporary theory, and to spell out a principled methodological practice. No matter either, as de Kock (1994:passim) has shown with consummate skill, that the way in which we have been represented in this context often bears little connection to what we actually do. This is especially paradoxical here: the anti-postmodernist gesture has, in its hurry to discredit postmodernism by metonymy, managed to prove one of its central claims: that authors are little more than a text written by their place in a discourse, not vice versa. For our own part, we still sustain the all too modernist hope that one day the work will be read in those circles with a close, not a closed, eye; with a view to its substance, not what it is held to stand for.

It is not only in South African anti-postmodern circles that we have provoked strong reactions. A yet more extreme one has come, for similar reasons, from an influential North American quarter: the senior Africanist historian Jan Vansina (1993:417f.). His is to be found in an ill-tempered review not of volume 1, but of *Ethnography and the Historical Imagination*, which he takes as exemplary of all our work. This he suggests is too dangerous, too misleading, to serve as a textbook for undergraduates. (*Pace* Vansina it was never intended as such.)[53] Even graduate students, he hints broadly, should be kept away from it. Only those "firmly grounded in their craft" ought to expose themselves to this work—and then purely to get a glimpse of what those exotics, "'fashionable' anthropologists from the Chicago school," do (pp. 419–20).

Let us take up this review briefly. We do so not just to reply to it—though that would be hard to resist—but with two substantive ends in mind. The first is to lay bare the way in which many positivist social scientists, in African Studies and elsewhere, continue to deal with post-positivist approaches; the second is to establish the ground for a constructive exchange with other interlocutors on the recuperation and interpretation of historical consciousness, especially when it is not expressed in words.

The review itself is notable for many things, not least the number of factual errors Vansina makes in excoriating us for a lack of respect for facts, archival and ethnographic; so many, indeed, that it gives cause for concern about at least one historian's craft.[54] And motives. But the logic underlying the critique is more interesting. It is based, implicitly, on a syllogism: "historical imagination" is "the rallying cry of postmodernists." Hayden White (1973) says that the "historical imagination" should not be fettered by evidence; we are postmodernists; hence we have no use for evidence. The mere (dare we say it?) fact that we argue the opposite is ignored. For an empiricist who, as we shall see, admonishes others to listen carefully to the natives, and to place their own interpretation of their actions above all else, this is hardly consistent practice. That our stated motive was to distance ourselves, in both theory and method, from what he takes to be postmodernism also is paid no attention. But then it is not clear that Vansina actually understands the theoretical issues involved,[55] as he seems to believe that postmodernism and neomodernism are the same thing. And to think—which would be a nice comic touch, if this fact-free diatribe were not so grimly serious—that a tough-minded, vocally *anti*-postmodern structuralist, Marshall Sahlins, co-founded the Chicago School of "postmodern (or 'neomodern') . . . 'historical anthropology'" (see n. 54).

This last is a particularly curious beast, since it does not exist. We should know: by Vansina's account, we are members (1994:295, n. 97). Natives. Whom he did not ask. Nor even read, since the two page references from *Ethnography and the Historical Imagination* given in support of the existence of this group mention nothing of the sort. Nothing. They are, bluntly, false citations.[56] Could it be that, for Vansina, listening to the natives may sometimes be a problem? Such as when, as one might infer from Werbner's (n.d.) acute review of his *Living with Africa* (1994), he is pursuing a political agenda? Then, it seems, respect for the evidence evaporates into so much hot air. For our own part, we would prefer to believe that Vansina's objectives were more noble: that this was merely another effort—misguided, perhaps, but well-intended—to warn his discipline, which he sees to be in transition, against the "great dangers of failure" that threaten an otherwise promising future (1994:221).

But that would be stretching credulity gossamer thin. For, more serious than any of this—and worth more attention than the insults handed out when one scholar decides that another should have written a different book[57]—is the attack by Vansina on interpretation itself. This is a matter that runs to the core of all historical anthropology done in the cultural mode and in a critical spirit, and anticipates our conversation with other critics as well. The argument here is straightforward, and a very old one indeed: that it is illegitimate to attribute "one's own interpretations, rather than those of the historical agents (or actors), to the phenomena observed." The "rather" here is misleading, of course. Only a very naive anthropologist does *not* include native exegesis, if it is recoverable, in her or his analysis. As Victor Turner pointed out years ago, it is a necessary aspect of any ethnography. But only a naive literalist would assume that it, in itself, gives a sufficient account of anything whatsoever. It is one version, one register, a datum which, far from explaining anything, has itself to be explained.

In castigating us for the sin of interpretation, Vansina takes one example from our work. It concerns a mute "madman" whom we encountered at a mental hospital outside Mafikeng, where we spent a great deal of time working in 1970 (see n. 54).[58] We describe his costume in detail, and then offer a symbolic analysis, showing how his attire composed an aesthetic commentary on the brute lineaments of the world according to apartheid. This, it is declared, was too "theoretically laden." A more plausible interpretation—by whose lights?—would have been there for the taking had we only asked the man himself and other locals what this uniform meant. (For the record, we say clearly that he chose to say nothing at all to anyone; he was famous for being mute. Asking him, therefore, would have produced a crashing silence. And we did speak at length to others, whose reactions are reported; page 173.) He wore a pair of miner's boots, a bishop's miter, and a sash with the letters "SAR" (for "South African Railways"): could it not be, Vansina asks, that he donned the boots simply because, like other ex-miners, he had them, and because they were "sturdy"? And are not SAR sashes used by company employees? In sum, was this not all about practical reason rather than cultural poetics? Whether his guesses are correct or wrong, adds Vansina, does not matter. "What matters is that the authors just threw their own interpretation unto the situation and left it at that."

Well, no, actually. It matters greatly whether "guesses" are correct or not. And how one arrives at them. Vansina is right about one thing, though: his *are* wrong. They are wrong, moreover, because, given his disinterest in and disregard for anthropological methods, he caricatures the ethnography—of which the miner's boots and the sash were but two elements, not the whole by any means—in order to disparage it. And to pretend that a simpler, more credible account was there if only we had looked with the eyes of a plainspoken empiricist (which, of course, is always easy if data are robbed of their contextual meaning, their "thickness"). In fact, all the information for a proper analysis is in the piece, available to anyone who reads it with care; it is obvious from our description of his costume, for instance, that the carefully stitched ceremonial sash and bishop's miter were hardly regulation handouts to black employees of the South African Railways. But, having blinded himself to the subtlety of a subtle symbolic act in the name of commonsensical simplicity, itself a profoundly pejorative gesture, Vansina chooses to pronounce our ethnography "bad."

As we have said, however, the attack is on interpretation itself; specifically, on the interpretation of less articulate forms of consciousness, forms that leave few textual traces. Which is why we have set upon such a small nut with such a large sledgehammer. Here, though, we change our interlocutor, and enter an altogether more serious dialogue with John Peel (1992, 1995) and Terence Ranger (n.d.[a]; n.d.[b]). These two scholars have also argued with us, if in different ways—the latter with greater reason and generosity, the former with greater passion and rhetorical bravura—about narrative, consciousness, agency, and the recuperation of the past; Peel (1992:328f.), in addition, questions the role we accord religion in our account, but that matter is dealt with substantively in chapter 2.[59] It is the more general argument which we address here, as it runs to some of the core problems of method in both anthropology and history.

Peel and Ranger challenge us on four grounds.[60] First, they allege, we are wrong to claim that Southern Tswana, in the precolonial and colonial periods, chose *not* to express their historical consciousness primarily in narrative form (or, more accurately, that they chose to express it in a wide range of other media, practices, and dispositions). Second, that by "denying" the Tswana "narrativity," we silence their voices and remove their agency, thus to authorize our own re-presentation of them and their history. Third, contrary to our opinion, narrative is indispensable in the articulation of historical (and, presumably, other forms of) consciousness; for Peel (1995:606–7), "narrative-as-lived"—life as text?—*demands* that there be "narrative-as-told." And, fourth (this from Ranger) that, by taking the postmodern view that narrative is inherently oppressive, we miss its liberatory potential; i.e., its capacity to empower those who seize it, whatever its provenance, for their own ends.

Before we address these points, let us be clear what we did say. For one thing, we did not suggest that Southern Tswana lacked a *capacity* for narrative—simply that, given the rich repertoire of media at their disposal, it was one that, *as a marked and specialized genre*, they seldom chose to use spontaneously, save in response to question or challenge. Nor did we ever imply that, historiographically speaking, "narrativity" was insignificant. To be sure, here as elsewhere, we squeeze everything we can out of the indigenous record, spoken and written. In short, ours was anything but a discourse of deficit. Notwithstanding Peel's grudging admission—"[The Comaroffs] do not deny the Tswana *some* form of historical consciousness"—we state, unequivocally, that they had it aplenty. It was by cultural proclivity, not by absence of choice, that they opted for genres distinctly non-Eurocentric. This generalization, we have noted, excluded Christian elites, which were to produce their fair share of carefully crafted narratives; although they, too, did not always resort to the latter to conjure with the past. From late last century onwards, those elites were also to spawn their own literati; their writings are quoted a great deal in the text below—as soon, in fact, as it becomes possible to do so. (Volume 1, recall, was about early encounters, about a period before cadres of literate Southern Tswana had arisen.)

At the risk of repetition: in speaking of the role of narrative in historical consciousness—it was in this *specific* respect that we said what we did, not in respect of all cultural expression—we had a restricted sense of the term in mind. Borrowing from our colleagues in anthropological linguistics, we understood it to denote a particular genre of storytelling and history-making: one in which past events are condensed into linear, realist accounts that make claims to authority and public currency, impute cause and agency, and so assert their own truth value. Admittedly, we did not offer an explicit definition. For a scholarly audience, we thought it would be didactic to do so. We certainly did not expect Peel or Ranger to take this quasi-technical usage to mean more or less anything "told" and, hence, to ascribe to us a position that we never intended; an absurd position according to which Southern Tswana could have no conventions of rapportage. Of the differences, more later.

Back, then, to the four grounds of critique. Were we actually mistaken, as charged, in claiming that Southern Tswana did not rely on narrative to give voice to their historical consciousness? Were they, as Peel (1995:586f.) implies they must have been, possessed of much greater "narrativity" than we allow? Did we really suggest that they lacked their own vernacular traditions of recounting the past? Between them, Peel and Ranger offer, as support for their skepticism, an odd mix of speculation and inference. Most convincing, at face value, is Ranger's comparative account of "narrativity," indeed a great deal of it, elsewhere in indigenous South Africa. If others all around have it, why not Southern Tswana?

Trouble is, though, that the exemplary cases on which Ranger draws, primarily the Khoi and Ndebele, shared neither a culture nor a language with Southern Tswana. And their historical predicaments were very different. On its own, rough geographical proximity is hardly a basis on which to pin the likelihood of shared expressive styles; were the same argument applied to Europe it would be regarded as ridiculous. Tellingly, when Ranger (n.d.[a]:13f.) comes to the Sotho, culturally the closest situation to ours, the evidence he gives of narrativity is the recitation of *lifela*. But this is a *poetic* genre, one in which laborers recount their lives and scenes in highly allegorical, non-linear, idiomatic terms. Its compositional form is owed largely to *likhoto*, epic praise poems—and is similar to that of the migrant poetics and royal praises which, as we have often noted, were also central to Southern Tswana evocations of the past. If *this* is narrative, so is anything uttered aloud: a Christian hymn, a Sotho initiation song, a Shakespearian sonnet, a children's nursery rhyme, a panegyric to a Tswana cow (see chapter 4). But it is not. It is the very opposite. In referring to a "*lifela* narrative," however, Ranger seems not to see the oxymoron.

In sum, the comparative argument simply does not bear scrutiny—in general or in its ethnographic specifics.[61] As Peel (1995:586, n. 21) should know, being an anthropologist, cultural forms are as likely to differentiate neighboring peoples as they are to be shared among them. An Africanist, he must be aware, for example, that Tswana practiced close agnatic (sometimes half-sibling) marriage, a form of endogamy not found anywhere close by, or much at all in sub-Saharan Africa (Comaroff and Roberts 1981:30f.); Radcliffe-Brown (1950:69), in fact, adjudged them "decidedly exceptional," even "an [anthropological] anomaly" (cf. also the singular form of mother's brother's daughter union found among Lovedu; A. Kuper 1975). If this is true of marriage—a fundamental cultural arrangement on which hinged all social reproduction—why not of expressive forms? So much for that argument.

For his part, Peel (1995:586f.) intimates that there really *is* substantive evidence for the "narrativity" we "deny" Tswana, evidence we "simply ignore."[62] He fails to mention that we were not alone in our perception. In all his work on Tswana history and society, Isaac Schapera, a gifted and tireless ethnographer if there ever was one, rarely writes of a historical narrative, of a full-blown annal or a kingly chronicle. Why? Did he miss them as well? Are his ethnohistories as fragmentary as they are because he, too, "simply ignored" the tales people had to tell? Is it not striking that, the moment he *does* adduce such stories, they come from those long exposed to Christianity? (As is the case, also, with Paul Landau's study [1995] of "the realm of the Word.") In volumes like *Tribal Innovators* (cited by Peel 1995, n. 26), Schapera lists chiefly acts and achievements elicited by asking old men; conspicuously, little of his material is derived from elaborated accounts of the past. Why not? Because his long-standing informants—who had made him privy to some very intimate things before (see 1940a)—deliberately withheld them? Many others, outsiders *and* insiders (see below), have drawn a similar blank. Are they all guilty of "denying" Tswana "narrativity," of failing to spot an indigenous narrative tradition? As it happens, Schapera (1965) has published a sumptuous collection of ethnohistories. But they exist in the form of praise poetry, a genre of great semantic and aesthetic richness. Interestingly, their beauty is held to lie partly in their language (page 23), partly in being "full of history" (page 15). Like Sotho *likhoto,* they are highly allegorical.

What is it, then, that Peel offers as counter-evidence? Not a lot, as it turns out. More a series of insinuations and leading questions:

> Are we really to accept that a "loquacious news-telling people," as the Reverend John Mackenzie called the Tswana, were strangers to narrative or that their politics of chieftaincy did not occasion arguments that turned on narratives of descent and succession? . . . [63] Did the first literate historians have no prior local narrative traditions to work from? In so far as the . . . case for the lack of Tswana narrative derives from its absence from "the nineteenth-century sources," it is a notoriously weak kind of historical reasoning, the *argumentum ex silentio;* and it is made weaker by the fact that the sources were largely those same missionaries . . .

Let us look at this purported counter-evidence. Take, for example, John Mackenzie's mention of the Tswana penchant for news-telling. Peel does not add that the Nonconformists often observed how, despite this interest in the intelligence of the moment, it was usually passed on in fragmentary, non-linear bits; how hard they found it ever to get a "straight story." Clearly he did not read Mackenzie, save in our text. If he had, he would have come across a reported exchange (1871:408) between the missionary and the Ngwato chief, who says, in conversation: "[W]hen a black man tells a story, he goes round and round. . . . [W]hen you open your mouth your tale proceeds like a straight line." But clues of this kind, here to an *indigenous* perspective on cultural differences in storytelling, fall outside Peel's purview. Neither are these the only clues in the documentary record.[64] At the conceptual level, though, there is a yet more basic point to be made: the recounting of news and the narrative representation of history are *not* the same thing. It hardly takes a literary theorist, or an anthropologist who would be a historian, to see the contrast—in tense, composition, intent and content—between them.

Nor ought anyone to have difficulty in telling apart historical narrative from so-called "narratives of descent or succession." What the latter refers to, of course, are *genealogies.* These, it is true, did play an important role in Tswana politics (J. L. Comaroff 1978). They served as a language of claims to position and authority; and, in articulating relations around officeholders, they communicated public information about the personnel in chiefly regimes—not unlike a party list in contemporary electoral systems based on proportional representation. As an expressive genre, however, genealogy is far from "narratological." It involves the recitation of names, implicitly positing kinship ties between them, *sans* allusion to events or actions. In the Old Testament, in fact, genealogical reckonings, signaled by the verb "begat," typically *interrupt* narrative. Clearly, whatever else it is, genealogy is not a *narrative* of descent or succession, save perhaps in the most unspecific sense of the term.

But what of Peel's other line of questioning? The one about early Southern Tswana literati and historians. Did they really have no prior narrative traditions on which to draw in their writings? The three who come most obviously to mind, since they are the best known, are Sol Plaatje, Modiri Molema, and Z. K. Matthews, all of whom belonged to an assertive Protestant elite of the kind Peel pays much attention to in his own Nigerian work. None of them, as it turns out, would have agreed with him. Molema (e.g., 1951:181–90), for one, went on at length about the absence, before the coming of Christianity, of anything that might be described as an indigenous narrative tradition, complaining also about the "mangled and corrupted" way in which "information" about "practices, usages, customs," and the like had been passed down the generations (pp. 189–90).[65] Had Peel familiarized himself with the writings of these men before invoking them, he might have come across such narratives about the "lack of narrativity." Perhaps he would have learned another lesson: that, having preached the gospel according to "native" voices, one cannot then ignore them.

He might also have been struck by the fact that, when Plaatje (1957) wrote the first black South African novel, *Mhudi,* it bore no vernacular imprint. (Nor did his later literary work, much of it journalism and translations of Shakespeare.)[66] Quite the opposite, says Stephen Gray (1993:8), he "spell[ed] out his message loud and clear in the language and in the form of the oppressor," a point made by Plaatje himself in the preface to the first edition. On the specific matter of "narrativity," moreover, he recalls, in the same place, that "by the merest accident, while collecting *stray scraps* of [Tswana] tribal history," he heard "*incidentally*" of some of the events at the core of the story; these he then had to take pains to "*elicit*" (our italics; S. Gray 1993:10). The events in question were not trivial: they involved the most traumatic war in Barolong memory. If these

Southern Tswana were prone to condensing their past in formal narratives, why would their most adept social commentator—a man who, working in his own tongue, spent years documenting their cultural knowledge—have had to rely on "stray scraps," often extracted by dint of sustained questioning?

This brings us to the alleged "weakness" of what Peel (1995) has decided is our *argumentum ex silentio*. In plain English: our claims about Tswana "narrativity" are flawed because they are based on a silence in the nineteenth-century sources; sources, in any case, not disposed to allow Africans their own history. We find the allegation specious. In the first place, as we have said, we focus throughout our work on what Southern Tswana had, on what they chose to do, not on what they lacked. And we offer abundant evidence, from archives of all kinds, of ways in which they spoke for themselves and argued with their white interlocutors. *Both* verbally and nonverbally. All the talk of absence and deficit is purely a figment of Peel's highly ethnocentric assumption that Tswana *ought* to have "had narrative" in a form recognizable to a late modern European sensibility; that, unless people communicate in this genre, they do not represent themselves; that other expressive media somehow do not count, are somehow lesser. (This, in turn, arises from confusing the truism that all humans have a capacity to narrate with the altogether more tenuous idea that all cultures privilege narrative.) It is only when this assumption is made that those who do not conform may be said to be wanting. Bluntly, then, it is not *we* who "reason" from the principle of *silencio*. It is he who—having decided what must have existed, and hence what the documentary record must hide—ascribes it to us.

And so we move on to the second major line of critique aimed at us by Peel and Ranger: that, by "denying" Tswana "narrativity," and by "bestowing it abundantly on the missionaries" (Ranger n.d.[b]:10), we rob the Africans of their voice and agency, thereby authorizing ourselves to represent them (cf. du Bruyn 1994). What we really do, says Ranger, is to document "the Tswana incapacity effectively to resist or to counter missionary cultural hegemony."

This critique is perplexing. For a start, it disregards our account of the failure of the evangelists to convert Southern Tswana or to remake them in their own image; also our account of the complex struggles set in motion by the effort to implant bourgeois European signs and practices on African soil. Our one mantra, repeated over and over, was that some Tswana responded to the civilizing mission by actively assimilating its ways and means; others by rejecting them entirely; and yet others by selectively appropriating them to their own ends, often amidst contestation and resistance. The point seems to have been perfectly well understood by most of those who reviewed volume 1. Many commented, usually positively, on the degree to which African agency featured in the study and, more generally, on the way in which the *dialectics* of the encounter were treated (see, e.g., Petersen 1992:21).

What is of greater import, however, is the fact that the critique is itself founded on two shaky theoretical assumptions. One is that *agency* may be equated with *voice*. This is a dangerous reduction. It is also—curiously, in light of the kinds of history which Ranger and Peel prefer—reminiscent of a brand of postmodernism that distills all social life into either talk or text. As we understand the term, following both Marx and Weber, "agency" does not translate as just anything people do or say. If it did, it would have no analytic specificity. Rather, it refers to meaningful activity: activity to which intention may be ascribed before or after the event; which has consequences, intended or otherwise; which may be articulate or inarticulate, poetic or prosaic, verbal or visual or sensual. As this implies, it has many modalities. To privilege one in writing the past is unfortunate; to privilege the one that has long enjoyed preeminent value in bourgeois Western thought (Mitchell 1986)—narrating in the realist mode—is simultaneously Eurocentric and profoundly elitist. It goes without saying that the production and circulation of narratives, especially publicly recognized ones, is not the prerogative of all persons alike; that the capacity to give voice and to be heard follows the disproportions of social power. That much has well established by revisionist histories of various sorts—part of whose *raison d'être*, remember, was to move away from the exclusionary, silencing tendencies of older paradigms, paradigms alas not yet lost. In this day and age, do we still have to remind ourselves that many of the players on any historical stage cannot speak at all? Or, under greater or lesser duress, opt not to do so? Surely, then, it is imprudent to assume that their "narratives-as-lived," Peel's (1995) unfortunate term for the unarticulated actions of everyday life, demand also "narratives-as-told" in order to have meaning.

The second dubious assumption is that there is such a thing as "African" or "European" agency, in the singular. Plainly put, this is a romance that reduces history to fiction. All Africans (plural) and Europeans (plural), past and present, speak and act. But, over time, they have done so variously according to their gender and age, their class and culture, their ideologies and idiosyncrasies, the (forms of) power they wield and the constraints they face. The point is to recuperate these patterns of variance—not to talk about "agency" in overgeneralized, vacuous, monologic terms but to trace out its specificities and multiplicities, its determinacies and indeterminacies.

We stress this, as it also lies at the heart of a current—in our view, misguided—debate about African Christianity. Some historians have taken to arguing that, far from being colonized by Protestantism or Catholicism, Africans seized these faiths and made them their own; that Christianity, never simply a "European" religion, was easily and comprehensively domesticated by them. This thesis lies behind the work of Sanneh (1993) and Landau (1995). It bears a resemblance to that species of neorevisionism which denies that Africans were ever victims of colonialism; that "African agency" ensured the appropriation of all European initiatives to local ends. Ironic this, as many black South Africans have written—either in celebration (e.g., Molema 1920:passim, 1951:181f.; Plaatje n.d.) or in reproach (Mphahlele 1962:192; *RRI*:4)—of the efficacy of Christianity in invading indigenous hearts and minds; but, as we have said, scholars sometimes shun "native" voices when they do not say what we prefer to hear.

Our point, though, is more fundamental. The reduction of the story of African Christianity to one of "native" appropriation alone is at once a mystification and a compression; one which, no less than the alternative that reads the story as a tale of unremitting domination, denudes history of its dialectics. The encounter between the mission and Southern Tswana, again, did not involve a monologic, undifferentiated quantum of indigenous agency. As we show in chapter 2, and have argued elsewhere (J. Comaroff 1985), some Protestant ideas and practices were actively taken up, in a range of *different* ways, by Africans placed variously across the social and political landscape; others insinuated themselves, influentially yet unnoticed, into *setswana*. To collapse this mutually determining, non-linear process to the terms of a linear equation, under the political chic-speak of appropriation and agency, belies and belittles its sheer complexity.

But how are we to reply to the *substance* of Peel's (1995:587f.) claim that, by virtue of our analytic practice, we deny Tswana all agency in their own history, thus to authorize ourselves to represent it? Listen first to the basis of his case. Narrative, he says

> empowers because it enables its possessor to integrate his [sic] memories, experiences, and aspirations in a schema of long-term action. The more potent narratives have the capacity to incorporate other agents, so that they become accessories to the authors of the narratives. To the extent that . . . narrative cannot be achieved, agency or self-motivated action— the hinge between the past of memory and the future of aspiration— becomes impossible.

Not a very clear statement this. It presumes, remarkably, that narratives empower human beings rather than the other way around; or, better yet, that humans and their narratives are reciprocally entailed in processes of empowerment and disempowerment. More immediately, though, to prove that we render Tswana impotent by "denying" them "narrativity"—that phrase again—Peel returns to the "madman" who so vexed Vansina. And he offers a disingenuous syllogism: (i) inasmuch as we (1987:191f.) claim to have learned our "most profound lesson about [historical] consciousness in rural South Africa"—i.e. about the possibility of its expression by non-narrative means—from a wordless encounter with this person, (ii) we elevate him to a "kind of paradigm" that (iii) "invites us to regard the Tswana as patients rather than agents in their history," Adds Peel, "the poor madman"—his patronization, not ours—"was, indeed, literally a patient." What he omits, irresponsibly, is the fact, specifically stated in the same essay, that the man was also a prophet and a healer with a large following; that his madness was a clinical definition imposed upon him by his white custodians; that he offered a compelling set of signs by means of which his compatriots, by their own account, could extend their understanding of the world around them. Peel also neglects to note that, in our account of the historical consciousness of older Southern Tswana males at the time—the analysis was painstakingly located in space and time—this character was juxtaposed to a second (see n. 39): a migrant laborer who expressed verbally, in another genre entirely, a different sense of the prospects that faced men of his ilk in apartheid South Africa. Neither madman nor migrant was "paradigmatic"; together they represented a grammar of possibility in reading the relationship between the past and the present, the here and there.

Why does Peel, usually a careful scholar, caricature our project? The answer, perhaps, lies in the final piece of his argument. Any (historical) ethnography that privileges dispositions over propositions, symbolic action over narration, lived culture over the spoken word, he suggests, "allows the anthropological object to be constituted" by the anthropologist, whose role as "gatekeeper to outside intelligibility is magnified" (p. 588). To the degree that "natives" do not tell their own story, it is the s/he who arrogates the right to represent them. Just as the evangelists did once upon a time. And so, indirectly, we become apologists for the colonial mission, on whose texts we primarily rely. But we also do the latter a disservice. Because the evangelists talk too unambiguously to have their own voices "denied" (yes, that once more)—the implication being that we would if we could—we engage in another kind of "scamping" (p. 589): we read their narratives for form rather than content. Unremarked here is the fact that detailed theoretical consideration is given to the relationship between form and content; that *all* actions, verbal and nonverbal, are read for *both;* that non-narrative materials are used in interpreting actions on every side of the colonial encounter. Peel, it seems, would have us attend only to substance. Why? So that the ideological message of the Protestants is heard without analytic intervention? In any case, we find it odd to be accused (i) of being complicit in the colonizing mission by privileging the accounts of the Europeans over those of Tswana *and* (ii) of not paying heed to what they said. But so be it.

We acknowledge all the problems of representation, of positioning and voice, involved in writing history and historical anthropology. We like to think, as de Kock (1992:260f, 1994) says, that both volume 1 and *Ethnography and the Historical Imagination* confront them head-on. However, Peel's intention is not to discuss these problems. It is to make the extraordinary assertion that histories based on narrative do not need decoding, or interpretation, in the same way as do those based on non-narrative sources (p. 588). To believe that any account is ever actually based on either narrative or non-narrative material alone is naive.

But to hold that the spoken word does not require interpretation in the same manner as any other form of cultural practice is quite breathtaking. As Paul Landau remarks,[67] underlining an old point made in college historiography courses, "People in works of history do not speak for themselves. Even if their voices are heard." And he asks a question that Peel might well ponder: "Is this," the suggestion that they do talk for themselves, simply a furtive "justification for a masterly narrative style?"

Is it even necessary to make the point? The reliance on narratives—which the historian selects and edits, which are not distributed uniformly across social space—is no less a gesture of representation than is any other kind of ethnographic reportage. Neither speech acts nor written texts are transparent in themselves. They do not reach readers without authorial intervention. Just as they were, or are, produced with intent, so they rarely come to the anthropologist or historian purely by accident; all recuperations of the past entail a collaboration of sorts. The question is *who* is heard, *how* they are listened to and represented. And to what end.

A similar comment was made, indirectly, during a recent internet discussion. Sparked by Ranger's (n.d.[b]) plea for a "return to narrative" in African history, it applies as well to Peel's intervention.[68] Offered Chris Lowe, "[R]ecall the reasons for the social historical turn in the first place: that there are many people in the past whose surviving traces don't lend themselves easily to stories of individual lives or events." Lowe clearly saw the tension between a call to narrative and a commitment to recuperate the agency of the inarticulate, of ordinary people, of the disempowered. He preferred, he said, to "define the issue as one of humanistic history—i.e. history which engages our human sensibilities and our imaginative capacities for . . . empathy with people in the past." We could not agree more. It is, as we implied, a short step from the stress on narrative to the history of elites, thence to elitist history. After all, few of us have at our disposal the bounty of private papers that Ranger (1995) had in writing his sensitive account of the powerful Samkange family in Zimbabwe; many of us are concerned with periods and places in which African narratives are no longer recoverable, even if they once existed;[69] not all of us work among peoples who, like Yoruba, have a culturally marked narrative tradition; only some of us choose to focus our gaze on *petit-bourgeois* and bourgeois Christian elites or church leaders. And none of us ought to use "narrative" as loosely, *sans* conceptualization or specification, as Ranger and Peel have done. Indeed, in our opinion, much of the argument arises from this: from the ill-defined contention that, because people everywhere have the capacity to narrate, narrative, as a marked medium, is universal. Not only does the very idea fly in the face of a good deal of anthropological evidence.[70] It is also founded on a palpable slippage between verb and noun, between commonsensical usage and a technical genre term. The moment, as we intimated above, that "narrative" becomes a synonym for any kind of telling, for almost any speech act or text, it becomes meaningless. For our own part, the point seems very simple really. Whether or not we write about it, Southern Tswana "have" a history. It is one that was made partly by them and partly for them, in complex proportions and through various forms of agency. It is a history, gratefully, that will long survive the arguments of white academics. Nobody can "deny" it to them, whether s/he wanted to or not. No scholar, least of all us, has that kind of authority. In this respect, we have never pretended to speak for Southern Tswana nor to represent them, whatever that could mean in the fraught political world of South Africa, past or present. They, plurally and heterogeneously, have always spoken for themselves, if not necessarily in the medium of John Peel's choosing. At times powerfully and articulately, at times by letting silence talk for itself. At times in the active voice, at times in the passive, at times by their embodied practices. We merely seek to understand their past as best we can—so that we may better understand colonialism and its aftermath, *tout court*. Others have done the same, and will continue to do so. In our own efforts, we seek not to simplify agency by rendering it singular or ethnic. Nor to fetishize voice, insisting instead that it takes many guises, *all* of which warrant attention.

It is for these reasons that we are assertively catholic in our methodological approach, seeking to capture the broadest possible spectrum of signifying practices in any lived world. Whether or not narratives, of any kind, happen to be significant in that world is an empirical question. Among the Yoruba and in much of twentieth-century Zimbabwe they clearly are. In other places and periods they are less so. When they are significant, they are not to be "scamped." As this suggests, we do not, as Peel and Ranger contend, evince a particularly postmodern suspicion of narrative per se. Quite the reverse. It is they who are, unwittingly, caught up in the effects of the culture of postmodernity. As David Atwell has put it: "You know you're in it [postmodernity] when narrative becomes the *sine qua non* of public culture."[71]

Nor do we see it everywhere, to reflect one of Ranger's (n.d.[a]) anxieties, as a tool of oppression. It may be that. It may also be an instrument of liberation. It can be mobilized in the cause of either—and of both at once. Or it may merely be a medium of self-discovery, self-expression, or self-delusion. But wherever it occurs, it *demands* interpretation. To be sure, all historical anthropology, all history, remains an interpretive art. So we interpret. Without pretending otherwise. Least of all, without pretending to be the conduits of other people's voices. And, yes, in doing so, we *do* read texts, especially those of the colonial in South Africa, "against the grain," trying not only to comprehend their motivation and their meaning but also how others speak through them— not to mention the social conditions that gave rise to them. Inevitably, their authors reveal more than they intended, giving glimpses not only of their own unspoken concerns, but also into the ways in which their African interlocutors engaged with them. We take this to be a self-evident procedure, fundamental to a critical reading of any text.

In this regard, we admit freely that our problem remains intractable. We simply do not have the kind of documentary record we should like, the kind in which many articulate voices course through time equally, leaving their echoes in profusion. Often we have no alternative but to work with a highly distorted, disproportionate documentary record. And so we have to make our own archive by disinterring Southern Tswana gestures and acts and utterances from the writings of non-Tswana; in particular, by reading these orthogonally and against each other. But we do not stop there either. We also look to whatever vernacular traces have been left on the landscape, whether they be narrative fragments or private correspondence, praise poetry or buildings, ritual practices or Tswana-authored history books; indeed any of manifold signs and artifacts that make their appearance in the three volumes that compose this study. In the final analysis, however, like all historians and historical anthropologists, we are confined by the evidence available to us. For this we make no apologies. Out of it we make the best we can.

SYNAPSES, SYNOPSIS

And so we pick up our story, moving on from its early phases to processes of the longer run; processes which, as we follow them toward the present in each chapter, take in ever more players and places, facets and forces. Its most prominent *dramatis personae*, like its primary conceptual themes, were introduced in the last volume. They remain the same, as does our qualification that their identities as historical actors were themselves shaped by the colonial encounter: (i) Southern Tswana, an ensemble of peoples living in what is now the North West and Northern Cape Provinces of South Africa (formerly, more or less, British Bechuanaland), and composed of the various Tlhaping, Rolong, and Tlharo polities; (ii) deeper into the interior, and secondary to our narrative, the Tswana inhabitants of present-day Botswana (once the Bechuanaland Protectorate), especially Ngwaketse, Kwena, Kgatla and the Ngwato; (iii) straddling the geopolitical and social space between Southern Tswana and the Cape Colony to the south, peoples variously dubbed Khoi, San, Griqua, and Kora, peoples themselves caught up in a complex colonial history and in ongoing political flux; (iv) emissaries of the London Missionary Society (LMS) and Wesleyan Methodist Missionary Society (WMMS), most of them from lower middle-class backgrounds in Scotland and northern England; and (v) other Europeans of the frontier. This last category grew ever more varied over time. It included the Boer settlers of the Transvaal and Orange Free State and, later, freebooters along the Bechuanaland borders; merchants, some of whom settled in Tswana communities; explorers, travelers, and "sportsmen"; and, after the discovery of diamonds in the late 1860s, capitalists, prospectors, labor recruiters, and urban traders brought into the South African heartland by the mineral revolution; with the coming of the colonial state, government functionaries and military men.

The terrain on which these people encountered one another was itself to undergo visible change over the course of the twentieth century. Although early European visitors sometimes described it as "wilderness," even as empty, it was hardly that. A mix of grassland and scrub, broken by trees, this landscape was relatively flat, its undulations interrupted only occasionally by hills, rock formations, and riverbeds, most of them dry for the best part of the year. A region of (often sparse) summer rainfall and dry winters, its eastern reaches supported viable agricultural and pastoral economies on bountiful red earth. To the west it became more parched, its soils sandy and porous, as it extended toward the Kalahari Desert and, southward, toward the Karroo, an arid plateau where only the hardiest of small stock survived. Indeed, as rainfall decreased in these directions, cultivation became concomitantly fragile, making animal husbandry the most reliable source of livelihood; everywhere the domestic economy was supplemented by the fruits of the wild and, until the game population was decimated, by hunting.

The Southern Tswana chiefdoms imposed themselves forcefully upon this ecology, their territories dominated by the large capitals that arose in the eighteenth and nineteenth centuries. These densely populated centers, some with thousands of residents, were surrounded by arable fields and cattle posts, typically interspersed with surface water sources; a few had outlying villages. The polity stretched as far as its chief and his followers could pasture and protect their stock. In the spaces between chiefdoms were tracts of "bush," broken in some places by small, scattered communities that, for one or another reason, were not part of centralized *merafe* ("nations"). The terrain was cross-cut by pathways that linked the capitals, serving as vectors of trade and alliance and, sometimes, of warfare and raiding. These pathways also bore goods and cultural knowledge over long-distance exchange routes.

With the arrival of ever more European settlers from the late 1830s onwards, and with the steady expropriation of Southern Tswana land, the region became increasingly populated, increasingly contested. White farms, trading posts, and villages began to dot the countryside. Along with the missions and their outstations—themselves augmented by schools, shops, and other structures—they asserted a visible presence on the landscape; inexorably, new roads and transport routes followed. After the mineral revolution, this presence made itself felt even further, especially with the rise of large mining towns at Kimberley and along the gold reef of the Transvaal. It was to these centers, just beyond the edges of their immediate world, that Southern Tswana would migrate in burgeoning numbers and in a variety of capacities.

MAP 1 *Southern Africa*

Finally, after the discovery of diamonds—which drew yet more land-hungry settlers inland and saw the deepening of territorial conflict—British overrule inserted the colonial state into the picture. Its structures and representatives located themselves either in the white towns at the hub of farming districts or in newly erected centers, from which nearby "natives" could be administered. Often these centers were sited close to Tswana capitals, and brought in additional Europeans, generally in pursuit of trade and business; the building of a railway line across the territory in the 1890s made it accessible to people and goods otherwise unlikely ever to have entered it. Hence there grew up, in what the whites liked to call "Southern Bechuanaland," a number of frontier communities that were dramatically divided along racial lines. Often the African population, concentrated on a royal court, sustained a palpably Tswana look. The (much smaller) European end of town, in many places across the railway track, was usually built in colonial style around its few public buildings and churches; although, as we shall see, a distinctly hybrid architectural style emerged in these places, one which bore the imprint of Africanity.

This, then, is the terrain on which our account unfolds. It does so themati-

55

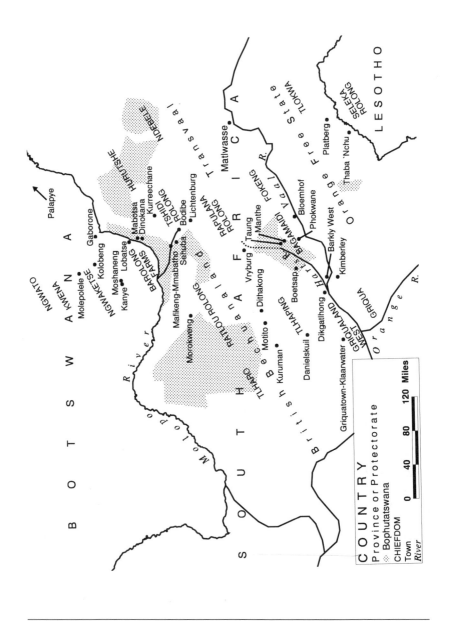

MAP 2 *The Southern Tswana World*

cally, as in volume 1: instead of offering an event history, chronologically ordered, we take a series of processes and follow each from the first years of the
colonial mission as far into the present as possible. We hope that, together, these
parallel pieces conduce to a compelling narrative, one whose very composition
illuminates the actions, intentions, and forces that went into making its subject
matter. In scripting it, moreover, we stress the continuities with those early moments described in the last book, to which we refer frequently and on whose
conceptual and contextual scaffolding we continue to rely. At the same time, we
have tried to render volume 2 readable on its own—which, alas, has made some
repetition unavoidable.[72]

Unavoidable, also, is its length. This for two reasons: because all our topics
are treated extensively over time and space; and because a story told, in dialectical terms, about the engagement of complex worlds is hard to tell in a few
words, at least without oversimplifying it. We are aware, of course, that long
books tend to raise more questions than do short ones; that the present volume
evokes more issues than it can possibly address; that we are more likely to be
taken to task for what we do not say than for what we do. We have, however,
attempted to make the account easily readable despite its size—and would like
to believe that the latter is justified by its substance.

Because of its scale, the present volume is differently constructed from the
first in one respect. While we try to write the dialectics of the colonial encounter
into the structure of each chapter, the dimensions of our *mise-en-scène* here create a descriptive tension. On one hand, we tell an expansive story of the long
run, a story which, despite its thematic composition, has necessarily to make
sense of chronology and events. On the other, we seek, above all else, to offer
"thick" descriptions of the social, symbolic, and imaginative processes that configured the "long conversation"[73] between Southern Tswana and their European interlocutors. This tension is not easily resolved. Perhaps it is unresolv-
able. Our strategy has been to fuse the two throughout: to move between "thick"
and "thin" description in such a way that each informs the other, thus to paint
as full a picture as possible.[74]

We open our narrative, in chapter 2, with an account of the religious dimension of the Nonconformist outreach to the Southern Tswana; religious, that
is, in the restricted sense of the term. Here, reprising and taking much further
the discussion begun in the last volume, we explore the theological concerns of
the colonial evangelists, the ways in which they dealt in spirituality, sin, and
salvation, the pragmatics of their attempt to make the world their parish. That
this aspect of the mission is treated first is, of course, iconic of its place in the
ideology and doctrinal platforms of the LMS and WMMS. In recuperating it
from the historical record, we show how the Protestant message was appropriated by Southern Tswana—of whom some joined the church, some became
leaders in it, some kept their distance or were kept at a distance from it, some

seized it and took it away with them to places near and far. All of them made it more or less their own, domesticating it according to their own cultural lights, their own social needs, their own politics.

These modes of appropriation did not compose a rigid set of "types," ideal or otherwise. Nor did they have neat sociological correlates. They were fluid, contingent expressions of African religiosity, a spectrum of *imaginative possibilities* through which people moved over time and space. They also had the effect, in different ways and degrees, of working themselves into, and transforming, local cultural practices. However, from the vantage of the missionaries, whose faith was also changed by their encounter with Africa, these alternative Christianities were syncretisms of which the Europeans did not usually approve—as if all Christianities before and after were not also syncretisms. To be sure, such arrogations of their creed underscored a fundamental contradiction for colonial evangelism. On one hand, it sought to bring a universalist orthodoxy to Bechuanaland; on the other, the Nonconformists spoke of creating communities of self-determining African Protestants, to whose everyday lives the faith ought to be relevant. But the lines of self-determination, like the limits of rendering Christianity local, were ambiguous and easily crossed, often to the dismay of the LMS and WMMS. Neither, in fact, allowed much autonomous "native agency" for many decades. Both saw "backsliding" all around them. And both declared that, measured in "true" conversions, their missions enjoyed only limited success—even when, especially when, large numbers of Southern Tswana actually entered the church.

This sense of failure underscores its own corollary: that, from early on, the colonial evangelists gave up—in practice, if not always in their public pronouncements—on the fragile distinction between salvation and civilization, between the theological and the worldly sides of their mission. In part, this was due to their conclusion, "in the field," that Christianity would make no headway here until the degenerate state of Southern Tswana had been improved; in part, it was due to the unreceptivity of many of the Africans to their theological message, their preaching and prayer. But, most of all, it was due to the fact that theirs was a pragmatic faith; a faith whose path to redemption was hewn in the here-and-now, whose theology was indivisible from its political economy, its legal sensibilities, its notion of embodied being-in-the-world.

From chapter 3 onwards, then, we look at the practical sides of the Nonconformist mission: at its campaign to effect "a revolution in habits" and at the dialectics of its encounter with the Southern Tswana world. All of this we do on the assumption that these were no less part of the religious initiative of colonial evangelism than was its strictly theological aspect.

Chapters 3 and 4 deal with "Christian political economy"; this not being our analytic term, but an ideological construct of the time. The first focuses on production: on the efforts of the LMS and WMMS to bring about an agrarian revolution. Their campaign—an endeavor at once material and cultural, social and aesthetic—was later exacerbated by the forces of colonial capitalism. It spawned complex processes of class formation and, with the seizure of economic initiatives by the rising upper and middle Tswana peasantries, transformed the local agricultural scene. The second traces the Nonconformist quest, also accelerated by processes unfolding elsewhere in this colonial theater, to alter local notions of value and patterns of consumption and exchange. This was done by introducing "refined" commodities, by disseminating the Protestant idea of self-possessed labor and the worth of wage work, and by essaying markets and money; the last being so significant that the LMS went so far as to mint its own currency, thus to persuade Southern Tswana to make conversions of all kinds.

In these domains, as in all others, the evangelists expected Southern Tswana to adopt "civilized" means and ends, if for no other reason, because of their "reasonableness" and the "comforts" they afforded. It was believed, too, that "natives" learned mainly by imitation—although some missionaries censured their brethren for encouraging Africans merely to "ape" their ways. In fact, the latter *did* sometimes engage in mimicry in the course of appropriating those ways. The misrecognitions here, again, point to the complexities of cultural exchange across colonial frontiers, and to the processes of hybridization to which they give rise. And so, in each of these chapters, as in the ones before and after, we look at the manner in which Southern Tswana took the forms presented to them by Europeans and refashioned them, how their doing so reciprocally affected the colonizers themselves, how new hybrid practices emerged.

One qualification here. We use "hybridization" descriptively, not as a theoretical construct; for, in the latter guise, it is misleading, implying that creolization occurs only along some frontiers rather than being, in varying degrees, an ongoing process everywhere. Thus we are concerned not merely with those cultural forms that arose on the fertile mid-ground between *setswana* and *sekgoa*, leaving the latter themselves untouched. Quite the opposite, we show that both were also constantly transformed and syncretized by the "long conversation" between Southern Tswana and Europeans. At the same time, we cannot deal equally with processes of hybridization on both sides of the colonial encounter. It is simply impossible, short of writing another book, to describe the impact of Africa (and other "others") on Europe in the same detail as we do the reverse. In this regard, any historical anthropology which attends to the dialectics of colonialism—or, indeed of the global and the local—is inherently unfinished, unequal, partial. But we *do* seek to show, by apt illustration, how deeply Europe and Europeans, both at the frontier and at "home," were affected by their confrontation with Africa. Even remade by it.

In the middle chapters of the book, 5 and 6, we again pick up the theme of consumption, aesthetics, and the materialities of style. Here we explore those

outer things—dress and bodily management in chapter 5, architecture and domesticity in chapter 6—through which the Protestants sought to remake the
inner being of Southern Tswana; how, by appealing to an economy of desire,
they set about re-forming vernacular habit, in both senses of that word, and its
habitat. The concentration of evangelical effort on houses and bodies was not
happenstance: the family home, centered on the conjugal chamber, was the
Mansion of the Lord, the domestic sanctuary in which the righteous Christian
was to dwell if s/he was to be redeemed; the body was the plane on which
the commodity met the self, where external civilities intersected with interior
proprieties and where inward virtue was outfitted for the world to see. The
endeavor to transform both brought the European fashion system to Africa,
where its designs were recommissioned, restyled, and drawn into the processes
by which local populations made and marked emerging social distinctions. Indeed, if there was anywhere that the Europeans lost control over the encounter
with Africa quickly and visibly, and were themselves tangibly affected by it, it
was here.

In light of the salience of the body and its management to the civilizing
mission, it is no surprise that health and hygiene would feature centrally in that
mission's outreach. As we show in chapter 7, which deals with the healing ministry, the Nonconformists were convinced, on good theological grounds, that
the treatment of physical ills would open the way to conversion. Yet many of
them displayed increasing reluctance to treat the sick, calling instead for trained
medical men—who, David Livingstone aside, were always scarce in South Africa. It was not only the lack of professional expertise that made this area of the
mission so fraught, however. For one thing, it was *too* successful. The evangelists found themselves the object of constant appeals for European medicines,
which were thought capable by Tswana of extraordinary effects; to the extent
that they worried about the disproportionate amount of time being given to
things corporeal—with little measurable spiritual effect. What is more, they ran
up against indigenous notions of healing, which were only dimly understood.
And, with the exception of Livingstone, deeply distrusted.

Most of all, though, it was in this domain that Africa, the "sick" continent
whose peoples seemed remarkably healthy, was least tractable, most difficult to
enter and alter—notwithstanding the appeal of European medicines. As a result, African physicality imposed itself on the consciousness of colonizers as a
fountainhead of mysterious, dangerous bodily forces, forces that threatened, as
they still are held to do today, other people in other places. At times, the South
African interior became a laboratory and a source of new medical cures; often
it served as a template on which such things as sexuality and gendered physical
processes might be projected and rethought; always it constituted a metaphysical space in which the putative biology of difference was objectified and interro-
gated. But healing was also the ground on which black and white bodies

touched, where mutual tears flowed, sometimes dissolving the cleavages of the cultural frontier.

For Southern Tswana, the healing ministry was a less vexed affair. Given their receptive disposition toward alien cultural knowledge, they saw no reason not to seize upon the forms of treatment made available by the evangelists. European medicine, it is true, did not address the social bases of their ills. But it could be absorbed into their repertoire of responses to misfortune—without, as they understood matters, challenging the foundations of their world. In this sense, the colonial encounter here reversed received stereotypes: turning Robin Horton (1967) on his head, it was Southern Tswana who evinced an "open predicament" toward things unfamiliar—and the evangelists, with their postenlightenment intolerance for the coexistence of different systems of knowledge, whose epistemic predicament "closed" them to alternatives (see n. 40). Over the long term, the confrontation yielded its own synthetic practices. In addition to affecting the healing technologies of both *setswana* and *sekgoa*, it shaped new modes of diagnosis, divination, and cure for a broad range of conditions. It also forged new ideas of the person in sickness and health.

Our last substantive chapter, chapter 8, follows personhood into an even more encompassing register. It explores the struggle—endemic to colonialism in general and to the civilizing mission in particular—over the making of the modernist subject. This struggle subsumes all the others with which we are concerned here: those set in motion by the crusade, on the part of the evangelists and other colonizers, to recast Southern Tswana patterns of production and consumption, their dress and domestic appointments, their aesthetics and architecture, their bodies, minds, and mundane routines, their orientations toward money and the market. All of these things came together in the construction of the right-minded, right-bearing, propertied individual; a being untangled from "primitive" webs of relations and free to enter both contracts and the church. As this suggests, the modernist self was embedded, imaginatively, in a culture of legalities, a culture then still very much in formation in Europe. In its export to Africa, it ran up against the brute contradictions of colonialism, the impossibilities of empire.

On one hand, the evangelists spoke of liberal individualism and universal citizenship, of membership in a moral community modeled on the nation-state. On the other, they persisted in treating Southern Tswana as premodern ethnic subjects in thrall to the primal sovereignty of their chiefs and customs. To the Europeans, these things did not appear inconsistent: the first described a promise for the future; the second, a prevailing predicament. But, in a colonial society founded on racial difference and material inequality, the worldview of the Nonconformists was unrealizable and unrealized; primal sovereignty, especially in the hands of the state, was to become an instrument of dispossession and disempowerment. It was in the fissures opened up by these contradictions, in fact, that various forms of black resistance were to take root. Even more palpably, the image of the self imported to Bechuanaland by the civilizing mission, with its discourse of rights and its discrepant conceptions of sovereign being-in-the-world, laid the foundation for a schismatic political culture, one which remains in evidence in South Africa. It is a culture in which the figure of the ethnic subject confronts that of the national citizen. Sometimes the confrontation is played out in the existential, artistic, or social construction of "new" personal identities, sometimes in electoral politics, sometimes in the violence that divides groups. Whichever, it is one place where the archaeology of colonialism, and of colonial evangelism in particular, has left its shards and traces.

Which raises one last set of questions. How, precisely, are we to delineate the role of the Protestant missions in the colonial encounter? How significant, in the final analysis, was the part played by them? And in what terms may we read its effects? While we seek to answer these questions in each of the chapters, we come back to them, summarily, in the Conclusion. There we revisit the problem of historical determination *sui generis*—and, with it, the analytic and methodological issues surrounding the way we might think about it from the singular perspective of a historical anthropology today. These issues involve, among other things, what it means to see colonialism in dialectical terms—and why it is worth doing so. They also compel us to give account of how it is that a narrative like ours, so detailed and narrow in its empirical canvas, might serve conceptual ends beyond the telling of its own story.

But such meditations remain a long way off. The story, its intricate unfoldings of the long run, has first to be told.

TWO

PREACHERS AND PROPHETS

The Domestication of the Sacred Word

Where the broad Zambezi floweth,
And its banks the Niger laves;
And the Pagan nothing knoweth
Of the Word that heals and saves,
Preach the Gospel
Unto poor benighted slaves.

Missionary Hymn (H. G. Adams 1870:xii)

T HE LONG CONVERSATION between the Nonconformists and Southern Tswana, as we noted in volume 1, played itself out, contrapuntally, in several registers—sometimes distinct, often overlapping. From the perspective of the missionaries themselves, the effort had two discrete dimensions. The one, aimed at securing converts, was dominated by the sacred narrative, the "good news" of the gospel. The other was the civilizing quest, which involved a struggle over the very fabric, and the fabrication, of everyday life. While the first centered most explicitly on the Word and the second on practice, both entailed a mix of utterance and action. Moreover, while separated in evangelical rhetoric, they were mutually entailed aspects of a single initiative; an initiative that turned on a particular kind of pragmatism.

As we pick up our story again, we begin on the plane of "direct influence": with the protracted dialogue between the Europeans and the Africans on the subject of religion. This is where the missionaries tried to win over believers by persuading them of the truth of the Christian message. In doing so, they ran up against a cultural contraflow, a stream of different ideas about being-in-the-world and, more specifically, about the divine and its place in human life. At issue was not merely a contrast, as the Protestants would have had it, between spirit and matter or between reflective and embodied ways of knowing; the Europeans were no less preoccupied with material enterprise or with things corporeal. What was in question, rather, were the appropriate relations among these aspects of human existence. And here cultural differences would have profound consequences.

Our account thus far has sketched the backdrop to the process: how the early nineteenth-century overseas missions, impelled by a heroic calling, grew out of the ferment of industrializing Britain; how the spirit of universal humanism that stirred secular reformers to exploration, and to "benevolent" imperialism, drove Men of God to extend His Kingdom to the "dark" places of the earth. This, after all, was the Age of Possibility, an epoch in which the moving spirits of Capitalism and Protestantism extended their horizons in new, global directions. The liberal imagination that dreamed of mass marketing could, and did, inspire a vision of wholesale revival, of the whole planet as a parish—just as the language of enlightened empiricism could be, and was, used to impress spiritual verities on an ever more skeptical, materialist world. True, it may be said that the story of the missions began with Abraham (Sundkler 1965:11). But the Apostles to Africa were also moved by historically specific objectives.

From their vantage, the gulf between the saved and the fallen was epitomized by the contrast between the civil and the savage. Consequently, conversion required not only that would-be Christians accept the gospel, but that they discard all marks of degeneracy and primitivism. Heathens had to be made to *acknowledge* their base sinfulness, so that they might be given the means of recovering themselves.[1] As it turned out, the coupling of salvation to civilization would complicate the meaning of redemption—and, with it, the practical theology of the mission. Among other things, it necessitated the counterpoint, the doubling of registers, in the dialogue between the Christians and the Africans. And it provoked endless arguments among the former over the relation of preaching to teaching and healing, of inner to outer being, of divine truth to local custom.

The efforts of the Nonconformists to resolve these ambivalences and arguments will receive due attention in the chapters to follow. Here, however, our purpose is narrower. It is to examine how the evangelists, and those whom they inspired, set about their highest calling; namely, disseminating the "doctrines of the Cross" in Bechuanaland (J. Philip 1828,2:356). As we have noted, these exertions met with limited success, especially in the early decades. Southern Tswana had a rather different sense of transcendent realities, realities left largely untouched by initial exposure to the gospel. But the dialogue, discordant though it often was, would continue within a dense field of verbal and material exchanges. Eventually, these exchanges, together, began to shift Tswana perceptions of personhood, power, and production—and, hence, their ideas about the numinous forces that shape human life.

While they might not have accorded with European notions of divinity, local gods were never jealous. They had long permitted an inquisitive and acquisitive attitude to the ritual techniques of others (*RRI*:162f.). Thus, while there was quite widespread indifference to mission preaching for much of the century, there was also, from the very first, a domestication of biblical texts and liturgical practices. What is more, the evangelists depended throughout on the help of African assistants, men who formed the kernel of new Christian elites. The ministrations of these "teachers" fed on vernacular forms of veneration, forging original religious styles both within the church and beyond.

We begin our examination of this register of the encounter by following the theological thrust of the pioneering proselytizers into the interior, into the heart of southern Africa.

THE APOSTOLIC COMMISSION

"Our beloved brother, go, live agreeably with the Word, and publish the Gospel of Jesus Christ to the heathen, according to your gifts, calling and abilities. In the name of the Father, and of the Son, and of the Holy Ghost." That commission, together with the "fundamental principle" from the Plan of the LMS, are the only statements of belief the Society has formulated.

Cecil Northcott (1945:38)

The evangelical movement that cut a swathe through Protestant denominations in the late eighteenth-century—and forged the great mission societies— was driven by a faith that all human beings were potential believers. Its theology was powered by a rediscovery of the gospel; of the unvarnished biblical truth of the "life, death, resurrection, and intercession of Christ" (Davies 1961:153). And its message was disseminated, first and foremost, by the act of preaching. The pulpit, says Chadwick (1966,1:442), was the revivalist's "joy and throne." From it emanated the "blast of judgement and the sweetness of promise."

This bespeaks the pragmatic orientation of the Revival, of its vision of truth, representation, and the religious subject. The evangelicals were concerned, above all, to give voice to the living word:[2] to make evident the revealed power of God in the here and now, so that the listener might be moved to seize control of his or her own spiritual destiny. Language was the privileged instrument of Divinity made manifest in experience. It was also the means of testifying to the reality of an empirical faith. A faith to be proven, that is, not assumed. Ideology to the contrary, the body was a vital medium in this process. Wesley had stressed that "sensible inspiration" lay at the core of Methodism, being its way of coming to know and believe (Dreyer 1983:14). Conviction, the fruit of inner reflection, was a matter of "feeling"; not of abstract reason or physical excitation, but of knowledge acquired through the senses, upon which human beings could exercise will. Wesley's skepticism of the role in conversion of "visions and voices, . . . fits and convulsions" (Dreyer 1983:15) was shared by most Nonconformists in the mission field—which, in turn, had consequences for the kind of "devotional self" (M. Shapiro 1993:12) they found acceptable and looked for in their converts.

Tswana spiritual life was also pragmatically oriented, of course; that much we saw in volume 1 and will see again. But not in the same way. The difference turned on a fundamental contrast in their understanding of religious being.

The evangelical emphasis on experienced reality, on the experimentalism of the senses, depended on a prior assumption: that speech acts had the capacity to conjure up the presence of God, thus providing audible proof of the power of the numinous. This is why revivalism invested so heavily in the reciprocal gesture of preaching and listening; why it exalted the "ear-gate" of the soul above its "eye-gate" (Davies 1961:236). The preacher was the vehicle of Truth as faithful representation; the believer, its sentient recipient. For Southern Tswana, on the other hand, divinity was rooted in an axiomatic yet tangible awareness of spiritual presence—this being reflected in the fact that direct communication between humans and the superhuman occurred more in deeds than in words. Deities did not require to be spoken to, or about, to make their reality felt. It was only when they seemed to have withdrawn that these beings were called upon at all.

As a result, Southern Tswana were not easily interpolated into the dialogic triangle of preacher, listener, and divine truth. Indeed, they would refer to mission sermons as "just talking" (Edwards 1886:91), as performance set apart from effective action in the world. The form and style of Protestant worship reinforced this perception. However much the evangelical pulpit took God to the masses, the Word was always contained in a framed ritual space, addressing everyday existence across a Cartesian divide. This act of invocation was theatrical in a profoundly modern sense: in its self-conscious awareness that exhortation was re-presentation; that the congregation was as audience; that a space existed between speaker and listener, a moral gulf to be breached. For Tswana, neither utterances nor sacraments alone could span this gulf. A distinctive local Christianity would emerge in the effort to close it, a Christianity that was itself a product of the multiple attractions and antagonisms of ritual practices colliding along the frontier. But this was yet a way into the future.

Preaching the Gospel to Every Creature

Let us return to the image of the evangelist "preaching from his wagon," an image that became emblematic of the African mission in the first half of the nineteenth century (*RRI*:232). The stance of this figure spoke volubly of the early outreach of the Nonconformists. For the LMS, Northcott (1945:41) notes, preaching was "the initial and sole purpose . . . the creative ground of all else— medical missions, education, social service, welfare of the peoples." The sermon was sovereign in preserving and proclaiming the beliefs of the Society (p. 38). It served as proxy for a statement of creed, a fact underlined by Northcott's own rendering of LMS doctrinal history as a string of quotes from memorable homilies. Given its pan-denominational nature, not to mention the minimal ed-ucation and training of many of its recruits, there was good reason for its call to proclaim the gospel by all available means. Short on exegesis, the evangelists tended to be impatient with learned speculation about what they took to be burning spiritual certainties.

It was a stress that would last: "The imperative of missions," declaimed Dr. Forsyth from a London pulpit in 1903, "is . . . in the urgency of the Risen Christ" (Northcott 1945:40–41). A similar emphasis obtained among early Methodists, who tended to assume that "charismata descend[ed] from heaven and needed no preparation" (Chadwick 1966:377). In fact, the lack of learning of many Wesleyan preachers was taken as a matter of pride in some circuits at home. No college education was required, wrote Whiteside (1906:23), for a carpenter, a smith, or a tradesman to "step from behind his counter and each in his way . . . testify: 'I have found peace with God; there is salvation in Christ for all.'"

The Nonconformists at the colonial frontier, many of them humble arti-sans, shared this orientation. Driven by a fervent, biblically rooted faith, they might occasionally have balked at their task. Some even gave up and left.[3] But, if their written traces are anything to go by, they wasted little time on spiritual reflection or doctrinal doubt. Nor were they much detained by the abstract theological debates—over pre- and postmillenarianism, Christian socialism, and so on—that vexed their more schooled colleagues elsewhere.[4] Once their initial hopes of mass conversion faded, they became ever more preoccupied with the practicalities of their civilizing quest, ever more caught up in quotidian de-tails as they battled patiently for souls.

Indeed, in the face of repeated proof of African resistance to their message, the faith of the founding generation in the redemptive power of the Word—at least, in and of itself—appeared touchingly naive to those who followed. And so, as the century wore on, the charisma of the missions among Southern Tswana gave way to routine. And to a concern with everyday entanglements.

Not only did the LMS and WMMS become embroiled in the affairs of the frontier; which, as their chronicles show, led them to ponder their place in the politics of "humane" imperialism. From the midcentury onward they tried, as well, to reconcile their spiritual objectives with such things as education and healing, which turned out to be their most effective activities; also to address the issues raised by these activities—among them, the proper role for "native agency" in the Bechuana church, and the responsibility of Christianity for ushering blacks into the world of colonial modernity. All of this suggests that, with the passing decades, both societies grew more self-conscious about their methods, and more intent on arriving at systematic statements of administrative policy. Even so, even across this broad historical sweep, the Nonconformists continued to preach, to spread the gospel by all available means, to draw anyone who would listen into the "kind conversation" of which Livingstone spoke (*RRI*:198). What changed over time were their evangelical styles, the content of their utterances, and the broader context in which they did God's work.

In the beginning, however, was the Word, plain and unvarnished: the gospel preached to the heathen by pioneer evangelists with heroic fervor, sanguine faith, and, in both senses of the term, spirited enthusiasm.

"My heart," declared Robert Moffat in 1817, impatient to be sent to the interior, "is panting after the salvation of the heathen."[5] His colleagues shared his conviction that, in their commission to carry the good news to the suffering, they were not merely heroes making history. They were also the apostles of a grand transfiguration that was rapidly expanding God's Kingdom on earth. Their early optimism—abetted, no doubt, by the need for inspiring testimonials from the front—led to claims that the gospel had worked "great and marvelous changes . . . [among] the Bechuana" (Broadbent 1865:203). The extent to which the Christians actually thought that this presaged the Second Coming is less easy to determine (cf. Stuart 1993:78). Moffat was apt, in the first years, to preach sermons so apocalyptic that his listeners feared the conflagration might descend there and then. But he also admitted (1842:302; *RRI*:231) that, in order to wrest Tswana attention from the "rubbish" that "paralyzed" their minds, he had to "make every subject as striking and interesting" as possible.

Not that drama and urgency were out of keeping with the pioneer evangelists' expectations of the work of the Word in the world (witness Read's vivid image of the gospel, on being heard, calling forth tears to wash "the red paint" from heathen bodies; *RRI*:214). These, after all, were children of the Revival. "God," said Hamilton, was "a wall of fire in the midst of Satan's Camp."[6] Faith in the capacity of the Cross to conquer was heightened here by the belief that Southern Tswana had once known divine truth;[7] that "sin [had] defaced the image of God in the soul, and blinded the understanding" from their minds (Baillie 1832:448). Recuperating that image, restoring it to the collective memory, seemed more promising than having to insinuate it *de novo*. As a result, opening exchanges on sacred subjects proceeded like would-be catechisms; perhaps the mere *sound* of the Truth might rekindle some vestige of a long-extinguished flame (Moffat and Moffat 1951:247f.):

> This afternoon, sitting on my fore chest, I entered into conversation with a young widow, who seemed more sprightly than wise. My first question was, what would become of her after death? She stared at me in the utmost astonishment. . . . Repeating my question, assuring her that death would spare neither of us, she at last answered, that she knew not. I gave her a plain scriptural answer, namely that she would go to hell if she died in her present state. I added that the wicked would be turned into hell . . . and pointed out that she was really of the number that forgot God. She looked at me, and added, "You are a man of wisdom, how can you talk that way?"

Such dramatically retold dialogues, of which there are many in the record, gave warning of the challenges ahead (cf. Etherington 1978:57). "Alas," sighed Broadbent, after a similar exchange, "they sit in thick darkness."[8]

But these conversations also affirmed the Nonconformist belief that rational exchange would persuade Southern Tswana to see the light. At first, their failure to respond was blamed on brute misunderstanding, caused largely by a lack of linguistic competence on the part of the missionaries. Hence the unsparing efforts to master Setswana, to translate the scripture and hymnal—hymns, says Davies (1961:201) were "sung creeds"[9]—and to preach in the vernacular; again, to do all they could to ensue that the divine verities might restore what had been erased. "The great principles of the Bible Society are exemplified here," Isaac Hughes wrote to Robert Moffat (1842:618); "the simple reading and study of the Bible will convert the world." Later commentators, like Sundkler (1965:56), would suggest that a "whole theology . . . [might] be built on the thesis that mission is translation." But the nineteenth-century evangelists in Bechuanaland regarded the matter much more literally: all human languages had the capacity to express the "good, pure salt of the Gospel" (Wookey 1902:58). And all intellects, if they roused themselves, could absorb its regenerating truth.

In short, while the Nonconformists acknowledged that Tswana had "a general aversion to the gospel," they were sure that "these prejudices [could] be conquered."[10] And so they set about preaching to whoever would listen. Their first regular "congregations" were captive audiences made up mainly of their own domestic employees: Broadbent, for example, describes how, in 1824, he addressed Seleka-Rolong servants in family worship at Matlwasse, speaking to them on heaven and hell, on God's love of righteousness, and on His hatred of sin.[11] But, in the early years, the missionaries also traveled widely, holding up, to uncomprehending African gatherings, the mirror of their benighted condition

(*RRI*:181f.). Some listeners were polite: in 1824, Hamilton proclaimed the message of John 3.16—"For God so loved the world that he gave his only Son, that whoever believes in him should not perish but have eternal life"—to "about 1000" people, assembled in "the greatest decorum" by the Tshidi-Rolong chief, Tawana.[12] Many local leaders grew less accommodating, however: in 1841, a resistant Tlhaping sovereign "[g]ot up a dance" around the self-same Hamilton in order to stifle his sermons (Livingstone 1961:9); much further north, the Kololo chief and councilors responded to Livingstone with "shouts and yells," mimicking his utterances and his singing (Chapman 1971:117).

In their early preaching, Moffat (Moffat and Moffat 1951:18) complained, the evangelists rarely moved beyond the "first principles of the doctrine of Christ"—which, he feared, could cause the mission entourage to lose its taste for "stronger food." Thus Baillie (1832:448), writing from Dithakong in 1830, reports that he "spoke of the character of God, to which they were very listless; told them of his goodness in sending his Son into the world to die for us; and by various methods tried to convince them of their state as sinners."

The essence of the gospel was conveyed in small, digestible bits, with the aid of key passages (John 3.16; Mark 16.15), affecting parables (the story of Jesus and Zacchaeus; the raising of Lazarus; the Prodigal Son), and "encouraging mottoes" from Proverbs and other sources. The Wesleyans also wrote inspiring verses onto the quarterly membership tickets that became emblems of Christian identity.[13] Here, and in their sermons, they were more inclined than their LMS brethren to range across the Old Testament, although they did so with a distinctly salvific emphasis.[14] Besides Proverbs, both societies drew heavily on Isaiah and the Psalms; all three, along with the Gospels, were translated by Robert Moffat (*RRI*:231).

From the 1830s onward, biblical tracts and extracts were printed for neophyte readers at Kuruman, Platberg, and Thaba 'Nchu. They also circulated widely beyond the evangelical community, stirring the imagination of many Southern Tswana, who put them to their own ritual uses. But the mission pulpit continued to be the main wellspring of scriptural snippets for the masses: John Mackenzie (1871:468–69) remained convinced that a careful selection of verses, giving audible expression to "what Christians must surely believe," was an effective way of edifying half-heathen congregations—much more so than was the "reading of a chapter." Perhaps it also was better suited to the talents of these Men of God. George Thompson (1967:76), a colonist who admired their work from close up (see chapter 3), reminds us that they were "persons of limited education, most of them having originally been common mechanics." Mind you, he added, it was not clear whether clergy of greater refinement would have been "better adapted to meet the plain capacities of unintellectual barbarians." For him, it seems, the theological prospects of colonial evangelism were less than promising. Better, in the circumstances, to get on with teaching Africans the practical arts of civilization.

When preaching to their own, the clergymen offered "enlarged" statements of Nonconformist doctrine. They also spoke a lot about "Christian warfare," the apostolic charter to fight the good fight for converts (Moffat and Moffat 1951:19). "The princes . . . of Ethiopia are crying like the men of Macedonia, 'Come over and help us,'" declaimed Hamilton.[15] And Moffat invoked the Gospel of John (5.39) in lamenting the reluctance of those who had "search[ed] the scriptures" to commit themselves to the Lord. Whatever theological shifts might have occurred within the LMS and WMMS over time, the Acts of the Apostles remained a lasting inspiration (*RRI*:231); this "missionary book" reflected their hopes and tribulations with enduring clarity. Their evangelism, it is true, would become ever more routinized, professionalized, and self-critical. And their pedagogy was to anchor itself in a distinctly this-worldly approach toward education. But the deeds of the disciples continued to personify the aggressive Christianity they advocated.[16]

Having declared war on unbelief, the evangelists tried to convince Southern Tswana of their depravity and damnation—and their urgent need for repentance. As we have noted, the Christian God was the God of the civilized, in whose eyes savagery was sin. Yet he was also the God of universal salvation and the father of all humankind. Moffat (Moffat and Moffat 1951:82) invoked James 1.18 in an early effort to impress listeners with the glory of the maker of all things: "Of his own will he brought us forth by the word of truth that we should be a kind of first fruits of his creatures."[17] What was more, He *loved* the world and all those in it. The point, here, was to tread the fine line between severity and compassion, threat and expectation. Hence, while the Nonconformists tried to temper African levity and "unruliness" with proper sobriety, they did not neglect the sweetness of promise, or the joy of Christian fellowship, that had colored the late eighteenth-century Revival. "Preached this morning from, '"Herein is love, &c,'" Archbell wrote (Broadbent 1865:179) in 1831, "[a]fter which I baptized a child of one of the members." Ever wary of overheated emotionalism, however, he and his brethren responded ambivalently to the unprecedented enthusiasm evoked by some of the early baptisms. Clearly, they were uncertain whether to celebrate or distrust these "outpourings" of "primitive Christianity" (Whiteside 1906:337; *RRI*:239).

While the evangelists favored preaching over communion as a vehicle of faith—they were, after all, products of the Dissent—the sacraments also had a role in extending God's grace and in forming Christian persons and communities. But it was a limited one. The Nonconformists remained suspicious of ceremonial, especially if visually seductive; again, this was not a matter of the presence or absence of bodily sensation, but of privileging one register (the ear) over another (the eye). Baptisms, burials, and quarterly communion were less an occasion for highly orchestrated rites than for extended, often extemporary, preaching and prayer—which, along with hymns, comprised the recurrent elements of their services.[18] Significantly, the rich symbolic potential of the sacraments was recognized and put to work, later on, by independent African church leaders; just as these rituals had been an object of struggle in the European reformation, so they would become a focus of contestation between dissenting black Christians and defensive white clergymen at the colonial frontier. In the meantime, however, the latter set about persuading Southern Tswana of their peril in the face of Judgment.

As the century progressed, the image of Divinity conveyed by the evangelists became more merciful, more life-affirming—and, concomitantly, more a focus of "kind conversation" than a figure of declamatory threat. This, we shall see in a moment, had a good deal to do with indigenous acts of translation. It did not necessarily imply a greater measure of common spiritual understanding. Still, there does appear to have been a degree of convergence across cultural boundaries. Whether or not they were "true" Christians, Mackenzie (1871:472) pointed out, the Africans grew to regard God, ever more explicitly, as the ultimate force in the universe, a final explanation for the inexplicable. Reciprocally, mission theology dwelled less on the eternal, more on the gradual extension of the Lord's kingdom-on-earth by practical, indirect means.[19]

There also began to emerge a more sober assessment of the efficacy of preaching at the Christian frontier. In 1869, John Moffat wrote to the LMS directors, telling them that he was calling on members of his congregation at Kuruman to exhort each Sunday. His goal was to have their fellows hear religious truths expressed in their own idiom. But why?[20]

> [I]t will help to rouse them out of the passive and dead-alive acquiescence with which they have been accustomed to listen to the sermons of their foreign teachers, intelligible or otherwise. . . . I fear the Pulpit as a Christian power has been grievously sinned against in this part of the Mission field. . . . I have been disgusted to find . . . to what extent the pulpit has been to them a mere *Nothing* as a medium of religious information. A law is not uncalled for to preclude any young missionary from "holding forth" until he can sustain at least five minutes rational conversation with a native in his own language.[21]

Moffat insisted that "public preaching in a foreign tongue" was far less compelling than were "private methods" of conveying the truths of the gospel. And, sure enough, systematic education, with a heavy emphasis on the schoolroom, would replace preaching, the instant pedagogy of the pulpit, as the primary medium of moral and intellectual reform. But it would never totally eclipse the sermon as a mode of spiritual instruction, not least because many African

Christians would make the medium their own. The latter were perhaps primed by a long-standing vernacular sensitivity to persuasive political oratory (cf. J. L. Comaroff 1975); contrary to the prejudices of some Europeans, a concern for rational argumentation was not a purely Western proclivity.

In the early years, the evangelists watched Southern Tswana intently for signs that they were hearing the Word; for evidence, as Mary Moffat (Moffat and Moffat 1951:292) put it, that they would "come out and be separate." Such signs were not often forthcoming, at least not in a form discernible to the Europeans.

At first.

Barriers to the Gospel

This indifference fed the discourse of racial inferiority that saturated Nonconformist understandings of the Fall: Africa's sin was its degeneracy, its descent into spiritual darkness. Still, if Southern Tswana could be "convicted" (LMS 1830)—made, that is, to recognize their cultural difference as a matter of individual guilt—they might yet redeem themselves. One by one. "The scripture," Robert Moffat (Moffat and Moffat 1951:40) insisted, "warrants us to expect *new creatures* from the effectual working of the Holy Spirit" (original emphasis). The state of these heathens might be deplorable, he reflected, but that merely aroused "a peculiar sympathy for their never-dying soul[s]" (p. 248). What is more, *pace* some doubters, the fact that they were "idle" and "dirty" rendered them no less capable of righteousness than people in "civilized countries." But they had first to plead guilty (Stuart 1993:383). The demonization of cultural difference—more even, the criminalization of custom—was an enduring feature of mission theology and practice. To be sure, it was the other side of the rule-governed regimes and legalistic idiom of the Nonconformist churches. And of a faith centered on statute, contract, adjudication, and the rights and duties of the self-willed subject.

Given the Nonconformist worldview, many Tswana social arrangements, many of their received cultural conventions, were bound to offend the colonial evangelists—and to be seen as "prodigious barriers to the Gospel" (R. Moffat 1842:251). Some, however, were taken to epitomize savagery, and were subjected to more than usual opprobrium. For example, while the (alleged) lack of "proper domestic order" was often bemoaned (Broadbent 1865:204; Livingstone 1959,1:70; below, chapter 6), polygyny loomed especially large as an obstacle (R. Moffat 1842:251; J. Mackenzie 1871:410f.); self-evidently, it violated the Christian ideal of marriage and family as the cradle of moral being. "Superfluous" wives had, therefore, to be renounced by those who would be saved—a stipulation that caused lasting argument between the missionaries and Tswana royals,[22] whose influence rested heavily on affinal alliance. Some local leaders, in fact, contested church rulings on the matter in public; Chief Sechele is reported to have challenged Robert Moffat to explain why Solomon and David were allowed many women when he was not.[23] And Chief Montshiwa put his name to a letter in the LMS newspaper, *Mahoko a Becwana*, defending *setswana* conjugal practices and the payment of *bogadi* (bridewealth).[24]

Similar struggles occurred in the realm of ritual. While all of their "absurd superstitions" and "profane ceremonies" were thought to hold the Africans in collective thrall, male and female circumcision (*bogwêra* and *bojale*) were treated as singular impediments to conversion (R. Moffat 1842:251). As we showed in volume 1, and as Mackenzie (1871:378) once said explicitly, the evangelists regarded these rites as the profane equivalent of baptism; Broadbent went a step further in describing them as a debased vestige of Old Testament practice, once more eliding difference and degeneracy.[25] Their public renunciation became a critical token of Christian sincerity; even, in a way, a rite of passage into the Nonconformist fold.

These sites of struggle were not arbitrary, of course. Both polygyny and initiation were crucially involved in the reproduction of socially situated persons and socially founded collectivities (chiefdoms, wards, regiments, towns, and the like). In defining them as private transgressions, the Christians struck at the *communal* construction of subjects and relations; at the "very being of a Mochuana," explained some elders to Archbell, their existential sensibilities clearly showing.[26] "God might burn them forever for the performance of them," the clergyman reported, "but they would not give them up." As this exchange makes clear, there were many Southern Tswana who argued openly with the missionaries and their message. To wit, the discord over initiation rites, marriage arrangements, and other elements of *setswana* continued well into this century.[27] And, in the process, Tswana became ever more fluent in the language of mission Christianity; ever more adept at redeploying its idioms; ever more able, if they were so disposed, to use its rhetoric in self-defense (*RRI*:199f.).[28]

While most of the Nonconformists had no difficulty in agreeing which Tswana customs (*mekgwa*) were unchristian abominations, there *were* dissenting voices. Setiloane (1976:103) notes that the WMMS emissary the Rev. John Cameron, for one, doubted whether mission perspectives and policies on the practice of polygyny were "likely to secure the happiest results."[29] And Livingstone (1857:166f.) questioned the association of initiation with heathenism: *bogwêra*, he asserted, was an "ingenious" mode of imparting discipline, not a "religious ceremony." Like Cameron, however, he seems to have thought it imperative that the church maintain a unanimous stance on such issues.[30] There was greater division in evangelical circles over the numinous aspects of Tswana spiritual life; most notably, over the existence of an indigenous divinity. Moffat (1842:243f.; *RRI*:202), recall, lamented the lack of legends, altars, or gods with which to do battle. "Their religious system," he wrote, "was like those streams in the wilderness which lose themselves in the sand." The Europeans, clearly, were wont to reserve the term "religion" for systems that accorded with a modernist Protestant sense of faith and worship. They preferred to see, in African "magic" and "ceremony," *pre*-Christian residues. Hence Broadbent's detection of Old Testament "vestiges" in initiation rites; similarly, the widespread tendency to perceive "rainmaking" as a form of pagan priesthood (*RRI*:208f.). There was a distinct reluctance on the part of most missionaries to recognize echoes of their own sacred orthodoxies—least of all a supreme being—in the Bechuana wilderness.

Not so others on the frontier. Certainly not those cultural brokers who plied the spaces between the Africans and the evangelists. They were much less reticent to see, and to make virtue of, resonances between different worlds and worldviews. John Mackenzie (1871:394) tells us, for instance, that the vernacular term which the missionaries came to use for the supreme being—*Modimo*—was originally chosen, without difficulty, by Dutch-speaking Tswana interpreters who had witnessed Protestant worship at Griquatown. This example is highly significant. It shows that the diffusion of signs within and across colonial borderlands far outstripped the efforts, or the influence, of self-consciously "civilizing" Europeans—in matters of religion as in all else. Translatability notwithstanding, however, most of the Nonconformists continued to insist on the contrast between their sense of divinity and "native" ideas of the life of the spirit. Among early commentators, Robert Moffat was probably the most influential—and the most categorical—in maintaining that Tswana had not even a residual understanding of the Lord.[31] *Modimo*, he said, meant "a malevolent *selo*, or thing," with no personal connotations. And *badimo*, "ancestors," implied "a state of disease," or of evil, especially associated with death and extinction (1842:261);[32] he used it as the word for "demons" in his Setswana bible (*RRI*:155f, 218).

Livingstone (1974:100f.) disagreed with Moffat, at least in part.[33] Tswana, he was convinced, did have knowledge of a supreme being "who made all things, and to whom all events not clearly traceable to natural causes were uniformly ascribed." What is more, this knowledge long predated the missionary presence.[34] Yet, both here and elsewhere (1961:62), he concurred that these were vague ideas,[35] "like broken planks floated down on the stream of ages from a primitive faith." They sparked no "curiosity" about divinity or eternity. This perception was later reiterated, with tenuous image intact, by Mackenzie (1871:394). *Modimo*, he said, was merely a name "floating" in Setswana, attracting no form of worship. All of which left Moffat's original views—themselves disseminated, implicitly, by his influential biblical translations—largely uncontested. In any case, like Europeans before and since, Livingstone sought religion in a formal edifice of sacral institutions, communal rites, and professed beliefs. And by that measure Tswana were repeatedly found wanting. As late as 1886, Alfred Sharp, a Methodist posted in Vryburg, noted that there was "no classical mythology, no gorgeous idol, no magnificent temple."[36] Naught here but superstition and barbarous practices with which to grapple.

From these assumptions, other misunderstandings would follow.

In light of their religious premises, the evangelists were ill-equipped to discern the intangible, yet ubiquitous, dimension of the spirit in the Tswana world. This dimension was personified in the ancestors—*pace* Moffat (1842:261), the *living* dead—whose reality was seldom proclaimed because it was never in dispute. *Badimo* participated with the "all-pervasiveness of vapour" in every aspect of the lives of their descendants (Setiloane 1976:64). Their power was both intimate and commanding. Disarmingly homely, they delighted in domestic sociability, and were placated by unceremonious words and common gestures of commensality in the daily round of the household. Yet they were also exacting alibis and agents of established authority. It was the very axiomatic quality of their presence that concealed it from the missionaries—themselves intent, ironically, on providing the Africans with a personal redeemer who, invisible but ubiquitous, defied all doubt.

So closely entwined were *badimo* with the rhythms of everyday existence, so heavily camouflaged in the quotidian, that they escaped the searchlight with which the Nonconformists scanned the cultural terrain for signs of "religion" (*RRI*:154). "One may spend years among [them]," Willoughby (1923:72) wrote later, and "never suspect that [Bechuana] worship their ancestors at all." The unobtrusiveness of these sensitive, superhuman forebears belied the fact that they were the very essence of the Tswana idea of divinity. Embodying both partisan protection and moral authority, they were gods "who know our faces" (J. Comaroff 1974:286). Their collective will was writ large in the fate of their children, eclipsing almost entirely the remote, inscrutable *Modimo*. Those who entered the church took these familiar guardians with them, almost like their own shadows. And in the shadows, largely unremarked by the whites, they would serve to mediate with the God of the missionaries.

The efforts of the early Nonconformists to "publicize" the gospel then, failed to engage the epicenter of Tswana religious life. To be sure, their own accounts tell a tale of repeated reverses and disappointments—this despite their energetic preaching against heathen practices, their painstaking conversational instruction, their unceasing attempts to (re)kindle the idea of Divinity by reciting the Christian narrative. What was conveyed to Eugene Casalis in 1838 by some Sotho might as well have come from their Tswana neighbors: "The poor missionary wastes his time to come and tell us about God," they said. "If he could show us God it would be better" (Setiloane 1976:133). That, of course, is what the evangelists thought they were doing in painting their impassioned word pictures. But words, here, seemed to distance people from the Lord. Of course, the evangelists also "showed" Him in their mundane "good works." However, Protestant rhetoric was contradictory in this respect, both claiming such "works" as instruments of virtue and yet valuing them less than the dissemination of spiritual truths.

While their "everlasting preaching and praying" left most of their early listeners indifferent (Livingstone 1857:25; *RRI*:236f.), the everyday labors-and-scenes of the missionaries impressed where least intended. Because Tswana recognized no sharp boundary between the sacred and the secular, what struck them most about the whites were their goods, their knowledge, and their technical skills. These things affirmed that they were the bearers of extraordinary powers, the wielding of which was taken to be the ritual core of their enterprise. In volume 1 we described the early Tswana endeavor to empower themselves by appropriating these techniques—and, simultaneously, to discover their hidden bases; we shall have cause to follow the process further in the chapters to follow.

For now, it is enough to say that African efforts to appropriate things European, as long as they were not sacrilegious, evoked an ambivalent reaction from the missionaries. On one hand, any interest in "refined" objects and techniques, like irrigation or manufactured commodities, was welcomed as proof of a desire for self-improvement—and, hence, as a civilizing impulse. On the other, any display of desire for commodities fed the fear that Tswana were unable to transcend the carnal, and unlikely to give a hearing to the Christian message unless there followed some temporal benefit (R. Moffat 1842:288; see chapter 3). This, in turn, convinced the evangelists that, however great their faith in the persuasive power of the Word, most of their energy would have to be devoted to what John Philip (1828,2:355; *RRI*:230) termed the "indirect" or "reflected influence" of the gospel. The tension between salvation and civilization, between the spirit and the flesh—which is how the ambivalence was usually glossed—was later seen by some as a creative spark at the core of the Protestant mission in the world (Warren 1967:90f.). But it haunted the Nonconformists in Bechuanaland, being perhaps the most immediate, most palpable instance of the impact of African values on Christian designs.[37] The LMS Foreign Secretary might have cautioned Mackenzie (1975:73) "never [to] fall into the fatal error of supposing that the people must be civilized before they can be converted to God." At the evangelical workface, though, everything declared otherwise.

But there were matters more unsettling to the mission than the tension between salvation and civilization, matters with important theological consequences. One was a species of Tswana behavior that fell into the uneasy space between the spiritual and the secular, hinting at both yet being neither. It was typified by the attempt of the Africans to persuade Europeans to part with "medicines" that appeared to instill superhuman powers; medicines that might instantly infuse them with new skills or even make their hearts pure (see chapter 7). Most challenging of all, however, were Tswana efforts to commandeer Christian worship itself, a gesture seen by the Nonconformists as downright blasphemous, not to mention insubordinate. We shall examine these in a moment. Before we do, it is necessary to turn our attention to an issue that would intervene directly in the encounter between mission Christianity and Tswana religious sensibilities: "native" evangelical agency.

ETHIOPIA EXTENDS HER HANDS[38]

Well trained Africans were, without doubt, the most successful missionaries [for the Methodist Church in South Africa]. Every effort should have been made to train and prepare such men and every encouragement should have been given for their ordination . . . [b]ut this was not done.

Daryl S. Balia (1991:45)

While they tended to write as if their stations were founded by their own solitary exertions, the pioneer missionaries relied heavily on the help of "native" assistants, often men with extensive knowledge of the local terrain (*RRI*:177). These frontier narratives, in fact, evoke the staging of Kabuki theater: while a few designated "players" are foregrounded, a large, darkly clad support cast moves efficiently about the business of making it all possible. Actors and audience alike are required to suspend disbelief, to "accept" the fiction that renders invisible those "offstage," thus permitting the pale protagonists to appear independent and self-automating. Such figure-ground inversions were endemic to European re-presentations of life at the edges of empire, of course. Like all acts of framing, all light shows, they refracted the dialectics of dependency on which was built the fantasy that colonial evangelists were self-propelled Men of History, each a lone bearer of the torch of civilization and salvation. Nowhere was this more evident than in the realm guarded most jealously by the Christians: the proclamation of the gospel.

"Native Agency"

The Africans with whom the evangelists made "first contact" in the deep interior—those they called Bechuana and painted as pristine, primitive heathens—had long been engaged in trade and other transactions with the hybrid peoples of the colonial borderland to the south. Already by the second decade of the nineteenth century, before the founding of the Kuruman station, Christian signs and practices were circulating beyond the margins of European control. In 1814 the LMS at the Cape had sent out several Khoisan converts to itinerate as "assistant preachers of the Gospel" in the Griquatown region (Moffat and Moffat 1951:18f.); here, Elbourne (n.d.:21f.) notes, the church quickly came to be a force in local politics. The first white missionaries to travel further north drew heavily from this and other colonial stations for the "interpreters" upon whom they relied so heavily. The latter, as their employers soon realized (*RRI*:216), did more than just translate the Word, often going far beyond the literal rendering of their masters' narrative, the master narrative of the New Testament. But there was little the Nonconformists could do about it. For a long while they had no option but to appeal to "native" mediation in communicating with African populations. This situation empowered indigenous cultural brokers. But it also cast them—sometimes awkwardly, always ambivalently—into the breach between Europeans and Africans, making them human bridges between worlds. Foreshadowings here of that celebrated subaltern of Central Africa under indirect rule, the "intercalary" village headman (Gluckman et al. 1949); foreshadowings also of that bridge in Zululand, immortalized by Gluckman (1968), which captured so well the contradictory relationship of colonizers to colonized. Like both, early African Christian interpreters were not merely vectors of communication between whites and blacks. They were also caught up in the symbolic construction of difference, in its objectification and in its violation.

Let us pursue this a little further. It will illuminate some of the crosscurrents, and cross-purposes, involved in the development of "native agency"—in all senses of that term.

At the turn of the nineteenth century, as we have said, the South African interior was a palpably diverse, fluid world. Not only were local polities home to peoples of mixed origin—Tswana chiefdoms, Schapera (1952) shows, have long been heterogeneous—but there was also considerable mobility among them. In addition, the exchange of ritual and practical knowledge was fairly common. If the documentation of early exploratory expeditions is anything to go by, ethnic differences were not especially salient (see Somerville [1802] 1979; Lichtenstein [1807] 1973; Barrow 1806). Totemic allegiances were recognized, it is true (Comaroff and Comaroff 1992:51f.; Schapera 1952). But, within the common—if sometimes fractious—humanity scattered across the landscape, cultural distinction appears to have been shadowy, evanescent, largely unremarked; except, that is, between the free citizens of political communities and those in servitude. In chapter 8 we shall return to the construction of collective identities. Here we have a more limited point to make.

It is this.

When the evangelists and other Europeans wandered into the African interior, they brought with them two Ideas. Both, we saw in volume 1, were very much tropes of the time. The first was a binary model of humankind, a model which not only opposed civility to savagery, light to dark, Christian to pagan, and so on, but also condensed all these contrasts into the polarities of a grand evolutionary telos. The second was a pre-anthropological image of sovereign social order. This assumed that the world was composed, naturally, of bounded, centralized polities; African kingdoms being the primitive forebears of the (then emerging European) nation-state. Wittingly or not, and with the implicit connivance of other Europeans, the missionaries imposed these two conceptual frames upon the hybrid socioscape beyond the frontier, slowly objectifying it for themselves into a terrain of clear cultural contrasts, sharp social distinctions, hard racial oppositions. Note, in this respect, their tendency to refer to "the Bechuana" as a "nation"; to speak of chiefdoms as if they were (nation-)states; and yet to regard "natives," one and all, as an undifferentiated other. Note, also, how easily social origins were parsed when people were referred to in the adjectival language of identity: Mahutu, for instance, the Tlhaping "queen," was well-known to be of Khoi origin (see chapter 3, n. 61). Yet she was usually described, even painted, as a Bechuana woman.

These cultural constructions had concrete consequences for the religious work of the missions. For example, they made plausible the Nonconformists' claim that "the Bechuana" merited a sacred literature and liturgy in their vernacular; although there did develop a *reductio ad absurdum* when some evangelists argued that "their" chiefdoms were distinct enough to warrant one as well. But, more generally, they were a condition-of-possibility for refiguring the frontier, first imaginatively and then materially, as a colonial society founded on an overlay of stark oppositions and dualisms; on the existence of coherent, counterposed identities and cultural "systems," each the distinctive, inherent property of a kind of social being. This, we repeat, in an epoch in which the culturally kaleidoscopic, politically fraught interior was far from stable.

In the circumstances, the role of "native" mediators could hardly have been untroubled: for the Africans, because they had to negotiate all the boundaries and cleavages put in place by the colonial evangelists; for the Europeans, because it compelled them to compromise the grammar of oppositions on which their worldview insisted. Was a black Christian—still black, after all—to be trusted with the gospel? Or would he (never she) taint it with savage superstition as he translated and/or taught it? These doubts, with which the missionaries constantly vexed themselves, were a product not of the actions of the Africans but of the imaginings of the Europeans. They would impede the project of seeding a self-sustaining black Protestantism in Bechuanaland. Nor did they take long to surface, manifesting themselves in the disposition of the Nonconformists toward their interpreters. Ironically, some of those people came from borderland backgrounds that defied the neat axes—white:black, colonizer:colonized, savage:civil—along which the missionary map was drawn.

Back, then, to our narrative. While the pioneer proselytizers of both mission societies capitalized on the willingness of the first Khoi converts to work as *bathusi* ("assistants"), especially in establishing schools and outstations,[39] they also kept a wary eye on them. Even the most enthusiastic advocates of "native agency," like Livingstone (1961:27, 81, 225f.; below), wrote repeatedly about the "impudence" and moral failings of early proteges. The latter, it seems, constantly found ways to flout church discipline and religious orthodoxy. Robert Moffat (Moffat and Moffat 1951:63f.) was particularly scathing about the "baptized Hottentots" who assisted him at Dithakong in the opening years. He cited "adultery, fornication, and incest" as their "reigning crimes," ascribing their immorality to the shortcomings of their faith. This, he said, was "founded on feelings and frames, visions and dreams." Not on self-reflective, rational conviction.

Greater yet were missionary misgivings about those converts—like the assistant preachers sent to the Griqua in 1814—who purveyed the gospel outside the circle of European oversight. Moffat was assiduous in bringing these men to heel (cf. Elbourne n.d.:23). In 1823 he reported disparagingly on the ritual ministrations of Cupido Kakkerlak, a Khoi who went among the Kora at Nokaneng,[40] and who had persevered valiantly under adverse conditions (Moffat and Moffat 1951:79):

> I told him that . . . he had better go to some place where he could earn bread for himself and his family, and no longer remain in his present situation, where he could not . . . but be a continued burden to himself and the missionaries. These remarks arose from a conviction that the character of him, and especially his wife, were in the highest degree detrimental to the cause.

The "appearance of his house and family," Moffat observed elsewhere (p. 18)— thus affirming our point about the lurking salience of African savagery—proved that Kakkerlak did not "intend to rise an hair breadth in civilization above them he pretends to instruct."

As the century progressed, the missions made more systematic efforts to regulate indigenous Christian evangelism in the interior; they also demanded, as a condition of everything they offered, strict conformity in rite and deed.[41] Ultimately, however, these constraints did not shackle the African religious imagination, even among those formally committed to the church. What is more, some who were quite orthodox in matters of worship were eventually driven by the paternalism of the Europeans, and by the reluctance of the latter to promote a "native" clergy, to contemplate institutional independence. Meanwhile, the majority of Tswana were simply not drawn into the immediate orbit of spiritual surveillance. They regarded the ways of the church with the same curious acquisitiveness that they applied to all other foreign ideas and techniques.

Over time, then, African mediation would have many modalities. In the late 1820s, when the Nonconformists claimed their own first converts among Southern Tswana,[42] the latter were encouraged, in true revivalist spirit, to hold prayer meetings in surrounding communities (LMS 1830:85; Whiteside 1906:333). Before long, newly baptized men were employed as "native teachers," working simultaneously as schoolmasters and catechists in the outstations.[43] All the "sanctified talent" available was put to the task of "multiplying" mission energies (Wright and Hughes 1842:42). This accorded well with the stress on "mass-marketing" then making itself felt in Britain—both in evangelical practice (Helmstadter 1992:10) and in the utilitarian push to educate ever larger numbers of poor children with the aid of student monitors (volume 3). Robert Moffat (1842:588), again:

> Hitherto our native assistants have been occupied only in their own villages; but there is little doubt that, after the Gospel has been introduced to a distant town or tribe by the missionary, these assistants will be enabled, with the help of a comparatively small sum, to follow him; and, by reading, teaching to read, exhorting, and a humble, devout deportment, prepare the people for greater advances in divine knowledge, and render them cheerful recipients of that civilization which the Gospel introduces.

Cheap and cheerful, perhaps, but these African assistants were expected to be faithful mouthpieces of verities that brooked neither critical reflection nor variance, so much so that preachers and interpreters often reproduced original sermons verbatim, complete with accompanying gestures (R. Moffat 1842:598),[44] a form of mimesis that came close to mimicry. None of the missionaries questioned the wisdom of being copied in this way; Moffat might have been the most patriarchal of the pioneers, but his orthodoxy in matters of religious discipline was shared by them all. "Nonconformists" at home, in Africa they demanded strict conformity. The stultifying effects of their insistence on dutiful obedience would return to haunt the next generation of evangelists, who complained bitterly of Tswana spiritual "apathy"; of what the skeptical John Moffat saw as a "dead-alive" subservience induced by the authoritarianism of his predecessors.[45] Certainly, this contrasted graphically with the animated forms of Christianity developed beyond the arc of the mission.

To the evangelists, one should add, a posture of conformity was a legible sign of "conviction," of a humble acquiescence before the elevating wisdom of the gospel. If they were to be faithful advocates of the Word, African teachers had to submit themselves to careful, prolonged training. Otherwise they would be incapable of giving the patient instruction required to revive a spirit long extinguished. Indeed, those prematurely cut off from the "voice"[46] of the European missionary had been shown to "conceive wild notions" (R. Moffat 1842:590). Here again we see the pragmatic cast of Nonconformist belief. It presumed a religious "sensibility" in all human beings; the possession of senses, that is, which were conduits to the mind and soul, and so could be used to reach into them directly. But reason had to bend these senses to her will. It was not enough that heathen ears be charmed by song, that heathen eyes see the benefits of Godly civilization, that heathen mouths taste the bread of Protestant charity, that heathen hearts be "touched" by the love of Christ. Only an untiring patrician vigilance, and painstaking teaching, ensured a properly "cultivated" appreciation of the Truth.

As this makes plain, the democratizing spirit of evangelicalism existed here in perpetual tension with the fear of African apostasy. The putative propensity of novices to slide back into paganism provided a ready rationale for the failure of the Europeans to promote baptized blacks to positions of responsibility in the church (Whiteside 1906:277; Balia 1991:45f.). Benign paternalism made congregants into perpetual pupils. More than twenty years after he arrived in the interior, for example, Robert Moffat (1842:589) declared that Tswana Christians were "still in their infancy." And too easily "puffed up" to be appointed as "official agents" of the LMS. On the other hand, as proof of the paradoxes of mission policy, he was already employing converts as "auxiliaries" to catechize, teach, and preach.[47] By 1842, six Africans were attached to his station in this capacity. The efforts of these men of "fervent zeal" (Mackenzie 1871:80) were, according to John Philip (1842:183), "the most remarkable work of God" he had witnessed. The Rev. Joseph Freeman (1851:264), Home Secretary of the LMS, who inspected Kuruman a few years later, was less rhapsodic. Echoing Moffat's pessimistic voice, he claimed that scarcely any of the "native teachers" would meet English expectations; none combined the intelligence, scriptural knowledge, and reading skills to convey spiritual knowledge effectively. His solution? No surprises here: rigorous training from childhood under close missionary supervision. Following Freeman's tour, the clergymen in the interior duly set about devising the first formal scheme for educating Tswana evangelists (E. Smith 1957:309).

The Wesleyans, in the meantime, had also put their converts to work. Giddy wrote from Thaba 'Nchu in 1839 that an intensive program of instruction was bearing fruit: "Thirty young men are employed every Sabbath day in itinerating and preaching to the neighbouring villages," he exclaimed, "and heathenish customs have received a mighty shaking."[48] What is shaken does not always fall, though, a fact that his successors would sadly acknowledge (Whiteside 1906:339f.). But, by the early 1840s, several "local preachers" were conducting day schools and services in and around Platberg and Thaba 'Nchu, and a cadre of class leaders were manifesting "due subjection to pastoral authority."[49] Cameron even suggested that two of these men might soon qualify as assistant missionaries. The enthusiasm did not last, however. As time wore on, the Methodists began to echo the LMS view that unseasoned converts tended to be "weak minded" and given to conceit (Whiteside 1906:277); this accusation being a sure sign that European authority had begun to feel itself challenged. In fact, white Wesleyans, citing "jealousy" and "limited attainments" among their Tswana agents, would argue, for decades to come, that the latter needed close oversight.[50]

Not all Nonconformists shared this opinion. Livingstone, for one, was a persistent advocate of the opposite view. With restless eyes straying toward vast, thinly populated regions up north, he held that minimally supervised "native" agency was the only practical means of provisioning Africa with "the bread of life" (1961:5). What is more, he professed to a strong sense that, if not kept on "perpetual leading strings" by European authority, blacks would make the most efficient evangelists, cultivating a robust, locally tuned Christianity (1974:106). Touching a chord seldom sounded by his peers, he offered (1974:106) that Tswana teachers had a "warm affectionate manner of dealing with their fellow countrymen"—and, crucially, a "capability to bring the truth itself before their minds entirely divested of that peculiar strangeness that cleaves to foreigners." Livingstone (1974:103) was dismissive of those who, like Philip, claimed that "true religion would disappear with the [withdrawal of the] missionary institutions." Sensing a rising sympathy among both clergy and statesmen for devolution and free trade, he argued for a largely self-propagating indigenous church.[51] Once sown, he insisted, the seed never died. Kuruman was a case in point. From there, the Word had been carried forth by various groups migrating to other places, several of which had set up vital congregations without the supervision of a white pastor (1961:147f.).

Many of the evangelists took exception to Livingstone's position. Some, he told his family in Scotland (1959,2:228), saw his views as heresy. Or, worse still, as worthy of the Plymouth Brethren. "There is no more Christian affection between most . . . the "brethren & me," he once quipped (1959,2:81), "than between my riding ox & his grandmother." Robert Moffat, while in sympathy with a number of his son-in-law's opinions, declared that his "remarks on Native teachers [were] exaggerated [sic] & some very erroneous."[52] But history was on Livingstone's side. Between the midcentury and the mineral revolution of the 1870s, a "ledger-keeping" laissez-faire (Whiteside 1906:337)—all too familiar to us these days—drove British statesmen to cast off some of their colonial dependencies; among them, with direct and dire consequences for Tswana, the Transvaal and Orange River Sovereignty (*RRI*:274). In a similar economizing spirit, the WMMS withdrew white pastors from three of its stations in the Bechuanaland District, leaving them in the hands of African teachers (Whiteside 1906:337); the LMS did nothing quite so drastic, but it, too, drew in somewhat on itself (J. E. Carlyle 1878:136). Making virtue of necessity, policymakers in late nineteenth-century European evangelical circles glossed this pull-back as a means to encourage local autonomy. They stressed the virtues of self-governing, self-supporting, self-propagating "native" churches (Sundkler 1965:40; J. E. Carlyle 1878:136).

Missionaries in South Africa itself greeted the call for devolution with ambivalence. Mackenzie (1871:79f.), for example, acknowledged that, where black Christians were "under the care of a native schoolmaster, more independent thought [was] begotten." Regrettably, however, competent instructors were thin

on the ground, notwithstanding the optimistic signs of earlier days: reports
from Bechuanaland revealed a mere clutch of "uneducated village teachers,"
who made a "feeble impression" (1871:80). The evangelists, worried about their
failure either to inculcate abiding religious orthodoxies or to produce capable
mentors, sought a remedy in ever more institutionalized schooling; as we shall
see in volume 3, pedagogy was to replace the Word, and hence preaching and
"kind conversation," as a panacea for the late nineteenth century. This, too,
failed to produce a sizeable indigenous clergy. But it *did* contribute to the rise
of a politically self-conscious black petite bourgeoisie.

It is instructive that Mackenzie (1871:80) took the lack of effective "native
agency" to be "the weak point of the Bechuana mission." His colleagues were
similarly prone to reducing the complex problems facing their enterprise to
inadequacies in local leadership.[53] This was overdetermined. As we have said,
the predicament of African mediators condensed the contradiction at the core
of colonial evangelism: the dissonance between its humanist universalism and
its Eurocentric chauvinism, its desire to localize Christian truth and its tendency to equate African cultures with primitive degeneracy. Inasmuch as they
embodied the effort to reconcile these incongruities, African apostles were eyed
with suspicion from all sides. To the clergymen, they personified the tension
between inert obedience and a vital, insubordinate domestication of the Word,
which is why there was persistent conflict between them and their assistants.[54]
To many Southern Tswana, black teachers were the anomalous emissaries not
only of the Europeans, but also of *sekgoa*, whose ambiguous powers were attractive yet threatening to indigenous authority.[55] As the mouthpieces of the missionaries, they were often subject, especially in the early years, to the same suspicion, even mockery, as their white mentors (Livingstone 1959,2:34). Perhaps
even more so as traitors to their "tradition."

In sum, then, few of the Nonconformists sustained Livingstone's
(1974:106–7) faith that African Christianity would bloom "in imperishable
youth" if "untrammelled by the wisdom of men." They tended, instead, to fear
the rank growth here of untutored, "wild notions." And they suspected self-
reliant local preachers of arrogance and apostasy; of what, toward the end of the
century, expressed itself in the rise of an assertive "Ethiopian" spirit. In 1899,
John Brown wrote from Kuruman:[56] "There is a grave danger threatening all
our churches, and especially our outstations. It is a movement known as the
Ethiopian Church . . . and its agents, I am told, are most zealous in their street
corner proselytising."

We shall return to Ethiopianism below. For now, let us note that, *pace* conservative clergymen, Christianity *was* sowing itself with vigor. But it did so in a
hardy, hybrid strain propagated some way off from the closely tended mission
garden. We should not be surprised that Southern Tswana moved by the Protestant spirit would strive, in various ways, to rupture the monopoly exercised over

it by European evangelists. Nor that they should be moved to find their own accommodations of the word to the world.

African Apostles: Domesticating the Word

They have well-formed heads, intelligent countenances, keen and penetrating eyes, with nothing vacant, absent, sullen, or unimpressible, and yet they remain heathen: reminding one of the affecting vision of the prophet, the valley "full of dry bones," till the Spirit of the Lord breathed, and the slain lived.

Joseph Freeman (1851:264)

What, precisely, did Southern Tswana make of mission Christianity? We put the question in these terms in order to stress both meaning and practice: How was the Nonconformist message *understood* by the Africans? And what did they *do* with it?

Our purpose in phrasing the issue thus is to suggest that the answer is to be found in historical *practice;* in words and actions that, simultaneously, (i) had a palpable effect on the world and (ii) gave voice, however refractory or provisional, to a particular sense of how that world was being reconstructed. By approaching the matter in this way we are not merely making analytic virtue of historiographic necessity, doing our best with a slim archive of salient narratives; indeed, the very slimness of those archives tells its own story. Southern Tswana, as we and others[57] have observed repeatedly, had a markedly pragmatic approach to religion. What they, singular and plural, made of Christianity is to be discerned and measured, therefore, by what they did to, and with, it.

In this respect, two preparatory points.

The first is obvious. But it bears repetition since its corollaries are crucial. Those Southern Tswana who made something of Christianity—who chose not to turn their backs on the theological assault of the mission—did so through a particular cultural lens. We cannot know, as we have said before, what they actually heard of the gospel. But it is clear that, insofar as they took the Nonconformist message into their everyday lives, the Africans did so on their own terms; in terms, that is, of their own prior spiritual orientations. The litany of "disgraces" of which they were accused by the clergymen often were the sins of a syncretic imagination. Indeed, these were the "hybrid" practices produced as Christianity was brought home. Home, where the ancestors resided, where compound families co-existed, whence youths went out to be initiated in order make them citizens of a political community.

Thus, for example, the "crimes" for which the "baptized Hottentots" were censured by Moffat (see above) grew out of a faith founded on "feelings . . . visions, and dreams." What the missionary probably misrecognized was the common tendency among African converts, Khoi and Tswana alike, to experience ongoing, occasionally dramatic, revelations from the living dead, a tendency that no doubt resonated with images of biblical inspiration and of the Holy Spirit (cf. Setiloane 1976:209f.; Sundkler 1961:250; Ranger, personal communication). Ancestors could not be banished from the world by European fiat. They continued to play a tangible part in the lives of Tswana believers, sometimes taking hold of persons (*go tsenwa*) and granting them the gift of special insight. All of this implied a more dynamic sense of divinity among Tswana than the Protestants were either able or willing to recognize; also a self whose openness to animating external forces was anathema to the mission, with its modernist ideal of a self-contained, self-controlled, self-willed Christian subject. Hence the discomfort of Moffat and his colleagues at African nonconformity, which spoke to them not of the persuasive power of cultural difference—to which they were largely indifferent—but of the sheer perversity of the savage mind.

The second point, whose relevance is less obvious but no less important, concerns "native agency." In the writings of the evangelists, and in most mission histories, the term refers to the activities of African converts who served one or another church as employees, paid or voluntary. This, however, is much too restrictive a delineation of both the practice and the role. Some salaried assistants worked not for but against the WMMS and LMS, finding fissures within them from which to subvert the European clergy and to appropriate Christian means to alternative ends. By contrast, many who were not on their books at all acted as "organic agents," seeking to disseminate the Word—often in quite orthodox form—from their own social and political niches; these organic agents, interestingly, included not only converts but also well-known heathens. Yet others fell in between, laboring officially for the church, but finding ways to spread the gospel in places and spaces of their own making. In order to throw light on what Southern Tswana made of Protestantism, let us explore instances of each of these variants. One thing, though, links them all. Native agency—paid or unpaid, formal or informal, Christian or heathen—always ran up against the ambivalence of the European missions toward the indigenization of their faith; the tension, that is, between their universal humanism and their fear of the degradation of Christianity at the hands of "others." In a very real sense, every African preacher and teacher, everyone who would traffic in the religion of *sekgoa,* had to arrive at some resolution to it.

One such resolution, which foreshadowed a number of similar cases in southern Bechuanaland, manifested itself first at the intersection of the LMS missions among Griqua and Tlhaping. It gives us our first glimpse of the emergence of a distinctly indigenous Christianity out of conflict and contestation between white clergymen and their black assistants.

In the late 1830s, a rumor was circulated to the effect that Robert Moffat had fathered a child by the wife of Paul, his African deacon (*RRI*:271).[58] Whatever the truth of the story, its conflation of adultery with miscegenation conjured up the worst nightmare of colonial evangelists, dramatizing the subversive possibility of racial and religious interbreeding across the frontier. Moffat was himself back in England between 1839 and 1843. During his absence, Hamilton and Edwards, who were left holding the fort, wrote in consternation to Peter Wright, LMS agent at Griquatown.[59] Two "native teachers" of his congregation working in the Kuruman district appeared to be keeping people away from Moffat's church. They had been especially successful at "Mothibi's place," the chiefly capital along the Vaal River to the southeast. What was more, these men were imposing ritual rules not "enjoined in the scriptures." In the "name of Christ," they had declared it sinful to "eat any and every kind of meat killed with gun or spear." Flesh, Hamilton and Edwards said, seemed to be more on their minds than any concern with a "holiness of heart and conformity to the revealed will of God."

Tension between evangelists at Kuruman and Griquatown was not new (*RRI*:269f.). And it was certainly heightened by the belief, on the part of those at Kuruman, that Griqua converts were spreading unsavory tales about Moffat in order to undermine his authority over his own domain.[60] But the dispute also brought to light deeper-seated resentments within the new black churchgoing elite, resentments against white control in general. Away from the oversight of the missionaries, African apostles had begun to elaborate their own synthetic Christianity out of signs and practices that resonated across cultural boundaries; among them, of course, Old Testament dietary proscriptions which spoke to the Tswana sense of food taboos—as, interestingly enough, the Griqua converts had understood. In later years, leaders of Independent denominations would institute similar taboos to define their spiritual communities (J. Comaroff 1985:218f.). There is also a foreshadowing here of a matter that would arise in secessionist church politics, starting with the first breakaway from the LMS in the area by the Native Independent Congregational Church at Manthe (near Taung): the alliance of congregation and chiefship against European dominance. Over the long run, it is true, some new elites emerging in the shade of the cross would challenge royal authority in the name of modernist Christian values. However, at the midcentury, many pastoral leaders were eager to apply their faith to the cause of local autonomy and communal reconstruction, a process in which rulers themselves were still important players.

Here, then, is the case of "native agents" in the employ of the LMS who sought to resolve the tensions of their position by creating an alternative Christianity *within* the purview of the church. To do this, they censured the missionaries, evaded their control, and persuaded their followers of a creed that fused elements of the gospel and the culture of European Christianity with familiar signs and practices.

A quite different form of "native agency" addressed the paradoxes of the Protestant presence, and formulated an alternative Christianity, not from within but outside the church. It was exemplified, in different ways, by one celebrated "backslider" and one influential "heathen," both of them chiefs.

The first was Sechele, whose singular fame as an African Christian and lapsed convert derived, in part, from the popularization of his spiritual biography by Livingstone and others. The Kwena chief, we are told (J. Mackenzie 1871:105f.; cf. Gulbrandsen 1993), was an avid scholar of the Bible.[61] Even after he was forced to leave the church on account of his "adultery," he was said to conduct family prayer and sermonize before his people each Sunday. In addition, he served as a self-appointed evangelist to his royal neighbors, "preach[-ing] regularly" in the court of Mzilikazi, says Mackenzie (1871:319), and teaching him "'pina ea sekhoa' (the white man's dance or religious service)." But Sechele also continued to sponsor "traditional" rites on behalf of his chiefdom; indeed, his ritual practice was, literally, an embodiment of cultural and spiritual fusion, of the workings of a dialectic of divinities. For him, there was no contradiction in participating in rainmaking ceremonies while praying to God. The Bible, he asserted in the face of the missionaries (see above), did not require him "to give up the customs of his ancestors." It enjoined him to believe in Jesus Christ. Which he did. Nor, owned Mackenzie (1871:106), was he at all unique in the perception that Christianity might co-exist quite comfortably with *setswana*.

Sechele, in short, solved the contradiction by refusing to recognize it. He drew on the scriptures to nurture his resilient spirit and on the church to empower his polity when it was threatened. But, in the end, he remained outside the compass of the LMS. What Mackenzie (1871:108) called his "chequered career" was a graphic instance of what social scientists would later term "syncretism," "particularization," "hybridity," or bricolage. It stemmed from an essentially relativist, open, pragmatic approach to foreign knowledge and practice. As we have said—and as is aptly illustrated by an enterprising Sotho royal diviner who invited the Rev. Casalis (1861:284) to go into partnership with him—this orientation permitted the incorporation of other ways of seeing and being without negating one's own. In their early opposition to the mission, interestingly, Tswana rulers often tried to make converts take part in collective rites, like initiation or rainmaking, as a condition of their religious *freedom*.[62] This, apparently, was intended not as a last-ditch "heathen" stand against the advance of revealed religion, as the evangelists thought. It was an attempt to ensure a continuing commitment to *setswana*—and to a Christianity that would live easily with it.

To be sure, while the mission, *qua* institution, constituted a threat to indigenous authorities—Macheng of the Ngwato termed it "another Chief in town" (Gulbrandsen 1993:54; *RRI*:261f.)—rulers often made use of its rhetoric and its rites, even as they held it at arm's length. Montshiwa of the Tshidi-Rolong, the second of our exemplary sovereigns, might have been regarded by the Europeans as "the most prominent heathen in the country."[63] And, early on in his reign, he might have fought bitterly with his Christian subjects (*RRI*:263). By the 1880s, however, he had appointed a "royal chaplain," made Methodism into his "state religion," and ensured that prayers were said at his *kgotla* (court) before all public ventures (Molema 1966:206).[64] Unconverted he might have been. But he insisted, as an affronted Rev. Lloyd put it, that "all his subjects be bound to him by ties ecclesiastical," and that all joined "his" (Wesleyan) church. He even tried, allegedly, to force an entire LMS congregation at the margins of his realm to switch its denominational allegiance.[65] At the same time, Tshidi oral history has it that he always surrounded himself with powerful *dingaka* (priest-doctors; sing., *ngaka*) and *baroka* (rainmakers; sing., *moroka*), and that his own ritual potency brought well-being upon his people.

Montshiwa's relationship to organized religion, and his very successful alliance with the WMMS,[66] is intriguing. On one hand, it obviously had a great deal to do with the pressures of contemporary frontier politics: as the colonizing forces of the late nineteenth century bore in on them, most Southern Tswana rulers arrived at one or another accommodation with the mission societies[67]— to the extent that, in the years after overrule, at least nominal church membership became the norm across Bechuanaland. Even so, that does not explain the Tshidi chief's propensity to "sandwich his conversation" with biblical passages, particularly from Isaiah (Molema 1966:206); or his participation in public worship; or his decision to ring a church bell at court every morning (*RRI*:264). These gestures, many of them unseen by white evangelists, went far beyond political necessity, far into symbolic surplus. In appropriating Protestant prayer, and placing it in careful parallel to *setswana* practice, Montshiwa did more than encompass the church. He encompassed Christianity itself, drawing it into his own spiritual mosaic; the pun, here, being suggestive. As all this indicates, religious commitment, among kings as among commoners, was not simply reducible to temporal self-interest. But neither was it a reliable guide to the substance of ritual practice. Just as Nonconformist worship found its way into predominantly non-Christian communities, so "traditional" rites continued in some "Christian" polities well into this century. As late as 1970, *bogwêra* was being sponsored, if sporadically, by the ruling Tshidi-Rolong line in the Mafikeng district (J. Comaroff 1985:106; cf. Schapera 1953:32).

As the guardians of communal ritual, then, Southern Tswana sovereigns were important vectors for the incorporation of Christian practice.[68] But their interventions rarely had the effect intended by the mission. A few, like Jantje of the Tlhaping (see n. 67), were "people of the Word," and gave the clergymen grounds for optimism in this respect. By and large, however, chiefs did not lead their people into the fold, as was first hoped (Livingstone 1961:149). Even those of whom the evangelists most approved did not always live in peace with them; indeed, it is ironic that Montshiwa and Sechele, the heathen and the backslider, were more supportive of Christianity and less subversive of its institutions than were many of their converted compatriots.

These sovereigns were not the only public personages who acted as "organic agents" in the Nonconformist cause. As long as rulers remained outside the church, others, typically junior royals, assumed leadership of *Bogosi yoa Kereste;* of the "Kingdom of Christ," that is, which came to exist alongside the chief*ship,* there to provide an alternative nexus of power, legitimacy, and mobilization. In volume 1 (pp. 261ff.) we showed how this fissure played into local politics. But its religious dimensions were also significant, not least from the vantage of the mission. These junior royal converts, many of whom were caught up in relations of rivalry with their chiefly kin (cf. Gulbrandsen 1993:58), were championed by the evangelists. Often, in fact, they were depicted as figures of noble enlightenment, saintly heroes forced to do battle with rude paganism (J. Mackenzie 1871:103, 410f.). Take, for example, Molema, the half-brother of Montshiwa (*RRI*:262), who was an especially celebrated character of this kind. Converted when his people were in exile at Thaba 'Nchu, he had returned with them to their former territory along the Molopo River, and had become an effective long-range emissary for the WMMS:[69]

Molema sends to me frequently to inform me how he is going on, and I have sent to him a large parcel of Scripture extracts, with directions how to proceed in teaching, holding the services, etc. He can read well and I have no doubt of his labours being blessed to the people. Thus have we in the wilderness, some 400 miles distant from our station, a society of Bechuanas and an unpaid native teacher zealously labouring among them . . . by means of whom we may reasonably hope the blessing of Christianity will be extended yet a stage further into the regions of heathenism and error.

The gospel was often effectively broadcast in the interior by such self-directed zealots (Livingstone 1961:147f.). But, while they were faithful to their calling, and quite orthodox in their Christianity, these men tended also to be independent of spirit; which is why they flourished beyond the reach of supervision.[70] The story of Molema is especially well-known.[71] Sent in the 1850s to establish an outpost at Mafikeng when his chiefly brother had to take refuge among the Ngwaketse (Molema 1966:35f.)—this as a result of Boer harassment—he became the assertive leader of the "people of the word." It was a role that brought him into conflict with Montshiwa, who accused him, from his retreat, of having set up a parallel polity of his own. Fraternal strife notwithstanding, Mafikeng grew into a strong, pious Christian community, marveled at by passing whites (e.g., Holub 1881,1:118f., 279, 294) and eulogized by the evangelists. Thus, for example, Mackenzie (1871:103) extolled it as a fine example of faith "not enervated by over-dependence" on European clergy. Yet the truth, as he later acknowledged, was that Molema "was by no means well disposed" toward the missionaries (Holub 1881:279). In fact, he made it extremely difficult for them to work among Tshidi—even when Montshiwa returned from exile, resituated his capital in the town, encouraged the WMMS presence, and placed "his" Methodist church at the center of the public sphere (Holub 1881:279; J. Mackenzie 1883:33). It was only after Molema died, predeceasing his brother, that the white Wesleyans felt comfortable in their own chapel here.

We shall have occasion to return to the church that Molema built. It represented one effective mode of dealing with the contradictions of colonial evangelism: mission Christianity *sans* missionaries. In the absence of white mentors, the Methodists at Mafikeng were not consumed by the problems of authority and autonomy in the Kingdom of God. Thus unburdened, they proceeded to work out their own accommodation of the Word to their world. While their theology and ritual bore the imprint of vernacular religious values, the mix was subtle, and free from bold, iconoclastic gestures. In fact, the style of worship and organization developed by such self-governing congregations within the Nonconformist mainstream remained closer than most to Victorian mission orthodoxy.[72]

Yet another resolution to the tensions inherent in "native agency" is to be found in the careers of two nineteenth-century LMS emissaries, Shomolekae Sebolai and Khukhwi Mogodi. Theirs was, in a sense, the inverse answer to the one contrived by Molema. While he created a mission without missionaries, they, to all intents and purposes, set themselves up as missionaries without the mission; although, by "without," we mean *sensu stricto* "outside." These men, both of commoner Southern Tswana backgrounds, pursued their vocation as pioneer evangelists along the frontier's frontier—in the "fever-stricken" swamps of Ngamiland, where several Europeans had died in an early attempt to found a station (Brown 1925:81). Shomolekae,[73] born in Kuruman in the early 1840s, became a model of patient black piety in the eyes of his mentors. He was also the subject of an "entertaining and well-illustrated" book for children, *The Apostle of the Marshes* (Brown 1925); British mission literature still tended to keep African heroes to the nursery (*RRI*:117). In a note appended to the copy lodged in the LMS archives, Wookey savored the irony of its reluctant protagonist as he patronized him: "A fine old chap," he said, but one who found writing "painful work" and was loath to relate his own "adventures." In fact, Shomolekae enjoyed little encouragement from the clergymen, who regarded him as an inept student.[74] They found no paid position for him until it was decided, in 1892, to revitalize the work in Ngamiland, where Khukhwi, a trained evangelist, already labored without remuneration. Independent of mind, Shomolekae appears to have relished preaching the gospel in far-flung places, with the Bible as his "sole teacher" (Brown 1925:8–9). He built a home and a church on an island in the marshes among the Yei, a subject people of the Tawana, whence he sent careful reports to his white mentors. These, however, were judged "not [to be] illuminating documents."[75] They seldom found their way into the chronicles of the LMS and have, as a result, left few historical traces.

The same could not be said of the correspondence of Khukhwi Mogodi, who had settled at the Tawana capital (Brown 1925:87). A keen writer, he authored a "regular letter" to the LMS monthly, *Mahoko a Becwana* (J. Jones 1972:115, 119).[76] His lively accounts of his trials, travels, and tribulations in the northwest swampland were in many ways a reprise, this time for black readers, of the narratives of discovery penned by early white evangelists. They provided pithy descriptions of local populations, heathen rituals, and fabled rainmakers. But Khukhwi's tone was dispassionate and often gently self-mocking: in one cameo piece, for example, he told how the Tawana chief had jokingly accused him of using medicine (the "water of faith") to make people into believers.[77] Like Shomolekae, he kept far away from Kuruman,[78] although his white overseers did recall him from time to time; once, remarkably, to censure his efforts to support himself through trade (see chapter 4). While they were commended for their "faithfulness"—and for that of their wives, described by one observer as deserving "at least equal honor"[79]—these African apostles virtually operated a Protestant outreach of their own. As with Molema, their religious practice, while self-propagating, remained fairly conventional in its content. It seems that the *further* they were from European supervision the freer they felt to essay an orthodox Christianity. Mission teleology, it appears, was sometimes turned around by "native" agency.

Taking Hold of the Church

By contrast to those African apostles who sought to domesticate the Word within the broad compass of the mission church, others, more radical in their riposte, broke away from it entirely. These movements, which originated under the noses of the evangelists,[80] were not only born of frustration with white Protestant paternalism, although that certainly played a large part in them. They were also a product of struggles involving the relationship of politics to religion in this fraught colonial theater. One was to prove a landmark in the early history of black "separatist" Christianity in South Africa, preceding even the rise of Ethiopianism: the formation of the Native Independent Congregational Church (NICC) at Manthe, which hived off from the LMS at Taung in 1885 (Sundkler 1961:38; Pauw 1960:47f.).

This secession occurred against a background of political instability: the southernmost Tlhaping chiefdoms, weakened by the effects of colonization, had divided several times previously during the century. In its own explanation for the split, the LMS offered that (South Africa 1925a:28): "[The NICC was] not so much a schism from the London Missionary Society . . . as a desire to have a tribal church distinct from that at Taungs, as the chief at Manthe sought for and ultimately received his independence."

Neither the documentary record nor oral histories belie this perception. The breakaway ruler, Kgantlapane Motlhabane, appears to have taken an active role in establishing the congregation and appointing its pastors.[81] Above all, he seems to have wanted a clergyman of his own, since men of the cloth had come to be the accoutrements, and often the agents, of sovereign rulers. To be the leader of a mere outstation, therefore, and to lack an evangelical presence, was a mark of subordination (Pauw 1960:53). In many places, the mission hierarchy was iconic of local political hierarchies—and, therefore, opened up a symbolic space for their renegotiation.

But the records suggest that something else, something rather more complex, was also unfolding. For a start, the Manthe secession was not an isolated case. Two others, similar in character, occurred in the area at the time. The first was led by the chief at Taung, where John Brown was stationed; by the very person, that is, from whom Motlhabane and the NICC were said to be asserting their independence. The second took place at Phokwane.[82] Although neither of the splinter congregations survived, and many of their members returned to the LMS after a while, their rise and fall were symptomatic of a deepening sense of disempowerment. Brown observed, plausibly, that these movements were one among several indications that "traditional" rulers were seeking to regain their autonomy. But he put it all down to parochial power struggles: "[T]he attempt of the head chief to assume the position of head of the church . . . naturally led to some of the petty chiefs making a similar effort."[83] The people would learn the folly of putting their trust in princes, he was sure: African sovereigns simply could not occupy the same position in relation to the gospel as they did with "rainmakers and heathen doctors." Understood thus, the mission was barely involved at all.

In point of fact, the mission was not nearly as incidental to the rise of these secessionist movements as Brown and others suggested. In their desire to drive a wedge between the ritual and political coordinates of the Southern Tswana world, as we saw in volume 1, the European clergymen had not merely subverted chiefly authority. They had spawned a legitimation crisis. This crisis was greatly exacerbated, in the late nineteenth century, by the impact of the mineral revolution in South Africa, by the expropriation of Tswana land and labor, and by efforts on the part of the state to weaken the chiefs; all of which made it hard for these sovereigns to exercise effective control over their subjects and/or to sustain centralized polities (see chapter 3). Predictably, in the circumstances, any attempt to recuperate a measure of self-determination was seen to require that things forced apart be put back together—beginning with the spiritual and secular axes of "traditional" governance. But the gesture was not confined merely to the restoration of political authority. The rupture of *bogosi* (chiefship), the tearing asunder of its ritual from its temporal dimensions, after all, also fractured the universe at whose core it stood. Hence, in taking hold of the church, and in domesticating Christianity, the point was also to put its potency to the project of communal regeneration. Significantly, at the same time as they built breakaway churches, rulers in the Taung district also tried to revive initiation rites, to set in train a variety of public works, and to introduce community-wide levies in "money or kine"[84] to fund the commonweal—all gestures directed, assertively, toward (re)building a public sphere in the face of powerful outside pressures.

On occasion, movements to take hold of the church also sought to dislodge and expel the missionary societies themselves. In this, they tended to be abetted by disillusioned "native" preachers who had, for one or another reason, been disciplined by the white evangelists.[85] For example, Chief Mankurwane of Taung took the opportunity created by the Bechuanaland Land Commission of 1885–86 to file suit against the LMS, in which he challenged its rights to the land occupied at Kuruman (Great Britain 1886a). Mankurwane had forbidden its clergy to hold services in his realm, but had seen his order summarily overturned by the colonial administration. Patently, he felt no affection for either the LMS or the state. Nor did Matsame, described in the documentary record as the chief's "teacher." This man had been a "native agent" at Taung for a spell, and was put in charge of the station while Brown was seconded to Kuruman in the early 1880s. The return of the missionary had led to conflict between them, and Matsame "lost the confidence" of the Bechuanaland District Committee. As a result, he was removed from his position and made to leave the church.[86] At the hearing of the Land Commission, he was an articulate witness in support of Mankurwane's (unsuccessful) case against the Society. The more general point is clear: the establishment of so-called "tribal churches" was an effort to seize initiative—often by using the white man's own means, his legalities, his spiritual resources—thus to turn back the encroaching forces of overrule. Among these, as we know, the mission was seen by many as a vanguard. The desire to excise it, then, signified a rejection of European authority in all its forms.

It seems not, however, to have signified a rejection of the Word, or the style of worship, of the Nonconformists. Even today, ritual and preaching in the NICC at Manthe, still the center of the movement,[87] shows surprisingly little deviation from the doctrine or demeanor bequeathed by the mission. Wookey's original hymnal is still in use, as is the book of *Christian Worship* [*Kobamelo ya Sekeresete*] of the United Congregational Church of South Africa. Indeed, a strong inclination toward orthodoxy has characterized this church from its inception; it is as if, in appropriating and redeploying the spiritual resources of *sekgoa,* of European power, the point was to keep them more or less intact. The NICC was one of the few independent denominations ever to be officially recognized by the Native Affairs Department in South Africa;[88] it continues to stress the formal training of its clergy and the constitutional grounding of its national organization (Pauw 1960:53). This, in turn, underlines another of its features, one that appealed both to its local founders and, later, to the apartheid government: its capacity to cultivate the ethos of a "nation at prayer" and so to promote ethnic consciousness (*RRI*:287f.). The alliance between the NICC and political authority has endured. Its president, the Rev. O. J. Kgaladi, served as Speaker of the "National Assembly" in Bophuthatswana; when his church was threatened by African National Congress comrades in the unrest following the demise of the "homeland" in 1994, he summoned no less a figure than Nelson Mandela to restore order in the district.

The theological conservatism of the NICC was thrown into relief when, in the late 1800s, a wave of "prophets" arose from within the mission communities of southern Bechuanaland. Far from accepting orthodox styles of preaching and prayer, these icons of iconoclasm improvised in various ways on the charismatic themes they found in the scriptures.

Prophets in Their Own Land

"Prophets," *baperofeti,*[89] the term often encased in anxious quotes by evangelists, made themselves felt in growing numbers as colonial incursion pushed Southern Tswana into ever more apocalyptic circumstances. While these visionaries drew on both *setswana* and Judaeo-Christian traditions, they addressed themselves directly to their compatriots. Many of the latter immediately saw a correspondence between, on one side, biblical prophecy and, on the other, spirit possession and oracular revelation. The Protestant missionaries, however, were inclined to dismiss their inspiration as heathen delusion (Willoughby 1928:113; Casalis 1861:284).[90] This was especially so after 1856–57, when the cattle-killing movement set in motion by the Xhosa seer Nongqawuse revealed the fateful force, and the anticolonial consciousness, at the heart of African millenarianism (Willoughby 1928:117). Thereafter, too, black charismatics were increasingly criminalized: Rev. McGee, for example, describes the truncated careers of two young men from Taung who claimed, in 1909, to be reincarnations of Jesus and John the Baptist. These "visitors from the Lord" promised that, if all cultivation ceased, God would destroy the whites and give the Tswana "everything"—indeed, "far more than they could desire."[91] The men were summarily arrested by the local magistrate and charged with sedition; their followers were publicly thrashed at the court of the Tlhaping chief.[92] Not all visionaries suffered the same fate. Some provoked the other standard reaction of modern authority to charisma: they were declared insane.[93]

In his account of the Taung incident, Willoughby (1928:121) failed to mention that the prophets had called on church members to "despise" the teaching of the mission.[94] To the whites, what was most unnerving about the seers spawned by the LMS and WMMS was the way they applied the idiom of Revelation to their own historical conditions; they had an unerring knack of using biblical rhetoric against the evangelists. But there was more to the actions of these visionaries than mere resistance and refusal. As Willoughby (1928:115) himself put it, "The Bantu [had] a natural aptitude for symbolism." And their ingenuity was fired by the frictions of the colonial frontier. In an effort to make a place for themselves on its troubled terrain, they drew freely from *setswana* and *sekgoa*—and set about reconstructing Nonconformist practice in their own image.

An early instance of prophetism, one which long anticipated the outburst after overrule, illustrates this process in some detail. We have already had cause to mention it in passing (*RRI*:248; also 1989:267–95). Described in the mission media as "Pretences of a Bechuana Woman to Immediate Communion with the Divine Being," this case occurred at the colonial edges of Southern Tswana territory in 1837. The events in question were related to the Rev. John Monro (1837:396–97) by two "exemplary" members of his church, "an apprentice and a Hottentot." Not only do they underscore the sheer inventiveness of ritual innovators here; they also introduce us to the symbolic repertoire that was to become popular among Tswana charismatics:

A Bechuana woman, who had been enrolled on our list of candidates, and who had made some progress in scriptural knowledge, first absented herself from the class of candidates, and then from the means of grace on the Sabbath. She prevailed on others to follow her example, by telling them that she had found out the way of enjoying communion with God. . . . One Sabbath-day she told her disciples, that now the time was come; and by her direction they met . . . about four miles from town, and at the stated hour *Sabina* commenced her vain devices, by placing a large earthen basin in a particular spot, using certain mystical words, and muttering indistinct sounds, while she poured water into the basin. Then taking out of a bag which hung by her side a number of square patches, (chiefly calico,) she put them down singly on a board one by one. She then took up one of the patches, which she held by the corners, and uttering a number of incoherent expressions, in which texts of Scripture, verses of hymns, and portions of the Lord's prayer, were jumbled together, she shook the patch with violence; then laid it down, and told her followers that this was the way to pray to God. She then took up another of the patches, and went through the same ceremony . . . until she finished her line of patches, after which she told them, that whosoever among them had acted according to her directions should *now* see the face

97

of God in the basin of water, and further, that, according to the sincerity of their prayers, God would speak to them out of the water.

We do not know whether God ever did speak to these Tswana out of the water. But we do know that the visionary persuaded them to follow her out of the church, to her well of inspiration in the wilderness.

Sabina, it appears, would not discuss her ministrations. She and her associates maintained a "sullen silence" (Monro 1837:396–97). But she obviously talked eloquently with her followers in a register intelligible to them. It was one whose inflections would be echoed by other Southern Tswana visionaries as they made Protestant Christianity their own. In an ironic recognition of the potency of Nonconformist worship, Sabina rent the sacred robe and deconstructed the Holy Service. And she recombined its elements into her own unique design; into a cultural cloth, so to speak, of shreds and patches. Her bricolage made concrete the logic of this recombination in a pageant of material symbols and verbal utterances. Bits of "jumbled" prayer became powerful spells as the captured force of Christian ritual was put to work, making tangible—quite literally, condensing—the numinous promise of the European deity, who had perplexed Southern Tswana by being pervasive and paternal, yet remote and uninvolved. This, clearly, was one effective way of "showing God" to the people (see above), of giving Him a palpable presence in their lives.

Sabina's liturgy also reunited words with actions and portentous signs. Note, in this respect, that the evangelists viewed "native" rites—with their stress on the indivisibility of the ear and the eye, of words, objects, and deeds—as "magic." As if in reply, the prophetess fused verbal elements of Christian prayer with the practical poetics of vernacular ritual to make her own strikingly animated, assertively syncretic service. Her bag of calico squares was reminiscent of the diviner's bag of dice, remade in white fabric. And, like many later visionaries, she expressed her spiritual powers, her ability to effect *collective* (rather than individual) salvation, in the idiom and with the instruments of rainmaking.

In particular, her basin of water would appear over and over again in the paraphernalia of Southern Tswana seers. One appeared in Platberg in 1843; she was promptly excommunicated by the Methodists.[95] Another turned up among the Rolong at Morokweng in the 1860s. A pied piper of sorts, he led the children around the town seeking to avert drought and annihilation by "singing songs and pouring out libations . . . from little pots which they carried" (Willoughby 1928:120f.). Yet another traveling prophet, Sencho Legong, who arrived in 1908 at the borders of the parched, politically sensitive Ngwaketse chiefdom, elaborated further the link between the *moroka* (rain doctor; plural, *baroka*) and the millennium. As an "angel" of God, he foretold not only torrential downpours and triannual harvests, but "absolute freedom from the white man's control and a return to all the old heathen customs of the past."[96] Great *baroka*, Schapera (1971:35f.; cf. Breutz 1956:77) shows, were often said to have the ability to charm enormous water snakes, reptiles that could draw rain down from the heavens. They also conjured up memories of miracles wrought by charismatics elsewhere, as when rods were turned into serpents before Pharaoh (Exodus 7.10). Sure enough, Tswana prophets also sometimes invoked these signs; although one puff adder, we are told, met an untimely death at the hands of a more orthodox Ngwato convert who was offended by tales of its sacred power (Willoughby 1928:107).

But, if they called forth life-giving waters, these prophets also brought down fire and brimstone. In order for there to be rain and plenty, there had first to be a cataclysm, a destruction of established order: the sweetness of promise, the harshness of judgment! In preaching the gospel, the Nonconformist pioneers had been eager to convey the urgency of their "news"; of the imminence of Godly damnation and, hence, the dire need for redemption. Like colonized peoples elsewhere, Southern Tswana seem to have been predisposed to hear the scriptures, told thus, as chronicles of epic struggle and portents of deliverance (Hebdige 1979:30f.; cf. Waltzer 1985). Under duress, some of the most avid of converts applied these lessons to their own predicament, giving a unique cultural twist to the more universal features of milleniarism (N. Cohn 1957). For example, Sencho Legong's many Ngwaketse followers, who included two preachers and an ordained African pastor, prepared for the end by burning their Bibles and hymnals. For his own part, Legong razed an LMS church in the Kwena chiefdom.[97] While the liberatory potential of their message had been internalized, the evangelists themselves had become palpable embodiments of a pervasive regime of occupation. Remember, from volume 1 (pp. 289–90), their growing realization, in the second half of the century, that many Southern Tswana had come to regard them as "deceivers"; worse yet, as "destroyers of the country" and "Agents of the Government." It was as if, by burning the texts and trappings that contained and concealed their distinctive power, they would free the might of *sekgoa* to fuel their own dreams.

This last point is vital. It is often misunderstood by those who see millennial movements merely as efforts to recapture a *status quo ante* (cf. J. Comaroff 1985:196f.). While these visionaries sought to sever the faithful from the signs of the invader—some insisted that their followers cease using European goods, or wearing trousers[98]—this was not a call simply to return to the past (cf. Willoughby 1928:115). If the charismatics wished to alter the terms of engagement that had insinuated whites into their world, they also hoped to distil the essence of *sekgoa* to remake that world. Legong, for instance, not only collected copious gifts of livestock from the hundreds he inspired. He also accepted a gun and a wagon, at once means and metonyms of a new material existence.[99] And, as the subversive Sabina demonstrates, prophetism sometimes challenged the male monopoly on divine mediation that prevailed in Protestant *and* precolonial Tswana ritual, if not elsewhere in black South Africa.[100] In playing with fire, an incendiary force in both indigenous and Judaeo-Christian iconography,[101] these "technicians of the sacred" (Eliade 1964) forged a fresh style of worship, taking charge of a flame kindled long ago in another wilderness of the human spirit.

The Nonconformists had no illusions about the gravity of the threat posed by these visionaries—and by the fact that they chose to defy the mission in a language over which it had no command. Whatever else they heralded, the prophets proclaimed the rise of a vitally transformed, Africanized Christianity. They also challenged temporal authority: Tswana chiefs would struggle to meet their fire with fire, even burning property in an effort to cauterize their presence (see n. 92). In the event, the apocalyptic moment passed. And the faithful recognized, reluctantly, that what had appeared to be the end was in fact a beginning: the beginning of a protracted age of colonialism from which there would be no immediate deliverance. Yet many of them clung fast to the lively promise of prophecy. As Setiloane (1976:209) notes, concerted missionary condemnation drove it underground in the orthodox denominations; although, even there, as we saw ourselves in the 1970s, it was never fully eradicated. Where it was to flourish most, however, was in the singular style of worship developed by the Zionist churches. This movement, an indirect but palpable heir to early prophetism, drew its inspiration largely from another millennial Christianity, this one in America, refracted it through the filter of local ways of seeing and being, and applied it to the circumstances of life in South Africa. In that context, too, the charismatic would be a conduit—and the vision, a fountainhead—of power, revelation, and healing. But that is another story, one which we do not tell here since it did not arise directly out of the encounter between the colonial mission and Southern Tswana; in any case, it has been fully dealt with elsewhere (J. Comaroff 1985).

Ethiopia, Free Thyself

Somewhere in the space between prophetism and more orthodox black Nonconformism, another movement took root: Ethiopianism. It, too, shaped its own brand of Christianity by seizing the signs and practices of evangelical Protestantism, domesticating them, and applying them to contemporary social and material conditions. The name of this movement derived originally from the Ethiopian Church, a secession from the Wesleyan Society in Pretoria led, in 1892, by one of its first ordained African ministers, Rev. Mangena Mokone (Sundkler 1961:39, 56f.). Frustrated by the racism in the Methodist church, Mokone found a charter for ecclesiastical self-rule in a verse much favored by the British missionaries themselves: "Ethiopia shall soon stretch out her hands unto God (Psalms 68.31; Sundkler 1961:39)."[102] This evocative image reverberated rapidly through the dense networks that were coming to link black Christian communities across the country. It suggested how "discrepancies" (Barrett 1968:268)—less euphemistically, contradictions—in the message of the master might be made the means of his own displacement.

The evocation of biblical Ethiopia linked an emerging sense of pan-African identity and diaspora to a disaffection festering in the hearts of mission converts (Chidester 1992:117). In doing so, it served well as an organizing trope for a cluster of newly independent denominations, most of them founded by leaders—educated commoners in the main—weary of the unyielding white control of an ostensibly universal church. But its rhetoric also gestured beyond the pulpit to oppression in the society at large. Nor were its implications lost on those in authority, sacred or secular. Already in 1893, members of the Cape Parliament had expressed concern. The editor of the *Cape Times* wrote that, in being simultaneously "of a racial, an ecclesiastical, and a political character," the movement paralleled the ambivalently regarded Afrikaner Bond, if with exactly the inverse aspirations.[103] Among evangelists, meanwhile, *any* indigenous challenge to their control was dubbed "Ethiopian," and was ascribed to "wily" outside instigators who were said to be "seeking entrances everywhere."[104] This was somewhat fanciful. True, Ethiopianism gave voice to a deep sense of discontent. But it required no outside instigation. Enough homegrown disaffection had been germinating for a long while.

Although the term "Ethiopian" was quick to gain currency, Southern Tswana adherents of the movement often disputed it, referring to themselves as *boikgololo*. Commented Williams, tartly:[105]

> I prefer the latter word as it meets the case better. It means "the free" i.e. free from the control of the White Missionary and verily it is so. Among the *Boikgololo* every man is a law unto himself. . . . Alas! Alas! That a word so grand in its ideals should be prostituted to such uses.

Derived from the verb *golola*, to "loose" or "outspan" (Brown 1925:79), *boikgololo* probably *did* capture more accurately the motivation, meaning, and cultural idiom of Ethiopianism in Bechuanaland. But Williams and his colleagues misrecognized one fundamental thing about the movement: it was not individual liberty that was at issue. It was the freedom to forge an authoritative moral order, a community of ethical and social commitment, to which black Christians could bind themselves. Both Ethiopian and prophetic leaders tended to found their churches on elaborate and explicit codes of conduct and rules of membership—although their legalism was inspired less by concerns with original sin than with the exigencies of interaction in the here and now (Pauw 1960:218–19; J. Comaroff 1974:63f.; cf. Willoughby 1928:388).

The evangelists might have misread the motives behind the movement among Southern Tswana. But they did recognize that the desire to break free of the mission had developed a good deal of grassroots support along the colonial frontier. John Brown was forced to admit, in 1898, that, "[f]rom a spiritual point of view . . . Kuruman is not dead, but sleepeth." He also observed that Ethiopian sympathy seemed to be sprouting vigorously on all sides:[106]

> Seele [Seile], the Evangelist at Khunwana, has . . . joined them. He has been in this and other districts, and the seed sown by him is, I am afraid, beginning to take root. I also fear that some of our Evangelists [in Kuruman] are in sympathy with the movement, and one, at least, in open defiance of all requests to the contrary, has shown public sympathy by allowing Seele to fill the pulpits in his charge.

In the language of "Christian warfare," a counter-invasion had begun. Ethiopia had extended her hands into the very heart of the Nonconformist mission. And she had her finger on the pulse of the disaffected—who, admitted Brown, were especially attracted to the movement, as were those who had been disciplined by the white clergymen. The latter told themselves that the Africans wanted a church without Europeans at its head because it would impose fewer "irksome laws," fewer demands for "purity and honesty in the lives of professing Christians." But Ethiopianism involved a more profound critique of colonial evangelism than this suggests, one born directly of the contradictions of the mission experience itself. What was at issue is illustrated by its most dramatic manifestation in Bechuanaland at the time (Chirenje 1987:94f, 144–45): the secession led by Mothowagae Motlogelwa, LMS evangelist at Kanye and a Bible School graduate of the ill-fated Moffat Institution at Kuruman (see volume 3).

In 1898, the court of Bathoen Gaseitsiwe, the Ngwaketse chief, rejected an overture to proselytize at Kanye by Seile, the Ethiopian who had so perturbed Rev. Brown. At the public assembly, one speaker accused Seile of merely "sprinkling heathens with water and taking them into his church." Bathoen himself declared that he "had been born in the London" and wanted no other society; he also reminded his people of all the practical benefits bestowed by the LMS.[107] Mothowagae had once shared similar loyalties. Having graduated from assistant teacher to Bible student, he had entertained hopes of being ordained as a Congregationalist minister. This was not unreasonable in light of the Nonconformists' long-standing ideology of self-advancement and their concerted efforts in the late 1800s to educate black leaders. But their good intentions were repeatedly compromised by their own entrenched Eurocentrism—typically expressed in a demand for proper "standards," measured in orthodox English terms, on the part of aspiring Africans. Consequently, they tended, over and over again, to find reasons not to elevate people of color to positions of authority.

Mothowagae was one such person. Instead of being promoted, he was posted to a remote Kalahari outstation. When he refused to go, he was dismissed by his white overseers. In the protest that ensued, many local church members, including the brother-in-law of the chief, demanded that he be ordained and installed in place of Edwin Lloyd, then the serving white clergyman at Kanye; Lloyd, it appears, was thought to have acted high-handedly in this and other matters (Schapera 1942:20). The protracted dispute that ensued drew in all the key players then involved in the struggle for the Tswana soul. In 1899, the Bechuanaland brethren had formally resolved not to recognize the Ethiopian Church. Now, a short time later, they feared that the followers of the dissenting evangelist would secede and ally themselves with that movement.[108] For their part, Ethiopian leaders in South Africa recognized his struggle as their own, and provided him with legal council. But Mothowagae did not immediately break his ties with the LMS, being more concerned at first to gain authority *within* the Society—the right to administer sacraments, perform baptisms and marriages, and so on—than to enter the expanding black national arena.[109] His efforts also implicated the Ngwaketse chiefship, to which he was by no means subservient, bringing Bathoen onto a collision course with the European clergymen. And this, in turn, sucked in the colonial state, which was eventually called upon to arbitrate as the conflict deepened.

We cannot pursue the details very far here. Suffice it to say that the records of the two-man delegation sent by the LMS to investigate the dispute point to an intractable gulf between the missionaries and Mothowagae. The latter was by then ministering to a breakaway congregation of no less than a third of the local Christians, and he expected to be accorded a degree of collegial respect. Far from receiving it, he was put down as "impudent."[110] To add fuel to the fire, he opened his own free school; Tswana instructors often ran one-person literacy campaigns beyond church walls.[111] This school seems to have thrived, and to have contributed to the popularity, even mystique, of Mothowagae himself. The local fee-paying LMS institution, by contrast, had floundered. This encouraged Chief Bathoen to intervene on his behalf—only to be reprimanded for meddling in church affairs. Thus rebuffed, the ruler granted the black evangelist first the right to hold services at his *kgotla* and then to build a chapel in Kanye (Schapera 1942:20). Here, to the dismay of the white clergymen, Mothowagae administered the sacraments to a growing band of followers.[112]

Royal patronage would be short-lived, however. True, Mothowagae had elicited Bathoen's firm support against the mission. Among his followers, moreover, he counted a growing number of the ruler's kin and affines, and a "large proportion of the heads of the tribe."[113] But relations between chiefs and Christian leaders were now more complex than they had been when independent "tribal churches," such as the NICC, had been content to restore ritual authority to local sovereigns (cf. Chidester 1992:116). For one thing, advances in communication had made places like Kanye less isolated.[114] And men like Mothowagae, their horizons expanded, had a markedly more universalistic view of the relationship between church and state. (Like all universalisms, though, this one had its own parochial expression: the movement was called the "King Edward

Bangwaketse Mission Church.") These men were also much more assertive about their role in the public sphere; Mothowagae's congregation, for example, became involved in power struggles surrounding the chiefship. Under such conditions, the evangelist was bound to fall foul of Bathoen. By 1903, the ruler, disturbed by his "insubordination," complained to the Resident Commissioner that he "treated him as an equal and not as a Chief" (Schapera 1942:20). The missionaries put this conflict down to the palace politics of the moment.[115] But that, once more, simplified matters. At issue here was an argument over the place, and the constitutional rights, of religious organizations in the society at large.

In the struggle that followed, the Resident Commissioner had to judge between two claims: Bathoen's that the "Ethiopian" was pursuing politics by other means and thus subverting legitimate chiefly rule; and Mothowagae's that his entitlement to freedom of worship was being compromised. It was an impasse that underlined, again, the contradictory implications of the opposition between the sacred and the secular imported into African communities by the colonial mission. The evangelist proved highly adept at exploiting the conflicting possibilities of Tswana and English law: on one hand, he used the rhetoric of British jurisprudence to assert his constitutional rights; on the other, he avoided chiefly banishment by appealing to the customary veto of the mother of the sovereign.[116] The Commissioner, thoroughly disconcerted, first decided to uphold Bathoen's request, then rescinded his own order. Mothowagae was finally made to leave Kanye for a remote corner of Ngwaketse territory in 1910. Here his congregation survived until well into the 1920s, their indefatigable leader constantly protesting their right to religious freedom—and making common cause with nascent Ethiopian groups in other Tswana towns (Chirenje 1977:221).

Unprecedented in the force of its challenge to white mission authority, Ethiopianism was the product of a particular phase in the rise of black consciousness in South Africa. This was the period that saw the emergence of an assertive African press and other supra-ethnic associations, and culminated in the formation of the South African Native National Congress (later ANC) in 1912. The connection between the independent Christian movement and African nationalism is usually said to have been limited (L. Kuper 1971:436f.; cf. Oosthuizen 1968). But the cultural content of both owed much to the long struggle with racism, both blatant and latent, within the Protestant churches.[117] Above all, though, Ethiopianism announced the birth of a humanist Christianity that insisted on uniting the word and the world, religion and moral action. Unrecognized offspring of the Dissent, these secessionists carried its practices far beyond the horizons of their mentors—and into the cauldron of colonial struggle. The first Ethiopians never recruited a great many members among

Tswana. In the north, especially, chiefs joined the mission societies and the government in reining them in. They were also plagued by the continuing subdivision that tends to bedevil such passionate democratism. But their salience to our story far outweighs their numbers.[118] For, in daring to unhitch the African spirit from the grasp of white Nonconformist hegemony, they pointed the way for generations of independent black Christians to follow.

The documentary record suggests that Ethiopianism shook the Bechuanaland mission to the core. Not only did it incur anger at Tswana "ingratitude." It also provoked a good deal of self-reflection.[119] In their public deliberations, the likes of Willoughby (1923:237f.) admitted that the pride and conservatism of the white clergy might have "left the reformers without hope." Yet he sought the "final cause" of the movement elsewhere: in the "nigger-hating nonsense" rife among "Afro-Europeans" (1923:241). Nonetheless, in the matter of African Christian independence, as in everything else, the missionaries were caught in the middle. The colonial establishment, they knew, charged them with "encourag[ing] their converts to think themselves brothers and equals of the Whites" (Willoughby 1923:241). Yet black "reformers" in their own ranks—Willoughby's usage identified them with an ancient Protestant tradition—accused them of failing to make brotherhood real in the church. Even the Native Churches Commission would cite the "colour bar" among European evangelists as a prime cause of separatism (South Africa 1925a:25). This liberal dilemma would continue to dog the Nonconformists as they sought to redirect their activities with the advent of the modern South African state after 1910. It was the kind of dilemma often faced by members of a "dominated fraction of the dominant class" (Bourdieu 1984:421; *RRI*:59), especially when they assume the role of moral mediators between oppressor and oppressed. Indeed, it would shape the history of struggle for much of liberal Protestantism throughout twentieth-century southern Africa (de Gruchy 1979; Villa-Vicencio 1988; Balia 1991).

More immediately, the debate among clergy and statesmen—later, scholars as well—over the "real" nature of Ethiopianism was dominated by one question: Religion *or* Politics? Was the movement truly "religious"? Or did it have, as the South African Native Affairs Commission (South Africa 1905:63) put it, "mischievous political tendencies"? The latter were eventually discounted after an official inquiry. But the question was never fully laid to rest, in part because, despite the assertiveness of their Christianity, the Ethiopians seldom *professed* doctrines any different from those of the parent churches. Even when absolved of "Politics," in the upper case, they were said to have been preoccupied with issues of authority in matters ecclesiastical and administrative (e.g., Oosthuizen 1968). But that rather misses the point. Pragmatic faiths of this kind typically defy conventional distinctions, not least that between the "religious" and the "political." They are always both—and therefore, strictly speaking, neither.

Ironically, efforts to reduce Ethiopianism to one or the other obscured the manner in which it was experienced from within. They also overlooked some of the more profound transformations of Protestantism effected in its practice.

We stress that Ethiopianism was not unique in the way it made Christianity its own, although its links with the African Methodist Episcopal Church gave it access to the different Nonconformist tradition of black America.[120] But the domestication of Protestantism occurred even in the mainstream mission churches, particularly as more of them were entrusted to Africans during the early years of this century (cf. Setiloane 1976:185f.). Subtle, slower, and largely unremarked, these shifts were a consequence of the impact, over the long run, of indigenous religious dispositions on Nonconformist teaching—a process which, as we shall see, was refracted along widening fissures of class. To wit, the spectrum of Christianities that took root in Tswana communities—from the most orthodox denominations, through the movement founded by *boikgololo*, to Zionism—was centrally implicated in the making of new cultural distinctions, new social differences.

At the same time, Christianity also provided a common language with which to think and speak about the relationship of local communities to worlds beyond, worlds of which they were rapidly becoming part. The way in which Southern Tswana used this language, this sacred legacy of words and images and texts, often ran against the grain of mission orthodoxy. It was not just that the tribulations of the Israelites, or the promise of Cush, struck a more resonant chord with black experiences of overrule than did the ambiguous commonwealth of the mission. It was also that much of British Protestantism—its conception of time and space, its contemplative mode of worship, it docile praying bodies—simply did not connect with the religious sensibilities of many Africans. Nor is this our reading into the past: we heard it repeatedly in the 1960s and 1970s from, among others, Southern Tswana Methodist, Anglican, and Catholic clergy.[121] In unyoking the Christian legacy and making it their own, African reformers seized its potential and put it to work in the attempt to nurture a sense of collectivity. The mores taught by the mission as a means of conquering sin, and the rites that promised individual redemption, were redeployed by independent congregations to fashion a shared communion in the here and now. Accounts of the first independent churches leave little doubt about the passion with which they set about this task. Their reformation-in-practice reshaped several of the core categories and principles of European Nonconformism—not least, the very idea of the sacred.

*****

The remaking of the interior as a colonial province brought a host of new ecclesiastical influences to bear on Tswana communities—including missions other than the LMS and WMMS. Already in 1865 the Anglicans had established themselves close to the Wesleyan station at Thaba 'Nchu;[122] later they also built a church at Kuruman.[123] After the mineral revolution, there was a gradual multiplication of orthodox denominations; eventually the first three were joined by, among others, Roman Catholics, Lutherans, Presbyterians, Dutch Reformers. Each opened up a more or less pliable space in which congregants might make their own spiritual accommodations—in both senses of that term. The independent movements diversified the field yet further, first with the formal arrival of the Ethiopian Church and then through an explosion of Zionist groups. On this much populated terrain the Africans found a wide range of sites in which to give expression to their spiritual sensibilities.

From the late nineteenth century onward, Southern Tswana began to join churches *en masse*. This does not mean that there was a mass change of heart; many of the new "converts," as the evangelists were aware, were no more than "nominal" Christians (Schapera 1958:passim). During this period, the church—in the generic sense of the term—became part of the taken for granted sociopolitical landscape; part, so to speak, of the establishment of an emerging colonial world. There is an irony here. In 1820, says Campbell (1822,2:139), Tswana traveling south "expected to find every white man in the colony a Missionary." Over the next eighty years that illusion was dispelled. Yet, by the end of the century, Christianity had indeed insinuated itself into the warp and weft of colonial society. It was not only that church affiliation was a *sine qua non* of advancement for blacks; for access to jobs and schools and a "better" future for their children. Even more, as we shall see in the chapters below, Christian moral and legal discourse, not to mention Christian political economy, came to pervade the very language of interaction here. The church, in short, became metonymic of civil society, framing the altered universe in which the Africans now found themselves. Entering it signaled a passage across the threshold of that universe; it was an emblematic gesture, an act of positioning. Indeed, we are not the first to have been struck by the disconnection between the mass "conversion" of Tswana and the apparent lack of purchase that orthodox Christianity, as a religion, had over most of their lives (see Schapera 1958).

Patterns of church affiliation had their own sociology, of course. They were closely related to class divisions whose social origins we shall encounter in the next chapter. Broadly speaking, the emerging elites of the new bourgeoisie composed much of the membership of the mission churches, and were their most stalwart, most orthodox members. Some of them stood out as staunch bearers of Protestant religious and moral sensibilities; they were also the most comfortable in taking on the ways of *sekgoa*. By contrast, the poorest tended to seek out the Zionist denominations, where the community of the church provided a social context within which to deal with the exigencies of a world run amok. And those in the middle found the independent churches, in the tradition of *boikgo-*

lolo and biblical Ethiopia, most appealing. But these were only broad correlations as people moved about—sometimes in search of healing and fellowship, sometimes in their own pursuit of the numinous.

TRANSPOSING THE REDEEMER'S SONG

How, then, to describe the *substance* of these African appropriations, these domestications, of European Protestantism?

We have already anticipated the answer. In fact, our entire account thus far has laid the ground for it; here we begin to bring together its various strands. Note that we do *not* address the problem by describing the rites or religious orientations of any of the numerous independent churches that emerged, or found a home, in Bechuanaland. Rather, we approach it schematically: by identifying generic forms and practices—and then by exploring, in broad comparative terms, how they came to be refracted across the ever enlarging terrain of Tswana Christianity. This for two reasons.

The first is evidentiary. In the mission churches, appropriations occurred surely enough; Christianity *was* domesticated, if in variable degrees and various ways. But, for the most part, this happened exactly where it would go unremarked and undocumented: in the interstices of routine rites, in the invisible depths of experience, in unsaid words and unrationalized actions. Radical religious movements and "organic" reformers, likewise, rarely left written signatures on historical processes. Early Ethiopian leaders, Chirenje (1977:222) reminds us, gave little account of their motives and commented even less on matters of faith or liturgy;[124] the same is true of most of the charismatics. And few contemporary accounts exist of any of their services or sermons or sacraments. In short, there is no archive, in the conventional sense of the term, to draw from. The creative impulse that drove these movements arose within the mission fold without consent, and persisted at the margins of white awareness. Not that this makes their legacy irrecoverable. Quite the contrary. It was writ large across the styles of worship that developed in Tswana communities, and has remained perceptible, though obviously not unchanged, through this century.[125] But, like the less visible transformations wrought within the orthodox denominations, it has to be recuperated from indirect speech, from dispersed recollections, from an archaeology of enduring symbolic practice, and from ghosts of Christians past that linger on the cultural landscape (see above, chapter 1).

The second reason is analytic. Insofar as Tswana Christianity may be said, heuristically, to have composed a continuum—from mission orthodoxy through Ethiopianism to Zionism—we might expect there to have been a closely correlated range of distinct religious beliefs and practices. Very broadly speaking, there was. And yet, as soon as we look closely and comparatively at the practical theologies of the various denominations—observe the shift here from form to pragmatics—predictable patterns decompose. Some features that ought, perhaps, to have been clearly differentiated across the continuum turn out to have been shared, or inflected hardly at all. Others even ran counter to expectation. Moreover, it becomes apparent that the way in which individuals inhabited the churches, and lived their spiritual lives, did not map neatly onto the denominational landscape. A schematic topology of practice, in sum, yields counterintuitive insights into the domestication of the Word in this part of the world—and, by extension, into the dialectical processes by which modern African religious sensibilities have been shaped.

Let us begin, then, by returning to practical theology. And by parsing it. First, the *practical* . . .

If there was one thing common to the way in which Southern Tswana reacted to the Christian message, it was the attention they paid to its pragmatic dimensions. In the long conversation with the colonial evangelists, they listened to the Word professed, but were moved by the word-made-flesh: by the promissory power of the Protestant God, as manifest in His emissaries, to heal and promote communal well-being. Thus did divinity "show" itself, and proclaim its ineffable presence, both as an ontological reality and as a force in the world. This orientation was not only given voice in acts of veneration. It was also expressed in the early insistence that the real potency of the white clergymen lay in their practical knowledge and their objects, many of which were regarded as "medicines." This is why Southern Tswana were wont to see evangelists as doctors (see chapter 7); why they tried to induce them to make rain or, at the very least, to hold prayers for it; why they constantly embroiled them in political schemes; why they often sought to gain possession of their commodities. Reciprocally, it was these reactions that prompted Broadbent, Moffat, and others to comment on the "carnal" tendencies of the "heathens," on their refusal to heed the gospel unless it brought some immediate temporal benefit. For the missionaries, this was a symptom of African degeneracy; for the Africans, it was a reflex of the indivisibility of the temporal from the spiritual aspects of religion. This is underscored by the fact that it was not only Europeans who were treated in this manner. *All* bearers of new cultural expertise were—as we know from accounts of the reception of ritual specialists, including Christians charismatics, when they visited Tswana communities. Even in the 1970s, stories were told, in respectful awe, of the capacities of Sarwa ("bushmen") practitioners and Zionist prophets to cure diseases resistant to Western medicine.[126] In short, it was not the whiteness of the evangelists that gave them their power. It was their disposable cultural knowledge. One corollary, though: what appeared most potent about the Christian message to the Africans often transgressed the bounds of what its European messengers themselves took their religion to be.

We stress that the indigenizing emphasis on practical faith was not confined to the early confrontation with colonial evangelism. The ethnohistory of

Southern Tswana religion, as recounted by clergy from the mainstream denominations in the 1970s, reiterated many of the same themes. And it insisted on their longevity. We were told over and over that their own orthodox, Eurocentric Christianity—"too" European was a phrase uttered often—had failed to "heal the whole man, help the whole man."[127] Added one Methodist minister, pointedly, it had lost a form of ministry that had been there in the time of the prophets, a form of ministry to which Tswana responded enthusiastically. These religious functionaries also volunteered, sometimes in self-criticism, that worship in their churches remained too abstractly verbal, too disengaged from the everyday concerns of ordinary people: "The church is a chatterbox," said the pastor of the AME church in Mafikeng in 1969, reflecting on the irrelevance of mainline Protestantism in the era of high apartheid (J. Comaroff 1974:220). A Catholic colleague noted that his congregants preferred to pray "with their feet"; when they did, it "brought up what was in their souls." Like many leaders of denominations of mission origin, he recognized that communicants attributed "magical" qualities to the sacraments. He also regretted that they went elsewhere in search of "ritual healing," a term used in more than just the corporeal sense. All of this merely reaffirms, in "native" voice, that the full-bodied, pragmatic ethos at the core of Southern Tswana spiritual life has endured over the very long run. The question, though, is *how* exactly was it made manifest, across the various denominations, as Protestantism was domesticated. We shall return to the answer in a moment.

Before that, . . . *theology*

For Southern Tswana, the presence of superhuman forces in the world, of divinity, was taken as axiomatic. So was the power of these forces to determine the way life was lived. They were experienced in two forms: *Modimo* and the *badimo.*

Whatever the spiritual archaeology of *Modimo,* itself left unresolved in the debate between Moffat and Livingstone, the supreme being became a key point of reference in conversation across the religious frontier; indeed, the mutual agreement that He[128] existed laid the ground for presumptions of a common humanity. Yet this agreement, and the discourse that established it, hid the fact that significant conceptual differences lurked in the silences on both sides. There is evidence, for instance, that the Protestant God remained a rather remote figure for many Tswana Christians—despite the best efforts of the evangelists to bring Him closer by casting Him as a stern yet compassionate father figure. This is not to say that His revealed presence, as evoked in the Bible and in acts of worship, inspired no reverence. Hardly. Dissenting black visionaries were drawn to the aesthetics and power of the "sacred service." Why, otherwise, deconstruct it and refigure its signs, as Sabina did, in order to persuade the Lord to speak to the living? Why, otherwise, use the Holy Book in apocalyptic preaching and divination, as did Ethiopian and Zionist leaders? For people accustomed to praise poets and enigmatic diviners, moreover, biblical psalm and prophecy had obvious resonances; just as, for those steeped in a rich legal culture, the Law of Moses and the Abominations of Leviticus made a great deal of comparative, quotable sense. Hence their invocation by Southern Tswana in debating with the European clergymen, and in seeking to give divine legitimacy to their arguments with colonial authorities.

Still, without some form of intercession, *Modimo* remained genially unconcerned with the affairs of his free-willed subjects. That is why prophetic figures had such lasting appeal to Southern Tswana: as messengers and intermediaries of God, they enabled Him to dwell among them in human form, and so made real the Christian promise. For, while the Africans had come to accept the supreme being as Lord of all in the universe—as the spiritual ground, in Horton's (1967) terms, of a global, macrocosmic awareness—none of them actually *lived* in the macrocosm; nobody ever does. Rather, they lived in a world in which relations among human and superhuman beings were personal and partisan. Under these cultural conditions, Protestant divinity left a void just where their religious imaginings were most active. The problem, for them, was *how* to tap the might of *Modimo,* how to bring it into palpable connection with their lives. Even then, it was widely assumed that He would only concern Himself with major events: drought, destruction, catastrophe, cataclysm.

This is where the *badimo,* "gods who know our faces," entered into the pantheon of a humanist, "down-to-earth" Christianity (Setiloane 1976:186). The ancestors, always a vital presence in Tswana experience, continued to stand by their descendants in the domain where the Protestant god was most remote, the domain in which mortals felt most in need of spiritual protection; all of which underlines our earlier point that their active participation in everyday life was the key to their numinous power. Not only did they accompany the living everywhere, but they were pressed increasingly to intercede with *Modimo.* In this capacity, they were the addressees of much heartfelt prayer—and the bearers, in dreams and visions, of divine inspiration. A respected elder and lay church leader told us in Mafikeng in 1969 (J. Comaroff 1974:269):

> I cannot simply approach the chief. I must approach him via the headman. . . . The chief cannot really recognize me (*ga a nkitse*). My wishes must be interpreted to him. With God it is as if he and I speak different languages. The ancestors know the language of God, and they are nearer to him. They have the right to approach him. But with me it is quite different. . . . [I]f I was to speak to him, he wouldn't know me.

Some Southern Tswana put it to us that the moral regime vested in *badimo* was not incompatible with Christian ethics; that, to the contrary, it had long anticipated them (J. Comaroff 1974:285).

As this implies, the figure of Jesus was often eclipsed by these more proximate mediators.[129] The senior Anglican clergyman in Mafikeng in the early 1970s, the Rev. Chipfupa, an eloquent advocate of a black theology, was wont to say that the received image of Christ made little sense to many Southern Tswana, himself included. Apart from being a pallid white man, who appeared no match for the devil, he was *God*'s son, not an African father, and therefore not plausible as a partisan intercessor. Once again, all this raised a problem for orthodox Christianity. While *badimo* appeared capable of rendering Protestant divinity more immediate, more interested, more responsive to a changing local world, they were not recognized in the mission churches. In the independent denominations, particularly those of a prophetic bent, their presence was more palpable; it was often glossed, generically, as *moya* (literally "breath"; like the Hebrew *ruah*), also the term for the animating force of the Holy Spirit (cf. Sundkler 1961:250).

But what does all this add up to? First, that colonial evangelism bequeathed Tswana a range of creative possibilities in the realm of the spirit; that these were taken, refracted through the prism of *setswana*, and, at times in open argument with the missionaries, condensed into the terms of revised, practical theology. Second, that in fashioning their Christianities thus, the Africans built on a series of common elements, themselves distilled from the encounter between the Protestant legacy and their world; and that, in doing so, they ran into a number of common challenges, common conundrums, in giving expression to their religious sensibilities on a transfigured spiritual terrain. Third, that each denomination, each movement, responded to those challenges differently, thereby arriving at its own living creed and repertoire of ritual practice; that this yielded a devotional landscape, a geography of numinous possibility, within which individuals might situate themselves—or across which they might move in the course of their lives.

We do repeat, however, that the coordinates of this landscape derived from a practical religiosity whose essential principles were widely shared. That is why, whatever their formal affiliation, people might, and so often did, attend churches other than their own (cf. Murphree 1969:140); why, to the enduring puzzlement of white observers, there was so little systematic doctrinal difference among the various Christianities, notwithstanding stark contrasts in styles of worship (Pauw 1960:107); why doctrine was so seldom made explicit at all. Because Southern Tswana placed primary emphasis on pragmatic ritual, it follows that denominational dissimilarities would be most clearly evinced in practice. To be sure, the manner in which mission orthodoxy was refashioned across the religious spectrum may be told as a story of *enactment/s:* of the diverse ways in which transformed notions of spirit, ritual, community, and the Word were played out, registers of feeling retuned, and the devotional self reoriented. It is here, in fact, that we find answers to the three questions posed along the way: How did the practical theology at the core of Tswana spiritual life manifest itself in the various Christianities? How was the force of *Modimo* engaged? And how were the *badimo* accommodated into Christian worship?

The most radical enactment, the most audible answers, were to be found in the independent African Christian movements. At the heart of these movements lay an effort to close the gap between the Christian subject and the master narrative of salvation, thus to make redemption tangible in scale, local in application, and accessible in experience. Petersen (1995:11) describes their orientation as *kairotic;* one which strives, in Tillich's terms, to make the eternal "transparent in the particular." From this ontological vantage God is immanent in the everyday. However else He might be imagined, his Spirit was made manifest, above all, in the human form, his chosen instrument. It was in the language of bodily signs, Setiloane (1976:219) says, that "Christ's work of Salvation of the individual person [was] understood."[130] And relived, again and again. For in the body, the telos of the gospel, its past marvels and its future promise, intersected with life in the present tense. Hence the portentous power of a biblical Ethiopia. Hence the possibility of a prophetic realism in which visionaries might step seamlessly into the *mise-en-scène* of the Old Testament and return to herald the millennium. Hence, also—if the body was the meeting ground of spirit and flesh—the salience of healing as the quintessential religious act, as a sacrament in itself.

The devotional self at the center of independent African Christianity was markedly different from the person presumed by Protestant prayer. The posture of piety required by the "white man's dance/service" (see above) showed itself in the sedate, "starchy" worshiper seated in a straight row, body reverentially subdued (Setiloane 1976:201). The very uneasiness of the phrase, the "white man's dance/service," calls attention to the fact that what was kept apart in *sekgoa* was indivisible in *setswana*. In the vernacular, the verb "to venerate" (*go bina*) also meant "to dance" and "sing" (RRI:241). The "native dance" had been avidly opposed by the evangelists. They had believed it to be the very antithesis of prayer, a profanity in which flesh overcame spirit, in which the hypnotic force of superstition stifled individual reason (Broadbent 1865:187; *RRI*:260).

In the different corporeal culture of Southern Tswana, the act of worship was "moving" in all senses of the word. The human frame became the sonorous instrument of the divine, whether in forceful preaching and responsive listening or in the making of "joyful noise." The production of rhythm and harmony compelled a body of people to move "in time." And it epitomized the pragmatic power of rites to effect a coherence of action—a communion—that instantiated transcendence as it "drew down the spirit" (Comaroff and Comaroff 1992:89). Especially in prophetic churches of the sort known as "wells of healing" (*didiba*), this distilled power was put to work; called upon to redress those afflictions caused primarily by the disembodied will of others, living or dead. *Badimo* were frequently acknowledged in such rites, and in the extemporary prayers that were part of them. Often uttered audibly by worshipers in a simultaneous stream of supplications, these prayers came together in a cacophony of community, of chaos made *kairos*.

Here, then, ritual was less a matter of individual consumption than of interpersonal production; less a vehicle of private, self-contained worship than the synchronized step of a community under the sway of the Holy Spirit. As time passed, preaching, which remained significant in many groups, especially those of Ethiopian origin, grew more experiential than scriptural in substance; often rich in its rhetoric, it grafted indigenous poetic traditions onto the animated dialogics of the black American pulpit. Prayer, dance, and song came together—and brought people together—in an act of devotion whose aesthetic and numinous power was at once awesome and embracing. This was most evident when, as they often did, intricately choreographed movements underscored the lyrics of hymns, whose own rhythms and harmonics marked the quickening pulse of vernacular spirituality. Interestingly, according to Mackenzie (1871:468), non-Christians sometimes referred to hymn singing as *go bokwalela*, to "utter the death-cry."[131] To members of the independent denominations, song, dance, and veneration were the life-giving media of a humanist faith, a faith centered on inspired social action. Measuring out the distance from early mission orthodoxy to an indigenized Christianity, *go bina* also pointed toward mass action yet to come; specifically, toward forms like *toyi-toyi*, the dance that was to galvanize practical resolve, to cry freedom, to sing of a "new" South Africa in the making.

But what of the mission churches, the mainstream Protestant denominations? How did Tswana in them make Christianity their own? These, after all, were sites of maximal surveillance, in which white clergy required that proselytes (*badumedi*, "those who agree," in Setswana, *RRI*:247) profess their beliefs and adhere to ecclesiastical law, that "backsliders" be struck from membership, that things hinting of African "superstition" be strictly disallowed. We know, already, that Tswana did not enter these churches in great numbers for most of the nineteenth century; also, that the evangelists often distrusted their conversions as "shallow-rooted" (*RRI*:243). But when they did join, they found ways of domesticating the Word. If we may recollect what we said in volume 1 (pp. 246–47):[132]

> Not only did the relativism of Tswana culture resist the universalism of [European] Christianity . . . [but] "conversion" was always mediated to some extent by the forms of *setswana*. . . . [P]rofessions of new belief belied the fact that older modes of thought and action were never fully laid aside.

This is not to say that there were no "true believers." There certainly were those among the emerging Christian elite who found European Protestantism appealing, and who identified strongly with its orthodoxies. Some, in fact, were fiercely protective of its rules and procedures, and, it seems, fearful of apostasy (cf. Werbner n.d.[a]). And some, more tolerant, saw no objection to the coexistence of mission Christianity with other religious faiths;[133] again, the relativist ethos of *setswana* made manifest. All of them, however, indigenized the signs and practices of Nonconformism to a greater or lesser extent. It could hardly have been different; *vide* the anthropological truism that, however global denotation may appear to be, however universal its pretensions, connotation, meaning-as-lived, is always finally local. And culturally constituted.

At the same time, obviously, the domestication of Christianity at this end of the spectrum was more subtle, often more difficult to discern, than at the other, where performance was itself part of the act of appropriation. Some impulses had to be concealed, of course. For a start, as we said a moment ago, *badimo* were not recognized here. One way of resolving that difficulty was to do as the evangelists had done: to ignore their very existence. Perhaps some *badumedi* did. We have no way of knowing. But we do know, from the self-reporting of modern-day Southern Tswana, that many did not; that dead forebears went with their descendants to church, albeit incognito. Elizabeth Maloisane, a staunch Methodist, told us in Mafikeng in 1970 how, in her silent prayers, she addressed God through those she saw with her "inner eyes" (*matlho a mo teng*), her ancestors. And, she added, through the ancestors of the Tshidi-Rolong chiefs, of whom she was a distant collateral descendant. This last addendum was somewhat singular; the practice itself, however, was not. It was acknowledged by young and old, male and female, rich and poor. For these people too, as the Rev. Chipfupa noted, the role of Jesus was ambiguous. Frequently invoked in ritual formulae, he often went unmentioned in spontaneous prayer. Elizabeth Maloisane readily explained that the red uniform of the Methodist Women's Prayer Union was a reminder of the blood of Christ. Yet she directed her own devotions to more familiar mediators.

The refraction of mission Christianity through the optics and acoustics of *setswana* occurred in diverse sites and practices. As a black clergy established itself, for example, preaching styles took on features both of vernacular and African-American oratory: didacticism frequently gave way to interactive exhortation, its rhetoric aiming to move listeners to a collective profession of deeply felt truths. And prayer and eulogy hinted at the rhythms and tonalities, if not the content, of praise poetry; likewise the other elements of *go bina*, song and dance. Hymn singing had been fostered by the evangelists in the hope that "sung creeds" would imprint themselves on reluctant hearts. The sounds of Sankey (RRI:241) endured, but were transposed into a different aesthetic key. Singing came to punctuate every part of every service, spontaneously cutting across sermons and making formulaic liturgy more responsive to the mood of the congregation. Familiar songs began to ring with a distinctly non-European sense of harmony, itself a product of a subtle sense of intersubjectivity. Dance was a little more complicated, given missionary attitudes toward it. While not an integral part of orthodox worship, it was not altogether absent either. In some mainstream congregations, women entered the church at the beginning of services, and exited at the end, in a coordinated shuffle step. Also, mimetic movement sometimes accompanied hymns; it was still popular among (mainly younger) Tshidi-Rolong Christians in the 1970s. But, frowned upon by some older congregants, it was largely confined to rituals conducted by voluntary associations. One favorite of the Methodist Young Men's Guild (*Makau*) was "His Hand Shall Write My Name." As it was sung, in English, the swaying singers made appropriate gestures with their right arms (J. Comaroff 1974:209).

There were yet other contexts, many of them quite unexpected, in which the indigenized signs of a practical theology took up residence in the crevices of Christian orthodoxy—or accreted at its edges.[134] Some were intensely personal, although their roots were patently social. Uniforms, for instance, were metonymic of church affiliation: the question "*A o apara?*" ("Do you dress/wear outer garments?") meant "Are you a churchgoer?" Members of voluntary associations seem often to have treated their regalia as if they were infused with sacral power. Prayer Union women sometimes recited Revelations (22.14) in this connection: "Blessed are those who wash their robes, that they may have the right to the tree of life." And they kept theirs scrupulously clean and starched. These outfits were also thought able to protect their wearers from evil and misfortune—and liable to inflict harm upon those who desecrated them. In similar vein, if somewhat later, Southern Tswana Catholic clergy began blessing the homes of congregants by sprinkling holy water around their perimeters. In so doing, they knowingly evoked the calendrical ministrations of a *ngaka* doctoring the boundaries of a property against malign forces (*go thaya motse*).

The picture will be clear. Even though the mainstream denominations did not appear particularly welcoming to them, vernacular forms found their own points of entry into the church. As we have remarked before, there were also areas of resemblance and consonance between evangelical Nonconformism and everyday Tswana life. Not only were both animated, if in different ways, by religious pragmatism; both were characterized by a highly developed sense of legality and taboo. What is more, the missionaries relied on a book much of whose imagery accorded well with locally lived realities, and whose narratives often served as a pre-text for changing local experience (cf. Werbner n.d.[a]). This allowed many indigenous signs to slide seamlessly, inconspicuously, into Christian practice. So too did the openness of *setswana*, whose ontology predisposed it to the tolerant appropriation of the ways and means of others. All of which, in turn, made it possible for those who found their way into the mission churches to domesticate the Word, and so to render European Christianity local and habitable.

CLOSURES, OPENINGS

There are one or two issues still to address. As it happens, they provide a bridge to the chapters that follow.

It will be clear, following our comments in the Introduction, that the question of the degree to which European Christianity colonized African religion—or, conversely, Africans appropriated European Christianity—is not reducible to a simple equation. Not here. The encounter between them was an intricate affair, a dialectic whose curious mix of determinations and indeterminacy produced a wide horizon of religious actions and reactions, and had a profound effect on everyone concerned. In this regard, one thing ought to be said. Recent efforts among historians and anthropologists to recuperate African agency have shied away from treating Africa as victim, Africa as cipher for the heroic histories of others. Which is as it should be. At the same time, Europe *did* colonize the continent, not the other way around, and in so doing perpetrated and provoked a great deal of violence, both physical and cultural. To acknowledge this fact, the fact that imperialism had very real effects, is not to remove agency. It is merely to refuse to trivialize it. The point of colonial evangelism, after all, *was* to erase what was indigenously African and to replace it with something different. It did work changes. In Bechuanaland, as we have seen, it drew forth a range of rejoinders, giving rise to a complex, increasingly fragmented terrain of religious faiths and practices, all of them some kind of hybrid of *sekgoa* and *setswana*.

Of course, this was not what the missionaries had intended. Nor was the indiscriminate entry of "nominal Christians" into the churches. Even by their most optimistic lights, the colonial evangelists had failed where they had most hoped to succeed: in their own judgment, many of the conversions they effected were, in their own judgment, "opportunistic" and "skin deep." There is no reason to restate our argument, spelled out in volume 1 (pp. 243–51), with the Eurocentric concept of "conversion" *qua* cultural category or analytic term: why it is ethnocentric, why it mistakes an ideological construct for a truth claim, why it distorts the religious experience and the everyday practice of the likes of Southern Tswana. Nothing we have read by way of critical counterargument or Christian apologetics has given us cause to change our minds.

We simply make the point again: "becoming a Christian" here was *not* a matter of making a spiritual choice among alternative, incommensurable faiths, as the evangelists insisted it should be. Nor did it entail a profession of one "true belief" in repudiation of all others; that would have made little sense in a relativistic world, a world in which the accretion of cultural knowledge and technique was not taken to erase existing verities. It is true, of course, that conversion, here as elsewhere, was a socially meaningful event, marking the (re)-construction of personal identity. But it remained a poor guide to the complex

117

processes that went into the existential making of a religious life. To the Non-conformists, with their universalistic worldview, none of this was easy to assimilate: *any* residual faith in the spiritualities and moral sensibilities of *setswana* appeared to be evidence of "insincerity." It is not surprising, therefore, that J. Tom Brown found the term—"insincerity," that is—applicable to the "lives of the bulk of [Tswana]."[135]

The fact that they did not succeed in gaining many converts, at least not many of whom they approved, underlined the missionaries' sense that they were not going to win the battle to save souls by "direct influences" alone. Or even at all. Not only was the number of followers acquired in the years before overrule disappointingly low; few of them could be said to have been persuaded by the sheer power of the Word. In the circumstances, the second front of their "Christian warfare," the civilizing mission, came ever more to the fore. They continued, it is true, to reassure the Great British public—and themselves—that salvation and conversion were their real business. But they also found ways to justify paying ever more attention to the pragmatic task of revolutionizing the fabric and the fabrication of everyday Tswana life. One of their most successful alumni, S. M. Molema (1920:220; below, chapters 3 and 4), recalling the debate as to whether "the *regeneration* of the Bantu is better achieved through *secular* or *ecclesiastical* means"—his terms, our italics—came to the same conclusion as did most of his teachers: while their final objective was "Christianization," European evangelists had to "stand first as civilizers." Their main duty, he said, was to see that the lesson of the gospel "sinks deep and soaks into everyday life." Therein lay their practical mission.

And so onto the terrain of everyday life we follow them.

Let us rejoin the Nonconformists, then, as they began to break African soil. Their effort to produce an enlightened peasantry was a first step in the campaign to export Christian political economy to Africa. It was also a means to an end: the conversion of Southern Tswana not just into a congregation of Protestants, but also into a modernist "nation" of propertied, properly embodied, right-bearing, right-minded individuals. There lay the way, "the way everlasting" (Psalms 139.24), from a revolution in habit to a revelation of the truths of the gospel.

THREE

CULTIVATION, COLONIALISM, AND CHRISTIANITY

Toward a New African Genesis

[C]ivilization . . . must originate and depend on the culture of the ground.

Robert Moffat, May 1825[1]

IN OUR EXPLORATION of the heroic age of the early mission, and in the long conversation to which it gave rise, we encountered three things over and over again. The first, reiterated at the end of the last chapter, was the evangelists' conviction that, if they were to remake the Africans in their own image, they would have to begin on the terrain of everyday practice. Of this the missionaries were reminded not just by the subversive sniggers and indecorous snores that frequently greeted their sermons,[2] or by incidents that "proved" how "indifferent [were the Tswana] to all instruction except it were followed by some temporal benefit" (R. Moffat 1842:288, 284). The point was more subtly reinforced, as we have said, by the absence of idols to overthrow and, worse yet, of a "rational" theology with which to argue. Add to this the Nonconformists' mistrust of the seductive power of ostentatious ritual, their puritanical commitment to personal self-improvement, and the result is John Philip's (1828,2:355) evangelical first principle. Recall it (*RRI*:230): "The elevation of a people from a state of barbarism to a high pitch of civilization supposes a revolution in the habits of that people, which it requires much time, and the operation of many causes to effect" (cf. J. Mackenzie 1975:72). That revolution, moreover, had to be systematic, methodical, total. It had to run to the very core, and to all corners, of Tswana social being: "[I]n the completeness of his daily life," Wilkie Collins ([1868] 1966:245) once observed of the evangelical obsession with mundane habit, "the true Christian appears."

Second, precisely because this world was not to be remade, or the missions to be established, by smashing idols and ideologies, the LMS and WMMS could not depend purely on didactic means to achieve their ends; that is, on such received technologies of conversion as the sermon or the formal lesson. The early evangelists might have continued to preach and pray. But, in the pragmatic matter of re-forming the Southern Tswana, they vested most of their hope in a prosaic theater of Protestant industry: an unceasing performance in which they set forth—by personal example, with accompanying conversation and exhortation—the mundane signs and practices of European modernity.[3] This show-and-tell was based on the faith that, while they lacked reflective minds, the Africans would be unable to resist the temporal benefits of civilization.[4] And that, being childlike and impressionable, they would learn readily by imitation.[5] Copying as a means of Christian improvement had deep biblical roots. Thus Ephesians 5.1, "Therefore be imitators of God, as beloved children." At the same time, as we have seen, imitation always ran the risk of degenerating into empty "aping," this being a tension that ran to the heart of Protestant pedagogy in general (see chapter 2; also *RRIII*).

Third, as this suggests, a recurring motif in the drama was its stress on things material. For evangelists and abolitionists everywhere, as has often been remarked, "commerce" was the very antithesis of, and an antidote to, both slavery and primitive communism; the latter term, interestingly, came as easily to Moffat and Edwards as it did to Marx and Engels. So, as we shall see in chapter 4, did a concern with the fetishism of commodities. The missionaries took it for granted that consumption and production were of a piece;[6] that, tied together by the mechanism of the market, they were indissolubly bound up in the workings of advanced capitalist economy and society. If the Tswana were to reap the benefits of a refined material and social existence, if they were to gain entry into the Christian commonwealth, therefore, *both* would have to be recast— each in relation to the other and both from the ground up. Literally from the ground up. Hence Moffat's call, quoted at the head of the chapter, to begin cultivating civility from the ground up. And Campbell's (1822,2:60) comment that

> Till the present system [of agrarian production] shall undergo a complete revolution, [the Tswana] population can never abound in grain, nor can it become an article of trade. The land that may fairly be claimed by each nation is capable of supporting more than twenty times the population, if the ground were to be cultivated.

The reconstruction of the Tswana "system," Campbell's "complete revolution," was meant to be at once conceptual and material; a matter of both culture and agriculture. Unlike some scholars of a later age, Nonconformist missionaries in the South African interior were not wont to argue the metaphysics of which came first, concrete practices or meaningful signs. From their perspective, such things were not usefully distinguished to begin with.

In this chapter, then, we look at the campaign of colonial evangelists to revolutionize patterns of production among Tswana, a campaign that shaped a new field of social and cultural distinction, a field of classes-in-formation. In the next, we broaden our horizons, examining the orders of value and entrenched practices—inscribed in money, commodities, trade, wage labor—on which that "revolution" depended. Thereafter, in chapters 5 and 6, we examine the LMS and WMMS campaign to refashion modes of consumption, especially those concerned with the human body, home, and health. In each instance we explore the exchanges evoked by these efforts, tracing both the short- and long-term impact of the missionary outreach. And also the historical processes—sometimes surprising, often ambiguous, inevitably complex—which they unleashed.

CIVILIZATION AND THE CULTURE OF THE GROUND

There, on their pious toils their Master, smil'd
And prosper'd them, unknown or scorn'd of men,
Till in the satyr's haunt and dragon's den
A garden bloom'd, and savage hordes grew mild.

T. Pringle (LMS 1828)

The centrality of agriculture to colonial evangelism in South Africa owed much to the close ties, both sociological and imaginative, that bound the missionaries to the displaced peasantry at home; it played on their nostalgia for the lost idyll of the English yeomanry, that rural myth turned all-purpose metaphor. But, even more fundamentally, the Christians were from a world in which cultivation and salvation were explicitly linked—and joined together, more often than not, in a tangled mesh of horticultural imagery, much of it biblical in origin (*RRI*:80);[7] so tangled that, at the evangelical workface, an accomplishment (or failure) in one was often taken as an advance (or reverse) in the other.[8] As this suggests, agrarian labors and scenes saturated spiritual discourses, and vice versa. For example, Robert Moffat (1842:500, 588), professional gardener and farmer's son, told his readers how he and his brethren "put their hand to the plough," preparing the arid African earth for a "rich harvest of immortal souls." In fact, there was more than just a poetic parallel in likening conversion to cultivation. For the Nonconformists, the worldly side of the civilizing mission, the major thrust of their work for many years, was sacralized almost as an end in

121

itself. And it was to have repercussions more profound than they could have foreseen.

But cultivation was not only linked to salvation. In the culture whence the missionaries came, it was closely connected to colonialism (Delavignette 1964:8) and civilization as well.[9] William Somerville (1979:144), leader of the earliest colonial expedition to the Tswana, wrote in his journal on 8 December 1801: "[G]reater benefit would accrue to Society as well as to themselves," and moral improvement would follow, were "the spade or hoe," not the catechism, to be put in the hands of Africans. The evangelists might have disputed Somerville's priorities, but they did agree about the importance of agriculture. Hear, again, Moffat (1842:616–17), now echoing the antislavery argot of Fowell Buxton:

> Let missionaries and schoolmasters, the plough and the spade, go to-gether, and agriculture will flourish, the avenues of legitimate commerce will be opened . . . whilst civilization will advance as the natural effect, and Christianity operate as the proximate cause of the happy change.

Nor was this a fleeting vision. If anything, it grew more elaborate over time. At his ordination in Edinburgh in 1858, John Mackenzie (1975:72),[10] an LMS evangelist of the next generation, said:

> As to civilization and the temporal interests of the people, I conceive that I am furthering both when I preach the Gospel. . . . In order to complete the work of elevating the people, we must teach them the arts of civilized life. If we exhort them to lay aside the sword for the ploughshare and the spear for the pruning-hook, we must be prepared to teach them to use the one with the same dexterity which they exhibited in wielding the other. . . . [W]e must teach them to till their own land, sow and reap their own crops, build their own barns.

It is little wonder that Thoreau (1908:32), from the critical distance of Walden in the 1850s, was to see in the adoption of Christianity "merely . . . an improved method of *agri*-culture." The italic smacks of irony, the hyphen of ill-humor. Both are his.

Given the African concern with cattle keeping, it may seem odd that the early missionaries seldom included pastoralism in their plans for the Tswana; even more odd, perhaps, in light of Braudel's (1981:124) observation that "it was . . . by opting for forage crops and livestock farming that eighteenth-century England achieved a revolutionary improvement in cereal yields" and, thereby, in its agriculture at large. Maybe some of the clerics were unaware of the part played by animal husbandry in their own agrarian history. We do not know for sure. But they certainly were not ignorant of the value of stock to Southern Tswana. Chiefs and commoners alike were quick to inform them. So, too, were other European visitors to the region.[11] In 1807, for instance, Lichtenstein (1973:80–81, 66) described indigenous ranching practices in detail. Beasts, he said, were of high quality here: they were treated with great care, were the subject of aesthetic pride, and were slaughtered only for ritual purposes. For "everything appertaining to cattle breeding," he added, "Bechuana . . . have a large vocabulary." Similarly, as we noted before, Burchell (1824,2:272, 347) took pains to explain that, among Tlhaping, stockwealth and power were synonymous. But the evangelists did not need to be told any of this. Their own writings make it perfectly plain that they knew just how significant were animals to the peoples of the interior.[12] To wit, Campbell (1822,2:210f.), whose ethnographic notes on the topic were extensive, recorded a case at a chief's court in which the ownership of oxen became, literally, a matter of life or death.

The stress on the civilizing role of cultivation—and the concomitant silence on the salience of cattle—flowed from an axiom at least as old as English colonialism itself. And as enduring. *Sedentary* agriculture, it was believed, was both a cause and an effect of civility and advancement, the fountainhead of productive society and moral community (Livingstone 1974:76). "[T]he way to increase the productivity of both land and people in Africa," Willoughby (1923:181) was to declaim in the 1920s, "is to cultivate each by means of the other." By contrast, cattle and culture, ranching and refinement, seemed almost inimical. As long as it had no fixed abode, was not tied to permanent pasture, or did not accompany settled tillage, pastoralism excited uncomfortable visions of shifting populations: of shifty, shiftless people wandering about *sans* property, propriety, or a proper place in the body politic; of a world, to return to Thoreau (1908:48), where "men are not so much keepers of herds as herds are the keepers of men."

Already at the turn of the seventeenth century, Edmund Spenser had blamed the barbarity and belligerence of the "wild Irish"[13] on their seminomadic, pastoral pursuits (Muldoon 1975:275; cf. Ong 1942).[14] In order to allay the threat they posed to England—and to bring them within the compass of its civilization—they had to be conquered, colonized, and made to cultivate; that is, to live *settled* agrarian lives. Similar schemes were later to be exported to the New World and Africa, since they accorded well with what bourgeois Britain came to regard as the natural development of its own superior social order. The Bible might have spoken of a chosen people who herded at least as much as they tilled, a point which was not to be lost on Tswana readers. But, to the modernist imagination, evolution depended on cultivation. In due course, the connection between them would find its way into both thesaurus and theory.[15] It lives on in anthropological typologies of economic systems,[16] in the historiography of great social revolutions,[17] in models of the modern world-system.[18] Of more immediate concern, however, is the fact that the evangelists in South Africa, like their contemporaries in England, absorbed the axiom that agriculture made men peaceful, law-abiding, and amenable to education—at once civil and servile. Indeed, Livingstone (1974:75–76) blamed the lawlessness of "the Boers," whom he likened to "the blacks" in some respects, on the fact that they "were more a pastoral than an agricultural race." Not for naught had Spenser ([1595] 1882–84,9:235) warned an imperially minded England that all who live "by [the] kepinge of cattel . . . are both very barbarous and uncivill, and greatly given to warr." And that Rome had fallen before the onslaught of barbarian nomads (Muldoon 1975:275).[19] From a purely evangelical perspective, too, mobile populations posed problems. The Rev. Philip is reputed to have told his pioneering colleagues that, as long as people had "no settled homes . . . it was easy for them to desert the means of instruction" (Macmillan 1929:76).

If the rude savage was to be refined, then, it would be tillage that would do it. As he sowed his fields, nourished his seedlings, and harvested his crop—all with enlightened techniques and tools—the African peasant would make himself anew; the gendered pronoun here gives early warning that, in the transformed Tswana world, the existing division of labor was to be turned upsidedown. (Note that the evangelists themselves used the term "division of labor"; see, e.g., Lloyd 1889:162f.) This agrarian revolution, as was often said, was intended to enable African converts to yield enough of a surplus to tie them through trade to Christian Europe (e.g., Mackenzie 1975:72; cf. Bundy 1979:39). Blighted no more, the dark continent would become a "fruitful field," a rich rural periphery of the metropolitan centers of civilization abroad (Broadbent 1865:204). No more would it call forth the "agonizing tears of bereaved mothers," the "orphan's cry, the widow's wail" (R. Moffat 1842:613). Not, that is, if their menfolk were restored to them as true *husbandmen*. Even in its most materialist moments, circa 1820–50, the civilizing mission continued to ring, not merely of biblical pastorale, but also of romantic naturalism and abolitionist moralism.

It also invoked many of the old tropes: Africa, savage and infantilized, devastated by slavery, its women dispossessed and its men laid low—all awaiting the white savior to regenerate them so that they might once more harvest their own crops and "sit under their own vine and fig-tree" (R. Moffat 1842:613f.). Confided Hodgson (1977:185), to his diary, on 3 August 1823:

> Oh Africa, long and much-neglected Africa, to what a state of misery art thou sunk, and who will afford the means of delivering thee from such wretchedness; surely England will yet do things for thee?

No matter that Tswana had never suffered bondage. In Nonconformist narratives of South Africa, *difaqane* (RRI:42, 167–69) served much the same imaginative function as did the slave trade further north.[20] This period of upheaval in the 1820s—usually ascribed to the rise of the Zulu state and the subsequent predations of displaced warrior peoples (*RRI*:42f.)—had ostensibly "desolated the whole Bechuana country." These predations were held to have robbed "the native population" of its moral manhood and its capacity for self-determination, and, further, to have left it "unprotected . . . without missionaries" (J. Philip 1828,2:146; also Edwards 1886:83f.; R. Moffat 1842:435). Some of the peoples of the interior, it is true, *were* badly disrupted by the turmoil of the times. Nonetheless, most Southern Tswana had managed to grow some crops in temporary places of refuge, to recoup their herds, and to keep intact their political communities.[21] But such subtleties went largely unspecified in the stark stories penned by the Christians. These told of soil strewn with blood and bones by "warlike, wild tribes," of a wake of women and children left to wander about, barely surviving on wild fruit, locusts, and "garbage"; even, added the horrified evangelists, on human flesh (e.g., Broadbent 1865:71). Here too we detect traces of the vision of Africa-the-Fallen, the degenerate, of its children as foundlings. In recalling their own travels across the backwash of *difaqane*, Broadbent (1865:37f.) and Hodgson (1977:123f.) tell how they came upon a young girl left to die without food or succor. We may guess the rest: the Europeans "save" this stereotypic victim of South African savagery. They "adopt" and raise her. And they "(re)name" her. *Orphina*.

Such accounts did more than merely confirm the florid portraits of primitive Africa circulated by late eighteenth-century philanthropists. They also justified the resolve of the clerics to "train [the Bechuana] up in the habits of civilized life" (Broadbent 1865:98); in particular, to teach them how to farm productively in the fields of God (R. Moffat 1842:613). Hence the essential gesture in the imagery of colonial evangelism, one to which we keep returning (*RRI*:Plates 3.1a and 3.1b; cover illustration): the missionary, a black male convert at his back, tending an "abandoned mother" in the bush.[22] In most versions of the tableau, the supine, supplicating female is being handed bread, the "bread of life," long a European symbol of *cultivated* food—and, not coincidentally, the stuff of the sacrament and icon of the Gospel.[23] (Note here, once again, Read's early comment[24] that those who had "tasted bread, long for [it]. . . . By this means the Gospel may get a footing"; *RRI*:185.)[25] Camporesi (1989:182) observes that sixteenth-century Italian Catholicism thrived on the specter of the "humble pauper, servile, . . . weak, relentlessly persecuted by misfortune," of "mutilated human forms, wrecks of every war, laden with starving children." The act of feeding the "bread of dreams" to these sufferers, he goes on, was put to powerful dramatic use in the service of the church. Nineteenth-century Protestantism might not have been as theatrical in its evocation of misery and poverty. But it also relied on their rhetorical force to conjoin the spiritual and material axes of the civilizing mission and to link both back to the theme of cultivation. Hear Moffat (1842:282):

It is easy for men to degenerate in religion and civilization, especially when compelled to lead a wandering life, which is by no means favourable to the cultivation of devotion in the soul. . . . In all ages "hunger and ignorance have been the great brutalizers of the human race;" and, if we look at the large tracts of barren country inhabited by some African tribes, it is not surprising that they are what they are.

And so the evangelists took it upon themselves to teach Tswana to "plough and sow, and eat bread-corn; and . . . become industrious, wise, and mighty." This, at least, is what a Tlhaping royal allegedly told a Cape merchant when asked about the impact of the civilizing mission.[26] The merchant was himself a member of the Commercial Exchange, a colonial business fraternity with its own agrarian designs: it hoped to introduce silk production among "bordering tribes" under the instruction of the clerics.[27] The scheme foundered. Not so, however, the Nonconformist campaign to cultivate Tswana in order that they might grow European cereals.

As it would turn out, the gift of bread was to be a decidedly mixed blessing. For it carried within it the germ of a new affliction. But we are running ahead of our narrative.

AFRICAN AGRICULTURE: SEEING, SEEDING, SOWING, REAPING

Superstition, Socialism, and Agrarian Aesthetics

The civilizing mission might have portrayed Africa as uncultivated, a metaphorical mix of virgin bush to be inseminated and fallen Eden to be regenerated. And yet, this iconography of emptiness notwithstanding, the early evangelists expatiated at length on Tswana economy, taking pains to underscore how much had either to be erased or remade. A good deal of their commentary may be characterized as a discourse of absence: it focused on the lack of ways and means taken for granted in European culture. Most notable, perhaps, were references to the want of money,[28] itself assumed to be indispensable to an advanced economy (see chapter 4); of markets, or anything beyond rude barter (e.g., Campbell 1822,1: 139f.); to the want of civilized crops, especially refined species of maize, corn, or vegetables (e.g., Campbell 1822,1:178; Moffat and Moffat 1951:187–88); of irrigation (e.g., R. Moffat 1842:285) and all but the simplest implements and technologies (e.g., Livingstone 1857:215f.; Crisp 1896:16); of privately owned land (e.g., Campbell 1822,2:150; Edwards 1886:87); of any native capacity for practical invention or for self-improvement by the exercise of reason. "[T]hey are *so* unaware of their own lack," W. C. Willoughby (1923:181) was to muse a hundred years later, "that they [still] desire no superior agricultural knowledge."[29]

Still more striking than this discourse of absence, however, was the discourse of irrationalities that permeated mission texts and conversations: Tswana economy was portrayed, for the most part, as a repertoire of illogical, impractical, improvident means and ends. Not even their consumption of food escaped comment. Thus Campbell (1822,1:248), a man rarely given to pejorative remarks:

> Their stomachs being capable of receiving almost any quantity, they never . . . consider a meal to be finished till all be eaten up. The man who could introduce economy in eating among the African tribes would prevent much misery arising from frequent scarcity of food, which is produced by their extravagant and improvident conduct.[30]

One noteworthy feature of this discourse of irrationalities was its obsession with the *aesthetics* of agrarian production and material life. Some evangelists were quite open in their disapproval of the "disorderly" way in which Tswana put nature to use "without regard to scenery or economy" (R. Moffat 1842:330), thereby destroying the "park-like appearance of the landscape" (Broadbent 1865:63). Throughout the century, moreover, many of them harped on the indigenous preference, in cultivation and construction, for the "sinuous" and "arc-shaped" over neat rectangular forms, a point to which we shall return in chapter 6.[31] Livingstone (1857:46) spoke of it with resignation,[32] Philip (1828,2:26) with clinical detachment; he once likened Dithakong and its environs to an "ant-hill" (p. 121).[33] But Mackenzie (1871:92) was most direct: "[Tswana] gardens and arable land," he lamented, "are laid out in a manner which offends the eye of a European."[34] Even as late as 1899, Willoughby (n.d.[a]:28) claimed that the Africans could not plough a linear furrow. A "straight line," explained the missionary-ethnographer, "is foreign to the native mind." At issue here was not merely taste violated. Beauty, after all, was truth. And truth beauty. Both demanded an internalized sense of proportion.

Again, the idea that civilization—and cultivation, *sui generis*—expressed itself in squares and straight lines ran to the core of postenlightenment British culture. In *The Return of the Native* (1963:181), for instance, Thomas Hardy contrasts the wildness of the imaginary Egdon Heath ("an uncouth . . . obsolete thing") to the "modern" countryside "of square fields, plashed hedges, and meadows watered on a plan so rectangular that on a fine day they look like silver gridirons." Even closer to home with respect to the South African mission was the effect of early nineteenth-century scientific "improvement" on the Scottish countryside, whence came Moffat and Livingstone. Here, with the application of Newtonian science to agriculture (I. Adams 1980:159), an open half-moorland was re-visioned, and then remade, as "an ordered, geometrical, fenced landscape" (Caird 1980:204, quoting I. Adams 1968:249). No wonder that Philip (1828,2:114), in praising the progress of the Kuruman mission (circa 1825), chose to stress the "taste" with which its rigidly rectilinear garden had been laid out. There was, he stated, "something very refreshing . . . and pleasing" in this place of "rising beauty" (p. 115). By implication, Tswana terrain was much less attractive, much less productive. Much more like farmstead Ireland, circa 1815, which Halévy (1961:210) was to dismiss, stereotypically, as "a disgusting sight . . . [there being] no vestige of a garden"—just a promiscuous admixture of muddy, murky shapes and forms.

But the putative irrationalities of Southern Tswana economy were described in terms that went far beyond the aesthetic. Among the things most commonly remarked and rued by the missionaries were (i) the prevailing politics of production; (ii) the unenlightened "selfishness" of the Africans; (iii) the savage "superstition" and "enchantments" said to saturate their world; and (iv) their "unnaturally" gendered division of labor.

The Nonconformists regarded it as utterly beyond reason that chiefs should orchestrate the rhythms of agrarian production; that the annual cycle should be punctuated by collective rites; that cultivation should be seen to depend on a ruler providing spring rains to inseminate the land; that women should not be permitted to plant before the sovereign "gave out the seed-time"; that each activity, from sowing to harvest, should begin with tributary toil on royal fields (*RRI*:146f.). The evangelists might have asserted, throughout the nineteenth century, that "traditional" authority was on the wane. But they continued to rail against the prevailing politics of production. As late as 1900, Brown was to write[35] from Taung that the local chief was still the channel "through which the rain flows to the people. He still exercises the right of saying when the ploughing shall begin. . . . Corn in some gardens may be fully ripe, and even wasting from ripeness; but the owners of these gardens dare not reap till the chief has given permission."

Although the chiefly capacity to enforce such "rights" *was* eventually to wither away, many communications from the mission field, written both earlier and later, tell similar tales: of women being punished for ignoring royal regulations, of energetic efforts being made to sustain centralized control over agriculture, of rulers extracting any form of tributary labor they could muster.[36] To the evangelists, this remained a form of bondage—and a major obstacle to the development of an agrarian economy based on private enterprise, commodity production, and free labor.

Another obstacle, equally irrational in the eyes of the Europeans, was summed up by the Rev. Willoughby (n.d.[b]), speaking in the timeless evangelical present. "The African," he declared, "lives a simple socialistic life, subordinating his individuality to the necessities of the tribe." Hence his antipathy to "healthy, individualistic competition," to the maximization of time and effort, and to self-possessed industry (Mackenzie in Dachs 1972:652). Tswana might have been crafty and duplicitous (R. Moffat 1842:254), suspicious and jealous of each other (J. Mackenzie 1871:402). And they might have been "keenly alive to their own interests" (Livingstone 1857:21); "under the influence," Hodgson (1977:157) put it, "of [the] selfish principle." But this was quite different from the kind of refined, *rational* individualism that the Nonconformists had in mind; the kind that persuaded people to "submit to the labour of cultivating the ground" (J. Philip 1828,2:356).

The allusion to rationality here picks up another theme in the discourse. Many of the evangelists spoke of the need to rouse the Tswana capacity for "reason," thereby to counter its natural antithesis: "savage superstition." The latter, held John Philip (1828,2:116), flowed "from confused ideas of invisible agency." These led the Africans to believe that successful cultivation depended on the observance of taboos (against the felling of certain trees, the castration of young bulls, and so on); that female pollution could cause the clouds or the crops to abort; that the fertility of fields might be increased by the ministrations of medicine men (see, e.g., J. Mackenzie 1871:385f.).[37] Much to the annoyance of the Christians, moreover, such beliefs had been placed as impediments in their way (J. Philip 1828,2:116): "Till lately, the missionaries have not been allowed to use manure for their gardens. It was formerly universally believed that if the manure were removed from the cattle-kraals, the cattle would die."

From the standpoint of the mission, the enchantments of savagery had yet another insidious side to them: they encouraged an irrational conservatism in the face of challenge and change. This, allegedly, made peoples like the Tswana reluctant to accept the most obvious, most persuasive proof of the superiority of civilized practices. Added Philip (1828,2:118),

[I]t was against their practice to deviate from the customs of their ancestors. When urged to plant corn, &c., they used to reply that their fathers were wiser than themselves, and yet were content to do as they did: they also regarded every innovation as an insult to the memory of their ancestors.

In fact, the evangelists knew well that Southern Tswana were often ready to experiment with alien cultural techniques—but on their own terms, and as long as it did not threaten to overturn their "whole system" (*RRI*:196). Missionary accounts over the years described many instances of the adoption of European practices by Africans. Nonetheless, the clerics tended to stress their conservatism.

But it was the division of labor—in particular, gendered relations of production—for which the evangelists reserved most of their opprobrium. Lichtenstein (1973:77) might have likened Tswana agriculture, approvingly, to that of the "Mosaic forefathers"; the Christians, who sometimes drew similar biblical parallels,[38] found the comparison altogether less happy. From their perspective, African economy was "topsy-turvy" (Crisp 1896:16). The men, whose herds were tended by youths and serfs, looked—to the missionaries, that is, not to *all* observers[39]—to be lazy "lords of creation" (R. Moffat 1842:505); their political and ritual activities were largely invisible to the European eye, their leather work did not appear to be work at all, and their exertions as smiths went largely unremarked.[40] Women, on the other hand, seemed to have been forced into doing what was properly male labor, building and thatching, digging and "scratching"[41] on the face of the earth like "beasts of burden" (Kinsman 1983:46, after Solomon 1855:44). "Cruel vassalage" is the term used by John Philip (1828,2:139), the abolitionist, to describe their status. (By contrast, long before French Marxism vexed itself with the theoretical question, Lichtenstein [1973:77] referred to these females as a "working class," but not a discontented one.)[42] Nonconformist accounts of women's toil were always tinged with disgust and were often highly emotive. Mary Moffat (see J. Philip 1828,2:139), for one, observed that

> The women cultivate all the land, build the houses [and so on] . . . while the men . . . never condescend to lend a helping hand to them. Picture to yourself tender and gentle women . . . bending their delicate forms, tearing the rugged earth . . . dragging immense loads of wood over the burning plains, wherewith to erect their houses, thus bearing the double weight of the curse on both sexes.

What is more, rather than till lands tied to the family home, they were sent to far-off fields for weeks on end—where, disconcertingly, they remained beyond the reach of the mission.

Occasionally, too, existing relations of production sparked conflicts between the sexes, conflicts that discomforted the Nonconformists and gave the lie to patronizing talk of "tender and gentle women." Speaking of Batlharo, Wookey wrote, in 1873:[43]

> [T]he gardens belong to [females]. The cattle, sheep and goats belong to the men. Well, amongst the Batlaro it seems some of the cattle had been troublesome in wandering into the gardens and destroying the women's corn. Accordingly, they determined to kill everything found in their lands. In doing this they were following a law to that effect made by a Batlaro chief; and for which also some women were cut off the church by Mr. Moffat. Numbers of cattle were hacked and killed in a most horrible manner, the women of the church taking a prominent part in the work.

It is obvious why such incidents, which had a long history, should have distressed the evangelists: hacking beasts to death, like heavy agrarian toil far from home, was not exactly their idea of a proper feminine activity. No wonder that the LMS and WMMS were so intent on confining Tswana women to house and hearth; on domesticating them, that is, within a world divided—socially and sexually—into public and private domains, sites of production and reproduction (see chapter 6).

The missionaries were under no illusions that this would be easy. One had already learned as much at the turn of the nineteenth century, when he tried to set up a station along the Kuruman River. His request met with resistance from the chief, who, having heard news of Khoi converts to the south, feared the civilizing lessons of the LMS (Somerville 1979:143). Why? Because, the ruler insisted, they led to indigence. And a "life of idleness" would not "suit" his people at all. "Leave us to work the ground peaceably and plant our corn," was his message to the mission (Somerville 1979:143). Twenty years later, Broadbent (1865:105) reported that, while Tswana listened to much of what he had to say, they would not hear his advocacy of European agriculture: its division of labor "opposed their ideas and habits." He might have added that, to the Africans, European material practices appeared just as "topsy-turvy" as did theirs to the evangelists. Remember from volume 1 how, in the very early days, some Tlhaping women offered—out of sympathy for the benighted Britons—to cultivate for them. It was an offer the Christians did not understand.

Nor did they always see quite how unreasonable was their own discourse of irrationalities; quite how full it was of counterexamples which gave a very different impression of Tswana economy. For instance, Campbell (1822,1:177)—himself, as we implied above, slower to condemn local practices than others—recalled that, while traveling across Rolong country in 1820, he came upon "several hundred acres of Caffre corn; many of the stalks were eight and nine feet high, and had a fine appearance." Earlier, at the edges of Dithakong, he and his companions had passed "extensive corn-fields on both sides of the road." Giving voice to the observation of one group of Africans by another, the evangelist said that the Khoi in his party, themselves familiar with agriculture in the Cape Colony, "were amazed at the extent of the land under cultivation, having never seen so much before in one place." Similarly, secular European visitors, both before and after, commented admiringly—often in the media of the day—on the quality and quantity of Southern Tswana horticulture.[44] Even in 1823, when the interior was astir with the upheavals of *difaqane*, Hodgson (1977:134) saw, among Seleka-Rolong, "a large quantity of Caffre corn in full bloom growing most luxuriantly with abundance of water-melons." All this in "uncultivated" Africa.

Moffat (1842:285) also offered counterevidence, albeit of a different sort. The Kuruman station, he noted, was situated on "light sandy soil, where no kind of vegetables would grow without constant irrigation," a costly and difficult business. By contrast, he added in passing, unirrigated "native grain . . . supports amazing drought." In this light, and in the ecological circumstances, the claims made by the Christians for the superiority—and rationality—of European agrarian techniques must have puzzled the Tlhaping. All the more so since whites from the Colony kept entering their territory to purchase their surplus cattle and, later, crops (see chapter 4). But *their* discourse of irrationalities is largely irrecoverable, save, as we have said before, from traces scattered inchoately between the lines of colonial texts—and from a variety of practical reactions, some of which we shall come upon as our account unfolds.

Metamorphosis and Disenchantment

Livingstone (1940:203) once wrote of a young chief who, eager for the benefits of civilization, wanted him "forthwith to commence the work of metamorphosis by means of enchantments." The missionary, the ruler knew, was a master of medicines. In fact, the first generation of evangelists *did* resort to a technology of enchantment—involving, among other things, their almost magical gardens—to impress the power of their presence on the Africans. But when it came to reconstructing Tswana material life over the longer run, the terms and techniques used by the Nonconformists were to speak repeatedly of *dis*enchantment. They would advocate the "rational" expenditure of effort, introduce such "scientific" instruments as the plough, and try to replace the "superstitious" practices of the vernacular ritual calendar with the secular logic of commodity cultivation.[45]

Given the recent fortunes of English agriculture, the evangelists might have given careful thought to its export to Africa. According to Lord Ernle (Prothero 1912:312),[46] the period 1815 to 1837 was "one of the blackest" in its history. "Prosperity no longer stimulated progress. . . . [V]anishing profits . . . crushed the spirit of agriculturists" (cf. Kitson Clark 1973:32). Some have questioned Ernle's now dated account, and have tried to amend the common view that these were years of deep agrarian depression (e.g., E. Jones 1968:10f.). But it is clear, from contemporary debates and government commissions, that the state of the rural economy was highly, if variably, precarious—and was popularly seen to be so.[47] The predicament of small farmers (in particular, ironically, those who did not raise livestock) was worst of all (see, e.g., Halévy 1961:220f.). It did not take Cobbett's *Rural Rides* (1830) to indict the condition of the countryside. Few could have believed that cultivation was a panacea for the peasants of England; and this notwithstanding the profitable years of the Napoleonic Wars, the zeal of the king and aristocracy for agriculture (Halévy 1961:224), the modernist rhetoric of enclosure, growing mechanization, and the rise, later in the century, of High Farming (see Caird 1849). Goldsmith (1857:13) had been prescient—unwittingly, no doubt—when, in 1770, he had rhymed: "But a bold peasantry, their country's pride // When once destroy'd, can never be supplied."[48] Perhaps it was this very sense of loss, even anachronism, that made small-scale arable farming appear such a suitable means for regenerating Africa. For many of the missionaries, after all, the demise of the English yeomanry, itself idealized by nostalgia, fueled the horticultural dream for Bechuanaland (*RRI*:75). And so they put their hands to the plough in the effort to produce peasants. Like some clergymen in England (Kitson Clark 1973:168f.), they had great faith in the capacity of a garden allotment—and hard work—to raise up the rude and to relieve their misery.

At the start, as we said in volume 1, the daunting task of cultivating the interior and its inhabitants was centered on the mission garden, itself a master symbol of civilization and Britishness.[49] For a while, this square of red earth stood between the Christians and hunger, perhaps even starvation (Wookey 1884:303). But it was always much more than just a source of food. It was also an exemplary appropriation of space (cf. Alloula 1986:21) and an icon of colonial evangelism at large, a means of material existence and an Idea. Represented as a triumph over rank nature—portrayed, for these purposes, sometimes as wilderness, sometimes as desert—it usually began as a vegetable patch, grew to include an orchard, and, in time, was expanded by the addition of fields of wheat and other crops; in short, not exactly a garden at all in contemporary English terms, but paradise to those who saw, in the creation of the first mission stations, an African Genesis.[50]

In the ideal Nonconformist scenario, this Act of Creation had to be played out, from the first, on land obtained from the Africans by purchase, *sensu stricto.* We shall return, in chapter 8, to the complex process set in motion by the evangelical campaign to transform "tribal" territory into the private property of modern, right-bearing subjects. For now it is enough to note that the gesture of purchase was meant to have two effects: (i) to establish missionary agriculture, from the ground up, on a bedrock of civilized practices, thereby (ii) to make it a palpable example to the Tswana of those very practices. In an optimistically spirited letter, dated 21 November 1823, Mary Moffat (Moffat and Moffat 1951:111) wrote: "[E]ach [Tlhaping] individual is to purchase his own ground, the missionaries having set the example." Although some chiefs agreed to "sell" plots, the evidence suggests that they could not make much sense of the Christian's actions—or their explanations for them. "[T]he particulars of . . . sale," Livingstone (1857:21) confessed, "sounded strangely in the ears of the tribe[s]." As Archbell's account[51] implies, the major effect of these exchanges seems to have been reflexive: they persuaded the Europeans, who sometimes feared for the security of their venture,[52] that the mission was firmly implanted on soil it actually owned.[53]

Aside from being vital to the worldly self-sufficiency of evangelical households, then, the cultivation of the mission garden played out the first scenes in the narrative of reconstruction. In this garden, the Nonconformists enacted the principles of material individualism: the creation of value by means of self-possessed labor and scientific technique, the forceful conversion of nature into private property, and the accumulation of surplus through an economy of toil.[54]

Robert Moffat's son, John, makes it clear that his father spent a good proportion of his daily round as a "farmer" (R.U. Moffat 1921:14; see also Elizabeth [Moffat] Price 1956:61); much of his own youth, it seems, was also given to irrigating Kuruman. The point, he implied later (p. 1), was to provide an "object lesson," a visible model for the Tlhaping to mimic (above, n. 5). No wonder that Edwin Smith (1925) was to describe Moffat Senior as "one of God's gardeners." Or that George Thompson (1967:96–97; see n. 27), a Cape merchant who spent some time at Kuruman in 1823, should admire "the example [the evangelists had] set before the natives of industry in cultivating the ground"— which, he added, "is not likely to be thrown away upon this ingenious race of men." Thompson was as impressed by the cultural openness and the resourcefulness of Tswana as he was by the "inoffensive, disinterested, and prudent demeanour" of everyday mission instruction.

The lessons of agriculture were to extend beyond the confines of the mission garden, flowing outward and fructifying surrounding communities. David Livingstone, for example, although professedly "ignorant of the scientific way of irrigation" (MacNair 1976:98), spent a considerable proportion of his time, at his first stations, supervising the construction of dams and extensive canal systems. At Dinokana, in the North West Province of South Africa, his extraordinary network of channels is still clearly in use. Even today it waters luxuriant fruit trees, winter wheat, and other crops.

Perhaps the most vivid insight into the didactic spirit of evangelical agriculture, however, is provided by Samuel Broadbent (1865:104–5). Note how the first Methodist emissary to the Seleka-Rolong chose to make his point in the form of a show-and-tell exchange:

> I and my colleague had each enclosed a plot of ground, which we had, of course, in English fashion, broken up and cleared of the roots of weeds, and then sown with Kaffir corn, which we had obtained from the natives, and with sweet cane and various kinds of beans, also melons and pumpkins. . . . [W]hat became the subject of wonder and remark was the notorious fact that these and other vegetables grew much more luxuriantly, and were more productive, in our grounds than theirs. One day a number of respectable natives came to ask the reason of this difference . . .
>
> My first answer was, "Your idleness." "How so?" they inquired. I said, "You have seen that we have dug the ground ourselves; you leave it to your women. We dig deep into the soil; they only scratch the surface. . . . Our seed, therefore, is protected from the sun and nourished by the moisture in the ground; but yours is parched with the heat of the sun, and, therefore, not so productive as ours." I added "Work yourselves, as you see we do, and dig the ground properly, and your seed will flourish as well as ours."

Here, in sum, were the four crucial lessons of the sacred garden.

The first presented itself, innocently it seemed, as purely technical: that successful cultivation necessitated digging "deep into the soil." This, of course, was only possible with the plough—not with the hoe, an artifact seen by the Europeans as exotic and primitive (e.g., Livingstone 1857:215f.; Crisp 1896:16). As we have noted, the fashioning of implements, in public at times, was an essential evangelical activity.[55] The objects so fabricated became iconic of mission cultivation at large; at once instruments of production and symbols with special meaning (cf. Volosinov 1973:10). Thus S. M. Molema (1920:119), the Tshidi historian and a devout Christian, was to write that "no single machine . . . [did] so much for the civilization of the Bantu than the plough." Like the irrigation ditch and the well, agrarian appliances were as vital to the construction of the Nonconformist worldview as they were to the material basis of the mission.

This is where the second lesson of the garden lay: in enclosure after the "English fashion." As Broadbent (1865:104–5) suggested, everything commenced with the founding of a fenced plot, itself the material core of the imagined African farmstead of the future. Within its rectangular confines—apparently the Old English root for garden, *geard*, actually meant "fence" and hence "enclosed space" (Darian-Smith 1995:402, after van Erp-Houtepen 1986:227)—lay the promise of great productivity. Which is why Robert Moffat was delighted to report that Kuruman had become an exemplary "Goshen to the surrounding country" (quoted in Northcott 1961:148): here five hundred acres had been brought under irrigation and neat smallholdings, allocated to those affiliated with the mission, had begun to appear.

The third lesson involved the contrast between idleness and labor, African indolence and European industry. The evangelists sought, by their own conspicuous efforts, to show that self-possessed toil was the key to a decent life. Profitable agriculture, which connoted the cultivation of "civilized" crops[56] for both home consumption and the market, depended upon it. The essence of this lesson was to be found in the Letter of Paul to the Thessalonians, often invoked in mission preaching: "[We] give you in our conduct an example to imitate. . . . If any one will not work, let him not eat" (3.9–10);[57] And in Timothy: "It is the hard-working farmer who ought to have the first share of the crops" (2/2.6). This celebration of labor, as we shall see, was integral to the practical theology, and to the theology of practice, at the core of colonial evangelism: "Work, the gospel of work, the sanctity of work, *laborare est orare*," to work is to pray, as Aldous Huxley ([1928] 1994:217) would put it at a later date and in a quite different connection.

But, and here was the fourth lesson, not all toil was the same. Or equal. The world of work envisaged by the Nonconformists entailed an entirely new division of labor. The relative value of male and female exertions could not have been more clearly stated. "Luxuriant" productivity, proclaimed Broadbent (1865:104–5), demanded mastery over field and furrow, not scratchings on the soil; like all the evangelists, he believed it "of great importance . . . to lead the minds of the Bechuana men to agricultural pursuits" (Moffat and Moffat 1951:113). The corollary: that, while their husbands became breadwinners, *house*wives ought to be confined to such "homely" tasks as cleaning, childcare, cooking, and sewing.[58] This invoked the same ideal of gentility that had enclosed bourgeois European women in the domestic domain. And, in so doing, it revealed a contradiction in the objectives of the civilizing mission. On one hand, the clergymen dreamed of a free and prosperous African peasantry. On the other, their values, firmly rooted in the age of revolution, presupposed the social order of industrial capitalism, itself centered on the urban, middle-class household. Few Tswana women were to be embourgeoised, of course. Quite the contrary: many had eventually to earn their livelihood as domestic workers in European settler homes, their servitude offering a bitterly ironic commentary on the evangelical model for the African family. Others were compelled to seek employment in the industrial, commercial, or agrarian sectors of the colonial economy, or were forced back into the arid fields of subsistence agriculture. But this was still a long way off. In the early nineteenth century, the vision of Tswana society built on a fusion of the genteel bourgeois home and the sturdy yeoman farm had not yet disclosed its paradoxes.

Re-actions of the Short-Run: From Mockery to Mimesis

What were the first reactions of Southern Tswana to the evangelical onslaught on their material practices? It is clear that they did not immediately take the lesson which the Christians tried to convey—namely, that the abundant yields of "modern" agriculture were the product of a particular regime of hard labor and enlightened technique. We have already mentioned two early forms of local response (*RRI*:chap. 6), both of them anticipated by our analysis of contemporary Tswana culture and society. One was to conclude that the bounty of the mission garden flowed from the innate potency of the whites themselves and the means at their disposal. Hence, for example, we are told that Rolong men vied to have their wives plant fields beside the visibly fertile plots of the Methodists;[59] apparently they thought that the fruitfulness of the WMMS grounds would overflow into their own, or that sheer proximity to the Europeans might give access to their mysterious agrarian powers. Given time to observe British horticulture, however, and the tenacity of the Nonconformists in essaying their methods, the Africans soon began to differentiate the alien means of production from the personal capacities of their owners.

The other reaction to the agrarian challenge of the mission came mainly from Tswana women. As some of the implications of European practices became discernible, they began to resist them by interrupting irrigation routines, damaging dams, and stealing the fruits of the garden.[60] Patently, if men took to the fields, it followed that their wives would lose control over agricultural production and its harvest, the very things on which rested the well-being of their houses. The clerics might have regarded the lot of African females as unduly arduous, even unnatural. But given prevailing hegemonies—and, in particular, their expression in the unmarked contours of everyday economics—there is no reason to expect that these women would have seen matters in the same light. All the evidence suggests that they did not. Why, otherwise, should the feisty "Queen" Mahutu and her Tlhaping companions[61] have offered to plant corn for the Christians in the early days, explicitly to save them from doing "women's work" (see *RRI*:203)? Why, otherwise, should they have tried in 1821 to take over *more* irrigated land to cultivate (Moffat and Moffat 1951:23)? And why, otherwise, even fifty years later, should Southern Tswana females have defended their gardens with such ardor, both mystically and materially, against the inroads of men and beasts? From their perspective in the social order, they had every reason to fear the innovations of the Nonconformists. Over the long run, their anxieties were to prove justified.

Pragmatic though their response may have been, it was also shaped by a particular cultural vision, a sense of the proper connections among production, gender, and human capacity (*RRI*:144f.). For a start, intensive agriculture involved hitching the ox to the plough. And this, in turn, required bridging the gendered gulf between cows and cultivation—marked by the taboo against women handling beasts—that ran to the very core of the Southern Tswana world in the early nineteenth century. At the same time, as we also saw in volume 1, the inhabitants of that world were remarkably open to practical innovation and the exchange of cultural knowledge. It is not surprising either, therefore, that the evangelists' methods, which yielded tangible results, should have elicited their attention. Or that some people would have begun to experiment with them.[62] Reported Lichtenstein (1973:80), very early on:[63]

A plough was something quite alien to them, till a missionary showed them one. They liked it very much and were also favourably impressed by various agricultural methods as they are employed in Europe. They were anxious to use these advantages and to learn how to handle the new implements.

Similarly, Broadbent (1865:104) claimed that his "gardening operations produced a strong and favourable impression on the people." He went on to add that the "public benefits" of the highly visible horticultural experiments of his colleague, Thomas Hodgson, "were so obvious, and acknowledged by the Chiefs and people, that they served to win their regard" (p. 106). This seems to have overstated matters somewhat. But there certainly were signs of gradual gains made by the mission as some Tswana contemplated, and then tried out, their methods. In August 1821, Moffat recorded Mahutu's efforts to expropriate a valley that he and his brethren had sown with corn, one that had proven manifestly fruitful (Schapera 1951:23; see above). True, he would greatly have preferred it had her husband taken over the farming operation. And he complained that she misused the land, watering it in the heat of midsummer when moisture was scarce. Also, as we observed a moment ago, her actions may have had more to do with the effort of women to sustain control over cultivation than with a desire to become a progressive farmer, European style. We have no way of knowing. Still, for the LMS this was one of the first signs of success.

More were to come. Philip (1828,2:118), who always took care to describe "the progress which rational ideas had made," tells how Tlhaping cynicism gave way to comprehension, mockery to mimesis. When, at Kuruman, his brethren began to cut their irrigation channel, the Africans were unimpressed, he says (pp. 113–14):

> Until they saw the water running into the ditch, they deemed it impossible, and treated the attempt with ridicule. But, when they saw it completed, their surprise was as great as their former scepticism. . . . The Bechuanas are, however, now convinced of their error; and some of them are leading out the water to make gardens and corn-fields on an inclined plane.

With the necessary cultural seeds planted, the agricultural effect could now follow. On his next visit to the station, in the mid-1820s, Philip (p. 118) "had the satisfaction to see [Chief] Mahuri, with his people, and other Bechuanas, applying to the missionaries for seed-corn to sow on the lands then under irrigation. In reference, also, to a promise of the missionaries to plough some land, and train a span of bullocks for him, he manifested considerable pleasure."

This, for the Nonconformists, was a real breakthrough: *men*, including a chief, were evincing interest in cultivation—indeed, in animal-driven *plough* cultivation. Soon after, the Seleka-Rolong leader, Sefunelo, approached the Wesleyans working among his people for seeds, "which he promised to sow" (Hodgson 1977:206).

Once the sparks of an agrarian revolution had been kindled, thought the Nonconformists, there was nothing to stop its catching fire. Or so it seemed in the late 1820s and 1830s. This "revolution" was not limited to those who had formally allied themselves to the church, and who cultivated mission ground. But the latter were under more direct European supervision, and featured more regularly in evangelical reports. Thus, in 1828, Mary Moffat commented that "[n]early all our poor people have reaped good crops of wheat . . . and some maize. . . . They also grow much tobacco, which they exchange for cattle, karosses, &c" (Moffat and Moffat 1951:292). "I am astonished," she added, "to see what the willing earth yields in so short a time." Her sanguine husband, in a letter written on the same day, offered that "[n]ext year the crop will be much extended, [and] the station will rise to some importance in a temporal as well as a spiritual point of view" (Moffat and Moffat 1951:290).[64] Note, again here, the insistence on the simultaneity of the secular and the sacred.

Nor were the evangelists alone in speaking optimistically of agrarian "improvement" around LMS stations. Bain (1949:154), for one,[65] wrote in 1834:

> The improvements at Kuruman . . . are truly astonishing! . . . What pleased me much . . . was to see large fields of yellow wheat belonging to the natives vieing with the crops of the Missionaries, having been cultivated and irrigated. This is a grand step towards civilisation.

Equally auspicious reports came from the Methodists, albeit a few years on. In 1842, at Platberg, Cameron observed that "numerous gardens . . . have lately been walled in," and were being brought under cultivation; at Lishuani, "sixty large gardens [had] been enclosed, and upward of two thousand trees planted." A new era, it seemed, lay just beyond the horizon.[66]

The economic revolution was farther off than the Europeans suspected, however. And it was not to take the course, or to occur in the spaces, that they anticipated. For one thing, sites of agrarian "progress" were very restricted at the time, being confined to the immediate surrounds of the mission stations— and to those Southern Tswana who fell within their sphere of influence.[67] For another, as Shillington (1985:18) has noted, not all of Bechuanaland was ecologically amenable to agricultural intensification; especially toward the arid, infertile west, people had little option but to rely throughout the century on their herds (and, to a decreasing extent, on hunting). What is more, the region had yet to feel the full impact of settler expansion, of unsettled subcontinental conditions, and of a mineral revolution.

As this suggests, the encounter between the colonial evangelists and the Southern Tswana had only just begun to play itself out in the "economic" register. Let us turn, now, to consider agrarian transformations of the longer run, transformations that were as much cultural and social as they were material.

CROPS, CULTIVATION, AND CLASS: TRANSFORMATIONS OF THE LONG RUN

In contrasting the semi-civilized state of the Bechuana of today with the uncouthness of eighty years ago, one must not overlook the important influence which acquaintance with the appliances and methods of European life has had upon them. The plough, the wagon, the horse, and the gun have changed the tenor of their lives. . . . The native races are not yet an industrious people; still, the unskilled manual labour of South Africa is entirely in their hands . . . and no inconsiderable portion of the produce that finds its way into the market is raised by them.

Rev. William Crisp (1896:53)

There was a sustained ambiguity in mid nineteenth-century Nonconformist accounts of Southern Tswana reactions to mission agriculture. On one hand, the evangelists continued to speak of a strong African tendency to cling to custom, and to resist enlightened self-improvement. On the other, they often suggested that the techniques of modern farming were making rapid inroads, and that an agrarian revolution was imminent. On the rare occasions when Tswana were canvassed for their views, their answers[68] seemed to justify both impressions at once. Thus, for example, a Tlhaping elder, brought to the Cape in the early years by Moffat (see n. 26), was asked whose ways and means, whose "manner of life" was preferable? (G. Thompson 1967:166): "He said, each was best for those who were used to it. He saw that we [Europeans] were a wiser and more knowing people than the Bechuanas; but from long habit, he preferred the customs and manner of life of his own country to ours." His British interlocutors might have been impressed by the man's tact. But, given their own sensibilities, they did not take well to his cultural relativism. So they plied him with "proofs" of the superior power of European agricultural *knowledge*—the italics were theirs—until the man conceded the point, "and promised to follow diligently . . . the instructions of Moffat . . . and become . . . like the 'Macooas'" ("white men"; G. Thompson 1967:166).

This counterpoint in missionary texts, the simultaneous talk of continuity and change, was not born of witting misrepresentation. Some features of the Tswana world did *not* give way easily; long-established hegemonic forms rarely do. Among these were the gendered division of labor, the concomitant separation of cattle husbandry from cultivation, the polluting effect of women on animals, and the difficulties this raised for hitching the beast to the plough. In addition, some categories of people *were* less disposed or less able than were others to experiment with European productive technologies. For instance, only those with sufficient livestock could consider using ploughs, or could profit from taking surpluses and trade goods to distant markets; the corollary being that the persistence of received practices among their more straitened compatriots might as well have been a function of necessity as choice (see below). As this implies, the immediate impact of colonial evangelism on Tswana agriculture was bewilderingly variable. It was the extremes of this variability, compressed in time and space, that are reflected in the ambiguities of contemporary mission texts. Quite simply, it is not possible to speak of *the* effect of agrarian transformation on *the* Southern Tswana. Its effects (plural) on Batswana (plural) have to be carefully disaggregated. But that raises the obverse, obvious question: Was there any pattern at all in the way in which European means of production took root, and worked their social effects, on this landscape? The answer is not straightforward. It is to be found in complex, drawn-out processes of class formation, social reformation, and cultural distinction. Before we explore these processes, however, let us begin by laying out a brief *histoire événementielle* of agricultural change during the middle and late nineteenth century. Not only will this demonstrate the variabilities of which we speak. It will also prepare the ground for an analysis of social and material reconstruction.

Passing Seasons, Eventful Years

As we have already intimated, the colonial evangelists saw the reconstruction of Tswana material life to depend, above all else, on the entry of men into (irrigated) plough cultivation. From this, they believed, would follow the privatization of the soil, the emergence of the nuclear family "farmstead," the ascendance of cropping over pastoralism; in short, the rise of a "true farming class" (J. Mackenzie 1975:110). Notwithstanding early mission reports of the adoption of European horticultural techniques by Tlhaping, however, this gendered transformation did not occur at once. It was only after *difaqane* had disrupted rural production, after the countryside had settled down in the wake of the turmoil, after the viability of hunting and foraging had begun to decline, that males began to take to the fields in earnest (Tilby 1914:193; Broadbent 1865:105; also Shillington 1985:17).[69]

Eventually, as Neil Parsons (1977:123) has observed, speaking of more northerly Tswana, the plough would displace the hoe everywhere, save *in extremis*.[70] According to John Mackenzie (1887,2:341), this was owed entirely to the LMS evangelists at Kuruman:

> Under the supervision of the missionaries, the natives learned a higher agriculture, and exchanged the hoe of their own ruder garden work for the plough and the spade. What had been done at Kuruman was imitated by the natives elsewhere.

In fact, it was not so much mimesis as culturally tooled pragmatism that commended the plough (and irrigation) to Southern Tswana. Its capacity to enlarge the scale and yield of farming[71]—especially in this dryland, dramatically unreliable ecology (cf. Schapera 1953:19–20; Shillington 1985:92)—was soon noted by a people keenly interested in the accumulation of useful knowledge. (It also had a down side, but more of that in a moment.) Among Tlhaping, for example, the harvests of those who went in for intensive agriculture grew markedly in the late 1830s; before that, there had been only three ploughs in the Kuruman valley. After 1838, when a trader settled on the station to cater to the demand for British goods (below, p. 185), there was a steady increase in the ownership of implements and wagons (Northcott 1961:148), most of them bought from the proceeds of grain sales (R. Moffat 1842:605). Much, but by no means all of this, involved members of the LMS congregation.

As productivity around this and other missions rose, some Tswana communities became regular exporters of European cereals; among them, notably, the WMMS stronghold at Thaba 'Nchu. In 1844, for example, the Rev. Ayliff wrote that Dutch farmers near the Orange River were "passing out of the colony with wagons . . . to purchase wheat of the Bechuanas" (Broadbent 1865:106).[72] Local produce was also finding its way to more distant markets (see chapter 4). At the same time, we do not know what proportion of Southern Tswana men actually moved into plough cultivation during these years. Many, some Christians among them, did not. Or—lacking the necessary beasts, access to human labor, and fertile fields—could not. Among those who did, moreover, the size and success of farming enterprises appear to have been distinctly uneven. As far as can be told, a large number of women throughout Bechuanaland continued, in the 1850s, to sow and reap as they always had done. According to Mackenzie (1887,2:168), who seemed here to contradict other things he had written on the topic, "two styles of agriculture" prevailed in the region: the "old" and the "higher." Even as late as 1865, he said, few ploughs were to be found in many parts of the country. Most gardens were "being cultivated in the old way by women with the hoe."[73]

When males did invest in intensive cultivation, they quickly seized control over the crop and its disposal. Females, however, were not banished to the "domestic" domain. Prosperous farmers, it seems, had servants and clients take over activities involving animals, but left the rest of the burden to those who once were mistresses of the fields.[74] Even men who ploughed small acreages, sometimes with borrowed beasts, relied on women for crucial tasks—and then sold their harvests to the market on their own account. In sum, to the degree that males entered the arable sector, the gendered politics of production were radically altered. And distinctions of wealth and status were greatly widened: because it was only stock owners who could plough extensively, and because plough agriculture yielded by far the largest returns on land and labor, the rich became steadily richer. Although they did not immediately become poorer— that would happen in time—other Southern Tswana benefited little from the agrarian innovations of the mission.

If the uneven impact of European agriculture was already discernible in the 1840s, reports from the midcentury onward disclose its ever more equivocal effect on Tswana life. On the positive side, they spoke of the general "improvement" of farming in many areas. For example, Mackenzie (1887,2:168) observed that, at Taung as at Kuruman, irrigated crops were being grown and sold with success. The Africans, he complained (1871:70), could still not make a straight fence or furrow. But they had taken great strides in adopting the means of modern agriculture. This, he added (p. 90), was having a number of beneficial effects: it was weakening the tenacious hold of custom on ordinary people; old forms of "vassalage," the class differences of the *ancien régime*, were now disappearing, abetted by the breakdown of royal trade monopolies (p. 131); and the authority of retrogressive rulers was on the wane.

But Mackenzie (1871:70f.) also recorded some of the unhappier corollaries of agrarian reform: among them, that the widespread use of guns, purchased from the proceeds of cropping, had so depleted the game population that hunting yielded almost nothing to those who still needed it; that, when drought and disease threatened the livestock economy, on which tillage increasingly relied, many people were forced to survive by gathering roots or "picking" at the ground; that, with ever more pasturage being brought under cultivation, politically powerful families were gaining control of a disproportionate amount of land. (This included the most reliable, irrigable holdings—"comparatively few in number and limited in extent"—around natural water sources; cf. Shillington 1985:62). The missionary might have noted another thing as well. The first signs were also becoming visible of the serious erosion caused by ploughs to earth whose shallow fertility was not well suited to them (cf. N. Parsons 1977:128, on the Ngwato). Broadbent was correct: these implements do "dig deep into the soil." What he failed to see was the despoliation they left behind. The material bases of both poverty and inequality were being inexorably reconstructed under the impact of European commodity agriculture.

By the 1870s, the decade that saw the onset of the mineral revolution and the growth of the diamond fields around Kimberley, Southern Tswana agriculture had become even more polarized. A few European observers, most notably Andrew Anderson (1888:81), reported glowingly, if rather too generally, on the local agrarian revolution:

> From cultivating little or no corn, which was the woman's work, they now go in extensively for ploughs, which the men use, and instead of growing mealies, which is maize or Indian corn, and a few melons, they now produce wheat, barley, and oats, which they . . . sell to traders for English goods, and in addition they breed herds of cattle, goats and sheep.

Then, in an singular passage (p. 83):

> The Bechuanas . . . also bring down from their homes, wood, corn, and vegetables for sale to the Diamond Fields, and are far more beneficial and useful in the country than the Boers. They are outstepping them in civilization, and if they had white skins, would be looked upon as a superior race.

Some Tswana, especially from the southern chiefdoms, were well placed to supply the Kimberley market with fruits, cereals, and vegetables;[75] wagon owners also did very well, for several years, from selling huge quantities of wood to the diggings (Shillington 1985:66f.). Of those who expanded their business ventures during these years, most were men who joined royal privilege—specifically, access to abundant labor and fertile fields—to techniques of cultivation and accumulation taught by the evangelists.[76] Others were commoner converts who, on becoming monogamous[77] and entering the church, had been given irrigable mission land, itself scarce and highly fecund. They had procured the necessary tools, adopted "modern" methods, and reinvested their profits in their farming enterprises. But the ideal of advancement via commodity production was being realized by relatively few. Holub (1881,1:120f.), for example, traveling across the back reaches of Tlhaping territory in 1873, discovered that a "good, useful plough" was a "rarity" (p. 125). So, too, was a substantial farmstead. Only a handful of families raised cereals or had "any transactions at the Kimberley market" (p. 120). Recall also Wookey (see n. 43 above), who observed in 1873 that, among the nearby Tlharo, gardens still "belonged" to women, a sure sign of the absence of animal-driven agriculture.

Those Southern Tswana who did not have the means to buy their own ploughs, or to irrigate their fields, were steadily reduced to economic dependency. A good number lost all access to productive land, which was taken over by their wealthier compatriots.[78] The latter set about indebting their less fortunate kin and neighbors (see *RRI*:140f.), extending loans of cattle, cash, or grain to them—and then sought recompense by having their dependents till their fields or serve them in various ways.[79] So much so that, among Tlhaping, says Kinsman (1983:39), "roughly two thirds of the formerly free, town dwelling population . . . succumbed to a clientship status" in the years after the discovery of diamonds. Others, caught between the extremes of wealth and poverty, made a sustained effort to continue farming on their own account, supplementing their incomes if necessary by hiring themselves out (cf. Shillington 1985:63f.). By the late 1870s, however, drought and the destruction of natural resources were driving more and more people into the labor market. While Southern Tswana were attracted to urban centers for many reasons, the flow of migrants was accelerated by events surrounding the annexation of Griqualand West to the Cape Colony—itself the culmination of a battle for territory around the diamond fields—which led settlers, speculators, and administrators to disempower chiefs and dispossess their followers of land and stock (Shillington 1985:99f.; *RRI*:chap. 7).[80] Not all the missionaries were upset that Southern Tswana were being drawn into wage employment in this manner. To the contrary, as we shall see in the next chapter, a few actually took pride in the fact that they had been so well prepared to enter the work force—especially as skilled farmhands (Mackenzie 1887,2:341).[81]

Some chiefdoms were less fractured, and less straitened, as a result of the agrarian transformations initiated by the mission. The Hurutshe at Dinokana, for instance, who retained only a small territory after Transvaal Boers had expropriated much of their land, raised some eight hundred (two-hundred-pound) sacks of wheat in 1875. And they were expanding their acreages under cultivation each year (Holub 1881,2:22). They also grew maize, sorghum, melons, and tobacco, and sold all surpluses "in the markets of the Transvaal and the diamond-fields."[82] As far as it is possible to ascertain, moreover, their productive and commercial successes were spread evenly across the population. But this seems to have been an exception rather than the general pattern in the Tswana interior.

More typical was the case of the Tshidi-Rolong. Among them, it was the industrious Christian community at Mafikeng, established in 1857, that made most use of the methods of intensive cultivation—without the permanent presence, recall, of a white missionary (see chapter 2). Its citizenry soon prospered, in large part from the introduction of European cereals and from marketing semi-irrigated maize to the Transvaal (Holub 1881,1:278–82; 2:22). By 1877, this town, with its "farmsteads" and "enclosures," supported considerable plough agriculture. The large, colonial-style houses of its richer residents (see below), signaled a level of wealth very different from that of the general population (Holub 1881,2:13)—much of which, as among the Tlhaping, was sinking slowly into penury and servitude.

This process of polarization was accelerated by external events. In the late 1870s, having returned from a period of exile to his former capital near Mafikeng (*RRI*:280), Chief Montshiwa ousted the Ratlou from lands that blocked his way to the diamond fields—declaring that he now grew "corn for the markets to get money" (Shillington 1985:129). The displaced Ratlou, joined by Boer freebooters with their own designs on Tswana land, responded by driving the Tshidi ruler and his people back to Mafikeng itself (Z. Matthews 1945:20), by looting their herds and crops, and by bringing the greatly enlarged population close to starvation (A. Anderson 1888:117). In time, the town would recover, but it never regained its past affluence. Further territorial wrangling and settler violence was followed by British annexation (1885) and the imposition of taxes. This, along with a series of ecological reverses and the shift of the industrial center to the Transvaal goldfields, added to the decline. While the local economy did not collapse altogether—Tshidi produced surpluses during the Siege of Mafeking, 1899–1900 (Plaatje 1973:60)—most families had become dependent on the labor market by the early years of the new century. Only the wealthiest survived the crises with their fortunes intact.

Elsewhere in the region, too, the 1880s and 1890s were decades of turbulence, transition, and yet further differentiation within Tswana communities.[83] Surveying southern Bechuanaland in 1884, Wookey (1884:303f.) confirmed that there was little hoe cultivation seen any longer, "men with their ploughs and teams of oxen having taken the place of the women at field labour of that kind" (cf. Conder 1887:86). What is more, some of those engaged in commercial farming were doing very well: "I am acquainted with a man who, just now, has bought a new wagon with mealies, valued at over 150 [pounds], grown on his own farm this year." All this, he added, had had commendable social implications: chiefs no longer enjoyed "despotic" power; "bushmen" serfs had largely disappeared; women, servants, and other bondsmen, like the poor and the aged, "[occupied] a far higher position than they did fifty years ago. . . . None are thrown away, as formerly" (p. 306). The Rev. Crisp (1896:17), who reiterated that the advent of the plough had led to the production of "an enormous quantity of corn . . . for the purposes of commerce," agreed that the burden of a Tswana wife had been eased. But, he added, "she has also lost her perquisite. The husband now apportions to her so much as is required for food; the rest is his to sell."[84] And sell husbands did, with an avidity that exceeded even mission exhortations. Freed from the communal obligations and cooperative arrangements that surrounded female cultivation in the past, themselves a hedge against ecological risk, most disposed of as much as they could; in 1888, thirty-five thousand bags of grain, each of two hundred pounds, were purchased by storekeepers around Taung alone (Great Britain 1889:53). Nor was this rush to the market confined to the wealthy. Men of more modest means often sold small amounts of corn and grain to meet immediate financial needs, and to invest in cattle and other capital goods, only to find themselves short of food and funds later on (see below). In the upshot, hunger became rife in many places, to the extent that some rulers felt it necessary to regulate the vending of crops, as they did in the Bechuanaland Protectorate some years later (Schapera 1933:647, 1943b:203).

Wookey (1884:304f.), who did not mention the problems arising from the rampant marketing of crops, went on to discuss other developments that obviously did worry him. Owing to the sale of wood to Kimberley, the country had been denuded of trees and bushes. And, as noted earlier, wild beasts had disappeared. But, most of all (p. 305):

> Work amongst the men has become more general; in fact, with many, it is the only means of subsistence. . . . The land question has become the pressing one of the day here, and some of the chiefs, in order to get out of their difficulties, have been giving away land to Europeans to such an extent that it is a serious question whether there will be any land left for the natives to live upon. . . . The country itself is capable of producing far more than it does at present. There are many fountains lying unused; and all are capable of doing very much more than they are at present.

Two forms of pressure were working away at the infrastructure of Southern Tswana economies: the expropriation of territory by settlers[85] and the concentration of much of the remaining fertile land in the hands of fewer and fewer families.[86] Consequently, arable acreages became scarce and valuable; although, as we shall see in chapter 8, this did not actually turn the terrain into real estate. Nor did Wookey's most dire prediction ever come to pass: there was to be at least some "land left for the natives to live upon." For most Southern Tswana, however, the conditions of production—in an arid ecology, on barren ground, lacking the wherewithal for intensive farming or for the cultivation of large acreages[87]—were not promising.[88] Moreover, as already noted, some of those who suffered privation were likely to be "eaten" by powerful men. Which is why increasing numbers of people in each chiefdom ended up laboring for wealthier neighbors, for whites, or as self-employed artisans.[89] A handful took refuge around mission stations which rented plots to tenants.[90] And some managed still to scratch out a bare subsistence from the soil. But many found themselves dispossessed of the means of a steady, independent livelihood.

Matters took a general turn for the worse in 1896, with the rinderpest pandemic that afflicted much of the interior of southern Africa. We shall return to this period of crisis, as it opened up a space into which the colonial evangelists tried to extend their own regime of value; it also saw the outbreak of armed hostilities between Tlhaping and colonial forces, the former deeply disaffected by the unremitting expropriation of their territory and their stock, by the imposition of punitive levies and restrictions on their movement, and by the actions of the state in robbing them of their independence (Shillington 1985:215f.). The pandemic itself decimated herds and led to several years of acute hardship. In its wake followed famine and illness, not helped by the fact that, in the hope of containing infection, the colonial government prevented "the natives of Bechuanaland" from selling poultry and firewood at the diamond fields[91] and from shooting game.[92] Not only were pastoral pursuits severely affected, but cultivation also ground to a virtual halt.

Both herds and horticulture would recuperate in time, but not fast and never fully. In 1899, Willoughby (n.d.[a]:29) reported that, in Chief Khama's country to the north, cultivation was once again being done by women—with hoes. And this in a chiefdom whose ruler had been assiduous in implementing the lessons of colonial evangelism: in facilitating the purchase of ploughs and wagons, in engendering a new division of labor, and in disseminating the methods of intensive farming (N. Parsons 1977:120).[93] How much more would people further south, less successful in their prior agrarian pursuits, struggle to recoup their losses? Parsons (1977) points out that, between the turn of the century and 1910, agricultural production, and hence economic recovery, was discouraged by "falling prices combined with restrictions on external markets, made worse by drought and disease"; although, in years when it rained, Tlhaping and Rolong took the opportunity to hitch "every available ox and cow and calf" to the plough.[94] The drop in the retail value of crops was accompanied by a soft market in cattle—of which, in any case, the Africans had few and would only sell if absolutely necessary. In the circumstances, it was not easy to re-establish a local economy.

The dawn of the new century, then, saw most Southern Tswana well on the road to endemic poverty and economic dependency. Their agrarian reverses had not occurred *in vacuo*, of course. They were part of a broader process in which black South Africans were drawn into the dominion of colonial South Africa (see *RRI*:chap. 7); converted, at least in part, into what Parson (1984) has called a "peasantariat." As early as 1878, Sir Gordon Sprigg, Prime Minister at the Cape, had toured the Colony telling whites of his intention to make "natives" into laborers (Comaroff and Comaroff 1992:199). The point, he said, in a dig at the missions, was "to teach them to work, not to read and write and sing."[95] Thanks to recent revisionist histories—and earlier writings by black South Africans, presently being recuperated[96]—the story is now familiar: how colonial capitalists, settlers, and statesmen, despite differences among themselves, found common cause in coercing large numbers of Africans into wage employment; how *tax Britannica*, the seizure of property, the manipulation of agricultural prices and conditions, and other blunt fiscal instruments conduced to make them reliant on supplementary cash incomes;[97] how all but the wealthy had to subsist on an uneasy mix of female peasant production and the income of low-paid male jobs, both being necessary, but neither sufficient, to nurture a family; how a carefully regulated labor force was reproduced by women "at home," the countryside being made to bear the cost of nurturing and sustaining a rising proletariat; how, in all this, the political economy of rural and urban, black and white, rich and poor, agrarian and industrial South Africa was integrated into a single, tightly meshed structure. We shall retell part of the story in the next chapter, albeit from a different perspective, since the evangelists had a crucial role in it. Indeed, some of them, *pace* Sprigg, were to take credit for provisioning the country with an abundance of well-primed, willing workers.[98] But more of that in due course.

There is one last piece to add to our *histoire événementielle*. Although drawn from the very end of the period with which we are concerned, it illuminates the contours of a social landscape long in formation. Here we see the lines of difference and distinction, of new configurations of class and identity, that had been emerging, and would harden, as the Southern Tswana world (re)formed itself under the impact of the agrarian revolution.

By the 1930s, the material existence of most Southern Tswana was only a little less precarious than it had been at the turn of the century. In a series of classic studies, Schapera (e.g., 1933, 1943b, 1947) has documented the economic predicament of the Bechuanaland Protectorate at the time. Across the border to the south, judging from the field notes of Z. K. Matthews, himself a Tswana ethnographer,[99] conditions looked a great deal worse. Writing in 1938,[100] Matthews told of the "dire poverty" he found among Tshidi-Rolong and others. Based on official figures from the 1936–37 South African agricultural census, on information from a local official, and on his own observations, he calculated that "the average family . . . possesses not more than 2.5 head of cattle, 1.5 sheep, 2.5 goats and produces a quarter of a bag of mealies [maize], half a bag of corn, hardly any beans, no vegetables, has practically no meat and very little milk." But for migrant labor and a range of cooperative arrangements among kin, there would not merely be

> serious malnutrition but actual starvation. . . . As it is their physical condition is very poor. Traditional foods are being replaced by foods . . . [which] must be bought with cash obtained as a reward for labour in industrial centres and on European farms. . . . [T]raditional economic activities suffer through the absence of the able-bodied, leading to worse poverty.

The picture that emerges from Matthews' matter-of-fact, scientific prose is desperately bleak. And affecting. It tells of humble people straining to eke out a living in "customary" ways, augmented by whatever European methods they could muster;[101] straining to sustain their division of labor[102] and nurture their herds; straining to keep their families intact and as independent as humanly possible. A few boreholes had been sunk by the government to improve the "very poor" water supply in the region. Three "native" agricultural demonstrators sought to improve techniques of cropping and stock raising, to persuade cattle owners to dip and vaccinate their animals, and to make the few implements at their disposal available to Tswana farmers. But they were fighting an uphill battle. During the following year, one of little rainfall, labor recruiting agents told Matthews that "never before had so many Barolong come forward and been so ready to take any type of work that was offering."[103] Shades here of the late 1920s, when a young demonstrator was sent to the Tlhaping *sans* resources or equipment in the midst of a drought. At a public assembly called to greet his arrival, the local chief was advised to tell the government "that the need at the moment is a rain doctor and not a ploughman."[104]

At the same time, in a handwritten narrative, Matthews describes the life of a wealthy elder and his family at Madibe, a settlement some fifteen miles from Mafikeng.[105] Leteane by name, the man was seventy-two years old, his wife sixty-five. Living with them were their twenty-seven-year-old daughter and her four children. Other offspring were away in cities and towns earning a living, although the financial situation of the household did not demand it. By this time, some youths migrated to urban centers as much to mark their passage into adulthood as a reaction to economic necessity.

Like his father before him, Leteane was a headman. He owed allegiance to Joshua Molema, the prominent Methodist leader of the Molema section at the capital, whose daughter he had married. An active member of the Wesleyan church himself, Leteane's descendants were to be respected teachers at the capital in years to come.[106] As Molema's representative, he wielded authority over members of the section who had cattle posts and fields (and, in a number of cases, residences) around Madibe. Attached to his household—as to "every important Barolong household"—were a clutch of servants who "act[ed] as herdsmen, [did] the milking, ploughing, . . . [and] all the more strenuous jobs" (p. 2). According to an insertion in the field notes, these people were not Rolong but Kgalagadi; with hindsight, we know this to be the ethnic label applied to some of those in Southern Tswana chiefdoms who, having lost the means of an independent existence, ministered to the wealthy.[107] They received no wages, but were fed and had stock earmarked for them every now and again. Added Matthews (pp. 2–3):

> Their treatment on the whole is not harsh. . . . The only disability from which they suffer is that of an inferior station. They may not marry or make love to the children of their masters; they do not handle the food of their masters except under exceptional circumstances and they are expected to show the utmost deference.

In fact, these servants labored under two major forms of disability. One was the absence of any right to recompense if a master or his sons impregnated their womenfolk, which happened "not infrequently" (p. 3); here, as in many places, sexual access marked out the directionalities of power. The other was a lack of economic and social self-determination. As Matthews himself points out (p. 3), if a family in servitude accumulated independent means, which some actually did, it immediately took off for elsewhere.[108]

We do not have details on the size of Leteane's herds or his fields; all indications are that they were extensive, although cattle were not as "plentiful" in 1938 as they had once been in the area (p. 6). Neither the headman nor his wife did any productive labor on their own account. He was said (p. 4) to have sat in the *kgotla* most days where, from dawn, he heard disputes and presided over public meetings. Together, they "direct[ed] the activities of the servants." Their daughter looked after her children, did some of the domestic work, and fed her kin. Unlike the poor households described elsewhere in this record, this one lived comfortably and ate well. Large quantities of porridge, fresh and soured milk, occasional meat (especially mutton), corn dishes, and wild fruits made up the bulk of its diet. This, along with the allocation of beasts to servants, suggests that the plough cultivation and animal husbandry done under the management of Leteane enjoyed high yields.[109]

Here, then, to end our event history, is the vignette of an affluent family; one whose position had been built on political privilege and access to land, on an alliance joined through membership of the Methodist church, and on the agrarian methods of the mission. Leteane was not, by any means, among the richest of Rolong in those years. But his household enjoyed a lifestyle far more comfortable than did most others. The very fact of this contrast affirms, if affirmation were necessary, that the agrarian history of the long run did not conduce to a single, monolithic outcome; that its end point was a field of social and material disparities, diversities, differences; that Southern Tswana were not all alike immiserated and reduced to a state of dependency. Nor, as we shall see, were *any* of them—prosperous, poor, or the middling sort—remade in the precise mold of the civilizing mission, the mold cast from the figure of the British yeoman farmer.

It is impossible, in retrospect, to quantify the overall distribution of wealth yielded by a century of colonial evangelism, of state intervention and settler expansion, of the machinations of merchants and the mechanisms of the market. But the broad lines of what was happening—processes of class formation and political transformation, of economic de-and reformation, of social distinction—are inescapable. Let us pursue these processes further. Their determinations, and their implications, turn out to be intriguingly complex.

Class Formation, Political Transformation, Social Distinction

At first blush, the agrarian history of the long run here seems to echo Colin Bundy's (1972, 1979) now classical account of the "rise and fall" of a South African peasantry. With good reason. For ordinary Tlhaping, Rolong, Tlharo, and others, the early successes achieved through a selective adoption of European ways and means were the tangible reward for their openness to alien forms of cultural knowledge—and evidence of the sheer dynamism of their economies. So, too, were the cash returns that many enjoyed as exporters of produce and fodder crops. But, as time passed, the rank and file experienced ever more difficulty in making a decent living: with their land disappearing, with the prices for their harvests low and their debts to European traders mounting, with strong "inducement" to enter the labor market, they found themselves less a sturdy yeomanry than a population of partly proletarianized workers, partly sub-subsistence farmers. In short, for the vast majority of Southern Tswana, incorporation into the political economy of colonial South Africa marked an end to their lives as independent producers; their "fall," that is, not just into poverty but also into a state of dependency on social and material forces beyond their control.

But this master narrative,[110] a narrative of mastery lost, had another side to it as well. An inside. Insofar as the colonization of Southern Tswana agriculture altered patterns of production and differentiation *within* local communities, it also evokes the story told by Lenin (1971:14f.) of the Russian peasantry under capitalism (see D. Ferguson 1976; cf. also Snyder 1981:282f., on the Banjal).[111] According to this story—we phrase it in its generic, not its concrete historical form—the growth of commodity production in the countryside leads initially to a general rise in levels of output as rural populations avail themselves of new technologies and markets. Soon, however, because of inequalities in circumstances, there begin to emerge three rural "subclasses," each with very different social and economic means and ends: a petite bourgeoisie composed of those who, being in a position to accumulate land and capital in the changed circumstances, become commercial farmers and, as they do, exploit the wage labor of others while diversifying their enterprises out of agriculture; a poor peasantry, which includes both small-scale producers and landless proletarians compelled to sell their labor power either locally or at distant centers; and a middle peasantry, which engages both in subsistence cultivation and, wherever possible, in the raising of marketable surpluses, but which does not depend for its income on the exploitation of others.

Of these "subclasses," goes the argument, the lower peasantry remains most dependent on noncommercial reciprocities and exchanges among kin. Its members, who face constant risk and whose agrarian yields are marginal at best, are typically coerced either into leaving the land or into the classical "peasant-proletarian" predicament; that is, of having to survive from a combination of subsistence gardening and wage labor, neither yielding enough to support the household. Middle peasants, while not in the same straits, are also in an endemically unstable position. Unable to purchase the most efficient means of production, they cannot grow surpluses large enough to protect themselves entirely from disaster; hence they always face the threat of downward mobility. Only the upper peasantry is (more or less) secure. Free of the uncertainties of agriculture, it gradually takes on the social and cultural characteristics of bourgeoisies everywhere, although its local color and collective consciousness, like its economic strategies, are shaped by virtue of its relations and struggles with the other two fractions. In this sense, all three are classes in the making, *not* simply socioeconomic categories.

A process of fragmentation of this kind occurred in British Bechuanaland from the mid nineteenth century onward. Three broadly discernible (if loosely bound, unstable) fractions steadily took form, each with its own social practices and productive relations, its stylistic preferences and ideological proclivities. Many practices and preferences continued to be shared, of course; *setswana* itself defined a common, albeit not an uncontested or unchanging, cultural field. As Volosinov (1973:23) puts it, classes typically share common signs; indeed, these often become an object of conflict among them. Yet they speak with very "differently oriented [and differently empowered] accents." So, too, with class fractions. The emergence of such fractions here did more than just lay the basis for future patterns of social distinction and ideological struggle. It also gave shape to the disparate ways in which the civilizing mission in particular, and colonialism in general, worked its effects on Southern Tswana economy and society. To that extent, the Leninist model, like Bundy's paradigm for the South African peasantry, is highly suggestive. The two, in fact, complement one another: the latter pays attention to the broad lines of domination and dependency suffered by indigenous populations at the hands of Europeans; the former, to the modes of differentiation that took root within their societies under the impact of agrarian capitalism. Neither, it is true, addresses the agency of local people/s, *their* capacities to alter, direct, affect their own destinies. Nor, for obvious reasons, does either describe the minutiae, or the indeterminacies, of specifically local processes. One, after all, was drawn from modern European history, the other from a quite different part of colonial South Africa. But they do frame the terms in which global forces entered upon Tswana terrain, there to play—dialectically, at once determining and determined, dominating and deformed—into a world with its own orders of value, its own social topographies and intractable realities.

One thing should be said immediately, though. No Southern Tswana, however they fitted into the emerging fractions of the peasantry,[112] ever lived an agrarian life anything like the ideal envisaged for them by the Nonconformists. None, even those most identified with the LMS and WMMS, simply embraced, in the manner of the mimic-man, the ways and means of European agriculture. To be sure, the neat, detached yeoman farmstead, an anachronism transposed from Britain onto the Bechuana scrublands, was never more than a chimera, a mirage that hovered just over the horizon of an unfolding history; likewise the image of the mission vegetable plot, with its surrounding fruit and shade trees, as a template for the domestication of the African veld. Eve Darian-Smith (1995:402–3), making a general point about the English garden as fantasy, quotes Pugh's (1988:130–32) observation that it has always been "a model for everything that reality is not." This was no less true of the version exported to South Africa. To whatever degree Tswana took over the forms of modernist horticulture, they adapted rather than adopted them, inserting them into social relations, residential patterns, tenurial arrangements, timetables, and rituals of their own.

Even the evangelists' most self-evident, purely technical truth—that advanced agriculture depended on rational procedures, hard work, and enlightened scientific methods—was never passively received. The Africans, notwithstanding differences of wealth or religious affiliation, saw the production of crops and cattle as a far more complicated, less neutral affair. For them, it involved social considerations, invisible forces, the intervention of ancestors, and the insidious actions of enemies. Theirs, remember, was a highly fraught world of agnatic conflict and interpersonal rivalry; one in which it was deemed necessary for people to protect their own fortunes by whatever means against the nefarious deeds of others. Thus, returning to Matthews's field notes on farming in predominantly Christian Mafikeng, circa 1938 (see n. 101), we are told that "every man" doctored his seed,[113] this "being designed not only to enhance his own opportunities of making a decent living but also at hindering the progress of his neighbours" (p. 12). The success or failure of crops was universally attributed, in the last instance, "to the practices of magic" (p. 14). What is more, Matthews commented, the "individual system of agricultural production," encouraged by the mission, had greatly exacerbated "private interest and competition" (pp. 12–14)—and, with it, the incentive to deploy *setswana* measures in order to get ahead at the expense of others. In the spiritual economy of ancestral protection, one man's gain was not necessarily another's loss, although success *was* often seen as a product of the ill-gotten gains of sorcery. "Tradition" might have given way to an economy of the limited good. But that economy, the bastard child of Adam Smith, was enchanted nevertheless. It was an economy of magical rationalism in which unnatural profit was, if anything, more palpable than it had ever been before.

Nor were its workings confined to cultivation. Cattle husbandry had a similar side to it (p. 9). For example, a medicine, *thiba-di-molekane*,[114] was boiled, ground, and sprinkled over both beasts and their byres by stock holders. This was believed to enlarge their herds and to prevent those of their neighbors, presumably their agnatic rivals, from multiplying. Bulls were also doctored both to facilitate the insemination of the cows of their owners and, simultaneously, to discourage them from mating with the animals of others; or, if they did, to make those animals sicken and die. As this suggests, even when European methods were taken on enthusiastically, they were absorbed into a local moral economy with its own regimes of value. Agriculture here was irreducible to an ensemble of material techniques. It was a profoundly social business, part of the politics of everyday life in the labile, enigmatic world described in volume 1 (p. 128f.).

If Southern Tswana were not passive proselytes in the face of the assault of the civilizing mission on their material lives, none was untouched by it either. *All* of them, as we have seen, were transformed by the introduction of the plough and by the commodification of agriculture, with everything it entailed over the long run. But not in the same way or to the same extent. Each of the three fractions of the peasantry engaged with the forces of agrarian capitalism differently. Each sought—out of choice or compulsion, or a measure of both— to domesticate these forces according to its own lights: to appropriate them, to turn them aside, or to accommodate to them.

Self-evidently, it was the most affluent sector of the population that came closest to the mission ideal in embracing the spirit, and the practices, of agrarian capitalism. This fraction, being relatively small, was scattered thinly across the communities of southern Bechuanaland, although it wielded influence far in excess of its size. It was made up, as we have intimated, of two components: the commoner Christian elite, men like Wookey's well-off acquaintance (pp. 145– 46) and the Methodist citizens of Mafikeng; and those members of ruling cadres who, in the manner of Joshua Molema and Leteane, combined the techniques of advanced agriculture with resources gained by "traditional" means.[115] Many of the latter joined mission churches in the early twentieth century—if they had not done before—when (at least nominal) membership of one or another denomination, orthodox or independent, became almost universal among Tswana (see chapter 2).

As Lenin's portrait of upper peasantries would lead us to expect,[116] these wealthy families farmed on an ever larger scale, almost entirely for the market, and with more and more advanced implements and methods.[117] It was they who appropriated the best acreages, at times, it is said in retrospect,[118] by devious means; who sought to gain exclusive control of scarce water sources, both natural and man-made;[119] who reinvested their profits most determinedly in their farms, enlarged their herds, and "modernized" their stock management techniques;[120] who recruited as much nonfamily labor as possible (see below), thereby allowing their womenfolk to become "housewives" rather than producers, and their offspring to enter the salariat (also, in a very few cases, the professions); who developed a monopoly over the long-distance carriage of goods and people by wagon and, later on, by motorized vehicles; and who, as the century advanced, bought mechanized means of production,[121] which they used both to increase their own arable operations and to rent out as a source of low-risk income.[122] It was by diversifying their interests, in fact, that this fraction of the population managed to survive, and recover from, the impact of the rinderpest pandemic. A number of them did so well from the sale of agrarian services, from transportation, by opening stores, and through other business ventures that they eventually scaled down their dryland cultivation, the most fragile of their enterprises. Silas Molema, for example, Joshua's younger brother, established himself as a commercial cattle breeder, a newspaper proprietor, a retail merchant, and a land rentier whose clients included white farmers in South Africa and in the Bechuanaland Protectorate.[123]

Where they took an active part in the life of their communities, which many did, members of the upper peasantry tended to associate themselves with the modernist ideals of the civilizing mission. Even those who were weakly affiliated with the church, or did not join at all, shared a Eurocentric, Protestant-oriented sense of improvement and development (*thutho*, "learning" or "knowledge," also "education")—albeit with a particular local inflection. They spoke of towns and villages graced with dams, schools, clinics, stores, cooperative farming services, and communal facilities.[124] And, in policy discussions at chiefs' courts, they gave articulate voice to an ideology of enlightened individualism; hence Matthews's comment on the conspicuous rise of an ethos of "private interest" among Rolong farmers. In their own view, those who invested capital in their arable land and their animals, who were successful in commerce and did "great works," were the source of the commonweal. So Sebopiwa Molema had written to his paternal uncle, in 1918, urging him to ensure that the people of Mafikeng buried their dead as "civilized people" do. "You always lead in modern improvements," he added.[125] Others, less fortunate, obviously saw matters differently: elites were often alleged to feather their own nests, accused of sorcery, and attacked by mystical means. And they often returned the compliment. The Protestant ethic clearly did not account for all that moved between heaven and earth.

In short, the upper peasantry—whether they were Christian believers, nominal members of the church, or people for whom the religion of *sekgoa* meant little—became the prime conduit of bourgeois values among Southern Tswana. This is not to say that there were no disagreements in their midst. There were. Or that their perspectives on social policy and the concerns of the public sphere were all alike. They were not. Apart from power struggles within their ranks, there were clear differences of opinion among them over the degree to which the "progressive" adoption of *sekgoa* ways should be tempered by the received practices of *setswana*, especially in respect of *mekgwa le melao* ("law and custom"; see Comaroff and Roberts 1977, 1981).[126] Still, these were differences of degree, not kind; the sorts of dispute that occur along the interiors of a broadly shared ideology. Quite how the evangelists managed to infuse the spirit of Adam Smith so pervasively into this fraction of the Southern Tswana population is itself an engrossing story. We tell it in the next chapter. And how that spirit expressed itself in distinctive modes of consumption and cultural styles we shall see in chapters 5 to 7.

As the upper peasantry set itself apart, as it diversified both its livelihood and its lifestyle, it slowly took on the shape of a local bourgeoisie. At first, though, a very local one; and, in the sense of keeping close to its patriarchal, agnatic roots, a virilocal one too. For, notwithstanding the enthusiasm with which it opened itself up to the ways of the civilizing mission and *sekgoa*, this fraction did not repudiate *setswana*. To the contrary. It persisted in—indeed, it initially built its fortunes on—received indigenous practices. Some we have already mentioned: a reliance on vernacular ritual techniques in pursuing agricultural, and social, ends; the founding of capitalist enterprises not on private property but on fields and cattle posts allocated under "communal" land tenure provisions; the recruitment of a work force not, by and large, through free wage labor—although a few employees were paid in cash—but through prevailing ("customary") forms of servitude and clientage. In many cases, moreover, their wealth depended on access to constituted positions of authority and, through them, to human and material resources. And that, in turn, necessitated dealing with competitive agnates, and mobilizing matrikin, in the effort to protect or negotiate genealogical rank.[127] As this implies, while several erected large, well-appointed residences,[128] and others lived in dispersed communities or at their farms (see below),[129] a large proportion kept their homesteads in the family groups and wards of their fathers and paternal grandfathers, not departing at all from the spatial and political arrangements that composed their world.[130] Far from sloughing off those arrangements, a number went out of their way to sustain the centralization of their towns and villages, even when pressures toward decentralization and dispersal grew.[131] This is a point to which we shall return.

At the other end of the spectrum, the lower peasantry, which made up the majority of the population, was at once most and least affected by the impact of the civilizing mission on the local economy. Most, because it suffered the greatest poverty and disempowerment. Least, because the technical "improvements" wrought by the evangelists reached it hardly at all. These were the kinds of people with scarcely a "good useful plough" between them; those who made a meager living from the "old" agriculture; those who later suffered "serious malnutrition." Among them, very few of the men were orthodox Christians. Women belonged to churches in larger numbers. But, if our Mafikeng histories are anything to go by, they found their way in increasing numbers, after the turn of the century, into independent churches; especially into small charismatic congregations which stressed pragmatic ritual, paid a great deal of attention to healing and material well-being, and formed close-knit social communities (J. Comaroff 1985:187f.; cf. Pauw 1960:221f.).

Poorer peasants did not farm for the market at all, though, *in extremis*, they might sell a little grain or an animal to a trader. As they lost access to fertile land, and had to raise crops or graze stock on less yielding soil, they curtailed (or ceased) their agrarian enterprises and/or toiled for others; either, depending on their circumstances, in servitude to wealthier compatriots or as wage laborers elsewhere. When they did cultivate on their own account, they did so with crude implements—hoes or simple wooden ploughs—and whatever beasts they, or their kin, could mobilize. Under these conditions, taboos against women tilling the fields with bovines eventually gave way. As men tended to be the ones to seek employment, and to be recruited by labor agencies, there was no option but for their wives to take responsibility for horticulture again (cf. Schapera 1933:638, on the Kgatla);[132] females were, in any case, discouraged by statute from accompanying their husbands to work away from their rural homes.[133] An ironic recension of "custom" this, wherein the division of labor was returned to its prior lineaments by the exigencies of poverty. Sometimes "tradition" is not invented or constructed, but recuperated as a function of material necessity, out of a brute lack of choice. Not that this was understood by contemporary European observers. In state circles it was all put down to native folly (Cape of Good Hope 1907:33): "The beneficial effects of improvements in cultivation they cannot, or will not, recognise, and hence they have made no material advance during this century or more they have been in contact with civilization." This, in 1907, from the resident magistrate at Taung—of a population that had marketed thirty-five thousand bags of grain just twenty years before.[134]

Once restored to the fields, women depended on their matrikin for help and support, and on cooperative labor arrangements to perform large-scale tasks.[135] Reciprocities among neighbors and relatives were widely attenuated as these people were thrown back repeatedly on their social resources and on the familiar practices of *setswana*. In the process, they turned less to the alms of the mission churches than to the more intimate embrace of an Africanized Christianity. Thus it is that they appeared, to Europeans, to sustain a strongly "collectivist" ethos; to be wedded to "traditional" forms of exchange; to be enmeshed in "socialistic" webs of relations; to be prone to "superstitious" ideas about the ways in which the rich grew fat by consuming their fellows; to be innately conservative, wanting in initiative, and unenlightened in their attitudes toward "refined" individualism. But, however elaborate their communal arrangements, however hard they worked together in tending their fields and herds, families of the lower peasantry inevitably came to rely on at least some earned income (see chapter 4). Always strapped, they were unable to fashion the kind of material existence urged on them by the evangelists—and, more and more, by the local bourgeoisie.[136] It is not, we stress again, that they lacked the desire. Quite the opposite. Many acquired more "advanced" means of production, engaged in commerce, and bought European commodities whenever they could, using them to invent distinctive styles of self-presentation. But their predicament was hardly a matter of volition. It derived, rather, from their location in a world of distinctly unequal social and political relations; a world in which rising, as it were, from rags to riches was very difficult to do.

Unlike the upper peasantry, the lowly favored decentralized living arrangements: they preferred not to reside in large towns but at their fields and cattle posts. In volume 1 we showed that Southern Tswana *merafe* ("nations") displayed counterposing tendencies toward concentration and dispersal, toward aggregating at political centers or scattering to agricultural peripheries. There is no need here to recapitulate their complex internal workings, save to say that, while ruling elites fought to sustain a pattern of centralized settlement—their authority depended upon it—the lower peasantry saw two advantages in taking to the countryside (*RRI*:147): autonomy from those who would subserviate them; and an opportunity, away from chiefly oversight, to maximize their harvests under ecological conditions in which the timing of arable operations was crucial.[137] If they were to have any prospect at all of an independent existence, without subordination to more powerful men or reliance on wage labor, dispersal was a necessary requirement. Not always a sufficient one, of course, but necessary.

Given this predisposition for scattering, the lower peasantry seems to have taken little part in the public sphere or in communal activities; unless, that is, they were coerced into it, which only a strong chief could do (see below). Hence they did not, by and large, offer an articulate counter voice to the ideology of the upper peasantry in local politics—although there *is* evidence that they resented those who had enriched themselves by seizing the best lands and by forcing many of them into servitude.[138] Even when they did attend assemblies at *kgotla*, voluntarily or under duress, they seem rarely to have spoken up.[139] But, as we shall argue, they expressed themselves volubly in other registers.

Just as the upper peasantry metamorphosed into a petite bourgeoisie, so the poorest segment of the population became a hyphenated class of peasant-proletarians. As such, it constituted a battalion in South Africa's infamous "reserve army of labor," the human scaffolding on which was erected the colonial economy. Occupying the space between it and the rural elite, if somewhat uneasily, was a middle peasantry. Of all three fractions, this one is the most difficult to characterize. For one thing, its membership was unstable, consisting largely of people who aspired upward but, as the Leninist model suggested, often found themselves pushed in the opposite direction. For another, its lifeways and material practices were inconstant, responding repeatedly to contingencies of one kind or another. But, most of all, being an interstitial category, it was defined largely by what it was not. And yet, as the evidence indicates[140]—and as is aptly illustrated by Setiloane's (1976:162ff.) sensitive account of his family history[141]—the existence of a middle peasantry of substantial size and significance, with its own discernible social and economic profile, is undeniable.

What, then, *were* its distinguishing features? As we might expect, and shall see later in respect of their cultural styles, middle peasants tended to draw, more than anyone else, from both *setswana* and *sekgoa* (cf. Setiloane 1976:174f.). On one hand, they were quick to adopt European agrarian techniques, typically investing in intensive agriculture and commodity production to the extent that their means allowed. Many of them, male and female alike, joined the mission churches early on, were members of voluntary associations and "improvement" societies, and took an active part in the public sphere.

At the same time, they faced real constraints in building up their enterprises. First and foremost, they found it hard—in the face of competition from the upper peasantry and of settler incursion—to obtain sufficient high-quality, well-watered land. Some of them, in fact, had no choice but to leave their towns and villages to pursue their economic objectives. Plaatje ([1919] 1996), for example, tells of a number who, unable to obtain fertile acreages within their chiefdoms, rented arable land and pasture on white farms in return for cash, produce, and labor (cf. Setiloane 1976:168, 173); on these holdings, he says, they did well, harvesting between five hundred and sixteen hundred bags of grain per year (at least until the Natives Land Act of 1913 debarred their tenancies; see chapter 8).[142] Second and almost as important, because most of them were not from families of long-standing prominence, they were unlikely to have many "traditional" clients or servants. Consequently, they had to recruit a labor force either by paying workers in cash and/or kind or by entering one or another exchange arrangement. Three more factors added greatly to the precariousness of their situation: (i) their business interests seldom extended beyond agriculture; (ii) they rarely had the most advanced (or, later on, mechanized) implements; which meant that (iii) they often had to hire them from wealthier farmers. These considerations, together, made them particularly vulnerable to stock disease, drought, and personal misfortune. It was they, not surprisingly, who found it hardest to regain their former economic position after the rinderpest pandemic.

If middle peasants shared an ideology and a range of material practices with the upper peasantry, they had two things in common with those below them. Both were partly a function of economic vulnerability, partly a matter of social value. One was a tendency, especially in bad times, to depend on reciprocities, in the received manner of *setswana*, with kin and neighbors; indeed, as emerged repeatedly in our own household histories from Mafikeng, commercial farming practices were frequently accompanied by a reliance on communal work parties arranged by women. The other was the preference for living away from the capital. Middle peasants took pains to avoid being consumed by those more powerful—and, by evading chiefly regulation of space, time, and tributary labor, to retain control over their own arable activities. One qualification here, though. Where men of this category ascended into the upper peasantry, they might try to convert wealth into political capital, vying for positions of authority (around those chiefships that remained viable), and even persuading rulers to create new offices for them.[143] If successful, the men concerned were likely to recenter themselves at the capital. But, along the way, of course, they had left the middle peasantry.

As all this suggests, middle peasants were a classical intercalary bloc. In their religious practices, for example, they frequently chose a middle way. Many found the larger, liturgically more orthodox independent churches particularly congenial: while they often resented the dominance of established elites in mission congregations, they were also uncomfortable with the charismatic Christianity of the lowly and illiterate. Moreover, they tended to respond to economic insecurities, to the pressures pushing them downward, by investing wherever possible in education (see volume 3). One practice, among many, demonstrates the degree to which they straddled the gulf between the other fractions, partaking of the values of each simultaneously. Like both the rich and the poor, to anticipate again what we shall say below, they placed enormous value on cattle. In common with the former, they sometimes treated beasts as capital, buying and selling them for profit or using them as a means to political ends. But, like the latter, they regarded their herds as much more than a mere conduit for cash transactions. They named their animals, parted with them reluctantly, and saw them as a social resource, as a mark of personal identity, as an insurance against disaster.

The fact that the middle peasantry shared values and practices with each of the other fractions highlights the complexities involved in processes of class formation here. To begin with, relations among these classes-in-formation were often ambiguous, rendered even more so by (i) the intricate lines of kinship, affinity, and political affiliation that cross-cut them; (ii) mutual mistrust between the new, self-made elite and poorer, more conservative royals; and, in some places, (iii) increasingly ambivalent attitudes toward indigenous ruling cadres (cf. Shillington 1985:69). But these were not the only sources of ambiguity. To the lower peasantry, both wealthier fractions represented a threat. Apart from having seized ever more communal resources and having put the autonomy of their compatriots at risk, they were bending the local world out of its recognizable shape in the name of their own interests. And yet, in times of attrition, they were a source of employment and aid—however costly in social terms—much closer to home than the alternatives. For middle peasants, the upper peasantry, as owners of the most efficient means of production, were the people from whom they might purchase the wherewithal to enrich themselves. But these people were also competitors and, potentially, creditors who could preside over their ruin. And the lower peasantry, although a reservoir of labor, were those into whose ranks they might easily fall. For the upper peasantry, both the middling and the poor were a fund of wealth: the former as a market for their agrarian services; the latter as recruits to their work force; both as a pool of (actual or would-be) clients. But both also showed a strong will to independence and dispersal, and hence resisted their schemes and machinations whenever possible.

Which returns us to the broader impact of the agrarian revolution on the internal dynamics of contemporary Southern Tswana polities. Recall again, from volume 1 and from our reiteration a few pages back, that all of them demonstrated opposing tendencies toward centralization and decentralization; that, at least since 1800, there had, at any one time, always been highly concentrated *merafe* and acephalous ones and ones moving between the two polarities; but that, because of trade and tributary monopolies, relations among ruling families, royal wealth, and other factors, conditions early in the century encouraged the reproduction of hierarchical communities with strong chiefships and large capitals. The agrarian revolution played into all this, but, inevitably, its effects were mediated by external events.

As we have said, new rural elites tended to favor centralization, against the counterpressures of the lower and middle peasantries. And they often bolstered chiefships in order to create an environment conducive to their material interests and their social values. Many of these people, it is true, had extensive holdings scattered far and wide; but even then, as Shillington (1985:20) notes, they sustained a presence in the capital. In the final quarter of the century, however, Southern Tswana rulers came under increasing pressure: they lost their trade monopolies; saw large tracts of territory seized, water sources expropriated, and herds diminish; lost whatever military might they had had; and, with overrule, relinquished a great deal of their authority. In the upshot, as they told Mackenzie (1887,1:76–77), they found it very difficult to hold the center. "Our people are now scattered over the country like the white men," one remarked. Among the southern branches of the Tlhaping, for example—annexed, in the late 1870s, as part of Griqualand West to the Cape Colony and dispossessed of much of their land—populations were quick to disperse altogether as their chiefs were disempowered for good and all. The Tshidi and Seleka-Rolong sovereigns sustained much more centralized chiefdoms, although their fortunes ebbed and flowed as well, and at times their polities showed signs of fragmenting. The Ratlou and Rapulana-Rolong and the more northerly Tlhaping fell somewhere between, also fluctuating considerably over the years—and veering, in the longer run, toward the decentralized mode.[144]

In sum, the period witnessed major changes in the Southern Tswana universe, many communities coming to look more like scattered peasantries elsewhere in the world than like "traditional" chiefdoms. Where political centers collapsed permanently, local bourgeoisies seem to have given up on them—as did even members of old ruling elites (Mackenzie 1887,1:76)—and moved to wherever it suited them best to live. And so, across the terrain were to be found farming populations of all class fractions bound very loosely, if at all, to established structures of authority. This while, not fifty miles away, there might be a *morafe* with an elaborate political order and a highly concentrated, tightly integrated capital; with a ruler who still regulated the seasons, who could fine those who took off to their fields without permission, and for whom tributary fields were ploughed each year; whose population was equally divided, but whose elites remained invested in sustaining the polity against the centripetal tendencies of the lower and middle peasantry.

This returns us, full circle, to the role of the colonial evangelists. As in many other aspects of the civilizing mission, there lay a thoroughgoing contradiction in their effort to recast the spatial coordinates of the Tswana world. On one hand, the Nonconformists were attracted by the existence of large towns here: it promised to make conversion easier than would have been the case with dispersed peoples. What is more, many of their major institutional projects, like the founding of schools and the building of elaborate churches, presumed centralization. So, too, did irrigated agriculture in this ecology, which was best served by the concentration of populations near the few reliable water sources (as at Kuruman) or along (preferably dammed) rivers.[145] Also, in the late nineteenth and early twentieth centuries, much of the active membership of the church was drawn from the upper peasantry, a good proportion of which was invested in the survival of sizeable capitals. And yet, on the other hand, the Southern Tswana future world, as the LMS and WMMS envisaged it, consisted in small, scattered, loosely articulated communities of individuated farmsteads, each on its enclosed lands; the preferred mode, that is, of the lower and middle peasantries. But it was the lower peasantry that was *least* drawn to orthodox Christianity. And, anyway, it lacked the means to live the kind of rural life of which the evangelists dreamed.

Contradictions notwithstanding, the missionaries encouraged decentralization with great vigor. Mackenzie (1887,1:77), for one, tells how, in doing so, he tried to assuage the fears of the southern chiefs: he suggested that they allow people "to remain at their farms all the year round," calling them twice per annum to assemblies of the whole nation. Nor did the evangelists confine themselves to the weakened rulers of Griqualand and British Bechuanaland. Further north and a decade later, Willoughby asked the powerful Khama to allow his subjects to disperse,[146] although he feared the proposal altogether "too revolutionary" for the sovereign. Again, on the face of it, the logic of the evangelist's case was less than persuasive:

> [T]his living in a large community is full of evil. The people have so much difficulty in getting necessary things . . . that they have to spend long periods of time in their gardens, and at their cattle-posts, and this is a great hindrance to education.

If this was so, patently, year-round residence at these scattered fields and cattle posts would have helped the cause of education even less. At issue here was something quite different, something much more fundamental: the disposition of people in space. The evangelists had sought, for a very long time, to unhitch Tswana from the yoke of centralized chiefly ritual control, all the better to draw them toward the church. Ironically, from the late nineteenth century onward, independent Christian leaders tried to detach their own followers from the orbit of the mission churches. Recall the term they used for these men and women: *boikgololo,* those outspanned, unyoked.

Of course, it was not just the agrarian revolution of the mission, its unleashing of the spirit of capitalism, that transformed and decentered so much of the Southern Tswana world. True, this is where some of the disempowered sovereigns put the blame. One of them—the one who had complained that his followers were now living scattered "like white men"—told Mackenzie (1887,1:76–77) as much, adding: "We accepted the Word of God in our youth, but we did not know what was coming behind it." From a different vantage, it is clear that a number of potent historical forces were converging on this world, especially as it found itself caught up in the mineral revolution and the insatiable appetite of mining and industry for cheap labor; in the schemes of the colonial state; in the land- and cattle-grabbing intrigues of the settler population. Still, the chiefs were not, in the final analysis, entirely incorrect either. The civilizing mission, as an ideological and cultural vanguard, *did* prepare the way for what "came behind it." It insinuated new forms of individualism, new regimes of value, new kinds of wealth, new means and relations of production, new religious practices. And it set in motion processes of class formation. All of which could not but alter, on one side, the internal workings of Southern Tswana economy and society, and on the other, the way in which the Africans—plural, sociologically speaking—embraced the European presence.

The issue of centralization and decentralization was to make itself felt for a long time to come. Not only did the evangelists continue to interest themselves in it. It also arose in the early development discourses of the colonial state in both the Bechuanaland Protectorate and the Union of South Africa (cf. Schapera 1943b:267ff.). The administration of the former, for example, took up the question in the early 1930s. In a report to the Secretary of State for Dominion Affairs,[147] it noted the views of the Principal Medical Officer. "Native" towns were unhygienic (see chapter 7), he believed; living enduringly in more scattered settlements near fields and cattle posts would be much healthier. The Chief Veterinary Officer was said to agree on the ground that it was impossible to "farm by proxy." By contrast, the report went on, the agricultural section of the Native Affairs Department in Pretoria favored large population centers: being the pattern among "all civilized . . . peoples," it facilitated industry, trade, education, better medical facilities, and community life—the very things that the LMS and WMMS spoke for when they were not essaying dispersal. While acknowledging that poor Tswana farmers had good reason to resist centralization, the Protectorate government came down for it, adding that "educated natives"—the Tswana bourgeoisie, that is—also preferred "the town system." Echoes here of the lines of division we have come across before. The matter was still being debated in Botswana, in governmental circles and among development agencies, in the mid-1970s (J. L. Comaroff 1977). It persists as a concern in the reconstruction of post-apartheid South Africa.

*****

In conclusion, while the agrarian revolution gave rise to a class of commercial farmers, indeed to an assertive bourgeoisie, it brought the majority a harvest of hunger. It also brought a world of very different, evanescent social, material, and spatial forms. Having come, many years before, to recreate the lost British yeomanry, and to re-seed their own roots on African soil, the Christians had, for the most part, contributed to making not an independent peasantry but an army of wage workers. Or, rather, a population of peasant-proletarians entrapped in a promiscuous web of economic dependencies.

As black intellectuals[148] and liberal missionaries were to point out, the dependencies were mutual, if desperately unequal. White colonial society had itself become utterly reliant for its survival on peoples like the Southern Tswana: on their many bodies and their mass buying power, on their taxes and their crops. Hence the Rev. Crisp's (1896:53) observation that "the unskilled manual labour of South Africa is entirely in their hands . . . and no inconsiderable portion of the produce that finds its way into the market is raised by them." Some of the Nonconformists, it will be recalled, saw this as an achievement on their part, although none of them took pleasure in the racist excesses of the colonial state or the conditions of the workplace. Their claim had merit, even if it was overblown. For, as we said at the start of the chapter, their economic revolution was not confined to agriculture. Agrarian production, in fact, composed only one dimension of the order of signs and practices, of material relations and values that they sought to reconstruct. Its other dimensions ran to the very core of the Protestant ethic and the spirit of capitalism. And they had an enormous impact on the way in which Southern Tswana oriented themselves toward the world of markets and money and commodities and commerce. It is to these that we now turn.

FOUR

CURRENCIES OF CONVERSION

Of Markets, Money, and Value

The double influence of the spirit of commerce and the gospel of Christ has given an impulse to the circulation of men, ideas and commodities over the face of the earth, and the discovery of the gold regions has given enhanced rapidity to commerce in other countries and the diffusion of knowledge. But what for Africa? God will do something else for it. Something just as wonderful and unexpected as the discovery of gold.

David Livingstone ([c. 1853] 1960:282)

Money is sacred, as everyone knows . . .

Barry Unsworth (1992:325)

IN THEIR EFFORT to transform African agriculture, the Nonconformists spoke of reclaiming the prodigal soul along with the wasted garden. The idiom of improvidence was neither accidental nor incidental. Saving the savage meant teaching the savage to save. It meant, too, that he be taught to recast his inefficient mode of production so that, using God's gifts, he might bring forth the greatest possible abundance. Only then would black communities be animated by the spirit of commerce that—along with the Gospel of Christ—promoted exchange on a worldwide scale. Only then might they be part of the sacred economy of civilized society. As this suggests, the early evangelists came of an age in which the notion of economy, *sui generis*, was central to the way in which the universe was seen to be constructed, in which human qualities were understood.

In its most general sense, "economy" described a metaphysical discourse, one concerned not just with the provident interplay of persons, properties, and things, but with the nature of value itself. Implicit in this discourse was a worldview in which a preoccupation with man's "horizontal" place in nature and society had replaced the presumption of divine hierarchy; of what Shapiro (1993:12) refers to as the "vertical" posture of the "devotional self" (*RRI*:98). Vesting the vital principles of life increasingly in human action and interaction, this "horizontal" orientation figured in several prominent paradigms of the period. For example, heroic medicine had come to define health in terms of an *animal economy* that entailed the endless flow of humors among transacting bodies within a particular physical environment (see chapter 7); and theorists of *political economy* conceived of wealth as a function of the circulation of commodities among contracting parties in a benevolent market. Economy, furthermore, was not opposed to the domain of the spirit, even if it was no longer a reflex of *lex dei*. They existed, rather, in a symbiotic relationship, which is why Adam Smith, and later David Livingstone, saw commerce as a means of moral improvement and virtue. It was also a proof of man's providential endowment.

Political economy, in sum, was a form of "secular theology" (Hart 1986:647). In a striking passage on the "animating spirit" of British capital before 1875, Jenks (1927:2) wrote:

> The investment of capital is . . . the essential act of faith of every man who enters business, buys a farm, or employs a laborer. Nor is it new. It was commonplace to the peasant folk to whom Jesus preached his gospel.

As an exact "science," Norman (1976:41) notes, political economy was not particularly popular among early nineteenth-century intellectuals, either in the church or outside. But its underlying ontology resonated with liberal Protestant social thought, and with the wider humanist impulses of the moment. Its impact was especially palpable among abolitionists and "improvers": "Christian Political Economy," Waterman (1991:6) observes, fused a belief in the beneficence of existing economic institutions with a whiggish desire for reform. As explicit theology, this position was most fully formulated within the established church. As a call to practice, however, it was most congenial to the spirit of the great evangelical societies. While political economy was seldom a subject of discussion among missionaries to South Africa, some did cite liberal theory as a charter for their labors: LMS Superintendent John Philip (1828,1:369), as we note elsewhere, quoted Adam Smith on the need to stimulate the indigent to industry; and Livingstone (1961:194) made mention, albeit irreverently, of Malthus on the subject of reproduction. But all of them were guided, to a greater or lesser degree, by some of its material and moral principles.

Economic reform, we argue, was not ancillary to the activity of the evangelists. It was always more than merely a profane means to religious ends. Although its theological status would remain ambiguous, economy here was a part of a sacred order that described the production of value and virtue in the world; an order in which individual exertion and righteousness gave shape to civil society and earned divine credit. In the mission field, this vision had pragmatic implications: converting heathens required changing their sense of worth—and their mode of producing it—so that they might lay up treasures on earth and in heaven. Drawing African communities into the Christian commonwealth meant persuading them to accept the currency of salvation, a task involving the introduction, along with the gospel, of market exchange, wage work, sometimes even a specially minted coinage. In this chapter we turn our attention to evangelical economics in the broadest sense of the term: the effort to recast indigenous regimes of value by teaching Tswana how to make good with goods, how to elevate barter into commerce, how to use money, how to commodify their labors. We trace the impact of these ventures on vernacular practices, and explore the hybrid media, the uniquely local notions of worth and wealth, they called into being.

Let us look, first, at the two distinct systems of value whose encounter opened up a new frontier of British liberal enterprise.

RELATIVE VALUES

Virtuous Endeavors: The Business of One's Calling

[The great evangelical societies] were conceived as pragmatically as the Manchester Chamber of Commerce. All these organizations operated in ways their members thought utilitarian, and some of them operated very much like business firms.

Richard Helmstadter (1992:10)

If early nineteenth-century political economy was a secular theology, contemporary Nonconformist teaching was, in many respects, sanctified commerce. During the "second reformation" of the late 1700s (*RRI*:44–45), British Protestantism had refashioned itself with cultural fabric milled by the industrial revolution. Helmstadter's (1992:8) telling portrait of the Rev. Andrew Reed, an enterprising London Congregationalist, shows how much the habits of mind formed by the evangelical revival paralleled those of the business world. It also suggests that the continuing interplay between the (never fully separate) realms of church and business produced a rich discourse about value and its production—a discourse, at once religious and secular, whose material and historical effects do not reduce to simple generalizations or determinations (cf. Hempton 1984:11; Waterman 1991:3f.).[1]

Eighteenth-century evangelicals, Rack (1989:385f.) claims, were more influenced by the language of practical reason than their espousal of scripture
and supernaturalism might suggest. For Wesley, "scripture, reason, *and* [our
emphasis] experience" were the keys to faith. The concept of experience—
which combined "spiritual sensation" with a Lockean sense of empiricism—
became ever more important in discerning truth and biblical meaning. Under
the impact of the revival, Congregationalists, too, would adopt an active, optimistic brand of Calvinism that gave honored place to human agency (Helmstadter 1992:15). This reorientation also connoted a shift, in immediate religious
concerns, from "future things" to the here and now. John Wesley, Dreyer
(1983:14) writes, came increasingly to focus on the "how," rather than the
"what," of Christian belief; on its materialities rather than its metaphysics. It is
not surprising therefore, that Warner (1930:138) long ago linked the "empirical
temper" of Methodist lore to the central place it accorded economics. Human
enterprise, by these lights, was not caught in a disabling conflict between this
and otherworldliness. The only inherent evil in the universe was the moral failing, the spiritlessness, of man himself.

As this implies, Wesley was an advocate of moral deregulation. So were the
Congregationalist clergy, whose "New System" Calvinism regarded everyone,
not just the elect, as candidates for salvation; they also sought to remove the
spiritual "ceiling" that the Anglican hierarchy put in the way of aspiring dis-
senters (Helmstadter 1992:15, 23). These men set all available means, including
economic ones, to work for their cause. Like most early champions of free trade,
Wesley saw nothing *intrinsically* unworthy or antisocial in riches (Semmel
1974:71f.). Quite the reverse. In this, his views were not very different from
those of the established church (cf. Norman 1976:33f.); he insisted, after all,
that he "lived and died" a member of the Church of England (Davies 1962:245).
In fact, the "lusty zest" with which he advocated the quest for gain went further
than most previous Puritans, who tended not to celebrate wealth but to condone
it as a necessary compromise with evil (Warner 1930:138f.); for Wesley, temporal "business" need not "interrupt communion with God." It was merely one
of its channels. "Business," in fact, seems to have served as a synecdoche for
human action in the world,[2] just as "usefulness" conveyed the sense of virtuous
efficacy (Helmstadter 1992:9). Not that commerce did not pose its own dangers.
As Outler (1985:264) has stressed, Wesley's economic teachings were, in many
ways, a lifelong effort to counter those implications of *The Wealth of Nations* that
he saw to be corrupting (below, n. 4). But therein lay the challenge: "Make
yourselves friends of the mammon of unrighteousness," he preached
(1985:266), citing Luke (16:1–2) on the duty to redeem the potential of wealth.

Like the liberal economists of his time, then, Wesley was preoccupied with
money as an instrument of worldly enterprise. His disquisitions on the topic
are not unambiguous (Warner 1930; Rack 1989:65), but our concern is less with

the immediate effects of his teaching than with what it reveals about Nonconformist notions of value—especially as they shaped the civilizing mission. In his sermon on "The Use of Money," he (1985:267–68) chides fellow Christians for acquiescing in an "empty rant" against the "grand corrupter of the world." The duty of the faithful was to deploy, to the greatest possible advantage, all that providence had provided. Money was a precious "talent"; the word evoked both biblical coinage and a sense of special, God-given ability:

> [It] is of unspeakable service to all civilized nations in all the common affairs of life. It is a most compendious instrument of transacting all manner of business, and (if we use it according to Christian wisdom) of doing all manner of good.

Money, he went on (p. 268), was "food for the hungry" and "raiment for the naked." Even "father to the fatherless"—surely one of the most genial images of cash in contemporary European discourse! As a compendious instrument, it was an *ur*-commodity, condensing in itself the essential quality of all good/s. Reciprocally, it could stand for all things, even the closest of human connections. Wesley seems to have seen coin as the servant of existing laws of value and the vehicle of trade; he subscribed to the "commodity theory" of currency shared alike by classic liberal theorists and by Marx (Hart 1986:643). Marx, of course, also stressed that money, as capital, was uniquely equipped to extract value from human producers. Wesley would himself inveigh against dishonest industry and fettered exchange, if not against the evil powers of cash per se. In his simpler moral economy, its poison was drawn if it was used in ways pleasing to God. And it made all virtuous effort measurable and commensurable, permitting the conversion of worldly enterprise into spiritual credit. In this sense, the most "precious talent" of money was its capacity to enable mortals to "trade up." Salvation itself became obtainable on free-market terms.

These fiscal orientations also suffused Wesleyan practice. "As a voluntary organization," says Obelkevich (1976:206f.), "Methodism . . . fostered in its members a new outlook, individual and collective, towards money." Finances were a constant matter of concern, and collections were taken up for many causes, not least the foreign missions. Here, as among African converts, a ceaseless stream of demands and appeals highlighted the meliorative qualities of cash. But "practical pietism" was not limited to the Wesleyans. According to Tudur Jones (1962:193f.), the early nineteenth-century Congregationalist fixation upon social usefulness expressed itself in innumerable schemes for turning a profit, from hawking religious tracts to advising the rich on how best to deploy their wealth. The great missionary societies were perhaps the clearest instantiation of all this. As Helmstadter (1992:10) shows, they were run like businesses, with men of commerce actively investing their resources and managing their affairs. In the field, the Nonconformists put their trust in the power of money to bring progress, and to place all things, even God's grace, within human reach.[3] True, LMS evangelists occasionally decried the excessive Methodist attention to profit (Livingstone 1959,2:152). Yet they themselves championed trade and, we shall see, went to great lengths to introduce cash into African societies (Philip 1828,1:205; Livingstone in LMS 1843).

The faith of the missions in the creative capacities of cash recalls Simmel's *Philosophy of Money*, perhaps the most refined statement of the nineteenth-century European belief in the power of coin. For Simmel (1978:291), man was by nature an "exchanging animal" and, by this token, an "objective animal" too: exchange, in its "wonderful simplicity," constructed both the receiver and the giver, replacing selfish desire with mutual acknowledgment and objective appraisal. Transaction, he went on, begets rationalization. And the more that values are rationalized, "the more room there is in them, as in the house of God, for every soul." Because of its unlimited convertibility (p. 292), money was uniquely capable of setting free the intrinsic worth of the world to be traded in neutral, standardized terms. And so it enabled the formation of an integrated, expansive society of morally dependent, but psychically self-sufficient persons (Simmel 1978:297f.).

While they might never have put it in just these terms, the Nonconformists devoted much of their effort to making Tswana into "exchanging animals," an enterprise in which cash played a pivotal role. They, too, nurtured the dream of an expansive civil society built not upon savage barter but upon transactions among self-possessed, moneyed persons. According to this dream, the liberation of Africans from a primitive dependence on their kin and their chiefs lay in the creation of a higher order, a world of moral and material interdependence mediated by refined, impersonal media: letters, numbers, notes, and coin.

There was, as we all know, another side to money: its long-standing Christian taint as an instrument of corruption and betrayal. In part, this flowed from the power of cash to equate disparate forms of value. It could dissolve what was unique, precious, and personal, reducing everything to the indiscriminate object of private avarice: the Savior, note, had been sold for thirty pieces of silver, monastic relics melted into gold. What was more, the ability of coin to transpose different forms of worth enabled profitable conversions to be made among them; in particular, it allowed the rich to prosper by using their assets to control the exertions of others. Parry and Bloch (1989:2f.; cf. Le Goff 1980) remind us that this sort of profit was anathema to the medieval European church, which saw productive work as the only legitimate source of wealth and condemned, as unnatural, the effortless earnings of merchants and moneylenders. Capitalism was to exploit the metabolic qualities of money in unprecedented ways, of course—especially its capacity to make things commensurable by turning distinct aspects of human existence, like land and labor, into alienable commodities. And Protestantism would endorse this process by sanctifying desire as virtuous

171

ambition and by treating the market as a realm of provident opportunity. Yet its medieval qualms remained. As Weber (1958:53) stressed, those Christians who most avidly embodied the spirit of capitalism were ascetics; they took little pleasure in wealth *per se.* For them, *making* money was an end in itself, a transcendental value. It gave evidence of ceaseless "busyness" and divine approval.

Inasmuch as money remained demonically corrosive, there was only one way to avoid its corrupting qualities: to let it go. If it was to generate virtue, it had to circulate visibly and constantly. Here the Methodist doctrine of stewardship was explicit. Hoarded wealth was "the snare of the devil" (Wesley 1986:233). It made men forsake the inner life for superficial pride, luxury, and leisure. Indeed, all forms of surplus accumulation were forbidden.[4] The Divine Proprietor required that his stewards put his talent to work by cycling it back into honest business or giving it in charity. The distrust of usury and moneylending—of "pariah" capitalism, the hidden, incestuous breeding of cash without exertion—was still strong (Wesley 1985:271, 276).[5] The proper movement of wealth, however, was something else, something creative and positive. And by those lights, exchange *was* production (cf. Parry and Bloch 1989:86). Nonconformists still held to a labor theory of value. But the notion of industry had changed. It was now cast in terms of manufacture and the market, of wage labor and fair prices, of the circulation of wealth and the productive character of capital.

For Nonconformists like Wesley, then, assiduous effort and ethical dealing—the market, literally, as a "moral" economy—were enough to curb the malignancy of money. Charity, itself a high-yield investment in virtue, was the main means of redistributing wealth, a way to "lay up . . . treasures in the bank of heaven" (Wesley 1984:629). Humble toil also paid moral dividends, but at a lower rate. As this implies, the opportunities for spiritual accumulation favored those with capital. Of course, all riches were ultimately the Lord's, from whom they could never really be alienated (Wesley 1985:277). In the here and now, however, Methodism tended to endorse existing labor relations; in the late 1700s, even child workers were said to profit from industrious discipline (Warner 1930:151). And the just wage *was* just, for exertion in one's allotted calling was its own reward. And so it behooved the faithful to strive ceaselessly to produce all they could; only by so doing could they redeem God's investment in humankind. This injunction, to realize human possibility by acting upon the world, sounded well with the expansive ethos of liberal economics.

Read in this light, it is clear that the economic emphasis of missionary practice in South Africa expressed more than a mere effort to survive or even to profit. It was part of the attempt to foster a self-regulating commonwealth, for which the market was both the model and the means; also, to induce what Unsworth (1992) has aptly termed a "sacred hunger,"[6] an insatiable desire for material enrichment and moral progress. As we shall see, the task proved onerous, for the "mammon of unrighteousness" was never easily befriended. By the mid-1820s, some of the more radical evangelicals in England were denouncing the wholesale reduction of human qualities to price.[7] And, in the mission field, the Nonconformists were caught, time and again, in the double-sided implications of money. Meanwhile, the kind of value carried by the coin would come face to face with African notions of worth, setting off new contrasts, contests, and combinations.

Wet-nosed Wealth: Other Forms of Value

On the surface of it, the Southern Tswana world of the early nineteenth century bore some similarity to the one from which the missionaries set out. Great stress was laid here, too, on human production as the source of worth. Here, too, communities were understood as social creations, built up through the ceaseless actions and transactions of people eager to enhance their fund of value. Here, too, exchange was conducted by means of versatile media that measured and stored wealth, and facilitated its negotiation from afar.

These parallels, we have argued (1992:127f.), are sufficient to cast doubt on the exclusive association of commodities and competitive individualism with industrial capitalism. Or with modernity. But, by the same token, apparently similar forms or practices do not necessarily have the same genesis, constitution, or meaning. Although Southern Tswana subscribed to a fundamentally humanist sense of the production of wealth, their understanding of value— and of the way it was vested in persons, relationships, and objects—was rather different from that of their European interlocutors. Thus, while the early missionaries thought they detected in "the Bechuana" a stress on active self-contrivance, a dark replica of Western economic man, they found, on closer acquaintance, that this person was a far cry from the discrete, enclosed subject they hoped to usher into the church. Indigenous "utilitarianism," Molema (1920:116) maintained, was quite different from that of "egoism"; the evangelists, as we know, referred to the "native" variant as "selfishness." Indeed, the progressive engagement of previously distinct economies on the frontier would reveal deep distinctions behind superficial resemblances. It would also give birth to a dynamic field of hybrid subjects and signs.

Let us recall some of the relevant details (*RRI*:140f.). The Setswana verb *go dira* meant "to make," "to work," or "to do." *Tiro*, its noun form, covered a wide range of activities—from cultivation to the forging of political alliance, cooking to the performance of ritual—which yielded value in the production and reproduction of persons, relations, and things. It also gave rise to "wealth" (*khumô*), an extractable surplus (of beer, artifacts, tobacco, stock, and so on) which could be further deployed to multiply worth. Sorcery (*boloi*) was its inverse, implying the negation of value (cf. Munn 1986) through attempts to harm persons and unravel their endeavors. *Tiro* itself could never be alienated from its context and transacted as mere labor power. Rather, it was an *intrinsic* dimension of the everyday act of making selves and others, and hence of all positive social ties.

This vision of the production of value, based on close human interdependence, was very different from that of the liberal economists, who saw the commonweal as the fruit of impersonal transactions among autonomous beings. For Tswana, wealth inhered in relations. Which is why its pursuit involved (i) the construction of enduring ties among kin and affines, patrons and clients, sovereigns and supporters, men and their ancestors; and (ii) the extension of influence by means of creative exchanges, usually through the medium of cattle, which secured rights in, and claims over, others. But, while these rights and claims were constantly negotiated, the productive and reproductive properties of a relationship, be it wedlock or serfdom, could not be alienated from the bonds that bore them (Molema 1920:125; cf. Schapera (1940b:77f.). Indeed, the object of social exchange was precisely *not* to accumulate riches with no strings attached: the traffic in beasts served to knit human beings together in an intricate weave, in which the density of living connections and the magnitude of value were one and the same thing.

Because they were the means, *par excellence,* of building social biographies and accumulating capital, cattle were the supreme form of property here; they could congeal, store, and increase value, holding it stable in a world of flux (Comaroff and Comaroff 1992:139). Not surprisingly, their widespread use as currency in human societies was noted by early theorists of political economy (Smith 1976:38; Marx 1967,1:183). While Adam Smith (1976) judged them "rude" and "inconvenient" instruments of commerce, he appreciated that they embodied many of the elementary features of coin, being useful, alienable, relatively durable objects. Although standardized as species, moreover, livestock come in different sizes and colors, genders and ages, and so might be used as tokens of varying quality and denomination. (Many African peoples have long engaged in a good deal of elaboration on the exquisite distinctions among kine.) True, cattle are not as finely divisible as inanimate substances like metal and tend, therefore, to be more gross, sluggish units of trade. But, as we shall see, Southern Tswana took this to be an advantage over cash, whose velocity they regarded as dangerous. Herds *were* movable, of course, especially for purposes of exchange, a fact stressed by Marx (1967,1:115); for him, the apparent self-propulsion of money was crucial to its role in animating commodity transactions. Affluent Tswana men made considerable use of this ambulatory quality, dispersing bridewealth to affines and loan stock to clients as they strove continually to turn their resources into control over people. They also rotated animals among dependents, and between their cattle posts, both as a hedge against disaster and as a way of hiding assets from the jealous gaze of rivals (Schapera 1938:24).

It is as exchange value on the hoof, then, that the pivotal place of cattle in Southern Tswana economies becomes plain. Their capacity to objectify, transfer, and enhance wealth endowed them with strange, almost magical talents— much like money in the West. The beast, goes the vernacular song, is "God with a wet nose" (*Modimo o nkô e metsi;* Comaroff and Comaroff 1992:127).[8] This is a patent instance of fetishism in bovine shape; the attribution to objects, that is, of value actually produced by humans. The commodity is not specific to capitalism. It is a form of connection between persons and things that may occur in other contexts as well. At the same time, the case of Tswana stock also shows that commodification need not be an all-or-none process. And that it is always culturally situated in a meaningful world of work and worth. Here, for example, while animals enabled rich men to lay claim to the labors of others, they did not depersonalize or objectify or efface productive relations among people. To the contrary. They drew attention to the social embeddedness of those very relations.

The complex qualities of bovine currency would intervene in mission efforts to transform the Southern Tswana sense of value. For beasts were enough like money to be identified with it, yet sufficiently unlike it to make and mark salient differences. On one hand, they could abstract value. On the other, they did just the opposite: they signified and enriched personal identities and social ties. "A fool who owns an ox," the old Setswana saying goes, "is not taken to be a fool" (Plaatje 1916:52). The capacity of animals in Africa to serve both as instruments and as signs of human relationship has long been noted (Evans-Pritchard 1940; Lienhardt 1961); the so-called "bovine idiom" is a particular instance of the more general tendency of humans to use alienable objects to extend their own existence by uniting themselves with others (Mauss 1954; Munn 1977). Both in their individual beauty and their collective association with wealth, kine were ideal—and idealized—personifications of men. A highly nuanced vocabulary existed in the vernacular to describe variations in their color, marking, disposition, shape of horns, and reproductive status (Lichtenstein 1973:81; Sandilands 1953:342f.). Named and praised, they were creatures of distinction. Not only did they bear their owners' identities aloft as they traversed social space (Somerville 1979:230). They also served as living records of the passage of value along the pathways of inheritance, affinity, alliance, and authority.

The intricate patterns of stock deployment among Tswana made it difficult for early European visitors to assess their holdings. Longer-term records suggest a history of fluctuations in animal populations, with cycles of depletion being followed by periods of recovery, at least until the end of the nineteenth century (Campbell 1822,2:112; cf. Grove 1989:164). But there is clear evidence of the existence, at the beginning of that century, of large and unequally distributed herds. Observers tended to be struck by blatant discrepancies in cattle ownership, and by the unambiguous association—Burchell (1824,2:272) used the word "metonymy"—of wealth in kine and power (cf. Lichtenstein 1973:76f.; Molema 1920:115; above, chapter 3). Thus the chief was the supreme herdsman (*modisa*) of the polity, a metaphor that captured well vernacular visions of value and political economy. Situated atop the *morafe* ("nation"), he controlled its largest estate, living evidence of the entitlements of birth, office, and tribute that ran together in his person.[9] Moreover, he presided over a domain marked not by fixed boundaries, but by an outer ring of water holes and pasture. The chiefdom itself, in other words, was a range (Comaroff and Comaroff 1992:141). Royal stock also built relations outside the polity, being used to placate, and sometimes to trade with, other sovereigns. They carried the ruler's imprint across his realm and beyond, naturalizing his authority and rendering it enduring (Burchell 1824,2:347f.).

But it was not only chiefs who mobilized cattle as a currency of power. Other men of rank and position also accumulated stock and set up networks of alliance and patronage. Ordinary male citizens, in contrast, depended on inheritance, bridewealth, and natural increase to build their modest herds. Some—serfs, and others laid low—had no animals of their own. They made up what Burchell (1824,2:348) termed an "ill-fated class," eternally dependent on their betters. The poor man, went the Tswana proverb, is *motlhola tlotlô a se tlo le ja*, the creator of treasures he will not consume.

In the bovine economy of the Southern Tswana, then, an indigenous "stock exchange" underwrote inequalities of class, gender, and rank. As the pliable media used to forge all productive relations, human and superhuman alike, cattle were the quintessential form of social and symbolic capital—and the very embodiment of wealth and aspiration. They moved men to intrigue, sorcery, and warfare, to deep contemplation about the nature of life and worth, and, as Somerville (1979:134) witnessed in 1801, to passionate poetry:

> The great amusement of the men consists in the return of the cattle from pastures about Sunset when they are constantly upon the look out and some orator is always prepared with a speech. . . . Every cow that lows is saluted with [a] harangue in praise of her Calf—or milk. Such is the passion for this species of public speakers, these Booshooanah Improvisators, that regularly every evening a party paid us a visit for the sole purpose of greeting our Cattle on their return.

One of Somerville's (1979:230) companions confirmed that praise poets were especially affected by the sight of their favorite cows or oxen (cf. van der Merwe 1941:309f., 321f., on Hurutshe cattle poems).

Cattle were also a prime medium in the exchange networks that, by the late eighteenth century, linked Southern Tswana to other peoples on the subcontinent (*RRI*:161), yielding beads from the Kora and Griqua to the south, and iron implements, copper jewelry, and tobacco from communities to the north and northeast (Lichtenstein 1930,2:409; Stow 1905:449, 489). Bovine capital also gave access to the ivory and pelts desired by white travelers, who arrived in growing numbers from around 1800 (Shillington 1985:11). And pack oxen[10] enabled the haulage of *sebilô* from its source in Tlhaping territory; the glittering hematite powder, a sought-after cosmetic, was traded widely in all directions (Campbell 1813:170; see *RRI*:162). But the earliest European observers already noted that Tswana were reluctant to part with their beasts in any significant numbers: Somerville's (1979:140) expedition to the interior failed in its trade objectives because of the "[natives'] decided unwillingness to part with their cattle." The Englishman found this "difficult to account for, since they convert them to no useful purpose whatever."

Nonetheless, regional exchange networks were active enough to persuade the Europeans that they had stumbled upon the "essential principles of *international traffic*," or "mercantile agency in its infancy" in the African veld (Burchell 1824,2:555; original emphasis). Andrew Smith (1939,1:251), in fact, suggested that chiefs managed production explicitly to foster alliances: the Tlhaping ruler, for one, prevented his subjects from growing tobacco so that they might purchase it from the Griqua in the interests of "friendly communication." Local sovereigns tried, as well, to monopolize transactions with foreign merchants and to control commerce across their realms; recall that Mothibi "demand[ed] a tax" from all outsiders who came to collect *sebilô* (Campbell 1822,2:194). He also limited his own people's access to the powder; possibly, Campbell (1822,2:194) speculated, to prevent its price from falling. Indeed, whites found Tswana leaders well aware of discrepancies in rates of exchange for such items as ivory, and keen to profit from them.[11] Notwithstanding the reluctance to sell beasts, opportunities to traffic with Europeans—in the early years largely for beads, later for guns and money—were eagerly seized. When Lichtenstein (1930,2:388f.) visited the Tlhaping in 1805, long before a permanent mission was established, he noted that a "general spirit of trade" was easily roused. Although the Africans showed "no idea of the ordinary usages of barter," he said, they kept up an energetic exchange until his party had naught left to sell.[12] A few years on, Burchell (1824,2:555) was struck by the existence of enduring trade partnerships (*maats;* Dutch) between individual Tlhaping and Klaarwater Khoi.

We shall come back, shortly, to the engagement of the civilizing mission with Southern Tswana commerce. Already, however, two things are clear. The first is that the Africans had long channeled their surpluses into trade networks which enhanced their stocks of value, bringing them a range of goods from knives and tobacco to widely circulating forms of currency. Of the latter, second, beads had become the most notable. By the turn of the nineteenth century,[13] they were serving as media of exchange that articulated local and global economies, linking the worlds of cattle and money (cf. Graeber 1996).

Along with buttons, which served a similar purpose (especially in the Eastern Cape; Beck 1989:214), beads were portable tokens that, for a time, epitomized foreign exchange value beyond the colonial frontier. They were "the only circulating medium or money in the interior," Campbell noted (1822,1:246),[14] adding that every "nation" through which they passed made a profit on them. Different kinds composed distinct regional currencies; Philip (1828,2:131; cf. Livingstone 1959,1:151) tells us that no importance was attached to particular examples, however beautiful, if they were "not received among the tribes around them." At the same time, says Beck (1989:220f.; cf. Somerville 1979:140), African communities showed strong preferences, in the early 1800s, for specific colors, sizes, and degrees of transparency.[15]

Even as they became a semi-standardized currency for purposes of external trade, beads served internally as personal adornments; in this they were like many similar sorts of wealth objects. Their attraction seems to have stemmed from the fact that particular valuables could be withdrawn from circulation for display, which was itself a form of conspicuous consumption.[16] But men of means also accumulated *hidden* stocks: "Their chief wealth," Campbell (1822,1:246) wrote, "like that of more civilized nations, is hoarded up in their coffers" (cf. Graeber 1996; chapter 5). Here it stayed, far from the eyes of jealous rivals, until favorable opportunities for trade presented themselves. Market exchange was, at this point, a sporadic activity, set apart from everyday processes of production, consumption, and distribution.

Some observers, like Campbell (1822,1:246), emphasized the monetary properties of beads: "They answer the same purpose as cowrie shells in India and North Africa," he reported, "or as guineas and shillings in Britain." But others were struck by the differences. For a start, aesthetic qualities seemed somehow integral to their worth. "Among these people," offered Philip (1828,2:131), "utility is, perhaps, more connected with beauty than it is with us." Simmel (1978:73f.) would have said that the separation of the beautiful from the useful comes only with the objectification of value: the aesthetic artifact takes on a unique existence; it cannot be replaced by another that might perform the same function. Such an artifact, therefore, is the absolute inverse of the coin, whose defining feature is its substitutability.

Among Southern Tswana, the increasing velocity of trade did objectify some media of exchange—first beads, then money—rendering them ever more interchangeable. But the process was never complete, and did not eliminate other forms of wealth in which beauty and use explicitly enhanced each other. Indeed, the longevity of cattle currencies in African societies bear testimony to the fact that processes of rationalization, standardization, and universalization are *always* refracted, locally, by social and cultural circumstance. In the cow, aesthetics and utility, uniqueness and substitutability existed side by side, coloring Tswana notions of value in general—and money in particular. Black wage laborers in early twentieth-century South Africa, Breckenridge (1995:274) notes, set special store by the physical qualities of metallic coins. In explaining their attitude, public intellectuals John Dube and Sol Plaatje contrasted "flimsy" paper money with "the good red gold we know and love." Beauty and usefulness play off each other in the West as well, of course; in much modernist design, after all, "form follows function." The Tswana appreciation of prized beads and beasts, similarly, expressed a sense of "attractiveness" that fused the perfect with the practical. Persons or objects possessed of it were thought to draw toward themselves desirable qualities dispersed in the world at large. Ornamental baubles or celebrated stock were the very epitome of attractiveness: held apart from the everyday cycle of exchange, they embodied precious potential in congealed form.

Objects that come to be invested with value as media of exchange vary considerably over time and space—a point vividly demonstrated by the emergence of new currencies as formerly distinct economic orders begin to intersect. Marx (1967,1:83) once observed that, when the latter happens, the "universal equivalent form" often lodges arbitrarily and transiently in a particular kind of commodity. So it was with beads, which had been mass-produced for rather different ends in the West, but turned out to serve well, for a while, as a vehicle of commerce beyond the colonial border. Marx also noted that, as traffic persists, such tokens of equivalence tend to "crystallize . . . out into the money form." So, once again, it was with beads. Campbell (1822,1:246) reports that, while Tswana would accept various articles as gifts, these were of "small value" in trade. "They want money in such a case," he wrote, "that is, beads." What was more, as transactions increased in volume, standards of value in the worlds linked by this new currency began to affect each other: merchants found that rates charged by Africans in the interior rose and become more uniform.[17] By the 1820s, Beck (1989:218f.) shows, the demand for beads at the Cape had driven up the price quite dramatically, to the extent that missionaries tried to secure supplies from England at one-third of the cost.

The bottom soon fell out of the frontier bead market, however (although not so further to the north; see Chapman 1971,1:127; Livingstone 1959,1:151). Initially, despite ever more direct contact between Africans and the colonial economy, that market seems to have been sustained by the dearth of fractions of the rix-dollar, the currency at the Cape in the early 1800s (Arndt 1928:44–46). But after 1825 the British government introduced its own silver and copper coinage in its imperial possessions, and paper dollars were replaced by sterling. Once the new supply had stabilized, and filtered through to the frontier, its effect on bead money was devastating. Andrew Smith (1939,1:250) wrote in 1835:

Schoon [a white merchant] informs me that when first he began to trade in this country about 1828, nothing was desired by the natives but beads, etc., but now they are scarcely asked for; indeed nothing is to be purchased by them[18] but milk or firewood. . . . They understand reckoning money quite well, and if told the price of an article . . . they reckon out the money with the greatest precision.

Ironically, as we shall see, while Tswana came to reckon in money by the 1830s, many traders preferred to deal in kind. But, even more important than changes in the cash supply, a shift was occurring in the structure of wants and in local notions of value. It was a change encouraged, above all, by the presence of the evangelists and by the entry onto the scene, at their encouragement, of a cadre of itinerant merchants and shopkeepers.

*****

Here, then, were two distinct regimes of value, one European and the other African, whose engagement would have a profound impact on the colonial encounter. To the nineteenth-century Nonconformists, economic reform was no mere adjunct to spirituality: virtue and salvation had to be made by man, using the scarce material resources bequeathed by providence for improving the world. Commercial enterprise allowed the industrious to turn labor into wealth and wealth into grace. Money was the crucial medium of convertibility in this process. It typified the potential for good and evil given as a birthright to every self-willed individual. The Tswana, upon whom the evangelists hoped to impress these divine possibilities, also inhabited a universe of active human agency, one in which riches were made and enhanced through worldly transactions. Exchange, in their case, was effected primarily through cattle. In contrast to cash, stock socialized assets, measuring their ultimate worth not in treasures in heaven, but in people on earth. We move, now, to examine how these regimes of value, already in contact in the early 1800s, were brought into ever closer articulation by the efforts of the missions.

EXTENDING THE INVISIBLE HAND

Civilizing Commerce, Sanctified Shopping: The Early Years

"You white men are a strange folk. You have the word of God, but whilst you are very quick about other things you are very slow about the word of God. You want ostrich feathers and in one year the whole land is full of white men seeking feathers. And what sort of men are they? Hark!" said he, pointing towards the quarter of the town where the traders were encamped. "I know what they are doing now. They are giving beads to the

*girls, for it is dark. They are corrupting the women of my people, they are
teaching my people abominations of which even they were once ignorant,
heathen as they are. Here are traders enough."*

Chief Sechele, 1865[19]

British observers in the early 1800s might have acknowledged that Southern
Tswana peoples showed a lively interest in trade. But they also stressed the
difference between "native commerce" and enlightened, rational European
markets. Burchell (1824,2:536f.), for one, noted that the "inconstant" relations
between Tlhaping and their neighbors were driven by "selfish views and the
prospect of booty"; that a "mercantile jealousy" had called forth competing
efforts to monopolize trade with the colony to the south.[20] He proposed a "regulated trade for ivory . . . with the Bichuana nations," to be vested in an authorized body of white merchants who would institute fair dealing in place of uncouth speculation—to the putative advantage of all (p. 539). His "free" market,
like that of liberal economists before and since, required careful management.

The founding evangelists, we have stressed repeatedly, shared this trust in
the civilizing force of trade. Some believed that the very "sight of a shop" on
mission ground did wonders to rouse savages to industry (Philip 1828,1:204–5).
The equation of civilization with commerce might have become one of the great
clichés of the epoch, but for the Nonconformists it was far from a platitude.
The point was not to create an exploitable dependency, although that did happen. Nor was it simply to play on base desire to make people give ear to the
Gospel, although that happened too. It ran much deeper. Trade had a capacity
to breach "the sullen isolations of heathenism," to stay the "fountain of African
misery" (Livingstone 1940:255; 1961:258; 1857:34). All of which made material
reform an urgent moral duty. Philip (1828,1:207) was quick to condemn those
concerned only with "talking from the pulpit"; those who deemed everything
connected with industry and the elevation of a people "carnal" and "alien to
the propagation of the gospel." Honest enterprise, however, was a sure means
of producing prudent subjects and civil societies. The optimism of the missionaries in this respect was to falter in the face of the stark realities of the colonial
frontier. The Christians had eventually to rethink their dream of a commonwealth of free-trading black communities, actively enhancing their virtue and
wealth. But they continued to hold that the liberal market would rout superstition, slavery, sloth. And this even when, later in the century, market forces brutally undercut their own idyll of independent African economies, compelling
"their" peoples to become wage-working vassals in their own land.

There was thus a good deal more to championing commerce among the
heathen than merely "making virtue of necessity," even though it was probably
true that many pioneer evangelists had to exchange to survive (Beck 1989:211).[21]
In fact, the most ardent advocates of free enterprise were often also those most

opposed to clergy themselves doing business. Livingstone (1857:39) held that, while missionary and trader were mutually dependent, "experience shows that the two employments can not very well be combined in the same person."[22] In his *Missionary Travels* (1857:40), he claimed never to have come in contact with an evangelist who traded,[23] and made disparaging mention of "two of the Wesleyan Society" who had left the church to become full-time speculators (Livingstone 1959:2,152). He was himself also to be accused of gun-running by the Boers. But then, on the frontier, the lines between prestation, purchase, and profit were very fine indeed. And often in dispute.[24]

Much has been made by some historians of the business activities of the first evangelists in the South African interior. One has even argued that the likes of Moffat instigated "wars" to enable them to traffic in slaves (Cobbing 1988:492; *RRI*:331, n. 48). Commerce with peoples living beyond colonial borders was forbidden by law. In practice, however, missionaries were exempt, except for the ban on selling liquor, guns, and ammunition.[25] The very first LMS emissaries to the Tswana, Kok and Edwards, were quickly embroiled in the ivory trade; Kok was subsequently killed by Tlhaping employees in a dispute over remuneration (*RRI*:190). Exchange between those who followed him and various African peoples also often went well beyond the procuring of necessities, involving considerable capital outlay. Competition and mutual accusations of dishonorable dealing among the brethren soon became common (Beck 1989:214f.). The danger of "losing the missionary in the merchant," as Philip (1828,1:206) put it, was obviously real enough—although, as he insisted, there were also cases of the reverse occurring, of men of business taking up the Christian cause (cf. Moffat and Moffat 1951:10, n. 37). By 1817, members of the LMS at the Cape had to confront the issue as a matter of policy. They agreed that, while trade was forced on them by the inadequacy of the Society's support, they should strive to make their stations self-sustaining through agriculture and handicrafts. The quest for profit was specifically discouraged (Moffat and Moffat 1951:216).

From the first, Southern Tswana seem to have associated the evangelists—indeed, all whites—with barter. Moffat (Moffat and Moffat 1951:18) reports that, when he and the Rev. Kay of the WMMS traveled among the Tlhaping in 1821, "the Bootchuanas flocked around us with articles for exchange." The first Methodists among the Rolong had similar experiences.[26] The clergymen tended to be less than open in their formal correspondence about their own dealings, however. In letters to his kin, Moffat (Moffat and Moffat 1951:62) did mention some of his transactions—like taking delivery of consignments of "goods." But he seldom described precisely what was done with them. He obviously used beads to buy ivory tusks and pelts (p. 266f.). And while he was wont to represent his "trifling" acquisition of karosses, cattle, and ivory as ceremonial exchange rather than business, the distinction was probably less than apparent to others.

Some of his colleagues thought him wealthy, although Livingstone (1959,2:173) indignantly dismissed this as a misapprehension; everyone in the interior, he said, was alleged to be rich.[27] But the missions themselves saw the hinterland as a source of riches: Campbell advised the LMS to participate in the lucrative ivory trade in the 1820s, thereby to raise funds for projects in the Colony (Beck 1989:217; Moffat and Moffat 1951:62). Cooperation between the Nonconformists and commercial agents was close: traders journeying beyond the Orange River tended to lodge at the mission stations and often accompanied the Christians evangelists on their journeys (Livingstone 1960:141; 1961:153). When first they arrived, the Wesleyans were dismayed that such activities had led Africans to regard all evangelists as merchants. But they too proceeded almost immediately to transact beads, axes, and spears for stock.[28]

The Nonconformists also gave out goods for purposes other than trade. Early on, they dispensed tobacco, beads, and buttons to encourage goodwill, only to find that prestations came to be expected in return for attending church and school.[29] Few Tswana seem initially to have shared the precise European distinction between gifts and commodities, donations and payments. Yet one thing *was* widely recognized: that whites controlled desirable objects. As a result, they soon became the uncomfortable victims of determined efforts to acquire those objects. Their correspondence declared that Africans of all stations, even dignified chiefs, were inveterate "beggars";[30] that they persistently demanded items like snuff, which the missionaries were assumed to have in large supply; and that their behavior violated Protestant notions of honest gain (Moffat and Moffat 1951:63). It took a while for the Christians to realize that "begging" was also a form of homage paid to the powerful (Price 1956:166; Mackenzie 1871:44f.). Burchell (1824,2:407) was less perturbed by these requests than were his clerical compatriots, having discerned that they were limited largely to a specific category of goods:

> In begging for any trifling gift or remuneration, they never asked for *sikháka* (beads); these being considered more especially as *money*, to be employed only as the medium of trade with distant tribes, and for the purchase of the more expensive articles; while *muchúko* and *lishuéna* (tobacco and snuff) being consumable merchandise, are, though highly valued, regarded as a less important species of property. (Original emphasis.)

A similar contrast between treasures and trifles seems to have obtained in the brazen "theft," in the first years, of the evangelists' belongings, especially their produce and tools. "Anything eatable requires a sentinel," recounted a despairing Moffat (Moffat and Moffat 1951:57), "and many useful utensils and implements are carried away." Previous visitors had remarked on the virtual absence of pilfering.[31] Lichtenstein (1973:75) was struck by the fact that only "a few bits of meat" and "unimportant household implements" were ever taken; again, items not considered as property in any meaningful sense. But Broadbent's account of the severe response of a Rolong chief to one such incident[32] makes it clear that the sudden presence of quantities of desirable goods had raised unprecedented problems of defining and maintaining ownership (see Campbell 1822,2:63 for another case). The missionaries tended to see this as a lack of respect for private effects; Hodgson (1977:336) mused, in 1826, on the "precarious tenure upon which the natives [held] their possessions." Obviously, conventions of acquisition, proprietorship, and remuneration were being tested on both sides of the encounter.[33]

In light of all this, we must qualify Beck's (1989:224) claim that missionary trading had a significant impact on the economies and cultures of African peoples beyond the colonial borders in the early nineteenth century. He is undoubtedly correct that the evangelists introduced more European goods than did any other whites at the time; also, that their dealings eroded the local desire for beads and buttons in favor of a more complex array of wants, primarily for domestic commodities such as clothes, blankets, and utensils. This transformation was certainly evident in Southern Tswana communities. But, as we have suggested, it entailed far more than the mere provision of objects by the Nonconformists. Changing patterns of consumption grew out of a shift in ideas about the nature, worth, and significance of particular things in themselves— which, in turn, was set in play by the encounter of very different currencies of value. Thus, even where their uses seemed obvious, goods were given meaning in ways not reducible to utility alone; often, moreover, they were put to purposes which made the Europeans uneasy. We explore this process in respect of specific items—such as apparel and furnishings—in the following two chapters.

Yet more basic than this was the fact that, as the century wore on, it was less the evangelists than the merchants they brought in their wake who were responsible for the supply of goods. Recall that the Christian enthusiasm for enlightened enterprise had been accompanied, from the start, by a distaste for the corrupting power of money. The prospect of men of God haggling over the price of trinkets remained unedifying (Beck 1989:213).[34] That is why most of them encouraged traders to settle on their stations. By the mid-1880s, Mackenzie (1887,2:341) was able to state categorically that he and his brethren were unconnected with trade—in 1881 they had reprimanded and transferred Khukhwi Mogodi, the "native" evangelist, for dealing in ivory after the LMS had withdrawn its financial support (Chirenje 1977:202; see chapter 2)—although their work "always led to the development of commerce." While storekeepers conducted their business within the compass of the mission, they were never under its control.

By the 1830s, then, both the LMS and the WMMS were seeking to attract merchants to their stations (R. Moffat 1842:605).[35] Philip (1828,1:204f.) had already publicized the success of his "experiment" to have one open a store at

Bethelsdorp: "The sight of the goods in their windows . . . produced the effect anticipated: the desire of possessing the articles for use and comfort by which they were constantly tempted, acquired additional strength on every fresh renewal of stimulus." Money, he added, had gone up in the people's estimation. They had begun, enthusiastically, to bring produce to the trader to exchange for goods. Bechuanaland soon followed Bethelsdorp. "A storekeeper has come from Grahamstown, and the people are delighted at the idea of being able to purchase what they may require," Archbell wrote from Platberg in 1831; "by him our strength will be increased."[36] Moffat (1842:605) was similarly rhapsodic about the services of David Hume, who not only supplied Kuruman with "British commodities," but volunteered his labor in building the mission chapel (Philip 1828,1:206). Mackenzie (1887,1:31) would later recall how, at Shoshong to the north, sales were first conducted only from wagons. Then "round huts were built for the traders by the native women as shops." Sun-dried brick houses followed, and finally large burnt-brick and iron-roofed establishments were erected to accommodate the brisk business of the "exceedingly well-disposed and able European traders." The introduction of stores in this manner—all the better to instruct non-Western peoples in "the economic facts of life"—was a high priority among British Protestants in many parts of the world; Miller (1973:101) describes similar ventures in the Argentine in the 1930s.

Time would mute the idyll of cooperation between missionaries and merchants. Already in 1841, Mary Moffat (1967:18), while reiterating the need to foster a desire for goods, bemoaned the "high prices" charged by local dealers for "worthless materials." A decade later, Livingstone (1959,2:152) was writing in acerbic terms about traders in general, and about Hume in particular. While they reaped huge profits, he complained, these men resented the evangelists, suspecting them of driving up the price of African goods; they raised an "outcry" if "they should see . . . any missionary buy a sheep or a kaross from a Native." Yet who, in fairness, had more of a right than the men of God to gain from the markets they themselves had made? Not, he concluded testily (1974:116), the "smouses" [itinerant traders], the "diploma of whom [could] be procured by any one who can count ten without the aid of his fingers." But there were also, he allowed, more "respectable" merchants, those who acknowledged their immense debt to the Christians![37]

While the whites squabbled over their dealings with Africans, Tswana sovereigns—witness the words of Chief Sechele—had their own reasons for being wary of traders. The latter paid scant respect to long-standing mores or monopolies, being ready to buy from anyone who had anything desirable to sell; the purchase of ivory and feathers from Rolong "vassals" in the Kalahari, for instance, cost the life of one merchant and his son (Mackenzie 1871:130). Beyond the confines of the mission stations, such friction was frequent, sometimes drawing in Griqua mediators and Sarwa clients (Livingstone 1959,2:86). But even when the merchants did their business under the eyes of the evangelists, their behavior often gave offense. On occasion this was unintended; like the commotion among women caused by James Chapman (1971,1:127) in 1853 when he tried to kill a crocodile near a Tswana village in which the species was venerated. However, brawling, theft, and sexual assault were also common; Sechele had to banish two storekeepers for an "indecent" attack on a Kwena woman in broad daylight near Livingstone's home (Livingstone 1974:120). No wonder that Tswana rulers developed a "well-known" reluctance to allow itinerant traders to pass through their territories (Mackenzie 1871:130). Or that, later in the century, strong chiefs would try to subject European commerce in their realms to strict control (Parsons 1977:122).

As it turned out, the Nonconformists would have to wrestle continually with the contradictions of commerce. In embracing its virtues, they had also to deal with the fact that the two-faced coin threatened constantly to profane their sacred mission. Yet the merchants, men of mammon among them, were indispensable in the effort to reform local economies by hitching them to the colonial market—and to the body of corporate nations beyond.

Object Lessons

For all the reasons already given, the merchants remained on the mission stations. And they prospered. Moffat (1845:219f.) reported that Hume was drawing Tswana trade from "far and near." This "medium of intercourse," he assured the Christian public, promised results "most beneficial to the cause." Storekeepers stocked all of the quotidian objects deemed essential to a civil "household economy" (R. Moffat 1842:507, 502f.): manufactured clothes, fabrics, blankets, sewing implements, soap, and candle molds; the stuff, that is, of feminized domestic life, with its scrubbed, illuminated interiors (see chapter 6). Shops also carried the implements of intensive agriculture, and the guns and ammunition required to garner the "products of the chase," increasingly the most valuable of trade goods. Colonial whites abhorred the idea of weapons in African hands. But, by the 1830s, "old soldier's muskets" were being sold for "6,7 and 8 oxen," and three or four pounds of gunpowder for a single animal (A. Smith 1939,1:232).[38] Even more controversially, the evangelists themselves sometimes supplied these goods (Livingstone 1959,1:113, 171; 2:238f.; *RRI*:274). After the midcentury, however, as Shillington (1985:13f, 21f.) shows, the ever expanding arms business was mostly in the hands of itinerant dealers and well-capitalized Cape entrepreneurs,[39] a fact that would have far-reaching consequences for game stocks and for the economic independence of Southern Bechuanaland.

Mission accounts from the late 1800s show, in both their rhetoric and their referents, that European commodities had begun to tell their own story in the Tswana world, serving as vehicles of significant new developments. As Wookey (1884:303) wrote:

Through the settlement of missionaries, and the visits of traders and travellers, the country became known and opened up. Cattle first, and then
ivory, feathers, and karosses, were the principal things brought by the natives for barter. They were exchanged for guns and ammunition, cows,
wagons, horses, clothes, and . . . other things. Today a trader's stock is not
complete unless he has school material, stationery, and even books for the
people who come to trade with him.

Ornaments, cooking utensils, and consumables—such as coffee, tea, and
sugar—were widely purchased, he went on. Foreign manufactures seemed everywhere in use. These objects, as we shall see, spoke of domestic reconstruction. At least in some quarters; the acquisition of commodities required a certain level of surplus production and disposable income, which was largely
restricted to the upper and middle peasantry. What was more, in spite of their
growing taste for European goods, many men remained reluctant, except in dire
need, to sell stock (cf. Schapera 1933:648; above, chapter 3).[40] The market was
particularly attractive to those excluded from indigenous processes of accumulation: as we have noted, client peoples were easily tempted to turn tribute into
trade—which is why some chiefs were increasingly unable to monopolize exchange. (Others were more successful; see Parsons 1977:120). Especially along
the frontier, steadily growing numbers of individuals, citizens and "vassals"
alike, entered into commercial transactions, and acquired manufactured goods
well before the mineral revolution and the onset of large-scale labor migrancy.
Small objects may speak of big changes, of course. Rising sales of coffee, tea,
and sugar mark important shifts in diet and in patterns of sociality and nutrition. And they link local histories to the production and consumption of commodities in other parts of the empire (cf. Mintz 1985). As George Orwell
(1982:82) once commented, in this respect, "changes in diet are more important
than changes of dynasty or even of religion."

But Wookey's account also points to a process that had veered out of mission control (1884:304):

> Changes, however, have taken place in the trade of the country. A few
> years ago many thousands of pounds' worth of produce annually changed
> hands and passed through to the colony. Now ivory has become scarce, as
> the elephants have been killed . . . [and] the [ostrich feather] trade has
> dwindled down. . . . But another door was opening for the people . . . I
> mean the Diamond Fields.

Proletarianization was an almost inevitable consequence of the Nonconformists'
economic revolution and the beliefs that informed it. We shall return to it in a
moment. Wookey went on to admit that the material developments promoted
by the mission had not been an "unmixed good"; in this, he anticipated the

concerns of African critics, voiced some years later, about the impact of sugar, alcohol, and imported provisions on the health of black populations (chapter 7). Not only had new diseases appeared, but drink had become "one of the greatest curses of the country" (Wookey 1884:304).[41] The most profitable and addictive of all commodities, its effects were a sordid caricature of the desire to make "natives" dependent on the market. Despite evangelical efforts to limit its distribution (Mackenzie 1871:92), brandy was being supplied in ever growing quantities to Bechuanaland by the second half of the nineteenth century (Shillington 1985:146; see n. 41).

Sorghum beer had long been part of the vernacular diet and was regarded, much to missionary chagrin, as food; indeed, as the essence of commensality.[42] Under the impact of monetization, women began to brew for profit; some of Willoughby's congregants told him that they did so to pay their subscriptions and to buy clothes.[43] Their activities swelled the tide of intoxicants flowing into local communities. The Ngwaketse, for instance, were described in 1877 as being "fast demoralized by drink from the Chief downwards." The successor to that chief, Bathoen I, would journey to England in 1895 as part of a delegation to protest the transfer of the Bechuanaland Protectorate to the British South Africa Company,[44] a move anticipated, among other things, to encourage the sale of European alcohol there—even though it had been banned since 1889. In 1895, too, Chief Montshiwa addressed the Queen and her Ministers:[45]

[D]o not let the Cape Government kill my people with their Brandy; we do not want it. [I]t will destroy us; it will cause fighting; it will fill our land with sorrow and darkness. We are living nicely without the whiteman's brandy. Please hold fast the hands of the Cape so that Brandy may never be allowed in our country.

The issue was not trivial. Several Tswana rulers had already tried to banish brandy from their realms, and Khama III expelled traders who failed to comply (Holub 1881,1:278; Parsons 1977:122; Schapera 1970:146f.). Plaatje (1996), using the black press, was to champion the Liquor Proclamation of 1904, a law prohibiting the purchase of "white man's fire water" by "natives" in South Africa. In Britain, Bathoen was moved to remark to the Rev. Lloyd (1895:170) that, while the chiefs had seen "the fountain of things" in England—of clothing, churches, houses, even the Word of God—they had not been shown "the fountain of strong drink." "Why do they not show us the fountain of brandy?" he mused. "Is it not because they are ashamed to show us such a fountain of evil?"

This image of a natural source of goods and evil spouting forth at the core of empire is powerful indeed! Unfortunately, the flow of brandy had already eroded the cultural and physical defenses of many frontier communities. Holub's (1881,1:236) account of his tour of Tlhaping territory belies Wookey's paean to the positive, "opening" effect of European commodities. It sketches a graphically dark picture of the corrupting force of the colonial market:

> [M]en, in tattered European clothes, except now and then one in a mangy skin, followed by as many women . . . and by a swarm of children as naked as when they were born, came shouting eagerly towards us. They were nearly all provided with bottles, or pots, or cans, and cried out for brandy. . . . They had brought all manner of things for barter for spirits. One man held up a jackal's hide, another a goatskin; . . . and some of them had their homemade wooden spoons and platters to dispose of to us. It was a disgusting scene. . . . [W]hen we attempted to drive on, their importunities waxed louder than ever. . . . One of the men made what he evidently imagined would be an irresistible appeal, by offering me a couple of greasy shillings.

In the nineteenth-century colonial imagination, as we shall see, "grease" evoked the clinging filth of savagery, the grime of uncontained bodies and unsavory associations. Money was meant to promote the kind of upright industry and lifestyle that would dissolve its dirt. But in this instance it had failed, merely adding to the muck of heathenism, its own nonstick surfaces becoming coated with the residues of depravity.

Accounts of this sort soon became more frequent. As the new center of mining and industry sprang to life around the diamond fields, the satanic face of commerce, its coercive underside, came all but to the Nonconformists' door. And, in doing so, it exposed their naiveté in hoping to befriend the "mammon of unrighteousness" by introducing Southern Tswana to the market in a controlled, benevolent manner. By then, in any case, the traders they had brought into their midst had already helped to set a minor revolution in motion, serving as agents of commodification in a double sense: they were both emissaries of European capital in African communities and the means whereby it actually began to work its magic upon them. That magic had ambiguous effects. It led, at one extreme, to the contrivance of a polite bourgeois life-world; as well, among ordinary people, to forms of creative consumption in which objects were deployed in new designs for living, newly contrived identities, all of them stylistic fusions of the familiar and the fresh. At the other extreme, it conjured up the "disgusting scenes" of poverty described by Holub and others. To be sure, the merchants had also given Southern Tswana practical lessons in the exploitative side of enlightened capitalism, in its capacity to impoverish hardworking families. From the very first and for a very long time these entrepreneurs engaged in the infamous practice of buying local produce for a pittance in cash or kind and then, when food was short, selling it back at exorbitant profit; in this century, at twice to three times the purchase price.[46]

The missionaries themselves had also played a crucial role in determining the ways in which Western objects and market practices had entered into Tswana life, however; as we have stressed, there is more to commodification than the mere provision of goods. The Christians set out to instill a specific form of desire, a "sacred hunger," that linked discerning consumption to a particular mode of producing goods and selves—and that encouraged continuing investment in civilizing enterprise. Above all else, this required a respect for the many talents of money.

THE OBJECTIFICATION OF VALUE[47]

The Meaning of Money

[M]oney's educational. It's far more educational than the things it buys.

E. M. Forster ([1910] 1992:133)

Insofar as colonialism entailed a confrontation of different regimes of value, the encounter between Southern Tswana and the missionaries was most clearly played out—and, the records suggest, experienced—through the media most crucial to the measure of wealth on either side: cattle, money, and the trade beads that, for a while, strung them together. Encounters of this sort, especially when they involved European capitalism in its expansive form, often ended up in the erasure of one currency by another. But they sometimes gave rise to unpredictable, unexpected hybrids, and to processes a good deal more complex than allowed by most theories of commodification (cf. Breckenridge 1995). For value is borne by human beings, who seek actively to shape it to their particular ends. Along the Cape frontier, cash and cows became fiercely contested signs and means, alibis of distinct, mutually threatening modes of existence. The Nonconformists were deeply mired in this struggle, at least in the early years.

To Tswana, it will be remembered, beasts were the major means of storing and conveying wealth in people and things, and of embodying value in social relations. In fact, control over these relations was one of the objects of owning animals. Thus, while cattle *were* sometimes dealt on the foreign market, the bulk of both internal and long-distance trade seems to have been directed toward acquiring more stock.[48] In ordinary circumstances, barter never drew on real capital; this is why Somerville's (1979:140f.) party failed, in 1801, to persuade Tlhaping to part with bovines in any number, or to procure a single milk cow. Beads, here, stood for worth in more explicitly alien and alienated form, circulating against goods on the external market, or those which had been freed from local entanglements. By being transacted with neighboring people for animals, they could also be used to convert value from more to less reified forms.

But this currency had its own logic. With the increasing standardization of the bead market across the interior in the early nineteenth century, the value of certain key resources in Tswana life was rendered measurable. And more easily negotiable. Articles formerly withheld from sale, or given only for cattle (such as karosses, made as personal property; Lichtenstein 1930,2:389), became purchasable (Moffat and Moffat 1951:262, 267). The Nonconformists, anxious to draw local economies into exchange, actively encouraged this process of commodification, although their real objective was the introduction of money. Hence they used the token currency themselves to put a price on hitherto inalienable things, such as land and labor. Not only did they pay wages in it, a fact to which we shall return, but, in 1823, used it to acquire (what they thought was) the freehold on which their mission station was built (Moffat and Moffat 1951:189, 113; see chapter 8). Beads were also bartered for agricultural surpluses by both missionaries and merchants. There is even evidence—*vide* Sechele's outrage—that some traders, operating under the aegis of the evangelists, offered Tswana women these baubles for sexual favors.

The effort of the missionaries to commodify African labor, land, and produce, and to foster a desire for everyday consumer goods, eventually helped to reorient the bulk of trade from the hinterland toward the Cape. This had the effect of limiting the viability of bead currency itself. The latter had served well as long as token transactions remained relatively confined in space and time; as long as they involved a restricted range of luxuries from a few external sources of supply; as long as exchange was sporadic and did not extend to the procurement of ordinary utilities. But once the ways and means of daily life began to be commodified, and increasingly to emanate from the colonial economy, a different, more standardized, and more widely circulating currency was required to traffic in them. Consequently, as Tswana engaged with a rapidly broadening range of manufactures, merchants, and middlemen in the 1830s, money quickly became the measure of value. This, in turn, posed a threat to internal regimes of worth and wealth, which had formerly been kept distinct from foreign exchange. Even where coin did not actually change hands, it came to stand for the moral economy, the material values, and the modes of contractual relationship propagated by the civilizing mission—and the world whence it originated.

While the pioneer evangelists had no option but to deal in beads, they sought, from the first, to teach the value of cash. Their early efforts, before the buying power of colonial currency spread to the interior, were not a success. Campbell (1822,2:140) describes the disappointment of some Tlhaping who traveled, with mission encouragement, to a market at Graff-Reinet in 1820, there to be paid in paper:

When . . . [they] received paper money for the articles they had to dispose of, they could not be made to understand its use; after farther explanations they supposed they could procure any things they chose for it, whether the paper was for one, two, or more rix-dollars. Their money being rejected as too little for the articles they wanted, they thought they had been cheated by the persons who had given them the paper, and gave it for any thing they could obtain, despising small pieces of dirty paper.

The Tlhaping seem not to have been alone in their distrust of this kind of tender. Between 1806 and 1824, rix-dollar notes were notoriously fragile, and were thought unreliable by many Europeans (Arndt 1928:44, 62). Later in the century, white dealers would pass illiterate Africans spurious bills—issued, in one case, by the "Bank of Leather," and entitling the bearer to "the best Value" in "London or Paris Boots & Shoes"[49]—in exchange for diamonds (Matthews 1887:196). As Breckenridge (1995) has shown, paper money would have its own complex history in relation to metal coins in South Africa. Meanwhile, Campbell (1822,2:140) went on to relate how the disappointed Tswana traders entertained the population of Dithakong with depictions of "mock sales," mimicking the auctioneer, and calling out in Dutch: "Once, twice, thrice! Who bids more?" In this manner the conventions of the market began to circulate beyond the site of sale itself.

But the evangelists did not always entrust the introduction of money, or the dissemination of its qualities, to the workings of the market. Given the uncertainties of the colonial currency, they occasionally took matters into their own hands. A few years earlier, Campbell had himself attempted something quite remarkable. On a visit to Klaarwater in 1812–13, part of a tour to assess the progress of the LMS in South Africa, he determined that the Griqua community merited consolidation both as a "nation" in its own right and as a base for expanding evangelical operations into the interior (Parsons 1927:198). Crucial to this venture was a proper coinage (Campbell 1813:256):

> It was likewise resolved, that as they had no circulating medium amongst them, by which they could purchase any small articles . . . supposing a shop to be established amongst them . . . they should apply to the Mission Society to get silver pieces of different value coined for them in England, which the missionaries would take for their allowance from the Society, having Griqua town marked on them. It is probable that, if this were adopted, in a short time they would circulate among all the nations round about, and be a great convenience.

God's bankers indeed! This mission money would be dubbed "one of the most interesting emissions in the numismatic history of the British Empire" (Parsons 1927:202; Arndt 1928:128). It was clearly intended not only to foster local trade, but also to establish a regional cash currency—and, with it, a sense of regionality.[50] A man of action, Campbell, apparently without consulting his fellow

LMS directors, set about ordering supplies of special coinage from a well-known English diesinker. We have record of four denominations, two each in silver and copper. "Griquatown" and the amount were inscribed on one face, the symbol of the Society on the other. The latter, a dove with an olive twig in its beak, aptly embodied the ideal of pacifying diffusion.[51] Aesthetic considerations were significant on both sides: the Griqua expressly asked Campbell to obtain only silver pieces for them. Consistent with their views of beauty (see below), Africans at the time preferred bright, shiny currency over duller coppers, a fact that seems to have had a tangible effect on the dissemination of this money (Parsons 1927:199). Shipped to South Africa in two consignments in 1815 and 1816, it established itself in limited circulation (*pace* Arndt 1928:127), a few examples turning up in places like Kimberley years later.[52]

The evangelists would also deploy other means to foster a respect for money. At issue, as we have said, was a moral economy in which its talents measured the output of enterprise and enabled the conversion of wealth into virtue. If there was no cash in the African interior it had to be invented—or its existence feigned. The evidence shows that, even when little coinage was in circulation, the missionaries used it as an invisible standard, a virtual currency, against which to tally the worth of goods, donations, and services. In 1828, a few months after establishing an offshoot from the main Wesleyan station at Platberg, Hodgson wrote of his new school (WMMS 1829–31:120):

> We pay for it four shillings and sixpence per month rent; which sum, however, is raised by the children themselves, most of whom subscribe one halfpenny per week each, which they obtain by bringing us milk, eggs, firewood, &c., for sale. . . . The first week produced three shillings and ninepence; (the children having been requested to bring one penny each;) the second, two shillings and twopence.

Penny capitalism was the first subject taught in the school, the missionaries trying to create a market *ex nihilo* by playing shop with the children. In a place devoid of money, merchants, landlords, or produce for sale, they paid rents. Amidst a barter economy, they reckoned their accounts with numerical exactitude. In their campaign to reorient perceptions of worth and to promote exchange, moreover, they often provided coin so that it could be returned to the church in measured subscriptions. Beck (1989:223) reports that, in the 1820s, the Methodists on the eastern Cape frontier encouraged offerings of beads and buttons that would be calculated in shillings and pence according to current "nominal" values. And Robert Moffat (1842:562) tells of Tlhaping contributions to his building fund in 1830, when "money was still very scarce" among them: a few gave cash, a few oxen, and a few, "some months' labor." By 1837, members of the same community were donating "more than a tenth of their whole property" to the cause (LMS 1838:42). Five years later, Livingstone (LMS 1843:202) related a case that he found especially edifying:

I have had a cheering illustration [of progress] in the conduct, upon a late occasion, of the person who guided my wagon into the interior on one of my journeys, for when I paid him eighteen dollars as wages, he immediately laid down twelve of them as his subscription to the Auxillary Missionary Society.

Financial exchange, here, facilitated the reciprocal construction of responsible African subjects and benevolent institutions. The stress on continuous collection, and on shouldering the cost of their own congregations, closely paralleled the "practical pietism" found in British Nonconformist circles at the time.

Also at issue in the small grinding of God's mills was the effort to encourage calculation. Counting—adding up, that is, the margins of profit and loss—enabled accounting, the form of stocktaking that epitomized puritan endeavor. The evangelists associated numeracy with self-control, exactitude, even reason; school arithmetic, for example, was taught mostly in fiscal idiom, the implications of computation being inseparable from the process of commodification itself. Numbers provided an impersonal calculus with which to equate hitherto incomparable sorts of value, pricing them, and permitting "unconditional" convertibility from one to another; echoes, again, of Simmel. Hence the frequent association of religious conversion in "modernizing" contexts with various forms of enumeration, with what Spyer (1996) has termed "conversion to seriality." Quantification was iconic of the kind of standardization and incorporation, the erasure of differences in kind, at the core of cultural colonization. But it was also salient to the expansive logic of evangelical Nonconformism, with its need to measure conquests and tally treasures. The emphasis on numbers cannot be taken to imply a trading of quality for quantity, however, as Simmel (1978:444) might have implied in arguing that the reduction of the former to the latter was an intrinsic feature of monetization. The Protestants, after all, were also preoccupied with the morality of money, with the exchange of riches for priceless virtue. They struggled ceaselessly to reconcile these two dimensions of value. For, just as time always entails space, quantity always entails quality, at least in the lived world (cf. Weiss n.d.:16).

Still, by promoting the commodification of the Tswana world—where, in fact, cattle had long been counted[53]—colonial evangelism spawned a shift from the qualitative to the quantitative as the *dominant* idiom of evaluation. This shift had important consequences for control over the flow of wealth, as men of substance were quick to grasp.

In effecting it, the Nonconformists were helped, and soon outstripped, by the European traders. While these men used monetary values to compute all transactions, they preferred actually to do business by barter (cf. Philip

1828,1:205f.). They "bought" ever larger amounts of local produce wholesale, giving back goods set at well-hiked retail prices, and often extracted additional profit by extending loans (Shillington 1985:221; Livingstone 1940:92). In 1835, just months after setting up shop in Kuruman, Hume's partner, Schoon, told Andrew Smith (1939,1:250) that they had collected "over 400 Rds," adding that they had swapped the items most in demand—clothes—for tobacco. He also reported that their African customers were well able to reckon in cash, and counted with precision. Among populations served by merchants, monetary conventions seem rapidly to have been internalized, and the operations of entrepreneurial gain clearly understood (cf. Parsons 1977:121).

In attempts, later on, to exert an influence over prices and profits, some Tlhaping farmers, on the advice of Chief Mankurwane, would persuade merchants to pay them a minimal rate in cash for their crops (Shillington 1985:222).[54] But coin remained scarce for a long time and struggles to elicit it from European entrepreneurs would go on well into this century in some rural areas (cf. Schapera 1933:649). Storekeepers reaped great benefit from conducting their business by barter, mediated through virtual money. By using goods as token pounds and pence, they also limited the impact of rising cash prices in the Colony on those they paid in the interior. This form of cash-in-kind, as we shall see, was a species of signal currency that had its (inverted) equivalent in Tswana "cattle without legs," or cash-as-kine. Such were the sorts of hybrid media of exchange born of the articulation of previously distinct, incommensurable regimes of value. They expressed the efforts of the different *dramatis personae* to regulate the conversion of wealth in both directions. We return to them below.

While familiarity with the value of money did not always translate into the circulation of cash, it did bear testimony to the growing volume of Tswana production for the market. Most lucrative were the fruits of the hunt. As they gained access to guns, African suppliers became ever more crucial to the highly capitalized colonial trade in feathers and ivory—until overtaxed natural resources gave out (Shillington 1985:24). But agricultural surpluses were also important, especially among the middle and upper peasantry. As we saw in the last chapter, these surpluses were sold, in steadily increasing quantities, to merchants and settlers, permitting the purchase of cattle, farming implements, wagons, and other commodities. With the discovery of diamonds, but before the territory was annexed by Britain in 1871, Tlhaping, Kora, and Griqua took part directly in the new commerce, finding stones and selling them to speculators for "exorbitant prices" in cash, wagons, and livestock (Shillington 1985:38; Holub 1881,1:242). Matthews (1887:94f.) writes that, once this trade had been outlawed, traffic was conducted in an argot in which gems were referred to as "calves."

Although Southern Tswana soon lost all claim to the diamondiferous lands, many remained implicated in the local economy that developed around Kimberley. It soon became apparent that, wherever possible, their profits were being converted into livestock. Indeed, a report in the *Diamond News* in 1873 voiced the worry that, in turning their cash into beasts, blacks were avoiding wage work (Shillington 1985:68). No less a personage than Sir Gordon Sprigg, Prime Minister at the Cape, would reiterate this concern to white audiences he addressed on a tour of the colony in 1878 (see above). "[L]arge troops of cattle and other stock . . . meant idleness," he declared, to cries of "Hear, Hear!"[55] Such anxieties were not altogether baseless. But they focused only on Africans of means, underestimating the impact of class formation and the growing impoverishment of much of the interior. While most resources, even water, now had their price in southern Bechuanaland (Holub 1881,1:231, 246), a high proportion of Tswana were in no position to benefit from new market opportunities. Those with stock and with access to irrigated lands might, with mission encouragement, have supplied the diamond fields. "The poorer classes," however, "who trust[ed] only to 'rain gardens,' [we]re often sadly disappointed."[56] Many had already begun to sell their labor either to rural employers or in the Colony.[57]

It has been said that God punishes mortals by giving them what they want. Recall that Livingstone, in trusting to the Lord, had hoped for something wondrous, like the discovery of gold, to speed the spirit of commerce in South Africa. The evangelists would soon find that Tswana were being drawn into mining and industry more forcefully than they could ever have foreseen. Nor did the terms of their involvement allow for the kind of benevolent self-enhancement envisaged by Christian political economy. Yet the Nonconformists did not, for the most part and for quite a time, see the proletarianization of rural blacks as damaging, either to their own long-term goals or to the welfare of African communities. On the contrary, they tended to welcome the advent of labor migration. Wage work was integral to their civilizing vision.

Labor: Learning to, Earning from

Seek the strays, child of the Makuka,
bring home the human strays;
do as with the cattle you've just sought.
Search for them by telegraph.
Some are heard of in the Cape;
write to the Commissioner of Cape Town
and say, 'Help us seek, we seek people'. . .
Most of them are in Johannesburg.
At Rustenburg women are increasing;
collect the women also, let them come.
Some women have left their husbands,

they've left the men who wooed them;
it's said they went to acquire cupboards . . .
send the chief's Machechele after them,
who know the corners [tunnels] of the towns.
Men stubbornly remain in White areas,
deserting the wives whom they wooed;
women and children worry the aged,
and make their grandfathers cry,
they do not dress, they are destitute.

Kgatla Praise Poem, 1931[58]

Labor was, in many ways, the ultimate commodity in the moral economy of modern Protestantism. By its grace, physical production, long the source of righteous worth for Christians, was enhanced through value added by the market. Diligent wage work had become a model for, and of, the believer's relation to God: it epitomized the voluntary contract and the just reward. It is hardly surprising, then, that the Nonconformists were quick to celebrate the readiness of some Southern Tswana to enter employment at the diamond fields. By doing so, Wookey (1884:304) wrote, the Africans both "enrich[ed] their white neighbours" and "better[ed] their condition." Their willingness, he maintained, was proof of the long-term effects of the civilizing mission. This may have overstated matters somewhat, but it was not altogether wrong. For, as we have seen, behind the unceasing efforts of the colonial evangelists to reform Tswana economy was one aim above all else: to teach the virtue of "honest" industry. The Rev. Lloyd (1895:169), echoing the views of many of his colleagues, lamented the fact that there was "much to encourage idleness in native life, such as the absence of any motive for working." Most Tswana, he added, "are 'independent gentlemen,' both socially and ecclesiastically." If they could be made to submit to wage labor, they might also submit to the will of God. Some evangelists spoke of this often in their long conversation with Southern Tswana—and in such a way as to make the conversation itself into a form of surveillance. Reported Alfred Sharp, a Methodist, "I enquire after their work, have they any or none?, impress upon them that idleness is sin, dissuade them from gossip, and they profit from all this."[59]

The campaign against "native idleness" had pervaded the daily lives of Nonconformist missionaries from the outset. On their stations they took every opportunity to convey the meaning of wage labor—not least, of domestic toil. The Moffats (1951:59), for example, hired three "maidservants" early on. Later, the regular household staff grew to at least five (Price 1956:60). Their efforts were not always successful, however: "If they are put to more work than what may be considered play, [the servants] immediately abandon us, even though nothing but starvation stares them in the face" (Moffat and Moffat 1951:59).

Clearly, money was not enough to persuade these employees of the value of working. Not, in any event, of working for Europeans.

As we shall see in chapter 6, the mission house was itself a microcosm of the gendered and pigmented colonial economy-in-formation; and it would be a prime site for teaching black women and men to toil and to earn their keep.[60] In describing the regime at his station at Chonwane in 1846, Livingstone (1940:92) revealed how much labor was required to maintain it, his own included[61]—and the extent to which it schooled local people in the practical skills of daily life, *sekgoa* style:

> As I write now my hands have the same aching sensation I had when spinning. My mind is often so exhausted by sympathy with the body I cannot write in the evenings. . . . We have a man and his wife as servants, and a girl as a nurse maid. The man is waggon driver and everything else he can do, his wife a servant of all work. These form our establishment. But these are not all we require. Grinding corn, baking, washing etc. are done by calling an assistant from the town. Mrs. L changes these assistants as soon as they have acquired some knowledge of household duties and operations. These supernumeraries are taught reading as well as washing etc. All sleep in their own homes. . . . They are paid in beads, a variety of which costs about 3/-a pound.

The constant change of employees was explicitly designed to allow as many people as possible to toil under the close supervision of Mrs. Livingstone; over the years, an increasing proportion of their wages were paid in cash (Livingstone 1959,2:234). The first Methodists also hired as many Tswana as they could, sustaining a regular staff of about a dozen (WMMS 1823–25:200). Workers were recruited, on most stations, as building assistants and interpreters, and, before long, as teacher and preachers.[62]

Instruction in the nature and benefits of self-possessed labor accentuated the need to recognize the value of time and to maximize it; to render the fruits of paid employment to their rightful owner; to temper immediate desire with discipline; and to pay due attention to longer-term rewards. Work was "proper" only when it involved a voluntary contract between employer and employee, specified terms and conditions, and was remunerated in cash or its equivalents. It is here that the historical specificity of the Nonconformist vision—its rootedness in early nineteenth-century liberal economy—becomes plain. Free labor, the evangelists believed, would deliver the Africans from what the Christians saw, somewhat contradictorily, as both "selfishness" and primitive communism. It was also, of course, the antidote to that other premodern evil, slavery. Livingstone (1974:70f., 88) and other missionaries (e.g., Freeman 1851:261) denounced Transvaal Boers as slaveholders, alleging that they had forced Tswana into servitude on their farms; this, they said, had prevented the blacks from seeking properly paid jobs in the Colony to the south.[63]

By the midcentury, the Nonconformists were drawing attention to the fact that Tswana were "most willing to labor for wages" (Livingstone 1857:46). More sought work, it seems, than the missions could hire—although, by and large, the Africans preferred to toil on their own terms and for their own purposes. The numbers actually employed were quite low in the early years. But, in the 1850s, the eyes of politicians in the Cape Colony, where workers were already in great demand, came to rest on the interior. A letter to the *South African Commercial Advertiser and Cape Town Mail* in 1854[64] noted that there were people who wished to solve the shortage by "break[ing] up the Missionary Institutions and dispers[ing] their inmates." The writer disagreed, however. "The most intelligent and the most experienced capitalists in the neighbourhood of such institutions," he observed, "regarded them as the great depots where labor may be obtained, and as most useful to the colony." All this more than a decade before the birth of the mining industry underscored the role of the evangelists in producing workers.

An incident recounted by Livingstone (1974:88) makes it plain that some Tswana were already journeying "thousands of miles" to the Colony in search of a livelihood by the 1850s. As we saw in the last chapter, increasing numbers were driven to sell their labor by agricultural failure, by the decimation of the game population, and by local processes of class formation; many, also, were drawn by the adventure and by a desire for specific goods (see chapter 5; Schapera 1947:115f.). Despite their espousal of a black yeomanry, the missionaries were not slow to note the positive side of this development: "The old habit of spending three months in hunting is happily coming to an end, through the game having been killed out," enthused Lloyd (1895:168). Man-the-hunter was an even less likely Christian subject than man-the-pastoralist. And if farming was inadequate, this too had compensations. "Of course all peasants are poor," John Moffat wrote, trying to quell his uneasiness about the state of the population around Kuruman in 1874; their salvation must lie in employment.[65] A few years later, Mackenzie (1887,1:30) reported, with more than a hint of approval, that ever more Southern Tswana men, women, and children were traveling to European farms and small towns to find jobs. In pressing his own plan to induce English immigrants to settle alongside African freeholders, thus to stimulate progress in Bechuanaland (*RRI*:294f.), he emphasized the abundant supply of workers who had "learned a higher agriculture" (1887,2:341). Tswana, he opined, were also "unsurpassed as stockherds." While cattle keeping by them on their own account had struck the evangelists as incompatible with a civil existence, it was acceptable as a form of wage labor.

With the mineral revolution, the *axis mundi* of wage labor shifted to the new industrial centers: first to Kimberley, and then, once gold was discovered in 1886, to the Witwatersrand. By then the campaign of the colonial evangelists to persuade Tswana to put their trust in the providence of the market was half a century old. Mackenzie (1887,1:80–81) reproduced a catechism on the subject for his European readers:

> 'But will you explain to me,' I asked [some intelligent natives], 'why it is that if a black man breaks away from his chief, he does not face northward like the white men, but goes southward?'
>
> 'He goes south,' was the immediate answer, 'because he knows he can get work and wages.'

But, in the years immediately after the discovery of diamonds, the laws of supply and demand gave no firm guarantees that work would actually be there when needed. Adequate jobs were *not* always available on demand.[66] The gemstone economy went through several periods of technical and financial crisis before it was consolidated under the control of a few major corporations. The LMS and WMMS had cause to lament the consequences of these fluctuations for Tswana: "[P]aying work is scarce in a country where there is so little European capital," commented John Moffat in 1874, as he surveyed the poverty of many in the Kuruman district.[67] Reports from Kimberley linked the shortage of employment there to the rapid rise of crimes against private property, notable among them being the burgling of traders' stores.[68] Holub's (1881,1:101, 212) account of "day laborers" and "servants" at the diggings in the early 1870s makes it clear that those migrants who did find positions tended to stay between three and six months; long enough, that is, to earn the money for bridewealth cattle or firearms, and perhaps for a few European commodities to take back home to communities in which the objects of *sekgoa* had already made inroads. These men were partial proletarians, working primarily with the intent of converting most of their wages back into the currency of rural production and reproduction (cf. Atkins 1993:29).

In time, the black labor force would grow, although Shillington (1985:125) shows that, between 1878 and 1884, the number of Southern Tswana recruited to the diggings still fluctuated widely. Government statistics indicate that, in addition to those contracted to the mining companies, many were engaged in casual toil (Holub 1881,1:101). This was even more so before the centralization of the industry, which led to underground excavation, tight regulation of the supply and conditions of labor, and closed compounds which drastically restricted black urban social and economic life (Turrell 1982). In any event, by 1884 Wookey (1884:304) claimed, somewhat expansively, that in Bechuanaland "there is scarcely a man, or a boy of any size, who has not been, either to work or for other purposes, to the wonderful diamond mines."

For their part, however, industrial and agrarian employers found the stream of black workers sporadic, uneven in quality, and dear throughout the 1880s. "The Barolongs," reported the Resident Magistrate at Mafeking in 1888, "unfortunately . . . are not a working class" (Great Britain 1889:51). A letter to the *Bechuanaland News* in 1892, signed "Stellalander," chided the government for not doing more to address the "labour question." The region was "teeming with natives" who "[lay] in the locations from year to year" (cf. Atkins 1993:2f., on Natal); unless they could prove that their stock provided a livelihood, these men should be treated as vagrants, regardless of what "negrophilists and missionaries" might think.[69] In point of fact, efforts *were* made to ensure a more reliable supply, both by appealing to desire and by applying pressure. In respect to the former, for example, the Tswana demand for guns and other goods was used blatantly by labor recruiters to lure them into work contracts; one Kgatla ruler, at war with a neighboring chiefdom, is said to have sent a regiment of young men to the mines so that their earnings might be spent on weaponry "for the tribe" (Schapera 1947:25–26; cf. Ramsay 1991:253; Turrell 1982:50).[70] But attraction gave way more and more to coercion during the closing decades of the century—especially when, after the annexation of Griqualand West and southern Bechuanaland, the material dependence of Southern Tswana on the colonial economy was increased: when their political autonomy began to melt away, under pressure from the state and forces set in motion by the evangelists; when, from the mid-1880s, hut tax was imposed. To many capitalists, and to settlers like "Stellalander," however, none of these measures was sufficient or specific enough to resolve the issue. In one regard, at least, they were correct. There is little evidence that taxation succeeded, of itself, in compelling Tswana to seek jobs on a more sustained basis than before; payment was resisted in some areas and collection remained uneven for a long time (Shillington 1985:73f., 180f.).[71] Whatever the demographic realities of the labor supply—or its "quality"—white colonists continued to believe themselves to have a problem.

In the Cape Colony, under whose jurisdiction most Southern Tswana now fell, the government eventually felt moved to address the issue by legislative means. The Glen Grey Act of 1894 linked the granting of land under individual tenure in designated "locations" to the mandatory provision of either tax or wage labor; its architects expressly used growing pressure on commonage (see chapter 3) to combat "African idleness" (Wilson 1971:65).[72] Some observers with close Nonconformist connections condemned the Act: there was no need to force black men to go out in search of work when pay was high enough, asserted Macdonell (1901:370), chair of the South African Native Races Committee.[73] And when it was not, government coercion was rightly resented as unfair. "The need of the hour" was "a free flow of cheap labour." Yet that flow remained irregular. Industrialists, he pointed out, portrayed blacks as "loafers" unless they toiled for whites (p. 372),[74] this being the "oldest argument for slavery" on the part of those unwilling to tolerate the "inconveniences" of a free market. It was true that "native" hands were prone to leaving "capriciously" once they had earned sufficient to acquire cattle for bridewealth (pp.370–71). But, for his part, Macdonell saw a high rate of remuneration as the "greatest civilizing agency" in South Africa,[75] even though it might result, in the short term, in "more wives [and] more cows."

Reports from the Bechuanaland authorities at the turn of the century indicate that, faced with acute land shortage and erosion, and then with the devastating rinderpest pandemic of the mid-1890s, more Tswana sought jobs in industry than they had before; many were employed on the Mafeking-Bulawayo railway. "Nearly all the young people are absent from the villages, at work at the Diamond, or the Gold Fields," Brown reported in 1898, adding that he was "constantly hearing of the money—very often small in amount—that they sent back . . . for the support of parents, or wives and children."[76] While some missionaries were sanguine that this would teach the masses a singular lesson in "the dignity of labor,"[77] others began to express disquiet at the depletion of once populous rural communities. They were saddened, particularly, by the loss of mission-schooled youth: "It is painful to me to hear of the young men and women who have left our Institution to go to Kimberley," Gould wrote from Kuruman, "there either to shovel earth or do mere labourer's work instead of learning some handicraft by which to earn a livelihood."[78] Means should be found to instruct the more "advanced and educated" in the industrial trades, an imperative that would loom large in the Nonconformist effort to redefine their pedagogic role in twentieth-century South Africa (volume 3).

Meanwhile, for most turn-of-the-century Tswana, employment continued to be more a means to specific ends than an induction into a full proletarian existence; this even when their material needs were most pronounced. Thus, for example, the Inspector of Native Locations at Taung complained, in 1908, that men "remained in their Locations the whole year and only went to work when pressed . . . for their Hut Tax" (Cape of Good Hope 1909:32).[79] Once the latter had been secured they returned home again. In better watered areas, where cattle were quite plentiful, migration remained low. "The 'Bathlapin' (sic)," the Inspector went on, "ceases to work as soon as he becomes the owner of a few head of stock." He implied, too, that the Southern Tswana rank and file were still investing, wherever possible, in things of local value, things *setswana,* things outside the market. In this they were quite different from the upper peasantry, whose habits and habitus were increasingly dominated by commodities, cash, and the object-world of *sekgoa.* Only coercion, his annual report hinted broadly, might make these reluctant Africans into proletarians.

While local functionaries and other colonists often argued that "natives" should be forced to work, the Native Affairs Commission of 1903–5 decided otherwise: that the recruitment of wage labor by coercion was unjust and unproductive (South Africa 1905:80–83). The theory that blacks were hopelessly indolent, it said, was belied by the fact that millions were capable of sustaining themselves beyond the market. Favoring a policy of "inducement without compulsion," the Commission recommended (i) that more attention be paid to the interests, safety, and hygiene of migrants, both in the workplace and in transit; (ii) that laws against vagrancy be strictly enforced and unrestricted squatting prohibited; (iii) that priority be given to employing "native women" for "domestic purposes," thus to release men for more "suitable" jobs and, simultaneously, to introduce "higher standards of comfort, cleanliness and order" into urban African home life. Almost in the same breath, it noted that females would be exposed in town to "the danger of moral ruin" (p. 83). But the risk was worth taking.[80] For, if male laborers could reside with their families, it might quell the "spirit of restlessness" that kept them from permanent employment.

This underscores, once again, how thoroughly moralized was the discourse on wage work in industrializing South Africa; not unexpectedly, of course, in a context where labor power was so obviously value to be extracted—and where its disposition was crucial to the shaping of everyday day life for all concerned. To be sure, the effort to sustain its supply on tractable terms, against all resistance, would present itself as a recurrent "problem" for the state and capital throughout the twentieth century. In seeking to resolve it, those concerned had to address the inseparability of the conditions of production from the social reproduction of the workforce. For the Commission, the answer was to gain hold of elusive black proletarians by moving their families,[81] whose well-being was the object of their exertions, securely into the orbit of the white economy. Once there, they might be situated according to its gendered lore: women in housework, men in mining, manufacture, business, the service of the state. As the ethical angst of the Commissioners suggests, this urban-based solution ran counter to the sense that towns were "special places of abode for the white men, who are the governing race" (Cape of Good Hope 1905:68); also, to the prevailing pattern of oscillating migrant labor which brought males, as contract laborers, to the center and relegated females, now subsistence farmers, to the ethnicized countryside (chapter 3).[82] Paying scant heed to the Commission, however, the newly unified South African colonies, no longer subject to the same degree of imperial control after 1910, opted for the migrant model. And it continued to do so ever more systematically, and coercively, as it headed towards the years of high apartheid.

Integral to this struggle over labor was another: a struggle over location and movement—or, more precisely, over the distribution of people in space and, concomitantly, their passage across the social landscape. We have argued that the evangelical effort to reshape agrarian production among Southern Tswana hinged on a redefinition of place and mobility; on persuading "shiftless" populations to root themselves on the land, to enclose their property, and to live, literally, within a private estate. Coming hard on its heels, and persisting for over half a century, the expansionism of the Boers, their territorial nationalism, handed the Africans another kind of lesson: the meaning of margins in modernist geopolitics. As one LMS observer put it (Freeman 1851:261), the tribes of the interior became increasingly "hemmed in" by ethnically assertive strangers who wished to siphon black labor onto their farms. Later, mining companies, too, would seek to confine them, to draw them away from their own terrain and hold them in closed compounds. Annexation and overrule further reduced their room for maneuver: colonial authorities pursued a vigorous politics of "location," fixing "native groups" on scheduled parcels of land near white centers, whence they could be mobilized for work. *Location.* The very term typified the attempt of the state to position blacks on its own topography of production. Not for nothing did the "pass" become South Africa's most infamous icon, rendering Africans legitimate travelers only by decree of a master and in response to the laws of supply and demand.

But the Africans sought to retain a measure of control over the rhythm of their movements across this changing national vista, especially with regard to labor migration. Even when in need, most continued to play off wage employment against agrarian production in an effort to regulate their passage between the two. To a palpable degree, and for a long time, many succeeded. As we have seen, while Southern Tswana often had want of coin and commodities, and often took up wage work, few were entirely captured by the monetary economy. It was precisely this independence, and the self-determination with which they pursued their own values, that made them seem such "restless" spirits to would-be employers. For the latter, it was imperative to convert vagrants into migrants. "Vagrancy," with its connotations of fitful mobility, was used in the criminalization of "homeless," unemployed blacks. So was "squatter," a category which became yet more salient when the Natives Land Act of 1913 formally debarred Africans (outside of the Cape Province) from purchasing or hiring land from whites.[83]

As more and more Southern Tswana journeyed to and from labor centers—particularly after the Land Act—"restlessness" did actually become a way of life for many. Their mobility posed new kinds of dangers to whites who sought to model South Africa on European civil society, imagined here as a landscape of tidy thoroughfares, settled communities, and orderly public spaces. Labor legislation would be directed, for decades to come, toward channeling the flow of this human traffic, a huge undertaking supervised by a burgeoning, byzantine bureaucracy and backed by vigilant policing. Mass transport, critical to the enterprise and capable of yielding vast profits, became highly politicized.[84] For their part, African migrants developed a popular culture rich in idioms of movement, capturing heroic journeys and harrowing exiles by road and rail (cf. Coplan 1994; Auslander 1997). Praise poets in Tswana capitals lamented the loss of these "human strays" (*matimêla abatho*), calling on rulers to seek them out in the "tunnels" of the towns (*dikunyane;* "holes in the side of a pit") and to herd them homeward "by telegraph" (see above).

As this implies, the politics of place and mobility were equally salient to Tswana constructions of South African labor history. In a moving description of the impact of the Land Act on black tenant farmers in the Orange Free State, Plaatje (n.d.:58f.) paints an unforgettable picture of evicted "Israelites," driven hither and thither with their herds in search of somewhere to settle, somewhere to make a livelihood on their own account. He describes an exodus without deliverance, much like that of the fleeing Rolong who encountered the first WMMS missionaries in the same spot a century or so before (n.d.:60):

[A displaced] native farmer had wandered from farm to farm, occasionally getting into trouble for travelling with unknown stock, "across [a white man's] ground without permission," and at times . . . being abused for the crimes of having a black skin and no master. [H]e sold some of his stock along the way, besides losing many which died of cold and starvation; and after thus having lost much of his substance, he eventually worked his way back to Bloemhof with the remainder, sold them for anything they could fetch, and went to work for a digger.

This allegory, one of many, tells of the loss of the stuff of self-determination; of forced entry into the labor market; of the relegation of a man of means to what was now, indeed, a "true" working class. Ironically, his attempted flight from the world of *mmèrèko*, of dependence on wage work, led back to Bloemhof. This was where, after the discovery of diamonds, Southern Tswana were relieved of much of their land by a colonial commission; also where some of them had had their first experience of wage labor.

Plaatje's narrative implies a "moral geography" (Auslander 1993:169f.), a sense of right and wrong in the sociospatial connections among mobility, property, possession, production, place. It was this moral geography that underlay the apprehension with which Southern Tswana regarded wage labor, especially on long contracts that exiled men to urban compounds; that shaped their preference for toil above rather than below ground; that disposed them toward the diamond diggings instead of the goldfields; and so on. Not that all these preferences were mysterious. They were often quite practical. For example, by the early years of the twentieth century, the conditions under which blacks were employed in the Witwatersrand mines were so appalling that African leaders repeatedly petitioned the British authorities to intervene;[85] so appalling, in fact, that the Transvaal government had to take action. But other things were less obvious. Of all workers, Southern Tswana seemed most reluctant to work beneath the earth's surface,[86] and not just because of the physical dangers. They clearly found the mines awesome—in all senses of the word.

Oral testimonies collected from migrants in Mafikeng in the late 1960s indicated that the pit had long been regarded as a predator; that those who toiled in it were reduced, perforce, to "beasts of burden," even "tinned fish" (cf. Alverson 1978:225). The fact that the mine was seen as an alien medium, hazardous to ordinary men, was underlined by its association with snakes;[87] in particular, with the large water serpents (*dinoga tse ditonna;* sometimes, *dinenebu*) that were once the fearful familiars of the mightiest of rain doctors (chapter 2). These creatures were thought to draw lesser mortals to certain death in deep, dark rivers or pools (those "one could not see to the bottom of").[88] Miners made a point of noting that, in the eery netherworld below ground, their feet were always under water (cf. Coplan 1994:130), a discomforting state for Southern Tswana, who, in the past, neither swam nor ate fish. Even in the 1970s, most still shunned the latter, tinned or otherwise, insisting that they were "like snakes," themselves taboo as food. Indeed, the two species share an "unnatural" mode of locomotion. And both inhabit dank, unlit depths—places, that is, closer to the realm of the ancestors than to the bright surfaces of the earth. That they aroused a mix of fear and disgust was observed, way back, by Philip (1828,2:117) and by Livingstone (1857:244), who described what he took to be "remnants of serpent-worship" in Bechuanaland.[89] Schapera's (1971:35) ethnography suggests that the rain serpents of yore often had their pools on bleak hills, whence they sucked moisture from the clouds, making rain amidst clashes of the elements. Snakes, in fact, were channels of elemental transformation. They also made sinuous connections among the living and the dead, yielding superhuman potency to those capable of grasping them (Freeman 1851:279). Like rainmakers, prophets sometimes wielded such amphibious signs of power (see chapter 2). And Zionist healers developed a whole iconography centered on the well (*sediba,* the same word being used for "deep pool") as a font of the Holy Spirit (Comaroff and Comaroff 1992:81f.). The sheer density of these tropes, then, points to the conclusion that the mine epitomized the industrial workplace at its most awesome and otherworldly, its most productive and also its most perilous.

Two summary, interrelated points here. First, this brief excursion into labor history, into the attempt by colonizers of various kinds to make Tswana into proletarians, confirms the general thrust of our argument: that Bechuanaland was undergoing a process of radical class differentiation during the late nineteenth century. Notwithstanding the emergence of an upper and a middle peasantry, the unfolding demographics of prosperity and privation were clear. While some contemporary white observers might have thought otherwise (see above), a burgeoning proportion of the population, described now as a "working class" in colonial media and state narratives,[90] found itself caught up in a cycle of want; that infamous orbit of rural poverty—wherein neither cultivation nor wage work was sufficient to support domestic reproduction—into which blacks in South Africa would be pressed for a century to come (Palmer and Parsons 1977). This, then, is the point: the workings of the colonial economy, of the very mechanism that was intended to "civilize" and enrich them, did more than just eat away at the material lives of most Southern Tswana. It also perverted the effort of the Nonconformist mission to instill in them a commitment to the bourgeois European idea of self-possessed labor, individualistic exertion, and enlightened commerce; to seed among them the persuasive hegemony of the market as sacralized place, practice, and process; to replace their "primitive communism" with a lifestyle centered on the refined domesticity of the nuclear family. Take just one dramatic illustration. In Taung, a white news reporter, obviously distressed, described a particularly tragic inversion of the ideal of prosperous trade.[91] Here desperately hungry women

> had to bring for sale articles such as empty grain bags, chairs, and in some cases crockery which had been bought by them at the stores in times of plenty.

Almost every one of the husbands of these women, it appears, was away working "for a very small wage" at the diamond fields, unable to feed his family at home. And so the process of making a world of domestic civility—a process marked out, at the behest of the mission, by the careful accumulation of commodities— was reversed, undone.

Second, despite their indigence, most ordinary Tswana remained reluctant proletarians, with strong views about the terms on which they were willing to sell their labor. Even when hunger was most rife, and jobs in Kimberley and at the River Diggings scarce, they were unwilling to work in the Transvaal mines, where there was a great demand for labor. Ill-treatment there (van Onselen 1972:486f.; Cape of Good Hope 1909:34; 1907:20), and a lack of rations, made lower paying work at the diamond fields a more worthwhile overall proposition to them.[92] Interestingly, too, while their wealthier compatriots had challenged merchants who traded only in kind, they distrusted earnings paid only in cash; that is, without the provision of food and other everyday necessities. In fact, observers noted repeatedly that migrant movements in and out of the workplace were simply not driven by brute necessity. Among other things, they were tied, as the Inspector of Native Locations said, to the state of cattle holdings; and, as we mentioned earlier, to the desire of Southern Tswana to invest, through various forms of stock exchange, in local social relations and political enterprises. It was precisely this, of course, that many years of colonial evangelism had been designed to transform.

STOCK RESPONSES
Cattle, Currency, and Contests of Value

From a missionary point of view the possession of large herds of cattle is a difficulty, and we should be glad to see the Bechuana sell their cattle and put the proceeds into the Government Savings Bank.

Edwin Lloyd (1895:168)

Cattle are our "Barclay's Bank."[93]

Mhengwa Lecholo, Mafikeng, 1970

By the close of the nineteenth century, Southern Tswana communities had become part of a hybrid world in which markets and migration were more or less prominent; in which money had become a ubiquitous standard of worth; in which coin undercut all other currencies—including cattle. For many, this last development was neither inevitable nor desirable. Turning cattle into cash was not, for them, a neutral act. It entailed the loss of a distinctive form of wealth and endangered their autonomy. Especially older men, whose power and position derived from the control of herds, sought to reverse the melting of everything to money. Even more, as we have said, they tried constantly to convert all gains from the sale of labor or produce into bovines. Their orientation contrasted with that of the rising Christian literati, for whom universalizing media—cash, education, consumer goods—promised entree to a modernist, middle-class commonwealth. Not that these families ceased to invest in beasts; the correspondence among Southern Tswana elites at the time makes frequent mention of transactions in kine. But, as Chief Bathoen of the Ngwaketse wrote in 1909 to Silas Molema in Mafikeng, he would be happy to take payment for an old debt "in cattle or money."[94]

The missionaries shared the sense that livestock enabled Southern Tswana to sustain their independent existence, to resist the invasive reach of Christian political economy. As Willoughby once put it:[95] "[T]he whole cattle-post system has been alien to our work. . . . [T]he frequent absence of the people at their posts has been a break in all their learning, as well as an influence of an alien order." Efforts to persuade men to harness their beasts to agricultural production might have been reasonably successful. But, for the most part, the missionaries had failed to displace, or even decenter, the "alien order," that enduringly resistant "barbarism," inscribed in animals. They had not convinced Tswana to dispense with their far-flung herds or the social relations secured by them. Quite the contrary: in 1881, in Kuruman, "[t]he people [were still] almost all engaged in pastoral pursuits—either being themselves the owners of cattle, or as servicing those who are."[96] What is more, their stock gave the Africans a potent resource—their own cultural expertise—in their dealings with whites. While they complained that merchants consistently used bureaucratic means ("papers") to cheat them, Tlhaping knew they could trump these men in the business of bovines (Mackenzie 1887,1:80). Here, to their obvious satisfaction, they were on home ground; here their own local knowledge gave them a clear edge; here, within the colonial economy, was one domain, one site of struggle, from which they might profit. The corollary? By investing in wealth that served as a hedge against the market, they made themselves less dependent, both conceptually and bodily, from the cycle of earning and spending on which the evangelists had banked to change their everyday lifeways. Through such determinedly ordinary deeds were grand colonizing designs eluded. At least in part. And for a time.

Other whites, in particular those eager to employ black labor, shared the uneasiness of the missionaries over the enduring African preoccupation with cattle. They, too, were aware that stock wealth permitted "natives" some say over the terms on which they engaged with the market economy; hence Sprigg's fighting talk of animals, idleness, and wage work. From the very start, the colonization of Southern Tswana society involved the gradual, deliberate depletion of their herds and the dispossession of their range; it was a process that gathered momentum, exponentially, through the century. Early on, Boer frontiersmen in the Transvaal tried to press Rolong communities into service by plundering their beasts, seizing their fountains, and invading their pastures. Later, in the annexed territory of Griqualand West and then Bechuanaland, settlers impounded "stray" African stock in such numbers that government officials were moved to express concern (Shillington 1985:99f.).[97] "Exorbitant" fees were charged for retrieving these beasts, cash that had to be borrowed from traders at the cost of yet further indebtedness. The Tswana sense that "money eats cattle" (Comaroff and Comaroff 1992:151) probably owes much to such experiences.

Apocalypse, Then: Rinderpest

Several of the evangelists working on the unsettled frontier protested the blatant expropriation of African stock.[98] At the same time, they did not mask their relief when the rinderpest pandemic of 1896 seemed, along with overstocking and deteriorating pasture, to deal a fatal blow to Tswana herds. The Rev. Williams's response was fairly typical:[99]

> If the loss of their stock teaches the people the value of labour it will prove a veritable blessing in disguise. The wealth of the people has always been a hindrance to progress. So long as a man had a cattle post he cared little about anything else. The cattle have gone and larger numbers of the people are away at the Diamond and Gold Fields.

Mary Partridge, a teacher at the LMS school in Molepolole, also saw the hand of providence in the pandemic. If it drove large numbers of men to the mines, she opined, "it would do them good."[100] Yet more auspicious consequences were perceived by Roger Price: "if it only leads to the complete breaking up of the tribes, . . . and the semicommunistic ways of tribal life," rinderpest would be a godsend.[101] Similarly sanguine colleagues elsewhere in southern Africa reported that stricken populations were seeking refuge at mission stations (van Onselen 1972:480f.). Many of the clergy cheered at the apparent demise of pastoralism. A few, though, pondered its implications for the lingering ideal of viable Christian communities in the countryside. While the scourge would probably help the Nonconformist cause, mused Willoughby at Palapye, it had reduced "the capital of the country" by some fifty to sixty percent. And it had deprived Tswana of their protection from drought, of their income from transport riding, and of their main means of locomotion.[102] From his vantage in the more heavily agricultural district around Taung, John Brown saw a revisitation of the days of Moses, when "all the cattle of Egypt died." Wagons and ploughs lay idle, and "women and girls, and in some cases men, [had] been busy picking [at the ground] in the old way" (see chapter 3).[103]

The Tswana experience of rinderpest was unquestionably apocalyptic. Stock owners large and small lost literally millions of beasts (Molema 1966:196f.; cf. van Onselen 1972:484). The herds of the southernmost peoples, who were already land-poor and widely dependent on the labor market, never fully recovered. Some communities in semiarid regions turned to agriculture for the first time, only to be struck by drought and locusts—a veritable rush, indeed, of plagues. "Not since the days of Moses," repeated the Rev. Williams, had there been a cataclysm like this; "*re hedile*," intoned a chorus of local voices, "we are finished!"[104] As we saw in chapter 2, it was not merely the evangelists who found these events to be of biblical moment. There were Tswana seers who also experienced the rinderpest as a time of *kairos*, an instant in which "the intimate connection between things is realized" (Untersteiner 1954, as cited in Petersen 1995:44; see chapter 2).

The impact of the devastation was inseparable from that of wider political and economic processes unfolding at the time; most immediately, from the protracted, sometimes violent, struggle of the Africans to withstand those who would deprive them of their wealth and autonomy.[105] Beasts were often implicated in acts of rebellion along the frontier; they became highly charged objects of contestation on both sides. For example, Burness, a farmer killed with his kin in an uprising in 1898 (*RRI*:290), was the keeper of an official cattle pound beside the Orange River. Such acts of insurrection led to yet further looting and confiscations, much of it in the name of the colonial state. As a result, African herdsmen were wary of European intervention in any matter concerning kine. When government agents sought, somewhat ineptly, to halt the implacable advance of the pandemic by shooting entire herds of Tswana stock,[106] they were met with acute distrust. And disaffection. An effort by the Department of Native Affairs to send a deputation of Africans, several of them indigenous healers, to experiment with herbal cures for the disease only heightened Tlhaping suspicions.[107] Rumors spread that the authorities had introduced the rinderpest to reduce blacks to servitude (van Onselen 1972:487). In the end, some rulers complied with the administration and received compensation; cattle-to-cash once more. Others, like the ruler of the Tlhaping at Phokwane, whose people had a history of resistance, did not. In the confrontation that followed, three white traders were killed and between 150 to 200 Tswana perished (Shillington 1985:235f.).[108] In the Langeberg Reserve to the west, another site of armed struggle, a constable on "rinderpest duty" was also put to death (Cape of Good Hope 1898:67).

Africans in the Cape called the rinderpest *masilangane,* "let us all be equal" (van Onselen 1972:483), a sardonic reference this, no doubt, to its leveling effects and to the power of beasts to make and break people. While the pandemic struck a devastating blow at Tswana, it did little to diminish the value of stock among them. Nor did it dislodge cattle from their place at the heart of the *setswana* world. Nothing of the sort. It enhanced the "bovine mystique" (Ferguson 1985). Exploiting the transport crisis caused by the shortage of live oxen, the upper peasantry began gradually to rebuild their herds—and, with them, the distinctions that comprised their social milieu (see chapter 3). The evidence suggests that their understanding of the economic forces at work was epitomized in the relation of cattle to cash: not only could cash eat cattle, but the replacement of the latter was impossible without the former. The association of beasts with banks became a commonplace, making animals synonymous with financial assets at their most secure (cf. Alverson 1978:124). In the upshot, coin came to be seen as the most fitting recompense for kine (cf. Schapera 1933:649); as we intimated earlier, they were alike special commodities. Both had an "innate" power to equate and translate different sorts of value. And to generate wealth. But they were also different in one respect that no European political economist could have anticipated: their distinctive colors, their racination. Money was associated with the transactions controlled by whites. It was the elusive medium of the trader, the hard-won wage paid to worker, the coercive currency of taxes levied by the state. It was also a highly ambiguous instrument. On one hand, it opened a host of new possibilities, typifying the universalizing culture of the mission and its object-world; and it made thinkable new materialities, new practices, new passions, new identities. Yet, in its refusal to respect particularistic personal identities, it also undermined "traditional" monopolies, eroded patriarchal powers, displaced received forms of relationship—which is why, in part, many Southern Tswana rulers found their authority weakened, the centralization of their chiefdoms giving way, the hegemony of long-standing political and economic arrangements in question (above, p. 162f.). "Money," the Tswana saying goes, "has no owner"; *madi ga a na mong.* In democratizing access to value, it put a great deal of the past at risk, sometimes, it seemed, in the cause of transitory desire. Formerly inalienable, intransitive values might now be drawn into its indiscriminate melting pot. And, in the name of debt, tax collectors could attach Tswana cattle and force men to sell their labor to raise cash.

Government Stock, Live Stocks

In the meantime, many observers—besides the evangelists—were announcing the death of African pastoralism. Somewhat prematurely, it turns out. The *Report of the South African Native Affairs Commission of 1903–5* (South Africa 1905:54), concluded:

> The desire to possess cattle has been in the past a strong incentive to Natives to earn money. Natives have often been heard to say that cattle were their bank and the means of securing their money in a visible and reproductive manner. The destruction of cattle by rinderpest and other cattle plagues has made the investment of money in the manner above stated more difficult. . . . Money is the great medium of business where formerly cattle were used.

The *Report* went on to note that, in order to encourage thrift in Africans, and to ensure the "safe custody" of their earnings in a postpastoral age, they should be encouraged to use government savings banks; this, as the Rev. Lloyd told us, was in keeping with mission opinion. But the matter was not so straightforward. In 1909, a resigned Rev. Williams wrote to his superiors that, to Tswana, cattle were *already* like government stock:[109]

> [T]he Native is very slow to part with his cattle . . . until he has exhausted every other method of supporting life. Too often he will see himself, wife and family growing thin, whilst his cattle are increasing and getting fat, but to buy food with any portion of them is like draining his *life's blood.* On the other hand if he wants a wagon, rifle, ammunition, horse or plough, he will not think twice about buying them even in a time of hunger. These are things which he can handle, see and regard as "property." Food must come from his gardens and if the harvest fails, well he must either work, or if he has grown up boys send them to the mines. . . . His cattle are like Government Stock which no holder will sell for the purpose of living on the Capital unless he is forced to do so. (Emphasis added.)

The reference to "life's blood" is telling. Williams seems to have understood that beasts, here, enabled a particular kind of existence. It was this, for Tswana, that made them capital in the first place. Indeed, any asset that did the same thing might be treated as if it were stock—even, as we shall see, coin. But all too often coin did the opposite, consuming cows and threatening the relations made through them. Ironically, it was referred to in Setswana as *madi*, an anglicism, and a homonym for "blood." But this was blood, or perhaps blood money, in a less sanguine sense. It connoted the alienable essence of the laborer, that part of her or him from which others profited. (Tswana themselves made this plain to us; see J. Comaroff 1985:174.) For cash was often earned in dangerous circumstances, ones that depleted workers and threatened their ability to ensure a future for themselves. As Williams implies, selling cattle under coercive conditions was tantamount to selling lifeblood.

The Rev. Williams went on to say that Christian teaching *had* made inroads into the Tswana reluctance to sell beasts. Many more were now willing to part with cattle when corn was scarce. But prices had fluctuated wildly on local markets: at the time of the rinderpest, a "salted" (disease-resistant) ox had fetched thirty pounds, and during the Boer War returns had remained good. By 1908, however, the finest animal fetched no more than six pounds. No wonder, Williams concluded, apparently contradicting what he had just said, that the "natives" were slow to retail their livestock. Returns on agricultural produce were also erratic. As a result, money was often scarce. Under these conditions, the capacity of kine to serve as the "safe custody" of wealth was underlined. They were a bulwark against the ebb and flow of other, less stable, stores of value. Hence their enhanced mystique. Hence, also, the fact that they were exchanged only against coin or other recognized forms of capital: the wagons, ploughs, and guns which had become the primary means of producing wealth in a receding rural economy. Hence their being likened to "Government stock."

But, and even more importantly, cattle were also shares—live stocks, as it were—in a social community and a moral economy whose reproduction they enabled. While overrule further eroded courtly politics in many Southern Tswana chiefdoms, patronage continued to be secured through the loan of cows; young, educated royals seem, in the early 1900s, to have used their cultural capital to shore up family herds.[110] Fines in local courts were levied in kine, and marriage involved the transfer of animals, well into the late twentieth century (Schapera 1933:639f.; Comaroff and Roberts 1981). Significantly, where bridewealth came to be given in cash payments, the latter was often spoken of as token beasts, "cattle without legs" (Comaroff and Comaroff 1992:148).

Livestock, in sum, were still the medium for making the social connections that, by contrast to more ephemeral contracts, formed and reformed a recognizable social world. These "signal transactions"[111]—in nominal animal currency at a rate well below prevailing prices—distinguished privileged exchanges from ordinary commercial dealings. Legless cattle were a salient anachronism, an "enclave" within the generalizing terms of the market. Counted in cows but paid in coin, they facilitated the give-and-take that made and marked the distinctive qualities of persons and local relations. This notional cash-in-kine was the inverse of the cash-as-kind deployed by merchants to compel Africans to barter at noncompetitive rates. Both virtual currencies served as modes of "surge control" that tried to harness the flow of value, if in opposite directions, by putting a brake on the rapid conversion from one form to another.

It was precisely because they experienced colonization as a loss of control over the production and flow of value that so many Tswana pinned their hopes on cattle in the early twentieth century. In them, it seemed, lay the means for recouping a stock of wealth and, with it, a sense of self-determination. This did not imply an avoidance of money, markets, or wage work. The Africans had been made dependent, to a greater or lesser degree, on the colonial economy; their access to beasts and other goods—not to mention cash—lay increasingly in the sale of their produce and/or their labor. Neither did it imply opposition to Christianity. By the turn of the century, as we have seen, most chiefs had joined the church, and many of their people followed suit, even if they were not, in the main, the pious, conforming converts for which the evangelists had hoped (cf. Schapera 1958; Fripp 1897:520; *RRI*:236f.).

The significant contrast in this world did not lie between Christian and non-Christian. It was between, on one hand, those for whom the values and relations inscribed in cattle remained paramount and, on the other, those more invested in the mainstream economy and society of turn-of-the-century South Africa. Cows, and the ways in which they were used, were the markers of this contrast. Rather than the bearers of a congealed, unchanging tradition, they were the links between two dynamic orders of worth. Thus, even where they served as icons of *setswana*, they were hybrid signs of identity in the here and now; identity that was itself a matter of shifting relations and distinctions.

Remember, in this respect, that stock wealth was not repudiated by those of more modernist bent; as we said in chapter 3, they tended to treat it like other forms of capital in a world of mercantilism, commerce, and commodities. It was they—the educated, fairly well-off children of old elites, the upper peasantry, and the petite bourgeoisie cultivated by the mission—who were heirs to the liberal vision of the early evangelists. Others, less able to ride the contradictions of colonial political economy and Protestant modernism, remained marginal to the conventions and the cultural practices of the marketplace. They sought to garner what they could of its wealth,[112] and to invest it in the social and material assets they knew and appreciated. This was to be an enduring strategy, visible even as the forces of global capital reshaped the post-apartheid southern African periphery in the late twentieth century. In August 1995, the *Gaming Gazette* of the Sun International Corporation carried the story of a man, apparently of modest means, from Ramotswa in Botswana. He had hit the jackpot on a slot machine at the Gaborone Sun hotel. Ralinki, his given name, would use his winnings to buy beasts. "In Botswana," he explained, "cattle are seen as a form of wealth, and it is traditional to have as many cattle as possible to pass on to your sons."[113]

REPRISE

We have moved, over the past two chapters, from the early evangelical campaign to effect an agrarian revolution, a new African genesis in Bechuanaland, to the impact on Southern Tswana of Christian—and then, more broadly, colonial—political economy.

While it was seldom narrated or explicated as such, a distinctive regime of value, an ideology at once ethical and economic, suffused the contemporary Nonconformist religious imagination. It also animated the modernist Protestant understanding of civilization and conversion. Aligned with bourgeois verities—although never completely, and never their mere creature—this ideology presumed the indivisibility of worldly endeavor from spiritual grace, giving a practical bent to the everyday work of redemption. It joined liberation to labor, salvation to saving, and good to goods; its sense of worth was vested, in important respects, in the commodity. For men like Moffat and Mackenzie, Hodgson and Broadbent, the circulation of manufactures was a means of disseminating Christian knowledge. Commerce, they believed, carried the truth across the globe in a digestible, consumable form. Despite their ambivalence toward mammon—and the fact that they constantly ran up against the two-facedness of coin—money and markets featured centrally in the effort to draw African societies into the hegemonic circle of European civility.

Of course, those African societies, replete with their own hegemonies and civilities, were home to rather different ideas of wealth and worth, of persons and objects. It goes without saying that their encounter with divers, often squabbling European colonizers—itself a diffuse and contradictory experience—set in motion a highly complex set of processes. For, far from merely bowing to missionaries or merchants, settlers or statesmen, their actions and reactions took on an autonomy, a historical force, all their own. And they had a counter-impact, both direct and indirect, on those who invaded their world, sometimes subverting imperial ambitions, sometimes appropriating them to their own purposes, sometimes abetting them, sometimes accommodating to them. Large numbers suffered wounding poverty, and occasionally brute violence, along the way; a proportion benefited greatly, according to their own lights; many found a middle course, hybridizing the habitus by raiding the world of markets and money and taking the spoils—sometimes the spoiled—to refashion their material lives.

Two things follow from all this.

The first is that, as we began to show in volume 1 and will demonstrate further, the encounter undermined the sureties of the civilizing mission, decentering the Christians and altering their own life-world. It was also to be implicated in the remaking of metropolitan Britain, then itself very much under construction.

The second is that the transformation of Southern Tswana economy and society departed from the Nonconformist scenario—from its great expectations, its grand narrative of history in the making—in some quite unexpected ways. At one level, to be sure, the LMS and the WMMS were successful in their quest. Even if they never actually created the yeomanry of which they dreamed, even if their agrarian revolution yielded a harvest of hunger, even if they did not persuade Tswana to plough in straight lines, they *did* alter African agriculture, changing its technology, its politics of time and tribute, its social stratification, its gendered division of labor. Even more, in ushering the Africans into a world of money, manufactures, and wage work—into, as we said, the hegemonic circle of European modernity—the evangelists *did* make advances in their avowed undertaking to colonize the consciousness of the heathen; to effect, as they put it, a "revolution in . . . habits." It was Molema (1920:119), after all, a key voice of the Southern Tswana bourgeoisie in the early twentieth century, who deemed the plough to have been the prime instrument in "the civilization of the Bantu."

But the effort to colonize Southern Tswana consciousness, like the campaign to colonize their agrarian economy, was never a straightforward affair. Nor did it affect all alike.[114] As we said in volume 1, hegemony—the taken for granted, naturalized practices that command any cultural field, empowering without appearing to do so, seeming to transcend historical time and human agency—is a matter of form rather than content. Over the course of the nineteenth century, all Southern Tswana were drawn into the net cast by the commodity *form:* all came to partake of relations and transactions involving money and manufactures, whether as wage earners, as consumers, as the sellers of produce, as taxpayers. Even poverty came to be perceived, in part, as a lack of cash, an incapacity to meet levies or pay school fees or, *in extremis,* to buy processed food. At the same time, the ideological disposition of Tswana toward coin and things European varied a great deal, being mediated, as we have seen, by the stark sociology of class formation and social fragmentation. Indeed, cash and cows, metonyms each of an order of values, were the prime tropes in a struggle over means and ends along the frontiers of an expanding colonial society.

They were not, however, binary points on a dualistic colonial map, a map constituted of just two sets of protagonists (European colonizer and Tswana colonized), two cultures (modernist *sekgoa* and traditionalist *setswana*), two political economies (colonial capitalism and the noncapitalist countryside). As ideological constructs, rather, they were icons of contrast and contestation in a world in which white and black were locked in indivisible embrace—but in which racial politics cut an ever deeper chasm between them. The contents of, and opposition between, *setswana* and *sekgoa* might have been evanescent, permeable, historically sensitive; just as, along the frontier, cleavages of color were constantly compromised and breached. But, as has often been said, the racination of colonial power—and at the edges of empire, of social class—has long represented itself in the imaginative argot of opposition. In South Africa this was especially marked. Not only was its cultural cartography mapped onto the axes of radical difference brought from Europe in the late eighteenth and early nineteenth centuries (*RRI*:chap. 3). Here, in the wake of the mineral revolution, the state, abetted by self-styled "capitalists," openly committed itself to the creation of a *native* working class. It would seem overdetermined then, that those who felt disempowered should have responded by creating their own tropes of contrast and difference. This, patently, was not the only riposte offered by Southern Tswana to the European challenge. But it was one way in which many of them sought to regain mastery, conceptual and material, over an increasingly refractory world.

One last point. It was not, of course, just the colonial evangelists who drew Southern Tswana into the commodity economy. Their quotidian actions, however—their exercises in penny capitalism and missionary monopoly—laid the ground for the entry of many Africans, however hesitant and experimental and partial, into the marketplace. Southern Tswana, as we have seen, sought out the objects and the currencies of imperial Britain long before they were coerced into wage work, long before taxation was imposed, long before overrule. This reprises one of our old themes: that ours is not, by any means, purely a narrative of domination. Nor, primarily, a tale of large visions and heroic gestures and epochal forces. It is, to paraphrase Njabulo Ndebele (1991), a story of life unfolding in the lower case. Of ordinary people in rather extraordinary times. Of their senses and sentiments; of their curiosities, fears, desires; of their notions of beauty and disfigurement. Of their will, finally, to make livable lives.

*****

As we have intimated throughout, the Nonconformist effort to revolutionize production, to introduce money and commerce, and to essay the virtues of self-possessed labor were only one side of the story. The other lay in the parallel attempt to transform indigenous patterns of consumption. It, too, had a palpable impact on the character of everyday life, engendering, simultaneously, new constraints and new sites for creative self-expression. Also for competition and resistance.

FIVE

FASHIONING THE COLONIAL SUBJECT

The Empire's Old Clothes

Christianity does not seem to be looked on [by the Bechuana] as a life to be lived, but rather as a garment to be worn, which may be put on or taken off as the occasion requires.

LMS, South Africa Reports, 1914[1]

I N SEEKING TO reconstruct the agrarian economies of Bechuanaland, the colonial evangelists might have conjoined cultivation to Christianity, the Bible to the plough. But they did not privilege production above all else. As we have stressed throughout, they set their sights on *total* transformation: on altering modes of exchange and consumption at the same time; on making subjects by means of objects; on "increasing artificial wants" in order to persuade Tswana of the benefits to be had by cultivating themselves and their land in a Christian manner (*RRI*:270). In this respect, the grand tautology of the Protestant Ethic gave an elegant circularity to their vision. Proper, propertied, prosperous agriculture and self-possessed labor might seed the Christian spirit. But prosperity was itself the reward of a pious heart and a disciplined body. Both—prosperity and piety—were therefore to be enjoyed, and to be measured, in sober, not too conspicuous consumption.

We move on, then, to the efforts of the LMS and WMMS to recast Tswana patterns of consumption. This the clerics took to be a task at once lofty and mundane. Their divine duty, as they saw it, was to elevate the soul by overdetermining the ordinary, to nurture the spiritual by addressing the physicality of everyday life.

It is hardly necessary to point out that consumption, as an idea and a species of activity, has to be understood here in its nineteenth-century British sense. As we saw in the previous chapter, there was a widespread faith in the positive attributes of the market, especially in its capacity to convert differences among objects and abilities, wants and needs, into a single order of negotiable values. This integrative function lay, of course, in the exchange of consumer goods and services through the standardizing medium of money. By its graces the social order was animated and shaped: an ethos of enterprise was induced in right-minded people; persons of energy and discipline were rewarded; the well-off were separated from the poor, and the various classes and estates found their proper level in the world. No wonder, in this light, that the civilizing mission was founded on the conviction that commodities and commerce might shape new desires, new exertions, new forms of wealth, even a new society (see Philip 1828,1:241f.); that civilization was to be promoted by the encouragement of discerning consumption, through which Africans would learn to want and use objects of European provenance in a refined Christian manner; that, by being drawn into the workings of the market, would-be converts might develop a healthily competitive urge to fashion novel identities.

In this respect, the evangelists in South Africa shared one thing with some other early European colonizers: an impulse not merely to make non-Western peoples want Western objects (Sahlins 1989), but to have them use those objects in specific ways. In many places across the expanding eighteenth- and nineteenth-century world, imperialists and their mercantile associates tried to conquer by implanting new *cultures* of consumption. Over the short and medium terms at least, they often focused less on extracting labor, raw materials, or exotic goods than on promoting trade that might instill needs which only they could satisfy, desires to which only they could cater, signs and values over whose flow they exercised control. The idea that cultures are (re)constructed through consumption is no mere figment of the postmodern or postindustrial imagination, as some have said (Baudrillard 1973; cf. Appadurai 1993). It is as old, as global, as capitalism itself.

A general point here: it may be argued that, over the longer run as well, early modern European empires were as much fashioned as forged or fought for (cf. E. Wilson 1985:14). As worlds both imagined and realized, they were built not merely on the violence of extraction, not just by brute force, bureaucratic fiat, or bodily exploitation. They also relied heavily on the circulation of stylized objects, on disseminating desire, on manufacturing demand, on conjuring up dependencies. All of which conduced to a form of bondage, of conquest by consumption, that tied peripheries to centers by potent, if barely visible,

219

threads and passions. Indeed, the banality of imperialism, the mundanities that made it so ineffably real, ought not to be underestimated. Cultural revolutions, not least those set in train by European colonization, usually root(ed) themselves on modest terrain, in simple acts of fabrication, use, exchange. Even the most elaborate social formations arise from such quotidian acts. Weber and Marx understood this well, to be sure. That is why the latter vested his mature account of capitalism in the unobtrusive career of the commodity, that "very queer thing" (1967,1:71) whose workaday production, distribution, and consumption built the contours of an epoch, a whole world.

But not all objects, nor all exchanges, are born equal in history; nor are they borne equally across the globe. For the colonial evangelists in South Africa, the most crucial realm of enlightened consumption hinged on the human form. It was on the body that the commodity came into physical contact with, and enclosed, the self. To a nineteenth-century religious sensibility—keenly attuned as it was to the moral, theological, even cosmogonic significance of cloaking the revealed anatomy—the treatment of the domesticated physique was an everyday sacrament. In cleaning it, housing it, curing it, and clothing it lay the very essence of civility. In this and the coming chapters, we examine these processes and their place in the colonial encounter. We begin, now, with the effort of the Protestant mission to cover African "nakedness": to re-dress the savagery of Tswana by dressing them in European fashions, by making them receptive to the ethics and aesthetics of refined attire, and by insinuating in them a newly embodied sense of self-worth, taste, and personhood.

Like consumption, "fashion" also had a wide fan of resonances in the contemporary European imagination. Not only did it epitomize the capacity of the commodity to envelop the self, to insert a culturally legible screen between human beings and the world. It insisted, too, on "pure contemporaneity" (Faurschou 1990:235; Simmel 1904, repr. 1971:296) *and* constant movement (E. Wilson 1985:3), situating those who kept up with the styles of the moment in the cosmopolitan here and now; those who did not, by contrast, were rendered "out of date," provincial, parochial. What is more, the very idea of fashion affirmed the modernist assumption that identity was something apart from one's person; something to be produced, purchased, possessed; something that had continually to be "put on" and "shown off" (Bowlby 1985:27–28; see J. Williamson 1992:106).[2] This rendered clothing the manufactured good *par excellence.* Hence its centrality in colonial evangelism: it made the "native" body a terrain on which the battle for selfhood was to be fought, on which personal identity was to be re-formed, re-placed, re-inhabited. At the same time, the Nonconformists in South Africa would be caught in a bind: on one hand, they were to appeal to the modernist potential of fashion to alter Tswana sensibilities, to individuate them; on the other, their stress on unaltering verities drew them to the "traditional" (unfashionable?) value of sober sameness and uniformity. The sartorial adventures of the mission did not occur *in vacuo*. They were caught up in the more general British effort to incorporate African communities into a global economy of goods and signs; this itself being a critical dimension of the rise of capitalism—which, Macfarlane (1987:173–74, after Weber) reminds us, had long been intimately tied to "the massive growth of the English cloth industry" (cf. Schneider 1989:180f.). The evangelists themselves, as we know, sometimes invoked the commercial interests of Great Britain in speaking of their own objectives. Livingstone (1857:720), for example, once said: "I have a twofold object in view, and believe that, by guiding our missionary labors so as to benefit our own country, we shall therefore more effectively and permanently benefit the heathen."

This "twofold object" was to be sustained for much of the century. McCracken (1977:31) cites an anonymous letter to the *Church of Scotland Missionary Record* which, in 1876, argued that colonial evangelism was "a grand outlying business investment." In making "savage men . . . realize their wants and needs, and thus awaken[ing] in them *healthful tastes*," asserted the writer, the missions were a palpably positive, profitable force "in our markets." One historian of religion has recently gone so far as to argue that there was a "clear parallel," perhaps even a symbiosis, between the great missionary societies and the magnates of Manchester, the former wishing to convert the world, the latter to clothe it (Helmstadter 1992:9).

But the Nonconformists were not simply seeking to dress up British mercantile interests in pious clichés. Their campaign to clothe Tswana in European manufactures—like all their interventions into colonial commerce—were intended to effect, as John Philip said, a "revolution in the habits" of the Africans (see above, chapter 3). Historically speaking, these exertions were no less significant for the fact that they focused on fashion and the aesthetics of embodiment rather than on the brute materialities of political economy; in any case, as we just said, cloth and capitalism were deeply imbricated in one another. Nor were they merely a representation, an outward expression, of a more "real" history being made by others elsewhere. The cultural exchanges that took place between Southern Tswana and the missionaries began, on their own account, to generate a new economy; an economy at once material and moral, social and symbolic, stylistic and sensuous. Both the Europeans and the Africans—and the traders, adventurers, and brokers of various backgrounds who plied the spaces between—invested a great deal in the objects fabricated by, and passed among, them. They encoded, in compact form, the structure of a world-in-the-making.

They were also to tell a story full of surprises, of mischievousness and misapprehension and misgiving. This chapter of the story recalls how many Tswana refused at first to "buy in" to the dictates and dress codes of the mission; how the evangelists themselves began to don garments not unlike those they denounced; how the fashioning of the South African frontier was implicated both in the "improvement" of the uncouth at home and in the development of the British idea of charity; how, in Bechuanaland, the import of Western styles gradually gave rise to parodic experiments in synthetic design; how, in time, these styles played into the making and marking of new social classes, new patterns of distinction, which ruptured existing communities of signs; how, despite their faith in the Gospels of Jesus and Adam Smith, the Christians were to learn that commerce and civility did not always go hand in glove; how commodities rarely produced converts, although they converted people to the global order of goods; how, over the longer run, Tswana self-presentation was altered in a colonial order that fashioned men into migrant laborers and led women to adopt the ethnicized "folk" costume of the countryside. All of which conduces to one conclusion: that the struggles over the way in which Tswana bodies were to be clothed and presented—struggles at once political, moral, aesthetic—were not just metonymic of colonialism. They were a crucial site in the battle of wills and deeds, the dialectic of means and ends, that shaped the encounter between Europeans and Africans. And transformed both in the process.

THE HEATHEN BODY

Clothes, as despicable as we think them, are so unspeakably significant.
Clothes . . . are Emblematic. . . . On the other hand, all Emblematic things
are properly Clothes, thought-woven or hand-woven: must not the Imagi-
nation weave Garments, visible Bodies, wherein the else invisible creations
and inspirations of our Reason are, like Spirits, revealed, and first become
all-powerful[?]. . . . Nay, if you consider it, what is man himself, and his
whole terrestrial Life, but an Emblem; a . . . visible Garment for that
divine Me of his, cast hither . . . down from Heaven?

Professor Teufelsdröckh, *Sartor Resartus*
(Thomas Carlyle [1834] 1920:62)

Durkheim (1947:115–16) observed long ago that the "world of representations" etched on the human body holds a special salience. Clothing, as "social skin" (T. Turner 1980), at once constructs subjects and contexts everywhere. The early evangelists to South Africa were from a society in which distinctions of dress had long been crucial in the work of "self fashioning" (Greenblatt 1980; Veblen 1934). Carlyle (1920) might have mocked nineteenth-century German logicians in his *Sartor Resartus*, with its pious parody of "the Philosophy of Clothes."[3] But the last laugh was on him. For his ironic defense of the sacredness of the sartorial, of the "Moral Teacher" as "Metaphysical Tailor" (p. 260), revealed a closeted fact: that while he, the cynical Carlyle, might have played with the bare truth, Christian cultures put clothedness next to godliness. To wit, it was easier for a camel to pass through the eye of a needle than for the improperly clad to enter the Kingdom of Heaven. This was to be amply affirmed by the LMS and WMMS missions among Southern Tswana.

A tension between inner and outer verities, between the enterprise of spirit and things of the sensuous world, lay at the core of the civilizing mission from the start. It would never be fully resolved. Clothes epitomized this conflict. On one hand, they were thought to be both an effective means of working on the self and a fitting medium for signaling its interior improvement; the evangelists, who took for granted the "impressionability" of Africans (Willoughby 1923:255), believed strongly in the capacity of proper dress to work profound changes in their sentiments and conduct.[4] Yet, on the other hand, as John Wesley (1986:261) had famously pointed out, raiments were the stuff of the flesh, of pride, vanity, lust, and anger.[5] Even more, fashion was "the mistress of fools," seducing them through the "desire of the eyes" to be gratified only by constant novelty (pp. 524–25, 235). Unless worn in such a way as to give evidence of moral awakening that was more than skin-deep, attire remained a mere overlay. Thus, while it could serve as the visible outer wear of a transformed soul, of the "divine Me," it might also be no more than a veneer. Worse yet, a deception.[6] At their most pessimistic, the Nonconformists used the sartorial to signify the superficiality of African Christianity as a whole. In a fit of disgust, for example, Robert Moffat (1842:285; *RRI*:237) once accused Tlhaping of treating the Word like an "old and ragged garment." Several decades later, as we noted under the title of this chapter, one of his successors at Kuruman complained that, to Southern Tswana, Protestantism was like a "garment to be worn, which may be put on and taken off as the occasion requires."[7]

The concern with dress pervaded both the poetics and the practices of the colonial evangelists in South Africa throughout the century. Often it revealed their failure to effect the simultaneous cultivation of body and soul, or even to impress their spiritual point on the Africans. Take, for instance, a dialogue recorded by a Lutheran cleric among the Pedi at Lydenburg in the Transvaal in 1875 (Delius 1984:32):

> *Evangelist:* The missionaries are like the men who give food to the hungry and clothing to the naked. But be warned: if you do not strive for the dress of baptism in earnest and through prayer, you will have to bear the burden of a further profound sin.
> *Native:* Why don't the missionaries bring me this clothing?

This kind of reaction confirmed the European view that Africans reduced "all spiritual things" to the crass and the carnal (Broadbent 1865:178). More significantly, by (deliberately?) misreading the metaphor of the missionary, the "native" riposte frustrated its ideological intent; that is, to press a connection between the clothed body and the converted soul. Such attempts to force analogic associations—thereby to address nascent contradictions in the Christian enterprise—often foundered amidst problems of translation and discontinuities of meaning. The cultural borderland between colonizer and colonized was a terrain of enigma and ambiguity even at the best of times. Still, the evidence suggests that many Southern Tswana *were* ready to acknowledge the ritual resonance of costume. But they did so from a perspective of their own; one that gave expression to a somewhat different understanding of the colonial encounter. As Tswana read them, the evangelists' gestures with clothes were irredeemably pragmatic and embodied.

These gestures began, and were at first frankly obsessed, with the covering of African "nakedness." A complex trope in this context, "nakedness" did *not* proclaim, to the evangelists, either savage innocence or nude nobility.[8] It evoked degeneracy and disorder, the wild and the wanton, dirt and contagion—all familiar signs and ciphers in European conceptions of the continent. Robert Moffat (1842:287), like many in the mission community, felt the danger posed by the rampant heathen body to the delicate order of relations built up along the evangelical frontier:

> As many men and women as pleased might come into our hut, leaving us not room even to turn ourselves, and making every thing they touched the colour of their greasy red attire. . . . They would keep the housewife a perfect prisoner in a suffocating atmosphere, almost intolerable.

No effort is made, in this uncomfortable passage, to disguise the distaste felt for the African intruders who breached the bounds of domestic privacy and propriety.

Moffat's prose here is not without precedent. The image of the "greasy native," oiled and unwashed, appeared in early Dutch accounts of the Khoisan peoples and in the texts of late eighteenth-century travelers, anatomists, and literati (*RRI*:104); for example, in his *Laocoön* ([1766] 1984:132–33), Gotthold Lessing, citing *The Connoisseur* (Chesterfield 1761:161),[9] a contemporary English weekly, suggested that the "dirtiness" of "the Hottentots," their "ugliness" and the "disgust and loathing" awakened in Europeans, derived from their perverse corporeal aesthetics—not least from their habit of "covering the whole body . . . with a layer of goat's fat, . . . [and] the hair . . . with grease."[10] By the mid nineteenth century this image, this figure of the "greasy native," had gained wide currency in popular literature.[11] The term itself probably arose from the use, especially in the hottest and driest regions, of animal lard and butter as a moisturizing cosmetic; the naturalist Burchell (1824,2:553), in fact, explained the practice as a necessary measure "to protect . . . skin from the . . . parching air." In much of southern and eastern Africa a gleaming skin was also seen to radiate beauty and status.[12] And sensuous delight: according to Somerville (1979:143), the Tlhaping ruler was worried that the missionaries would stop his people from smearing their bodies with cosmetic fat—and thereby "rob us of the greatest pleasure we have in the world."

But, to the evangelists if not to all Europeans,[13] even the epithet—"greasy native"—carried prurient, lascivious connotations. It suggested stickiness, a body that refused to separate itself from the world, leaving red, "greasy marks upon everything" (Religious Tract Society n.d.:85). Little could have been further from the contained, inward-turning person of the Protestant ideal, a self "discreet" because "discrete." As we shall see shortly, in the threat of ruddy pollution, of uncouth substances invading bounded beings and spaces, lay the very essence of the Nonconformists' notion of disease. It menaced the mission, always liable to undo its islands of order, to return it to the wilderness.

The bogey of bestial bodies was firmly rooted in the British imperial imagination. First the Irish, then Native Americans, then Africans had been portrayed as dirty primitives garbed in animal skins (Muldoon 1975). Thus, in his now much-quoted description of a "Bushman" who had "been exhibited about England for some years," Charles Dickens ([1853] 1908b:229; see also n. 11) drew particular attention to "his festering bundle of hides, . . . his filth and his antipathy to water, and his straddled legs, and his odious eyes shaded by his brutal hand." Nunokawa (1991:149) comments that, in this text, "the body itself composes the spectacle that inhabits the dark landscape of Africa." True. But, as in Ireland and in America before, the trope of embodied savagery here was yet more finely tuned to the tenor of its times.

In the imagery of the Nonconformist mission, the "lubricated wild man of the [African] desert" stood opposed to the "clean, comfortable and well-dressed believer," as did "filthy" animal fat and hides to the "cotton and woollen manufactures" of Europe (Hughes 1841:523). Most of the evangelists, remember, came from parts of Britain where the textile industry predominated. Their dreams of dressing the naked heathen in refined Christian garb were fashioned accordingly. As a sometime piecer in a mill, Livingstone (1857:291, 720) scanned the countryside of the dark continent with an eye to growing cotton and to introducing "Manchester goods"—as if this would harvest civil, clothed persons. At first, few difficulties were anticipated: the evangelists simply assumed that the Africans would jump at the chance to wear "proper" attire. Indeed, while Moffat (1842:348) could understand why Tswana might initially refuse the Gospel, he thought it only "natural" that they would adopt Western dress—"for their own comfort and convenience."

But such appeals to practical reason ignore their own cultural and moral provenance. Rybczynski (1986:21f.) notes that "comfort," far from describing an autonomic physical state, was a construct born of the eighteenth-century bourgeois experience of domestic order, civility, and amenity. Of course, *all* the assumptions about physicality and clothing made, respectively, by the missionaries and the Tswana arose out of historically specific, often clashing, cultural milieus. And they were implicated in a history of the senses in which very different "structures of feeling" ran up against one another. Each was located in a body attuned to the sensation of a particular mode of attiring and presenting itself; to a particular ensemble of postures and gestures, modulated by gender and age and status, that constituted a specific sort of being-in-the-world.

Thus, to the Nonconformists, on whose bodies only refined fabrics and manufactured textiles felt proper, skin garments were not clothing at all; leather was the issue of the wilderness, unwoven, ill-fitting, and immodest. Early on, it is true, John Philip wrote of Tswana "elegance" and the "neatness" of their dress (LMS 1828). But, in evangelical circles, this view seems to have been unusual and short-lived. Much more common was Robert Moffat's (1842:348) opinion. "Strictly speaking," he once admitted, Tswana were "neither naked nor obscene in their attire." Nevertheless, he described their scanty dress as "disgusting," a term of vehement, almost physical aversion. To underscore his point he put into the mouth of a heathen chief words he apparently could not bring himself to utter (1842:503): "We," said the unnamed ruler, "are like the game of the desert." And like game, it is implied, bereft of any sense of cultural refinement. Or shame.

It is to be stressed, in this respect, that the colonial evangelists were themselves heirs to a moralistic language that had long waxed eloquent on the issue of shame and modesty. The frequent irruption of corporeal images in staid mission prose suggests a preoccupation with the erotic.[14] It also lends credence to the claim that, in order to extract power from the repressed body, modern Protestantism has had constantly to evoke it (Foucault 1978:115f.). A metaphysical battle waged within each beleaguered believer as Puritan preachers made him or her graphically aware of carnal urges to be overcome. E. P. Thompson (1963:365ff.) offers stark evidence of the emotional tone of British Revivalism, of the way in which it harnessed a heightened sensuality to the rigors of self-discipline.

It is hardly surprising, then, that we find traces of the same thing in the mission fields of the nineteenth century. We saw, for instance, how the Word was meant to "melt the flinty hearts" of Tswana, to bring forth penitent, passionate tears from their eyes, to "wash away all the red paint from their bodies" (*RRI*:214). Again redness and rudeness were symbolically fused, this time also with body paint; the daubed physique invoked a brace of associations, from the "rouge" of Western female depravity to "Red" Indian warpaint. (Decorating the skin was, after all, a basic Judaeo-Christian taboo.) That these symbolic associations were driven by prior European images of scarlet sexuality, rather than by the perceptual logic of the color spectrum, seems evident. For the ocher used in vernacular adornment[15] was of a terra-cotta hue; it may not even have appeared "red" in British eyes. Note also that, in the vision of revelation and purification presented here—of melting hearts and washed bodies—inner and outer transformation go together. Both were to be effected by the sheer power of spiritual emotion.

In order to account for those flinty hearts and unwashed skins, for the alleged immodesty of Africans, early evangelists tended to look to diabolical intervention. If satanic reverses were to blame for the bodily state of Southern Tswana, it followed that the latter had immediately to be made aware of their brazen nakedness, of their wanton sinfulness, and of the embrace of the devil. And if they were to be saved, to become vessels of the Holy Spirit, their corporeality had to be reconstructed: confined, channeled, turned inward, and invested with self-consciousness and a sense of shame. Western clothing, the social skin of civility, was to be both a sign and an instrument of this metamorphosis. In time, it would also be advocated as conducive to good health. During the late 1840s, David Livingstone (1961:129) declared, with medical authority, that conditions like inflammation of the bowels, rheumatism, and heart disease declined with the adoption of "decent dress." As we shall see in chapter 7, this opinion was informed by the tenets of humoral medicine. But it also revealed the connection between "indecency," dirt, and contagion in the physical culture of early evangelism.

To European and African alike, then, Western attire would become the most distinctive mark of association with the mission (cf. Etherington 1978:116), a fact graphically conveyed to the British public in pictures sent from the field. Return once more to our illustration of Robert Moffat ministering to the "abandoned mother" (*RRI*:111). In the engraving, the evangelist's black assistant, a male convert, stands attentively behind his mentor, replicating his dress in almost every detail. The heathen, on the other hand, lies in tatters in the bush, her breasts flagrantly bare. Absent altogether from the scene is the mission wife, who, as it would turn out, was to take the lead in the campaign to clothe Tswana in the European fashion.

African Adornment

It is difficult to know what sense Tswana could have made of the idea of nakedness brought to Africa by the Christians. Apart from all else, it bore with it a particular conception of bodily being, nature, and culture—and a great deal of biblical baggage besides.[16] Notwithstanding our own naturalistic assumptions, both nakedness and nudity are historically specific tropes: they have varied widely in their referents and rectitudes, even in recent Western usage. It may be true, as Beidelman (1968:115f.) says, that, in most societies—even those "not much disposed toward clothing" (p. 130)—people suffer shame and disrespect as a result of being unclad ("naked") in inappropriate circumstances (see n. 40);

also, that states of prescribed undress ("nudity") may be a potent element in some rites, having the capacity to dissolve and remake social status.[17] But that is not the same as saying that either "nakedness" or "nudity" is a transcultural construct. John Hay (n.d.), for one, argues that the nude did not figure in classical Chinese representation because "the body" was not understood as a finite object apart from the clothing and drapery that configured its presence in the world. There was, so to speak, no bare truth to be revealed; interestingly, Perniola (1989:258–59) shows that, in fifteenth-and sixteenth-century Europe, anatomical drawings pictured the body itself as a garment, its skin folded back like fabric. In South Africa, what the missionaries took to be indecent exposure was anything but that in indigenous eyes. Although Tswana dress and grooming might have seemed scanty by European standards, they conveyed, as they tend to everywhere, subtle distinctions of gender, age, social standing, and identity. In their outward "nakedness," the Africans went about fully clothed.

A number of contrasts between European and Tswana (un)dress were especially unsettling to the evangelists. First, there was the matter, already noted, of materials; specifically, of the difference between refined fabrics of English manufacture and the "raw" animal hides from which indigenous outfits were sewn. In fact, the Nonconformists would themselves resort to wearing tailored skins, as would other missionaries in Africa.[18] But that is a part of the story to which we shall return later. More fundamental was a sense of unease that arose from the place of clothing in the Tswana world at large—itself quite unlike the role of costume in the moral economy of modernist Britain. At the time, Europe was increasingly pervaded by a commodified fashion system in which consumption—now set off from production as a gendered, female domain—was a major index of social standing, at least for the rising middle class. Women's newly accentuated demesne centered on a display of adornments that signaled the success of their male providers, whose own attire, as befitted their earnest endeavors, was more sober (T. Turner n.d., after Veblen 1934; but cf. E. Wilson 1985:33f., 52f.). Moreover, while men of the bourgeoisie controlled the manufacture and marketing of apparel, the labor which made textiles and garments was largely that of poor women, who were excluded from the play of stylish self-production that engrossed their privileged sisters. Among Tswana, on the other hand, females, royal and commoner alike, built houses and cultivated crops; their husbands "ma[d]e the dresses" for everyone (Campbell in LMS 1824). That women should sow while men sewed struck the evangelists as decidedly peculiar.

They were also disturbed by the fact that Tswana female garb, although marginally different by rank, seemed all the same to their (naked?) eyes; no distinctions of male wealth or status were immediately apparent on the bodies of women. Men's attire was of somewhat greater importance in signaling social standing (cf. Kay 1834,1:201; J. Comaroff 1985:219–20); their more varied out-fits drew comment early on, as did the languid "idleness" and the almost dandy-ish appearance of a few nobles (LMS 1824, 1828). Even so, the overriding impression of the Europeans, at first, was that vernacular costume was unremit-tingly rude and rudimentary, undifferentiated and undistinguished. For the most part, people of the same sex and age appeared to dress more or less alike (cf. Schapera 1953:25). No wonder, then, that clothing was such a morally charged medium for the missionaries, speaking volubly about (im)proper social distinctions. Or that the effort to refashion Tswana dress was seen to necessitate two things: a restructuring of relations of production in general, and of the division of labor in particular; and the creation of a distinct, and distinctly femi-nine, domain of domesticity and discerning consumption, naturalized as "taste" (see chapter 6; cf. also Gaitskell 1990).

In due course it became clear to the evangelists that indigenous clothes *did* serve to mark status and difference, albeit in a register not their own; that there was more to be seen by an informed eye than they had imagined. This is con-firmed not only by their own texts, but also by the earliest reports of white travelers (Somerville 1979:119f.; Lichtenstein 1973:67f.) and by a retrospective "native" account—of one John Mopharing—recorded earlier this century.[19] In contrast to infants, who were dressed in nothing besides medicated ornaments, citizens of both sexes wore skin cloaks (*dikobò;* sing., *kobò*) that reached toward their heels. These garments were significant "sign(s) of wealth" and status (Campbell in LMS 1824; cf. G. Thompson 1967:165).[20] According to Lich-tenstein (1973:67), who appreciated Tswana styles more than did the Noncon-formists, they took a "great deal of craft, time and trouble" to make (cf. A. Anderson 1888:82);[21] Mopharing, in fact, details how the skins were rendered "soft as cloth" by being soaked with water, treated with animal brains boiled in milk, trampled, and tinted with the roots of a "fern-like plant." Cloaks were first donned toward the end of initiation rites, denoting the onset of sexual and jural maturity; during periods of withdrawal from adult social life, such as oc-curred at bereavement, *dikobò* were put on inside out. Royals had especially fine ones, often incorporating the pelts of wild beasts, although that of the leopard was usually reserved for chiefs (J. Philip 1828,2:126; G. Thompson 1967:86; Theal 1910:237). As one missionary linguist later noted, the term for "persons of value" was *bakobò ditelele,* "[those with, or wearing] long cloaks."[22] *Bakobò dikhutshwane,* "[those with] short cloaks," referred to people of lesser means (Sandilands 1953:352).[23] The skin cape was to prove highly durable in this econ-omy of signs, surviving amidst a riot of market innovations to give a distinctive stamp to Tswana "folk" style. And it would live on, in the shape of the blanket, to become part of the "ethnic" costume of these and other "tribal" peoples in twentieth-century South Africa. Enduring also would be the gender specific mode of securing the cloak. Men fastened it at the shoulder, so as to leave the right arm free, while women pinned it in a more constraining fashion across the chest (see plate 5.1).

Beneath their cloaks, according to Mopharing (see n. 19), adult males wore hide loincloths; sometimes, it seems, these were shaped into a "kind of trousers consisting of a three-cornered piece of leather made from the skins of young goats" (Lichtenstein 1973:67; cf. Burchell 1824,2:319f.; Somerville 1979:120). Females covered themselves with at least one "small apron before, and a larger one behind" (LMS 1824; Campbell 1822,2:219f.; Burchell 1824,2:563f.), although they might put on additional skirts of varying shapes and lengths.[24] People of both sexes went about with sandals on their feet (LMS 1824; A. Smith 1939,1:226; Mopharing [see n. 19]). The evangelists, like other European observers, made minimal mention of the clothing of children. But Schapera (1953:25; 1940a:47f.) notes that a skin flap was used to cover the genitals of small boys; a brief skirt of leathern fringes served the same purpose for girls. As we shall see, juvenile dress was to alter hardly at all for a long time to come. It was the most persistent of all features of vernacular attire, a fact that would have telling significance amidst the many changes of the late nineteenth century.

More elaborate, distinctive garb was worn by those, such as warriors, initiates, or rainmakers, who participated in rites of passage, communal observances, and other collective enterprises (Mopharing [see n. 19]).[25] In these contexts, the clothes themselves took on pragmatic power: like other symbolic media, they were thought to affect the social and physical condition of the people who donned them (J. Comaroff 1985:87f.; Schapera 1953:25; cf. Schwarz 1979:28). Tswana rulers, for example, when seeking to reassert authority in the face of growing European incursion, often enjoined ceremonial costume and its attendant public ritual. The potency ascribed to ritual attire probably contributed to the enthusiasm with which many Tswana took to church uniforms later introduced with much the same intention; namely, to regain a measure of control over a universe endangered by alien forces.

Hairdressing was an integral and intricate aspect of Tswana apparel, alike in ritual and in everyday situations; it was, in fact, an important mark of social and sexual maturation. The cosmetic used in precolonial styling, lead hematite (see chapter 4), was mixed with animal fat to make the iridescent gel *sebilo*. This preparation was applied by all adults, but especially by females, who rubbed it on to their neatly trimmed heads to give the appearance of a sparkling metallic cap, a coiffure adopted after initiation as a sign of nubility, and of sociability in general (cf. Mopharing, [n. 19]). Only at times of seclusion, after childbirth or bereavement, did people go unanointed. Early nineteenth-century styles all but vanished under the impact of the civilizing mission. But the adoption of modest scarves by Tswana matrons implied a similar end: to constrain their hair and the physical potency it embodied. Both men and women liked to don headgear

of skin and grass (Schapera 1953:25), the former typically sporting "caps of jackal or cat fur" (Lichtenstein 1973:67)—although sometimes they wore more varied and "fanciful" hats, incorporating ostrich and crane's plumes (LMS 1828; A. Smith 1939,1:225; cf. Theal 1910:236). These, too, would disappear, but male fashions in headgear always remained less regimented than those of females. As the trade in beads from the colony gained momentum, adults worked short strings of them into their coiffure, a practice which did not appeal to the evangelists.

Nor were they enamored of Tswana jewelry. By their own lights, African "ornaments"—made from grass, leather, ivory, and base metals—were unattractive and unclean. By no standards did they measure up to the precious finery of Europe. Even John Philip (1828,2:127), with his unusual regard for indigenous aesthetics, described two Tlhaping royal women as "covered with a profusion of ornaments, which added nothing to their personal attractions."[26] Others offered more detail, among them Campbell (in LMS 1824): "[T]he legs and arms of the women are loaded with rings, of ivory, copper, leather, &c. and the *fashionables* at Kurreechane[27] wear four or five heavy copper rings round their necks."

The Nonconformists, as we know (*RRI*:170, 184f.), were to take advantage of the Tswana fondness for finery, having brought glittering "baubles" to captivate local rulers, thus to speed the work of the Gospel. They hoped that such "trifles"—which, it was said, played on the heathen penchant for sensuous superficialities—would be cast off as people joined the church and put on respectable garb. But their efforts to encourage Tswana self-improvement would stimulate a more avid interest in fashionable display than the evangelists anticipated. These efforts also evinced a greater liking for the "outward" charms of certain commodities than they might have wished. All of which left some of them deeply ambivalent about their role in the traffic in trinkets. What the Europeans did not fully grasp—and what made these goods appealing in the first instance—was the fact that precolonial adornments had a particular potency for their wearers. Jewelry and clothes, fabricated within households, were personalized objects which, when properly treated and worn, protected the body against attack. Necklaces, anklets, and waiststrings often contained medicine (*molemò*) and were imbued with the substance of their owner; so much so that they could stand for the latter, metonymically, in rites aimed to harm or heal. At death, they passed to the deceased's maternal uncle, a very special kinsman who became the executor of the departed spirit (*RRI*:134f.).

Early accounts indicate that, well before the arrival of the missions, Tswana were adept at making ornaments with the beads and buttons that found their way into their hands (see, e.g., Lichtenstein 1973:68). These objects, as we have seen, became a transcultural currency in the early nineteenth century, linking monetary to non-monetary economies across South Africa. Such tokens have often served alike as units of exchange and as items of display; their capacity to congeal, conceal, and reveal value lies in their being, simultaneously, a means and an end (cf. Graeber 1996). This was true in Bechuanaland, where they were sought avidly, if not indiscriminately, both to facilitate trade and to fashion new forms of finery; according to Campbell (in LMS 1824), in fact, Tswana men, women, and children were as fond of their bead necklaces "as any miser is of gold." Adults also experimented with strings of buttons, although it was some time before they showed any interest in the "bags" to which these were sewn, and into which white men insisted on putting their legs (Religious Tract Society n.d.:83). It is not surprising, then, that, in a book of "traditional" proverbs compiled a century later, Plaatje (1916:52), an acute cultural commentator, would include one, *Loare go bona sesha lo se eka-eke lo latlhe segologolo sa lona,*[28] which he translated as: "At sight of new styles you always discard your old customs and nurse the new."

At the same time, however, Tswana expressed strong tastes in respect to objects of adornment.[29] Not all baubles were equally valued. Those thought to be beautiful enhanced the status of their wearers, radiating their personal identities, their potential for social extension beyond themselves, and their powers of attraction (Mopharing [see n. 19]). Others, like worthless currency, were disdained. The Africans favored shining surfaces, in line with their liking for glossy cosmetics and glinting coins—and in sharp contrast to Nonconformist aesthetics, which eschewed "flashiness" for dull restraint and inward reflection. In one regard, though, their inclinations *did* converge. Campbell (LMS 1824) went on to say that he discovered Tswana, circa 1820, to "greatly prefer . . . [beads of] dark blue"; even earlier records show that neighboring peoples associated them with trade in blue beads (Saunders 1966:65; chapter 4, n. 15).

This is intriguing: dark blue, particularly that of indigo-dyed fabric, was to be advocated by LMS and WMMS for the dress of converts;[30] in blue prints, so to speak, lay a blueprint for refashioning Bechuanaland. If Campbell was correct, their chosen color had a fortuitous precedent, having been associated, from before their coming, with foreign objects of high worth: beads of this hue were globules of foreign exchange value, imaginatively sedimented into local designs. Note that blue had no significant place in vernacular art; patterns on housefronts, pottery, and ritual artifacts relied on black, red, and white (J. Comaroff 1985:114). It seems, rather, to have become the pigment of exogenous powers and substances; of the mission and European materials as well as, in Tswana poetics, the pale, piercing eyes of whites. By contrast, red, as adjective and noun, was to denote "traditional" practices and peoples in the wake of evangelization elsewhere in South Africa.

CIVILITY, CLOTH, AND CONSUMPTION

*[I]n this day the angel of Democracy [has] arisen, enshadowing the classes
with leathern wings, and proclaiming, 'All men are equal—all men, that is
to say, who possess umbrellas'.*

E. M. Forster ([1910] 1992:58)

The campaign to introduce European fashions into Bechuanaland might
have appeared "trifling," explained Robert Moffat (1842:507, echoing Wesley
1986:248) to his British readers. But decent clothes were "elements of a system
. . . destined to sweep away the filth and customs of former generations." As this
implies, some of the Nonconformists set great store on the need to force African
bodies into the straitjackets of Protestant personhood. More than just demand
"civilized" garb of those who would enter the church, they sought to scramble
the indigenous code of body management in its entirety—and then to reform
it inside out. For their part, Tswana were not slow to grasp the potent role of
Western apparel in the colonization of their world. When, for example, Chief
Montshiwa began to perceive a challenge to his legitimacy from the Christians
in his realm (*RRI*:262f.), he ordered his daughter "to doff her European clothing, . . . to return to heathen attire," and to leave the Methodist congregation
(Mackenzie 1871:231). His royal counterparts in other chiefdoms did similarly,
sparking several bitter style wars and struggles over freedom of dress.[31]

From the first, Southern Tswana appear to have treated Western adornments as signs of exotic forces; as quintessential *sekgoa* (things white; Burchell
1824,2:432, 559; cf. Somerville [1802] 1979:109). Some European clothes had,
like beads and buttons, preceded the mission into the interior,[32] where they are
said to have been regarded as "a badge of the highest status" (Burchell
1824,2:432). An early report from Kuruman tells how the Tlhaping chief addressed his warriors prior to battle in a "white linen garment," his heir wearing
an "officer's coat" (R. Moffat 1825a:29). In a published account of the incident,
Moffat (1842:348) says that the garment was a chemise of unknown origin, and
included a picture of the ruler "cutting capers" in it before the "Bechuana Parliament" (plate 5.2);[33] this as evidence of the "absurd" use made by heathens of
civilized attire. Such items of dress might have derived their potency from their
alien provenance, but they resonated with vernacular symbols as well. White,
for instance, the color of the baptismal gown—itself much like a chemise—was
also the color of the concoctions and fibers placed on the body in indigenous
rites of passage (J. Comaroff 1985:98). Likewise the military uniforms borne
inland from the Cape Colony by Khoi soldiers: their mystique was probably
heightened by their association with a mobile frontier people regarded by
Tswana with a mix of awe and fear.[34] Yet the interest they evoked seems to have
been fed by long-standing local concerns with the magical properties of battle

PLATE 5.2 *"The Bechuana Parliament" [from Moffat 1842:348]*

dress. Observers were to remark the unusual, even parodic, deployment of Western attire, most notably petticoats and hats, by Khoi (e.g., Campbell 1822,2:64f.).[35] This, too, must have communicated itself to Tswana, who, as we know, had their own proclivities for playing with the power of embodied objects—and who, according to Burchell (1824,2:432), accorded these "Hottentots" the highest prestige precisely because of "their Colonial dress." In the upshot, as elsewhere in southern Africa, European garb took on great value, value inseparably material and metaphorical.[36] And it increased dramatically, in the 1820s and 1830s, with the coming of the evangelists (Baillie 1832:447; Hughes 1841:523; see below).

Western dress, in short, opened up a host of imaginative possibilities for the Africans. It made available an expansive, expressive, experimental language with which to conjure new social identities and senses of self, a language with which also to speak back to the whites. In the early days, before missionaries had been very long in permanent residence—and before they began to present a palpable threat to chiefly authority—royals tried to monopolize the garments that traveled inland from the Colony. These were often worn in an iconoclastic fashion, most notably for ceremonial audiences with visiting Europeans. Thus John Philip (1828,2:126–27):

> Having erected our tents, we paid our respects to the family of Mateebè. . . . Mateebè was dressed in a pair of pantaloons, a shirt and waist-

coat, with a cat-skin caross over his shoulders. . . . [The queen] wore a
printed cotton gown, which had not been much used, a large and rather
handsome shawl, and her head was covered by a handkerchief, neatly tied
behind. The young women were dressed in gowns[37] . . . and above these,
each of them wore a jackall-skin caross, which served as a covering by day,
and a blanket by night. They were covered with a profusion of ornaments.

Already visible here are the signs of a synthetic style that was to be much in
evidence later on; among them, the overlay of European garments with skin
cloaks.[38] This was an aesthetic fusion abhorred by the evangelists, who tended
to describe it as if it were a particularly disgusting form of sartorial miscegenation. They never managed to eradicate it.

From the time they arrived to find Tswana "naked," or wearing an indecent
mix of garments, the missionaries expended a remarkable amount of effort and
cost on altering the appearance of their would-be converts. The task was made
difficult, at the outset, by the distance of colonial markets and by the infre-
quency with which traders passed through the country. But the Nonconformists were determined, as Robert Moffat (1842:505) put it, that the Africans
should "be clothed and in their right mind." The phrase itself—which crops
up in evangelical narratives from other parts of South Africa (Seif 1995) and
the world (e.g., Langmore 1989:168)—is from Luke 8.35.[39] Tellingly, it refers
to a man who had been possessed by demons, like Tswana allegedly afflicted by
the devil, and who had long gone about naked.[40] Healed by Jesus, he is said to
have dressed and regained his reason at the same time. The irony here, however,
is that, as Western apparel became more closely associated with Christian control, it became more equivocally regarded—to the extent that, in some quarters,
sartorial experimentation ceased entirely. Most senior royals turned their backs
on *sekgoa* garb and identified assertively with *setswana*. At least for the time being. In due course, they would don European dress once more. Meanwhile,
though, the few who persisted in wearing trousers and the like were "ridiculed
and even abused for adopting the white men's customs and laying aside those of
[their] forefathers" (A. Smith 1939,1:337; cf. Campbell 1822,2:64). One was
prevented from joining in a communal rite until he took off the offending attire.

As we have noted, the campaign to clothe the Africans was inseparable from other aspects and axes of the civilizing mission. In order to dress
Tswana—or, rather, to teach them to dress themselves—the Nonconformists
had to persuade women to trade the hoe for the needle, the outdoors for the
indoor life (Gaitskell 1990). This intention was visible in some of the earliest
episodes of the mission encounter. Thus Broadbent wrote, in 1823:[41] "Two
women came into my hut, one of them belonged to the King. . . . I let them
taste my tea and presented each of them with a needle, thread and thimble."

In this domain, however, the Nonconformists, creatures of their own culture, relied largely on the "domesticating" genius of the "gentler sex" (cf. Hunt 1990b; also chapter 6); most of their wives and daughters started sewing schools at once (Mears n.d.:46; R. Moffat 1842:505). These, in turn, provided a felicitous object for female philanthropists back home. They sent the pincushions and needles with which to stitch together the seams of an expanding imperial fabric (R. Moffat 1834:124; cf. Gaitskell 1990). Because the production of leather clothing had previously been a male preserve, the schools had limited appeal at the outset. In the early years, too, they lacked a regular supply of materials, despite British charity. But by the late 1830s some Tswana women were already taking in sewing for payment (M. Moffat 1967:17); this being another area in which the Christians stimulated commerce well before the arrival of colonial markets in goods or labor. As important, however, the industry of these women marked them, and those who consumed their wares, as church people—thus producing a means of signifying difference in communities with a Protestant presence.

Even if the evangelists had succeeded immediately in persuading large numbers of Tswana to outfit themselves in European garb, local manufacture would have been unable to meet the demand. Hence the mission societies made further appeal to the generosity of the Great British Public. The growth of the factory and fashion systems, each encouraging obsolescence, had by now provided a copious supply of used apparel for the poor and unclad at home and abroad (cf. Genovese 1974:556, on the American south). And so, when the Moffats returned to Cape Town from a visit to the United Kingdom in 1843, they sailed with fifty tons of "old clothes" for the Kuruman station (Northcott 1961:172). These garments, it seems, were not exactly cut out for the social and physical conditions of Bechuanaland: Livingstone commented scathingly about the cast-off ballgowns and starched collars given by the "good people" of England to those "who had no shirts" (Northcott 1961:173). But a letter from Mary Moffat (1967:17–18), written in 1841 to a woman well-wisher in London, shows that she had thought carefully about the adaptation of Western cloth and clothing to just these conditions. Charity was mediated by culture:

The materials may be coarse, and strong, the stronger the better. Dark blue Prints, or Ginghams . . . or in fact, any kind of dark Cottons, which will wash well—Nothing light-colored should be worn outside. . . . All the heathen population besmear themselves with red ochre and grease, and as the Christians must necessarily come in contact, with their friends among the heathen, they soon look miserable enough, if clothed in light-colored things. . . . If women's Gowns will not be too heavy work for you, they may be made with bodies to fit very stout women. . . . *I* like them best as Gowns were made 20 or 30 years ago, or rather I should say *as the fashion is now,* except the tight sleeve, which would be a great misery in a warm climate. . . . For little Girls, Frocks made exactly as you would for the Children of the poor of this country, will be the best. (Original emphasis.)

While any European clothes, even diaphanous ballgowns, were better than none, more somber, serviceable garb was ideal. Dark blue attire, especially, resisted the stains of a red-handed heathenism that might "rub off" on the convert. Black Christians, Mrs. Moffat suggested, were like the British poor: neither had the ability yet to produce the wealth or wherewithal to gain entry into the world of fashion—and, hence, were marked by the drear, dismal uniformity of their dress. Not that these Tswana were as undeserving as the underclasses at home. Added Mrs. Moffat approvingly (pp. 18–19): they "wisely condemn any gay thing, if *flimsy* . . . [and] are economical in their clothing, taking all possible care of it . . . as long as it can be made to hold together" (original emphasis). Taken to excess, of course, such frugality also offended the Protestant ethic: "Whereas it is the duty of poor women to be shy of ostentation in dress," declared the *Evangelical Magazine* of 1815, "it is most certainly not the business of wealthy women so to behave" (Tudur Jones 1962:194; cf. Wesley 1986:249f.).[42] By extension, neophyte Christians, in pursuit of material and spiritual self-improvement, ought to be stirred by a desire for modestly fashionable, refined apparel. To this end, it was important that they be moved to participate in the civilizing exchanges of the colonial marketplace.

The fact that Mary Moffat's letter was addressed to a woman was itself predictable. Ready-made garments, as well as haberdashery, were moral tender in a rising domestic economy that was thoroughly feminized. Recall that, in England, middle- and upper-class Christian wives, largely excluded from the workplace, had become mistresses of consumption (Davidoff and Hall 1987); they were also the primary purveyors of charity and noblesse toward the poor. By sending their cast-offs to Africa, these gentlewomen sought to dress and domesticate the bare bodies of the benighted abroad, making this their special contribution to colonialism. Their munificence was intended to display virtue and, presumably, to elicit gratitude (cf. Genovese 1974:555). It was also meant to draw peoples like the Tswana into the global order of British Christendom. But largesse carried its own dangers: it could inhibit ambition. Due care, therefore, had to be taken not to promote indolence. Here the missionaries and their benefactors trusted to the sheer charm of commodities. Clothes from the center of civilization, they hoped, would awaken a desire for self-enhancement, for a life of righteous earning and careful spending. Mary Moffat (1967:19) concluded:

Those who have property, are inclined to lay it out very sparingly, sometimes more so than we could wish, but by our sometimes being able to supply in a *measure* the necessities of the poor, they are stimulated to make larger purchases, least [sic] the poor of the people should look better than themselves! I have often been pleased to see this effect produced, as they by such means make more rapid advances in civilization. (Original emphasis.)

Thus it was, mainly through the exertions of mission wives, that the germ of the European fashion system arrived on the African veld. With it would come the peculiar conjuncture, in the culture of capitalism, of competitive accumulation, symbolic innovation, and social distinction (Bell 1949). But its export to this edge of empire also underscored a deep-seated ambiguity in the Protestant ethic. Among Tswana, where Christians lived cheek by jowl with heathens, the industrious were encouraged to procure commodities in order to set themselves off from the "indigent." Yet, given their strong puritanism, the evangelists could not but worry that the drive toward sartorial civility and consumption might degenerate into vain acquisitiveness. As late as 1877, for example, the Rev. Hepburn's joy at baptizing six "servants" in "decent" clothes at Shoshong was vitiated by his fear that the men would become "puffed up with self-importance."[43]

Ascetic angst focused most sharply on female frailness, however. For, insofar as women were the prime subjects and objects of fashion, femininity was associated with things of the flesh. Willoughby was not alone in grumbling, toward the end of the century, that many Tswana matrons were in thrall to ridiculous hats and costly garments;[44] much earlier, one of his colleagues expressed relief that "our native ladies have not yet adopted the crinoline, that social abomination of which they have been shown bright exemplars."[45] It was a matter of time, he thought, until they would—all of which made it imperative to keep tight bounds on the sartorial self-expression of those who joined the church. Again, while the Nonconformists sought to produce an elite driven by virtuous wants, they were also heirs to a creed that accommodated the lower classes at home; theirs was a doctrine that sanctified poverty and contained physical pleasure in the cause of eternal grace. The early evangelists resolved the dilemma by portraying their mostly humble adherents, in contrast to the "carnal" heathen, as sober, deserving recipients of Christian charity. And they clothed them in the cotton prints whose color and texture would become a hallmark of the mission—and, later, of a rural "folk" style that typified the status of Tswana peasant-proletarians. It was a style that some literati of empire found profoundly ugly, blaming it for the erasure of "native" beauty.[46]

As the years wore on, the LMS and WMMS directed their energies increasingly toward the creation of a black petite bourgeoisie. But, throughout the century, they advocated improvement and self-reliance as an ideal for all: hence their efforts to bring traders and, with them, the goods needed to make civilized subjects. In chapter 4 (see n. 35) we saw how Archbell tried to induce a merchant to settle at the Wesleyan station among the Seleka-Rolong in 1833; how,

by 1838, Robert Moffat (1842:605) had persuaded David Hume, a factor catering to the "demand for British commodities," to establish himself at Kuruman.
The Nonconformist clothing campaign played a large role in stimulating that
demand, not just for garments but for all the elements of the European sartorial
economy (Hattersley 1952:87). Much, for instance, was made of the fact that,
unlike "filthy skins," garments of refined manufacture needed to be washed and
maintained, binding wives and mothers to an unrelenting regime of "cleanliness"—a regime epitomized, to this day, by the starched uniforms of black
women's Prayer Unions (Gaitskell 1990). It was a form of discipline that the
missions monitored closely, ensuring brisk sales of soap and other cleansing
agents both personal and domestic (cf. Burke 1996). Thus Wookey, in 1888:[47]

> One has to preach to the people about things which would sound strange
> to English ears. For example, . . . one has to take up the subject of cleanli-
> ness, and give them a sermon on washing themselves and their clothes.
> The consequence has been a sudden run on the soap at the stores.

Moffat (1842:507), alive to the interests of his bourgeois audience, claimed that
such activities opened up "numberless channels for British commerce," especially in personal requisites, "which but for the Gospel might have remained
forever closed."

This claim was echoed by others. From 1830 onward, mission narratives
speak, with pleasure, of the "decent raiments" worn by loyal members of the
church. They also note, as we did above, that more and more Tswana evinced a
desire to possess European apparel—and that the garment trade was flour-
ishing (Baillie 1832:447; R. Moffat 1842:219; Read 1850:446). By 1835, in fact,
one merchant reported that Tlhaping were "particularly anxious for ready made
clothes," where before "nothing was desired [by them] but beads." In just two
months he had sold more than a hundred shirts. "They even purchase with
avidity waistcoats," he added, obviously surprised (A. Smith 1939,1:250). The
clothing of the heathen had begun in earnest.

The fact that people were buying Western attire did not mean that they
would necessarily wear it in the manner favored by the mission. Anything but,
as the Nonconformists were to report, with regret, for many decades to come;
we shall return to this in a moment. Nonetheless, they found much to cheer
them: the sedate style of an Anglophile Christian elite was taking shape—and
becoming visible (e.g., Hughes 1841:523). Read (1850:446), who had accompanied Campbell into the interior in 1813, returned in 1849 to find

> Many of them . . . [are] not only well, but respectably clad in English man-
> ufactured clothing: the men, many of them with surtouts[48] or coats, waist-
> coats, trousers, Wellington boots, polished, starched collars &c to their
> shirts, beaver hats, and here and there watches: almost, if not every man

with a wagon. The women in gowns, shoes, stockings, and good shawls; mostly with caps and bonnets. . . . Surely this also is not a failure.

While modesty forbade mention of underwear among the faithful,[49] we might assume that the Christians sought to lay the outfits of their followers over a decent foundation; one James Liebmann (1901:163) referred to the "dear, good ladies [of Exeter Hall] who spen[t] their time in making, and embellishing with beautiful embroidery, flannel nether garments for the poor, benighted blacks" of South Africa. "Bloomers"—female drawers here—became a staple of nee-dlework classes in South African schools for all races in the early twentieth cen-tury; they must have had their antecedents in mission sewing circles. Further, they are listed in Schapera's (1947:230) Bechuanaland merchant inventories for the 1930s as "an old line, but increasingly in favour"; these lists also show men's cotton undervests and short underpants to have been "popular" (pp. 229, 231). Because they were invisible to the eye, it is impossible to know for sure how and by whom such intimate apparel was actually used. Not so in the early nineteenth century, however. The "unmentionables" worn then by Tswana often intruded upon the gaze of white observers. The idea that such finely wrought items of clothing should be hidden from view might have expressed mission notions of concealed virtue. But it conflicted with the Tswana sense that beauty was for display. Such garments, clearly, were not being put on in ways intended by their European makers.

Self-fashioning on the Frontier: The Man in the Tiger Suit

Western dress had an effect on Southern Tswana quite different from that in-tended, or envisaged, by the evangelists. Some turned their backs on it entirely until they could do so no longer. Others put it on enthusiastically, and in a manner recognizably orthodox. But the most immediate and visible response— and, for many decades, that of the great majority—was somewhere in between: a synthetic, syncretic style which, to European eyes, appeared absurd. And, when not actually promiscuous, faintly comical (R. Moffat 1842:506):

> A man might be seen in a jacket with but one sleeve, because the other was not finished, or he lacked material to complete it. Another in a leath-ern or duffel jacket, with the sleeves of different colours, or of fine printed cotton. Gowns were seen like Joseph's coat of many colours, and dresses of such fantastic shapes, as were calculated to excite a smile in the gravest of us.

Some years later, as Willoughby's notes indicate,[50] a similarly fantastic array of styles were no less in evidence—and regarded as no less absurd:

> Boboyan[51] in celluloid collar and very heavy boots. Sometimes trousers big[52] enough to contain all the furniture in the wearer's house, as well as

the limbs that are thrust through them. And sometimes hardly reaching the ankles. Coat that Abel wore with patches of nearly every material in my wife's wardrobe. Hats that look as if they might have covered the heads of several generations . . . generally soft felt, but occasionally bell-topper. Very common to see boys wearing nothing but a shirt, which they have bought at a local store for a shilling. Occasionally a second-hand ulster that has got too shabby for its European owner. But the women's hats are most amusing—such hats! Silks and satins are not rare among the wealthy. Many women spend as much on clothes in a year as would keep my wife well-clad for ten years; and when they have bought their expensive garments, their last state is worse than their first. Intermixed with all this, the suffocating fur-robes which are the sign of wealth among them, and the absurd straw bonnets, that are almost like bee-hives.

Several things emerge clearly from this fragment: first, and most obvious, that the Tswana penchant for unconventional styling increased over the years, especially among those who could afford it; second, that the wealthy were spending considerable sums of money on fancy clothes; third, that their less affluent, younger compatriots also wore store-bought items—if, on occasion, little else; fourth, that some had to make do with shabby hand-me-downs, often obtained from Europeans. Elsewhere in his notes, Willoughby adds that a few older, poor Tswana had "nothing" to cover them, intimating that they continued to wear only the sparse garments of *setswana*. His own reaction to all this? That those who put on these clothes looked much the worse for their wear. This was not purely an aesthetic judgment. It expressed, beneath the amusement, a sense of disgust at the expense, extravagance, and insobriety of Tswana fashions—and at their non-Christian spirit.

Like Moffat (1842:506), Willoughby wished for a congregation of "well-dressed believers." But both discovered that this was not an easy objective, given the self-willed cultural reaction of Tswana to their outreach. What is more, as both also found out, the sartorial contrast between convert and heathen was not always as clear-cut as some of the earlier accounts (e.g., Hughes 1841:523) might have suggested. True, those who repudiated *sekgoa* were easily distinguished from those who donned modest Christian garb. In the spaces separating these extremes, however, there developed a good deal of convergence and overlap. Take, for example, a ceremony that occurred in January 1868.[53] John Mackenzie (1871:461; 1883:268), who orchestrated this event—the opening of a new church at Shoshong—and who sought to ensure that it would be attended by Christian and non-Christian alike, described their dress in detail:

Heathen men with hoary heads . . . came, leaning on their staffs. Full-grown men—the haughty, the cunning, the fierce—came with those younger in years. . . . As to their clothing, the heathen dress admits of little variety. But many appeared dressed partly or wholly in European attire, and here there was variety enough. We had the usual members of the congregation, some of whom were neatly dressed. But sticklers for "the proprieties" would have been shocked to see a man moving in the crowd who considered himself well dressed, although wearing a shirt only; another with trousers only; a third with a black "swallow-tail," closely buttoned to the chin—the only piece of European clothing which the man wore; another with a soldier's red coat, overshadowed by an immense wide-awake hat, the rest of the dress being articles of heathen wear, etc. etc.

To the evangelists, such dramatic moments offered a disconcerting reflection of the process, the dialectic of style and self-fashioning, they had set in motion. But the "eccentric" attire adopted by the Africans—redolent, as it was, of anomaly, anarchy, impropriety—was not only visible on the ceremonial stage. As the century wore on, it became an ever more quotidian feature of Tswana life. And it caused the Christians more than just passing anxiety. As Douglas (1966) would have predicted, these hybrid outfits came to be seen as dirty and contagious, a concern later echoed by state health authorities, who blamed the partial adoption by "natives" of "our style of dress" for their susceptibility to disease (Packard 1989:690; see chapter 7). For another, by flouting British dress codes, they called into question the normative authority of the LMS and WMMS. Where mission "uniforms" were introduced to mark the compliance of those who entered church schools and associations (see volume 3), the colorful, home-made creations of others cried out in obvious counterpoint: the former signaled an acceptance of the Protestant ethic and its aesthetic, the latter parodied both.

In not conforming to Nonconformism, the riotous *couture* contrived by so many non-Christians implied a riposte to the symbolic imperialism of the mission *tout court.*[54] It spoke of a desire to harness the power of *sekgoa*, yet evade its control. A similar tendency manifested itself in respect to domestic architecture. In both domains, the bricoleur contrasted, on one hand, with those who rejected everything European, and, on the other, with those who identified with the church and its values. In broad terms, this tripartite division corresponded, as Bourdieu (1984) and Volosinov (1973) might have anticipated, to the embryonic lines of class formation encountered in the previous chapter: the nascent petite bourgeoisie stuck closest to the polite norms of Christian fashion, the poorest tended to adhere most strictly to *setswana*, and those between were most likely to experiment with fusions of the two. This, as we shall see, does not exhaust the grammar of colonial aesthetics. But it does make the point that style was deeply implicated in the active construction—not the passive reflection— of radically new social distinctions; distinctions that, over the long run, eluded the schemes and dreams of the civilizing mission.

From the midcentury onward, as Southern Tswana were drawn more tightly into the regional political economy, the means for making those distinctions were increasingly provided through commercial channels—and affected by market forces—beyond the control of the evangelists. As a result, the fashioning of the frontier took a series of new turns. Apart from all else, the sheer volume of goods pumped into Bechuanaland rose markedly. On a visit to Mafikeng in 1875, Holub (1881,2:14) noted that, aside from the small elite and from youths dressed in *setswana* outfits, the population persisted in its patchwork of styles. But the makeup of the mixture had subtly altered. Items fabricated from "skins, either of the goat, the wild cat, the grey fox, or the duyker gazelle" were worn with "garments chiefly of European manufacture" acquired from traders—without, it seems, the moderating intervention of the mission and its stress on things plain, blue, and uniform (cf. Willoughby 1899:84). Mafikeng might then have been a nominally Christian Tshidi-Rolong town, lacking any white presence. Yet store-bought commodities comprised a growing proportion of its cultural mélange.

What is more, British aesthetic conventions themselves were being used in ever more complex ways. Both in the honor and in the breach they marked widening social and economic differences. Sometimes they did so in unexpected ways. This was evident, for example, in the changing garb of "traditional" rulers and royals. As we noted above, they had responded earlier to the missionary challenge by reverting, assertively, to *setswana* costume—and by insisting that their Christian subjects do likewise. Nor was this reaction confined to Southern Tswana communities. In his effort to win the chiefship of the Ngwato in 1885, one pretender, Khamane, sought the backing of "the old heathen men" by pledging to resume circumcision and rainmaking. To underscore his point, he "gave orders to the young regiment to strip off all European clothing [and] to meet naked in the chief's court." Adult males, including converts, were then commanded to prepare the "warcap," which had been part of the ritual paraphernalia of battle. When the Christians refused—arguing that this spelled a resurgence of "charms, circumcision, idolatry, and a whole army of attendant evils"—Khamane accused them of political disloyalty. Did not English soldiers also wear uniforms?[55]

By the late nineteenth century, however, with the colonial state closing in, few but the most far-flung Tswana sovereigns (H. Williams 1887:111) harbored any illusions about the habits of power. Some tried to make the best of a difficult situation by seeking, ambitiously, to encompass all sides of a fragmentary world. John Mackenzie (1871:105) records the fascinating case of Sechele, who, in 1860, had a suit tailored from "tiger"—that is, leopard skin, all "in European fashion."[56] According to the missionary, many Kwena thought that their ruler wished "to make himself a white man." But the matter was surely more complex. In refashioning the skin, itself a symbol of his office, he seems to have been

PLATE 5.3 *"Royal Visitors" [from Holub 1881,1:289]*

signifying an intention to transform and extend his authority: to legitimize it simultaneously in *setswana* and *sekgoa*, in terms of both European *and* Tswana political cultures, thus to contrive a power base greater than the sum of its parts. Mackenzie (1871:106) added: "His position . . . [was] that Christianity might be engrafted upon heathen customs, and that the two could go together." Although he might not always have succeeded, Sechele was adept at playing games of parallel politics, and at navigating cultural borderlands. Other rulers, most notably the Tshidi and Ngwaketse sovereigns (Holub 1881,1:291), took another tack. They dressed, for a time,[57] in ostentatiously fashionable European garb, whose opulence set them off not merely from non-Christian commoners, but also from their less extravagant Christian subjects (plate 5.3). Among the latter, it appears, they counted the evangelists. Seeing that the trappings of "tradition" could not secure their privilege or position, these men, like other Tswana royals, set out to acquire the signs of the order that engulfed them. This form of royal dandyism involved only male dress (cf. J. Comaroff 1985:219; J. Mackenzie

245

1975:42). Later, though, the Christian bourgeoisie would display its status as did its European counterparts: through the attire of its women.

Through the Looking-Glass, Again

Our central claim throughout has been that colonialism in general, and the civilizing mission in particular, was never a monolithic process of domination or a one-sided cultural crusade; that it was, rather, an encounter in which local and global forces, Africa and Europe, interacted on multiple levels and in subtle, polyphonous, mutually determining ways.[58] This was no less true of struggles over sartorial styles and bodily management than of any other aspect of the imperial enterprise. Far from merely being molded by colonial evangelism, Tswana fashions were to develop in complex, often unpredictable directions. And, inasmuch as they expressed desires to which colonial manufacturers and markets felt it necessary to react,[59] they had a palpable impact on the economy of the English heartland (cf. Sahlins 1981; Nielsen 1979, on West Africa).

But what of the most immediate theater of engagement? Did Tswana dress have any impact on the missionaries? True, these Europeans sought to protect themselves against the stains of savagery. But did they succeed? Or did their encounter with African aesthetics leave visible traces on their bodies?

The evangelists wrote reams about the physical and spiritual privations of life in Bechuanaland. Yet they gave only patchy account of the everyday minutiae of their own material existence. We learn quite a bit, in the first years, about the ingenuity with which they extended meager technical resources by using local substances and skills, particularly in their agricultural and architectural pursuits. But domestic matters, such as diet and dress, seem to have been too mundane to mention. Some details did find their way into correspondence, especially family letters, and into private journals, often those of mission wives. And a few descriptions were provided by British visitors from the Cape, who came to witness how the Christian pioneers were "roughing it." For the rest, we are compelled to fill out our collage from glimpses and fragments. Fortunately, however, these conduce to a fairly coherent picture of the reciprocal impress of Tswana self-fashioning on the Europeans.

The maintenance of methodical personal routines, as we have noted, preserved a fragile sense of civility and survival among frontier missionaries. So crucial were these routines that the Moffats once sent their laundry more than a hundred miles when denied access to water (*RRI*:208). Exemplary self-presentation was essential not only to their morale, but also to their evangelical outreach. It expressed the conviction—encountered repeatedly in chapters 3, 4, and 6—that the Christian family had to establish itself as an attainable model of sensible, sober, sanitary living.

Nevertheless, the Nonconformists modulated European convention during their sojourn in the African interior. This they did in response both to local practice and to the exigencies of life beyond polite society. Mary Moffat (1967:17), in describing the dated, dark, durable garb appropriate to Tswana converts, shared the fact that the missionaries had themselves adopted similar attire. They "would never think" anymore of wearing delicate or light-colored clothes, she said, having themselves to bear the imprint of the heathens around them. In general, their self-presentation seems to have shifted subtly from the refined to the rugged. Telling, in this respect, were portraits of Robert Moffat (see *RRI*:111), some by travelers to the interior, which accentuated his shaggy beard and hair,[60] making him an icon of the pioneering pilgrim. His relative unkemptness—as Barthes (1973:47f.) notes of "The Iconography of Abbé Pierre"—marked the distance from metropole to frontier.

That distance, as displayed on the bodies of the evangelists, was also numbered in temporal terms. Chiding the director of the LMS in London for the unjustly small budget allowed to the Tswana mission, David Livingstone (1961:197) grumbled: "We were a queer looking set when we came to Cape Town [on a visit in 1852]. Clothes eleven years out of the fashion. We all needed being clad anew." The European sense of fashion, with its stress on contemporaneity, made garments into finely gradated gauges of time, history, and social (dis)location. This put the missionaries in an ironic position. Here they were, trying to clothe Africa in the dress of civilization. Yet, owing to their own sojourn in the "wilderness," they had themselves become stylistic anachronisms: their outfits were now more like those they first brought to the Tswana than anything currently worn in the refined world they sought so avidly to represent.

These, however, were the negative signs, the signs of disruption, wrought on the lives of the evangelists in Bechuanaland. Their appearance also bore positive marks of African influence. Despite speaking often of their disgust with skin clothing, for example, many missionaries came to make and wear it (see n. 18). Reported Campbell (1822,2:76) of his early encounter with a Tlhaping headman, who "[seemed] desirous of imitating," rather than selectively adopting, "the dress and manners of civilized life":

> He wears a jacket and trowsers made by himself. Referring to these articles, he told me they were only made of skin, for he was a poor man! I then remarked that the only difference between his vest and mine was, the one being made from the skin of the sheep, and the other from that of the tiger.

The "tiger" [again, leopard] skin vest, added Campbell in a footnote, had been made for him by Mary Moffat at Dithakong.

This passage is fascinating on a number of counts: it suggests that local leather workers were learning quickly to adapt their craft to European forms; that Tswana were keenly aware of the extent to which skin clothes, whether or not they had been tailored in Western mode, were devalued by the whites; that hides, worn on the body, were becoming a mark of the lowly, even though the animals that provided them remained signs of wealth. But most striking of all, for present purposes, is the revelation that the evangelists were themselves experimenting with African couture. Campbell's own adoption of the latter was partial and selective: he had put aside his coat of woolen manufacture for a vest made of indigenous materials. Vests, of course, were not "basic" items of apparel in the mission wardrobe, in that they did not cover nakedness; like neckties and cravats, they were among the few pieces in the male ensemble that might be made of a decoratively patterned—distinctly signifying—fabric. These, in other words, were garments by means of which men exercised choice and showed off their personal predilections. Campbell's souvenir of his stay in South Africa, sewn by a woman who had become a symbol of refined European womanhood-in-the-wild, was not stitched from just anything. Leopard pelts, as we know from Sechele's suit, were the prerogative of chiefs alone. They were highly valued, in part, because the beast itself was at once fierce, stealthy, hard to kill. In doffing his native dress to don one—the European counterpoint to what Tswana were doing in making their bricolage of *sekgoa* and *setswana*—Campbell engaged in an old local practice: the appropriation of exotic substances from others to empower one's own cultural designs. Could he have hoped that the skin might invest him with some of the strength attributed by the clerics to their African adversaries? Sechele's outfit, it is said, "surprised" Mackenzie. But, for its precedent, he ought to have looked to the Christians who went about Bechuanaland before him. On the back of the "tiger"—a tiger that did change its spots—two stylistic traditions had met, there both to be refashioned.

Campbell, as we intimated, was not alone in venturing into African aesthetics. He was merely an early example, and not a particularly extreme one at that. Much more memorable is the case of Robert Moffat, largely because he railed so against Tswana dress. In a letter written to his elder brother on 12 April 1823—*not* a text for public consumption—he offered a remarkable, if terse, description of his appearance (Moffat and Moffat 1951:72):

> "I often wear a Bichuana cap made of fox skins. Trousers of a prepared antelope skins. . . . Last winter I had a waistcoat and tucket made of tiger skin for the cold weather."

Only his footwear, which he made himself from local hides, "quite resemble[d] English shoes." Was Moffat's clothing bred of necessity? Had his supply of European clothes simply had been exhausted? Those brought from England, he says, were indeed no longer serviceable. But he *had* obtained adequate supplies from the Cape "from time to time." Also, at the date of writing to his brother, in April, he had just received a "large chest containing valuable articles of [British] clothing" (Moffat and Moffat 1951:72). And yet, in June, George Thompson

(1967:80), a visitor to the region whom we have encountered before, saw Moffat at Griquatown "dressed in a jacket of leopard skin." The missionary, it seems, was fond of his skin clothes and cap, and chose to put them on when he might have done otherwise. As de Kock (1993:215) suggests, quoting Northcott's (1961:116f.) biography, he often "dressed himself in veld-going, home-made leather trousers and jacket," his own "tiger" outfit having apparently given way at some point to a less flamboyant replacement. On one of his travels, moreover, he relinquished those hide trousers to an African to use as a model for mass duplication. The refashioned leopard pelt might have been the garment in which those who dressed for power met one another across the cultural frontier. But the likes of Moffat's synthetic suit—which seems to have resembled that of the man in sheep clothing—did for more common people, destined as they were to seek their stylistic fusions in humble materials and designs. And they did for many of the evangelists in Africa who, no longer part of the "pure con-temporaneity" of European fashion, had slipped through the looking glass—and had begun to appear ever more like those around them. Save for the color of their skins.

MIGRANTS, MERCHANTS, AND THE COSTUME OF THE COUNTRYSIDE

European clothing, which is coming more and more into general use, has not been an unmixed blessing.

South African Native Affairs Commission,
1903–1905, p. 51

Urban Outfitters

Colonial Europeans in South Africa had insisted, from first contact, that Afri-cans with whom they associated should adopt minimal standards of "decency"; that they should, at the very least, cover their "private" parts. In this they were not unique. Britons venturing to the margins of empire commonly made the same demand (cf. Cohn 1989:331, on India). As a result, Tswana women who became attached to white households, settler or missionary, hid their breasts and discarded their skin aprons for skirts. Men, in parallel circumstances, re-placed their *loincloths*[61] with trousers (Shaw 1974:101f.)—although later many had, at the insistence of their employers, to don shorts and aprons, a form of dress that they found at once feminizing, infantilizing, and humiliating (cf. H. Kuper 1973:357). As the century progressed, those who journeyed to the new towns and industrial centers had no option but to conform to the rules of re-spectability pertaining to public places. All the while, of course, the evangelists were working away to refashion indigenous bodily wants and needs. And they had succeeded in considerable measure. As we know from the observations of Willoughby, Mackenzie, Moffat, and others, there had developed a widespread demand for Western garments, if not necessarily for Western styles. By the early twentieth century, says Schapera (1947:122), speaking of transformations of the long run,[62] "European clothing was worn by all who could get it, although costumes varied widely in completeness."[63] Elsewhere (1934:45) he argued that "the desire to purchase special goods, such as . . . clothes" was a powerful motive—albeit a secondary one, the primary cause being economic compulsion[64]—for the migration of Tswana to the cities. A spell away from the countryside, he went on to report (1947:116f.), came to be regarded in Bechuanaland as a form of initiation into manhood (see chapter 4): males who had been to urban centers were preferred in marriage over those who had not, the latter being said to "[lack] self-respect, 'because they have *nothing to wear but their loinskins*' instead of *working for decent clothes*" (our italics).

This suggests that, from the late nineteenth century onward, it was labor migration and the urban experience that had the greatest impact on Tswana dress styles—in both the country and the city. Those who traveled to towns were immediately met by an array of "Kaffir Stores" which pressed upon them a range of "native goods" designed for neophyte black proletarians.[65] Advertisements placed by wholesale suppliers in the *Diamond Fields Advertiser* in Kimberley give a sense of this range. They also illuminate the symbiosis between British manufacturing interests and the shaping of local demand. A typical example, from 6 September 1878, reads:

> TO KAFFIR STOREKEEPERS—Storekeepers who deal with the dusky native should attend Mr. Alexander Levy's Sale tomorrow.

On offer were "oilman's clothing, hats, boots, slippers, shirts, half-hose, undershirts, blankets and handkerchiefs." Mr. Levy's stock, it appears, was made up almost entirely of men's apparel. Earlier, on 6 April, another insertion had announced the arrival of "stock specially selected for this Market:"

> Amongst other lines may be enumerated CLOTHING of all descriptions, including:
> Jackets, Coats, Suits, Reefers, Tweeds, Cotton Cord and Bedford Cord Trousers, Woollen, Oxford and Cotton Shirts, Hats, etc.
> Boots of various makes and quality.
> Handkerchiefs, Braces, Belts and Sundries.
> All the Goods will be found very suitable for the trade of Kimberley, and are worthy of the attention of Buyers.

These commercial notices attest to the fact that clothes were by far the most significant commodity sold by urban storekeepers, although domestic goods, stationery, and furniture sometimes appeared at the bottom of stock lists. The sheer volume of business at the time indicates that migrants were devoting a major proportion of their disposable income to outfitting themselves. What is more, they were being subjected to the fashion *system* of industrial capitalism; subjected to it as both a mode of seduction and as a cultural grammar. Advertisements, shop windows, magazine features, and store displays distinguished work from leisure, the manual from the nonmanual, blue from white, weekday from Saturday and Sunday, daytime from nighttime, indoors from outdoors, the secular from the ceremonial; signs and portents, all this, of the structural logic of Roland Barthes's (1967) *Système de la mode.*

But, on the streets of Johannesburg and Kimberley, these categories and contrasts were conveyed in an altogether more practical language. It was in an effort to "educate" consumers and move merchandise that vendors contrasted hardy "oilman's clothing" and other plain working garb—the garments that laborers bought first—with "fancy" attire, special dress, and luxury accoutrements, for which there was also a growing secondary market. The latter in particular (the half-hose and slippers, the underwear and handkerchiefs, the belts and braces, umbrellas and sundries) were presented as essential accessories of a civilized existence. They were the means by which one might, through refined consumption, contrive respectability and personal distinction in urban colonial society. And by which the eye was trained to recognize the fine contrasts that made up its different fractions. Similarly the genteel styles and fabrics of bourgeois British taste: Bedford cord trousers, tweeds, Oxford shirts, even formal shirt collars. These were held up to blacks as an entrée into the idealized world of whites—as if differences of race and class consisted in little more than a collar bar.[66] It was an illusion that added much to the coffers of English manufacture and imperial trade. The moral economy of the mission and the material economy of the marketplace had finally merged into one another.

For all the advertising and the energetic efforts to sell British wares to them, black South Africans were not, we reiterate, passive consumers of European commodities. As newcomers to the labor market, it is true, they were receptive to certain articles, apparel among them. For this they had been prepared by a mix of indigenous values, mission ministrations, and the impact of an invasive colonizing society, powerfully present in particular goods. Ames (1978:21, cited by Schlereth 1991:xv) reminds us that "objects were prominent parts of Victorian everyday life precisely because Victorians themselves were fascinated with material culture." This enchantment communicated itself to Southern Tswana. But once European artifacts found their way onto African soil, they were redeployed in a cultural field whose signs were very much in flux. In the event, whatever ready-made garments might have meant to their purveyors and purchasers in town, they served rather different ends as soon as they were taken "back" to rural areas. Apart from all else—as Schapera (1947:122), and Holub (1881,1:291) before him, noted—the very ownership of clothing from the city separated those with urban experience from their less worldly compatriots. But this was only the start.

Rural Transformations

In rural areas, too, important transformations were playing themselves out. If we take up the story where we left it—with dress styles becoming caught up in processes of class formation and social distinction—we find evidence, toward the end of the century, of a complex array of emergent fashions. One source is especially revealing. It is the first published collection of photographs of *Native Life on the Transvaal Border*, something akin to an early coffee-table book, produced in 1899 by W. C. Willoughby (n.d.[a]); this was the same LMS evangelist, amateur ethnographer, and future head of the Tiger Kloof Native Institution (see volume 3) on whose unpublished notes we drew above. In a moral exploration intended to acquaint "those . . . at home with the more distant parts of the empire" (p. 4), Willoughby let his camera linger on the civilizing efforts of the mission, piecing together a portrait of pious, peaceful people and slowly improving communities. Through its lens we are afforded some intriguing insights into the development of local material culture, not least in respect of dress and domestic design.[67]

The grainy, gray pictures make it clear that the patterns discernible a couple of decades back had undergone changes. Wealthy royals remained the most expensively clad (plate 5.4). But it had become hard to distinguish them from the Christian elite,[68] of which a growing proportion of rulers were in any case now members; that elite was wearing fairly elaborate, if sober, versions of contemporary English fashions (plate 5.5). This convergence reflected the impact of overrule: the expansion of the colonial state had further eroded chiefly authority while enhancing the status of those educated by the missions. (Nonconformist schooling set great store by sartorial reform; see below.) What is more, church membership now extended to most Tswana, including senior nobles. While many of the latter continued to invest in bovine rather than bookish values—and were, in the eyes of the evangelists, merely "nominal" Christians—they bought their clothes from the same purveyors as did the rising Protestant bourgeoisie. Consequently, the costume of the relatively rich and privileged, whatever their religious beliefs or affiliations, had become more uniform. Some differences still obtained, however. Among those who identified with the mission, social standing was increasingly expressed in the garb of women.[69] It also entailed competitive expenditure on ritual dress: church weddings and funerals, which signaled gentility but did not necessarily displace indigenous rites, involved the punctilious, often extravagant, reproduction of European *haute couture* (plate 5.6).

The salience of fashion in sedimenting the status of Southern Tswana literati is clear from these and other sources as well. Take, for example, a photo-

No. 13. MILLY, ONE OF KHAMA'S DAUGHTERS.   SEKGOME, KHAMA'S ONLY SON.   No. 14

PLATE 5.4 *Children of Khama, circa 1899 [from Willoughby n.d.[a]:15]*

PLATE 5.5 *"Cottar's Saturday Night—Secwana Version," circa 1899 [from Willoughby n.d.[a]:48]*

253

PLATE 5.6 *"Native Bride," circa 1899 [from Willoughby n.d.[a]:25]*

PLATE 5.7 *Staff of Koranta ea Becoana*, circa 1901 [Molema-Plaatje Papers, Collection number A979, item Feb 1, University of the Witwatersrand]

graph of the staff of the first Tswana newspaper, *Koranta ea Becoana* (plate 5.7): the impeccably middle-class outfits of the journalists contrast sharply with the garb of the printers, who bear in their hands the tools of their trade. The signifying role of dress was evident, too, in the content of the vernacular press. For a long while, the front pages of the popular *Tsala ea Becoana* and *Tsala ea Batho* were dominated by three-column advertisements for trousseaus; these included imported lace veils, dresses, nightgowns, and, sometimes, sewing machines for brides-to-be (plate 5.8).[70] By the early years of this century, the same papers were printing regular reports of "society" weddings, replete with descriptions of the gowns of the bridal retinue.[71] Here, as elsewhere, class distinctions were being tailor-made. Style did not just represent new Southern Tswana social cleavages and alliances. It was part of their very fabrication.

At the other end of the social spectrum, the crowd scenes in Willoughby's pictorial archive give little evidence of "heathen dress" being worn anymore by fully grown men and women. But it did remain common among youths and unmarried girls (plate 5.9; cf. Conder 1887:87). Such clothing, now regarded as primitive and childlike, might still have been put on by adults in areas not yet

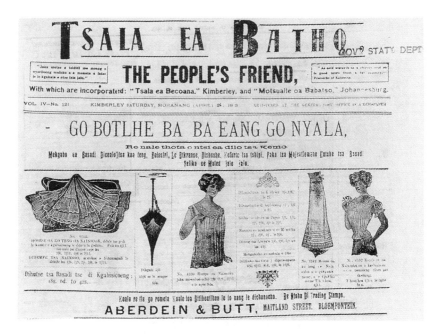

PLATE 5.8 *Trousseau Advertisement [Tsala ea Batho, 26 April 1913, p. 1]*

penetrated by the white gaze. But, in the era of overrule, these were becoming few and far between. Many chiefs, furthermore, mindful of the stigmatizing implications of "backwardness," themselves insisted that their subjects dress in European mode, however mean or ragged; all of which allowed the evangelists to testify happily that "traditional costume" was virtually extinct (Willoughby 1899:84). By the 1930s, Schapera (1936:230; 1962:363) could state definitively that Sotho-Tswana had, one and all, adopted Western apparel. In contrast, among Nguni—where, for specific historical reasons, conversion to Christianity was an "all or none" matter—"traditional" people still marked themselves off from "schooled" church members by wearing blankets treated with red ocher (Mayer 1961:24f.).

Feminizing the Folk on the Ethnic Periphery

The most memorable of Willoughby's photographs, perhaps, are those that capture the middle ground between elite attire and "heathen" garb; the clothing, that is, of ordinary men and women. By now, as we know, the Tswana rank and file, most of them (again, "nominal") members of one or another church, had been drawn into a political economy dominated by commodities. Yet they seem to have crafted a distinctive sartorial style, a bricolage that tailored industrial materials to a heightened awareness of *setswana*. Neither straightforwardly Eu-

PLATE 5.9 *"Rising Generation," circa 1899 [from Willoughby n.d.[a]:49]*

ropean nor "authentically" vernacular, this style combined elements of both to signify a novel sense of anachronism: that of being citizens of a marginalized, "ethnic" culture. Like other indigenous peoples in South Africa and elsewhere (cf. Mayer 1961:25f.; Tolen n.d.), these Tswana found themselves refigured as quaint premoderns, as "natives" at the exploitable fringes of empire. In conjuring up their costumes, they opted for a form of dress that reworked imperial designs—and constrained the impact of white markets and morals.

Notwithstanding local variation, this style, in its generic form, has become readily identifiable. It is the "folk costume" of those peoples who have been socially and spatially peripheralized as the world has become ever more dominated by a largely Eurocentric[72] cosmopolitanism. Its greatest elaboration has often been in the garb of women,[73] though this is not invariably so. For example, in much of colonial and postcolonial West Africa—where bodily adornment appears to be much more elaborate than it is in southern Africa[74]—male dress has perhaps been the more finely wrought bearer of cultural identities. Here elites have long gestured not only to Christian Europe but also to the Muslim north and east.[75] Southern Africa, by contrast, has followed the more common pattern: by and large, ethnicized apparel has tended to be a female preserve.

Why? Why is there such a widespread tendency for "folk" costume to be feminized? The answer appears to lie in the *manner* in which the ("local") peoples of Africa, Asia, and Latin America have been incorporated into, and have acted toward, expansive ("global") orders. By now it is commonplace to note that this process has congealed the very line of cleavage between the local and the global, mapping frontiers and borderlands onto hitherto unbroken, fluid conceptual scapes; that, in redirecting flows of material and cultural exchange, it has set in motion the complex encounters and struggles, the geometries of difference and inequality, that pervade contemporary world history; that, while it has transformed social arrangements across the planet, it has also reinforced vernacular cultural practices everywhere, often reinventing them as tradition. Viewed in this light, European imperialisms might not have managed, untrammeled, to recast others in their mold. But they did export their *own* contradictions. In many places, for instance, South Africa among them, colonizers set out, on one hand, to seed modern European techniques and relations of production among subject populations; yet, on the other, they often sought cheap, well-regulated labor for purposes of farming, mining, and manufacture—which led them to exploit and perpetuate, not close, the gap between the "primitive" and the "civilized."

Let us explore this a bit further, since it puts our case into comparative perspective. Whether or not colonizers encouraged the "modernization" of local economies, they rarely waited long before extracting labor from them for their own purposes. Typically, most such labor involved males in the first instance,[76] but it did not usually remove them from their communities, even if it did detach them from prevailing relations of production. With the rise of colonial capitalism, the demands of economic "development" made it necessary that these men be "persuaded," in ever larger numbers,[77] to migrate as contract workers to industrial and mining centers, settler farms, or sites of road and rail building. At the same time, the parallel movement of women was frequently discouraged, if not actually prevented: many colonizers feared the entrenchment of assertive urban or agrarian proletariats.[78] Because male wages were often kept low to sustain a flow of cheap labor, and had to be subsidized by female cultivation "at home," the countryside tended to be feminized. As a result, women were made into "subsistence cultivators"—and, simultaneously, into the icons of a "tribal" center far from the reaches of modern economy, society, and history.[79]

And so, in the signifying economy of empire, black women often came to embody rural tradition. Sometimes portrayed as the premodern counterpart of working-class European females, most of them remained, willingly or not, in increasingly impoverished domestic enclaves, far away from "modern" centers of production and public life. This, patently, describes the process we have been following in southern Africa. Here, in "reserves"—later termed, literally, *home*-lands—Southern Tswana wives and mothers took control of production and reproduction. And here they became the prime bearers of a cultural identity

PLATE 5.10 *"A Couple of House-Boys," circa 1899 [from Willoughby n.d.[a]:51]*

that fixed the place of their people among other peoples of color on the subcontinent. However creatively fashioned, the lifestyle of these women bore the signs of their marginality: their "folk" attire marked out the rural, ethnicized half of the hyphenated condition of the "peasant-proletarian." Complementarily, the neutral working garb of their husbands and sons bespoke the status of ordinary Tswana men as poor, anonymous migrants, whose raw labor commanded low wages in the cities and in the mines.

All this is illuminated, once more, by our photographic evidence from Bechuanaland at the turn of the century. By contrast to the "fashionable" outfits of the small urban-oriented elite, the apparel of the male rank and file was limited largely to khaki jackets, shirts, and trousers. This was the uniform of a growing proletarian army, worn throughout southern Africa, that made no ethnic or other distinctions (plate 5.10; see plate 5.11 for an example from the 1920s). Schapera's (1947:228ff.) inventories show that, both as migrants and back home, Tswana men continued to live in khakis during the 1930s and 1940s—as they did in Mafikeng until the 1970s (plate 5.12), even though there was also a trade in old-fashioned clothes. Their womenfolk, on the other hand, wore tight-bodiced dresses of indigo cotton print, with full skirts drawn over several petticoats and appliqued patterns of darker blue fabric around the hem; blankets or shawls, wrapped about the upper body at all times, save during

PLATE 5.11 *Rural Men, Mochudi, circa 1929 [from Duggan-Cronin 1929, plate 7. Courtesy McGregor Museum, South Africa]*

PLATE 5.12 *Crowd Scene, Initiation Rite at Mareetsane [J. L. and J. Comaroff, February 1970]*

PLATE 5.13 *"Pounding and Sifting Corn," circa 1899 [from Willoughby n.d.[a]:32]*

strenuous labor; and dark twill headscarves, referred to, in Afrikaans, as *doeke* (plates 5.13, 5.14).[80] Some aspects of this costume were transformations of pre-colonial dress: of skin aprons and skirts that fell to mid-thigh, and of cloaks, put on in colder weather, that encased much of the upper body (plate 5.15). Other aspects derived from LMS and WMMS innovations. For example, Mears (1934:95), himself a missionary historian, noted the "long dresses and innumerable petticoats" favored by Tswana women, as well as the "bundles of cloth" tied around them. This outfit evoked the ideal of European feminine domesticity, an ideal essayed by the Christians—and distorted by the colonial economy.

This composite female costume, in sum, was the product of a specific conjuncture, a particular pastiche of African and European elements. It captured nicely the paradoxical calculus of similarity and difference, closeness and distance, that remade colonized peoples into diverse "ethnic" groups. Characteristic of such styles—indeed, crucial to their historical meaning—is a putative "conservatism"; putative, because it harks back not to the customs of an *ancien régime*, but to practices born in times of radical change, often in the relatively recent past. As this implies, we have more in mind here than the allusive anachronism of "invented traditions." The synthetic styles of which we speak are a

F I V E

PLATE 5.14 *"Using the Flail," circa 1899 [from Willoughby n.d.[a]:30]*

repeated invocation of the very process of articulation that encompassed local
identities, reified them, and redefined them in Eurocentric terms. In this, we
would argue, lies a crucial feature of "folk costume." Speaking of the Xhosa,
Mayer (1961:26) observed some years ago that

> School Xhosa have combined [White-derived elements] into a dress
> which is obviously of White-inspired type but . . . [is] obviously a 'folk'
> costume too. As in other parts of Africa the women's dress has been
> frozen in styles current among local Whites many years before.

"Frozen," of course, implies the very antithesis of the constant innovation, the
"pure contemporaneity," of the European clothing market. The accompanying
description of a dark blue outfit, with its Victorian outlines, recalls Tswana rural
couture of the late nineteenth century. Its form was as different from high Western fashion as it was from ruddy "tribal" garb—although both "fashion" and
"folk dress" were part of a more inclusive system of contrasts, a mutually intelligible language of style.

   Tswana rural costume, like its Xhosa counterpart, was to prove remarkably
lasting in the twentieth century, especially among older women of modest
means: in the 1920s, according to Duggan-Cronin's (1929) photographic studies,[81] most females were wearing "respectable," full-skirted frocks and headscarves in familiar country prints (plates 5.16, 5.17); in the 1930s, indigo cloth
still accounted for 75 percent of the fabric trade in Bechuanaland, with cotton
and woolen blankets, shawls and scarves making up most of the rest (Schapera
1947:228f.); in the 1960s and 1970s, throughout the Mafikeng District, turn-of-
the-century styles in dark materials still predominated (plate 5.18), although

PLATE 5.15 *"Bechuana Women in Winter Attire" [from Plaatje 1916, opp. p. 8]*

they had begun to make way for mass-produced garments and used clothes cast off by the affluent. As this suggests, some changes *did* occur. Outside the confines of the rising bourgeoisie, however, they tended to be slow and subtle, altering details rather than basic forms.[82] After the early phases of sartorial playfulness, the Tswana proclivity for experimentation, hedged about by the material and cultural realities of the colonial state, found its outlets ever more constrained. Indeed, the hallmarks of "folk" style—the matronly print skirts, the closely tied headscarves, the blankets—remained long in evidence. What is

PLATE 5.16 *Tswana Women's Rural Dress, Kweneng (i) [from Duggan-Cronin 1929, plate 12. courtesy McGregor Museum, South Africa]*

PLATE 5.17 *Tswana Women's Rural Dress, Kweneng (ii) [from Duggan-Cronin 1929, plate 14. Courtesy McGregor Museum, South Africa]*

PLATE 5.18 *Crowd Scene, Initiation Rite at Mareetsane [J. L. and J. Comaroff, February 1970]*

more, this style came to mark an assertive order of values, and was worn with pride by women who saw themselves as guardians both of a distinctive identity and of domestic virtue. Even in the 1980s, many younger women in rural South Africa were still improvising upon it.[83] Its fundamental lines and designs persist to this day.

So, too, do the connotations of traditionalist conservatism associated with all folk costume. Yet, far from being the creature of a timeless tradition, or being outside history, this style of dress—more broadly, this mode of embodiment— was (re)produced by particular historical forces; the same historical forces that consigned its wearers to a peripheral position within colonial society. For those wearers, though, their clothing was something other than a mere mark of penury. Just as it signaled a social identity, so it seems also to have connoted stability in a world of movement and flux. In this respect, it was, curiously, the female counterpart of cattle. In its relative lack of innovation, its refusal to allocate scarce resources to ceaseless self-fashioning, it was the very obverse of "modern" *couture*, which responds to the perpetual motion of the metropole and to middle-class aspiration. Fashion, it goes without saying, is better for business (cf. H. Kuper 1973:363). Shopkeepers in Mafeking in the late 1960s never tired of telling whoever would listen of their attempts to introduce new fabrics and styles to the mass Tswana market. And of their mixed success among people whose apparently "irrational" tastes often challenged the logic of bourgeois consumption.

Clothes, Colonialism, and Cultural Assertion

This sartorial history reveals some of the complex cultural dynamics at play in the colonial encounter. The exposure to Western commodities and modes of consumption encouraged peoples like the Tswana to deploy new objects in diverse ways. But these objects were embedded in practices and forms of relationship destined to transform their world. Clothes, and the domestic regimes they implied—being both signs and instruments of incorporation into the subcontinental economy—indexed the manner in which wider political and material forces came to rest on individuals. European norms of dress and comportment pervaded the public sector, laying out an aesthetics of civility and an order of values that positioned whole populations in a hierarchical socioscape. Indeed, the effort to fix black identity, to inscribe it in backward "ethnic" cultures, was central to the very construction of colonial society; of a society in which class divisions were fragmented and realigned along racial lines, with a concomitant curtailment of the scope for African political self-expression.

And yet, far from being a simple narrative of colonial domination, the story of Tswana "folk" *couture*—like all the other stories of cultural encounter we have told—has a paradoxical, ambivalent, even contradictory character. At two levels. First, to the extent that it took on the dated, dark shapes and colors and textures preferred by Mary Moffat and her ilk, this "traditional," ethnicized costume owed much to Nonconformist influence. But, insofar as it did, it turned its back on the other side of mission ideology: the injunction to aspire to newly individuated identities through (ever more refined) consumption and sartorial self-fashioning. Second, as a reaction to colonial evangelism, female folk dress seems to have spoken, simultaneously, in opposing registers. On the one hand, it appears, outwardly, to have accommodated to the ideology and moral regulation of the mission. On the other, it gave voice to a form of symbolic self-assertion, albeit modest and muted. For, even as they put on Christian garments, most Tswana women insisted on retaining distinctively non-European—distinctly *setswana*—elements of style in their dress. And this in the face of active discouragement on the part of the church.

Let us explore this last practice further, since it underscores some of the symbolic complexities of the colonial encounter. It also illustrates quite how subtle may be indigenous responses to the European outreach. And quite how much by way of African self-assertion may be missed by inattention to the silent practices of the everyday lives of ordinary people.

It is clear, from both merchant records and Victorian photographs, that store-bought cotton and woolen blankets became an integral part of Tswana costume during the second half of the nineteenth century. These objects were called *dikobò*, Setswana for the skin cloaks that had once been so important in marking social identity (by contrast to coats and jackets, which were known by their Dutch term, *baatje* or *baki*).[84] Here, as elsewhere in South Africa, they were a key ingredient, among the motley mix of African and European elements, in the creation of a specifically "ethnic" garb (Tyrrell 1968:93). Nguni women in the eastern Cape, for instance, dyed them with ocher and made them into skirts, breastcloths, and capes, the stuff of a refurbished "native" style; it distinguished those who wore it, as "red" or "blanket" people, from members of the church (cf. Shaw 1974:102; see above).[85] This defiantly self-conscious use of the blanket as a sign of so-called "tribalism" was quite unlike that found in Sotho-Tswana communities. There it was put on as an outer mantle over European garments, by Christians and non-Christians alike, completing the everyday peasant ward-robe—and enclosing all its wearers in an outer layer of *setswana*. The difference between the two usages[86] seems to have echoed fundamental dissimilarities in the way in which these populations were drawn into the regional political economy (J. Comaroff 1985:30).

For many Tswana, the mode of fastening store-bought blankets replicated earlier, gendered practices. As with karosses, men's were secured at the shoulder, women's across the breast—albeit with the all-purpose safety pin (cf. Tyrrell 1968:93). While there is little information on the colors favored by Tswana in the late nineteenth century, later records show that they preferred fancy patterns, especially those incorporating white and red. These contrasted with the sober blues and blacks that still dominated the rest of their attire (Schapera 1947:228, 230). Comparative evidence, most notably from among Southern Sotho, suggests that blankets disclose much about aesthetic volatilities. Some time back, Tyrrell (1968:93) noted that, while their basic function had varied little over the previous century, "fashions" in shade and design had shifted a good deal. Balinese imports, introduced by a German trader, were popular early on, only to be eclipsed by the "Victoria" line, which depicted the "beloved" British queen. It is ironic, in light of this history, that Moshweshwe, the heroic Sotho king, once declared his people to be as close to the English sovereign "as the lice in her blanket" (Tyrrell 1968:91). Manufacturers have often used historical images in their efforts to shape local taste: airplanes and bombs commemorated World War II; the crown and scepter marked a royal visit to Basutoland in 1947; more recently, "Freedom," "Lesotho," and "Independence" have been included in various motifs. How precisely these signs were, and are, interpreted remains uncertain; although it has been said that, in the past, African consumers have read them differently from the way their producers anticipated, paying more heed to color and overall effect than to imagistic detail (Tyrrell 1968:91).

Among Southern Tswana, factory-produced blankets had all but replaced skin cloaks by 1900. And they continued to be worn late into the twentieth century in both ritual and everyday contexts (plate 5.19). This in spite of the

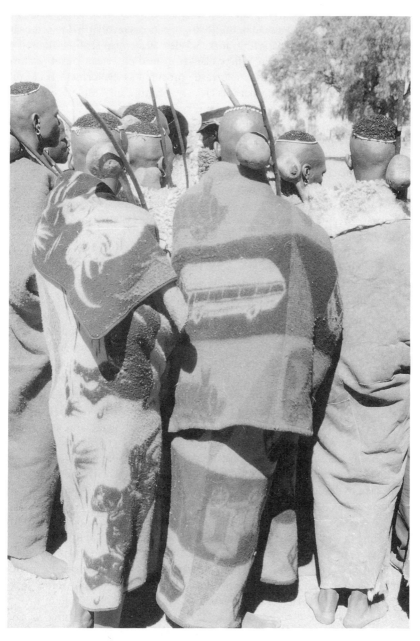

PLATE 5.19 *Blanketed Initiates, Mareetsane [J. L. and J. Comaroff, February 1970]*

269

opprobrium of the evangelists, who objected to the blanket just as they had done to the kaross; as Wookey noted in the 1880s, they occasionally tried to proscribe its use entirely:[87] "We have had to make a rule that no man shall be allowed to the ordinances who comes in a dirty blanket instead of a clean jacket or shirt. The latter, except for laziness, are as easily procured as the former." If cleanliness was next to Godliness, what was clean was European! Aesthetic ethnocentrism masqueraded, here, as moral virtue.

The battle over the blanket was, truly, a cultural struggle. Blankets shared one attribute, above all others, with skin karosses: their versatility. That is why they offended the missionaries, for whom the refinement, civility, and aesthetics of dress depended on the functional specificity of particular garments: on their being put on in a particular manner, at particular times, by particular people, over particular parts of the body, for particular activities. That is also why the Christians were so amused and irritated when Africans wore articles of clothing—indefinite rather than definite articles, that is—in ways for which they were not designed. And why *dikobò*, coverings of assertively undifferentiated form and function, could not but appear primitive in their eyes. For the Tswana, by contrast, it was their very capacity to serve as an all-purpose, enveloping mantle that commended these objects. Notwithstanding earlier evangelical efforts, ordinary people had neither the desire nor the means for a wide range of highly specialized manufactures. They purchased a limited number of commodities, *dikobò* among them, with which to craft ensembles that had to serve many ends; ensembles that varied little with season or occasion. Blankets, having the virtue of flexibility, could be worn as warm, yet easily removable, apparel—a second might be pinned around the waist in cold weather—and could also be wrapped about the upper body to cradle babies. In addition, they provided bedding on the road and ground sheets on which to sit, and were sometimes tied to poles or leafless trees for shade. So they were regarded as indispensable by labor migrants, of whose predicament they were iconic: *dikobò* were put to one set of uses en route to town, another while in the city, and yet another on return to the rural reserve. Not surprisingly, vehicles of mass transport were popular motifs (see plate 5.19).

Here, then, the topography of contrast. On one side, a European sensibility according to which, broadly speaking, the more specific the use to which something was put, the more refined the object, the more cultured the practice, the more civilized the person. On the other, the old Tswana penchant for multifunctionality, which associated versatility and plasticity with use-value, social worth, and, often, beauty. These two poles—both tendencies, of course, neither of them simple lived realities—charted the terrain of everyday practice. All Tswana, according to their means, abilities, backgrounds, and tastes, found themselves navigating that terrain, ever more so as the colonial world hemmed them in. Nor was this confined to the domain of cloth and clothing, fabric and fashion. As we shall see in the next chapter, it expressed itself as forcibly in the realm of architecture and domestic life.

*****

In sum, while Tswana elites followed the dictates of European fashion, seeking to master *sekgoa* in the cause of *embourgeoisement* (plate 5.20), the dress of ordinary people was a product of cultural patchwork. Cultivated against missionary opposition, their bricolage was wrought in increasingly confined spaces, with mass-produced materials garnered through an imperial market that pervaded their lives. As the early African creations, so bizarre to the foreign eye (cf. H. Kuper 1973:335), gave way to a more lasting colonial "native" style, Tswana men put on their khaki clothes, took up their blankets, and moved between country and city in growing numbers. A few youngbloods, home after contracts, sported flashy wardrobes bought at urban stores. But most migrants lacked the means for such purchases, even if they had wanted to make them. For the majority, only blankets domesticated the prescribed uniform of the workplace, distinguishing the garb of African peasant-proletarians as fringe citizens of the modern world order.

Their womenfolk, on the other hand, refashioned the dress of *setswana*, wearing a costume that fixed them on palpably "ethnic" ground. Some of its features would endure for decades. This style bore the imprint of Christian moral discipline,[88] yet it retained, in its blanketed elegance (plate 5.21), a sense of distinct origins, even an aura of independence and reserve. While Tswana females had internalized many of the signs and dispositions of *sekgoa*, they drew on them to give voice to their own condition. They had been absorbed into a nation-state in which they were not citizens; into a city-centered world that refused them a permanent urban home; into a universal "civilization" that depicted them as tribal, parochial, different in kind. Although they had to work with materials bequeathed them by the colonial political economy, they did not just buy into the ready-made persona offered to them. In this, their attire was symbolic of their general situation. And through it they represented themselves volubly: fabricated largely from foreign materials, it nonetheless expressed a locally tooled identity that elaborated on the vicissitudes of their history. The apparent conservatism of their costume echoed the fact that they had, in many respects, been made hostage to a newly politicized "tradition." But it also spoke of the effort to conserve a particular mode of life. And, like the continuing Tswana attachment to cattle, it implied an unwillingness to be seduced by the restless dream of social advancement through endless consumption.

Just after the turn of this century, at a time when more and more Tswana were donning their new uniforms of class and color and gendered ethnicity, Georg Simmel (1904, repr. 1971:305) observed: "It is peculiarly characteristic

PLATE 5.20 *"Mr. and Mrs. W. Z. Fenyang of Rietfontein" [from Plaatje 1916, opp. p. 8]*

PLATE 5.21 *"Entertaining Friends under the Baobab Tree," circa 1899 [from Willoughby n.d.[a]:11]*

of fashion that it renders possible a social obedience, which at the same time is a form of individual differentiation." In a single sentence, Simmel captured the original intent, and the ideological imperative, behind the mission effort to re-dress Tswana. His genius was to see how intricately connected were style and stratification, individualism and social interdependence—and how the delicate balance between self-expression and collective constraint was mediated, in ev-eryday life, by such things as the cut of one's coat. What he could not have grasped in full, however, is just what happens when these connections and pro-cesses cross cultural frontiers, there to become the object of other kinds of poli-tics and social assertion. In Simmel's own cosmopolitan milieu, the lines of class and distinction were well-grooved; the fashion system ran along familiar con-tours, even if it sometimes moved in mysterious ways. In colonial South Af-rica—where cultural exchanges and struggles were part of a society under con-struction—style did not *reflect* existing realities. It was part of their very making, part of the fabrication of a world divided along newly sharpened axes of discrimination and difference. And, today, of ethnic pride. Which is why its significance endures, if in altered form, in the current world of positively val-ued identities.

M A N S I O N S   O F
T H E   L O R D

Architecture, Interiority, Domesticity

If their homes can be revolutionized in a generation, so can their hearts.

A. M. Chirgwin (1932:28)

WE HAVE NOTED the parallel, in mission discourse, between attire and architecture, the unclothed body and uncontained space (*RRI*:172f.).[1] Attempts by colonial evangelists to reform the housing and interior design of Tswana life were, in many respects, the clothing campaign writ in clay, stone, and thatch. Each was a crucial site of domestication, each presumed the other as its metaphorical counterpoint. As John Mackenzie said in 1858:[2]

> [A Christian] cannot continue to live in the habits of a heathen. The African who believes that Jesus is preparing for him a glorious mansion in Heaven, will endeavour to build for himself a decent house on earth; and he who anticipates being hereafter attired in the pure white robe of the Redeemer's righteousness, will now throw aside the filthy garments of the heathen.

It is no accident that redemption should have been signified by building a house or furnishing its interior. This gesture, after all, fused biblical iconography, Nonconformist theology, and the contemporary social concerns of middle-class Christians.[3] Protestant ideology had long grounded moral improvement in the elementary forms of life, especially in the seemly domesticity of the Godly family (see *RRI*:68f.). As John Philip (1828,1:223–24) wrote, from the evangelical frontier, the "private and domestic situation of mankind is the chief circumstance which forms their character." What is more, he added, "the state of religion" in any missionary field was reflected in "the domestic condition of the people." Spirituality, domesticity, and moral refinement, in short, were all of a piece. Nor was this opinion restricted to colonial evangelists. By the mid nineteenth century, would-be historians of empire were finding its animating genius in "the holiness of the domestic circle" (Bruce 1851:41).[4] By contrast, savagery had no fixed abode. It was measurable by a lack of "natural" familial connections, of deep homely affections centered on cultivated femininity, of a rich interior life (see, e.g., Broadbent 1865:9f.; Livingstone 1960:253): foreshadowings, here, of the late twentieth-century concern that the death of "family values" spells the end of civil society.

Several studies have argued that "the home," as both place and precept, was a crucial site of European efforts to colonize Africa (e.g., Hansen 1989; Gaitskell 1983; Cock 1980);[5] in particular, to instill "Western family values" (Hunt 1990a:449). This is undoubtedly correct. At the same time, it is important to remember that contemporary British ideas of domesticity—and of its proper social and physical architecture—were themselves relatively recent in origin; they were anything but a secure, consensual, uncontested feature of the cultural landscape. As Rybczynski (1986:49) reminds us, the "private family home" only began to seed itself as a generic European social arrangement in the seventeenth century—and then primarily among the emerging bourgeoisie (Gallagher 1985:113f.; C. Hall 1990:47f.). In its modernist form, the "domestic" had two planes, one socioeconomic and the other architectural. It denoted, first, a social group (the family) sanctified in matrimony, possessed of property, recognized in law, and structured by a gendered, generational division of labor. Second, it presupposed a fixed physical space (the residence) set off from the world outside and divided inside into rooms dedicated to specific activities. At the intersection of these planes, and conjoining them, was the principle of privacy, as both adjective and noun: private property, private life, the privacy of home and person. Its obverse: privation.

But there was more to the middle-class model of domesticity than this. Rybczynski (1986:75) goes on:

> Domesticity has to do with family, intimacy, and a devotion to home, as well as with a sense of the house as embodying—not only harbouring—these sentiments. . . . [H]omely domesticity depended on the development of a rich interior awareness . . . an awareness that was the result of the woman's role in the home.

Home connoted a commensality of feelings, of refined emotions, of devotion. And sacred, marital sexuality (see, e.g., Perrot 1990a:123f, 180 [after Foucault

1976:143]; Mason 1994; Porter 1994:5).⁶ Connubial intimacy, femininity, and interiority were the tropes that, along with enclosed privacy, held it together as an imaginative construct,⁷ and gave it its sanctified moral status, its physicality and its spatial form. Still, we repeat, none of this ensured that, as lived practice, the ideal of domesticity was widely realized in British society at the time. Flora Tristan, a remarkable French feminist, suggested in her *London Journal* (1980:192), circa 1840, that any such claim would have been "far removed from reality." More an aspiration than an actuality among the wealthy, this vision of home and family still had limited purchase on the working people of urban Britain.⁸

Historians and sociologists now observe, as commonplace, that the development of a domestic domain—associated with women, unwaged housework, child raising, and the nuclear family home—was a corollary of the Protestant ethic and industrial capitalism;⁹ that, as a social construct and a tenet of middle-class modernity, it matured, in the age of the factory system, with the reconstruction of relations of production, personhood, class, and gender.¹⁰ Oakley (1974:42), echoing Tristan, points out that the "doctrine of (female) domesticity" had not spread far beyond the bourgeoisie before the 1840s. Only after 1841, with the call for the withdrawal of women from industry (p. 43), did this doctrine begin "to permeate downwards to the working classes" (p. 50; cf. C. Hall 1990:75f.).

Of course, there remained great variation in actual patterns of family organization within and across the social strata of Europe (e.g., Pawley 1971:6). There still does. But that is sociology. The struggle to naturalize the doctrine of domesticity was, from the first, part of the bourgeois endeavor to secure its cultural ascendancy. It was a struggle, Gallagher (1985:*passim*) notes, that reverberated through the literary discourses of the age. We use the term "naturalize" pointedly here. The effort to disseminate idealized images of domestic life was deeply indexed in nature, in its valuation and violation. As Oakley (1974:43–46) herself shows, *The Report of the Royal Commission on the Mines* (1842), for example, spoke of women workers as "disgusting and unnatural"; Engels (1968:160–61) added that factory toil deformed their bodies, making mothers liable to miscarry; and, in another genre, Charlotte Tonna's *The Wrongs of Woman* (1844) decried female employment for having "reversed the order of nature." This process of naturalization was an element in the forging of a coherent moral order, a silent edifice in which family, home, and marriage served as mechanisms of discipline and social control. Vested in dispersed regimes of surveillance (cf. Foucault 1978), in the texture of everyday habit, and in the shapes of lived space, the doctrine of domesticity facilitated new forms of production, new structures of inequality. It was also buttressed, increasingly, by the authority of church and state. Still, we repeat, it did not prevail immediately or without resistance. Nor everywhere in just the same way.

This brings us to the most general point we seek to make in the present chapter: that colonial evangelism played a vital part in the formation of Victorian domesticity *both* in Britain and overseas; that metropole and colony each became a model for, a refractory image of, the other. We argue throughout this volume that the encounter with non-Europeans was central in the development of Western modernity. This was particularly so with the modernist idea of "home," whose architecture was very much in formation at the time.[11] Scenes of distant battles with savages became the currency of a moral offensive against the urban "jungles" (Hebdige 1988:20f.) and "uncouth" rural villages (Fussell and Fussell 1953:172f.) of nineteenth-century England, where the poor were regarded in much the same light—or, rather, dark—as the most beastly blacks in the bush.[12] Here lay the basis of a *dialectic* of domesticity, a simultaneous, mutually sustaining process of social reconstruction at home and abroad.[13]

The bourgeois ideal of the family home might not have been universally established in Britain. But the colonial evangelists had few doubts about its propriety; which, given their theological orientations and their social position, is hardly surprising (see n. 3). Whatever else they argued about among themselves, or with others, they did not dispute the sanctity of properly housed, properly gendered domestic life (cf. Gaitskell 1990). It was taken as a Christian axiom that the family home was "the most sacred shrine of our temple" (J. B. Brown 1868:585–86). "Domestic society," announced John Philip (1828,1:224), was "esteemed sacred" in "all civilized nations." As this implies, the Nonconformists were avid bearers of Western family values to the outposts of empire— and were well-suited to serve at once as cultural colonizers and as conduits of a dialogue between Europe and Africa.

In this regard, moreover, they agreed with Chirgwin (1932:28) that, "if . . . homes [could] be revolutionized . . . so [could] . . . hearts"; that the proper domestication of Africans would bring true belief in its wake. Hence Philip's statement about the reciprocal connection between domesticity and religiosity. Over a century before Bourdieu (1977, 1979), de Certeau (1984), Giddens (1985), and other theorists of everyday practice (see Lawrence and Low 1990:469f.; Pader 1993:114), the evangelists took it for granted that houses, and the routines they inscribed, constructed their inhabitants.[14] The architecture of civilization should, therefore, be an effectual means of insinuating hygienic, Godly habits into heathen life. As they did in respect of economics, the Nonconformists put their faith in African mimesis: if appropriate models could be laid out for the Southern Tswana, they were sure, in time, to be copied and internalized. And, as they did in respect of clothing, the Europeans assumed one cardinal principle above all others: that the gauge of a civilized abode was the degree to which its interior spaces were rendered functionally specific and distinct. A residence with no internal divisions, no rooms given over to particular kinds of activity, signified savagery, almost animality; all the more so if that residence was not enclosed on its own grounds. On the other hand, the making of decent dwellings—with living and dining rooms, bedrooms, kitchens, pantries—might give access to the Mansion of the Lord. But it was not only the form of these dwellings that drew the attention of the civilizing mission. So did their contents, their innards. In this respect, too, colonial evangelists were creatures of their time. John Lukacs (1970:623), writing about the "external character" of medieval European life, remarks that the elaboration of domestic furnishings in the West was attendant on a sense of home as the context for an emerging inner life (see Rybczynski 1986:36): "The interior furniture of houses," he notes, "appeared together with the interior furniture of minds." Each was taken to fashion and reflect the other.

Similarly, the Nonconformists in South Africa saw new domestic appointments as a means by which to free Southern Tswana from a base, "unreflective" dependence on the external world.[15] Their Protestantism was a religion of interiority. For them, exteriors were merely surfaces which reflected an inner state of being; these required apertures to let in light from the outside, as windows to the soul. So it was with their architecture. On the inside of simple, square abodes—in their spaces and their furnishings—was a terrain on which Christianity might work its revelatory way, illuminating the recesses of the "native mind": in particular, its capacity for self-reflection. This, as we shall see, expressed itself as tangibly in practical construction as in religious instruction, as much in the effort to introduce panes of glass as to instil a spiritual sensibility.

*****

The importance of architecture in the grand narrative of European colonialism is now well recognized (cf. T. Mitchell 1991; Lawrence and Low 1990:486f.). As Salman Rushdie's *Midnight's Children* (1981:94f.) suggests, ruling cadres have often believed that fine habitations breed good habits. And accommodating conformity. The Raj, even in retreat, hoped that the houses left behind would reform Indians in its own image. According to Rushdie, they did. "We make our buildings," Winston Churchill once observed, "then our buildings make us" (Crook 1992:21). Construction was integral to other European imperialisms as well. Wright (1991), for instance, has shown how central was the design of colonial cities to the politics of French expansion; unlike most large-scale human settlements (Kostof 1991), such conurbations were often planned in their entirety. Not so in the world with which we are concerned, however. Prior to overrule, the efforts of Britons to establish themselves in the South African interior relied little on raising huge edifices—other than the occasional church or school of more than usually ambitious proportions. The early evangelists, long the only colonizers who sought to effect permanent changes on Tswana terrain, were perforce organic transformers, not the master builders of an imperial state. Unlike colonial administrators, they were denied the fantasy that their civilizing structures might be erected on bare ground. In the event, they concentrated, rather, on residential architecture and the contours of small communities. For all their modesty of scale, the fruits of these exertions were to be far from insignificant.

VERNACULAR ARCHITECTURE: OF ARCS AND ANARCHY

Symbolically, the war of the civilized man against the savage has always been the attack of the line against the irregular. . . . It did not always work.

Andrew Sinclair (1977:102)

European eyes appear to have beheld nineteenth-century Southern Tswana architecture and domestic life in quite disparate ways. The testimonies of early white observers vary markedly in both tone and texture: some spoke approvingly, others disapprovingly; some described in detail the constructions and social scapes they saw, others dismissed them in a few words. Yet others wrote as if there had been nothing at all in the "African wilderness" before European intervention had made places of its open spaces (cf. Carter 1989:9, 17, 27f.),[16] before the European gaze had invested it with meaning (*RRI*:174).[17] Until the establishment of the Kuruman station, declared the *Evangelical Magazine* (LMS 1840:142), what is now Bechuanaland was an empty land "where once the moral wilds presented a scene more sterile than the neighbouring desert."[18]

For all the variation among Western accounts, there was, with few exceptions, a high degree of homogeneity in those of the evangelists. Their representations of vernacular architecture and domestic life fixed on the point of intersection between ethics and aesthetics, morality and materiality. Let us look into these representations at two levels: at portrayals, first, of Southern Tswana towns and, second, of homes and dwellings. Wherever salient, we set them, contrapuntally, against other early European reports; also against our own account, in volume 1, of prevailing arrangements. This will make clear precisely what it was that the mission sought to transform.

Townscapes: Heaps of Huts Jostled Together

The earliest evangelical explorers, those who beat a path into the interior to lay the ground for missionization, sent home quietly favorable accounts of Tswana towns; if nothing else, these put the prospects for spreading the Gospel in the best possible light. In 1813, for example, Campbell described Dithakong (Lattakoo) in congenial terms.[19] His descriptions of Kurreechane (1822,1:222f.)[20] almost a decade later were as positive. John Philip (1828,2:121) also found Dithakong, regarded from a distance, "a very agreeable object to the eye"—although, as we noted in chapter 3, he likened its form to that of an "ant-hill." What Campbell and Philip had in common was that both were itinerant visitors to the Tswana "field," not sedentary evangelists. The latter were less complimentary. The Rev. John Cameron, of the WMMS, to cite just one, was less than overwhelmed by his first impression of Thaba 'Nchu:[21]

> Here [one] sees a vast assemblage of houses teeming with inhabitants. This, though a very delightful and animating sight in the solitudes of Africa, is, nevertheless, widely different from a European town. No splendid fanes, or spires, no public buildings to serve the ends of either justice or benevolence, greet the heavens; a heap of Bechuana huts jostled together without any apparent order, and their indispensable appendages, cattlefolds, make up the scene.

After traveling "for weeks . . . without seeing anything to be called a town" (see n. 21), Thaba 'Nchu might have offered a "delightful" vista. But, when all was said and done, Cameron found it somewhat disappointing. A disordered jumble, this urban scape appeared to lack the divisions and contrasts of a civilized place: the separation of humans from animals, the private from the public, high from low. The town proclaimed no elevations of spirituality,[22] none of the heights of social justice or the visible accomplishments of civil society. (The term was used by the missionaries themselves; see J. Philip 1828,1:220.) Since the chief's court was a stone semicircle in the open air, rather than a vertical structure reaching toward the sky, it did not break the flat planes of the settlement. And so the latter presented itself to the Nonconformists as an unending honeycomb of concentric circles, folded in on one another in secretive, serpentine involutions; hence Philip's image of the ant-hill (1828,2:121). Like crude garments and crooked furrows, such towns betrayed the tangled disarray of the lives of their inhabitants. Their lack of enclosure implied a lack of private possession. Even when picturesque, they had a "wild-African appearance."[23] Worse yet, having been "put down without regard to plan, and with no idea of streets,"[24] they were difficult to comprehend. Or control. Campbell (1822,1:255) once lost his way alarmingly in Kurreechane, so tortuous were the lanes of the Hurutshe capital. It is no wonder, as Sinclair (1977:102) reminds us, that "geometry and reason" were associated with "the authority of man"—European Man, that is, both upper case—"over the contours of nature." Added Livingstone (1960:272, 244) of African aesthetics, "civilization alone produces beauty" in both objects and people. All else "tends to the production of deformity and ugliness."[25]

The arcane, anarchic forms of Tswana urban architecture were sometimes taken to be more than just unappealing. They could actually be unhealthy (J. Philip 1828,1:209). Of Shoshong, John Mackenzie (1883:222–23) wrote, one summer in the early 1870s:

When viewed from the adjoining mountain, the town thus clothed in green is really beautiful. But however charming in the distance, it is not at all pleasant to thread those narrow, winding, and gourd-shaded lanes. . . . I found the atmosphere of the town to be quite oppressive, and constantly wondered that cases of fever were not even more numerous.

The feeling of dis-ease—to give way, in the early twentieth century, to the notion that Tswana towns were "unhygienic"[26]—seems to have emanated from the cloying profusion of an alien aesthetic. As we shall see, the Nonconformists tried to replace these secluded, sinuous lanes with "clean lines" and direct, accessible thoroughfares.[27] There was, in their effort, an echo of the Gospel of Luke (3.4–5; after Isaiah 40.3–5; our emphasis), among the earliest biblical translations into Setswana:

> Prepare the way of the Lord,
> *make his paths straight.*
> Every valley shall be filled,
> and every mountain and hill shall be brought low,
> and *the crooked shall be made straight.*[28]

The distress of the evangelists at the nonrectilinear form of African settlements was somewhat ironic. They were themselves from places hardly known for their square lines or their orderliness. Many of the northern British villages and towns whence they came were—still are—every bit as irregular as their Tswana counterparts. Neither have they ever been thought of as especially healthy or well regulated. The impulse to impose the orthogonal shapes of civilization on "savage settlements" spoke more of desire and absence than anything already accomplished in Britain. Nor, indeed, was the idea of the rectilinear city uncontested in Europe at the time. The struggle between competing visions— the urban scape as Order or Labyrinth, altar to the practical, or work of art— had not been, would never be, resolved.[29] All these visions, and others besides, had their protagonists among people of different sociopolitical persuasions. Charles Dickens ([1842] 1972:145), for one, inveighed against grid-like cities. After walking about one for a while, he "would have given the world for a crooked street." In London, of course, not Lattakoo.

The "primitiveness" of Tswana urban architecture was also conveyed, visually, in depictions of the contrast between indigenous settlements and those idealized by the mission. These were printed repeatedly. One, by Baxter (plate 6.1), appeared in Robert Moffat's *Missionary Labours* (1842:560), on the title page of the *Evangelical Magazine and Missionary Chronicle* (LMS 1840:141), and, slightly amended, as a frontispiece to a biography of John Campbell (R. Philip 1841). In the foreground stood an LMS station—a square-lined, well-ordered village—in the image of Kuruman. Behind it, receding into the distance, lay a

PLATE 6.1 *"Birds'-eye View of the Kuruman Station" [from Moffat 1842:560; LMS 1840:141]*

"native" town, a wild array of small, featureless huts scattered across the countryside. Africans, it asserted, lived in rampant disorder, all over the place. Something else too: the move from background to foreground was a figurative passage from past to future. It spelled out, at once, the objectives of the mission and the teleology of colonial evangelism.

As we saw in the previous volume (pp. 130f.),[30] Tswana towns were culturally complex structures, capable both of enduring for many years and of undergoing rapid change. Produced, reproduced, and transformed in the context of everyday social practice, they sometimes grew very large and highly concentrated; at other times, they showed a tendency toward fragmentation and dispersal. At their most centralized, as several of the missionaries themselves realized,[31] these towns were composed of nesting administrative units with an intricate internal organization (Schapera 1943b:68ff.), elaborate patterns of rank and relationship, and a proclivity for producing fractious struggles. What is more, when chiefdoms moved, they recreated their physical arrangements on arrival at a new site (J. Mackenzie 1871:370), thereby rendering space into place according to their own political priorities. Hardly a jumble of homesteads dotted all over the landscape!

In point of fact, other European visitors to Tswana towns were less quick to voice aesthetic or moral disapproval. Burchell (1824,2:513f.) might not have discerned any great "regularity of arrangement" in Dithakong. But he seems to have been charmed by the place, and spoke of his high regard for its dwellings (see also G. Thompson 1967:84); these, he decided, were "perfectly suited to every want and fitted to every circumstance" of life here (p. 522). Lichtenstein (1930,2:373; 1973:67), similarly, commented on the "pretty wide street" by which he entered a Tlhaping village, and on the "artistic way" habitations for humans and animals were built.[32] But the most striking of all accounts—because it inverted the iconography of the mission—was written by Anthony Trollope (1878,2:279f.) some years later of Thaba 'Nchu, the Seleka-Rolong capital that had so underwhelmed Rev. Cameron. This "native town" struck Trollope as captivating and unadulteratedly exotic. He was especially taken by its quaint sense of "municipal regularity." A striking contrast, he averred (pp. 275, 278), to the scatter of European homes on the plain below.

Huts and Homesteads: Earthen Spaces, Empty Nests

Let us reverse, here, the order of telling. Most secular European observers wrote appreciatively of the aesthetics and architecture of Tswana homes. "In elegance and solidity," stated Barrow (1806:393), they were "as good as the *Casae . . .* built in imperial Rome." They were also superior "in every respect" to most Irish habitations. Lichtenstein (1973:69f.; 1930,2:377f.) added that, besides being "artistic," these houses were built with "great care and exactness." They were commodious, cool, durable, free of "bad odour," and, again, ideally suited to the environment.[33] Burchell (1824,2:521) and George Thompson (1967:84–85) agreed.[34]

These accounts do more than just commend Tswana domestic architecture, however. They also show that it involved a complex internal division of space. Burchell (1824,2:515f.) explained that each Tlhaping homestead consisted of a round house—with inner and outer chambers, a veranda, and a store for everyday supplies—abutted by a hut for servants and by elaborate corn jars (cf. Stow 1905:441). Outside, within a strong perimeter fence, were front and rear courtyards, their smooth floors made of clay infused with cattle manure, and a cooking hearth. Such dwellings could be larger or smaller, with less or more internal partitions. But, overall, their design did not vary a great deal. Burchell went on to reflect on the fact that all houses were built on a circular plan (p. 517). "[W]hether derived from ancient custom or from natural judgement," he said, this "shows a distinct and peculiar taste."

[T]heir own observation or experience, has taught these people . . .
the axiom that a circle comprises a greater area than any other figure of
equal circumference; or, as we may suppose their mode of expressing it

would be, that a greater number of men or cattle may be contained in an enclosure of that shape, and that thus, the making of the outer fence, or the walls, is performed with as little labor as possible.

Instead of lamenting the aesthetic of the arc, or seeing savagery in the circle, Burchell found practical reason—and cultural sense —in them. Not only that, he discerned a great deal of functional specificity in the interior organization of domestic space: sleeping chambers were set off from sites of sociability, cooking from storage, servants' quarters from those of the family, long-term corn caches from everyday food pantries.

Burchell, again, was not alone in his observations (see, e.g., Lichtenstein 1930,2:377f.; A. Smith 1939,1:242–43). How, then, did the missionaries come to describe "traditional" habitations as rudimentary, one-roomed huts? Partly because this is what they saw—or, at least, what second- and third-generation evangelists thought they saw—albeit, ironically, for reasons of their own making. As the century wore on, many Southern Tswana abandoned the designs of the past, removing the interior chambers from their houses. Why? In order, primarily, to accommodate the bulky furniture encouraged by the Nonconformists! In 1933, in fact, the Kgatla regent, Isang, would speak to a gathering at the University of the Witwatersrand of "the anomaly of having a square bed in a round hut" (Schapera 1980:54). Tradition, so-called, was remade by hollowing out the content of past practices.

But this, we repeat, was later on. And it was only part of the story. There was more to the mission reaction against Tswana housing, especially in the early years, than a historical farce about bedroom furniture. The colonial evangelists had to acknowledge, from the first, the existence of an indigenous domestic architecture centered on the homestead (*lolwapa;* Schapera 1943a:84–85). Many of them knew that dwellings were internally divided, various interior and exterior spaces being allocated to different, and differently gendered activities;[35] Stephen Kay (1834:199), a Wesleyan missionary, for example, described the four compartments of Tlhaping habitations in much the same terms as had Burchell. Some of his LMS and WMMS colleagues were also aware that, like the *lolwapa,* the "house" (*ntlo*) had enormous conceptual and political significance in the Southern Tswana world (see, e.g., Campbell 1822,1:226; J. Mackenzie 1871:364). Many read what other European observers had written of the clean, neat, orderliness of "native" abodes (e.g., R. Moffat 1842:223–24).[36] But they perceived them differently, deciphering many of the same signs in strikingly dissimilar ways.

Take, for example, the compartmentalization, and functional specification, of homestead design. Far from seeing in this an enlightened architecture, or an aesthetic of domestic life with deeply textured interiors, the evangelists did one of two things. Either they ignored it, preferring to characterize Tswana houses by reference to stereotypic conventions ("the rude skin-clad Pagan in his circular hut"; J. Mackenzie 1871:475). Or they took it to bespeak an animal-like instinct for replication. "As birds of the same species always form their nests alike," opined *Missionary Sketches* in 1824, "so do each of the African tribes build their houses."

We shall return to the metaphorical twinning of birds with uncouth beings. The association of home making with nest building[37] here flowed from the evangelists' perception that Tswana dwellings were constructed from "raw," natural materials: the clay of the earth, the feces of cattle, the branches of trees, the wild grasses of the bush. Devoid of the signs of cultivation, these dwellings were said to have no "proper" windows or doors, nothing to let in light or lock out unwanted intruders, nothing to mark off private space. No furniture, or other "necessities," graced their interiors. Lacking manufactured materials in their making, they displayed none of the elements of design that Europeans took to set off human art from animal fabrication. The fact that their female inhabitants were, in a manner of speaking, transhumant—moving to their fields for the agricultural season—robbed them of perennial feminine domesticity. All of which added up to the impression that "native huts" were more like the impermanent abodes of creatures than the homes of cultured humans. This impression was underscored by Nonconformist descriptions of the epoch before the arrival of the mission (R. Moffat 1842:507): "Hitherto when they had milked their cows, they retired to their houses and yards, to sit moping over a few embers; . . . at night, spreading the dry hide of some animal on the floor." "Moping over the embers," rather than reading by lamplight, captures well the entropy, the vacuity attributed to African domestic life. And "spreading the dry hide of some animal"—apart from underscoring the absence of furniture—bespeaks an existence close to the earth.

Note here the unspoken parallel, in mission discourses, between the "huts" of the Southern Tswana and their "filthy skin cloaks." Both were unrefined, both were natural in provenance, both were marked by an absence of functional specificity. And both were said to teem with infestation. "The houses are generally not very clean," proclaimed Willoughby (1899:84–85), revealingly, in an LMS magazine for British youth. "After a year or two, creatures that the editor will not allow me to name become so numerous that even the thick-skinned natives have to clear out." Although published at the end of the century, this account, with its heavy-handed humor, implied that vernacular housing had always been this way; that, since time immemorial, Tswana dwellings had been the kind of places that only the "thick-skinned" could bear.

Robert Moffat (1842:399) went one better. Using a favorite literary device, he damned Tlhaping housing by affecting a conversation with the (rival) Ngwaketse chief, Makaba. In the passage, the two men appear to collude in condemning the "barbarous manners," the base building skills, and, most of all, the lack of cleanliness of the Tswana to the south. No matter that other Europeans[38] had stressed the "neatness, good order and cleanness of [the] dwellings" of these very same people.[39] For most evangelists, African dirt and degeneracy had a different derivation: it signaled an offense against the moral design of the mission. "Cleaner . . . better houses" make for "*happy homes*," said Wookey (1884:306). The emphasis was his. Behind it lay the conviction that Tswana domestic life was an altogether miserable affair.

For a start, the Africans were believed to have no sense of personal privacy—and, by extension, no appreciation of the division between the private and the public. Recall how put out were the Europeans by the Tswana propensity, in the early years, to make uninvited calls. The evangelists seem, *in extremis*, to have regarded it as a form of promiscuity, a practice that polluted their own intimate world: dirt, once again, as a transgression of the moral order of the mission. In an account of Moffat's labors (Religious Tract Society n.d.:85), rewritten for the young, the anonymous author comes clean:

> The dirty Bechuanas would come in and stay. They did not see that their missionaries did not like so many visitors. So all day long they were there; touching the furniture with their fingers, and leaving red, greasy marks upon everything they handled and wherever they sat. They would squat down and have a chatter; they would lie down and take a nap on the floor and afterwards go away, carrying with them . . . anything.

Nowhere in the published record is there a more frank statement of the discomfort occasioned by radically opposed values of sociability and property. Nowhere do we feel as palpably the rupture of "private" space, time, and possessions. Nowhere does difference emerge in quite so tactile a form. To many of the evangelists, this kind of interaction was proof perfect that the Southern Tswana had no idea of domestic order.

There were, in their view, further "proofs" as well, some of which we have met with before. Broadbent (1865:96f.), for one, denied that there was any "natural affection" between husbands and wives or parents and children.[40] Marriage barely existed. It implied no moral obligation to be faithful; men "bartered" their womenfolk at will, much like cattle. This view was extreme, it is true. But other evangelists were as quick to speak pejoratively of Tswana conjugal and familial relations. While they agreed that polygyny was by no means widespread, some went to great lengths to show that it conduced to immorality, to the "[destruction of] all family affection," and to the "internal strifes" endemic to "the ordinary life of a Bechuana community" (J. Mackenzie 1871:410–11).[41] The predicament of females—whose role in the division of labor was often deemed unnatural (see chapter 3)—was also likened to that of servants or slaves.[42] And, while the women "build and thatch, . . . make the fences, dig, sow, watch and reap the fields, cook the victuals, and bring up the children, . . .

[w]hat do the men do?" Nothing, most of the time. "They seem to resemble dogs, in their being able to sleep when they please" (LMS 1824). Under such conditions, decent family life, clearly, was impossible.

On one hand, then, Southern Tswana were sometimes alleged to lack domesticity altogether. Close to the earth, tolerant of its dirt, they resembled animals. And yet, inside the circles-within-circles-within-circles of their settlements, inside the groups to which they were tied, they were said to lead lives interconnected by dense, if debased, relations of consanguinity, affinity, obligation, and reciprocity. For the missionaries, it was crucial to free Tswana from these social entanglements. Only then could nuclear families be founded on a proper marriage contract between consenting individuals. Only then could civilized lives, suitably housed, be contemplated. Only then would the breeding grounds of savagery be domesticated.

*****

It is hardly necessary to remark again, in light of our account in volume 1 (pp. 126–69), that the colonial evangelists misrecognized the complex processes at work in the construction of family and domestic life among Southern Tswana. Such misrecognitions, after all, were mutual. But even if the Europeans had grasped these complexities, they demanded for the most part to be ignored. How, otherwise, to justify implanting on African soil the modernist ideal of Christian domesticity and its architecture without regard for what flourished there already?

RIGHTING ANGLES, SETTING SQUARES: RECONSTRUCTING THE ARCHITECTURE OF THE EVERYDAY

[T]he Bakwains [Kwena] have a curious inability to make or put things square. . . . In the case of three large houses, erected by myself at different times, every brick had to be put square by my own right hand.

David Livingstone (1857:26)

The right hand of reason would find it hard to straighten out the contours of Tswana social life. Its circular, erratic forms—the shapes associated with rank nature and "primitive" mentality (Comaroff and Comaroff 1986:13; cf. Lévi-Strauss 1972:204)—did not submit easily to the square set of civilization. Not that this deterred the missionaries. Determined to effect what we might call a syntactic "[re]distribution in space" (Foucault 1979:141), they were to manifest a very general modernizing impulse in the West. "Improvement makes straight roads," wrote William Blake (1975) from the depths of his experience. Just as

Thomas Jefferson saw fit to organize the American wilderness—even before it
had been mapped—in terms of Euclidian geometry (Sinclair 1977:102), so the
evangelists in Bechuanaland set out to subsume the unruly figures of African
existence in a grid of gentility. And to do so with similar dispatch. John Philip
(1828,1:240) recalls that, on arriving among the Khoi, Charles Pacalt "drew out
a ground-plan of his intended village, which he laid out in two open streets
parallel to each other." After persuading some of the local people "to build more
decent habitations for themselves" and to surround them with fenced gardens,
he went about enclosing the village itself in a substantial wall, six feet high. To
the extent that Europeans saw manmade boundaries as marks of civilization,
Pacalt's fortress must have been an impressive sight indeed.

The effort of the evangelists to work their transformations on Tswana architecture and domestic arrangements had two sides. One, couched in the subjunctive mood, was exemplary; the other, cast in the indicative, was more directly interventionist. In the first instance, they set out to create models for the
Africans to admire, desire, and emulate. In the second, they sought, by their
own deeds, actively to intrude their designs onto the local terrain and into local
habits and habitations.

The Mission as Model: (i) Home and Family

As we noted earlier, the evangelists believed that their own dwellings and family
lives ought to be held out as a visible ideal to Tswana. "The life of the missionary," according to John Mackenzie (1871:466), had to be at once desirable and
attainable enough to "be copied by his flock." This extended to the outer form
and inner design of his abode, the manner of its construction, its appointments,
and the domestic routines of its occupants. The notion that their dwellings
ought to serve as a *transparent* model—an example of "Godly domesticity . . .
open to all eyes" (Langmore 1989:85)—did not always sit easily with the Nonconformists' concern for their own privacy. But that was an unavoidable cost of
their calling.

While all the evangelists put up some form of temporary habitation when
they arrived at a new site, many tried, from the first, to build in a manner be-
fitting a "decent" existence—however stripped down. The mission house, as
they saw it, was the core of civilization in the wilderness, the nucleus from
which a Christian community had to start. It was also the most visible sign of
their presence. Edwards (1886:101) gives us a sense of the humble beginnings
of a station, this one among the former "Mantatees":

At Umpukani . . . we had to live in our wagons or in 'hartebeest' houses.[43]
Here also we had a reed and pole structure put up for a place of worship.
. . . We then got put up a little place containing two small rooms and a
kitchen, the walls being built of sun-dried bricks.

One of the two small chambers, he added regretfully, had initially to serve as both sitting room and dining room; it had also to accommodate visitors. The other was for sleeping. As time passed, this structure was enlarged and refined; eventually it became a "good-sized" house (Whiteside 1906:336). Close by, at Matlwasse, the Rev. Broadbent began more ambitiously (Tilby 1914:192): "He built himself an ample wooden house, whose single story was divided into bed-room, general living-room, and store-room for food and books." Broadbent (1865:61) himself stressed that his store room was partitioned, the pantry being set off from the depository for books and tools. He implies, too, that the living room, the largest chamber, was apportioned into "sitting" and "dining" areas. Like moral reformers in Europe, the missionaries in South Africa insisted that Christian propriety was impossible for families living "all in one room"— whether it be a hovel in underclass Britain (Jephson 1907:31), a hut in the African bush (Willoughby 1911:70), or a transient mission house in Bechuanaland.

In sum, Edwards, Broadbent, and other early evangelists might have seen themselves as ascetic pioneers, far from centers of gentility. But—as these texts underscore by remarking the unremarkable—they took pains to lay out the architectural principles of a civilized life inasmuch as they could: to set off private spaces from spaces of sociality; to divide apartments into discrete areas for cooking, sleeping, sitting, dining, storage, and so on; to make all rooms "quite square" (Moffat and Moffat 1951:59). Even in their wagons, en route to the "field," the most basic of these principles had been respected: enclosed familial interiors, home to women and children, were securely curtained off from the public exterior, where the missionaries engaged with black laborers, dealt with animals and natural obstacles, and interacted with the world at large.

As they settled into more permanent, ample houses, the evangelists elaborated yet further the domestic domain in which they lived, partitioning spaces by gender and generation, by mode of activity, and by the degree of closure and intimacy appropriate to them. Where possible, separate rooms were made for girls and boys, placing them beyond the conjugal chamber and its sacred altar, the marital bed (cf. Perrot 1990b:124); nurseries, studies, and guest rooms were added; eating areas became dining rooms; and so on. These may have been small apartments. But separation, not size, was the point. When the Moffats' new house at Kuruman was completed in 1826, it had, in addition to a kitchen and a pantry, four rooms plus a hall; an adjoining cottage was being built for visiting evangelists on their way to other stations (Moffat and Moffat 1951:231, 190). Similarly, Livingstone's (1959,1:105) dwelling at Mabotsa, erected in 1844, included one bedroom (there were no children yet), a pantry, a study, and a sitting room; its kitchen, tended by a Tswana servant, was outside (plate 6.2).[44]

Equally important were the fixtures and fittings of these houses. Windows and doors had at first to be improvised (Broadbent 1865:62; E. Smith 1957:176). But frames were typically installed, in the European mode, with hinges, latches,

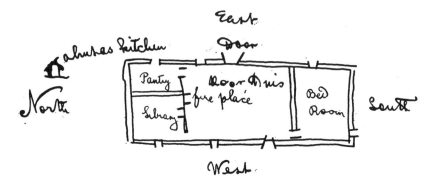

PLATE 6.2 *Sketch Plan of David Livingstone's House, Mabotsa [from Livingstone 1959,1:105]*

nails, and screws brought from the Cape Colony. Later, more elaborate iron castings were used (e.g., Livingstone 1959,1:105); some were forged locally at mission stations, some imported, along with other building materials, by traders who made their way into the interior. Shutters, too, were fitted, and, where possible, inside and outside walls—made of brick and stone rather than clay[45]— were whitewashed. Floors were a problem, since they had to be fabricated from local products, and, as many of the evangelists agreed, indigenous techniques were by far the most effective. Likewise roofs, which were usually thatched in much the same manner as were those of Tswana dwellings. This resort to vernacular styles and methods is a point to which we shall return.

Of all household fittings, however, perhaps the most important were locks and glass. The missionaries insisted on doors that could be properly secured and on windows that let in light; indeed, these were essential to their very idea of home. While latches and bolts ensured the sanctity of private possessions, personal space, and familial intimacy, windows were apertures of enlightenment. Recall volume 1 (pp. 181f.): glass was, to the early modern imagination, an important medium of civilization, permitting enclosure yet translucence. Once upon a time the privilege of the church (Braudel 1981:296–97), its illuminating properties had long been commonly (and inexpensively) available to house builders. The evangelists brought together its hallowed and domestic aspects: they encouraged Africans to open up the dark interiors of their lives— and to make within them a place for such edifying pursuits as sewing or reading.

And a place for furniture. Household furnishings, like fixtures and fittings, began modestly on the evangelical frontier: Broadbent (1865:61), again, tells how he contrived his first bed from "poles and leather straps," on which he laid a "hair mattress" (see also Moffat and Moffat 1951:59). Most ambitious, perhaps, was Price, at Molepolole, who fashioned a bed, a table, cupboard, bookshelves, and a couch out of packing crates and other odds and ends (E. Smith

1957:176). But these were strictly temporary measures. The objective was to fill indoor spaces with manufactured effects, the kind of domestic commodities that Southern Tswana might covet and, in due course, buy. Hence, once permanent stations had been established in the interior, most of the evangelists brought some furniture with them; usually beds, tables, and chairs. All gradually acquired more—wardrobes, cupboards, dressers, sofas, and the like—often imported by wagon from the south. Sooner or later, mission houses were filled with Victorian appointments; with the embroidery, bric-a-brac, photographs, cushions, pianos, and other necessities of a suitably feminized British middle-class home (cf. Langmore 1989:85).

Never, we stress, was the intention merely to erect and furnish a commodious mission house—even though personal comfort and bourgeois self-construction *was* a matter of concern to many of the evangelists.[46] As important was the demonstrative aspect of the gesture. Building a residence was a definitive and dramatic statement of values, of purpose, of resolve. It was also an early opportunity to put before would-be converts a concrete vision of prospect and possibility; the prospect of a different kind of existence in which heathen hardship might be replaced by the "purer and sweeter" trappings of civilization (J. Mackenzie 1871:465). Here was yet another effort to instill in Southern Tswana a new sense of want and need. That is why, when Read received permission to work among the Tlhaping (*RRI*:201), he immediately set about constructing a house that would be a "wonder to all"; why he was so quick to report that many came "flocking" to see it; why he promised to erect an identical one, presumably as publicly, for the wife of the chief. Explained David Livingstone (1857:46), if the Christians wanted their works "to be respected by the natives," they had to have houses of "decent dimensions, costing an immense amount of manual labour." It is unclear whether the Africans shared the labor theory of value advanced by the evangelist. But they do seem to have declared themselves impressed by the European accommodations. So much so that the missionaries believed their exertions to have been successful. John Mackenzie (1871:467), for example, reported that "[a]fter being shown, at their own request, some of the rooms of our house, a party of the wives of petty chiefs at length broke out, addressing Mrs. Mackenzie: 'Happy wife and happy mother! You have a "kingdom" here of your own.'" Mackenzie was as delighted that the Tswana women had *asked* to see the mission house—itself proof of its exemplary power—as he was to tell of its impact on them. Both affirmed that this dwelling, its interiors suitably appointed, had in fact served its purpose.

The Nonconformists appear to have understood their architectural quest as a truly spiritual one. Livingstone (1960:297), who did a great deal of didactic construction early on,[47] wrote of a dwelling completed at Kolobeng in 1848: "That house is an evidence that I tried to introduce Christ's Gospel into [Kwena] country." The house in question had been put up for Sechele. Like

Read, Livingstone (1961:113) believed that building homes for chiefs had a salutary effect on them, brought the evangelists "into closer contact with [their] people," and ensured that the seeds planted by the mission would "ripen into glorious fruit." He was gratified when, the work done, Sechele asked that a regular prayer meeting be established in his new habitation. Domestic architecture had yielded a House of God—albeit a transient temple inhabited by a polygamist who, for all his lively interest in Christianity, found it easier to accept monotheism in principle than monogamy in practice. Livingstone (1959,1:157) thought, nonetheless, that the building had a real effect on Sechele.

Livingstone and his colleagues also had another point in mind in stressing the need to erect substantial mission houses. For them, the cultural worth of a dwelling lay in the fact that it congealed a civilized, Christian act of construction. This act, in turn, bore within it a set of practical teachings. The first, and most important, had to do with a properly refined, appropriately gendered division of labor. European edifices, palpably, were made by males (even if Tswana females sometimes helped them with floors and roofs). It was the divinely ordained duty of men to house and provide for their families—and, at home, to do all the outside manual work. The role of their womenfolk was to decorate the finished interiors of their dwellings, to apply their "domestic arts" to its "tasteful" furnishings, and then to minister inside over its everyday routines.[48]

The second lesson was a respect for specialist building skills, which the missionaries learned and/or hired craftsmen to perform (see n. 45) in the hope that Tswana would take their lead.[49] It was their fond wish that, inspired by watching work in progress and perhaps by toiling alongside the Europeans, a cadre of "native" artisans would be formed. In the short run, this hope proved groundless. As Livingstone (1857:123) once commented, testily:

> They observe most carefully a missionary at work until they understand whether [for example] a tire is well welded or not, and then pronounce upon its merits with great emphasis, but there their ambition rests satisfied. . . . It was in vain I tried to indoctrinate the Bechuanas with the idea that criticism did not imply any superiority over the workman.

And in vain that he tried to indoctrinate them with the Protestant work ethic itself. Here lay the third lesson of missionary mimesis, one that we encountered in chapter 4. By employing men—at first, men from the Colony—to help them build, the Nonconformists sought to demonstrate the worth and the workings of wage labor, time, and money:[50] the object again being to tie the rewards of enlightened consumption, via the immediate purchasing power of cash, to the act of production.

Once built and furnished, the mission house became a diorama. On its stage was displayed, for all to see, the domestic round of "the exemplary married couple" (Jolly 1989:234).[51] So, at least, we are told. Many narratives of the

South African interior, especially those aimed at mass Christian audiences, described a "typical" day in the life of the evangelical family.[52] These accounts implied—optimistically—that much of this day was lived under Tswana scrutiny. No doubt idealized for popular purposes, it typically began with an early rise, ablutions, and family worship. For wives, this was usually followed by one or more instructional activities. Thereafter, they would attend to their own domestic chores. Their husbands, meanwhile, taught the older children and adults, and then did their manual and agrarian labor. All of this was interspersed with pastoral, medical, and charity work, and with public religious services. Evenings were devoted, where possible, to such "improving" activities as reading, embroidery, and prayer. The entire daily cycle was punctuated by regular, sustaining meals and modest refreshments taken *en famille*—and occasionally, in later years, with royals (Price 1956:395). Southern Tswana might first have encountered Protestant production in the mission garden. But it was in the mission house that they were shown how to dispose of its fruits, how to nourish bodies and minds through "responsible" consumption.

The Mission as Model: (ii) The Christian Community

If the mission house was meant as a model of Christian domesticity, the mission station was set up as a template of Christian community. The former condensed the private domain of the enlightened citizen; the latter, the public sphere of civil society.[53] Even the most rudimentary evangelical outposts laid bare the basic design principles of the Nonconformist world. As they evolved, these settlements, whose ground plans varied little, became microcosms of an imagined social order of ever more embracing, ever more complex proportions. Together, they made concrete—or, rather, cast in stone—the effort to place African terrain on the coordinates of a new map unfurling across the interior. This map was a product of the Archimedean eye of empire builders, albeit empire builders who could not build imperially. Along its frontiers, local spaces were converted into Christian scapes. Lauren Derby (1994:490), after Febvre (1973:208), reminds us that "*frontière*(s)"—about which we had much to say in volume 1—"originally derived from the French *front*, an architectural term denoting the facade of a building." The nineteenth-century mission was at once the visible frontage of empire and a cultural borderland in which Africa and Europe faced up to each other.

Each station came to include all the essentials of a "civilized" community: houses, gardens, a school, a church, smithies and workshops, watercourses, retail stores, and, later perhaps, a meeting hall and a sports field. These were situated on a grid of square blocks, spaced along broad, parallel "streets"—as in Pacalt's early Khoi village—and adorned with cultivated trees. While residential buildings anchored the rectilinear planes of the settlement, and manual and mercantile establishments filled out its center, the public edifices of the mission stretched up toward the heavens. They broke the horizontal surfaces of everyday lived space, conveying cogent images of power, municipal order, and social community. These were the so-called "splendid fanes" and "spires" of "justice [and] benevolence" which, Cameron lamented, had no place in Tswana towns.

Of these public edifices, the earliest, not surprisingly were churches; structures that easily dominated their surroundings, with their lofty roofs and distinctive bell towers, their large doors and glinting windows. In 1831 at Kuruman, for example, Robert Moffat began erecting a stone mammoth capable of holding nine hundred people (LMS 1840:143).[54] At the time he had made just seven converts. This towering "act of faith," we are told, was regarded as a marvel far and wide (H. Thompson 1976:37). It probably was. With walls two feet thick and huge ceiling beams, the building was T-shaped. In this respect, if not in all others, it recalled the design of many contemporary English Nonconformist chapels—although, as Horton Davies (1962:47f.) makes clear, the architecture of religious dissent in Britain was itself beginning to undergo complex transformations at the time. The construction of the Kuruman church was a spectacle in which many took part and even more came to see (LMS 1840:143). When, finally, Moffat dedicated it—in 1838, almost two decades after he established himself among the Tlhaping—his following had grown, but only to 150 less than solid members (LMS 1840:143). Nonetheless, the LMS was determined to radiate its influence from this epicenter, thus to extend its visible presence across the veld.[55]

Kuruman, of course, was *the* model Nonconformist station in the interior, the most celebrated token of its type: *la cité chrétienne à l'écart*, "the Christian city at the periphery," as Zorn (1993:376, after Jeanne-Marie Léonard) described Beerseba, its Paris Evangelical Missionary Society equivalent among Sotho. It was, John Mackenzie (1871:69) said, "one of those 'marks' in the country which would remain to testify to the skill and power as well as Christian perseverance of its founders." Both its "higher moral and spiritual structure" and its "solid . . . walls" inspired his own architectural exertions (see n. 55). An earlier visitor, the scientist Burrow (1971:33–34), described Kuruman as a "village," comprising superior stone buildings, "thatched in the Devonshire style." His diagrammatic map of the place (plate 6.3) lines up all the European structures—church, wagon house, smith's and carpenter's shop, school, printing office, merchant establishment, residences, and fenced gardens—along a straight main "street"; it is this horizontal axis that commands and focuses our gaze. Far to the rear is a scatter of small, faintly sketched circular huts. They seem to rest lightly on the veld. "Native town" is written beside them. Burrow's drawing, though quite different, evokes the much published one by Baxter alluded to above (plate 6.1); the one that captures the teleology of colonial evangelism and its architectural endeavors. Both put Africa into European perspective: disarrayed and in the

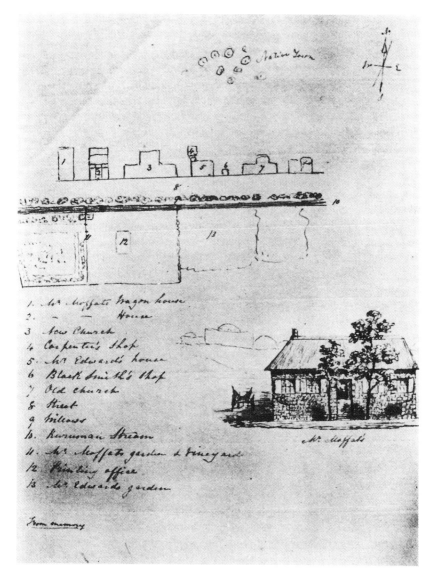

PLATE 6.3 *"Sketch Map of Kuruman, from memory" [from Burrow 1971:34]*

distance, behind the enclosed fields and well-aligned buildings of the LMS. As Tswana habitations fade into the background, the passage and priorities of history on this terrain are graphically reoriented. Alike on the earth and on the page, the shapes of the mission townscape begin to dwarf Tswana life, casting over it the long shadows of an encroaching frontier.

There were times when the wrong shadows were cast, when the moral order of mission architecture went awry. Trollope's remarks about Thaba 'Nchu point to one case. Perhaps the most unforgettable, however, comes from further north and later: the Bechuanaland Protectorate in the 1890s. When the Rev. Willoughby, who inherited the Palapye station from Wookey, arrived in 1893, he noted with dismay that the "W.C."—a rather large toilet—was "the most prominent object to any visitor approaching the station."[56] His predecessors, it seems, had been too delicate to mention sanitary arrangements. Willoughby, whose own initials were "W. C.," was not. He immediately proposed resituating the facility, substituting "movable buckets" for the existing cesspool. As we shall see, sanitation was to become a contested site of institutional regulation whenever colonial evangelists took control over the intimate details of African life (e.g., in boarding schools). But, in the moral architecture of the mission station itself, toilets belonged in the private sector, not in the public eye.

Mission buildings would later be joined by other European edifices on African soil. Aside from settler farms and towns implanted forcibly on expropriated land, the colonial state began, in time, to populate the Tswana world with its own dominating structures: "public facilities" such as administrative offices, "tribal" centers, communal halls, schools, clinics, labor recruiting posts, police stations, and gaols. Their construction was less neat than that of the missions, less rationalized, often at once perfunctory and peremptory. But, then, these structures were not meant as models or moral lessons; at least, not of the same sort. Even more than the Nonconformist stations, they gave off signs of alien authority. Even more than Christian institutions, they were to become sites of struggle in the twentieth century. But that is a story for later.

Practical Interventions: Teaching Tswana to Build a World

Let us move, now, from the subjunctive to the indicative, from the making of models to active interventions in Southern Tswana architectural and domestic arrangements. We have already anticipated some of these interventions. The most general, if diffuse and indirect, lay in the Nonconformist effort to reconstruct the local economy from its roots: in particular, to reform the division of labor, relations of production, and the nature of work; to initiate processes of commodification and encourage the use of money as a generalized medium of exchange; and to disseminate European patterns of consumption. All were intended, as well, to have an impact on spatial arrangements and everyday family life; all were part of the seamless campaign to "[get Africans] to build houses, inclose gardens, cultivate corn land, accumulate property" (J. Philip 1828,2:72–73), thereby "to turn the[ir] world upside down!" (R. Moffat 1842:236).

But there was a paradox at the heart of the campaign by the colonial evangelists to rebuild the habitus and habitations of Southern Tswana. On one hand, they worked actively to introduce their domestic designs. They often wrote optimistically of making vernacular dwellings into "marks" of self-improvement, of replacing African "huts" with "family homes" appointed in refined European style. Yet, at the same time, many of them evinced a detectable reserve, an awkwardness, about their efforts in this domain. It was as if they sought to reform the spatial and social interiors of Tswana life from a distance. Most appeared reluctant to intrude upon those interiors, even on spiritual business. Save in the case of the sick or the dying (see chapter 7), neither missionaries nor their wives were wont, by and large, to visit ordinary African abodes. As Alfred Sharp confessed,[57] "Pastoral visitation is not on the lines that it is done at home, we do not just look in and chat about the weather, the babies, the crops, the neighbours, and read and pray with the family and depart." Convinced that "jostled huts" and "sinuous pathways" bred promiscuity and disease, they tried to draw people from their homesteads onto public terrain. Rituals of building and agricultural production were performed in the clear light of day, in places to which the LMS and WMMS had formal claim. It was here, beyond the "web" of heathen superstition, that the evangelists tried to work their influence. At best, they hoped, converts would move into "decent" homes on secured mission ground. If not, those who drew close to the church might at least return to the "native town" resolved to better themselves, to influence others, and to transform their communities from within.

Missionary efforts to re-house Tswana also ran up against pragmatic difficulties. English dwellings could not be imported into the country like fabric or thread or other commodities. They had to be erected from the ground up, a collective, labor-intensive exercise impossible on large scale—unless, of course, the exemplary efforts of the evangelists sparked a spontaneous aesthetic revolution and prompted a mass indigenous impulse to build anew. But even if Tswana aesthetics had been protean enough to mutate of their own accord, the wherewithal to put up "decent" houses was not easy to obtain. Before the arrival of traders and British hardware, the best the evangelists could do was to encourage the Africans to substitute local for European materials—and to do their best with clay, wood, oxhide, and powdered anthills (Tilby 1914:192; Broadbent 1865:61f.). When, eventually, mass-produced merchandise did become available, it was fairly expensive. Hence the stress on the mimetic power of the mission-as-model rather than on mission-led building campaigns. Whatever other ends this strategy served, it also made virtue of necessity.

In sum, then, the colonial evangelists regarded the reconstruction of Southern Tswana housing and domesticity with ambivalence, as an endeavor of the long run; they seem to have accepted, from early on, that their impact would be indirect and slow. In this respect, they anticipated Braudel (1981:267) by many decades:

[A] 'house,' wherever it may be, is an enduring thing, and it bears perpetual witness to the slow pace of civilizations, of cultures bent on preserving, maintaining and repeating.

But this did not mean that reconstruction was impossible. Or that it should be easily given up on.[58] Hence, in addition to their reliance on teaching by example, the missionaries intervened into Tswana life on several fronts at once. For a start, they preached and conversed, this being their most routine manner of infiltrating local streams of consciousness. But the evangelists did more than just talk.

We have already noted the effort of some of them to build houses for chiefs and other royals. This had the dual purpose of making European dwellings into palpable signs of status, and locating them, as objects of desire, at the center of local communities. *Sekgoa* objectified, they were, to extend Allan Pred's (1985:335) visual pun, things to see-and-be-scene. In fact, few chiefs ever actually lived in replicas of mission houses. And when they did, they were not simply re-cast, or re-caste, by doing so. More usually, they domesticated their abodes according to their own aesthetic and social lights.

Another familiar sphere of missionary intervention, more to do with domesticity and interiors, was the introduction of house wares through the agency of traders and merchants. In chapter 4 we encountered the Nonconformist notion that "savage people" had to be taught "a relish for the decencies and comforts of life"—if necessary by filling shop windows with objects to tempt them (J. Philip 1828,1:209, 205).[59] Such goods were meant to *re*place the unrefined possessions of the Tswana; those "inexplicable objects," as Graham Greene (1963:61) once put it, that Europeans took to be the "the fingerprints of Africa." By the 1880s, Wookey (1884:303) noted, no "native store," rural or urban, was complete unless it carried a wide range of domestic items, all of foreign make. At the turn of the new century, Tswana mission alumni joined in the effort to sell these items: advertisements in vernacular newspapers, produced by members of the Christian elite, essayed the virtues of gleaming brass bedsteads (those for which the interior walls of homesteads had had to give way) made up with snowy linens.[60] Certain objects, especially, took on the moral weight of "home": double divans and mattresses, closets, candles, and soap became privileged signs of respectability (Schapera 1936:247; Burke 1996).[61] Sometimes, though, these very commodities appeared to mock the means and ends of the colonial evangelists. In the 1930s, as we saw earlier, a Kgatla poet would grumble, in verse, that women were going off to towns, departing their villages and husbands, "to acquire cupboards" (Schapera 1965:117). And not coming home.

The form of intervention most directly related to architecture itself was, as we have said, the employment of Tswana in construction work. In part, this was an extension of the general effort to introduce wage labor and money into the local economy. But it was also meant to implant the idea of charity. Most public building required voluntary assistance of various kinds, which the missions elicited and then blessed as virtue. Indeed, charity began at church, thence, it was hoped, to end up at home. Sometimes converts offered to put up chapels or classrooms on their own philanthropic account (LMS 1830:85; Livingstone 1959,1:210, 212).[62] To what degree they were "encouraged" is unclear, but a good deal of surplus labor was extracted in this way. At Boetsap (WMMS 1829–31:120), for instance, a WMMS school was built by "the people"; primarily, that is, by pupils who "assembl[ed] at the sound of a tin horn" each morning to "give" an hour before lessons. The upkeep of these edifices—like mission stations—entailed a long-term commitment that had to be met by the donation of goods, labor, and cash.[63] By urging communities to erect and look after them, the evangelists tried to instill a material identification between people and public property. They also hoped to inculcate the idea that buildings, fabrications of enduring value, objectified human beings and their "works."

It was not only in public building that the Nonconformists hired Southern Tswana in order to change them. The private interior of the mission house, the domain of the evangelical wife, was another site. As we saw earlier, women were engaged as servants so that they might be instructed in the arts of domesticity.[64] This "informal domestic training," argues Mafela (1994:87), played a "much more crucial role in the missionaries' 'civilizing' agenda than formal (domestic) education." And it was "much more ideologically far-reaching." Perhaps the most extreme case of parlor pedagogy and kitchen-sink schooling involved Elizabeth (Bessie), the Moffats' daughter and second wife of Roger Price. She set out to teach her employees "to do everything—even the 'superfluities' of civilized life— . . . in the household department" (Price 1956:393). Of the Prices' labors at Molepolole, Edwin Smith (1957:276) wrote a remarkable passage:

> Apart from her classes, Mrs Price's chief contribution was through her servants. She made a practice of taking young girls into the house for training. Her husband trained young oxen, she said, and she trained young women: and hers was not the easier task. They were wild little creatures . . . [but] in the house learnt the Christian domesticities.[65]

No doubt. Besides housewifery and child care, the crafts taught in mission houses across Bechuanaland included knitting, sewing and dressmaking, and the preparation of European foods, a form of refinement paid little attention in other contexts.[66] In due course, with the development of mission schools, the practical, everyday instruction given by the evangelists and their wives was augmented in the classroom (cf. Gaitskell 1990, n.d.; Mafela 1994); not surprisingly, domestic science and training in masonry and construction featured prominently in their curricula.[67]

There is one last register in which the practical efforts of the evangelists to reform Tswana architecture and domesticity made themselves felt: the reconstruction of time through the reorganization of space. The building of Christian towns composed of private houses and public buildings, of secular and sacred places, of sites of labor and leisure, implied a reconfiguration of temporalities. As Edward Soja (1985:94) has written, in a theoretical key:

> Spatiality and temporality, human geography and human history, intersect in a complex social process . . . which gives form not only to the grand movements of societal development but also to the recursive practices of day-to-day activity.

It is clear that the reordering of Southern Tswana spaces and places *was* meant to affect their quotidian routines. As horizontal and vertical planes spelled out new perceptual contrasts, so the activities conducted within them were supposed to take on new, and newly differentiated, rhythms. That, at least, was the intention of the colonial evangelists. For them, worship was opposed to ordinary, everyday pursuits; toil to rest and recreation; political and social endeavors to domestic life. Together, these elements comprised a bourgeois schedule, a schedule measured in hours, days, weeks, months, and years. They also presumed a *calendar*—rather than the "monotonous sameness of savage life"—in which local events were assimilated into the grander horizons of a Eurocentric world. In his first letters from the field, Broadbent (1865:86f.) had complained that, for Tswana, "every day was alike." In less than a year, he noted with pride, Sunday in Matlwasse had become as quiet and still as in England.[68]

Not that such things happened of their own accord. As we have noted, temporality was literally built into LMS and WMMS churches from the start, their chiming clocks soon being supplemented by the school bells and hooters that punctuated the daily round (cf. M. Wilson 1971:73; Oliver 1952:52); such were the sonic markers of fungible, commodified time and labor. In due course, too, the secular routine of the British schoolroom would complement the sacred order of Sunday services, weekly classes, quarterly communions, and annual feasts (see below). It was as if the countryside itself testified to this divine scheme:[69]

> Instead of the lonesome Karroo which never heard the sound of the church bell, these rocks and these dales ever smile when the Sabbath appears; . . . a goodly company who dwell on high, join together in calling on the name of the Lord, and in shouting his praises from the tops of mountains.

Through their efforts to reshape the landscape, then, the Nonconformists broke into the flow of events and the cycle of seasons that gave continuity to indigenous social existence. But in what measure did their mimetic models and their practical interventions actually succeed in remaking Southern Tswana architecture and domesticity, space and time?

IN BRICOLAGE AND MORTAR: THE IMPACT OF MISSION ARCHITECTURE

[W]hen anything is exposed by the light it becomes visible, for anything that is visible is light.

Ephesians 5.13

The Early Years, 1820–1850

Inasmuch as they measured progress by the extension, across the landscape, of four-sided frames, fences, and furrows, the missionaries must have felt disappointed in the early years. But then, as we know, they expected their advances in this sphere to be slow. Most Tswana seemed resistant to rectangular rooms, internal doors, dedicated spaces.[70] They were also resistant to the European idea of the nuclear household. With some exceptions, they continued to build round earthen dwellings for extended families; homesteads whose interiors remained versatile in form and function—and whose external style changed little.[71] For their part, the evangelists took every opportunity to report, if rather guardedly, the few optimistic signs to be read off the terrain. Several of these came from the WMMS. "About twenty European cottages built of stone," wrote Cameron in 1842 of some people settled near Platberg, "testified . . . to their industry and to their taste."[72] In these secured spaces, these square "cottages," families and their goods were enclosed in "indoor" privacy, safe from heathen promiscuity.[73] Six years later, William Shaw, Superintendent of the Bechuana District, said, of the same place (Broadbent 1865:200):

> The village is greatly improved since I was last here; the people have built themselves very good and substantial houses, after the colonial fashion. A large number of gardens and orchards are well enclosed; and hundreds, if not thousands, of fruit trees give the whole a very interesting rural appearance.

He was less rhapsodic about Thaba 'Nchu—the town he described as having a "wild African appearance"—whence he had just come. All he could laud there was "the erection of stone walls" around the "conical-shaped dwellings" (Broadbent 1865:199).[74]

On occasion, in these early years, other European visitors painted an altogether more sunny portrait than did the workaday evangelists. Thus Steedman (1835,1:228): "Observe how the proclamation of the Gospel hath clothed the mountain side with smiling cottages, and brought out and directed the energies of industry, and introduced the comforts of civilized life." Observe how different this was from the world according to Wookey, by whose account Southern Tswana settlements had altered hardly at all, even by the 1880s:[75]

> The style of architecture remains the same as it was generations ago. A square or oblong house seems to be much too much for most of them to manage. . . . The doorway is the only opening. . . . No window, no chimney; . . . a little partition now generally marks off the sleeping place.

Towns, he added, were still "put down" without discernible order. If there had been any "progress," it was confined to small Christian communities situated in or around LMS and WMMS stations.

This state of affairs, as we have seen, had to do in part with the practical obstacles encountered by the evangelists in reforming Tswana construction, in part with their reluctance to take on African domestic architecture from within. Also, unlike among the more scattered Nguni peoples—for whom joining the church implied being rehoused on mission ground[76]—the concentrated organization of Tswana settlements made it hard, save in unusual circumstances,[77] for the Nonconformists to set up discrete communities. Here there were no isolated Christian "Salems" of the kind described for West Africa (see Berman 1975:31). Most Christians lived at home (*RRI*:205) and "went to" church, a passage that transected the deepening divide between the worlds of *sekgoa* and *setswana*. These worlds were neither disconnected nor unchanging, of course: each was a condition of possibility for the other, each part of a single, if evanescent, historical reality. But they *were* domains of difference, domains of contrasting style and design, domains ever more perceptibly marked off from one another. Under such conditions, it was difficult for missionaries to insist that their followers erect new abodes, *sekgoa* in form, in the midst of a culturally assertive *setswana* milieu. Not that they doubted the impression left on Tswana by their own buildings. Edwin Lloyd (1889:162f.), the man who tried to change their division of labor by involving an entire community in putting up a church, told of the impact of the exercise on a "venerable old heathen." Note how the "house" of God had become an icon of colonial evangelism at large (p. 165):[78]

> Great was [his] marvel to see what [he was] pleased to term "such a big house." . . . Suddenly he turned [to his compatriots] . . . and said: "Men, you are all whites (or English) to-day; you are no longer Bechwana. . . . When I die I will tell [the ancestors] that they know nothing at all; . . . for my part, I have seen a house."

But it was a long way from the awesome to the ordinary, from orchestrating marvels to persuading Tswana that they should rebuild their mundane world. While the transformation of townscapes and domestic architecture was very gradual in these years, the furnishing of interiors was another matter. Already in the early nineteenth century, Tswana began to experiment, increasingly, with the new household commodities that found their way to the colonial frontier—just as they experimented with all other European objects. As trade with the Colony expanded, more imported goods were procured; goods, the missionaries hoped, that would change the nature of private space and the daily routines carried on within it. "Formerly," recalled Robert Moffat (1842:507), "a chest, a chair, a candle, or a table, were . . . unknown." Now they graced many Tlhaping dwellings. And one thing led to another: "They soon found to read in the evening or by night required a more steady light. . . . Candle moulds and rags for wicks were now in requisition, . . . an indication of the superior light which had entered their abodes." Almost every white visitor to Bechuanaland noted the accumulation by Tswana of domestic items of foreign manufacture— and the often iconoclastic uses to which they were put. Especially during the first half of the century, it was bric-a-brac rather than brick-and-mortar, housewares rather than house design, that fed the Southern Tswana propensity for bricolage. In the great cultural exchange along the colonial frontier, the missionaries might have been anxious to insinuate their moral architecture *tout court*. But Southern Tswana were more interested in their material artifacts, in European objects with which to augment their own interiors. And their courts too.

Transformations of the Longer Run

Over the long run, however, indigenous architectural and domestic arrangements were not to remain unaffected by the civilizing mission.[79] As time went by, some Southern Tswana—not least those trained in European construction by the LMS and WMMS—began to appropriate British designs and materials, to refract them through their own aesthetic and social lenses, to play with their logic, and, in differing degrees, to incorporate them into vernacular built forms. As early as 1820, reports Campbell (1822,2:81), one chief, iconoclastically ahead of his contemporaries, erected a homestead with two houses: a primary residence put up in "the fashion of the country," and a secondary "one behind, constructed after the European manner."[80] It was by such gestures of encompassment and appropriation that the Africans spoke back to the colonizers. But, in the process of thus seizing the initiative, Southern Tswana were themselves altered.

In the process, too, the proportional relationship between the reproduction and transformation of vernacular design underwent subtle shifts. Which is why the imagined contrast between *setswana* and *sekgoa* was so protean, so difficult to grasp. Take just one manifestation. What, by the late century, was known as a "Tswana house" typically had doors, windows, fences, and other Western accoutrements, features that would have been seen as *sekgoa* in earlier times; conversely, "flats"—square, *sekgoa*-shaped structures with corrugated iron roofs—were (and, in the 1990s, still are) often built of red earth, their facades adorned with geometric patterns regarded as distinctively local in Tswana communities (cf. Schapera and Goodwin 1937:146). Such hybrids and fusions, configured as much by African meanings and materialities as by alien ones, imply (i) that shifts were occurring in the *practical* production and understanding of space-as-lived (cf. Lefebvre 1991:31f.); and (ii) that the contours of architectural change, the making of "tradition" and its modernist alternatives, were more complex than they first appear, more complex than allowed by either the dejected Wookey or the optimistic Methodists. Each reported, perfectly well, what they saw. But each beheld fragments of a more embracing reality in construction.

Taken as a whole, in fact, the documentary record left by the second generation of colonial evangelists, circa 1850–80, suggests a pattern of bewildering diversity. At one extreme were those villages described as unchanged, as wallowing in the torpor of tradition, even by the 1880s.[81] At the other were places like Mafikeng, which had been built anew, and Likatlong, now composed of industrious "farmsteads arranged symmetrically in rows," the streets between them "full of life" (Holub 1881,1:118–19).[82] Other towns presented a more mixed picture. Some thirty years before, in Kuruman, a number of prosperous Christians had erected "good houses of stone, stone-walled gardens and cornfields" (Read 1850:446). These dwellings were furnished with British domestic wares and gave evidence of the accumulation of a "family estate." All around them, however, were "mud huts" arranged in semicircular wards. This pattern—a few European abodes amidst a large concentration of *setswana* homesteads—would be widely sustained for many decades to come. Long after the precolonial dress of Tswana adults had disappeared, round earthen houses still predominated in most communities (cf. Schapera 1943b:83).[83] But the proportion that was rectangular, and contained *sekgoa* features, seems to have been highly variable. Sometimes it was the chief or his kin who first built in European style (see Holub 1881,1:320),[84] often not. Trollope (1878,2:279f.), for example, wrote that royals in Thaba 'Nchu, while "dressed like whitemen," lived in simple huts surrounded by circular brush fences.[85] At the time, local Christians were beginning to put up residences of *sekgoa* design. And the wealthy were buying English bedsteads and mattresses (if only for show; cf. Schapera 1936:247, 1980:53).

Is it possible to make sense of all this? Is there any regularity to be picked out amidst the diversities? The answer, of course, is yes. It was anticipated in our analysis of processes of class formation and cultural implosion at work along

PLATE 6.4 *"Chief Bathoen's Homestead," Kanye, circa 1899 [from Willoughby, n.d.[a]:19]*

the frontier. Those processes, as we showed in respect of clothing, made themselves manifest in the politics and polarities of style. They were to become visible, too, in the architecture of domesticity—if not in precisely the same way.

In order to make our point, let us return to Willoughby's *Native Life on the Transvaal Border*, which provides a photographic record of Tswana domestic construction toward the end of the century. As we might expect, the author searched African architecture for signs of moral and material betterment. Like Wookey before him, he was disappointed (n.d.[a]:19): "Notwithstanding the number of European houses . . . dotted here and there, the natives have done but little to improve their style of building."[86] Their "huts" were "poor affairs," even though many were now made of sun-dried brick and had doors and windows (n.d.[a]:18). Of those that broke the mold, not all did so in commendable ways; change was not necessarily improvement. For instance, a large dwelling owned by Chief Bathoen of the Ngwaketse (plate 6.4) failed Willoughby's test of enlightened aesthetics. Put up by Transvaal Boers, it looked more like a frontier farmhouse than the kind of English residence favored by the mission. "[I]t is hard," commented Willoughby (n.d.[a]:19), "to say what style of architecture has been adopted." Shades of iconoclastic royals who flouted the dress code of the mission!

Among the "European houses . . . dotted here and there," those that appealed most to colonial evangelists were the abodes of the emerging Christian elite, the "small native gentry." Said to be unpretentious (Willoughby n.d.[a]:20), these cottages evoked rural England (plate 6.5)—although, increasingly, they resembled workers' housing in the Cape Colony.[87] As their owners prospered through self-possessed labor, such modest habitations were expected

PLATE 6.5 *"Improved Native Dwelling" #1, circa 1899 [from Willoughby, n.d.[a]:20]*

to grow into more substantial family homes. In due course, some would—even if, like Bathoen's, they were more likely to mimic settler ranches than English Victorian residences. Another species of "improved native dwelling," typically erected by well-off non-Christian royals rather than by commoner church members, were elaborately synthetic. Adobe and thatched, abutted by smaller round huts and enclosed in reed-fenced compounds, their overall aesthetic was assertively *setswana*. Yet they were rectangular, large, and internally divided, and boasted *sekgoa* fixtures and fittings, including shutters and chimneys (see, e.g., plate 6.6).[88]

Still, lamented Willoughby (n.d.[a]:19), "improved" dwellings, Christian or *setswana*, were the exception, not the norm. Interestingly, the evangelist himself looked to the colonial state for a remedy against the resistance of "ordinary" Tswana to European built forms. Perhaps, he mused, the newly imposed hut tax, which assessed each building within a homestead, might induce Africans to erect proper houses with more than a one internal room under a single roof (n.d.[a]:21). In fact, the tax, never efficiently administered, failed to have that effect. But Willoughby's musings point to one of several domains in which the objectives of the Nonconformists and those of the government converged. They also point to a bitter irony. Colonial capital, abetted by the state, was already deforming Southern Tswana families through migrant labor, thus preventing their embourgeoisement in the manner desired by the mission. Yet Willoughby sought a panacea in a levy imposed by the state, at the behest of colonial capital, intended specifically to coerce more men to work away from home.

In sum, then, Willoughby's photographic essay points to a three-way distinction in evolving built forms. At one extreme were "traditional" earthen

PLATE 6.6 *"Improved Native Dwelling" #2, circa 1899 [from Willoughby, n.d.[a]:21]*

structures. Conical in shape, they lacked windows, doors, or other Western features. While we cannot be sure of their use at the time—some seem to have
accommodated the very poor, the infirm, and dependents of the politically powerful—they would increasingly be put up in the shadow of "improved" habitations (plate 6.6), there to serve as storage or as sleeping shelters for younger
children and servants.[89] These, in fact, became the architectural counterpart of
"heathen dress." At the other extreme were the large *sekgoa* houses of Christians
with the capital to invest in family dwellings that proclaimed them as pillars of
the community. These houses, often indistinguishable from those of white settlers (plate 6.4; see also n. 84), were fully furnished with British commodities,
appliances, and fancy goods. While they never became quite like Victorian residences in England itself, their owners did strive to replicate the social and cultural patterns of bourgeois English family life—including, inevitably, such ritual observance as tea time.[90] Less affluent Christians could not normally afford
to build, or to live, on this scale. But, if their means allowed, they erected small
colonial-styled cottages which partook of the same paradigmatic design—and
in which the same social models were followed.

Between the two extremes were the synthetic structures of the majority:
fenced compounds of multiple clay-brick buildings, each with its hearth and
courtyards. These buildings, which came to house families of diverse composition,[91] might be round or rectangular, large or small. Most lacked internal
walls—although a few were divided into apartments and even single-rooms
were partitioned. All incorporated some fittings and furnishings of foreign
manufacture.[92] And all were home to a domestic existence fashioned in the space
between the idyll of the mission and the *setswana* world of days past. This synthetic architectural genre, this range of fusions of *sekgoa* and *setswana*, was, like

"peasant" dress, a colonial hybrid. And, like ethnicized attire, it was to prove remarkably stable during the century to follow (see n. 83). It, too, underscored the distinctively marked position of Southern Tswana at the fringes of South African economy and society.

The transformation of Southern Tswana architectural and domestic arrangements is epitomized by the "spatial history"—Paul Carter's term (1989:xxiii)—of the Christian town of Mafikeng. We have mentioned this town before; it was founded by Molema at the behest of his half-brother, Chief Mont-shiwa. The sovereign, then in exile with his people at distant Moshaneng, seems to have proposed the plan both to separate a voluble band of Methodists from his loyal following and to put a stop to Boer incursion (*RRI*:342, n. 9). European passers-by observed a striking contrast between Moshaneng and Mafikeng. Where the first had "no buildings in the European style," the homesteads of the second were detached on their own lots, those of "upper class residents" being "fitted up in the European mode" (Holub 1881,1:279, 294; 2:13); where the first was described as a "village," the second, though much smaller, was referred to by the Dutch term "*stad*" (town). In architectural terms, Mafikeng was the most thoroughly transfigured settlement in all of Bechuanaland at the time. And this despite the fact that there was no European missionary presence there.

When we first visited the place in 1969, we were struck by a cluster of dilapidated Victorian houses, some very large, at what had been once the Christian core of the *stad*, nearby but just outside the chiefly ward. Spaced out on fenced lots, they stretched along one of the few radial roads between the old Methodist chapel and the Elite Hall, a tellingly named Christian communal facility, since destroyed by fire. These battered buildings bore forlorn testimony to the vain bourgeois dream brought by the mission: that mastery of Western cultural forms would ensure enduring prosperity and access to white privilege.

Just as that dream was buried in the political detritus of apartheid South Africa, only lately to be reborn, so its built forms languish in the debris of the Mafikeng landscape. After Montshiwa returned with his followers from exile (1876), and eventually made Molema's *stad* his capital (1881),[93] its Christian nucleus was quickly enveloped by circular, clay-brick wards of *setswana* de-sign—that of the chief at their epicenter. Subsequently, as Z. K. Matthews was to report and we were to see, the town expanded further to accommodate the motley buildings of a burgeoning population of peasant-proletarians, many of them immigrants from other places.[94] By 1969, its relentless, low-rise advance had extended south and east as far as the eye could see.[95] It was dwarfed, in turn, by the aggressively postmodern skyline of the Bophuthats-wana capital, Mmabatho, which rose to the north during the 1970s and 1980s. In one of the expensive hotels of the new city, a careless tourist pamphlet on places of local interest described the *stad* as an "African iron-age village" with "traditional Tswana 'biblical' accommodations."

Within this topography of contrast and continuity, the distinctions of cultural style palpable in Willoughby's photographs, and in the documentary record, remain visible.[96] Descendants of the Christian elite of bygone days, many in reduced circumstances, still occupied the aging Victorian edifices; newer *petit bourgeois* dwellings, also *sekgoa* in design, stood nearby them and elsewhere in the *stad*, although the most successful middle-class families had moved away, to erect sumptuous houses outside "tribal" territory. The majority, however, continued to live in the wards of the old town, where homesteads comprised several single-roomed buildings, some round and some square; a few "mud huts" of earlier vintage were dotted about the place. Windows and doors, metal gates and wire fences were widely in evidence. Iron roofs were almost as common as thatch. Yet earthen exterior walls were frequently finished in hand-patterned local designs, and yards inside them were ornamentally smeared with mud and cow dung. Many people kept chickens and small stock, seldom in pens. Domestic life, *pace* orthodox Christian ideology, tended to take place outside, around the hearth and within the sheltering ambit of the compound. The "typical" household domiciled within that compound conformed neither to the nuclear family model of the mission nor to the agnatic ideal of the *setswana* past. Long affected by high rates of labor migration, domestic groups were diverse in composition, often containing three generations of women in addition to others too old or young to work away.

In short, Mafikeng, in its spatial aspect, asserts a distinctive experience of history. While it clearly bears witness to life in industrial, apartheid South Africa, the town appears also to shrink from the forces imposed on it both by the state and by the market. In 1990, a network of (mostly unpaved, dusty) roads traversed it, giving access to Bophuthatswana police and officials, traders and labor recruiters, tax collectors and the like. Apart from the residences of the petite bourgeoisie, most homesteads refused to line up with these thoroughfares, as if tangential to the influences they bore. In the late 1960s and 1970s, preceding the establishment of Mmabatho, Montshiwa Township had been built, across the national highway from the *stad*, to accommodate people imported to administer Bophuthatswana. Its scores of square, largely two-roomed "family" houses, each on a barren, fenced lot, seemed like a cynical caricature of the idyll of mission Christianity. The majority of Tshidi abhorred its very presence. The architecture of "separate development" flouted their sense of socialized space. In these places, they said, people were "naked," isolated behind wire barricades without kin, animals, or crops.

Living in such barefaced dwellings has been the fate of many black South Africans this century, alike in rural and urban areas. Yet not even the highly disciplined architecture of apartheid managed to construct them in its own image. Instead, state designs were reworked, their outlines softened, their infrastructures made to accommodate forms of domestic life never intended. Frugal brick boxes were augmented by local bricoleurs—often with the flotsam of the white world—to create space for the fluid kinds of household that arose in reaction to a notoriously coercive regulatory regime. It is an ironic history, the one set in motion long, long ago by colonial evangelism: over nearly two centuries it spawned domestic arrangements, physical and social, further removed from the European bourgeois ideal than anything first encountered by whites on the African frontier.

DIALECTICS OF DOMESTICITY: FROM THE AFRICAN FRONTIER TO THE WILDS OF ENGLAND

We promised earlier to show that the mission campaign to instill a particular idea of home was only one side of a dialectic of domesticity. The other side had two foci, one at the frontier, the other at the metropole. These were somewhat at odds with each other. The first involved the impact of vernacular forms on the European evangelists themselves and, later, on other colonizers; the second, the effort by bourgeois reformers to mobilize Africa in the cause of remaking the underclasses in Britain.

At the Frontier . . .

It will be recalled how, in putting up their dwellings, especially early on, the evangelists relied on indigenous construction techniques; how most of them thatched their roofs, usually with local help, and had Tswana women make their floors in *setswana* style. But the reliance on vernacular design went yet further. Broadbent (1865:61–62), for instance, in a hurry to start work at Matlwasse in the 1820s, decided "to build a house in the manner of the natives, though of a different form." The difference, as he perceived it, lay in its division into rooms. Little else. Had his account appeared in a contemporary "scientific" text, with pronouns altered from "we" to "they," it could as well have been a description of "native house-building":

> [W]e dug holes in the ground at proper distances, in which we set up perpendicular [wood] posts, well fastened by ramming the earth in around them. We then placed horizontal beams along the top, and fastened these and the rafters with thongs cut from the hides of oxen, which, being used while soft, became, when dry, hard and firm. The intermediate space between the main posts was filled with smaller spars, crossed with woodbines, and the squares filled up with clay.

And so on.

Much later, at Shoshong in the 1860s, John Mackenzie's (1871:247) first house—he called it a "temporary hut," but lived in it for several years—was built on land allocated by the chief, according to "the custom of the natives."

Its structure "was more picturesque than symmetrical, [being] made of poles, plastered [with clay] on both sides, and thatched with reeds." Although the interior was partitioned, the "kitchen," like the cooking area in all Tswana homesteads, was outside. Other than having windows of calico, in fact, it must have been largely indistinguishable from the surrounding dwellings.

As this suggests, the tendency to mimic African housing styles was not confined to the pioneering generation of evangelists, with its urgent need for shelter. And it was not limited to the erection of "temporary huts." The Nonconformists might have been untiring in their condemnation of Tswana construction—and in their insistence on the virtues of the right angle, the straight line, and the square. Yet, when they put up their own permanent homes, all over Bechuanaland, they continued to depend on local designs, techniques, materials, and artisans (E. Smith 1957:177).[97] Nor was this grudgingly done. As de Kock (1993:213–15) observes, the Christians often developed a taste for indigenous domestic practices—admitted in their private letters, if not in their publications—and quickly overcame their squeamishness with the "filth" of "native" life. Some mission wives, for example, saw to it that their houses were smeared with cow dung once a week; in a few cases, they did the labor themselves.[98] Mary Moffat, in fact, made an enthusiastic pitch for the healthful, aesthetic qualities of "fine clear green" animal excrement as a floor covering.[99]

As it was on the other side of the dialectic, so here too: the impact of *setswana* on the evangelists is tolled less through their words—for all that they said a lot—than through their works. Like other whites in southern Africa, they were greatly affected by the practical aesthetics of African architecture. The primary evidence? A set of sketch plans of mission houses across the country, circa 1876, accompanied by a water color of the Rev. Williams's residence at Molepolole (see n. 44). With its terra-cotta walls, its yellowing, ragged-edged thatched roof, its veranda bounded by vertical poles across the front, this dwelling is reminiscent of a large contemporary Tswana abode—notwithstanding its chimney and oblong shape. Like Mackenzie's "hut" and Livingstone's Mabotsa home (plate 6.2), the house at Molepolole, and the others for which we have plans, also had detached exterior kitchens and stores.

There is secondary visual evidence as well. Willoughby's *Native Life* has two pictures of older mission residences, one at Kanye and another, a derelict, at Shoshong (n.d.[a]:43, 6). Both were adobe and thatch structures, again very un-English in style. The L-shaped Kanye homestead, with its enclosing earthen wall, also resembled a *setswana*-style compound. A feature that the photograph hides, but that we know of from the sketch plan, is that it had "outhouses" for cooking and storage; nothing is disclosed—anywhere—of toilets. A third photograph (p. 53), of a merchant's dwelling at Palapye, shows that other whites in Bechuanaland were building in much the same mode as well. Clearly, a synthetic architecture was emerging. It was a frontier style that fused European outer shapes and inner partitions with a range of Tswana design elements and materials.

Sometimes the accommodations of Europeans in the interior were yet more visibly Africanized, losing even their rectangular shape. One form, later known as the "rondavel" (from the Dutch *rond,* "round")—a circular, one-roomed building with thatched roof—became widely favored. It afforded cheap, pleasant, practical housing. Writing from northern Bechuanaland in 1894, Willoughby reported of two British female teaching assistants:[100]

> The ladies are better off in point of accommodation than we are. . . . I have spoken of their "two huts." They are huts, but they are really good huts, and will be quite comfortable for many years. . . . They have a decent kitchen fitted up in the courtyard. . . . You need not be anxious about their health on the score of their accommodation.

Note the volte-face: round huts, in African style, were now made out to be healthy, congenial, and long-lasting. And outdoor kitchens had become "decent."

Rondavels were to prove a convenient answer to the residential needs of the mission, especially in housing people of relatively humble status within the Christian community (women teachers, "native" evangelists, and the like). Sometimes they served other purposes too. The first English church at Palapye, for example, was a round hut "bought" by the LMS (Willoughby n.d.[a]:58; plate 6.7). Surrounded by a classical Tswana brush fence, it looked as "traditional" a building as one could have imagined at the end of the nineteenth century. Willoughby (n.d.[a]:59) joked, caustically, that it was "such very early English" in style—that is, so unrecognizably primitive—that a notice board had to be nailed to a nearby tree to explain what it was. Nonetheless, as a House of God, it seems, its sole drawback was that it became unpleasantly warm during the evening service.

In due course, the rondavel would mushroom all over white southern Africa—and not only among the humble. Today it appears in contemporary farmhouse architecture, in public buildings, hotels, and resorts ("nature" and "game" parks notably among them), and, on occasion, within compound urban homesteads. Its basic design has been elaborated in various ways over the decades. The circular nucleus is often doubled or trebled. It may even be made oval. But the essential form persists. The conical clay and thatch structure that began as a white man's bricolage, a redeployed African (de)sign, has become a generic *southern African* style, one that now transcends ethnic particularity.[101] A splendid example, ironically, is St. Marks Anglican Church in Lobatse, a border town in Botswana.[102] Erected in 1934 and often refurbished, this light-brown stone edifice has been made to look as if it were constructed of earth. The effect is heightened by the yellow translucence of its small windows. Its thinning grass

PLATE 6.7 *"First English Church, Palapye," circa 1899 [from Willoughby, n.d.[a]:58]*

roof is woven, *setswana*-style, into a tight, oblong coiffure, and the sandy ground around it is raked clean of leaves and dirt. Flanked by a smaller round "hut," and enclosed by a hedge of dry brush that resembles a thorn fence, it looks for all the world as if it has been carefully set down in a *lolwapa*, a homestead compound.

Over the long run, then, the mutual appropriation of aesthetic forms, as much by Europeans as by Tswana, led to a steady convergence in frontier housing styles. Nor was this merely a convergence of facades. It entailed the way in which space was constructed and experienced; lived, so to speak, in the round. Or oblong. At the same time, this convergence, this evolution of a distinctly hybrid architecture, did not complete itself. The dialectics of colonial encounters never do. They are never fully resolved. Just the opposite. Their very logic lies in an eternal counterpoint of fusion and distinction; of promising to erase difference even while insinuating it into the practical consciousness of all those involved. To be sure, there would always remain a clear, if shifting, conceptual line between *setswana* and *sekgoa;* between African and European social and material designs. This cleavage—however inchoate to the eye—imprinted the politics of racial caste onto the imagined contours of the built environment.

There is, yet again, an irony here. It was to be the Dutch-speaking settlers of the interior who were to be most emphatic in enforcing the opposition between things African and things European. Perhaps this was because they were themselves regarded by the British—not least by colonial evangelists—as an undomesticated and antimetropolitan people who regularly transgressed cultural and racial frontiers. These "low grade" Boers, Livingstone (1974:75–77) remarked disparagingly, lived "in houses without chimneys," were unsanitary, and had such unrefined customs as "sleeping in their wearing apparel" and "soaking . . . [themselves] in solutions of tea and coffee." They had become "a shade darker than Europeans" and tended to breed profusely. It was their heirs who would make racial and cultural cleavage the ideological cornerstone of the colonial state. And of apartheid.

. . . And on the Home Front

In the effort to remake their own underclasses, bourgeois reformers frequently held up the "dark continent" as a mirror to the "dark masses" of "heathendom" in Britain.[103] The similarity of the benighted back home to the unenlightened abroad was repeatedly stressed, alike at the colonial workface and at the metropole. At times, especially in the early years of the century, the parallel was based on a vision of universal sameness, even optimistic progressivism; later on, the analogy was more likely to emphasize racialized difference and degeneracy (see below). Said Dr. Philip (1828,2:316–17), in the 1820s:

> We are all born savages, whether we are brought into the world in the populous city or in the lonely desert. It is the discipline of education, and the circumstances under which we are placed, which create the difference between the rude barbarian and the polished citizen—the listless savage and the man of commercial enterprise. . . . [In South Africa] we see, *as in a mirror*, the features of our own progenitors. (Our italics.)

Barbarians and savages, progenitors of Civilized Man, were, according to many social commentators at the midcentury (see n. 103), still to be found in disturbing numbers across both the countrysides and the cities of the British Isles.

Many rural places, says the careful social historian Kitson Clark (1973:xiv), were notable for their isolation and backwardness, for the sheer "savagery" of farm laborers, and for the awful state of their habitations. Indeed, country parsons in Britain, if they had any missionary zeal, found themselves as challenged as their brethren abroad by "rough, uncivilized" people. They were also challenged by housing conditions "deficient in almost every requisite that should constitute a home for a Christian family in a civilized community" (Kitson Clark 1973:173, 221; see also 1962:116).

But it was within the exploding Victorian city that bourgeois Britain met with undomesticated "savagery" at its most extreme. The poor of London and Liverpool, went the common lament, were far closer to rude barbarians than to refined burghers.[104] Some of them, it is true, were respectable and hard-working, and had humble, decent homes;[105] the line between "respectability" and its antitheses (indolence, indecency, animality, brutality . . .), as we know, had great social and moral significance at the time. For the most part, however, the undersides of England were portrayed as violent and gross, torn asunder by alcoholism, promiscuity, prostitution and (self-inflicted) misery. What was worse, the fetid, fitful lives and filthy habitations of the "lower classes" threatened to contaminate the citadels of the middle class, to pollute everything sane, safe, and sanitary.

A profusion of texts, diverse in voice and genre, attest to the widespread alarm caused by this threat. Among the more notable were Charles Girdlestone's pious "Letters on the Unhealthy Condition of the Lower Class of Dwellings" (Kitson Clark 1973:209); Mayhew's (1851) celebrated report on London labor and Booth's surveys of various parts of the urban sprawl (e.g., 1891); a number of subethnographic narratives of exploration (see below); and the assorted essays in Viscount Ingestre's *Meliora* (Shrewsbury 1852), which described, sometimes in melodramatic terms, the bleak circumstances which the indigent, victims of their own "gross misconduct," had to endure (pp. 18, 23). Most adverse of all, though—at least to bourgeois sensibilities—was the fact that these people had often to live "all in one room." Under such conditions even rudimentary standards of decency were impossible; "the consequences," wrote Henry Jephson (1907:31), chief sanitary engineer of London, "were always disastrous." No wonder, then, that a number of improvement societies, charities, and housing schemes—many under the aegis of the established church—were formed to address the problem from the 1850s on (Owen 1964:371f.).

Hebdige (1988:20) notes that, amidst the urban blight, the scourge of polite society was youthful "nomads," street "urchins" who were often compared to African savages. This resonates with Mayhew's (1851) classic description of costermongers (traders, usually very poor, who sold fruit and vegetables from barrows in towns and cities). Younger costers wore beaver hats and moleskin collars—just as, according to contemporary accounts, Tswana wore greasy animal hides and caps.[106] Both alike shunned "refined" dress. Furthermore, "eyewitness" reports (e.g., Garwood 1853; Hollingshead 1861) suggest that the lack of a settled home life among these youths made them seem like the "wandering tribes" of "unknown continents" (Hebdige 1988:21); their plight contributed to "the growing moral impetus towards the education, reform and civilisation of the working-class masses." Echoes of colonial evangelism in Africa could not be more audible. Interestingly, James Greenwood's popular travels in *The Wilds of London* (1874) were, in large part, guided by a missionary, from whose house in the dark innards of the uncharted city radiated the light of Christianity. The cleric's effort to "improve" slum people, especially their domestic lives, surfaces as a dispersed subtext in the narrative. Nor was Greenwood's cleric unusual. The figure of the civilizing evangelist appears in many tales of urban Britain, voyeuristic adventures and philanthropic manifestos alike. We shall return to him.

Those who authored "realistic" accounts[107] of inner-city Britain, such as Mayhew (1851) and Greenwood (1874), were wont to position themselves as social explorers.[108] The former, in fact, introduced himself as a "traveller in the undiscovered country of the poor" (p. iii). This evoked the geographical mission abroad: the scientific project, discussed in volume 1, in which Europeans "discovered" remote parts of the outer world, thus to bring them within the compass of intellectual and material control. Hence Stedman Jones's (1971:14) portrayal of the poorest districts of London as seen through the eyes of the middle classes: "a *terra incognita* periodically mapped out by intrepid missionaries and explorers who catered to an insatiable demand for travellers' tales." Recall that the goal of the Association for Promoting the Discovery of the Interior Parts of Africa, formed in the late eighteenth century, had been to "penetrate the *terra incognita* of the globe" (the *Monthly Review*, 1790(2):60–68). Recall, also, that the textual harvest of its expeditions, most famously Park's *Travels* (1799), fed the same middle-class penchant for stories of adventure, exoticism, and the pornography of others' suffering. These, as we said before, paved the way for mass-circulation abolitionist and evangelical writings: the writings through which the progress of Africans, guided by heroic Christians, became part of the popular literary fare of "respectable" Britain.

The intercourse between accounts of Africa and those of the poor in England varied in explicitness and elaboration. Often the pointed use of verbal metaphors in otherwise unconnected descriptions conjured up potent parallels: talk of urban jungles—in which the "dark" masses lived, like "wandering tribes," in "warrens" and "nests"—brought the "dark" continent disconcertingly close to home (e.g., Hollingshead 1861:8, 165). Sometimes, however, the parallelism was less a matter of lexicon than genre. A striking instance is to be found in another text by Greenwood, published before *The Wilds*. In his *Seven Curses of London* (1869:20), he describes a "strange observance" in the vicinity of the Cow Cross Mission. The evangelist there had seen many "instances of this strange custom; but even he, who is as learned in the habits and customs of all manner of outcasts of civilization as any man living, was unable to explain its origin." The "strange observance" was the prominent display of a marriage certificate on the living-room wall of many homes, sometimes under a time-piece. Given the low incidence of wedlock among the poor, the centrality of the conjugal family in bourgeois morality, and the role of the clock in marking work time, the symbolic logic of the practice hardly seems mysterious. The purposeful joining of these tokens of respectability gives graphic evidence of the impact of philanthropic efforts to reform domestic values; not least, to place legitimate marriage under the regime of responsible self-regulation. But even more salient here is the fact that this passage might easily have been written by Moffat or Broadbent or any number of other missionaries. It bears all the signs of literary "othering" (Pratt 1985:120). Its distancing, objectifying style, its synthesis of the tropes of ethnography (habits, customs) and evangelism (civilization), of science (learning, explanation) and moralism (outcasts), conveyed a transparent message: the British poor were as much "other" as any African aborigine.

Little wonder, then, that Mayhew (1851:iii) prefaced *London Labour*, itself modeled on the ethnology of South Africa,[109] with the remark that less was known of these inner-city unfortunates "than of the most distant tribes of the earth." His readership was left in no doubt that they were urgently in need of improvement. The charter for the civilizing mission at home—indeed, for the cultural colonization of underclass England—rang clear: the bourgeois burden in Britain was yet more pressing than the white man's burden abroad. The case was argued by a number of literati of the period; perhaps most cogently by Dickens (1908a; 1908b; see *RRI*:51f.). And it was supported by growing "scientific" evidence to prove that the lot of the very poor was as dire and dangerous as anything depicted in the most lurid novel or preachy political tract.[110] If this was not enough, foreign "savages" were sometimes made to bear the message, itself an ironic inversion that pressed home the parallel between the benighted of England and Africa. Thus Bosanquet (1868:1f.) tells of a "young Caffre" from South Africa who, after visiting London, recounts his experiences to his compatriots. "Many are rich and many are poor," he says. "In such a great place there is all that is beautiful and all that is bad."

The drawing of imaginative parallels between the "dangerous classes" (Stedman Jones 1971:11) at home and savages abroad, in sum, lay first and foremost at the level of unmarked imagery; of more or less direct intertextual and lexical references that wove a tapestry across the genres of travel, scientific, and missionary literature, fusing moral homily with homeric adventure, evangelical zeal with exotic didacticism, fact with wonder. This was epitomized, with particular reference to domesticity, by two popular texts: Thomas Archer's *The Pauper, the Thief, and the Convict* (1865) and Thomas Beames's *Rookeries of London* (1852). The undertitle of the former, "Sketches of Some of Their Homes, Haunts, and Habits," brings together, in avid alliteration, a hint of the naturalist's notebook, the traveler's tale, and the erotic eye. Archer begins by insisting that "there is little of the picturesque in poverty" (p. 1). In this, he evokes the evangelist to Africa who begs us, before laying out his romance, not to be romantic. And then, like the same evangelist, he takes us with him on a pilgrim's progress—save that his unknown land is Bethnal Green, with its "ruinous and dirty" maze of thoroughfares, its "teeming and filthy rooms," its "ragged, dirty children" and "gaunt women" (p. 10). Archer's Africa-in-London is a "social crime." Its streets give way to "blind," windowless courts, at the end which are "a number of black and crumbling hovels, forming three sides of a miserable square, like a foetid tank, with a bottom of mud and slime" (p. 11). Here, as in Bechuanaland, the wilderness is unnamed, unmarked, uncharted. Archer assures us that this is "as foul a neighborhood as can be discovered in the civilized world" (p. 10). The verb, in juxtaposition to its object, discloses the essential spirit of the voyage. So does the parenthetic comment that follows: "[S]avage life has nothing to compare to it."

Thomas Beames went yet one further. He likened the "pauper colonies" of London to the nests of rooks, the "lowest" of birds. That the term "colony" was used to describe underclass urban districts is itself striking. But even more so is Beames's portrait of these "colonies" (pp. 2–4):

> [Paupers] belong to the . . . section of the social body . . . descended to the lowest scale which is compatible with human life. Other birds are broken up into separate families—occupy separate nests; rooks seem to know no such distinction. So it is with the class whose dwellings we describe. [These colonies house] the pariahs, so to speak, of the body social, a distinct social caste.

And so the poor become a distinct race, the untouchables of bourgeois society.[111] How similar this rings to the missionary notion that Tswana lacked properly bounded families; that, being enmeshed in unhealthy "communistic relations," they showed no natural affection or individuality. In both cases, the sensibilities of pious humanitarianism served to devalue the dispossessed.

The parallels drawn between darkness-at-home and darkness-abroad often had an expressly political purpose. Rymer, for instance, explained that the object of his *The White Slave* (1844), one of several similar novels published at the time, was "to convince the public that there were white slaves in London a great deal worse off than the black slaves in Africa" (see Gallagher 1985:131). But the moral spirit, the ideological offensive, that animated the writings of this tradition[112] was articulated most sharply in Hollingshead's *Ragged London* (1861:vf.): "With all our electro-plated sentiment about home and the domestic virtues," he said, "we ought to wince a good deal at the houses of the poor." The qualifier here is revealing: electroplating, the coating of domestic tableware with shiny silver by electrolysis, was a brilliant symbol of the newly acquired, skin-deep sensibilities of the bourgeoisie. Those sensibilities were offended by thoroughgoing misery. True, the poor, with their "drunken indulgence" in "child-breeding," might themselves have been to blame. But the point, concluded Hollingshead, was to ameliorate the situation. This is where the analogy with Africa took on practical salience: what was required was an army of missionaries who would reform the needy from the core of their very beings. "In no part of the world—not even in the remotest dens of the savage wilderness—is there such a field for labour as in our London courts and alleys" (p. 221). Resonances, again, of Dickens.

The circle is closed. The wilds of London and Africa differed little. They were equally "other," equally un*domestic*ated. The primitive and the pauper were one in spirit, one in spiritlessness. And so the sacred task of the colonizing mission was to rebuild the homes and domestic lives of both in the name of universal civilization. John Philip (1828,2:316–17) was correct: the "dark continent" *was* a metaphorical mirror through which to reflect on the similarities and contrasts between savagery and civility, the past and the present, middle-class refinement and its obverse, all good things English and all bad. There was in this, as well, the quiet maturation of a national imagining, an imagining in which bourgeois civility and the cultural commonweal were homogenizing themselves into one and the same idyll. But that story of hegemony in the making has already been told by others.

The encounter with savagery was deployed, in the dialectic of domesticity, in two distinct ways, two modalities of discourse and practice. One was negative, the other positive. These followed upon each other conceptually and, broadly speaking, chronologically. The first has permeated everything we have said so far: namely, the invocation of Africa as a *camera obscura*, a counter model of bourgeois civility and, hence, a point-zero from which to begin campaigns of reconstruction. The "indescribable" disorder of Africans, their closeness to animal nature, became a measure against which to evaluate conditions and classes back home, thence to frame suitable social and evangelical policy. *Nomadic* costermongers, *wandering* paupers, the *teeming, filthy* poor, those *styed promiscuously* in their *haunts, hovels, dens*, and *nests*, it seemed, were no better than the undomesticated savages of the dark continent. And, inasmuch as this was true, they called into question Britain's own self-image, its claim to stand at the pinnacle of modernity and civilization. It was thus the common duty of the liberal middle classes to help them improve their homes and habits: to create the conditions for—and an attitude of—"cleanliness," thus to achieve a world in which all matter, beings, and bodies were put in their proper places; to reform sexuality by encouraging legal, Christian marriage, thus discouraging "drunken indulgence" in "child-breeding"; to spread the ideal of private property and to reconstruct the gendered division of labor. To the extent that such efforts fell short, however, the poor, like their African counterparts, were held responsible for their own "moral degradation, ruin of domestic enjoyments, and social misery" (P. Gaskell 1836:89).[113]

Note, here, the talk of "misery." We have encountered it before: the word appeared often in Nonconformist descriptions of African home life (e.g., Broadbent 1865:204).[114] Also favored by British abolitionists and philanthropists, it made the "other" out to be an inert, suffering victim. (Of precisely what or why, of course, was a matter of debate.) And it gave an alibi for Christian intervention and healing, a topic to which we turn in the next chapter. How could anyone cultivated, anyone morally responsible, ignore the plight of the ailing, the distressed, the tormented? So it was that the metaphors of affliction coursed through the literature on outcast London, a call to alms and to action on the part of all citizens with a social conscience. Some, it is true, found the call unpersuasive. E. M. Forster (1992:58) was to have Henry Wilcox, his arch Edwardian capitalist, assert that "the very poor . . . are unthinkable, and only to be approached by the statistician or the poet"; not by the practical reformer. But this was in later, more cynical times. And it probably represented a minority view even then.

The other manner in which the dark continent was deployed in the dialectic of domesticity, especially toward the end of the nineteenth century, expressed itself in the positive voice. Africa came to stand as living proof of, and a model for, the universal possibility of enlightened self-improvement. This "proof" was erected on a blatantly racist syllogism. Under the impact of the Protestant mission, went the argument, some savages had bettered themselves, built decent homes, learned the arts of domesticity, and enjoyed their just spiritual and economic rewards. If these blacks—people with inherent moral, material, and mental limitations—could climb the ladder of civilization, so might the most lowly of white Englishmen.

Such was the implication—sometimes stated, sometimes not—of any number of "eyewitness" reports of African life framed in optimistic terms: of Trollope's portrait of Thaba 'Nchu; of Holub's sketches of Mafikeng and Likatlong; of several of the missionary texts we have quoted in extenso, starting with Read's (1850:446) account of the Christians of Kuruman. Willoughby's Native Life made the point visually. His photographs, laid out in evolutionary sequence from the most "primitive" African "hovels" to the most "advanced" European-styled residences, beamed an unmistakable message at his British readership: among Bechuana, once the most backward of humans, there were individuals who had shown themselves capable of personal cultivation and domestic refinement. These "sable brethren" stood out as a humiliating example to every lower-class Englishman and woman who spurned civility and still lived, unmoved and unimproved, in the rookeries and recesses of the urban wasteland.[115]

CODA

This story of colonial domesticity, of the effort to domesticate the lowly at home and abroad, underscores our most general theme. Far from being a one-sided affair, British colonialism was always two-sided, dialectical, in at least three respects.

First, the old point: colonized peoples everywhere influenced the manner in which colonizers acted upon them. Their reactions and resistances placed effective limits on the means by which—and the measure in which—their worlds might be invaded. These reactions took many forms: willful misunderstandings, both mute and voluble; assertive refusals to listen or engage; subtle attempts to decenter and distract; gestures of determined destruction, of misinformation and misappropriation, of counter-violence. And, at some times and places, enthusiastic experimentation with things foreign. It goes without saying, too, that colonizers varied in the degree to which they were prepared to impose their wills, to resort to brute force, to intimidate and dominate at any cost. Indeed, it was in the spaces where the two axes of determination met—where the will of the colonizer ran up against the willfulness of the colonized—that colonial struggles took place.

Second, just as European cultural forms took root on African ground, so African cultural forms insinuated themselves into the everyday routines, the aesthetics, and the material lives of the Europeans. At times the latter had little choice: their knowledge and resources simply ran out along the frontier. At other times, local ways and means appeared more rational, more sensible, more capable of explaining and responding to prevailing conditions. Now and then, the adoption by Europeans of African practices presented itself as a deliberate choice, and was openly justified. But often it seemed just to happen, almost unnoticed, and became the subject of embarrassed rationalization (de Kock 1993:213f.).

And third, in seeking to cultivate the "savage"—with, as we have said, variable success—British imperialists actively sought to domesticate those of their own underclasses who eluded bourgeois control. From this perspective, cultural colonialism was a reflexive process, a double gesture, whereby "others" abroad, the objects of the civilizing mission, were put to the purposes of reconstructing the "other" back home. The two sites, the two impulses, went hand in hand. British colonialism was always as much about making the center as it was about making the periphery. The colony was not a mere extension of a modern society. It was one of the instruments by which that society was made modern in the first place. The dialectic of domesticity was a vital element in the process.

This returns us to the question of domesticity itself. Given that the seeds of cultural imperialism *were* most effectively sown in the contours of the everyday, it is no surprise that colonial evangelists paid so much heed to the physical and social architecture of "home." But the inculcation of the modernist model of domestic life was much more than a matter of spreading the "Western ideology of family." It always is. As most missionaries understood, the construction of the "private" domain was fundamental to the propagation of a particular kind of public sphere—not to mention a Protestant, middle-class worldview. Within it were contained all the elemental relations of gender and generation upon which proper social reproduction depended. As modernity took shape in Europe, moreover, the nuclear family became the point of articulation between civil society and the (ostensibly) free individual, the ideological atom upon which the bourgeois world depended.

In seeking to recast Africa domesticity in the same mold, then, colonial evangelists hoped to bring about a New Society, a New Civility. So, too, did those of their brethren who toiled among the lowly of London and Manchester and countless country parishes. As creatures of their time, these social reformers took for granted what was to take social scientists many decades to learn: that existing forms of domesticity and the dominant social order of which they are part depend on one another for their construction and reproduction. Hegemony begins at home.

SEVEN

THE MEDICINE OF
GOD'S WORD

Saving the Soul by Tending the Flesh

*[If y]ou admit, from an appeal to the example of Christ, that healing the
sick is one of the best means of benefiting, and therefore one of the best
means of reaching and influencing the hearts and sympathies of men . . .
you [will] grant the conclusion we seek to establish, viz., that the combination of healing and preaching is the best method of introducing
[Christianity].*

W. Burns Thomson (1854:10)

S HOULD HEALING BE regarded as a mere thing of the flesh, a
carnal palliative to the heathen sufferer? Or as a God-given instrument to be wielded by foot soldiers of the Lord in the cause of
Christian conversion? This conundrum dogged nineteenth-century
Protestant evangelism in Africa. Throughout the continent, nevertheless, missionaries were the most important—and, almost everywhere, the most eagerly
sought—purveyors of European medicine (cf. Northcott 1945; Ranger 1982b;
Etherington 1987; Vaughan 1991:55f.). Not least in South Africa: healing was
to be a critical site here, a space of ongoing existential and cultural exchange in
the encounter between the Nonconformists and Southern Tswana.
    And yet it did not merely replay the dialectics of that encounter in another
key. For it was in the domain of healing that the distances and distinctions of
the imperial frontier were most often breached; that all parties to the long conversation seemed most receptive to innovation from "the other"; that the hy-

bridizing effects of colonial evangelism were perhaps most fully realized—although, by the late nineteenth century, the rise of biomedicine would put limits on this process for bourgeois Europeans. Even at its most rationalized, however, healing remained, in large measure, a tactile process, one in which the physical separations of the civilizing mission were most often ruptured—and where feelings of recognition, even compassion, flowed across the cleavages of a racially divided society.[1]

The pioneer generation of Protestant missionaries to Bechuanaland was born of an "age of anxious, ardent philanthropy" (Thomson 1854:5), an age in which reformers strove hard to press Africa's afflictions on the public awareness (*RRI*:115f.). Their voices were visceral, their imagery organic (R. Moffat 1842:616):

Africa still lies in her blood. She wants . . . all the machinery we possess, for ameliorating her wretched condition. Shall we, with a remedy that may safely be applied, neglect to heal her wounds? Shall we, on whom the lamp of life shines, refuse to disperse her darkness?

This was the voice that would beckon the most legendary of all crusading doctors, David Livingstone, to the Tswana field. It echoed a tradition of Christian restorative rhetoric made newly relevant by abolitionism in the eighteenth century: a rhetoric in which images of healing and social amelioration infused each other, in which the blighted body served as a graphic symptom of moral disorder. Physical affliction suggested a "sin-sick soul" (Lowe n.d.:218). It seemed especially effective in arousing the conscience of those who saw themselves as humane imperialists, universal Christians. The call to save the heathen, on a continent so violently despoiled by slavery, was a plea to "heal wounds" that were, in most palpable respects, Europe's responsibility. Thus a poem by one "W.E. of Wimbledon," written for the *Evangelical Magazine* in 1834:

Yes; the negro who weeps on the shore,
Whose colour has doomed him a slave,
Precious balms in his wounds I will pour,
And tell him, "there's One that can save."

The drive to remedy moral and material disorder might have taken the missionaries into many different realms of everyday activity. But healing was a prime site for them, particularly in the opening decades, since it gave clear, easily justified motives for intervening into local lifeways. In addition, although medical assistance self-evidently addressed itself to the flesh, its evangelical significance had been roundly endorsed, through personal example, by the Greatest of all Teachers. And somewhat more recently, if less directly, by the publication of John Wesley's *Primitive Physic* (1791).

As we shall see, like elsewhere in the non-European world, there quickly arose a vigorous demand among Tswana for European pharmacopeia and medical treatment—which reinforced the view held by many in LMS and WMMS circles that healing the sick offered a ready physical means to their spiritual ends. Consequently, the early evangelists came to assume that ministering to the African body was part of their overall calling, an essential aspect of the civilizing mission. Moffat (Moffat and Moffat 1951:25, 44), for instance, confided that he took every opportunity to give medical aid to the Tlhaping—and to impress the Word of God on those whom he treated. Similarly, Broadbent reported that, when approached by Tswana doctors for his counsel on "what was good for a certain disease," he lost no time in trying to "instruct" them. By his own admission, he failed. "Alas!" he confessed, I "could not impart to them . . . the knowledge of things spiritual." Nonetheless, several of his Nonconformist brethren sought their first conversions on the sickbed;[2] we shall encounter several cases as we proceed. At the same time, these men were left largely to their own devices in deciding how precisely to respond to the clamor for their cures. Open debate over the place of medical mission work, within and outside the evangelical societies, would only come later, toward the midcentury and after (see below).

Between 1820 and 1920, the period that directly concerns us here, Western ways of curing changed profoundly, of course—and did so in a manner that had major effects on the mission. What began the period as an explicit discourse on moral economy ended it, at least in hegemonic form, as biomedicine; what was formerly couched in terms of Christian well-being came to be spoken of in the assertive language of science. This transformation was implicated in significant, epochal shifts in the nature of knowledge, authority, and sovereignty. It was to make medicine into the archetypal profession, and enable it, with the backing of the state, to replace the church as the guardian of "health," public and private. For a good part of the nineteenth century, though, there was no simple distinction to be drawn between the pioneers of scientific healing and those purveyors of the Spirit who also treated afflicted bodies. Nor was there an easy distinction between the reformist ambitions, respectively, of medicine and the colonial mission. Notwithstanding their (steadily growing) ideological and institutional differences, they had sprung from the same historical ground. At the frontiers of the European world, moreover, they often worked hand in hand, bolstering each other as they wrought changes on human subjects. But this was before British medicine was thoroughly professionalized, before a national register of practitioners was established, before a central council was set up to govern qualifying examinations (Reader 1966:44ff.).

As the century drew on, and medicine grew more specialized and regulated, there was a concomitant tendency among evangelists to see healing as a unique sphere of competence. Unqualified missionaries in South Africa became increasingly uneasy about treating the sick, in spite of undiminished appeals to do so. As late as 1895, it is true, the (untrained) Edwin Lloyd (1895:167) told an LMS convention in Britain that he and his colleagues still "seek to commend the Gospel to the Bechwana by means of our medical work." But many of those colleagues showed their reluctance by repeatedly asking the LMS directors to send out Christian medical men. To little avail. While the LMS had dispatched a few to China and India, Livingstone was to have no immediate successor in Bechuanaland (Northcott 1945:155, 157).³ The evangelists, as a result, had to continue doing their best to meet demands for their assistance. Eventually, to the apparent relief of some of them, they could do so no more; not legally. With the advent of the colonial state and the appointment of medical officers of health, lay healing was restricted.⁴

Prior to this denouement, however—prior, even, to calls from Bechuanaland for qualified doctors—there arose, in the evangelical world, an organized response to the question of treating the sick: an independent, institutionally based, professionally disposed medical mission. Although it was not to send practitioners to the Tswana, it was to affect the conditions under which all evangelists toiled. Before we turn to its development, however, let us first look briefly at the state of scientific medicine in Britain in the early nineteenth century. For it is here, in large part, that the narrative of the healing ministry begins.

THE AGE OF HEROIC MEDICINE

At Home: Contemporary British Medicine

The term "heroic" was often applied to British healing in the early nineteenth century. At its most sanguine, this evokes a vision, fanciful in hindsight, of daring exploits, intuitive genius, and virtuoso performance; not of routinized procedures, a systematic body of knowledge, or workaday expertise. Although there was no "homogeneous body of theory and practice answering to the name 'medicine'" (Porter 1992a:1), and many different kinds of practitioner sold their services (Wear 1992:17), the field is usually said to have comprised three major divisions, each associated with a distinct social estate. Physicians, gentlemen all, were trained only at Oxford and Cambridge and hence were members of the Church of England (Reader 1966:16). Surgeons were from less elevated backgrounds, as were even more humble apothecaries. They learned largely by apprenticeship. Each division exercised a modicum of control over its membership and modes of practice, but there was little overall regulation. Before the Medical Act of 1858, for example, almost anyone could assume the title of doctor (E. Turner 1959:153; Seeley 1973:76).

While a host of competing theories and techniques flourished on this unrestricted terrain, most of them were rooted in popular assumptions about the body and its humoral economy. These assumptions were *not* limited to medical practitioners, but "part of the common culture of gentlemen" (Jacyna 1992:225); indeed, of ordinary people as well. A doctor like David Livingstone—he referred to himself as a surgeon[5]—did not harbor etiological ideas markedly different from those of his untrained brethren. Although there was growing interest in biological complexity in university circles, the humors were still thought to mediate the impact of the environment on human physical equilibrium (see *RRI*:107f.). Bodily functions were also tempered by climate, gender, race, and moral disposition. Thus, in its opening passages, an LMS booklet on *The Means of Preserving Health in Hot Climates* (LMS 1819:7; emphases added), stated:

> There are *moral* as well as *medical* means of preserving health; and the former are hardly less important than the latter . . . especially in climates which render the duration of health even more dependent on habits and associations, than it is in colder countries.

James Read, one of the earliest LMS emissaries to the Tswana, owned a well-thumbed copy of the booklet,[6] which gave point by point instructions on maintaining an "evenness of feeling." This was necessary, it advised, to counteract the "nervous state of body" and "torpid state of the bowels" brought on by stressful work at "high temperature of atmosphere" (1819:8–9, 38–39). The constitutions of non-European peoples, and of women in general, were seen to be particularly dependent on external conditions; they were easily "destabilized" by heat and humidity.

Illness, as this implies, was a state of imbalance, a matter of excess or deficiency; treatment, an act of restoring equilibrium (C. Jones 1988:9). Toward the midcentury, contending causal theories of disease were being published at a giddy rate. But medical intervention remained remarkably consistent, conservative, and formulaic, resting on the "antiphlogistic regimen" of bloodletting, drastic purgatives, and emetics (C. Jones 1988:2–3)—as well as on the compensatory management of diet, dress, and exposure to volatile winds. More plebeian therapies looked even less to theory, relying largely on pragmatic, herbal remedies. Nevertheless, assumptions about persons and their physical economies were widely shared. Jordanova (1989:46) has noted, in this respect, that the environmental influences held to act on human beings were of two sorts: fixed forces of nature and habits susceptible to modification (cf. Vaughan 1991:35).

In its heroic age, British healing furnished colonial evangelism with a potent vocabulary. (Clinical biomedicine would resonate with colonialism in other ways; but that is a topic for later in the chapter.) Humoral thinking validated a grammar of stark contrasts. It opposed well-being to suffering, stability to riot, healthful temperateness to sickly heat, hygienic order to harmful filth, savage affliction to the comforts of refinement; all of which brings to mind Coleridge's distinction between those civilizations blessed with "the bloom of health" and those beset by the "hectic of disease" (R. Williams 1961:121). What is more, this conceptual economy—with its notions of depletion and excess, of balance and chaos—was also a moral economy; it was preoccupied with the steady production and free flow of worth, wealth, virtue. In regulating the motility of blood, food, wind, or effluent, its doctors addressed the interdependence of the body corporeal and the body social. This was most strikingly done through bleeding, which aimed to relieve feverish overaccumulation, or to stimulate systems that had been depleted or improvidently used (C. Jones 1988:123f.).

None of these things, as it would turn out, was incompatible with Tswana therapeutics (see below). To be sure, the confrontation, along this frontier, between Western and African medicine was not, in the first instance, one between "primitive" [witch]doctoring and a developed biological science (Vaughan 1991:56; Seeley 1973:77). Contrary to received conceptions of colonial encounters *sui generis*—and of medical encounters in particular—a mature system of knowledge and practice was not simply exported to the edges of empire, there (depending on your point of view) to be bestowed or imposed upon indigenous peoples. In the early nineteenth century, British medicine was rudimentary, unsystematic, often unsure of itself; perhaps no more developed, and maybe less coherent, than its Tswana counterpart. Hence the respect with which David Livingstone—and Henry Callaway, medical missionary among the Nguni (Etherington 1987:77f.)—listened to local specialists, the attention he paid to their techniques, his hope to learn cures that had eluded British physicians. This, also, is a matter to which we shall return.

With the gradual coming of age of the clinic, European doctors lost their sense of humors. Heroic healing gave way to an ever more technicist biomedicine, humanist art to the universalizing abstractions of rationalist science. Not entirely, of course. Homeopathic herbalists, for instance, continued to ply their now devalued trade. And, even at its most scientific and abstract, clinical practice never abjured all connection with humanist concerns or with the moral economics of bourgeois modernity. It merely relegated them to the nether regions of its unspoken ontology. The broad lines of the story, thanks in part to Foucault (1975), are now familiar. Not only did there follow paradigmatic shifts in theory and technology, especially with the development of germ theory and antisepsis, but the practice of biomedicine itself underwent cumulative rationalization, regulation, and regimentation. It became, *sensu stricto,* a discipline, taking on the ethos of professionalism which, in the words of a contemporary observer, helped "the great English middle class . . . maintain its tone of independence, keep up to the mark its standard of morality, and direct its intelligence" (H. Byerley Thomson in Reader 1966:1). In doing so, British science shut itself off from non-Western knowledges, denying them any value and refusing even the possibility of learning from them. Parochial in its universalism— and, *pace* Robin Horton (1967), "closed" in its "predicament"—it reduced African therapeutics and pharmacopeia to "magic" and "herbs." Thus, by the end of the century, Dr. J. Rutter Williamson (1899:9), an energetic advocate of "Clinical Christianity," could dismiss non-European practice with withering disdain: "Native doctors," he declared, "are absolutely ignorant" of even the rudiments of science. In point of fact, those native doctors were rather more open in their worldview. Some of them, the evidence shows (cf. also Etherington 1987:81, on the Zulu), were quite ready to learn from their encounter with the healing ministry.

Abroad: The Rise of the Medical Mission

In the middle years of the nineteenth century, conditions in Britain fostered an enthusiasm for evangelical healing. Although medicine was already in the throes of transformation, and was on the way to becoming a more self-consciously coherent discipline, it still remained open to the language of moral and spiritual reform (Garlick 1943:126). For their part, the mission societies were being influenced by the same mood of professionalism that was changing clinical practice. A drive for rationalization was evident in their growing anxiety to formulate systematic policy and vocational training. In the imagery of the period, too, the pioneer evangelist *cum* intrepid amateur explorer was being displaced by another kind of celebrity: the specialist. Doctors and scientists, who embodied the triumph of reason over nature, loomed larger and larger as the heroic figures of European fiction (cf. Jordanova 1989); thus, in Jules Verne's (1876) novel of whites in the Bechuana interior, set in 1854, the cast of characters included three Russians and three Englishmen, all distinguished astronomers and mathematicians. In this transition—in the fading out of the dashing, dilettante superhero in favor of the dedicated, masterful professional—David Livingstone was an especially compelling icon. Livingstone himself had been impressed by early appeals for *qualified* Christian healers: a pamphlet issued from Canton in 1833 by the philanthropist Karl Gützlaff—seeking recruits for China—is said to have crystalized his own resolve to become an evangelical physician (Gelfand 1957:16; Livingstone 1857:5).[7]

The penchant for medical work expressed itself as a distinct initiative within British evangelism; one which led to the establishment of specialist organizations with their own connections to the biological sciences. This initiative encouraged the tendency of the long run which we remarked earlier and will return to again: the growing reluctance of medically untrained missionaries—themselves reliant on piecemeal, plebeian techniques—to treat the sick. The mainstream societies sustained close relations with those dedicated to Christian healing, although they often fell into conflict. The division between them followed a familiar fault line, a dualism then deepening in European culture: they were often characterized as champions, respectively, of the "spirit" versus the "body," of "preaching" versus "practice."

329

One major bridging institution was the nondenominational Edinburgh Medical Missionary Society (EMMS), founded in 1841 by a group of philanthropic physicians to ensure "the settlement of Christian medical men in foreign countries" (Lowe n.d.:202). Taking every opportunity "to advocate the claims of this new and interesting department of missionary service" (Lowe n.d.:204), the EMMS published lectures, held essay competitions, and supported the education of doctors for the various evangelical associations. Predictably, Livingstone was invoked as patron saint. It is unclear whether the EMMS actually gave him material aid—although an offer of support *was* made (Livingstone 1959,2:81)—but it proudly claimed him as a corresponding member. In 1877, Robert Moffat laid the foundation stone of its Livingstone Memorial Missionary Training Institute in Edinburgh—a school situated, we are told, "in the very midst of the moral and spiritual wastes of our home heathenism" (Lowe n.d.:218). Once more, the counterpoint: that insoluble connection between the dispossessed, the dark, the diseased in the colonies and the spiritual wasteland "at home."

The double-barreled crusade of biblical Christianity and biomedicine was irrepressible. A stream of propaganda, variously nuanced, emanated from the EMMS. Toward the end of the century it was augmented, at one extreme, by the journal *Medical Missions at Home and Abroad*—later renamed, revealingly, *Conquest by Healing*—and, at the other, by the enduringly popular *Jungle Doctor* fables. In the latter, insightfully analyzed by Vaughan (1991:155f.), the white physician becomes another in a long line of supermen seeking to save Africa from self-destruction. In point of fact, the medical missions did flourish. They enjoyed a great deal of success, by their own lights, throughout much of the continent. Buoyed by the rising international status of Western science, their emissaries provided a high proportion of all available biomedical care well into the twentieth century (Headrick 1987; Hunt 1990b; Vaughan 1991:55f.).[8] By 1918, companies like Burroughs Wellcome were producing "medical outfits" designed specifically for "dispensing in the mission field." Tellingly, their advertisements replayed, in a clinical key, the essential evangelical gesture of healing: a Christian physician, helped by his "native assistant," prepares to tend to the prostrate Other (plate 7.1).

But the theological rationale for Christian curing was most clearly set out in a series of publications in the 1850s; these also reveal the ambiguous place of medicine in the broader civilizing mission. Their tone is nicely captured by a prize essay written in 1854 for the EMMS by W. Burns Thomson, later superintendent of the Society's training institution. In arguing that the Church ought to help "solve the great problems that concern the progress of humanity," Thomson (1854:5) presumed a metaphysical understanding of religion. He acknowledged faith as the "motive-power" of all improvement, but urged Christians to seek practical means—"incidental and indirect agencies," he called

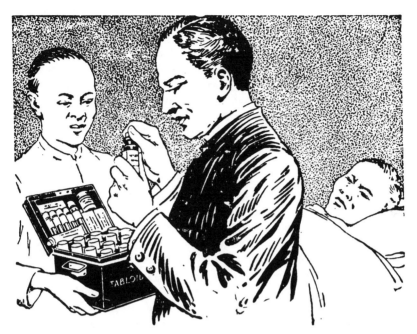

DISPENSING in the MISSION FIELD
greatly simplified by

TRADE
MARK
'TABLOID' BRAND

Medical Outfits

Reliable doses ready-to-take. No weighing or
measuring ; no deterioration ; no loss by breakage.

List of Outfits of all Chemists and Stores

BURROUGHS WELLCOME & CO., LONDON

xx 1893   COPYRIGHT

PLATE 7.1 *"Dispensing in the Mission Field" [from LMS, January 1918, back cover]*

331

them—through which to regenerate the world. Such a Christianity, far from being threatened by the Promethean rationalism of the age, accommodated it well. Divine provision had been completed in the world. It was now up to human beings to apply their energy and ingenuity in extending it, most of all to sites of "unreclaimed heathenism pleading for aid" (p. 7). Although bereft of miraculous powers, Godly Victorians had a worthy substitute: applied science. True, curing was not expressly included in the injunction to "preach the Gospel to every creature." Yet, as recent debates about the "Sabbath question" had shown, said Thomson, apostolic usage could be taken to supplement divine decree. And the evidence here, aptly provided in St. Matthew's Gospel, was unequivocal. It amounted to an "emphatic utterance,—Heal *and* Preach" (p. 17; emphasis added). He might also have invoked Luke 9.1–2: "And he called the twelve together and gave them power and authority . . . to cure diseases, and he sent them out to preach the kingdom of God and to heal."

Thomson (1854:20) went on to insist that pragmatic, bodily preoccupations should never supplant the supreme calling of evangelism; namely, the cultivation of the Spirit. Still, experience among laborers at home and heathens abroad had proven that "simple" people were highly susceptible to corporeal benefits. Like many of his brethren, therefore, he agreed that healing was an effective, justifiable entree for the gospel among those who had to be "taught as little children are . . . by object lessons" (Lowe n.d.:9). Stalwarts of the established mission societies were wary, however; their official policy statements, guarded. While acknowledging the efficacy of Christian curing among the "uncivilized"—*only* among them—they stressed that it had ever to remain subordinate to "spiritual work" (Garlick 1943:137).

Advocates of the medical mission responded by asserting its beneficial "sub-influences" in the evangelical field. Argued J. Rutter Williamson (1899:55), the same man who spoke so pejoratively of "native healers":

> It pioneers education, it stimulates scientific methods; it inculcates sanitary principles and introduces plague precautions and deals with epidemics. Again and again it becomes of political importance; its weight is thrown on the side of benevolent undertakings; while all the time it is raising in estimation the value of human life and the sacredness of womanhood.

We shall come back to the issue of evangelical healing and the value of womanhood. More immediately, however, as this homily suggests, medicine was becoming, literally, the cutting edge of civilization—as well, in some eyes, as its most effective vehicle. At home, extravagant claims were soon to be made for the power of doctors to heal social ills in unsanitary British cities (A. Adams 1991). Abroad, as participants in the LMS Founders' Week Convention of 1895 were told (LMS 1895:273), "medical missions have often acted as a key to un-lock the hearts of many. . . people . . . the world over."

Christian curing, it is true, did "act as a key" in the encounter between colonial evangelists and Southern Tswana. But its impact was not to be quite what the Nonconformists had in mind. Not only did contradictions arise be-tween the modernist ontology of medicine and the ideology of the mission church. The Africans, presumed beneficiaries of both, had their own ideas about well-being, affliction, and physicality. Healing held a pivotal place in their conceptions of power; apart from all else, it was the site, *par excellence*, of media-tion between the human and the divine. Here, once more, the missionaries would be hoist by their own poetics: from the beginning they were heard to be promising dramatic relief from death, disease, and affliction. Consequently, Southern Tswana were predisposed to regard them—*all* of them—as "doctors." Indigenous medicine centered on the manipulation of material objects and es-sences, words and things thought capable of harnessing diffuse, invisible forces. In its light, the evangelists—who proclaimed the power of prayer, of the Word, of the Bible—would be seen as ministers of strong substances, even of danger-ous magic. Shaped by a language that did not divide symbols from instruments, most Southern Tswana refused to separate the practices of priest and doctor. By contrast, the mission, following the general cast of Western thought, would insist on differentiating them. In the process, as we have already said, it was to open a breach in which a distinctly pragmatic African Christianity would take root. But we are running ahead of ourselves.

THE CURE AND THE CROSS: MISSIONARY
MEDICINE AMONG THE TSWANA

Medicine [is] . . . a handmaid to the Gospel.

K. G. Cameron (in Gelfand 1984:21)

As we have seen throughout the previous chapters, the Nonconformist ideal of Christian reconstruction was at once material, moral, and aesthetic. Partly contained in explicit dogma and formal knowledge, always conveyed in embod-ied, everyday ways of doing and seeing and being, its focus was the self-made subject: a subject whose refinement, self-possession, and righteous accomplish-ments were regarded not merely as "good" and "proper," but also, increasingly, as healthy. The Foucauldian observation that health was to supplant salvation in the "moral order of moderns" (Taylor 1989:11) may not have found expres-sion in LMS or WMMS theology. But the colonial evangelists, even while bent on persuading Tswana of the ultimate value of life eternal, gave evidence that they understood this-worldly order and *well*-being in medical terms. Quite early on, John Philip (1828,1:209), speaking of "Hottentots" (Khoi), summarized the chief challenge of the South African mission as follows:

Little can be done towards [the] . . . general improvement [of a savage people], till you can get them to exchange their straw cabins for decent houses. Their miserable reed-huts are unfavourable to health and morals. Great numbers of the Hottentots die of consumptions, partly from this cause. Continually enveloped in smoke, sleeping on their earthen floors, and covered in filth, they are almost always sickly, and are frequently cut off in early life, having the appearance of old age before they arrive at their fortieth year.

Not only is the association between health and moral order—indeed, between morality and mortality—made explicit here. So, once again, is the connection of both to "decent" housing (chapter 6). What is more, the causal link between living in straw huts and illness ("consumptions") is presented as if it were a "medical" fact—even though subsequent research cast serious doubt upon it.[9]

Remember, too, that Livingstone (1961:129) also pronounced Tswana clothing "unhealthy," claiming that endemic diseases declined as "decent" Western apparel was put on; others later went so far as to blame high rates of tuberculosis among African migrant laborers on their partial, improper adoption of European dress (see below, n. 32; also Packard 1989:49). Propagandist materials continued to play on this theme for a very long time. Livingstone's vision of the curative power of clothes was to be revisited, a century afterward, by the founders of a hospital in his name at Molepolole in the Bechuanaland Protectorate. In a publication intended partly to raise funds, "African Poverty" is portrayed as generic cause of disease. And it is embodied, photographically, in the tattered figure of an "*ill*-clad" man, dejected and self-incriminating, his "charm" necklace visible above threadbare attire (Shepherd 1947:16, our emphasis; see plate 7.2).

The correlation drawn by the evangelists between indigenous "customs" (*mekgwa*) and ill-health went yet further, reaching deep into *setswana*. Some offered lurid accounts of diseases and deaths caused by such "loathsome and horrible" rites as circumcision.[10] Others told of physical distress suffered by women and children as a result of the absence of a "real marriage relation" (Broadbent 1865:97–98); of the "bloody sickness," a fatal condition brought on by the practice of sorcery (J. Philip 1828,2:119); of the killing of babies in the instance of twin births (Campbell 1822,2:206). It is not surprising, therefore, that clarion calls to the civilizing mission, calls for the replacement of old African ways with the ways of European modernity, should have rung with medical metaphors.

PLATE 7.2 *"African Poverty: A Breeding Place for Germs" [from Shepherd 1947:16]*

Grease, Again: Contiguity, Contagion, Cleanliness

If "health" endorsed the rationality and comfort of Western political economy, affliction was taken to be endemic to the life of Africans; it was an unfortunate corollary of their social arrangements, their moral condition, their "animal ecology."[11] In the early years, as we showed above, the rampant, uncontained black body, often marked as female and "greasy," served widely to symbolize heathen disorder. At least it did for the evangelists; some Europeans, like Lichtenstein (1973:65), found most Tswana radiantly healthy in appearance. Livingstone (1857:20) referred to the principal wife of the Kwena chief, Sechele, as "an out-and-out greasy disciple of the old school"; she had shown herself unwilling to adopt European ways and means. This recalls Robert Moffat's (1842:287) comment that everything touched by Tswana, in their "natural" state, was tainted by the "colour of their greasy red attire"; that, when they departed the company of whites, they "left ten times more than their number [of lice] behind—company still more offensive."[12]

The menace of spreading contagion, of the infectious imprint of the savage, infuses such texts. Although their world was not yet informed by bacteriology, the evangelists often spoke of noxious organisms harbored by Tswana bodies and blankets, organisms that threatened to invade the hard-won order of the mission. To them, disorder, dirt, and pollution all spelled depravity, a sinful lack of self-containment and spirituality. Grease, it seems, was the opposite of Grace. What is more, it was deemed acceptable actually to punish those who were unclean, for cleanliness was, above all else, a righteous "duty" (see n. 12). But cleansing, as anthropologists are wont to say, is the management of "matter out of place "(Douglas 1966). And British Nonconformists found little more disorderly, hence unhealthy, than human bodies pressing upon each other, mingling their substance (R. Moffat 1842:503):

> The [Tlhaping] child . . . is carried in a skin on the mother's back, with its chest lying close to her person. When it requires to be removed from that position, it is often wet with perspiration; and from being thus exposed to cold wind, pulmonary complaints are not unfrequently brought on.

The warm closeness of an African mother's body did not protect or nurture. It was a source of sickness.

The management of mundane bodily functions in the name of order, health, and cleanliness was a major feature of European social engineering throughout the nineteenth century—both at home and overseas. Many grand imperial movements took material form in small, sanitizing gestures: in the daily ablution regimes established at mission schools, in the rules of hygiene enforced at colonial workplaces, in the policing of domestic space under regimes of public health (e.g., Jephson 1907; MacLeod 1988; Burke 1996; Thomas 1990). Conversely, some of the most visceral acts of resistance on the part of the colonized were to proclaim that, from their perspectives, such European practices were themselves "filthy" (see volume 3).

For the pioneer generation of evangelists, then, the very idea of healing was inseparable from that of cleansing. "Every one that would preserve health," Wesley once wrote, "should be as clean and sweet as possible in their houses, clothes and furniture" ([1791] 1960:30). But first it was necessary to reorganize African bodies in space, thus to create stable, discrete persons and properties; in short, fit habitations for the restoring spirit. All the missionary efforts to reform Southern Tswana economy and society partook of this purifying process. As late as 1886, Alfred Sharp, a Methodist posted at Vryburg told how he regularly[13]

> examine[d] their dwellings, [gave] a scrutinizing look at their dress and their faces, urge[d] upon them the necessity of cleanliness. In one instance I felt it necessary to order a number of about twenty to pack up their bundles and resort to a river close by with a little soap.

But, from the start, there was also a second, narrower sense of healing at work, one whose concrete point of reference was the sound human body. The Tswana and the Christians, as it turned out, had rather different understandings of what the latter might mean. Yet for both, the practice of doctoring in this more specific sense was part of an embracing moral economy. Indeed, struggles over medicine were often emblematic of the broader cultural confrontation at work in the colonial encounter (Comaroff and Comaroff 1992:223f.).

The Healing Ministry

I am exceedingly gratified to observe the confidence which has been inspired into the minds of the Bechuanas of the efficacy of our medicines. . . . I feel thankfull [sic], and hope it will by the blessing of God enable me to win their attention to a much more important topic than the preservation of their bodies, even the salvation of their immortal souls.

David Livingstone (1961:4)

Although their ministrations varied both in scope and in the willingness with which it was offered, all missionaries to the Tswana gave some form of medical treatment. With one notable exception,[14] they did not build hospitals or clinics. But "the medicine chest, with its glass stoppered bottles and its drawer below for pestle and mortar and small boxes" was a regular item of evangelical equipment everywhere (Northcott 1945:153). So, it must be assumed, were one or more of the standard manuals of the period, such as William Buchan's *Domestic Medicine* (Porter 1992b:216f.), itself, apparently (Hill 1960:20), a "largely elaborated copy—though unacknowledged" of John Wesley's *Primitive Physic*. That Tswana found curing the most attractive aspect of the Christian outreach is plain from the narratives of the Nonconformists—who themselves felt ambivalent about it, particularly because, when they spoke of salvation, they often elicited, by their own accounts, disinterest or incomprehension. Of course, what their patients actually took them to be saying about things spiritual cannot be known for sure. But they could not mistake the zeal with which their medicines were received, and other aspects of their activities taken to have therapeutic benefit.

Robert Moffat (1842:591), for one, soon found out that, in the interior, "it was well known that [he] performed some cures." On his travels, consequently, he was often brought "dozens" of patients and plied with demands for medication; although the fact that he was asked for books as well should alert us to the ways in which white power was being objectified in the local imagination (see *RRI*:229; below). In like vein, some people are said to have walked over a hundred miles to seek Livingstone's treatment (1940:30). When he journeyed to different villages, his "wagon was quite besieged by [the] blind & halt & lame." Nor was this a passing enthusiasm. John Mackenzie (1871:43) relived the experience a generation later. Having prevailed over a serious wound inflicted by a leopard near Kuruman, he discovered, during "the following travelling season, that [his] fame had preceded [him] . . . and all sorts of cases were brought, some for delicate surgical operations." All of the latter, he added cautiously, "I declined." The Methodists met with similar requests and reactions. They too were constantly approached to deal with a wide range of afflictions (above, n. 2).[15]

But the Africans did not merely wish to be healed by the evangelists. They also sought actively to acquire new remedies from them. As we have noted repeatedly, Southern Tswana had long been adventurous in searching out cures to enhance their own therapeutic repertoire (Campbell 1822,1:307f.). In one celebrated instance, a formerly barren woman attended by Livingstone (1857:146) produced a son, which led to rumors that the missionary had a treatment for sterility; soon he was besieged by men and women, some from very far away, hoping to "purchase . . . [for] any money . . . the 'child medicine'." Another case, altogether less fortunate, occurred among the Wesleyans when some local men seized a bag of gunpowder and proceeded to perform an experiment in the mimetic manufacture of European pharmacopeia. Having observed that whites ingested nothing much raw, they "cooked" the "seeds" in the hope of producing a potent distillate. In the upshot, which was very potent indeed, gunpowder came to be known as *"More oa sethunye . . .* the exploder's medicine" (Broadbent 1865:165; R. Moffat 1842:423). Tswana also had a tradition of importing expertise by encouraging healers from elsewhere to practice among them (Schapera 1971:44; Livingstone 1857:144). This extended beyond missionary circles: several European physicians who visited the country—such as the Czechoslovakian Emil Holub (1881)—were urged by local chiefs to remain with them as resident doctors (Seeley 1973:120). And explorers in the interior were sometimes asked to perform operations and cures. One of them, Andrew Smith (1939,1:282f.), there in the 1830s, found the Africans "very partial to medicine . . . [and willing] to take any with avidity which may be given to them."

What precisely—in these days before the Pasteur revolution, before germs or microbes or antisepsis—were the white men offering? Why was it so enthusiastically received?

By and large, the nineteenth-century evangelists confined themselves to humoral and herbal remedies and to straightforward surgical measures: to dressing wounds, promoting the excretion of "unhealthy" substances, curing eye ailments, bloodletting, applying tourniquets, treating boils, doing occasional amputations and excisions, lancing the pustules caused by such conditions as anthrax, and, especially as the intake of sugar had increased, pulling teeth (Seeley 1973:78; see R. Moffat 1842:436–37). They also performed inoculations during smallpox epidemics (see n. 35). Not all of this was new to Southern Tswana. Their doctors were, for example, familiar with inoculation techniques (Campbell 1822,1:307),[16] with lancing, and with cupping (i.e., piercing the flesh to extract blood; Livingstone 1857:143; Moffat and Moffat 1951:26; for an illustration, see A. Smith 1939,1:plate 23). Although they did not do operations on any major scale, and had limited surgical skills (Livingstone 1857:144), these doctors practiced *sedupe*, the removal of noxious matter from within the body by sucking on the skin.

Among the early missionaries, only Livingstone possessed and regularly used professional surgical instruments in large number.[17] He continued to order new ones from England, selecting them from the medical journals that sustained his links to the centers of science.[18] Most medicines, primarily purgatives and emetics, were also supplied from Britain, but were usually financed by the evangelists themselves (Seeley 1973:80); this being a further indication of the ambivalence with which healing was regarded by their societies. As a result, many of them felt it necessary to charge for their services (see, e.g., Price 1956:444), though some also saw in this an opportunity to teach a practical lesson in the value of goods and services (see n. 21). In 1844, Livingstone spent almost a third of his salary of one hundred pounds on pharmacopeia, and, like others before and after him,[19] pressed the directors for an annual allowance to cover such costs. He was successful. Two years later, the LMS agreed to send him drugs, purchased by a physician in England.[20] But the relationship of medicine to cash remained a vexed one. The LMS was uncomfortable about its emissaries "appropriat[ing] to their private use money received for . . . treatment," especially after a District Surgeon had been appointed in British Bechuanaland.[21] For their part, Tswana had long paid in kind for divination and curing. They learned quickly enough to pay for evangelical healing—as they did for many other Christian services.[22]

The provision of medical care was clearly consistent both with a rhetoric of salvation and with the stress on hygiene in European conceptions of socio-moral order; that point had been won by W. Burns Thomson and other protagonists of the healing ministry. But even more, treating bodily ills appeared, to the Christians at this evangelical frontier, a tangible way of "convincing the people that we were really anxious for their welfare" (Livingstone 1857:144, 47; cf. J. Mackenzie 1871:265f.). Which is why most of them continued to do it, despite their qualms. It was in this cause that they gained entry into African homes; that intimacies were exchanged and bodies touched; that, when medicine failed and words ran out, mutual tears flowed.

Given that Victorian sensibilities viewed medicine as a form of moral "theater" (Barker 1984:73ff.)—and were well attuned to the drama of the deathbed scene (RRI:236)—healing might also have seemed a felicitous arena in which to act out the purpose of the mission before the heathen. Moffat (Moffat and Moffat 1951:26) writes of his treatment of the wife of a Tlhaping "chief":

> At midday I returned, and found the women just commencing a cutting about the neck with a sharp bit of iron, with a view to extract blood in the way of cupping. I just arrived in time to prevent it. I gave her some diluting drink, and bathed her feet in warm water, when she began to show some symptoms of animation by opening the eyes. . . . The attendants, who were not few, and who had borne the look of sadness, now seemed quite overjoyed. I conversed some time with them on death and immortality, and the necessity of faith in Jesus Christ, in order to escape the punishment due for sin and obtain an everlasting salvation.

The redeemer, bathing the feet of the meek? This tableau condensed the evangelical ideal of medicine-at-work: a kindly but firm intervention in the savage abuse of the sick, dramatically restoring the vitality of the sufferer before an audience of awed, joyous witnesses. And all merely as a mundane prelude to the real lesson of spiritual healing; that is, the bestowal of life eternal. (Later, at Molepolole, Elizabeth Price (1956:445), would give "picture lessons," illuminated biblical instruction, to the patients of her husband, Roger; see n. 14.) Unremarked in the scene is an accompanying play of gestures, speaking every bit as loudly as the words—and, to the participants, perhaps more meaningfully. It is the spectacle of a white man, not declaiming from a pulpit, but on the ground in an African abode, amidst females, gently tending an ailing woman.

As healers, in fact, male missionaries were sometimes given access into otherwise intimate, exclusively female domains. Livingstone (1857:145) describes his first intervention in the field of obstetrics:

> [A] medical man going near a woman in her confinement appeared to them more out of place than a female medical student appears to us in a dissecting-room. A case of twins, however, happening, and the ointment of all the doctors of the town proving utterly insufficient to effect the relief which a few seconds of English art afforded, the prejudice vanished at once.

Gender prejudices in British medicine were to prove much more enduring, both inside and beyond the dissecting room!

The very success they enjoyed in treating the sick, however, was a cause of concern to the evangelists. For, in the absence of any parallel gains in disseminating their spiritual message, it merely underscored the great distance between African ideas of healing and the Protestant objective of salvation; between, in fact, two different perceptions of the exchange in process. To be sure, the missionaries *were* caught in the clutches of a contradiction. On one hand, their theology joined the redemption of flesh and spirit. On the other, being creatures of their own secular culture as well, their everyday practice distinguished doctoring from preaching, body from soul. By treating one as a means and the other as an end, they made it easy for Tswana to engage with the former and ignore the latter. They also made matters extremely frustrating for themselves. Even Livingstone (1961:46–47), the personification of inspired healing, soon muted his first enthusiasm for the medical mission:

> While here I could generally find a sufficiency of work by attending to the wants of the sick, who come in crowds from great distances as soon as they hear of my arrival. But as I believe the expenditure of much time and medicine is not the way in which in this country I can do most for the Redeemer's glory, I usually decline treating any except the more urgent cases.

Palpable, in this letter, is a restless spirit yearning for more heroic challenges; Livingstone went on to announce, to the LMS in London, that he felt called to "move . . . onward" into the interior to set up a new station. Still, his statement poses well the paradox of all Godly healing at the time. It was as doctors that the evangelists made most sense to indigenous peoples; through curing that their humane intent—their divine motivation, even—was most powerfully communicated in both word and deed (Seeley 1973). Yet, by devoting much of their time to healing, they merely seemed to drive a deeper wedge between the corporeal and the spiritual—and, in spite of their stated objectives, to traffic most effectively with Tswana in a commerce of bodies and objects. Writing of Central and East Africa, Megan Vaughan (1991:73) suggests that, "far from reiterating the post-Enlightenment soul/body division," missionary medicine "constantly referred to their indivisibility." In the early nineteenth-century Tswana context this was somewhat less straightforward. Here evangelical rhetoric and practice were often at war with each other. Especially in light of (i) the effort of colonial evangelism to make modernist subjects of Africans, and (ii) the non-dualistic, socially embedded Tswana view of curing, the Nonconformist commitment to the unity of body and soul was repeatedly compromised and ruptured—laying bare the Cartesian rifts that lurked uneasily beneath it.

In the end, Livingstone himself resolved only to intervene in difficult obstetric cases, and did so occasionally,[23] albeit sometimes with spectacularly unexpected results. Other evangelists learned to live with the contradictions of the healing ministry. Some felt that they simply could not refuse to treat the sick and, notwithstanding their appeals to their societies to send out medical men, continued to give assistance to Tswana. A few also attended Boer women in childbirth.[24] The latter, in fact, enlisted the aid of British missionaries even after colonial District Surgeons were appointed, itself an interesting instance of the way in which medicine bred unconventional collaborations within colonial society.

If success sharpened the dilemmas of the healing ministry for the evangelists, so too did the misrecognitions that often followed in its wake. While dramatic cures may sometimes have brought Tswana into the church,[25] all the evidence suggests that medical encounters did not, in themselves, make converts. If anything, they seem to have led mostly in another direction: away from Christian metaphysics, back to concrete realities and the banality of bodies. And when they did not, the theological discussions that ensued rarely had the intended effect. Robert Moffat (1842:403–5) again:

> One of [Chief Makaba's] men, sitting near me, appeared struck with the character of the Redeemer. . . . On hearing that he raised the dead, he very naturally exclaimed, "What an excellent doctor he must have been, to make dead men live!" . . . [T]he ear of the monarch caught the startling sound of a resurrection. "What!" he exclaimed with astonishment . . . "Will my father arise?" "Yes," I answered, "your father will arise." "Will the slain in battle arise?" "Yes. . . ." Makaba, then turning and addressing himself to me, and laying his hand on my breast, said, ". . . I do not wish to hear again about the dead rising! . . ." [Raising] his arm, which had been strong in battle, and shaking his hand as if quivering a spear, he replied, "I have slain my thousands (bontsintsi,) and shall they arise?"

Once more are mission poetics abruptly re-versed. The evangelists appear not to have considered the possibility that there were people who might prefer the dead to remain so. Among contemporary Tswana, the ancestors already enjoyed eternal existence and were accessible to the living in various ways (*RRI*:153f.). The Africans did not experience, in the same manner, the Stygian gulf that separated life from death in the West, a gulf into which evangelical healing often fell when it was accompanied by talk of life everlasting.

Treating the Social Body

[E]very misfortune, every calamity and every fatality was ascribed to . . . perverse and malignant forces, manifested through and directed by human agencies. . . . The whole business of life became one long sustained effort to overmaster, defeat or frustrate, avert, escape, humour or propitiate these sinister forces.

S. M. Molema (1951:185–86)

What concerned Southern Tswana, much more than just mending bodily ills, was the meaning of suffering: how, that is, to read affliction in terms of prevailing social relations. It was precisely this that the modern clinic threatened to erase, reducing symptoms to a grammar of physical dysfunctions *within* the skin of the corporeal individual (Foucault 1975); precisely this that Christian curing, with its stress on *personal* sin and salvation, had underplayed. For the Africans, by contrast, healing sought to reveal and reverse the harmful forces that flowed among the bodies and beings of socially connected people. Misfortune, to them, really was inseparably moral and material: the enmities that fueled it, and the utterances and medicines that turned hatred into hurt, themselves had tangible effects. Doctoring, the quintessential ritual act, always addressed dis-ease through its diffuse signs. It cured by interpreting and treating illness as an embodiment of the intensely human passions, properties, and perversities that made and unmade local communities (R. Moffat 1842:437; Livingstone 1857:25). Its means were inseparable from its ends.

In introducing the Tswana world of the early nineteenth century, we commented on the nature of ritual action and on the practice of *bongaka* (specialist healing; *RRI*:156f.). Healers, like the sorcerers they opposed, acted by manipulating media—words, substances, gestures—capable of condensing powers otherwise dispersed in the world (J. Comaroff 1985:84; Munn 1974). The physics at work in their ministrations were the same as those that underlay all life forms and processes—from the fall of the rain and the growth of plants to the flow of human blood and the maturation of the body. If *any* of these processes went awry, *botlhoko*, affliction, would follow; the term also implied "to be sour." Hence the *ngaka*, one skilled at transforming states and relations, could as well treat a field as a person or an animal. What is more, his powers were not limited to restoration (*go alafa*). He might also be called upon to protect and enhance (*go thaya*) or even to destroy (*go lòa;* to practice sorcery). There was no more deadly adversary than the doctor of an enemy.

Southern Tswana medicine, in sum, was not limited to the workings of material substances. Its chemistry extended as well to natural and social processes. This is crucial. For, in spite of the apparently sharp contrast between *setswana* practice and Western science, the former had clear parallels with the humoral theory that underlay early missionary healing; even with the unspoken moral economy that would later inform biomedicine. Like their British counterparts, Tswana doctors worked to restore equilibrium, if not always in precisely the same manner. They cooled bodies inflamed by conflict, warmed ones chilled by bereavement, steadied relations disrupted by human carelessness and greed (J. Comaroff 1980; cf. Seeley 1973:77f.). *Tsididi* ("coolness"), a state of tepid balance, was the basis of all well-being. It described, at once, the proper temperature of matter and of social ties. Anger, rivalry, sorcery, and adultery unleashed destructive heat, which was as likely to parch the heavens as to dry up a cow's udder, as likely to scorch crops as to scald blood. Here physics met functional sociology: the vitality of persons and productive processes, alike, flowed from the correct—for which read "hegemonic"—alignment of categories and connections in the world. As it is everywhere, "health" was a representation of the normative; affliction was a "standardized nightmare," made not merely by inverting the conventions of moral order, but by playing upon their contradictions and ambiguities. Thus Tswana saw sickness as arising most typically from the sorcery of agnatic rivals and from the anger of the disenfranchised dead. But it could also result from excessive female fertility, itself both the spark of life and the source of the most searing pollution.

When they addressed the symptoms of sickness, then, Tswana doctors confronted signs with multiple, socially situated resonances. Divination cast disease in causal idiom. Its dice or "bones" (*ditaola*) served as oracular tablets, intended to reveal the hidden sociomoral roots of disorder (Livingstone 1857:470; see Werbner 1973 on the complex semantics of similar practices among Kalanga). The *ngaka* enlisted a rich range of tropic devices to characterize an affliction and to reverse it. His actions were always rooted in the poetics of the concrete, in the application of substances whose names, textures, tastes, or effects held the key to their curative qualities; these were "medicines" (*more* or *ditlhare;* literally, "trees" or vegetable matter). But healers drew as well on the concreteness of the poetic. They used various forms of wordplay—what the evangelists termed "spells"—to actualize otherwise abstract forces and properties (*RRI*:225f.). It followed that their *modus operandi* was not parsimonious or exclusionary. Medicines tended to include several ingredients designed to have similar, reinforcing effects. Likewise, different forms of physical treatment (cupping, inhalation, lancing, bathing, and the sucking out of noxious matter through the skin) often repeated the same formula over and over. The more the medication, the greater the number of effective techniques, the better. This additive, synthetic approach to therapeutics underlay, also, the eclecticism with which Tswana, specialists and lay alike, appropriated the *materia medica* and rites of others—not least those of the mission.

Refrain: The Medicine of God's Word

> One of the missionaries was fortunate to cure some ill people quickly by giving them something to make them vomit. They were surprised that so little medicine could give so much relief. By trusting his ability they went so far that when on some other occasion the emetic did not bring the expected result, they blamed him for his bad intentions and nearly illtreated him.
>
> M. H. C. Lichtenstein ([1807] 1973:71)

Two things, each a reprise of themes introduced before, should now be abundantly clear. One is that Southern Tswana were predisposed—indeed, eager— to avail themselves of whatever medical techniques Christianity offered, thereby expanding their own repertoire. The missionaries might have meant their cures to be signs of eternal restoration, portents of a God to whom was owed exclusive fealty. For the Africans, however, healing was not only, or primarily, a metaphor of invisible forces; nor was it the province of a parochial deity. It acted, rather, upon immediate, immanent social concerns. That is why, despite the fact that the clergymen treated local doctors as "inveterate enemies" (R. Moffat 1842:305), the opposite did not occur. European therapies were rarely regarded as a challenge to *setswana*. Quite the opposite: they were seen to complement it. Significantly, David Livingstone was widely known as *Ngaka* Livingstone, his title blurring any hard distinction between the *setswana* and the *sekgoa* for doctor/diviner.[26] Like their brethren on the eastern Cape frontier and Natal (Reyburn 1933; Etherington 1978), evangelists among Southern Tswana were often asked by local rulers to make rain, one of the major tasks of royal ritual practitioners (Holub 1881,1:281; R. Moffat 1842:468; *RRI*:209). But their wouldbe converts soon realized that, in spite of possessing powerful medicines, the missionaries had no aptitude for divination. Neither were they interested in diagnosing the social causes of affliction (J. Mackenzie 1871:381). In this respect, Moffat (1842:384) recounts an incident more revealing than he appears to have realized: "My books puzzled them," he wrote. "They asked if they were my 'Bola,' prognosticating dice."

This leads, in turn, to the second point. Not only were Tswana enthusiastic about evangelical healing. For many years they saw medicines as the source of all that was particular and powerful about the mission; *vide* the reference, earlier, to gunpowder, "the exploder's *medicine*." The Nonconformists themselves came from a society in which "taking one's medicine" meant facing something distasteful; Broadbent, interestingly, once tried to dissuade some Seleka-Rolong women from tasting his soup by adding essence of peppermint to it and calling it "medicine."[27] He miscalculated. As Livingstone (1960:223; cf. Seeley

1973:90f.) quickly discovered among the Kololo: "The people have an uncon-
vincible belief that all we do is by means of medicine. The . . . medicine of the
book must be taken or [the book] will never be understood. There is no convincing them to the contrary." Such perceptions were common among Tswana
as well. Livingstone (1857:279–80) was himself asked for gun medicine by
Sechele, to which he responded, ambiguously, by offering some sulphur;[28]
the Kwena chief had originally sought a missionary, he said (Livingstone
1959,1:132), to "help him in sickness, mend his gun, teach him to read, &
'nthuta botlale' [*nthuta botlhale*, 'teach me wisdom']." More than thirty years
later, while traveling in the Kuruman district, Rev. Howard Williams (1887:115)
received similar requests for preparations almost immediately on arriving in
outlying communities. "Faith in the white man's decoctions is in some places as
vigorous as ever," he noted. He then proceeded to exploit this faith—in a manner, he owned, "more politic than scientific"—in the service of the mission.

Little wonder that, for all the declarations of goodwill by the evangelists,
the secret of their powers—at once promising and threatening—should have
seemed to remain hidden, withheld. Little wonder, too, that Tlhaping should
have feared the infusion of the "medicine of God's Word" from the mission
station into the river whence they drank (*RRI*:228). Or that local people should
have tried to harness that medicine for their own ends. On more than one occasion the Nonconformists were petitioned for a "physic" to instil instant knowledge of reading (e.g., R. Moffat 1842:599; volume 3); Hepburn (1895:53) was
approached by a Tawana royal with a yet more subtle version of the same request, namely, for "medicine to give people to enable their hearts to understand
the books." That Protestant pharmacopeia could change hearts and minds was
not in doubt. "I wish you would change my heart," said Chief Sekgoma of the
Ngwato to Livingstone (1961:20) in 1842, "I wish to have it changed by medicine, to drink it [and] have it changed at once, for it is always very proud and
very uneasy."

The Rev. Howard Williams (1887:115), among other evangelists, believed
that "unless the native can see, taste, and feel, he was inclined to regard [a] dose
as a mere sham." But there was more at stake here than a traffic of drugs with
tangible effects. In Tswana medicine, to reiterate, substances and words were
thought to distill inchoate forces at work in the world, and to direct them toward
ends at once sociomoral and physical. This some of the missionaries soon realized (see R. Moffat 1842:599). Yet they were less ready to recognize that their
own activities could be seen in much the same way; that their own "greatness"
might be understood to lie simultaneously in portentous utterances and objects
(the book, the sacred communion, the gun, captivating commodities); that the
ultimate object of Tswana interest was the hidden power—the fetish, the "medicine of God's Word"—which animated these very things. The secret was to
remain tantalizingly preserved. Like other colonized peoples, some black South

Africans would speculate that another Bible existed, one kept by the whites purely for themselves (Sundkler 1961:278; Comaroff and Comaroff 1992:260). The quest for medicine, in other words, was part of an effort to reach into the evangelist's control over the production of value. It was a quest for the "magic," the *deus ex medicina*, that lay behind the European power gradually enveloping a local world. It was a profound, poignant quest. For it strove—as we do here, albeit in different terms—to comprehend the unseen sources of the colonizers' might. What Southern Tswana wanted was the secret of skills not just potent and elusive, but skills that appeared to be intrinsic qualities of the humans who possessed them: an ability to "understand" (*go utlwa*, to "hear") the content of books and to tap into their manifold riches; a facility for speaking persuasively; the competence to use firearms without inflicting self-injury;[29] the capacity to heal and to effect a "change of heart."[30] If these were attributes of bodies and beings, it followed that the medicines which condensed their essence had to be obtained and imbibed. They had to be made part of the self.

All of this simply compounded the problems of the missionaries. For a long time, their healing ministry seemed doomed to misperception; or, more accurately, to appropriation by Tswana. This forced the pilgrims' progress somewhat off its original theological course. As a result, many of them felt torn. On one hand, they persisted in trying to keep Christian salvation separate from pragmatic pursuits; on the other, they saw good reason to tie both the meaning of human suffering and its treatment to God's Word (see, e.g., J. Mackenzie 1871:380). And so, while medical assistance was rarely denied those who asked for it, it tended to be accompanied by increasingly mixed messages. (Apart from all else, the Nonconformists preferred to offer prayers for the sick, and later encouraged their African evangelists to do the same thing.) The mission did, however, deny Tswana what they *most* wanted—indeed, what they would eventually build their own dissenting churches for: a ministry that addressed soul and body together, that regarded misfortune as a social condition, that healed affliction by seeking to restore ruptured moral and material relations.

FRONTIERS OF PATHOLOGY: HEALTH AND DISEASE IN THE INTERIOR

There seems reason to suppose that the physique of the Bechuana tribes in the south is steadily deteriorating. This is due clearly to the influence of the whites . . . and to the introduction of bad brandy and syphilis.

Captain C. R. Conder (1887:80)

Before we address the longer-term legacy of the medical mission, it is necessary to turn first to a prior issue: the material realities of "health"—as it is conventionally understood in Western terms—at the imperial frontier. How, precisely, was the physical condition of the various parties in this colonial theater affected by their encounter?

Diseased Continent, Healthy Africans

"Healing" might have been, for many "humane imperialists," the most compelling rationale of colonial evangelism. And yet, gauged by any criterion, the physical well-being of local populations deteriorated significantly as a consequence of the civilizing mission (cf. Hartwig and Paterson 1978). Among Southern Tswana, this seems not to have been a result, initially, of the introduction of foreign infections—save for sexually transmitted ones (Plaatje [1921] 1996).[31] S. M. Molema (1920:311–12), himself a doctor, ascribed the decline in their health to the intake of European edibles and the adoption of European habits.

> Civilization brings with it . . . over-eating and over-drinking. The Muntu [black South African] has good teeth and is free from toothache until he takes to eating sweets and sweetmeats. Originally he lived in the open air. . . . So long as he lived thus *naturally*, his span of life extended to seventy, eighty, and ninety years. . . . The net result of . . . [the] use of European habitations and wear—in hot or cold, dry or wet weather, and in all manner of occupations—is disease. [Emphasis added.][32]

Support for Molema's observation is not hard to find. Evidence abounded in everyday life, sometimes in unexpected places. In his Setswana-English phrasebook, for example, Wookey (1904:20–21) found it necessary to devote a long section to "Ñaka/Doctor." In it he included such phrases as "My tooth hurts," "Do you pass water?" "Is your stomach in pain?" and "[My] lungs are diseased."

But the negative impact of the civilizing mission on the general health of Southern Tswana was not solely a result of new patterns of consumption—serious though this was in respect of sugar, refined flour, and especially alcohol, the spirits of capitalism in liquid form (see chapter 4, also below; cf. van Onselin 1982,1:44f.). It came, even more, of the drastic effect on nutrition of efforts to transform the local agrarian economy—and to engage "rural natives" in processes of commodification—an exercise, as we have seen, that encouraged uneven accumulation, altered the division of labor, set in motion processes of class formation, impoverished a great many people, and sent a burgeoning stream of blacks to cities, towns, and farms in search of work (cf. Etherington 1987, on missions in Natal).

This process has by now been extensively documented (see e.g., Marks and Rathbone 1982). Here we simply note one of its corollaries: that rural privation and disease were linked, ever more inescapably, to urban industrial conditions distressingly harmful to the welfare of migrant workers.[33] The missionaries were not unaware of this. An apt illustration is provided by a despatch from

Wookey (1884:305), quoted earlier. Writing of "South Bechuanaland" at a time when labor migration to the diamond fields was expanding rapidly, when small-pox had just broken out at nearby Kimberley (Turrell 1982:60f.), and when settler incursions onto Tswana territory were at their height, he observed:

> Political changes have been taking place. . . . Work [for wages] amongst the men has become more general; in fact, for many, it is the only means of subsistence. . . . The land question has become the pressing one of the day here. . . . Diseases formerly unknown have come in. Drink has become one of the greatest curses of the country.

Wookey went on to express the hope that British annexation—being actively pursued at the time by his colleague, John Mackenzie (*RRI*:292f.)—might "put matters right."

The destructive forces lurking beneath the myth of humane imperialism in South Africa were particularly visible in the sphere of acute physical affliction. Notwithstanding contemporary clichés about the "diseased continent"—about "this miserable quarter of the globe" (Barrow 1806:405)—it is unquestionable that the European presence created more serious illness than had hitherto occurred among black peoples of the interior. In this sense, "the suffering African" (Barrow 1806:405) was a colonial construction as palpably material as it was figurative. Livingstone (1857:141–42; cf. Gelfand 1957:39–40), who took a precise, professional interest in the health of Tswana populations, declared himself surprised, at midcentury, that "diseases" among them were "remarkably few":

> There is no consumption nor scrofula, and insanity and hydrocephalus are rare. Cancer and cholera are quite unknown. Small-pox and measles passed through the country about twenty years ago, and committed great ravages; but, though the former has since broken out on the coast repeatedly, neither disease has since travelled inland.

He was also struck by the absence of syphilis (cf. Somerville 1979:148; Lichtenstein 1973:71; A. Smith 1940,2:25), and concluded that the disease was "incapable of permanence in any form in persons of pure African blood any where in the centre of the country." Prevalent, instead, were conditions then associated with sudden changes of temperature: pneumonia, "inflammation" of the bowels, stomach, and pleura, as well as endemic ailments like rheumatism and "disease of the heart."[34] Even so, it is not difficult here—as in other accounts by whites before and after (Somerville 1979:148; Lichtenstein 1973:70f.; Willoughby n.d.[a])[35]—to detect surprise at the robustness of African populations. "The catalogue of their disorders [is] but short," noted Burchell (1824,2:580) of the Tlhaping. "[N]or did I see a cripple or a person of deformed figure."

Livingstone's optimism was sadly misplaced, however. Venereal disease, far from being "incapable of permanence" in "pure" Africans, paid no heed to racial difference. In due course, it would follow the path of labor migration to and from the sprouting mining and industrial centers to the south and east, beginning at the Kimberley diamond fields.[36] So would other illnesses, their incidence increasing all the time. By the late nineteenth century, in fact, Southern Tswana chiefs were pressing the colonial state to treat the syphilis, tuberculosis, and "fevers" that had spread alarmingly among their people without respect for status or wealth (Laidler and Gelfand 1971:454).[37] By then, too, the black work force was being described by whites as a dangerous cesspool of sickness in "their" towns and cities;[38] just as "unhygienic labour"—the term is Joseph Conrad's—was seen as a threat to the social order of affluent Britain.[39] This history speaks to the fracture of local ecosystems that, while never in static equilibrium or free of ills, had developed in symbiosis with a particular physical and cultural environment. It also traces the toll taken by colonialism on black bodies.

Another thing here, where the material and the imaginative meet. The observations of Livingstone et al. reveal plainly the contradictory place of African "nature" in nineteenth-century European thought—a theme with which we began our account in the previous volume. On one hand, the trope of the "healthful native," uncontaminated child of a relatively unspoiled Eden, lingered on almost until *fin-de-siècle.* Inland, we are told, unlike at the disease-ridden coast, the air was pure and "salubrious," and the blood of the inhabitants, untainted and resilient (Livingstone 1857:141f.; also Broadbent 1865:119, 184).[40] And yet old bromides about the "diseased continent," about the unhealthiness of the savage wilderness and the living arrangements of its indigenes, repeatedly justified efforts to re-form the architecture of everyday life—from modes of production, through dress and housing and habitual activities, to the orchestration of bodies in space.

African Fever, White Death

In the early years, it was often ill evangelists—some of them tended "with devotion" by blacks (R. Moffat 1842:113; Broadbent 1865:119f, 153f.; Gelfand 1957:276f.)—who expatiated most on savage suffering. West Africa might have been a "white man's grave."[41] But the South African interior, which proved less than "salubrious" for the first generation of missionaries, claimed its share of lives as well. It was to be a burial ground, as well, for their wives and children (Broadbent 1865:7);[42] hardly a family escaped without loss. As this implies, the bold, heroic chronicles of the evangelical frontier bore within them another narrative. Often told in quieter, less assured tones, it was not one of epic battles with beasts barring Christian's progress (*RRI*:176, 112f.). Instead, it gave details of humdrum discomfort and persistent depression, of trying pregnancies, frequent miscarriages, and protracted, painful deaths.[43] In the *Quarterly Chronicle of Transactions of the LMS* (LMS n.d.:221), for example, Dr. Philip wrote of a routine visit to Kuruman in 1825:

I found Mr. Hamilton in good health; Mr. and Mrs. Moffat were suffering in body and mind, by the recent illness and death of a child; and Mr. and Mrs. Hughes we had met on our way to Lattakoo, on a journey to Griqua Town, for the benefit of Mr. Hughes's health. She herself had been dangerously ill with a fever, but was now so far recovered as to admit of his making this experiment in the hope of preventing a relapse, and of renovating his exhausted frame.

The letters and journals of Hamilton, Moffat, Price, Livingstone, Broadbent, Hodgson, Edwards, and others all included copious, often worried, comments about their moods, body temperatures, digestion, levels of energy, the confinements of their partners,[44] and the sickness of their offspring. Their reports of physical and nervous "exhaustion," and of other debilitating conditions, often blamed the intemperateness of both the African climate and its inhabitants.[45] Although there is evidence of mission wives standing stoically alongside husbands overcome by chronic despondency and illness (see, e.g., Schapera 1951:xxix; Moffat and Moffat 1951:passim; Broadbent 1865:119f, 133), European females were thought to be most susceptible to the hazards of the natural and human environment.[46] And when they fell prey to these hazards, one common reaction was to return them to the "centers of civilization" in the south.[47]

The affliction of women and children, being the underside of the Christian march into Africa, made for heartrending stories, stories that were highlighted for different audiences. Take, for instance, one particularly graphic text "designed for the young" by the Religious Tract Society (n.d.:238–43). It tells of two LMS families, the Prices and the Helmores, who set out from Kuruman in 1859 to establish a station among the Kololo on the Zambezi River far to the north. One of the evangelists, both wives, and several children and servants would fall desperately ill and die in the attempt, their agonies memorialized in gothic detail. An excerpt:

Mr. and Mrs. Price were . . . very ill, but they could still crawl about, and wait upon . . . their own little sick baby who had been born since they left Kuruman.

The first who died was little Henry [Helmore]. He had been lying on the same bed as his brothers and sisters outside the tent door, and their mother was by their side . . . unwatched, except for their heavenly Father and His holy angels. . . . [His mother] was so very ill, that she took no notice when told that her precious boy was dead. . . .

[Little Henry had actually been preceded by Malatsi, a Tlhaping driver, and was followed by two other Tswana laborers, one of the Price infants, and then, in order, by his own sister, mother, and father. All of them died at the Kololo capital. Mr. and Mrs. Price eventually decided to abandon the venture and retreat to the south.]

You do not wonder that Mrs. Price soon died [en route]. Her husband dug her grave under a large tree standing alone upon a wide
plain. . . . It had been very painful to watch her suffer as she had done
. . . [and he] could not help grieving; he felt left quite alone.

This narrative was to become a paradigm of personal sacrifice in the South
African interior. It was retold, not always so melodramatically but always poi-
gnantly, in most contemporary mission texts. John Mackenzie (1871:186ff.),
who was close by, blamed the "unhealthy atmosphere," the "rank vegetation,"
and the "hot sun" for causing the "*African* fever" that felled the party (p. 188).
At an adjectival stroke, brute European suffering—most bitterly the deaths of
white mothers and infants—was given an autochthonous etiology. Resonances
here of *African* AIDS, a trope of our own time in which lethal affliction and the
continent again become synonymous (see, e.g., Patton 1988, 1990; Watney
1990). Also of an ingenuous comment, made toward the end of the colonial
epoch, by Joyce Cary (1953:9). "The African setting," he said, "needs a certain
kind of story, a certain violence and coarseness of detail, almost a fabulous treatment to keep it in its place" (see Killam 1968:6).

In fact, the Price-Helmore story was more complicated, less fabulous, than
many of the published versions suggest. Mackenzie had himself written to the
LMS directors, in 1859, warning them that the Kololo capital was rife with
malaria.[48] He suggested that a "bachelor expedition" should travel there first,[49]
and that the Kololo themselves ought to remove to a more healthy site before a
station was established among them. Mackenzie was not alone in the view that
Linyanti was a particularly dangerous place. Or in attributing the tragedy to
fevers contracted there. Livingstone (1861:184) concurred. If they were correct,
the deaths of both white and black members of the expedition were due to specific local conditions, not to the generically unhealthful "nature" of Africa.
Nonetheless, it was the latter that became the key trope of the tale as it circulated back to England.[50]

Roger Price himself blamed the misadventure on a much more mundane
cause: poison administered by the Kololo leader, Sekeletu. For reasons we cannot go into here, his explanation was not altogether implausible; nor were the
symptoms suffered by the victims inconsistent with it. But this version, dismissed by John Mackenzie (1871:193f.), gained no currency. The Nonconformists, it seems, found more credible a story in which the foe was an anonymous,
threatening "Africa," whose sickly regions continued to lay waste to martyrs
like Mrs. Price and Mrs. Helmore.[51]

Some mission wives reacted to the physical difficulties of the frontier in
ways less susceptible to elegy than did these women. A few, in fact, tried to put
a stop to male heroics in the name of female well-being. Mary Moffat, for one,

making it clear that her husband had attempted to silence her, condemned David Livingstone for exposing his pregnant partner and small children to a journey among "savage men and beasts" in "sickly regions," all for the sake of an "*exploring* expedition" (Livingstone 1960:70–71, original emphasis; see also 1961:188–90). "Cruel" and "indecorous" were the terms she used to describe the actions of her son-in-law. Shocked reports also reveal occasional acts of resistance on the part of mission spouses, acts that appear to have hit their mark. They included sexual impropriety, taunting impiety, and threats of desertion (Moffat and Moffat 1951:23; also Schapera 1951:xiv).[52] Hear the Rev. Cameron, in 1844, on the infamous case of Mrs. Giddy:[53]

> Mrs. Giddy has been called to exchange worlds. Her death alas! was not that of a Christian. It is painful to be obliged to say so of a missionary's wife, but it is needless to hide from you a fact which is notorious here. The committee should be extremely careful not to send any married man out as a missionary, whose wife is not as truly devoted to the work as himself. . . . I do not mean by a good wife a woman that will take her husband's work out of his hands; but one who so far from counteracting that work will by every quiet and unobtrusive means assist him in its performance.

Devoted, quietly unobtrusive, models of Victorian modesty and righteous comportment. Much was expected of missionary wives. It was as if their health and moral condition were synonymous with the state of the mission itself. Fragile to begin with, both clearly endured mixed fortunes at the edges of empire; although, as the decades passed, the Europeans became ever more resilient, ever more likely to survive their ills—especially after 1880, when medical defenses against fevers were more readily available.

The lot of these women was contradictory in many respects, to be sure, but perhaps nowhere more so than in the sphere of health and disease. It was they who nursed the sick and dying; they who were responsible for catering to everyday bodily needs in "the field"; they who were taken to be most at risk in Africa. But, in the evangelical enterprise, it was saving souls, their husbands' work, that was given highest value. Just how anomalous was their position in shouldering the "white man's burden," and just how gendered was the civilizing mission, became plain as soon as females showed any signs of evangelizing in their own right (cf. Hunt 1990b). Their "sex" shackled them to reproduction, biological and social: much like Africans, they were said to be unduly susceptible to external sensory stimulation and, hence, inadequately in control of their own physicality. Intuitively moral yet unstably passionate, their role was largely restricted to preparing the domestic terrain for more significant spiritual work.

DIALECTICS, DOCTORS, AND MEDICAL
DISCOURSES OF DISEASE

As it played itself out in the domain of physical health, then, colonial evangelism reversed the grand narrative of European history; of history, that is, as it was supposed to happen. The Nonconformists expected to find a "diseased continent" and heal it. Instead, they found relatively healthy indigenous peoples and set in motion processes that assailed their well-being—thereby making Africa more diseased than it seems previously to have been. On the other hand, the early missionaries, most of them perfectly well when they left Britain, would typically fall ill soon after their arrival in the interior. And then, if they survived, which they did in increasing numbers, they would become ever more robust. Out of this dialectic of health and disease, the mission fashioned a medical discourse—a discourse of bodies and pathologies, contagion and cure—that would feed the production of scientific knowledge at home.

As we might infer from the concern of the evangelists with the health and physical condition of their wives,[54] that discourse focused heavily on procreation and reproduction. Like contemporary Western medicine at large (Jordanova 1989), mission medicine found a ready object in—even more, was fairly fixated on—female bodily processes, especially black female bodily processes. It was here, in fact, that colonial evangelism had a palpable impact on medical science; here that accounts from the Tswana field fed into comparative, universalizing biological arguments. As is now well recognized, there existed a privileged relationship in the Victorian era between the imperial and the empirical, between the spread of empire and the rise of scientific biomedicine (MacLeod 1988:2f.). The growing mastery of the *terra incognita* of the gendered human body by biology became the paradigm of positivist knowledge *sui generis* (Foucault 1975): it fed the imagination of those who sought to comprehend their expanding world, both inner and outer, all the better to exert control over it.

As comparative anatomy and physiology developed, and took hold of African bodies, two things followed. Both were deeply rooted in the signifying economy of colonialism. First, like much early travel writing, the new discourse eroticized the "dark continent," often reducing it, in the clinic, to the ostensibly excessive reproductive organs of its women (*RRI*:98f.). And, second, as the medical gaze moved into the unknown interior, it treated the black female physique as a natural site for explorations in pathology. This was especially marked in researches on the relationship between disease and unruly fecundity, a relationship quintessentially associated with Africa (Gilman 1985; cf. Vaughan 1991:129f.).

Influential in this respect, of course, were the writings of David Livingstone, who, it will be recalled, continued to treat difficult obstetric cases even after he lost enthusiasm for healing. Livingstone's fame as an explorer of "African nature" ensured him a wide audience, both specialist and popular; since he reported as well on the medical discoveries of his brethren, he was also a vehicle through which their knowledge was conveyed back to Britain. Livingstone may have been more tolerant than other evangelists of *setswana* practices, many of which he regarded with a benign relativism (*RRI*:210f.); his observational urge was certainly more intense than most, his descriptive style more influenced by the conventions of contemporary scientific journals. But, given the state of British medicine at the time, his training did not equip him with notions of etiology very different from those of his untutored colleagues—which is why he could so easily serve as a metonym of the medical mission. All of them saw illness as a product of the effect on human bodies of external pollutants and stimuli (cf. A. A. Young 1978). And all translated the relationship between bodies and environments, in the African hinterland, into a familiar range of ethical and aesthetic preoccupations: with ill-clad and indiscrete bodies, interracial sex, and the unrestrained fertility of women.

For his own part, Livingstone was intrigued, in particular, by childbearing among Tswana, and disseminated ideas about it that have a decidedly modern ring. To wit, they could have been—although there is no real evidence that they were—read as critical of birthing in "civilized countries." He commented (1857:145), for example, that

> women suffer less at their confinement than is the case in civilized countries; perhaps from their treating it, not as a disease, but as an operation of nature, requiring no change of diet except a feast of meat and abundance of fresh air.

Unlike others, he did not attribute any of this to the "fact" that African women were *themselves* somehow closer to nature. It was due, rather, to the manner in which they chose to treat a "natural" bodily function.

Livingstone (1960:47, 24) was struck, too, by the relatively low mortality reported of African women from malaria. This he also associated with their reproductive processes. Like John Mackenzie (Seeley 1973:80), he ascribed it to "excessive menstrual discharge," which expelled the "poison" from their systems. Where to from there? Into the tide of effluvia, presumably, that bore the disease to less resilient victims: black males and whites of both genders. According to the humoral pathology then prevalent in Britain, all fever (including malaria) was a symptom of excess, and menstruation was seen as a natural form of bleeding (C. Jones 1988:81). Livingstone (1960:24) appears to have thought that dark female bodies emptied themselves into the rivers of pollution traversing the continent: "The flow [of their blood] is very profuse and prolonged . . . [and, they complain,] more profuse etc. among the rivers than elsewhere."[55] That, perhaps, is why the exposure of Europeans to the "climate of the riverline," in this "animal economy" (see n. 11) was said to be particularly dangerous and deleterious (Meller [1864] in Gelfand 1957:320); why, also, a prime object of healing, and of the spread of civilized habits, was to regulate the sensual physicality of black women. Livingstone (1960:24) concludes one of his discussions of etiology with a revealing ethnographic tidbit: in indigenous belief, he says, for which there is an Old Testament precedent, "women may kill a man by not telling him when he approaches that they are menstruating."

One woman's fertile heat is another man's fatal poison; especially a white man's. Hence the uneasy coexistence of the fecund and the fetid, the two sides of nature so palpable in Livingstone's prose. Hence the historically particular, yet mythically transcendent, manner in which European etiology found multiple meanings in the surplus sexuality of African womanhood. Hence the fact, as Gilman (1985:231) reminds us, that black females were held accountable for sexually transmitted disease in the late nineteenth century.[56] Nor did it end then. As Vaughan (1991:129f.) shows, the putative link between female sexuality and syphilis in Africa has persisted through this century—augmented, more recently, by AIDS. For their part, the colonial evangelists among the Tswana worried a great deal about the "loathsome disease." As a form of pollution, it was the ultimate union of sin and sickness. Despite Livingstone's (1857:142) faith in the resilience of "pure African blood," interracial cohabitation was taken to be potentially lethal—a piece of "medical" wisdom that gave scientific imprimatur to colonial politics, whose structures of inequality had come to rest on the impermeability of racial caste. Here, too, the horizons of the medical mission reached from the local to the global. Miscegenation was emerging as an increasingly ominous source of pathology in European thought at the time. Linked to the decline of white populations everywhere, its perils, vividly spelled out in a number of popular Victorian novels,[57] were later to be given the alibi of science by eugenics (Gilman 1985:237). Under these conditions, the biomedicine of the evangelical frontier provided a welcome font of knowledge and authority. It also legitimated a reality very much under construction back home.

The horizons of the medical mission in southern and Central Africa were not entirely confined to female physicality, however. As Gelfand (1957:5–11) and others have noted, David Livingstone—like Henry Callaway in Natal (Etherington 1987:79f.)—insisted that European science might learn from vernacular knowledge and practice (e.g., 1857:694). He submitted himself to the ministrations of Tswana specialists (e.g., 1857:206; 1940:208) and sought from them fresh remedies and pharmacopeia (e.g., 1963:40f, 469);[58] so did some of his associates, albeit less frequently or systematically. Using Africa—and his own body—as a laboratory, Livingstone did careful experiments on the utility of medical instruments, the etiology of illness, and the effects of new therapeutic substances on humans and animals. Some of this work contributed to the development of curative techniques in Britain and in other parts of the empire. He also published accounts of a range of African diseases; several were to be of lasting professional significance (*British Medical Journal* 1913; Gelfand 1957:9; 297–321).

The afflictions that most engaged Livingstone were cholera and malaria, and he pioneered the use of quinine and purgatives to fight the latter; his treatment, the "Livingstone Pill" or "Zambesi Rouser," came to be widely applied by the midcentury.[59] But his understanding of the pathology of these fevers resorted back to the interplay of temperature, humidity, airborne pollution, other environmental forces, and human bodies. "The unhealthiness of the westerly winds," he says (1857:473) in one account, "probably results from malaria, appearing to be heavier than common air, and sweeping down . . . from the western plateau." But whence the malaria in the first place? Livingstone concurred with the prevailing theory of "noxious miasmas." According to this theory, fever was caused by breathing in emanations from "marshy miasmata"— the "effluvia, poisons, and human ordure," including female discharge, that fermented into a current of contagion under moist, densely vegetated conditions. (Even when fevers first came to be associated with germs in India and Africa— as a comic colonial story by Rudyard Kipling recalls—those germs were held to propagate themselves as they flew through the "muggy atmosphere" and lodged in the branches of trees.)[60] Certain parts of Africa were said to be particularly hospitable to dank putrification (Livingstone 1861:185): "Around every village in this country there is a very large collection of human ordure [that] . . . is swept into the rivers by the heavy rains" (see n. 55). The point of these observations, again, was expressly comparative. A parallel was drawn between the "natives here" and the "natives" who lived along squalid portions of the Thames (1861:185; cf. Carlson 1984:38). The conclusion? That the "origin" of the affliction was the same in Britain as it was in Africa; that remedies developed abroad ought to be "applied to some of the fevers at home that arise in unhealthy localities."

*****

Read as a saga of heroic science, the medical mission put prevailing European constructs to work on black bodies and climes. Then it returned them, transformed, to a voracious, voyeuristic public—as well as to professional audiences—with some fanfare and a few surprises. But the longer-term significance for Europe is not adequately measured in terms of "discoveries"; of triumphal revelations and authoritative advances either in the domain of therapeutic technique or in the discipline of comparative physiology. These occurred, of course, and were important at the time. The enduring legacy of the medical mission lay, rather, in something much more subtle: in its quiet impact on European consciousness during an age when parochial paradigms of knowledge and practice were undergoing reformation, an age when Europe was caught up in constructing the modernist self. This self, a biological individual/ist with an enclosed physique and discrete parts, was knowable, in the first instance, by contrast with its sable opposite: the uncontained, unrestrained African female body. But the latter was more than just an imaginative mirror image, a negative reflex. Its unsettling power to procreate, pollute, and destroy had to be controlled if the modern white male was truly to be a world conqueror, a maker of his own health and history.

The racial physiology of colonial evangelism, its theories of contagion and uncontainedness, would have more tangible consequences in late nineteenth- and early twentieth-century South Africa. It was to underlie the kinds of public health regimes set up by the state, and to inform the way in which bodies were classified, diagnosed, and treated. Of more immediate concern here, though, is another issue: What was the legacy of the medical mission as seen from the perspective of Southern Tswana?

THE LONG-TERM LEGACY OF
MISSIONARY MEDICINE

Like all aspects of the civilizing mission, the healing ministry had unintended consequences, not all of them confined to bodily matters; some we have come across already. Conversely, many of the most corrosive forces that impinged upon the health of Southern Tswana were not medical in origin; they were born of political and economic processes large in scale and long in duration. Mission medicine here controlled no institutions and organized none of the mass vaccination campaigns that engraved colonial power onto black bodies elsewhere (Vaughan 1991:47f.; Headrick 1987). What is more, it never succeeded in erasing the credibility of *setswana* therapeutics—although it was to render them, in the eyes of a modernist, black bourgeois sensibility, "primitive" and "traditional" (J. Comaroff 1981). Still, the healing ministry—with its oft-spoken concern for physical strength, the prevention of death, and life everlasting— entered an existential space critically salient for Southern Tswana. As such, it was an important dimension in the effort to colonize their world: in the struggles over form and substance set in motion when the Europeans tried to press their sense of health and well-being onto African bodies and minds.

Southern Tswana, as we have seen, regarded European medicine as a vital, integral aspect of white potency. The worth placed by them on church membership, on schooling, and on the evangelical presence might have fluctuated with the tenor of frontier politics over the course of the nineteenth century. But the demand for Western remedies never let up. At the same time, these were not simply taken over, displacing indigenous counterparts. From the first, the two therapeutic traditions were imbricated in a complex equation of exchange and synthesis. The result: a rich, hybrid field of healing techniques, refracted, as we would now expect, along the lines of social difference taking shape at the time. Nor, we stress, was this hybrid confined purely to the Tswana. It was to have growing appeal among whites living on farms and in small towns around the fringes of local chiefdoms.

Already in the 1830s, charismatic bricoleurs began to arise from among Tswana affiliated to the church. Unlike their counterparts in precolonial times, these architects of the enchanted were often women. They applied the power of Christian rites to ends shaped by vernacular ideas of healing; among them, divination, rainmaking, and the husbandry of wealth and well-being. Such charismatics—like Sabina (in around 1836) and the Prophetess of Platberg (about 1843)[61]—caused the evangelists no end of anguish as they tried, sometimes ingeniously, to redeploy the symbolic practices of the mission; we discussed them in chapter 2. For now, we simply reiterate that they foreshadowed a host of inspired figures who later fashioned an independent African Christianity, a Christianity of ritual pastiche, pragmatic theology, and sociosomatic healing. Few of its adepts or adherents were to come from the elite: membership of "Zionist" or charismatic churches was confined largely to the ordinary, the lowly, the marginal (J. Comaroff 1985). But these churches became fonts of enormously creative, vibrant energy. Their healing ministry—which sought to tap diverse forms of power, to invigorate persons "laid low," to redirect history toward a commonweal—was less a replica of mission medicine[62] than an effort to appropriate it. And, having done so, to meld it with the techniques of *setswana*, thus to traffic with forces which appeared to have the capacity to make the world anew.

This was not the only legacy of colonial healing, however. A more accommodating attitude toward European biomedicine—and the cultural *forms* presupposed by it—disseminated itself among Christian elites. Note that two of the most visible Southern Tswana figures on the national political scene earlier this century, both mission school graduates, trained in Scotland as doctors: S. M. Molema, also a popular historian and essayist, and J. S. Moroka, later president of the ANC (Willan 1984:186; Murray 1992:194f.; Molema 1951:195). Similar career paths were followed by other upwardly mobile Christians elsewhere in the country at the time.[63] Not surprisingly, public health became an important dimension of the nationalist vision then being forged by critical black intellectuals. By 1911, Sol Plaatje, the influential editor of *Tsala ea Batho* and soon to be first corresponding secretary of the South African Native National Congress, was reporting regularly on medical issues in his bilingual newspaper. The proud product of a mission background himself—and an in-law of Dr. Molema—he wrote almost weekly about the evils of profiteering from liquor and the connections among black alcoholism, ill-health, and the "scandalous" working conditions of migrants on the Witwatersrand.[64] He also censured the mission and "native" presses for their sensationalist advertisements of "quack"

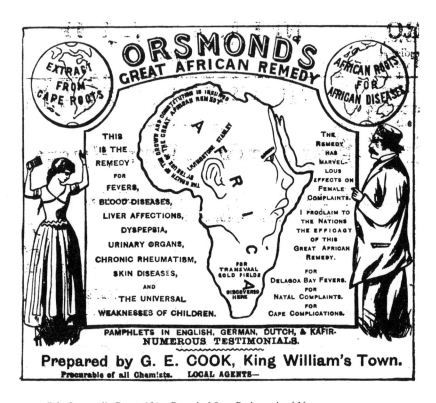

PLATE 7.3 *Orsmond's Great Africa Remedy [from Bechuanaland News,*
16 January 1892, p. 2]

patent medicines; no class of publication was without such notices, some of
which marketed a distilled "African" essence to both blacks and whites (plate
7.3).[65] But, most of all, Plaatje castigated the South African state for perpetuat-
ing the poverty and poor physical condition of his compatriots. And for its sheer
callousness. He was particularly galled by the appearance in the locations of
"well-paid scientists . . . preaching the laws of health to a proletariat who
earn[ed] not enough money for food and raiment, let alone soap."[66]

The public health discourse of black intellectuals, itself fixated on sanitizing self-improvement, was shot through with missionary moralism. In this, it
bore all the signs, all the autonomic reflexes, of the hegemony sown by colonial
evangelism. Plaatje's weekly, for instance, also featured regular columns on the
Native and Coloured Health Society (based at the Victoria Hospital, Lovedale
Mission).[67] In 1914, the managing committee of the Society published a sample
of its quarterly paper in *Tsala ea Batho,* outlining "what to do while awaiting the

doctor" in the event of nosebleeds and burns, suffocation and sprains, fits and faints, even swallowing a marble![68] Underlying all this is the assumption of a modernist order of material and social relations: a world of toys, toothpicks, footbaths, and physicians. And of biologically discrete, self-motivated, self-disciplined citizens of empire.

Comprehensive moral improvement, measured in clean living and healthy ways, was the primary aim of the Society. Appended to the same report was the following appeal:[69]

> The Society is . . . trying through its literature . . . to enlighten people who are in danger because of their ignorance. . . . The dangers today are those connected with the new civilization that has come upon South Africa. New kinds of food, new sorts of clothing, new habits of living, new occupations and new diseases, town life for many instead of country life. . . . It is the work of this Health Society to warn the people where the dangers lie. . . . To the whole people it speaks telling them plainly that many diseases are the result of dirty and careless living.

This, then, is early black Christian philanthropy, a call to the conscience of liberal, literate, salaried individuals to pay their dues, thus to enable the elevation of their "native and coloured" compatriots. The spirit of Moffat, Livingstone, and other evangelists is audible: the "appalling death rate in the town locations," declared the Society, results from "sin and moral uncleanness." It is, therefore, "every man's duty and every woman's duty to keep their own bodies healthy."

And yet, even at its most medically and morally orthodox, the concern of black intellectuals with public health revealed cracks in the hegemony of the civilizing mission. More sensitive to social and political forces than their white counterparts—they had closer experience of inequality and exploitation—these "subalterns" were quicker to blame the afflictions of poor people of color on conditions in the mines and urban locations.[70] They were also less ready to castigate the victim. But this was a matter of degree, not kind. After all, liberal medicine everywhere, Africa included, tended to anchor its etiology in the demise of "healthy country life" (Vaughan 1991:57). And Plaatje et al. never gave up exhorting their compatriots, as individuals, to better themselves.

Both biomedicine and European Protestantism were well capable of formulating critiques of colonial exploitation. And sometimes they did. When it came to everyday health and healing, however, their ontologies coalesced easily into a rhetoric of pathology and personal hygiene. This rhetoric tended to eclipse collective action and the broader social dimensions of disease. It envisaged, instead, a society of self-improving subjects, of corporeal individuals living out the middle-class model of domesticity encountered in chapter 6 (cf. Vaughan 1991:57). This was all quite different from the ministry of the independent African churches, which stressed healing by the intervention of the Holy Spirit in an epic struggle between forces of good and evil, a struggle that involved laying on hands and building a *community* of congregants through rousing dance and other rites (cf. Gaitskell 1992:178–80). It was also very different from the practices of *dingaka*, healers who relied on a range of indigenous means, but had a taste for bricolage; whose *materia medica* might be doled out in capsules and pharmaceutical bottles; whose paraphernalia sometimes included stethoscopes; who often divined using Bibles; who were likely to name God, alongside sorcerers or ancestors, as the cause of misfortune. Their remedies also reacted to new experiences in African life. But they dealt most directly with the (ego-focused) social relations of their patients (J. Comaroff 1974); in particular, with the superhuman harm suffered by persons engaged in competition over the scarce resources of being-in-the-world. Their sense of person, cause, and effect were the very oppposite of the bourgeois ideal.

The spectrum of therapeutic practices forged in the colonial arena, which was to widen yet further this century, implied a diversification of cultural orientations; of notions of agency, personhood, power, and—because subjects presume objects—social contexts and horizons. This heterodoxy was not random or infinite. It paralleled the production of differences, encountered earlier, in economy, aesthetics, architecture, and attire; processes wherein hegemonies and hybridities of style played into emerging lines of social distinction to create schisms in a universe of shifting values. Just as the nascent middle class was caught up in the orthodoxies of clinical biomedicine, so poorer Southern Tswana preferred to put faith in *dingaka* and iconoclastic African Christian healers. Not that these people ever turned their backs on European medicines, even the "quack" ones against which *Tsala ea Batho* warned. But to this day— despite the fact that many are members of mission churches and most make use of doctors and clinics—they continue to visit *dingaka* in pursuit of sociosomatic explanations and remedies for affliction. And a high proportion, as we have said, attend African healing churches in search of effective means to act on their ailing, fragmented world.

*****

There is a final piece to this narrative of health, the medical mission, and the Southern Tswana.

The imprint of the colonial encounter on the consciousness of the colonizers may be parsed into two parts; although, in the unfolding history of the everyday, they were closely linked. One was the *mediated* effect of that encounter: the effect, that is, of evangelists' representations of the medical mission on their own world, its ways of knowing and seeing and being. This we have already addressed, in discussing how a gendered Africa was mobilized in modernist discourses of pathology, bodiliness, and personhood. The second was the *di-rect*—often decentering—impact of the words and wisdom, the practices and possessions, of the "other." Many examples come to mind: how the counterar-guments of Tswana doctors against the claims of Western medicine forced Liv-ingstone and some of his colleagues to question the sureties of positivist, univer-sal knowledge; how, with the passage of time, the missionaries were compelled to see that the treatments of *dingaka* were sometimes more effective than their own in dealing with affliction; how the Europeans began to adopt vernacular styles—not least in architecture and dress—because they seemed more healthy and comfortable under prevailing conditions; how the realization dawned that indigenous reproductive procedures were successful in dissociating birthing from illness. But there is yet more to say about this.

In spite of the dismissive stance of the mission—reinforced by both the state and the Tswana elite—a fascination with indigenous medical practice has been discernible among whites throughout the twentieth century. This phe-nomenon has not been restricted to South Africa. In many places, the cultural knowledge of people marginalized in the name of modernity—or, more dramat-ically, suppressed as "primitive"—has been empowered by its very exoticiza-tion. Sometimes, as Taussig (1987:99) shows, the curing techniques of such peoples, rendered potent by being mystified, are sought even by those who most despise them. In the postcolonial epoch, more generally, with doubts growing about the supremacy of Western biomedicine, there has been a new attitude of open curiosity toward alternative healing. For example, *Time* magazine,[71] that global medium of middle-brow populism, ran a cover story in 1991 on the dis-appearing world of non-Western medical knowledge: a rescue narrative of eth-nographic journalism, it argued for the utility (and respectability) of recuperat-ing the practices of others made insignificant by colonialism and imperialism.

A history of the impact of *setswana* therapeutics on whites in South Africa is clearly beyond our present scope. However, since it is the other side of the dialectic of the long run, we cannot but exemplify the phenomenon. Two frag-ments will have to suffice.[72]

First, the attractions of exotic knowledge and hybrid "others." For many years, Dr. S. M. Molema had his medical practice at Mafikeng; he built a clinic at the edge of the Tshidi-Rolong town, on the side nearest the white settlement across the railway line which divided *setswana* from *sekgoa*, and kept apart those segregated by law. Here he treated the lengthy lines of local people who at-tended him each day. Here, too, he saw a large number of whites. Hundreds, it was commonly agreed, counted themselves among his patients, even if they had, as many of them did, another doctor in "European" Mafeking. His appeal for these patients lay precisely in the fact that, by their account, his healing com-bined biomedicine with *bongaka*. His pills, which he dispensed in large contain-ers, they said, were especially effective. (Recall the Rev. Williams, who believed that Africans only saw efficacy in medicine if they could *feel* its effects, the stronger the better?) Dr. Molema was referred to, affectionately, in Afrikaans, as "Die Doktor van die Groot Bottel," the "Doctor of the Large Bottle." When he died, in the mid-1960s, his practice was taken over by Dr. David Tsatsi, a highly respected physician and the eldest child of one of the most widely reputed *dingaka* in Southern Tswana territory. Dr. Tsatsi inherited many of S. M. Molema's white clientele (and acquired more of his own)—several of whom visited both father and son on a regular basis.

Second, and even more striking, is the entry of "traditional" practice into South African popular culture. In the late 1960s, many whites who lived along the perimeters of Rolong, Tlhaping, and Tlharo communities admitted to being intrigued by Tswana divination. They saw it as an unusually, almost eerily, potent technique of fortune-telling, water dowsing, mineral prospecting, and the like. Some consulted backyard bone throwers—recruited, ironically, with the help of their employees. It became clear, from questioning both practitioners and clients, that this had been going on for decades throughout the region. A number of the clients, moreover, set great store by *setswana* herbal remedies, some of which they purchased directly from healers; the rest were bought from tiny, unkempt shops, usually situated in those gray areas of small towns where "European" trade gave way to commerce of legally indeterminate color.

This fascination with indigenous medicine has imploded in the "new" South Africa; so, too, in Zimbabwe, where it is now possible to buy a mass-produced Shona "*hakata* [oracular] package," styled as "a fascinating parlour game based on the time-honoured principles of African divination" (van Binsbergen 1995:131–32). Vernacular doctors—both the Sotho-Tswana *ngaka* and the Nguni-speaking *sangoma*—have become familiar figures of popular culture. Newspapers and magazines now advertise "Dial-a-Sangoma" and "Dial-a-Ngaka," phone-in divination services aimed at both white and black.[73] (Note that the terms are no longer italicized. They have entered into the super-lingo of the multilingual nation, a lexicon that occurs in all tongues.) The media frequently carry stories about well-known black "witch doctors" and their multiracial clientele. And now the final denouement: the emergence of the full-service *white* ngaka and/or sangoma. Several of these healers have become well enough known, and been successful enough, to have had feature articles written about them in both the local and overseas press. By many accounts, they have growing, lucrative practices. For some white South Africans, it seems, "traditional" medicine—deracinated and culturally appropriated—has become one of the possibilities of their postcolonial modernity; "part," as van Binsbergen (1995:132) puts it, speaking of divination, "of the generalised, trans-ethnic contemporary culture of . . . Southern Africa."

EIGHT

NEW PERSONS, OLD SUBJECTS

Rights, Identities, Moral Communities

I am in deep distress. The Government and the Administrator have taken away my rights and those of my children and my people, when they took away [the] farms . . . which I had apportioned to them long ago. . . . Is it according to law to deprive people who are without strength of their inheritance? Why should there be a difference so that the white people shall get their farms, but I and my . . . people do not get theirs? Is this right in the sight of God?

Chief Montshiwa, March 1886[1]

I T HAS BECOME commonplace to note the centrality of law in the colonization of the non-European world: commonplace to assert "its" role[2] in the making of new Eurocentric hegemonies, in the creation of colonial subjects, in the rise of various forms of resistance.[3] In all this, the subject of rights, and the rights of subjects, has been a recurrent theme. The reasons are not hard to find, as we have been told repeatedly by historians of modernity. They have to do with the forging of the nation-state, conceived as a moral community, in the late eighteenth and early nineteenth centuries; specifically, with its reliance on a culture of legality—built on rights of person and property, of constitutionality and contract—in imagining the body politic. At its core was the modernist self: the familiar figure of the right-bearing, responsible, "free" individual whose very condition of possibility was the nation-state itself.

Given its salience at home, the figure of the modernist subject was obviously going to feature centrally in the colonial encounter. Indeed, the effort on the part of colonizers, plural—and, singularly, of evangelists—to implant this subject on African soil subsumed all other aspects of the crusade to change "native" habit and habitat; all those things, such as production and consumption, spirituality and embodiment, with which we have dealt so far. At the same time, precisely because postenlightenment European personhood envisaged the citizen as a socially and legally endowed being, it was bound to be more or less incompatible with the political realities of a racially divided colonial society; bound, also, to be a focal point of continuous tension and struggle. This is why we have kept the present discussion to the last; it serves as a summation of our account. Let us be clear, though: we do *not* suggest that modern personhood is, constitutively and exclusively, a creature of the law. What we shall argue, rather, is that the European template for making the savage into a civilized citizen of empire, and of Christendom, was cut *imaginatively* from a culture of legalities. The very fact that it was, and the fact that it ran up against a rather different conception of selfhood and its moral underpinnings, illuminates all the contradictions and limitations of the colonizing gesture.

In order to situate our own analysis, let us begin with a brief observation about the comparative treatment of law and colonialism, with particular reference to the question of rights.

The legal anthropology of colonialism in southern and Central Africa has long treated property, landed property most of all, as the quintessential context in which rights were constituted, conjured with, contested, and called into question. For good reason. As Chanock (1991:62) notes, after Bentham (1838), "Property and law are born together and die together."[4] He goes on to argue, again with justification, that European colonizers took possessive individualism[5] to be the foundation of civilized society; the corollary being that private property was unknown in "savage" Africa. These colonizers encouraged the idea of individual rights in the name of modernity, thus to effect the "evolution of human societies from status to contract" (1991:63). Henry Maine (1861) might have given a scholarly gloss to the idea, even stating it as a "law of progress" (1986:164–65); but it had long been taken as a practical axiom by cultural reformers and imperial functionaries. In due course, though, colonial governments did a *volte-face*, claiming that communalism and customary law, not individualism and a law of contract, were more "naturally" African; that these "traditional" institutions ought, therefore, to be recognized and fostered. The reasons usually given for the change of heart? If individual Tswana or Zulu or Ngoni or whoever had no conception of rights, only premodern "customs," it was easier to dispossess them of their land, easier to extract their labor power, easier to legitimize their subordination to a superior European law (cf. Snyder 1981:298 et passim; Stamp 1991). In short, the embrace of communalism and custom, and the concomitant erasure of rights, was "hugely convenient" for the colonial state (Chanock 1991:66; cf. also Moore 1986).

The general argument, which has struck a resonant chord with many anthropologists and historians, echoes more than just a persistent tendency to regard colonialism as, first and foremost, a matter of political economy; to identify its prime agents as states and statesmen, capitalists and corporations; to view other players on the imperial stage as members of its supporting cast(e), important perhaps but always secondary. It also reflects a continuing propensity to treat the colonial encounter itself as a linear, coherent, coercive process involving two clearly defined protagonists, an expansive metropolitan society and a subordinate local population; to locate its essence in the technologies by which the former imposed its axioms, ideologies, and aesthetics on the latter through a series of (relatively) calculated, never more than partially resisted, actions; and, once more, to hold that law, broadly conceived, was a vital part of this process.

These generalities have been questioned, amended, and modulated.[6] Still, they evince remarkable tenacity in the face of increasing counterevidence: patently, the way in which legal sensibilities and practices entered into colonizing processes, into their dramatic gestures and prosaic theaters, was a good deal more ambiguous, less audible, murkier, than has typically been allowed. What is more, there has long been an *un*remarked rupture in the received narrative of the connection between colonialism and law in Africa. On one hand, we are told how, over the long run, European overseas administrations denied Africans the very rights they themselves essayed as the *sine qua non* of modernization and civil being—enforcing, instead, a custom custom-built for the purposes of political control, direct and indirect. We are shown, too, how "the" state contrived discourses of modernity, and invented tradition, in order to shape reality to its material advantage. And yet some (again, see Chanock 1985) have observed how other agents of empire—most notably, but not only, missionaries—inculcated ideas about private property and possessive individualism; how these liberal reformers, intent on "cultural conversion," introduced new notions of ownership, citizenship, testamentary and civil rights (Mann and Roberts 1991:14–15).

Surely there is a paradox in all this? In the fact that, while colonial functionaries perpetuated the "premodern" by eschewing individual rights for Africans, their righteous compatriots sought to do the exact opposite in the name of civilization? Apart from all else, this should put paid to any last traces of the illusion that "colonialism" was a monolith, a machine of pure domination; or that "*the* colonizer" may plausibly be portrayed as a coherent, unitary historical agent. But the paradox runs deeper still, at least in South Africa. For there was also an unwitting ambiguity, an unresolved dissonance, at the core of the civilizing mission here: notwithstanding the clarity of their stated purpose, the evangelists set about, simultaneously, (re)making two quite antithetical forms of African person—one a modernist citizen, the other an ethnic subject—each endowed with different generic characteristics—and species of rights. This, we shall argue, was not a trivial hiccup in the imperial project, a superficial tear in its otherwise seamless fabric. To the contrary: it reveals many of the inherent contradictions of colonialism; many of the indeterminacies with which it was shot through; many of the disjunctures that were to play into the formation of modern Africa, its structures of ethnicity and nation, gender and generation. It also says much about the process of building new identities, individual and communal, of navigating newly imagined worlds of possibility and political reality, in those complex force fields found at any colonial frontier.

In short, the campaign of the Nonconformist mission to refashion modern African personhood, and to insert itself into the struggle over individual and collective rights, is a study in ambiguity, contradiction, and the sheer perversity of the unintended in history. It also provides apt illustration of the way in which colonizing gestures might, and often did, escape the control of colonizers—and might, and often did, have a profound impact on colonized peoples even while being disregarded and resisted by them. In interrogating these processes, we fill in the final pieces of our narrative, drawing together the themes set out in the Introduction and reaching the conclusions toward which we have steadily been moving. We begin, once more, by returning to Great Britain in the early nineteenth century. Let us look briefly at the culture of legality and the conception of right(s) which the evangelists took with them to Africa.

FROM SPIRITUAL AUTHORITY TO SECULAR LEGALITY

To employ all the faculties which He had given them, particularly their understanding and liberty, He gave them a law, a complete model of all truth.

John Wesley (1985:6)

The early Nonconformists were born of a world preoccupied with the nature and the uses of the law, both sacred and secular. The collapse of ecclesiastical dominion in the 1640s had begun a long decline of spiritual sovereignty which, among other things, promoted a growing separation of *lex Dei* and *lex naturae* (*RRI*:76f.). Within the Protestant tradition, the breakdown of doctrinal hegemony manifested itself in a series of ardent theological controversies. One, exacerbated by the Revival, pitted legalism against antinomianism: the first posited the moralistic view that salvation depended on doing good works and being law-abiding; the second held Christian faith to exist apart from, indeed to supersede and "void the law."[7] Many influential preachers, not least Whitefield and Wesley, attempted to maintain a balance between the two positions, even where they differed on other issues (Davies 1961:152; Outler 1985:1). But, as a practical matter, evangelical ethics were drawn to legalism: "One in a thousand may have been awakened by the gospel," Wesley (1985:22) declared, yet "[t]he ordinary method of God is to convict sinners by the law, and that only." This view was widely endorsed by South African Nonconformists, whose mission was to convert by evoking, at once, the social, legal, and ethical sensibility of each potential believer. Dedicated to extending His Kingdom, these emissaries of the Lord labored to bring about the "moral revolution" that, they believed, had to precede the redemption of the individual savage (J. Philip 1828,2:370).

This revolution, as we have seen, was complicated by the fact that salvation, and subjection to divine law, had become fused with the imperatives of "civilization." And "civilization" had been suffused by, and inscribed in, an impersonal legal system in which people were defined as citizens of a secular, liberal nation-state. Its ethical touchstone, far from being theocentric, drew on the temporal model of the unfettered economy, a model that presumed the protection of the right to enter into contract and to engage in enterprise by free individuals (chapter 4). "Right" in the sense of "good" was elided into "rights" in "goods," the "properties" of subjects into the subject of property. That is why property rights were the prototype on which other human rights, conceived as private possessions, were founded. The eighteenth-century expansion of trade and industry, of the circulation of commodities and their paper equivalents, had generated a raft of statutes concerned with the unencumbered ownership, transfer, and protection of objects. Closely related to this is the fact, noted by Hay (1975:29f.), that criminal law eclipsed religious authority as the dominant sanctioning force in England in the 1700s; in so doing, its rituals, judgments, and "secular sermons" took on the "righteous accents" of divine decree. Reciprocally, Christian metaphors of justice began to invoke the courtroom ever more frequently. Sin was increasingly cast as crime by clergy who delivered homilies on proper stewardship and commercial practice, on the management of money and the making of wills.[8] In the process, Christian and secular legalism merged into one another to make for a powerfully law-centered worldview.

It is not surprising, then, that, in the effort to recast Southern Tswana personhood—and to introduce their preferred forms of subjectivity and identity, citizenship and moral community—the Nonconformists would tune their teaching to the language of legalism and rights. On the face of it, we might have expected that this would have resonated closely with Tswana sensibilities; after all, they too had explicit notions of citizenship, moral community, personal entitlement, contract, and constraint (*RRI*:chap. 4; also below). But the story was to turn out more complicated: the whole issue of rights and legalities was to feature contradictorily in the civilizing mission, and in the colonial encounter at large. For it played itself out simultaneously, polyrythmically, in two antithetical registers. One may be dubbed the register of *radical individualism*, the other, the register of *primal sovereignty*. The first had to do with the construction, by the Europeans, of the modernist African subject and his/her equivocal status as a citizen of South Africa. The second, which defined people by virtue of membership in "customary" political communities, concerned the attribution, again by whites, of "traditional" collective being to "natives." It would express itself in the ascription of primordiality, of an ineffable, essential primitivism, to such ethnic categories as "the" Tswana, "the" Sotho, "the" Xhosa.

The relationship between these registers, indeed why they should have existed at all, will become clear as we proceed. So, too, will the fact that their *co*existence had some less than obvious consequences. For one thing, it laid a practical basis for the material and political subordination of black South Africans: while promising to incorporate and enfranchise them, it afforded white colonizers a means to legitimate and naturalize their command over an ever more racially divided world. And yet it also created the various spaces and the diverse terms in which the colonized peoples could refigure themselves, mobilize, and strike back. As this implies, and as we shall show, it is to the dissonances of the colonial discourse of rights, and the struggles to which it gave rise, that we may look for the seeds of contemporary identity politics in South Africa.

RIGHTS STUFF: AFRICAN SUBJECTS AND PAPER PERSONS

> *"But why don't the white men stay in their own country?" said some intelligent natives to me one day. . . . "Perhaps it is [the Queen] who sends them. Some say this is the English mode of warfare—by 'papers' and agents and courts."*
> *This was said with contempt.*
>
> John Mackenzie (1887,1:80)

In seeking to re-form Southern Tswana personhood, the Nonconformists called upon the full range of "civilizing" techniques and "indirect influences" at their disposal; as we said above, this aspect of their endeavor subsumed all the others. And it rested on a particular vision of being-in-the-world. The terms of this vision are familiar, being part of the modernist European cultural heritage; though, at the time, we stress, they were more contested, less firmly rooted in everyday practice than our collective "memory" often allows (see *RRI*:60f.). Among them, three themes—ontological principles, really—featured with special clarity. We have encountered them before in different guises. Here, therefore, we deal with them summarily, and only insofar as they impinge on present concerns.

The first was the figure of the Promethean individual at the core of liberal modernism. In volume 1 (pp. 61f.), we spoke of its social archaeology; also, of some of its—or, rather, since it was profoundly gendered, *his*—generic characteristics: his capacity to construct himself and his world by virtue of his own willful actions, and thereby to make and narrate history according to his lights; his autonomy and disenchantment; his possession not just of private property but also of a divided, hyphenated self that could be, in different measures, self-conscious, self-righteous, self-indulgent, and, as Foucault would have us remember, self-disciplined (cf. Fraser 1989:44f.). Here, however, we seek to highlight a point made by, among others, Charles Taylor. "What is peculiar to the modern West," he says (1989:11), and especially to the "bourgeois ethic" (p. 214), is that the respect accorded to human beings came "to be [formulated] in terms of rights"; specifically, of *universal* "subjective right[s],"[9] a form of "legal privilege" enjoyed by "disengaged subjects" (1989:11–12).[10] As John Philip (1828,1:xxvi) wrote from the evangelical frontline, even the "wanderer in the desert" ought to have

> a right to his life, his liberty, his wife, his children, and his property . . . to a fair price for his labour; to choose the place of his abode, and to enjoy the society of his children; and no one can deprive him of those rights without violating the laws of nature and of nations.

Note the patriarchal, familial character of the fantasy (cf. D. Barker 1978:256). Note, too, that the larger this image of a universal, right-bearing Man loomed in the discourses of English modernity (Corrigan and Sayer 1985:183 et passim)—and in the utopian dreams of colonial evangelists—the more *un*African it became; or rather, the more that African personhood was construed as its obverse. Almost all of the early missionaries, for example, told tales of Tswana dispossessed or put to death at the summary command of an uncivil king (see, e.g., Campbell 1822,1:211–12). Not only did the premodern monarch have a whim of iron. His subjects, more vassals than citizens, were said to have no legal protections, no entitlements, no rights to call their own. Not even to life and liberty.

This picture of an Africa lacking all civility, citizenship, and civil rights was to persist for a long time in much of white South Africa. In 1925,[11] over a century after the evangelists arrived among Southern Tswana, a parliamentary committee was set up to consider "Masters and Servants" legislation. Its members challenged Selope Thema, a highly respected black journalist and national political figure:

> Of course, you have read the history of . . . Chaka and Dingaan. Did the natives have any right to life or property under these [nineteenth-century

Zulu] chiefs?. . . These people [living under "tribal" conditions] would have had no rights except the chief's will.

Thema replied that Zululand had indeed once been "democratic"—until Shaka "learned . . . militarism" from white men. "And then," he added, "the history was written by Europeans."

The modernist ideal of propertied, right-bearing, personhood—the model subject of the civilizing mission—was securely founded on the principle of "reason"; its absence among "savages" being taken as proof of the point. Writing in a philosophical key some fifty years ago, Margaret MacDonald (1949, repr. 1984:29) echoed a view shared by nineteenth-century missionaries:[12] "[O]nly at a certain level of intellectual development do men claim natural rights. Savages do not dream of life, liberty, and the pursuit of happiness. For they do not question what is customary." Observe, again, the taken for granted antimony between right and custom—and its association with the opposition between civility and savagery.[13] It followed that only self-interested, reasoning human beings might be, in both senses of the term, right-minded. Premoderns, by contrast, lived in unreflective "thralldom." Imprisoned, even possessed, by "uncanny" forces, they could be neither disengaged nor self-regulating (Taylor 1989:192). It was not that they were inattentive to their own well-being. To the contrary, Europeans often remarked that Tswana were highly acquisitive, "selfish." But this, we repeat, was not *enlightened*, rational self-interest (Molema 1920:116). Just greed. What is more, their concerns lay in the wrong kinds of things, the wrong sorts of subject/s. Like their "selfish" gods, they were too partisan, oriented too personally toward self, family, and sovereign. For which, read: they did not dignify their own private pursuits by portraying them as the source of a greater commonweal, let alone the wealth of a nation.

As this suggests, the British idea of selfhood demanded a social setting—without which it made limited sense. Indeed, the kind of society in which the autonomous subject ought properly to be situated, and with which individual liberty was most compatible, long remained an issue for Victorian thinkers (Francis and Morrow 1994); but some form of sovereign political community was the presumed answer. Here lies the second theme of salience to the colonial mission in respect of modernist personhood and the discourse of rights: the emerging European nation-state. Conceived stereotypically (if not altogether accurately) as a secular universe of citizens who were free and equal before the law, it was held to share language and culture, territory and history, values, sentiments, and interests. This, of course, is the "imagined community" (B. Anderson 1983) of which so much has been (re)written lately: the modernist polity that, as an ideological formation, came to maturity in the age of revolution, 1789–1848. Indifferent to (or rather, intolerant of) internal difference, it was itself the product of a "cultural revolution," as Corrigan and Sayer (1985) remind us. And it was constituted as a state in the double sense of being both a political order *and* a condition of mind-and-being (*RRI*:5). As such, it had become the taken for granted context in which the right-bearing citizen was implanted.

The nation-state, in fact, was seen as the ultimate guarantor of individual rights, the guardian of propertied personhood, the garrisoned space in which modern subjectivities paraded as sovereign subjects. All of this was invoked by the missions when they called on Britain to protect the interests of indigenous peoples—and to underwrite their own (*RRI*:292f.). Founded on a social contract and codified law rather than on status and custom, it was the model against which other, more "primitive" political orders were measured (e.g., R. Moffat 1842:248; J. Philip 1828,2:132f.). After all, declared Philip (1828,2:317), "the character of a people depends on . . . the laws and government under which they live." By this criterion, unsurprisingly, Southern Tswana were said to be lacking: Edward Solomon (1855:46), in specifying what was particular to their "government" in the mid nineteenth century, offered sadly that they "have no regular code of laws, . . . [but] customs . . . to [which] they rigidly adhere." Some colonial evangelists, it is true, understood that the Africans *did* have a "law" which was "[far from] ridiculous or oppressive" (Campbell 1822,1:197f.). But, once remarked, this was rarely ever mentioned again.

This, in turn, moves us to our third theme, the remaining ontological principle behind the evangelical effort to colonize Tswana personhood: a positive, anti-relativist conception of knowledge (*RRI*:244f.). Expressed less in the abstract than in statements of faith and everyday action, this conception of knowledge held to a number of well-worn axioms: that the word and the world, fact and theory, the concept and the concrete were separate from one another, and ought never to be confused or confounded; that God's truth, like civility itself, was subject to absolutist standards; that wisdom was cumulative and irreversible; that, by extension, no two *systems* of knowledge, no two orders of cultural practice, could coexist (see, e.g., Livingstone 1857:19ff.). Taken together, these axioms composed the canonical, confident bases of a universalist epistemology, an epistemology that only allowed for one possible construction of the civilized subject, one discourse of rights, one telos of modernity.

*****

These three principles, then, were to figure with special force in the campaign to recast Tswana being-in-the-world, to implant the modernist, right-bearing subject on African soil—whether it be as Christian convert, faithful spouse, upright property-holder, *nouveau-riche* merchant, industrious yeoman, or disciplined laborer.[14] It was here that the first register of the discourse of rights, the register of radical individualism, was to play itself out.

The Politics of Personhood

The Christian campaign to reshape African personhood began, of course, with the "Bechuana" body: the "right-minded" subject was, first and foremost, an embodied, bounded, biological individual. The evangelists were quick to grasp the salience, for pedagogic purposes, of the management of the gendered physique; quick to sense the link, analogical and substantive, between bodily politics and the body politic. It was John Philip (1828,1:386), not Emile Durkheim, who first commented that the "different members of a state [are] beautifully represented by members of the human body." And Wesley (1985:17) who had described God's law as a mode of "empowerment" from "our Head into his living members." Much was to be made of this fortuitous symbolic connection: if the body personal was metonymic of the body politic, the reformation of the second might follow from the refashioning of the first. What is more, this objective, the reworking of bodily practices, was best achieved by intervening in the mundanities of Tswana life, and so fitted well with the Nonconformist tradition of methodical improvement.

It was here, in fact, that the Puritan legacy converged with the bourgeois ethic. Just as the former took "ordinary life" to be the major plane of effectual activity in an increasingly man-made universe (above, chapter 1), so the "affirmation of the everyday" (Taylor 1989:214–15) was integral to the modernist idea of the new civility. Thus it was that the evangelists expended great effort, day in and day out, on persuading Southern Tswana to dress in European garb, so that they might close off their bodies from one another (chapter 5); to put their energies to the task of earning their own incomes, so that they might harness their physicality and distinguish themselves through acts of refined consumption (chapter 4); to disseminate "modern" notions of hygiene, health, and illness, so that they might renounce the charms of local healers and free themselves from their faith in intrusive social and spiritual forces (chapter 7). Thus it was, too, that the clergymen spoke to the Africans of the merits of monogamy, so that they might control their sexuality and "unnatural" affections; of the vices of bridewealth, so that they might recognize the freedom of all God's creatures to enter into contracts of their own free will; of the moral benefits of living in nuclear families, so that females might confine themselves to hearth and home while men did an honest day's work in the field (chapter 6).

Where more appropriately to address all these concerns at once than in the context of marriage (cf. Snyder 1981)? The documentary record shows that, throughout the nineteenth century, the missionaries tried unceasingly to reform Tswana matrimony, transposing it into the language of legalism and rights. As we shall see, some black Christian literati, like Sol Plaatje (1996), would later object, pointing to the contradictions in this effort, among them that the insistence on lawful wedlock debarred many from the church. But, for the evangelists, "custom" was sinful—and increasingly criminalized—while legality was virtuous. It was an equation that ran to the moralistic core of their creed. In a letter to London on the topic of marriage in 1884, Roger Price wrote that "it will be some time yet before we can dispense with *law as a schoolmaster* for our Bechuana" (E. Smith 1957:276f.; our italics); interestingly, Wesley (1985:16) had used the same words to stress that law "drove sinners by force, rather than drawing them through love."[15] Likewise, in matters of conjugality, Africans had to be kept mindful of God's exacting judgment. In short, the point was to do more than merely induce men to wed monogamously, in church, and without "buying" their wives. It was to have them treat the marital bond as a sacred contract, an ensemble of enforceable rights and duties, and to inculcate a legalistic view of selfhood *sui generis*. To the Christians, moreover, matrimony and the family—being at the epicenter of the social and moral division of labor—were also the key to those other vital sites in the struggle for modern personhood: property relations and material life.

It was here that the lessons of radical individualism were most avidly taught; here that the "communal" tendencies of "the" African were most fiercely fought. Once the principles of private ownership and title to property were properly inculcated, believed the evangelists, all the other bases of right-bearing citizenship—the right to life, liberty, wife, children, and property (J. Philip 1828,1:xxvi)—might take root (J. Mackenzie 1975:72). But first the heathen antipathy to "healthy, individualistic competition," to the maximization of time and effort, and to self-possessed industry had to be overcome. So, too, had the Southern Tswana propensity for brute "selfishness."

It had been with a view to demonstrating the meaning of private property that the Christians sought to purchase the terrain on which to establish themselves, their churches, and their gardens. That is why Hamilton "bought" land from a Tlhaping man in 1820, ostensibly the "very first" transaction of its kind in Bechuanaland (Campbell 1822,2:149–50). And why Robert Moffat (Moffat and Moffat 1951:189, 113) insisted on acquiring the ground for the LMS station for forty pounds of beads, the equivalent of five pounds in cash; not nearly as good a deal as Manhattan, in view of the location, but still cheap at the price. As the agreements made by the Wesleyans underscore (see Mears 1970:36–41 for early examples), the evangelists insisted on "absolute" possession and clearly explicated rights; it was, says Moffat (1951:189) a *condition* of taking the territory from Chief Mothibi. Their title had to be clearly given, clearly gained, clearly grasped by the Africans, so that they might learn to do the same. Recall Mary Moffat's (1951:111; italics added) exact words, written in November 1823. They are telling: [E]ach [Tlhaping] *individual* is to *purchase his own* ground, the missionaries having set the *example*." The five points of emphasis capture, in a clause, everything the civilizing mission set out to do in this domain, and how: its grounding of refined individualism in exclusive rights of ownership over fixed assets, obtained through enlightened exchange; its gendered aspect; its reliance on achieving its objectives by example and mimesis. We noted in chapter 3 that the gesture was largely unintelligible to Southern Tswana, a fact which Livingstone (1857:21), for one, appreciated. As Schapera (in Moffat and Moffat 1951:110, n. 23) points out and Tlhaping chiefs were later to argue, Mothibi "regarded [these payments] as nothing more than tribute for use of the land" (see below). No matter. Once they had it in their possession, the evangelists went about investing themselves in it, a performance intended to dramatize the process of Protestant self-production:

Act I, the forceful conversion of nature into private property;

Act II, the cultivation of a fruitful field by means of material improvements and self-possessed labor;

Act III, the harvesting of wealth to be enjoyed as a just return on capital input and virtuous toil.

The missions also set up holdings for allocation to Christian inquirers who proved themselves worthy by virtue of their monogamous marriages and moral probity (see chapter 3, n. 77). There were, it seems, always candidates to take possession of such irrigated acreages as were available, especially in times of drought and poverty; they were highly fertile and very valuable. But the scale of the operation remained limited. These were not holy haciendas or evangelical estates. Just modest exercises in cultural engineering.

Beyond the compass of the mission stations, where the evangelists did make modest progress,[16] neither the privatization of commonage nor rights of ownership gained much purchase. If anything, they still appeared as senseless to Southern Tswana as they had at the time of the very first Nonconformist efforts to buy land. Neither arable fields nor pasture was scarce here. They had no exchange value, and were held and distributed by chiefly favor. Well-watered gardens, it is true, did have the potential to be turned into property; but, given the semi-arid ecology, there was never any prospect of introducing irrigation on a very large scale. Later, toward the end of the century, there *would* be a move in some quarters to introduce individual title; and wealthy families would try to purchase farms for themselves outside of "tribal" territories. But this was only after settler expansion had transformed the worth of real estate in the interior, after the mineral revolution had reconstructed the regional economy, after overrule had made the Africans ever more vulnerable to dispossession. By then, though, as we shall see, the very idea of rights to landed property for blacks had become a hotly contested issue throughout colonial South Africa.

In the meantime, and in spite of the benign bafflement that greeted their efforts and explanations, the missionaries did not give up. As the years passed, they continued, both by example and by "kind conversation," to encourage

Southern Tswana to enclose their fields, to invest in and improve them, to build houses alongside them, and to regard them as freehold farms. They also took their campaign to the colonial state, especially after the discovery of diamonds, when "native" landholding arrangements became embroiled in struggles over territory across the interior. The most tenacious among them was undoubtedly John Mackenzie, who worked tirelessly to make Bechuanaland into a Wordsworthian[17] paradise of enlightened, propertied yeomen (*RRI*:294; chapter 3). He and his brethren wrote innumerable letters, and made repeated appeals, in pursuit of their objective—which was to put in place a tenurial system that might, simultaneously, ward off settler encroachment and facilitate the rise of a propertied class here. One letter, written in 1878 to the Administrator of Griqualand West about the Tlhaping under Chief Jantje, captures well the style and substance of evangelical rhetoric in this regard (J. Mackenzie 1975:111–12):

> If . . . people would quietly settle down [on land with long leases] and pay an annual rent for their farms . . . the "native question" would be for ever settled. . . . A class of native yeomen would arise, which in some cases might merge into that of landowners, for it would be well to put it in their power to buy their farms after they had occupied them and improved them for some years. The less thrifty and capable . . . [would be allowed to] sink to [their] own level among the inferior labouring class.

Herein, then, lay the magic of private property. Not only could it alone secure a permanent basis for Christian industry. In so doing, it would also sort out the wheat from the chaff, producing classes of landowner, yeoman, and laborer, each according to his own abilities, his own virtuous industry. Thus would the relative, and morally proper, rewards of Protestant political economy become legible in the sociology of the Tswana countryside—yielding at a stroke an "inferior labouring class" to toil for Europeans while preserving enough land for those who needed and deserved it. And so it would settle the "native question"; the vexed problem, for whites that is, of how black South Africans should be allowed to live in a colonial world in which others sought to appropriate their land and labor. Interestingly, the tripart stratification envisaged by the evangelist was not all that different from the fragmentation of the peasantry we have already observed. Except that his version was offered as a desirable outcome of the introduction of individual property rights.

Mackenzie did not confine his efforts to South Africa. In visits to England and in his *Austral Africa*, he set out to persuade the British parliament and public that every African, other presumably than the "inferior" laborer, "ought to feel that his house and his cornfield are his own, and not mere 'Government-land' . . . which can be sold at any time over his head" (1887,1:30). Mackenzie was convinced that, by the 1880s, Southern Tswana had *already* developed a nice understanding of property—in the European sense of the term. He supplied evidence (1887,1:76f.), some of which we cited in earlier chapters, to prove that many now saw disadvantages in "traditional" tenurial arrangements; and, concomitantly, that they showed a willingness and a propensity for more civilized ways and means. Given the introduction of private holdings, and release from chiefly command, might not Bechuanaland become a haven of African modernity? Even if they had not all absorbed the lessons of the mission, he added (1975:20), the proceedings of the Bloemhof Arbitration Commission of 1871 (see chapter 4; *RRI*:283) had "taught . . . [Tswana] the meaning of land-titles, and the laws and customs of the white men as to buying and selling land." Bloemhof had been a hard school, of course, and had ended with vast acreages of "native" land in the hands of others. It had persuaded the Africans that "English" justice was "warfare" with "papers."

The fact that the colonial frontier was changing so rapidly merely affirmed the evangelists' belief—understandable at the time—that the salvation of the Tswana, so to speak, lay in privatization and in land titles officially sanctioned by the state. The likes of John Mackenzie told this to the chiefs at every opportunity. And, as they did, the proportions of their message changed. Where before they had stressed the civilizing capacities of property rights, and had spoken incidentally of protecting the territory from further incursion, their priorities were now reversed: primary emphasis was placed on the need to elicit the backing of the state against settler avarice, although the subtext—the positive value of property—remained audible. Take this fragment of a reported conversation between Mackenzie (1887,1:7–8) and a Tlhaping ruler:

> "You should fully face the change that has come and is coming. In the olden time you had all your gardens and cattle stations, and no one interfered with the one or the other. Now you see the coming wave of white men. . . . Where they find open country they will build and put in the plough, and will tell you that the unoccupied country is God's and not yours. But white men respect hard work, and if you improve your houses and your lands you may depend on it no English officer would dispossess you. . . . Why not meet together once more as a tribe . . . and introduce a better custom as to land? Every fountain or farm should be apportioned to him who cultivates it, and he should have a title to it acknowledged by the tribe."
> "But would he not sell it?" I was asked at once.
> "Fools might sell," I answered, "but the men of the tribe would not."

For "men of the tribe," read "socially responsible individuals," those who combined private interest with the public good.

> "But there is great deception about papers,—the agents deceive stupid people," said one of the men.

Here, over the issue of dispossession, is where the liberal idealism of the mission ran up against the facts of life on the colonial frontier, up against the brute realities of realty. And where the Nonconformists found it necessary to modify the kind of propertied personhood of which they dreamed—or leave their would-be converts open to the rapacity of other colonizers. And so:

"I have thought of all that,"

Mackenzie replied, allowing himself a great deal of prescience.

"You ought to have individual rights and title-deeds, but it ought to be printed on every one of them, 'Not saleable—not transferable.'"
    This was a new idea—individual titles, but unsaleable. It was declared on all hands that this would exactly meet their case . . . [the] idea of individual right to land beyond the power of the clever agent.

How this form of title differed from existing tenurial arrangements—other than being committed to paper—is not obvious. It may have consoled the evangelists by sustaining the fiction of private property. But, notwithstanding the enthusiasm put into the mouths of his interlocutors by Mackenzie, it is unclear what the Africans had to gain from it. Without the intervention of the state, dispossession would go on, as indeed it did, with or without title deeds. Many Southern Tswana seem to have been quick to grasp this, insisting that it was the very language of "papers," the transposition of territory into text, that enabled and legitimized its appropriation by the whites. And true enough, as Mackenzie's own account shows (1887,1:78–80), it *was* through the unscrupulous manipulation of claims to right and title that Africans were being relieved of their land, often with the connivance of colonial courts and commissions. Against such forces, the liberal worldview and the good intentions of the mission had little chance. But more of that later.
    Mackenzie's efforts underscore several things about the discourse of rights. The first is the simple fact that, while the Nonconformists set about remaking Southern Tswana property and personhood in their own image, they were not the only Europeans on the colonial stage who sought to do this. Nor were they fully in control of the physical environment in which they enacted their drama. Both considerations, as it turned out, diverted the impact of their exertions. Note our choice of term here: diverted. These factors did not negate the effect of the civilizing mission on the Southern Tswana world; as we shall see, they altered and redirected it. As did the actions of the Africans themselves. Second, although the broad outline of what the evangelists wished to accomplish here was clearly and repeatedly stated, the actual terms of its realization were left much more ambiguous. This runs to a general point made by John Stuart Mill (1965,2:253):

[T]he very idea of peasant proprietors is strange to the English mind. . . .
Even the forms of language stand in the way: the familiar designation for
owners of land being "landlords," a term to which "tenants" is always understood as a correlative.

Mill's observation—that freehold peasant proprietorship was an alien concept
to the British bourgeoisie—had echoes at the outposts of empire. Amidst all
the visionary calls for a propertied African peasantry, the precise terms of the
dream were never really spelled out: How might community life and governance
be organized? What labor arrangements should prevail? How was it possible to
prevent the alienation of land and still treat it as a privately owned commodity?
As a result, the discourse of rights fell silent on many of the issues that counted
most. At the same time, rights talk had begun to resound everywhere in the
interior. Indeed, it was rapidly becoming the lingua franca of negotiation across
the colonial frontier. Much more is yet to be heard of its resonances.

The lessons of radical individualism were not restricted to the domain of
landed property; nor did they extend only to marriage and bodily management.
As we have already seen, they also occurred in many other places: in the effort
to construct a domestic sphere, at "home," founded on the European model of
the family as an ensemble of right-bearing persons; in the representation of the
church as a rule-governed, voluntary community made up of spiritually autonomous members, each with an inalienable right to freedom of belief, each paying
her or his dues, each responsible for his or her own moral career;[18] in the establishment of schools in which pupils were encouraged to improve themselves,
and were dressed, addressed, and disciplined as serialized individuals; in the
dissemination, through a variety of contexts, of modernist notions of time and
money, of free wage labor and the private estate, of refined consumption as a
reward for virtue; in the expectation of responsible participation in the moral
and political community; and so on and on. Although these lessons merged, for
the most part, into the fabric of everyday life, on some occasions they burst
dramatically onto the public stage. The most notable, perhaps, occurred when
missionaries and Tswana Christians confronted chiefs, publicly, to demand that
converts be allowed to behave in accordance with their consciences rather than
be made to follow "custom." The assertion of this right resonated closely with
European ideas of citizenship: as loyal subjects of their rulers, church people
would obey the law, would pay their taxes, and would give tribute to their sovereigns. But they were entitled to pursue their own spiritual activities unopposed,
and also to be excused from participating in "heathen" rituals. That this demand often led to bitter conflict merely confirmed the lessons of radical individualism and universal rights that the colonial evangelists had tried so hard to
teach.[19]

In what measure, then, did the Nonconformists succeed in the task they set themselves? How much might they be said to have made modernist subjects out of "selfish" beings? In addressing this issue, it is necessary to keep in mind an obvious yet crucial point, one that the evangelists tended to ignore to their cost: Southern Tswana had their own constructions of personhood, possession, and entitlement, all of which were integral to what became known, in colonial times, as *mekgwa le melao ya Setswana*, "Tswana customs and laws." This body of norms was seen by the Africans themselves, ever more explicitly (*RRI*:129), to regulate both the flow of daily life and the terms in which disputes were defined and dealt with. In a world known for its rich culture of argument, a world wherein discourses of the everyday were to be heard almost every day in the public domain, they also afforded a language with which to discuss matters of collective concern. *Mekgwa le melao*, as is well-known, have been the subject of several scholarly studies.[20] What is important for present purposes is the way in which they shaped vernacular understandings of those aspects of *setswana* under challenge from the civilizing mission.

Southern Tswana are often said to have had a highly "legalistic" world-view—albeit not, as in the case of the Nonconformists, a moralistic or theocentric one. They also had an elaborate conception of selfhood (see *RRI*:142f.).[21] Like its Protestant counterpart, the Tswana person was situated in a historically forged social milieu, a milieu, remember, that appeared at once highly ordered and yet fluid: on the one hand, people were securely situated in a hierarchy of well-defined social and political constituencies; on the other, rank and position were open to constant redefinition, the onus being thrown on individuals to "build themselves up." This, in part, is why the Europeans perceived the Africans to be "selfish" and "cunning." What they did not appreciate, though, is that individuality here depended on self-construction through the husbanding of relations, a labor that involved the negotiation of both personal status and the indigenous equivalent of contracts; Tswana had a well-developed range of voluntary forms of exchange and reciprocity whose infraction was actionable in court (Schapera 1938:239f.). As this suggests, *pace* Maine, everyday life here was shaped by a complex hybrid of status and contract, both understood rather differently than they were in contemporary Britain.

Personhood, then, was a matter of pragmatic, ongoing fabrication; adult males here *were* self-made, but in ways and by means quintessentially social, engaged, and, quite explicitly, interested. Rank and position were contrived and/or consolidated, with respect to others more senior or junior, by accumulating wealth in people, objects, and animals—primarily through marriage and affinity, patronage and clientage, political alliance and material exchanges. The self, consequently, was not a state of being but a process of becoming, as were all the relations of which it was composed; inertia implied social death and the possibility of being "eaten" by others. Only at the end of life was that process arrested, temporarily, as the deceased passed into the ancestral realm, there to be remade yet again by the actions of descendants.[22] That is why status was constantly renegotiated: it expressed, in the public language of social position, the relative worth of an individual at any given moment. All of which must have made European personhood, as it was presented to Southern Tswana, difficult for them to accept. Various traces of the long conversation suggest that they saw the modernist subject as undersocialized, an ensemble of contractual ties and "paper" relations defined less as things becoming than as things being.

Southern Tswana being-in-the-world also involved membership of a political community—not merely, as the missionaries were wont to say, blind personal submission to a sovereign; and sovereignty itself was hedged about by constitutional constraint (Schapera 1938:53f.). Different classes of citizen were recognized, but all enjoyed the protection of the *mekgwa le melao*. Non-citizens did not. Their rights of residence and movement, of person and possessions, were severely restricted.[23] As this implies, the Tswana self-as-citizen connoted autonomy, entitlement, a sense of identity, and property. Without the last, in fact, neither personhood nor full citizenship could exist. For the *sine qua non* of affiliation to a *morafe* ("nation") was access to residential land, arable fields, and pasture without payment—other, perhaps, than tribute;[24] only nonsocial beings were denied it. Rights in this land might be held in perpetuity and were transmitted to heirs through a variety of devolutionary arrangements (Comaroff and Roberts 1981:70f.). But they depended finally on use rather than on an abstract notion of titled ownership. If fields fell into extended disuse they might be forfeited—they were not saleable—although *melao* to this effect were not everywhere the same, and changed in many places after overrule (Schapera 1970:97f.). Landholdings could also be taken from an individual banished for such antisocial crimes as witchcraft or subversion. Conversely, when people were divested of all their property, for whatever reason, they faced social death and, *in extremis*, loss of citizenship.

It will be clear that these nineteenth-century Southern Tswana notions of personhood and property, like the indigenous idea of spirituality, were strongly oriented toward the performative. Being was becoming, and both were a matter of doing. This unspoken principle underpinned the conceptual scaffolding of their world. And it served as a prism through which they read and reacted to the civilizing mission—in this sphere as in all others. But their responses were not all alike: there was no single "native" ear or eye, just as there was no one "native" voice. As we would expect by now, the impact of the evangelists was refracted through, and mediated by, various orders of difference. To be sure, the way in which the modernist subject took root on Tswana terrain was itself part of the sedimentation of social and cultural distinction in the second half of the century. In order to make this point concretely, let us focus, by way of example, on just two of the aspects of personhood and property with which we have been concerned: land and matrimony.

For most Southern Tswana, and certainly for the lower peasantry, the idea of real estate, as purveyed by Europeans, continued to make limited sense. Until overrule, while land was plentiful, access and tenure were guaranteed under *mekgwa le melao* without need for papers. Afterwards, with increasing poverty, settler expansionism, and the concentration of holdings in the hands of the upper peasantry, the situation changed. But ownership, in the manner of *sekgoa*, still did not have much positive meaning. For these people, purchase was not a prospect. And title merely enlarged the possibility of dispossession at the hands of speculators. The fact that it did, and the fact that ever more of the rank and file were becoming landless amidst the worsening economic conditions of *fin-de-siècle* (above, chapter 4), led many rulers to proscribe all transfers—and simultaneously to affirm that only tenure under *mekgwa le melao* was permissible. Nor was this restricted to southern Bechuanaland. John Mackenzie (1975:44) notes that Khama, for all his Christian zeal for reform, "proclaimed that the presence of Europeans in the country had not altered the Bechwana law as to land, . . . that ground was inalienable; that no house could be bought or sold." In due course—in British Bechuanaland, after the Land Commission of 1886— the colonial state intervened to make landholding within "native reserves" subject only to "tribal" law, thereby putting an end to the evangelical dream of a landed class of yeomen. As we shall see, there was to be a final irony here: some rulers, having insisted earlier on "customary" tenure to prevent alienation, were now to push for private title, either to protect their realms from incursion or as a reaction to their own loss of authority and resources (cf. Shillington 1985:175–76).

Among the middle and upper peasantry, and especially among the new Christian elite, there was a much more positive reaction to the idea of real estate. Recall chapters 3 and 4: as they became more affluent, people of this class fraction, many of them royals, began to buy farms *outside* their chiefdoms. It is difficult to track down the dealings of the period, but there is also evidence that territory once thought of as "tribal" ended up in individual hands; in any case, some wealthy men, including sovereigns, took to leasing land to whites (and even, on occasion, to their compatriots), thus becoming a small cadre of rentiers.[25] These men tended to hold acreages under both "traditional" tenure and by private title, and at times fudged the difference between the two.[26] All this, however, changed after 1913, at least in much of South Africa,[27] when the Natives Land Act severely limited ownership by blacks outside the reserves.[28] By then, the European sense of private property had made deep inroads into this segment of the population, as had the language of rights altogether. Indeed, this language was already being used as a matter of course by Tswana leaders in their effort to protect the assets and interests of their fellows and followers (see below).

Over the long run, then, all Southern Tswana were caught up in a world dominated by the authoritative rhetoric of rights—even though, for most of them, those rights were experienced primarily by their absence or their removal. Different fractions of the population reacted differently toward the conception of property essayed by the civilizing mission, just as they had in respect of other matters social and cultural, spiritual and material. Still, none could escape its implications. Or the political realities that accompanied it.

The modernist, right-bearing subject was not inscribed in landed possessions alone, however. S/he was invested in a *total* social persona. And this, by turn, brings us to marriage. For it is in the conjugal process that property and propriety, status and contract, came together in the formation of mature social beings. Indeed, if any one context was likely to reveal the inroads made by the Protestant person it was this. What, then, *does* the archaeology of changing matrimonial arrangements tell us of the effect of the civilizing mission on Southern Tswana selfhood?

A fair amount, according to the Rev. John Brown.

In a review of mission work at Taung, written in 1900, Brown cited shifting marital practices as indicative of the "quiet" but cumulative impact of Christianity in the district. He wrote:[29]

> The desire to be married in church seems to be growing. During the seven months we were shut in by the Boers,[30] I married more than forty couples. I . . . hope that this desire is indicative of a stricter observance of the marriage vows, and more permanence in the marriage bond. Some of the knots tied by the missionary are soon unpicked; and those who have been united in church quarrel and separate. In spite of this fact, however, the growing tendency to formal marriage must help to make native home life purer and happier.

Plainly, both the rite and the rights entailed in Christian unions had become important in the construction of relations and identities here; and this in a place known for its resistance to the mission. But, as Brown acknowledged, there was another, more disquieting side to what was happening, one which led him to wonder why Tswana should have had any "desire for marrying according to law" at all. Now that only "legal" wedlock was recognized by church and state, matrimony was becoming a matter of contract rather than morality or social commitment. Neither minister nor magistrate, he noted, could refuse to marry a "single" man, even if he had deserted a string of common-law wives. What was more, first marriages apart, legalized unions required legalized dissolutions. "Before the law came," Brown went on, "clear proof of infidelity or desertion was all that was needed before marrying again the party sinned against." Now a relict Christian woman who could not meet the cost of divorce was unable to remarry in church. And if she merely "allowed herself to be taken," she would be expelled. "The law," he opined, should not "seem to make right living more difficult than it was when heathen customs prevailed."

But often it did, especially for those without the resources needed to exercise the rights that had come to define legitimate personhood in South Africa. In 1903, writing in *Koranta ea Becoana,* Plaatje (1996) condemned one of the many "obnoxious disabilities" suffered by blacks in the Transvaal, a handicap which, he said, impeded the spread of Christianity: the three-pound tax on "legally" performed religious marriages. This tax, which amounted to the annual income of Africans working on white farms, created a "class" of persons who, though wed by "Native rites," could not afford the ceremony required of those admitted to full church membership.[31]

There were other material implications to "legal" marriage, of course. For example, men and women who entered into it, and assumed its contractual obligations, found that their estates also became subject to the law of the land. In the event, and as they were encouraged to do, many of them employed attorneys to commit their wealth to paper and to draft wills. This did not put an end to the arguments over succession and inheritance long associated with the politics of Tswana family life (Comaroff and Roberts 1981:175ff.). But, as bequests might now be contested in the courts, matters were made much harder for those who lacked the resources or the social knowledge to do so. When such cases did occur, they often took on a distinctly local flavor. Even the most devout and elevated of Christians rarely entered only one union during a lifetime; serial monogamy or, as Brown hinted, the coexistence of "legal" and other unions was more usual (cf. Comaroff and Roberts 1977). Under these conditions, suits hinged either on the relative seniority of the children of the various unions, or on the "legitimacy" of heirs born to women who had been wed, according to "custom," by men with "Christian" wives as well.[32] Patently, rights in property, in the European sense of the term, were being re-formed by the effects of the rite kind of marriage on Tswana personhood.

All of this underscores the extent to which matrimony was a node of articulation between the making of persons and the hardening of social distinctions. It often is. Among elites, "Christian marriage" had become the norm; which suggests that, in the early 1900s, the church *was* civil society in many respects.[33] Not that this erased *setswana* rites, centered on bridewealth and other exchanges. Marital histories collected in 1970 show that more than half the unions contracted by religious ceremony over the previous forty years had also involved prestations of stock or token currency. While the range of kin taking part in these exchanges had narrowed, nuptials were seldom joined by two individuals alone; for all ritual and practical purposes, families remained more extended than the missionaries might have liked.[34] Still, "legal" wedlock had become *the* sign of respectability among the prosperous—who, in championing an ideology of enlightened self-interest, saw matrimony as a means of consolidating alliances among their households (cf. Pauw 1960:7).

For those who could afford it, moreover, weddings became major rites of conspicuous consumption. Their trappings—elaborate gowns, invitations, gifts, feasts, photographs—were modes of configuring and displaying identities and relations. Members of the middle peasantry, who were more strapped, scrimped and saved to pay for simpler versions of the same rites; often they were helped by the informal credit societies that sprang up largely for such purposes as funding "decent" nuptials and funerals. Like their counterparts among the English poor (above, chapter 6), these people tended to hang their marriage certificates prominently in their homes. But, with or without ceremonial display, matrimony in the nontraditional mode became a mark of elevated status. A high school English student in Mafikeng wrote of the matter thus in 1969:[35]

> People who are married enjoy the privilege. They plan for their future. A wedding is advantageous since the children will grow up in a Christian life. The parents . . . send them to school . . . even if there is hunger, the children will be safe. [Marriage] helps people take care of their pence.

As an afterthought, she added, "[A] wedding is a form of bondage that permits freedom." It was not, however, an option open to all. Among the very poor, the prospect of a formal union, Christian or otherwise, presented a daunting challenge. So much so that, over the course of this century, there has been a steady decline in *all* forms of marriage among the lower peasantry—who have long given poverty, unvarnished and unqualified, as the reason.[36] Conversely, there has been a notable rise in informal unions referred to as "*vat en sit*," Afrikaans for "take and settle," and in female-headed households. The implication is obvious: those who lacked property found it well-nigh impossible to achieve "proper" personhood for themselves and their offspring, either in the civil or in the religious domain. The two, as Plaatje's comment made plain, were closely interconnected. Without the necessary assets it was difficult to marry formally; this meant exclusion from full membership in the mainstream denominations, made it impossible to secure places for children in "good" schools and training institutions (J. Comaroff 1974:157),[37] tended to foreclose access to such "civil" rights as were available to blacks in South Africa—and put great hurdles in the way of the kind of salvation offered by the orthodox churches.

Here a pause and a change of register, so to speak.

As we said at the outset, the evangelical discourse of rights was not restricted to the register of radical individualism, nor just to the politics of modernist personhood. It was to resonate, also, in the mythos of primal sovereignty.

The Politics of Primal Sovereignty

The progenitors of those who now know themselves as Batswana first appear in European records less than a decade after the earliest white settlement at the Cape: in the journal of Jan van Riebeeck for 1661 (Saunders 1966:62). Over the next century there were various reports of people whom the Nama referred to as "Briqua" and the Khoi called "Berinas," people who lived in "cities," worked in metal, and were active in trade.[38] Captain Robert Gordon, who traveled along the Orange River in 1779, substituted the term "Moetjoaanaas" for "Briqua"— it is not clear why—but he seems to have used it only for Tlhaping, not for the "Barrolo" to the north (Saunders 1966:69). Early nineteenth-century narratives make it evident that there was no idea of the existence of a "Tswana" nation; nor even a shared name. Solomon (1855:41), for one, described a number of independent chiefdoms, each denominated for its ruling line. An acute observer, he remarked no common cultural or political identity among them. Concluded John Mackenzie (1887,1:22):

> The name Bechuana is a word used at an early period by white men to denote the tribes of Batlaping and Barolong, with which they first came into contact. These people do not use the word of themselves, or of one another; nevertheless, they accept of it as the white man's name for them, and now begin to use it themselves.

Perhaps, perhaps not. Mackenzie *was* probably correct in one regard, though: that the use of "Batswana" [Bechuana] grew out of early encounters and exchanges among all the dramatis personae of the colonial frontier; also, that its narration into common usage owed a great deal to the pioneer evangelists. Prior to this, the autonomous polities and confederations of the interior were seen primarily to consist in the followings of their ruling dynasties. Together, these polities (*merafe*) formed a constellation of interacting peoples (*batho;* human beings), their humanity distinguished from non-Tswana *banna ba ditshaba* ("men of the tribes"; Maingard 1933:599f.; *RRI*:244).

For their part, the evangelists came to perceive and re-present the "Bechuana" with reference to a social geography that divided them into "tribes," and ascribed to them a primordial identity based on common ancestors and origins, language and lore, culture and customs, sentiments and interests (cf. Harries 1988).[39] Most nineteenth-century evangelical volumes came to include an elementary classification of tribal groups and clusters, a word list, and material on economy, society, religion, government, and "natural" characteristics. This material later found its way into mission ethnographies and anthropological writings on the Tswana (e.g., J. T. Brown 1921, 1926; Willoughby 1905, 1923, 1928, 1932; into dictionaries (e.g., J. T. Brown [1875] 1987), grammars (e.g.,

Crisp 1905; Sandilands 1953), maps (e.g., Campbell 1822) and typologies of languages and "dialects" (e.g., J. Mackenzie 1887,1; Broadbent 1865); and, of great significance for the formation of a modern ethnic consciousness, into vernacular school texts (e.g., R. Moffat 1842:570f.; see volume 3). It also foreshadowed the cultural and political cartography of modern southern Africa, the ethnoscape on which colonial rule (and later apartheid) was to be built. The organization of the evangelical field itself gave living expression to the emerging ethnology of the frontier: divided into "Griqua," "Hottentot," "Bechuana," and other missions, its districts and stations paralleled the ethnic and tribal categories it had helped to formalize.

Ethnic consciousness, we would argue, has its origins in encounters between peoples who signify their differences and inequalities—in power, economic position, political ambitions, and historical imaginings—by cultural means. Typically, it is the subordinate, not the dominant, who are first marked and named. (Hence it is that, prior to the British colonial presence, peoples in servitude to Tswana were ethnicized and labeled, while the latter remained relatively unmarked and unnamed.)[40] As this suggests, collective identity is everywhere a relation, nowhere a thing (Comaroff and Comaroff 1992:51). Viewed thus, the construction of "*the* Bechuana" as "a people" (see, e.g., R. Moffat 1842:236), the genesis of their own ethnicity in its modernist sense, occurred in response to the (increasingly unequal) terms in which they were engaged by significant others along the colonial frontier. European evangelists played an especially important role in this process. Their challenge to those whom they called Bechuana took many forms: apart from all else, they insisted that the Africans give coherent account of their own practices; that they hear their "custom" (*mekgwa*) condemned by Christian teaching, itself couched in the universalist language of reason and enlightenment; that they agree to the fact that "native" ways were degenerate and backward, and ought forever to be put aside. The teleological cast of the civilizing mission, as we noted before, did not welcome the possibility that two systems of knowledge, each with its own ontology, might coexist or be spliced together. Consequently, Southern Tswana found themselves being asked, in various ways, to objectify their own culture, *setswana*, by contrast to "European ways."

As we have seen throughout this and the previous volume, the documentary record is replete with dialogue, transcribed by missionaries, about the differences between *setswana* and *sekgoa*. These accounts are decidedly equivocal. And revealing. On one hand, recall (*RRI*:245), the evangelists often wrote that Tswana saw the ways of the whites to be clearly superior; on the other, we are told that they "could not see . . . anything in [European] customs more agreeable . . . than in their own" and, sometimes "laughing extravagantly," would "pronounce [ours] clumsy, awkward, and troublesome" (R. Moffat 1842:247–48). In truth, the Africans seem to have been more bemused than amused. They certainly made clear their difficulty in understanding why *setswana* and *sekgoa* should not coexist and comingle, why one should be adjudged better than the other; hence the Tlhaping elder who said to the burgers of Cape Town that the ways of "each [were] best for those who were used to it" (G. Thompson 1967:166; above, p. 140). Here were resonances, once again, of the confrontation between a universalizing and a relativizing worldview. As the colonial encounter took its course, Southern Tswana would give living expression to theirs: they would cull new cultural forms, large and small, from the fusion of the two worlds. Meanwhile, however, they responded in varying ways to the demand to choose between knowledges, traditions, deities. Those closest to the mission often *did* distinguish themselves from heathenism in the ways called for by the clergymen; others combined a public Christian persona with the private practice of *setswana*. But many more responded by not recognizing the duality at all.

It goes without saying that the *content* of any ethnic identity is a product of complex, drawn out historical processes: being a heterogeneous, fluid ensemble of signs and practices, a living culture is forged not merely in conversations, but also in the minutiae of everyday action, in the inscription of linguistic forms and material relations, in the course of struggle, contestation, and creative self-assertion. Here, however, we wish to highlight four points about the manner in which "Bechuana" identity was re-presented by the evangelists back to Southern Tswana themselves—in their schools, courts, churches, and other contexts—and, then, to the whites of colonial South Africa.

First and foremost, "the Bechuana" were portrayed as a people governed by the primal sovereignty of their "custom" (*mekgwa*, the concept now had vernacular denotation; see above). No matter that they had different chiefs and lived in different polities. No matter that they lacked any overarching identity hitherto, nor seem to have shared a proper noun. Every one of them, allegedly, was bound together by a common, ineluctable attachment to the ways of their ancestors. By their very "nature," moreover, they followed their traditions with little question (e.g., J. Philip 1828,2:118). This, the clerics told themselves, was why it had proved so difficult to sow the seeds of rational self-interest among them; so difficult to make all but a few "separate themselves," thus to become citizens of God's Kingdom. Even when attracted by aspects of mission teaching, they did not easily put aside their old ways. Even when they took on the trappings of civilization, they still "prefer[red] the customs in which they [had] been brought up" (J. Mackenzie 1871:397). What is more, Robert Moffat wrote (1842:249–50; emphases added):

> [T]he national council [is] the stronghold or shield of the native customs, in which speakers have, in masterly style, inveighed against any aggression on their ancient ceremonies, threatening confiscation and death to those who would arraign the wisdom of their forefathers.

Evangelists continued to report the stubborn hold of *mekgwa*—such as bride-wealth (Jennings 1933), initiation,[41] and "taboos" (Willoughby 1928, 1932)—well into this century, long after most Southern Tswana had joined the church. These reports, like the notion that "the Bechuana" were unreflectively submissive to ancestral usage, might have been based on a misreading of processes of cultural exchange and transformation. But that is beside the historical point. For the Europeans, the primal force that bound these people together, the sovereignty of *setswana*, was inherently and self-evidently conservative, communal, antimodern. By very virtue of being ethnic Bechuana, in sum, they were benighted subjects in a kingdom of custom. Shades here of an idea which, until recently, had wide currency in Anglo-American social science: that ethnicity, especially expressed in "tribalism" and/or "traditionalism," is inimical to modernity. Also its corollary: that the removal of difference is a *sine qua non* of the worldly progress toward universal civilization (see Geertz 1963; cf. Gellner 1983, 1987).

Moffat's reference to "the *national* council" is also telling since, strictly speaking, none existed.[42] It presaged the vision, which spread largely unremarked among colonial evangelists, of a (supratribal) Tswana ethno-nation. The germ of the idea, of course, was implicit both in the term "Bechuana" and in the imputation of a shared allegiance to the primal sovereignty of *mekgwa*. Here lies the second of our four points: that, increasingly, "*the* Bechuana," in the singular, were re-presented as a grouping with common concerns above and beyond those of the "tribes" (i.e., chiefdoms) which formed their everyday political communities (see below). At times this entity was made out to be much like a modern European nation. Witness, again, Jules Verne's novel, written in 1872, about a scientific expedition to South Africa. Taking its ethnographic background from early mission texts, it tells of the arrival of the scientists at a Tswana capital and of a ceremony in which they and the local ruler pulled each others' noses "according to African custom." All of which, Verne (1876:47) said, turned the Europeans into "naturalized Bechuanas."

This romance reminds us of something else as well: it was in their encounter with others, real or imagined, that nineteenth-century Europeans refigured and refined their own images of nationality and moral community. In this process, Africa, and the evangelical enterprise, assumed considerable salience (Stuart 1993:379). The mutual nose-pulling—sometimes also leg-pulling—makes the point well: the construction of collective identities here was not a matter of one party imposing its own, mature form of ethnicity or nationhood on another. It was one in which both participated in the reciprocal gesture of fashioning self and other. As bodies touched so did bodies politic. Each recognized the other, in both senses of that term, and both were transformed—if not, in the long run, equally or in the same way.

For the evangelists, in the meantime, it was a short step from the conclusion that Tswana shared a collective identity to the assumption that they "naturally" shared rights and interests. And so, from the 1830s onward, the missionaries refer repeatedly to what might harm or advance the commonweal of "*the Bechuana people*." Here as elsewhere, the road from primal sovereignty to the "rightful" claims of an ethnic group was tarred with myths and mirages. But it was also paved with good intentions. Many of the Nonconformists saw themselves as "protectors of the natives" against the predations of other colonizers.[43] In this role, as we know, a number of them became deeply involved in imperialist politics. Joseph Ludorf's representation of the Southern Tswana at the Bloemhof Commission, and his subsequent manifesto for a "United Barolong, Batlhaping and Bangwaketse Nation" (*RRI*:283–86), was only one dramatic instance—although it was particularly illuminating since he proposed the founding of an independent ethnic nation-state with a legislature, a system of courts, a charted territory, a militia, and a constitution that fused *setswana* and European statecraft. A few years later, two "Bechuana" polities *were* established, albeit as "possessions" of the United Kingdom: the Crown Colony of British Bechuanaland (later absorbed into South Africa to become, under apartheid, Bophuthatswana) and the Bechuanaland Protectorate (after 1966, Botswana).[44] There is no denying that the exertions of the evangelists contributed much to making these ethno-national polities thinkable in the first place. They also prepared the ground for the colonial state to sow its own special brand of tribal politics.

To the extent that it was shaped by the encounter with Europe, Tswana ethnic consciousness was also the product of other, less overtly "political" exchanges. As the chiefdoms became part of the British Empire, their shared identity was given substance by fusing received signs, styles, and images with new ones—many of missionary provenance. Some of the latter transcended the boundaries of the parochial: Christian elites, for example, gathered under the banner of the cross, distinguished by their English clothes, and uniformed converts came to see themselves as citizens of the "Nation of God." Yet, at the same time and in counterpoint, the rise of "tribal" churches—like the folk dress of the countryside—expressed a visible sense of *setswana*, positing it as one among many rural ethnicities in southern Africa.

So, too, did the development of print media. Both the WMMS and the LMS made initial efforts to establish vernacular newspapers in the late 1850s, and a monthly was produced in Kuruman between 1883 and 1896; according to Plaatje (1916:5), it enjoyed a wide readership among "peasants in Bechuanaland and elsewhere." The titles of these publications—*Molekoli oa Becuana* (The Bechuana Visitor); *Mokaeri oa Becuana* (The Bechuana Instructor); and *Mahoko a Becoana* (Bechuana News)[45]—all presumed a similar *national* audience, albeit in slightly varying orthographies. It was no accident that they emerged during the second half of the nineteenth century in these and comparable African communities along the colonial frontier (M. Wilson 1971:74). To the evangelists, news-papers served as tools for shaping self-conscious, "informed" civil communities. As Benedict Anderson (1983:63) has argued, they were significantly implicated in the imagining of modern national identities, both colonial and metropolitan. By refracting world events into the universe of local readers, they generated a sense of common experience, of a "solid simultaneity through time." Yet these very media also made some nations seem more worldly than others, others more parochial and tribal. The image on the masthead of *The Bechuana Visitor*, for example, showed a "civilized" party of Europeans, complete with its national colors, stepping ashore on a generic "native" beach.

The mission monthlies were a mix of religious exhortation, announce-ments, and letters from African readers within the church and beyond. They also reported on current events, not least on skirmishes between warring parties along the frontier. In so doing, they helped to create the very social identities they presupposed. It is not surprising, then, that the first Setswana newspaper to be owned and published by blacks in Bechuanaland should have been called *Koranta ea Becoana*, "The Newspaper of the Bechuana."[46] Or that its proprietor and editor should have been prominent mission school alumni. Between 1901 and 1908, *Koranta* wrote with pride of achievements in Tswana language and culture, and printed arguments in defense of "national" interests and entitle-ments. Significantly, it also voiced the distaste felt by educated elites for the primitive connotations of tribal labels. And it spoke out, at times, for a more modernist African nationalism, one centered on the universal rights of individ-uals, irrespective of race, culture, or creed.

But—and this leads to our third point—there was an anomaly here. While "the Bechuana" (singular) were being conjured up as an ethno-nation with its own rights and interests, these peoples (plural) inhabited a world in which ev-eryday political processes occurred within and among *local* chiefdoms. (Note that *morafe*, Setswana for "polity," was rendered in mission dictionaries as "tribe" *and* "nation," and was used to describe both a chiefdom and "the Bechu-ana" at large; *RRI*:306.) In acting on behalf of "the natives," furthermore, evan-gelists usually represented specific sovereigns and their subjects, not the ethno-nation at large; it was mainly to this lower level, in fact, that their day-to-day interventions in affairs of state were confined. As we saw in volume 1 (pp. 306f.), it was also in this context that Southern Tswana were instructed in the language of legality and governmentality; that they learned the parole of colonial politics and collective self-representation; that they were encouraged to see their "tribes" as antecedents, in miniature, of the European nation-state. We noted there too that Tswana rulers were quick to absorb the ethno-speak of imperial diplomacy, if not always to use it with great conviction (cf. Ramsay 1991). Thus it was that, in 1884, Chief Montshiwa agreed to a treaty with the Crown in the argot of constitutional nationhood;[47] that he wrote, or had written, a string of letters in similar vein claiming legal entitlements and protections for his people;[48] that, in 1903, his heir asked the Colonial Secretary, on behalf of the "Barolong *Nation*,"[49] to recognize "our rights and privileges as loyal citizens." In short, once the terms of this discourse were internalized, they became part of collective imaginings—and self-assertion—at *both* the levels to which the term *morafe* had come to apply.

Take just one example, which is revealing precisely because it had little to do with colonial diplomacy or dealings with whites. Sometime during 1917 or 1918 there arose a "Barolong National Council" with its head offices in Johannesburg. In April 1918, it called a meeting of "All Chiefs, Leaders, and Headmen of the Barolong People," to be held at one of the rural capitals. On the agenda were a "discussion of the constitution"; arrangements for collecting "national funds" with which to buy stock, a farm, "and other landed property"; and a consideration of anything "deemed advisable to the general welfare of the people."[50] "National" identities of this kind were reinforced, in South Africa, by the deployment of tribalism in the system of "native administration" that evolved after 1910. In the Bechuanaland Protectorate they became part of the structure of indirect rule. They survived into independent Botswana, where they correlate broadly with the district administrative divisions. Minorities in the country today protest that this excludes people who do not fit into the Tswana *merafe*. Or into the ethnology, developed during the colonial era, that remains the basis of collective entitlement (Durham 1993).

Fourth and finally, parallel to the construction of Tswana ethnicity went the progressive erosion of chiefly dominion. As we have seen, most evangelists, especially early on, treated local rulers with respect, abetted them in their dealings, and promised not to interfere in matters of state; some, by contrast, subverted those who opposed the gospel; one or two came to see the chief*ship* per se as an obstacle and urged its disestablishment (Dachs 1972). Conversely, sovereigns varied in the degree to which they succeeded in using the mission to their own ends, those to the north doing notably better than those closer to the frontiers of white settlement (Gulbrandsen 1993). Over the long run, however, such differences were relatively inconsequential. By forcing a wedge between the secular and the sacred, and by introducing alternative bases of empowerment, the presence of the church itself wrought wide-ranging changes in vernacular politics. This was exacerbated by the colonial state: both in South Africa and in Botswana—albeit much more so in the former—"native" legal jurisdiction was narrowed, indigenous potentates were made into tax collectors and civil servants, and the scope of tribal administration was redefined. And so, ironically, the more Tswana discovered and asserted a collective identity founded on "traditional" affinities, the less any "traditional" political figures had the wherewithal to represent their concerns. There were exceptions, obviously. A number of royals remained influential well into this century, especially in Botswana. And a few, on occasion, took it upon themselves to act for "the Bechuana"—most famously the three chiefs who traveled to London in 1895, accompanied by Willoughby, to protest the transfer of Bechuanaland to the British South Africa Company (see, e.g., Maylam 1980; Ramsay 1991; chapter 4).[51] But such things occurred less and less as the colonial state undermined local authority and divided as it ruled: the objectification of "the Bechuana," as an ethnic group with an awareness of its own objectives, unfolded amidst a deepening legitimation crisis in South Africa and a gradual process of corrosion in the Bechuanaland Protectorate.[52] It was against this backdrop that new forms of political association, action, and representation—the congress and union movements, parties, and the like—would emerge during the twentieth century.

Drawing all this together, then, the discourse of primal sovereignty played into the refiguration of "the Bechuana" as an ethnic group with inalienable rights: the right to perpetuate itself, to speak its own language, to occupy its own territory, to follow its own leaders and customs, to husband its own interests. At the same time, however, *setswana*, the "stuff" that made these people what they were, was said by European colonizers to be inescapably parochial, persistently primitive; it had to be erased if individual Africans were to be remade into African individuals and, as such, into citizens of the modern world. The fact that Southern Tswana had their own elaborate repertoire of rights, their own ideas of sovereignty, their own practices of personhood and property, went largely unrecognized. Further, because everyday vernacular politics were "tribal"— they were translated into the refined language of English civics only to be ceded to the Crown—the capacity of "the Bechuana" for autonomous self-representation was being eroded even as they were emerging into modern nationhood.

In the colonial discourse of rights, as this suggests, the attribution of primal sovereignty had a paradoxical quality. Apart from all else, it was erected, to use the argot of critical postmodernism, on an impossibility: in order to make "the Bechuana" into civilized moderns, it was deemed necessary to unmake what it was that made them Bechuana in the first place, to remove the differences that made them different; yet, because "they" had been objectified into an ethno-nation with primordial roots and collective rights *in perpetuity*, this was literally undo-able. Here, however, is only where the incongruities begin. Colonialism, *sui generis*, is widely acknowledged to have led to the invention—or, at least, the self-consciousness—of groups that did not exist before, groups that were said to have rights which were only made palpable by virtue either of their absence or of their being given up. It was only because "Bechuana" land was being seized by Europeans that "Bechuana*land*" was said to exist by right and to require protection (if only so that it might "voluntarily" be alienated, as a "possession," to British control); only because indigenous authority was being superseded by the state that a right to sovereign autonomy was articulated (if only so that local rulers might formally "petition" for overrule); only because the language of command had become English that the right of self-expression in Setswana was essayed (if only so that Tswana might submit to the Crown in their own tongue). Here in short, was a world of virtual realities, a world in which things existed primarily by the recognition of their nonbeing.

To those who lived within that world, however, its realities were far from virtual. Indeed, they were *made* real enough to become the basis of a self-constructed, assertive identity, a charter for a different history, another form of sovereignty.

The civilizing mission had not set out to contrive a world of virtual realities, of course, nor to abet the machinations of the colonial state. To the contrary, it had dreamed—naively, perhaps; paternalistically, for sure—of a very different kind of political landscape, a very different kind of moral community. Nonetheless, these were the implications of the processes in which it had involved itself. And they had a deeply sinister side to them. Since peoples like the Southern Tswana were held to have rights as a consequence of their membership in an ethnic group, it was also possible to remove those (or other) rights on the same basis—and, by appealing to legalities in doing so, to make it appear entirely legitimate and reasonable. As we shall see, because of its ostensibly "premodern" infrastructure, primal sovereignty was used to dispossess and disenfranchise black South Africans from the time of colonial overrule through the age of apartheid. But more of that in a moment.

CONTRADICTION, CONSCIOUSNESS, CONTESTATION

Others, besides the Crown . . . and the Plough of the Transvaal, have also rights. Alas! for the wrongs and the blood that cry to heaven against the souls of certain Europeans! Certainly, the great day of account is not far! The African races will yet be free under the banner of Christ.

Montshiwa, Bakhobi, and Moikechoe, 1870[53]

Contradictions, Recognized and Unrecognized

Most of the evangelists saw no contradiction, no disjuncture in the discourse of rights, between the register of radical individualism and that of primal sovereignty; indeed, they did not explicitly distinguish them at all. The effort to implant modern, right-bearing individualism might have pointed toward a society of *universal citizens*, while the conjuring up of a primordial Bechuana identity gestured toward the creation of *ethnic subjects*. From their perspective, however, the two were part of a seamless campaign to rework the indigenous world, one describing that world as it ought to be, the other as it was. The former, in short, was a narrative of becoming, of revealed "civilization" and increasingly, as the twentieth century dawned, of "modernity"; the latter was a narrative of being, of congealed "tradition."

In fact, for the mission, the universal citizen and the ethnic subject, liberal individualism and primal sovereignty, were conditions of each other's possibility—if for reasons not readily reflected on by the Europeans at the time. British colonialism, and colonial evangelism, was everywhere a double gesture. On one hand, it justified itself in terms of difference and inequality: the greater enlightenment of the colonizer legitimized his right to rule and to civilize. On the other, that legitimacy was founded, ostensibly, on a commitment to the eventual erasure of difference in the name of a common humanity. Of course, had the difference actually been removed, the bases of overrule would themselves have disappeared. It was not; they did not. Colonialism, in short, promised equality but sustained inequality; promised universal rights but kept the ruled in a state of relative rightlessness; promised individual advancement but produced ethnic subjection. In church and in state. In South Africa as elsewhere, the discourse of radical individualism and modern personhood bore the promise; the discourse of primal sovereignty and ethnic subjection, the *realpolitik*. It was by virtue of the latter, too, that "the Bechuana" were engrossed within a larger, more inclusive form of marking, of coloration and devaluation: that of race, in which all shades of non-European ethnicity, all kinds of colonial otherness, were finally submerged. The evangelists might have seen themselves as "friends of the natives." But, like their compatriots, they tended nonetheless to view Africans as inferiors, as rude beings only now entering "racial adolescence" (Willoughby 1923:239). They might not have taken black inferiority to be an immutable fact of nature; yet, to most of them, Tswana were, by and large, still a long way back on the great evolutionary road of Universal History (see volume 3). Had this not been so, the civilizing mission would have had no reason to be.

We said that *most* evangelists at the time did not see the disjuncture between liberal individualism and primal sovereignty. One or two did. John Mackenzie's dreams for "Austral Africa" sought to overcome it by envisaging a colorless citizenry in which "natives" would eventually be indistinguishable from anyone else (*RRI*:293). There ought to be no reservations, he argued, no tribal protectorates, no special entitlements for ethnic or racial groups (see Holmberg 1966:55f.; K. Hall 1975:102; Lovell 1934:48f.). Just imperial subjects with equal rights. For Mackenzie, this was the only way to deal with the antinomy between universal citizenship and traditional attachments, between the perpetuation and removal of difference—though, patently, he would not have put it this way. There is an instructive lesson in his exceptionalism. Mackenzie, the most vociferous imperialist among the clergymen, seems to have realized that the rhetoric of primal sovereignty would be used against the Tswana by white colonials as long as their rights depended on their ethnic and racial identity. He wrote (1887,2:456):

> There is nothing in the superstition or the customs of these tribes to disqualify them from exercising their rights as subjects of the Queen, when education enables them to do so. . . . There is nothing whatever in the character of the South African native to deter us from trusting him with the exercise of . . . 'rights' after the manner of the English constitution.

To withhold these "inherent rights" on the basis of color or race, tribe or nation, he added (1887,2:461), "is a deadly delusion."

Double Consciousness, Double Standards, and the Denial of Rights

As we have already intimated, the language of primal sovereignty was to be used, over the long run, to disenfranchise and disable blacks in South Africa,[54] thwarting their efforts to become free, right-bearing, propertied citizens. In this respect, recall our earlier point that Southern Tswana, one and all, had been familiarized with the *realpolitik* of rights on the frontier; that some discerned in it the "English mode of warfare"; yet that many, most notably the rising elite, had internalized the Protestant ethic and, with it, an idea of community based on the spirit of liberal individualism. It was predictable, then, that "the Bechuana," both as an incipient ethno-nation and as a congeries of chiefdoms, should fight the implications of overrule in the language of entitlement, invoking it to protest against their loss of autonomy, the seizure of their territory, the imposition of taxes, the conditions of wage labor, and so on. It was also to be anticipated that, in this struggle, both they and the colonizers—statesmen, settlers, manufacturers, mine managers—would exploit the contradictions between individual and communal rights, between the rights of private citizens and those of ethnic subjects.

Let us give just one, especially pertinent example drawn from the history of contestation over rights in this colonial theater. It concerns the Land Commission set up by the British authorities in 1885, soon after the establishment of the Bechuanaland Protectorate and British Bechuanaland, but before the latter was absorbed into the Cape Colony and then South Africa.[55] Like many such commissions, its mandate was to clear up conflicting territorial claims among local "tribes," and between them and white settlers, thus to pave the way for Pax Britannica. Its more self-interested aim, arguably, was to gather intelligence and lay the geopolitical foundations for overrule in the interior.[56]

Among the disputes heard by the commission was a minor wrangle between the Tshidi-Rolong and the Ngwaketse over some 432 square miles of remote pasture that lay in their shared borderland. Montshiwa, the Tshidi ruler to whom it was awarded, used the occasion to press for the introduction of individual land ownership, with registered title. A canny non-Christian chief—

but a strong ally of the WMMS in his later life (above, chapter 2)—he had learned well the language of liberal individualism. In particular, he was aware of the salience of private property to British notions of civility and modernity. Montshiwa held that, if freehold were granted and deeds lodged with the government, the latter would have to protect Tswana proprietors from settler expropriation. According to Tshidi informants many years on, he also thought that the creation of individual property rights might prepare the ground for other kinds of rights as well; but there is no documentary trace of any of this. What we do know, however, is that Montshiwa, strongly backed by his advisers, put the case in a manner that would have done the early evangelists—and John Stuart Mill—proud: those who had occupied the land, he said, deserved to own it because they had "improved" it. And they would do so even more if they had secure, permanent, heritable possession.[57]

As it turned out, other chiefs followed the line taken by Montshiwa and, for much the same reasons, also made the case for individual title. But the commission rejected their argument: the Southern Tswana were simply "not ready" for it. Shillington (1985:174) stresses how cynical[58] was the blanket denial of African rights to private ownership. Notwithstanding the recommendations of Mackenzie and several "native" spokesmen, the *Report* (Great Britain 1886a:12) said that sovereigns ought still to hold the land "according to native custom" as trustees for those using it on "communistic" principles; until "the people" requested it, a better system of tenure under "separate . . . deed" could not be introduced. But the people *were* asking for it. Or, at least, their royal representatives were, for the latter were fully aware of how "customary" tenure was being used to discount their holdings, personal and collective. As one Tlhaping ruler insisted, the *only* way to ensure that his "farm" did not become a "location" was to secure it by title (Shillington 1985:176). He and his compatriots were told, however, that the "communal system" was better protection against the alienation of their land. In a final, parenthetic irony, the rhetoric of custom was turned back on the whites: Chief Mankurwane, as we said earlier (chapter 2), used the commission to challenge the LMS ownership of land and water resources at Kuruman. Despite the claim of the evangelists that they had bought these holdings, he insisted that they could only have been granted leave to use sites which had never been saleable under tribal law. But, unlike the chiefs, the LMS won its case.[59]

Montshiwa protested the outcome to the colonial authorities, contending that customary arrangements in his own realm had been flagrantly and repeatedly violated for the sake of white interests. But history had turned the received script inside out: here was a "heathen" chief invoking universal rights and arguing for the introduction of private property, only to be held to his own "custom" by Europeans who posed as agents of enlightened modernity—but insisted on the primal attachment to tradition of a people who were explicitly demanding to set it aside. A subsequent commission, the influential South African Native Affairs Commission of 1903–5,[60] was to declare that "the Native population as a whole *instinctively* cling to and cherish the communal system" (South Africa 1905:26; our italics). Moreover, it went on (p. 27),

> [while] it is largely held to-day, that individualism is ultimately conducive to greater industry, enterprise and production, . . . our limited experience has not in all cases furnished proof of this.

Having been told for almost a century that "healthy individualism" was both the means and the measure of their move toward modernity, black South Africans were to be informed that, even if they no longer "cherished" their communal ways, *their* kind of individualism was somehow different, lesser. More immediately, however, in dismissing the Tshidi case for private tenure, the Bechuanaland Land Commission simply ignored the fact that most of the intended recipients of titles were highly educated mission school alumni and members of a propertied elite. To wit, the commission never deigned to ask *who* the landowners would actually be. Their rationale for rejecting the request— the tacit appeal to the sovereignty of custom—did not admit a discourse of individuation. Even more, it actively denied it. After all, the nub of primal sovereignty is the notion that, in their "natural" (instinctive?) attachment to their ways, ethnic subjects are all alike.

In the end, Montshiwa won a compromise: the territory—which was to fall into the Bechuanaland Protectorate (not British Bechuanaland, thence South Africa)—could be divided up into farms and leased, on an annually renewable basis, to individuals. But its ownership had to remain, "according to native custom," with the ruler and the chiefdom. Interestingly, after these farms were distributed, the terms of their leases were never enforced. They were treated by everyone concerned as if they were freehold. The nature of their tenure was to remain ambiguous until Botswana became independent, whereupon its government declared the matter finally resolved: the Barolong Farms, as the territory was called, was "tribal" land.

The Commission of 1885, like innumerable others to follow it, did not just deny the possibility of private property (and other) rights in the face of indigenous demand. Nor did it merely obstruct a move in the direction of liberal individualism. It also frustrated the *collective* capacity of a community and its leaders to remake their own world by due process. Until overrule, Tswana chiefs regularly legislated changes in social policy, often transforming institutional, residential, and material arrangements in response to historical contingencies and shifts in popular opinion (see, e.g., Schapera 1943c, 1970; J. L. Comaroff 1973). Prior to the British presence, there was no reason why Chief Montshiwa should not have introduced some form of individual tenure through internal legislative procedures, provided that there was sufficient support for the measure. Certainly, other sovereigns had made laws (*melao*) in the spirit of liberal modernity. But the colonial state effectively put paid to that possibility by asserting the sovereignty of custom above all else. At a stroke, the historical dynamics of Southern Tswana politics were severely debilitated.

This, we stress, is just one example. There are many more. From the notorious Land Act of 1913 through a series of laws and other enactments, "non-Europeans" were cumulatively denied individual rights or prospects of citizenship. The process began when the Commission of 1903–5 recommended that blacks should only have limited, indirect franchise (South Africa 1905:97). And it culminated in the thoroughly racinated culture of apartheid, which was legitimized by direct appeal to primal sovereignty: to the notion, first, that "natives" naturally preferred their own traditions to the alien practices of European modernity, and ought therefore to live by them; and, second, that they lacked the enlightenment, as individuals, to determine their own being-in-the-world. But that is a well-known story, a narrative that runs almost up to present.

*****

Colonialism in South Africa, then, from its genesis in the civilizing mission to the age of apartheid, bequeathed Southern Tswana a double consciousness to match the two-faced character of the discourse of rights itself.[61] One and all, they were encouraged to embark on the road to modernity, to fashion themselves into citizens of the civilized world. At the same time, as black Africans, they were made into ethnic subjects, ineluctably tied to their fellows, to their primal origins, and to *setswana*, a body of custom which marked them as premodern—and which was invoked to deny them the kind of personhood to which they were exhorted to aspire. Precisely because of the paradoxical, polymorphous nature of the discourse of rights, as we said before, Tswana came to know themselves, and their objectified "tradition," at once by attribution and erasure; by virtue of a positive construction of identity and by its negation. *Setswana*, to those who shared it, was a highly valued possession, the cultural product of a proud history. It still is. Yet, through much of the colonial epoch, "the Bechuana" had to hear that it was better set aside. Is it any wonder that they should have contested European domination sometimes by asserting their universal rights as citizens of empire, sometimes through rebellions that seemed at once to embrace and parody the fierce communalism attributed to them? These forms of politics—which gave voice to the double consciousness of the colonized, ethnic subject—have not been confined to South Africa. Ethnicity everywhere at once constructs people, placing them definitively in space and time, and effaces them, submerging their individuality and opening them up to the stigmatization of otherness. In some circumstances, it also affords them a basis to protest the contours of the world as they find it—but often, in doing so, confines them to an ethnicized Tower of Babel, a universe of competing identities. Clearly, the discourse of rights is one of the terrains on which all this occurs, both under colonialism and after. For Southern Tswana, it was central in shaping their sense of themselves, past and present.

And future.

Contestation: Back to the Future, 1992—?

In the contemporary struggle for South Africa, the two dominant styles of formal black politics—represented by the African National Congress (ANC) and the Inkatha Freedom Party (IFP)—are each heir to one of the registers in the colonial discourse of rights. A sizeable communist membership notwithstanding, the ANC has always stuck close to the ideology of liberal modernism first implanted by the Nonconformists; it grew out of the South African Native National Congress, formed in 1912 to protest the Land Act, and was led largely by mission school graduates. The SANNC spoke the language of civil and constitutional rights, relying heavily on rhetorical styles learned in the mainstream churches. Thus, for example, when its leaders fought against the Act, they argued that it had deprived "natives" not only of the right to individual title, but "of the bare human rights of living on the land, except as servants in the employ of whites" (Plaatje n.d.:28). In its dealings with successive governments, moreover, the SANNC took a position more notable for its progressive individualism than for its populism. While it envisaged a nonracial democratic South Africa, its spokesmen (they *were* all male) argued resolutely that blacks who had improved themselves ought to enjoy all the entitlements attendant on their achievements. Ethnicity was deliberately ignored: the SANNC was steadfastly supra-tribal, even pan-African, in its composition and its horizons, and avoided any hint of identity politics. It was also emphatically British in orientation and nonviolent in its technologies of protest. As we all know, its efforts were not rewarded. Although there are some important differences,[62] the ANC, which has always had a substantial Tswana following, retains much of the disposition and political ideology of its predecessor—albeit oriented energetically toward the present. It continues to talk the language of rights and universal citizenship; as Hobsbawm (1992:4) recently intimated, it has sustained its commitment to a classically European form of nationalism and nationhood (see J. L. Comaroff 1996). Significantly, in negotiating the future, its leaders have paid painstaking attention to the promulgation of a liberal democratic constitution—despite having been pushed to concede collective rights and protections along ethnic and racial lines.

By contrast, the assertively Zulu-centric IFP owes its origins to the politics of primal sovereignty; in particular, to the creation, under apartheid, of "homelands" for tribal groupings congealed during the colonial era. The ideology and political style of Inkatha have always been ethno-nationalist in tenor: since cultural identities run deeper than any other kind of attachment, goes the familiar argument, their bearers have a "natural" right to determine their own affairs and to be ruled by their own ("traditional") authorities. If a South African nation is to exist at all, then, it ought to give ethnic communities a high degree of autonomy, reserving to the state only those functions that cannot be devolved downward. The objective here is to secure collective entitlements—rather than unencumbered universal suffrage or individual rights—in a federated, pluralistic polity. The kind of politics that pursues this objective is typically fought along lines of ethnic cleavage, often with so-called "cultural weapons" both rhetorical and military. It is also inconsistent: the IFP leadership is ardently pro-capitalist and, when it is deemed appropriate, will resort to the distinctly nonindigenous vocabulary of modernist, free market political economy.

Inkatha, of course, is primarily a Zulu phenomenon.[63] But similar claims were heard, before the first free national elections in 1994, in some circles within Bophuthatswana and other "homelands"; also among white conservatives. So much so, in fact, that a "Freedom Alliance" was formed, in the run-up to the elections, among parties led by homeland "leaders" and right-wing Afrikaners. Underlying this coalition was a shared belief in primal sovereignty and the "natural" rights of ethnic groups. For those accustomed to reading South African history purely as a narrative of racial struggle, the establishment of this *Freedom Alliance* must have been an irony of cosmic proportions. Politics by parody, almost. After all, it brought together long-standing racial enemies in common commitment to an ideology of race. One last, closely related point here. Most of the recent violence in South Africa, and in other places torn by similar forms of struggle, has not been perpetrated between just any "tribes" or ethnic groups; between, as the popular media and populist stereotype would have it, irrational people caught up in an irrational desire for the blood of others. While it certainly *has* perpetrated horrific acts of cruelty and obliteration, and *is* often justified in the idiom of cultural difference, this violence has tended to occur very specifically across the line, the epistemic abyss, that divides primal sovereignty from liberal individualism; between, that is, two contrasting ontologies of personhood, polity, subjectivity, modernity (J. L. Comaroff 1994). The colonial discourse of rights—its contradictions, paradoxes, and perversities intact—continues to make itself felt as a new dawn rises on the South African postcolony.

CONCLUSION

It goes without saying that colonizing processes did not work out in exactly the same way throughout Africa. In British Tanganyika (Sweet 1982) and French West Africa (Snyder 1982), for example, the state encouraged individual landholding and private property more than it did in South Africa and other places with large settler populations. Nonetheless, the colonial encounter *does* appear everywhere to have involved a discourse of rights—a discourse in which local peoples were cast as ethnic subjects, racinated, and engaged in an often agonistic dialectic of construction and negation.

We reiterate, as we rejoin our larger story, that colonization was never a monolithic movement through which an expansive Europe imposed itself, systematically and inexorably, on peripheral populations. It may have been a world-historical process. But it played itself out in multiple registers and in disconcertingly ambiguous ways. Never just, nor even mainly, an affair of states and governments, an epic orchestrated by heroic figures, it was carried on in thousands of contexts, both mundane and magisterial, by castes of characters with different means and ends. As we have seen, moreover, it was often a messy business, wherein Europeans—settlers, evangelists, capitalists, administrators, army men—fought among themselves in the effort to impress their wills on the bodies, the being, the terrain of others. These differences among colonizers, to be sure, did not do much to ease the experience of the colonized. For despite the complex dialogues and exchanges it opened up, the power of overrule lay in its (relative) capacity to reduce complexities to brutal, black-and-white contrasts. And, sometimes, to brute coercion. But visible differences in the master class *did* create an awareness of ruptures and incoherences in European control; ruptures at which local resistance was directed, and in which new hybridities could take root.

Note, too, that many of the "civilized" practices exported from Britain to the colonies were hardly uncontested at home—not least rights to property, to fair work conditions, to the franchise. As even a cursory reading of John Stuart Mill (1965,2) makes clear, peasant proprietorship and private smallholding were not deeply entrenched in the English countryside, despite efforts to essay their virtues by, among others, Mill himself (cf. Holt 1992:322–23). Some contemporary "condition of England" novels, like Disraeli's *Sybil*, actually rehearse the arguments for and against individual tenure ([1845] 1980:91–94); this text, itself a strident polemic for the "rights of labour," also suggests that struggles over civil and constitutional rights in the colonies were implicated in debates about the situation of the British working class (p. 343). As in the case of the bourgeois home, the imperial frontier was not a place where a mature ideology of rights was presented, fully tried and tested, to premodern Africans. It was a space in which the unfolding sociolegal and political histories of Britain and Africa met—there to be made, reciprocally, in relation to each other.

One final observation here. It returns us to the *ur*-theme of this volume, now moving toward its close. For all its association with legalities, the introduction of a modernist discourse of rights to "the Bechuana" and other African peoples was not merely a matter of law. Inasmuch as it bore within it an elaborate ideology of personhood, of social contract, of material relations, it involved, as some of the missionaries themselves understood (J. Philip 1828,2:355; J. Mackenzie 1975:72), a cultural revolution. The fetishization of rights, in short, was itself part of an embracing worldview, one in which, self-evidently, the language of entitlement appeared liberatory. That is why colonial evangelists saw liberal individualism as an emancipation from the enchantment of custom and communalism, from the tyranny of tradition and the chiefship.

For Tswana, the promise would prove more equivocal—as it tends to be from the perspective of the colonized. Endowed with a culture whose faiths and fetishes were not the same, they were quick to learn that "[without] equality . . . all rights are chimeras" (Fuentes 1992:211–12). They learned, too, that law was very much a two-edged sword. On one hand, it was a devastating weapon of warfare, like no other in its capacity to annihilate and dispossess without being seen to do anything at all. And yet the appeal to rights was a means that, over the long run, came to be used by black South Africans in self-protection. Not always successfully, but not always in vain either. More to the point, it often seemed to be the *only* real means to hand, since it was part of the technology of rule on which rested the inequalities and disablements from which they suffered. This is why the language of the law is reducible neither to a brute weapon of control nor simply to an instrument of resistance. The inherently contradictory character of the colonial discourse of rights, the multiplicity of its registers and the forms of consciousness to which it gave rise, ensured that it would be engaged, on all sides, in the effort to forge viable moral communities, identities, modes of being-in-the-world. It still is. Everywhere.

NINE

CONCLUSION

*Generally speaking, there has been a complete revolution from the abject
condition of existence [of earlier times]. . . . A new way of life, with new
deeds, new thoughts, new vision, and new orientations, new physical, mental and spiritual possibilities and capacities has been* revealed *to the African. . . . This complete* revolution *has, in the first place, been due to the
quiet, patient unobtrusive missionary, the mainspring of African evolution.*

S. M. Molema (1951:191–92)

W E BEGAN VOLUME 2 with the closing scenes of a colonial
drama. We end it, writing from Mafikeng-Mmabatho in the
"new" South Africa, at the opening of the postcolonial epoch.
As we said in the Preface, "real" beginnings and endings are
never very neat. Nor is "real" history ever respectful of clean epochal breaks.
Yet this seems an appropriate juncture, a moment of transition, from which to
reflect one last time on the story we have told; also, on the terms in which we
tell it. Even more appropriate is the site, this hyphenated city on whose landscape has arisen a living archaeology of the South African past: founded at "the
place of rocks" (*mafikeng*) by a Tswana Christian, it remains the terrain of a
long-established chiefdom, was made internationally famous by an imperial
siege, became the capital of a colonial protectorate, was built under apartheid
into the toy-town hub of an "independent homeland," and is now a provincial

center under the political control of the ANC. Here history meets the present, chronology and context intersect, the future is being set in motion.

Given its situation in space and time, this vantage seems especially apt. For the "revolution" that brought down Bophuthatswana in March 1994, culminating in the killing of cadres of the *Afrikaner Weerstand Beweging* (the Afrikaner Resistance Movement), was understood to settle a score with history: with a history of deeply drawn, racinated lines of opposition, a history of protracted, intermittently violent struggle (Lawrence and Manson 1994:447, 461). In actual fact, local relations among the peoples of the region, not to mention the distinctions and conflicts among them, were always much messier, more inchoate than this suggests; less black and white, less sharply dualistic, less recalcitrant and clear-cut. But, at moments of crisis, such subtleties tend to dissolve. Old cleavages, real *and* imaginary, reassert themselves. Thus, while the popular uprising in Mmabatho pitted itself against a black ruler, it was directed, finally, at the regime for which he stood. President Lucas Mangope had long been seen by many as a "sellout" to, an icon of, apartheid. A "dog of the Boers" (Lawrence and Manson 1994), he was long known, too, for courting conservative Afrikaner nationalists—some of whom scurried vainly to his rescue. The vast majority applauded his fall; though there are those, not limited to the bourgeois bureaucracy he cultivated, who now lament the benefits that passed away with his reign.

In short, beneath the tangled play of events lay a genealogy of contrasts and antinomies, finely etched in the perceptions of those involved, between settlers and indigenous peoples, colonizers and colonized, ruler and ruled. Such distillations of the past, in which the record is purged of many of its nuances, cleansed of much of its untidiness, is intrinsic to the ways in which human beings imagine and inhabit the present. As Edmund Leach (1954) observed a long time ago, it is as necessary to the models of social actors as it is to those of the social scientists who study them. In this sense, the recent academic preoccupation with the evils of essentialism, valid though it is, often misses a crucial point: that all representations of social life must limit its infinite variety and fix its flux; that all depend in some measure—and sometimes for tactical purposes—on "working" essentialisms, on "as if" constructions (Leach 1954). The crucial question is how this is done, to what degree and effect; also, whose interests are served, whose subverted. Empiricists notwithstanding, even the most unvarnished descriptions entail editings of a kind: they compress and classify, smooth and simplify, parse and proportion. As we all know, a great deal of debate turns upon the various strategies and models deployed in scholarly efforts to order the world by arranging it into meaningful fragments. And upon the dangers of confusing representations of reality with reality itself—or with the processes of reification by which it is produced.

Likewise, to return to the historical context with which we are concerned here, in life-as-lived along colonial frontiers, inside imperial borderlands: in these messy, evanescent worlds, human beings construct themselves and others, subjects and objects, by means of working essentialisms, by compressing and editing dissimilarities, by fixing the flux of everyday existence.

During the nineteenth century, recall, Southern Tswana condensed the colonial world, for perceptual and practical purposes, into the opposition between *sekgoa* and *setswana*. As we have seen, they—depending on their class, age, gender, and so on—ascribed dissimilar values to the things for which these terms stood; sometimes they argued openly over them, sometimes they differed in silence. But the antinomy itself distilled a highly ambiguous, fluid field of relations and practices into a pair of working essentialisms, ideological tropes with tangible consequences. This antinomy did *not* exhaust the multiple, polymorphous ways in which people lived their lives. Nor did it pay heed to the ways in which the content of *setswana* and *sekgoa* changed, hybridized, and were contested over time. To the contrary, the very point of imaginative dualisms lies precisely in reducing the inchoateness of everyday experience. Of course, such compressions usually have some basis in existing realities. And, tautologically, they dispose human beings to make social facts in their mold. Tracing the production and circulation of these imaginative constructs thus throws light on historical questions of the longer-run. Here, for example, it makes sense of an issue that long puzzled us: why it is—despite all the twists and turns of past actions, events, and attitudes, despite complex patterns of relationship, resistance and alliance, despite the irreducibility of the past to black-and-white— that coarse-grained oppositions and antagonisms remained salient to Southern Tswana for well over a century. Or, more accurately, *remain*. In 1996, Tswana graduate students at the University of the North West, talking articulately about their own history, continued to insist on seeing it, above all, as a narrative of domination. Of an uneven struggle, with lines clearly drawn, between colonizer and colonized.[1]

In seeking to discern patterns and processes amidst the dense interactions—of persons, objects, signs, practices—that constructed "Bechuanaland" in the nineteenth century, we have perforce made editorial decisions of our own. One was to tell the story at several levels simultaneously. At the most general, we take the *leitmotif* of this period of Southern Tswana history to be their incorporation, under the European *imperium*, into a global order of capitalist relations (*RRI*:4). But we have argued that the way in which it occurred was not overdetermined either by its outcome or by the social physics that brought it about. Looked at up close, the dynamics that drove colonialism and the rise of modernity, although usually spoken of in the language of universalism, were always particular in their workings. And they were domesticated in various ways, depending on local contingencies. At this level, where the lines of sameness and difference were redrawn, colonization was not a matter of abstract forces. Its course was shaped by the quotidian: by words and signs and things exchanged, by gestures understood or misrecognized, goods rejected or consumed, tastes and identities subtly altered. Hence our focus on the manner in which Christian images and rites were received and redeployed in everyday contexts; how plows were put to work, transforming agrarian production and relations among producers; how money changed senses of value; how cotton dresses, brass bedsteads, and window panes were implicated in the refashioning of people and their habitations; how discourses of individual and collective rights refigured personal and political being. How, that is, for the likes of S. M. Molema (above, p. 405), a new world of possibility was revealed, a quiet revolution effected.

These quotidian processes linked Tswana to factory hands in Lancashire, indigo producers in Bengal, and proletarians elsewhere across the empire; to captains of industry, colonial merchants, and charitable churchgoers among the bourgeoisies of London and Liverpool. Mediated by the market and caught up in the global logic of class formation, all alike were encouraged to situate self and other with reference to a putatively universal grid of difference: as civil or savage, modern or primitive, European or native, Christian or heathen, cosmopolitan or tribal. We have entered into the flow of transactions and interactions involved in this history through a singular window: that opened up by the long conversation between Southern Tswana and Nonconformist missionaries, themselves vanguards of a sustained British presence in the South African interior and self-styled standard bearers of a cultural revolution. The encounter, we have suggested, provides an especially revealing vantage on the dialectics of colonialism, on the making of European modernity, and on the exchanges through which colony and metropole constructed one another.

This vantage only gives access to part of the story, however (see *RRI*:6). We have never claimed that Protestant evangelism, alone, *determined* the processes we describe. Quite the opposite, the case of the missionaries, wilful agents in the making of history, is itself used to explore the limits and complexities of historical agency. Thus, for instance, we have shown that their niche in the imperial division of labor constrained their political effectiveness (*RRI*:Chap. 7). Even as moral reformers, their influence depended largely on the cultural and material baggage that, wittingly or not, they took with them to the frontiers of Christendom. The goods and values they proffered had strings attached, strings capable of binding Africans to the hegemonic forms of British capitalism, its commodities and its culture. The LMS and WMMS saw it as part of their crusade to promote those ties, to usher in money and merchants, to instil the kinds of knowledge and dispositions that anticipated colonial economy and society—and, above all, the labor market. The forces set in train by their actions eventually escaped their control, sometimes to their palpable discomfort. By the late nineteenth century, the modes of civility championed by them—possessive individualism, commercial production, wage work, contractual relations, ethnicized identity—were also being pressed on black South Africans by other colonizers, usually with less Godly intentions. What would have happened, we have been asked,[2] had Protestant missions never established themselves among Southern Tswana? Would not the same processes have occurred, if more brutally, as a result of colonial capitalism alone? The question is useful, but not for the obvious reasons; rather, because it underscores how we differ from those who would see colonialism primarily as a product of political and/or economic forces, forces merely qualified by cultural factors. In our view, it is always to be understood, *at once*, as economic and cultural, political and symbolic, general and particular. Indeed, colonialism was intrinsic to the rise of modernity in Europe, itself a historical movement whose universalizing ethos was indissolubly material and moral, secular and spiritual. We have tried to show, after Weber, just how integral to early British industrial capitalism was Christian political economy, and *vice versa*. Subtract Protestantism from the equation and capitalism, if it had evolved at all, would have been something altogether different, something perhaps more like the various capitalisms that developed beyond, if not independently of, western Europe. We would argue the same for colonial capitalism in nineteenth-century South Africa. Without the civilizing mission, it would not have existed in the way we know it; just as the mission, and the humane imperialism that propelled it, could not have taken the shape it did without the rise of industrial capitalism in its modern, bourgeois form.

This does not mean that the relationship between the Nonconformist mission and colonial capitalism was simply one of functional complementarity or common cause. It was not. Drawn from different class fractions within a complex, changing, and conflicted social order both "at home" and abroad, those associated with the church, business, and the state often found themselves at loggerheads over specific issues and interests. Nonetheless, there was also a profound resonance, over time, in the modes and consequences of their activities; the spiritual, financial, and civic ends that each pursued, in their own ways, were closely interdependent. All were driven by the theology and practices of the free market. All ostensibly conducted their enterprise under the authority of the nation-state. All alike were products, in sum, of the elective affinity, the reciprocality, between Protestantism and industrial capitalism—from which arose many of the distinctive cultural forms of modern bourgeois Europe.

Here, in treating the connections between the Protestant mission and colonial capitalism—as in dealing with the impact on each other of Africa and Europe—we stress the analytic salience of *dialectical* processes, processes of reciprocal determination (above, Chapter 1). Some scholars, working with a more orthodox idea of the dialectic, have seen our appeal to the concept as unwarranted, especially in light of our insistence on the open-endedness of the colonial encounter. Elizabeth Elbourne (n.d.:13f.) for example, a considered and careful interlocutor, remarks on the fact that we rely on a "dialectical model . . . *despite* . . . so often and so valuably underscoring the indeterminacy of meaning" in our historical narrative (our italics). She concludes that the model, when and how we use it, proves "excessively rigid." This shortcoming, allegedly, is not ours alone. It is shared by other cultural and literary scholars; specifically, those preoccupied with "the self" and "the other," definite articles both, who, having read Hegel in improperly materialist terms, reduce his master-slave interdependency to innate psychological processes and/or concrete political relations.

As we noted in volume 1 (p. 14), we are ourselves uneasy with most literary critical approaches to colonialism, although we see their problems to lie in something more than a vulgar reading of Hegel. To the degree that they envision history as a matter of representation, and culture as text, they tend to make the study of colonialism into an exercise in the analysis of discourse and dialogics, of European self-fashioning through the prosaic refiguration of others. All of which occludes social practices and institutional forms, material conditions and the realpolitik of everyday life. Our own approach eschews the existence of psychic forces cut free from their cultural, political, and economic contexts. "Selves" and "others"—always plural, indefinite articles—are precipitates of the meaningful practices and power relations that configure colonial societies. From this standpoint, social worlds cannot be the products of conversation alone, however cogent the latter may be as a heuristic metaphor (see Chapter 1, n. 73). To be sure, metaphors are *not* analytical constructs; the conflation of the two has subverted some of the most suggestive work of literary critics-turned-social theorists. In our view, as we have said before (1992:11), the historical anthropology of colonialism ought to address itself to dialectics rather than just to dialogics; "dialectics" again, *pace* Elbourne, understood not to refer to tight teleological processes, unfolding according to one or another rigid historical "law," but to the mutually transforming play of social forces whose outcome is neither linear nor simply overdetermined. Defined thus, it is hard to imagine how colonial history could be regarded as anything else.

The identification of our approach with literary criticism, even postmodernism, by some historians (see pp. 39f.) points to a deeper disquiet with the methods of historical anthropology: a sense that we rush in with "theory" where more patient chroniclers fear to tread, imposing premature order on the "full complexity" of the documentary record. We *do*, it is true, seek to abstract broad outlines from a messy profusion of events "on the ground," although we also try to capture something of their richness and complexity. How otherwise to account for them in more general terms? How otherwise to rise above the purely idiographic which, as anthropologists, we are committed to do? We find no contradiction in discerning dialectics amidst apparent disorder, or determinations amidst indeterminacies. That, if anything, is our objective. Even more, it is how we understand history to be lived. As we said above (Chapter 1; cf. *RRI*:21f.), not all signs and meanings are ever drawn up into its critical processes; not all become terms of consensus or contestation. Nonetheless, the happenings with which we are concerned here had a palpable logic: structures of inequality and exploitation were established, racialized distinctions were inscribed on the landscape, hegemonies emerged that turned hybrid realities into discriminating dualisms, elites and underclasses in Europe and Africa became implicated in each others' lives and identities. These are common characteristics of colonial encounters—whose mix of shared and unique features is crucial to grasp as we confront the yet more perplexing blends of sameness and difference that compose postcolonial worlds.

There is a real distinction, then, between the kinds of question we engage and those that detain more conventional historians of colonialism. It is a distinction that evokes long-standing disciplinary differences: differences between the ideographic and the nomothetic, between the effort to arrive at the fullest possible description of events in their infinite particularity and the desire to pick out general principles across space and time. The latter, patently, demands a certain boldness of abstraction; it is inherently risky. And while, in practice, most histories and historical anthropologies hover somewhere between the two extremes, visible contrasts of emphasis and expectation remain.

To wit, some historians would like us to have paid less attention in volume 1 to dialectics and determinations, more to the minutiae of events and actions involved in the making of colonial Bechuanaland; to the endlessly complicated "fudging[s] across the fault lines" of its social landscape and the "messy struggles" for control over its cultural exchanges.[3] The present volume has taken up some of these issues. But it remains the case that this is neither an event history of "the colonisation of the Southern Tswana" nor a chronicle of the indigenization of Christianity; each, after all, is the subject of an earlier study (Shillington 1985; J. Comaroff 1985). Rather, it addresses what was, when we began, a relatively neglected dimension in the historical anthropology of colonialism, one that raises very broad theoretical issues: how modernity, rooted in the development of capitalism in Europe, took on its particular forms in Africa and elsewhere; how those forms emerged out of the interplay of religion and political economy, meaning and power, both "back home" and abroad; how the metropole was itself affected in the process of its confrontation with "others"; how this process gave rise to cultural struggles, accommodations, hybridities, and new hegemonies. In relation to these issues, and to our central thesis, the kind of details called for by a more conventional historical sensibility, as Elbourne (n.d.:23) herself says, would merely have complicated our narrative. Not discounted its claims. We believe, obviously, that they would also have confirmed yet further the conceptual arguments laid out at the beginning of this work and elaborated in each of the chapters along the way.

More generally, by way of closing comment, it is our own view that there is ample room for a variety of approaches to the study of colonialism in South Africa. None of them will ever exhaust the interrogation of this, or any other, aspect of the past. As the nation enters the post-*apartheid* epoch, there are many fresh histories to be written, many old ones to be revised. The advent, in the late twentieth century, of a newly proportioned global order, and of a further stage in the life of capital, makes this all the more urgent. If we are to grasp the continuing present and its histories-to-be-made, it is crucial that we comprehend the forms of economy and society that preceded it, forms that came to maturity in the age of empire.

*****

And so we move on to the third and final part of our study. It addresses the place of education, broadly conceived, in the encounter between the Southern Tswana and the Nonconformists; indeed, in the colonizing process as a whole. Modern Protestant evangelism was impelled by a faith in the universal human capacity for improvement. If the whole world was its parish, it was also its classroom. The civilizing mission was above all a pedagogic crusade. As we pointed out in volume 1 (pp. 233f.), schooling was the model for conversion, conversion for schooling. What is more, education in its modern, secular form—as a privileged means, that is, of producing bourgeois selves and national subjects—arose partly in consonance and partly in dissonance but always in dialogue with Protestant instruction. While the state took control of mass schooling in Britain during the nineteenth century, in South Africa missions long remained *the* major source of Western learning for indigenous peoples. This, in turn, had significant implications for the disposition of the black intelligentsia that emerged in the early 1900s; also for the formation of African national consciousness *tout court*.

As the evangelists in the interior passed from an era of pioneering optimism to one of sober routine, pedagogy became ever more central to their labors and scenes. Schools were the most condensed loci of their effort to change hearts and minds and mundane habits. Places of careful design and anxious investment, they were made to serve as windows onto a world beyond parochial horizons. Tswana valued much of what was offered in the Christian classroom, and saw to it that skills like literacy circulated widely beyond its walls. But they also had their own ideas of socialization and the acquisition of cultural knowledge. European *thutho* ("learning"), and the universe it proposed, were regarded with ambivalence by many. That ambivalence deepened during the late nineteenth century as educational institutions were ever more implicated in colonial overrule itself. Emblems of a new order in the making, these institutions became charged points on a disputed frontier: sometimes bastions, once quite literally a fortress, sometimes outposts of an insidious affront on local self-determination. In the upshot, schools were often turned into sites of strident struggle, sites where lives were put on the line. And so they would remain—portals of promise and places of dispossession—through the *apartheid* years to the Soweto uprising of 1976 and on into the new South Africa. Where, as we write, old enemies battle still over the almost magical power of pedagogy to bring hoped-for futures into being.

It is these portals that we enter in volume 3.

APPENDIX

The first impression of volume 1 contains several errors. Most are simple typographical mistakes not caught (or in some cases, especially in the Index, not corrected) before that volume went to the printer. They include the misrendering of Mackenzie as MacKenzie (pp. xviii, xix); of Mafikeng as Mafiking (p. 5, map I); of Gcaleka as Galeka (pp. 204, 402); of Cory as Corey (pp. 269, 344, 361, 400); of Richard Elphick as Robert Elphick (pp.364, 401); of M. H. C. Lichtenstein as W. H. C. Lichtenstein (p. 374); of David Brion Davis as Peter B. Davis (pp. 362, 400); of the Setswana term *bogosi* as *bokgosi* (pp. 129, 148–49, 257, 261–62). In addition, on p. xix (line 3), the word "formerly" should read "formally"; on p. 345, in n. 61, the date given for the Shineberg reference in parentheses should be 1971, not 1961 (it is correct in the bibliography). In the index, Ashton is misrendered as Asthon (p. 396); Berlin, Isaiah as Berlin, Isiah (p. 397); Khoisan as Khosian (p. 404); Mankurwane as Mankkurwane (p. 406); Moffat, Robert as Moffat, Robert U. (p. 408); Molema (Tshidi-Rolong headman) as Molema (Tshidi-Rolong chief) (p. 408); Montshiwa (Tshidi-Rolong chief) as Montshiwa I (Tshidi Baralong chief) (p. 408); *Nkosi Sikelel 'iAfrika* as *Nkhosi Sikel iAfrika* (p. 409); Peel, John D. Y. as Peel, John D. W. (p. 409); Philip, John as Phillip, John (p. 409); Sontonga, Enoch as Sothongo, Enoch (p. 412); and Turner, Terence S. as Turner, Terrence S. (p. 413). Also, the dates after "Anglo-Boer War, First" (p. 396) should be "(1880–1881)" not "(1880–1901)." In the Bibliography, the pagination for Comaroff, J. and Comaroff, J. L., 1989, "The Colonization of Consciousness in South Africa," *Economy and Society,* 18, should read 267–96, not 267–95 (p. 360); and the entry under Trexler, Richard C., 1984, should read "We Think, They Act: Clerical Readings of Missionary Theatre in Sixteenth Century New Spain" (p. 390). Finally, on p. 69 in the text, our phrasing suggests that George Whitefield was an eighteenth-century Methodist; he did, in fact, have strong connections with Wesley and Methodism, but died a Presbyterian. Most of these errors have been eliminated from later printings of the volume.

An altogether more substantial mistake, albeit not of our making, appeared (and remains) on p. 74, where we reproduce a lithograph (circa 1841–45) attributed to Henry Alken. This picture came to our attention in Asa Briggs's *Iron Bridge to Crystal Palace: Impact and Images of the Industrial Revolution* (1979:6); indeed, it was to differ with Briggs's interpretation that we included it in the first place. In 1989 we wrote to the Iron Bridge Gorge Museum Trust for permission to reproduce the work from the Elton Collection, and asked for a photograph. In doing so, we specifically identified it (sending along a photocopy) as the Alken drawing, and duly received both the photograph and permission. A year later, we visited the Elton Collection for the first time and, to our great surprise, found the illustration (under the title "Rail Triumphs over Road") ascribed to George Leighton (1826–95), previously "an apprentice to the famous printer Baxter." We have no idea how the trail of misattribution began or was perpetuated; as it happens, it makes little difference to our comments on the picture. However, we record the error—which is repeated in our list of illustrations on p. ix—for the sake of scholarly accuracy.

NOTES

WE FOLLOW THE same conventions as we did in volume 1. All primary materials are annotated in endnotes; so, too, are newspaper articles. Published writings, other than newspaper articles, are cited in parentheses in the text itself (by author/year), and listed in the bibliography at the end. (References to *RRI*, accompanied either by a page or chapter number, are to the previous volume.) Wherever possible, archival documents are located by author/source, place of writing, date, and storage classification (category, box-folder-jacket; or, if applicable, just box). Note that CWM is the Council of World Mission, whose papers (which include all the records of the London Missionary Society [LMS]) are housed at the School of Oriental and African Studies (SOAS), University of London. So, too, are those of the Wesleyan Methodist Missionary Society (WMMS). The correspondence and reports of the Paris Evangelical Missionary Society (PEMS/ SMEP), at the Bibliotèque Nationale in Paris, could only be read from microfiche. In this case, documents are located by author, place, date, microfiche category and number; see the *Guide to the Microform Collection, Paris Evangelical Missionary Society Archives 1822– 1935* (Départment Evangélique Français d'Action Apostolique, 1987). The papers of Tswana communities, kept in their so-called "tribal offices," are listed by chiefdom, capital, file name, date and, if possible, title. References to the Molema-Plaatje Papers, in the Library at the University of the Witwatersrand, follow the listings in the inventory compiled by Marcelle Jacobson (1978). Unfortunately, the Willoughby Papers, at Selly Oak Colleges, Birmingham (U.K.), are less than systematically catalogued; they are identified as best as possible in each instance. All other unpublished sources are fully annotated where they are cited and/or quoted.

Four further points of explanation are also in order here. They concern our references to early mission British publications and newspapers. First, some of these publications—for example, the *Evangelical Magazine and Missionary Chronicle* and *Missionary Sketches*—often printed articles, *sans* authors, in which communications from one or more evangelists were excerpted or summarized by anonymous editors. We cite these under the missionary society that published them. Second, the *Missionary Magazine and Chronicle* appeared in two forms: as a journal in its own right and as an enclosure within the *Evangelical Magazine and Missionary Chronicle* [EMMC]. In its first guise, it had its own volume numbers and pagination; in its second, it was included within those of *EMMC*. Hence the same reports, letters, and articles may be referenced in quite different ways. In general, we cite the versions in *EMMC* as they tend to be more accessible in libraries. Third, a few of the missionary society journals—for example, the *Chronicle of the London Missionary Society*—were not given volume numbers at all. In these cases, in addition to the year of publication, we add the month in parentheses before page numbers. Fourth, we discuss a large number of pamphlets, broadsheets, primers, and the like that were printed at the Tswana stations for local distribution and use. Since these were not strictly publications, and cannot be obtained save at a few reference libraries, we annotate them in endnotes along with other evangelical archives; they are not included in the bibliography. Articles in contemporary local newspapers, similarly inaccessible, are treated in the same way for much the same reasons. They, too, are annotated in our endnotes.

O N E

1. The name referred most immediately to the dam, itself a popular recreation spot, alongside which the park was located. It memorialized Lotlamoreng Montshiwa, chief of the Tshidi-Rolong between 1919 and 1954.

2. Mutwa describes himself as such in the foreword to his controversial book, *Indaba, My Children* (1966:xiii), written to "tell the world the truth about the Bantu people." His mother, he says, descended from "an unbroken line of Zulu witchdoctors"; his father was a Catholic catechist in southern Natal. Mutwa was hired by Lucas Mangope, then President of the putatively independent "homeland" of Bophuthatswana, to design and build the Lotlamoreng Cultural Park. He made his home in Mafikeng and seems to be enjoying a new career as "prophet, poet, psychic, and story-teller" in the new South Africa (Hazel Friedman, "Sounds of Celebration," Weekly Mail Internet Domain, usr/spool/ftp/wmail/9504/950428/).

3. Tom Nairn, "Nationalism Is Not the Enemy," *Observer Review,* 12 November 1995, p. 4.

4. Advance publicity gives a sense of the motives in the minds of its planners. The park seems to have been designed to appeal to a cross-section of consumers, both black and white (many of whom visited Bophuthatswana to revel in the "pleasures"—from gambling to interracial sex—denied them by the apartheid state). The marketing of leisure in this "homeland" was dominated by the South African businessman Sol Kerzner, whose Sun City complex, with its Rider Haggard fantasies, has more humble echoes in Mutwa's creations.

5. Observe the use of the present tense. It underscores the fact that the ideal-typical, rather than the historical, is the conceptual dimension in which this model was (and occasionally still is) framed.

6. Sometimes claims of this sort are made less in ideal-typical terms than with putative historical precision. Jameson (1990:44f.), for instance, argues for the coincident emergence, in 1884, of "the new imperialist world system" and cultural modernism—and for the demise of both with the formal end of colonialism. Thus he discusses James Joyce and the Irish colonial situation almost entirely as a function of a contemporary global moment, as if there had been no past to the English presence in Ireland.

7. Like many terms in the literature on colonial and postcolonial discourse, *neo-imperialism* has antecedents in earlier writings on the encounter between the West and its others; in this case, in the analysis, by such Marxist theorists as Amin (1974) and Leys (1974), of neo-colonialism. Likewise, *hybridity* recalls *syncretism; double consciousness,* which has its own African American genealogy, evokes *schismogenesis;* and so on.

8. And this in spite of Horvath's (1972:45) comment that the "academic establishment possesses no widely accepted theory of colonialism, nor does any substantial

agreement exist upon what colonialism is." We were made aware of this statement by Julian Go, a graduate student in sociology at the University of Chicago; we should like to record our debt to him. In an excellent essay on imperialism and colonialism, Go notes that, even "in the most recent wave of 'colonial studies,' [it is hard to find] explicit definitions."

9. The phrase is Fuentes's. It is a fragment from *The Orange Tree* (1994:5): "Observe then, . . . how decisions are made when time presses and history suppresses. Things could always have happened exactly opposite to the way the chronicle records them. Always."

10. A number of scholars—among them Raymond Williams (1976:131f.) and Etherington (1984) himself—have tried to resolve the problem of defining imperialism (i) by excavating the archaeology of the term and (ii) by recognizing that its very contestation is part of its meaning (see below, n. 24).

11. This was central to all species of Marxist theory, of course (see, for just one overview, Phillips 1989:5ff.); in fact, our very phrasing here evokes Magdoff (1978:118f.). But even those who did not themselves agree that colonialism necessarily involved exploitation (e.g., Lüthy 1964:27f.; Fieldhouse 1981:7f, 1982:380f.; cf. Gann and Duignan 1967)—or who, like Nadel and Curtis (1964:3), agreed only reluctantly and with qualification—often accepted the fact that it had come to be seen in this light.

12. For obvious reasons this was especially true of theories of imperialism and colonialism that focused on the political (rather than the economic) dimensions of overseas expansion (see Nederveen Pieterse 1989:15f.); it still is. But it was commonly a feature of popular conceptions as well—hence the familiar image of the world map, circa 1870–1945, covered in the red of imperial Great Britain.

13. The question of the difference (indeed, the relationship) between colonialism and imperialism is more complex than this suggests. However, because we are concerned primarily with the former, and because so much of a specialist nature has been written on the topic (see, e.g., n. 26 below), we do not pursue it further here.

14. The words quoted are from the *Penguin Concise English Dictionary* (1991:147); see also the *Oxford Paperback Dictionary* (1983:121) and Delavignette (1964:9), who, some thirty years ago, observed that "'Colonialism' is a fairly recent term signifying 'an imperialist policy of exploiting colonies to the profit of the mother-country alone.'" Dictionary definitions tend also to embrace the settlement of emigrants from the metropole, a matter to which we anthropologists pay less heed in our conceptual discussions (see n. 11 above).

15. Because these features are discussed in most works on colonialism (including those listed here), there is no need for citations. But Delavignette (1964:8–9)—whom we mention several times precisely because his is an older, more conventional text—stressed all of them at once. He noted that colonialism usually took the form of *political* expansion; necessarily became "a matter of State"; involved exploitation for material profit; was built on physical, ethical, and sociological distance; and was centered on a "metropolis."

16. In a recent grant proposal, George Steinmetz, our colleague, argued that, with a few exceptions, scant attention has been given, in colonial historiography, to *theorizing*

the state—or to relevant conceptual writings on the topic in sociology and political science. And this in spite of its (presumed) centrality in colonialisms everywhere. The point, which is also cogently made by Phillips (1989:10), Kaviraj (1994:23f.), and Nederveen Pieterse (1989:xiif, 8f.), is well taken.

17. Given the large body of writing on the topic, it is hardly necessary to point out any longer why colonialism cannot be explained as a reflex of the rise of capitalism. Or why Marxian models of underdevelopment were flawed. (For an impressively concise, yet insightful summary, see Phillips 1989:1–13.)

18. As Hechter (1975:8–9) points out, the concept itself was not new. He dated it back to Lenin and Gramsci, and noted that it had recently been used by sociologists in Latin America; more importantly, it was being deployed in the 1960s by ethnic minorities in the U.S.A. to define their own situations (p. xvi; cf. Blauner 1969).

19. "Internal colonialism" was the phrase chosen by Ken Saro-Wiwa to characterize the treatment of the Ogoni people by the Nigerian state. He was hung at Port Harcourt in November 1995, ostensibly for murder but in fact for his political activism on behalf of the Ogoni cause. His *Detention Diary* (1995), in which the comment is contained, was not yet published at the time of our writing this; we came across it in a version excerpted by the *Observer Review,* Sunday 3 December 1995, pp. 1–2.

20. The general point has been made by, among others, Stoler (1989:passim; 1995) and Thomas (1994:12f.); the former makes it with particular cogency. It is reinforced by Saro-Wiwa's accusation (above, n. 19) of internal colonialism against the Abacha regime in Nigeria.

21. For just one vivid example, see Livingstone (1974:75); other parallels drawn between blacks and Boers are mentioned in volume 1 and in chapters 3 and 6 below. (See also Ranger 1982a, who reminds us that Britons in South Africa also likened Portuguese to Africans.) Interestingly, in *The Master of Petersburg,* J. M. Coetzee (1994:180), who is familiar with English representations of Boers in South Africa (see 1988:29f.), elides class and coloration in a quite different context: late nineteenth-century Russia. He speaks of the lowly of St. Petersburg as the "black poor."

22. This cannot be put down merely to differences of historical perspective, to ideological struggles, or to disparities of the imagination, important though they are. As we are reminded by Cain and Hopkins (1993:6), among others, colonial situations *did* vary. Colonies were subjected to a range of governmental arrangements and to greater or lesser measures of direct violence; they did not share the same constitutional status, and suffered or enjoyed—depending on one's vantage point—markedly dissimilar material conditions.

23. There already *is* a vast review literature, of course; yet another addition to it, from us here, is in any case unnecessary. But our point is more principled: because we hold that a general theory of colonialism is impossible, our engagement with efforts to arrive at one could only be negative. And there is little profit in that.

24. Kemp (1967:1) makes a similar point about the scholarly effort to define imperialism, itself an ideological and political act: "To attempt a definition," he offers, "is already to adopt a position." It is one of a species of politically and intellectually problem-

atic terms, adds Tomlinson (1991:4, after R. Williams 1976), *all* of which are contested and can only be understood with reference to the discursive contexts, the "real [political] processes," of which they are a part.

25. We mean, for these purposes, the period initiated by the age of revolution, 1789–1848. The colonization of South Africa has a much longer history, of course (see Chronology), although the European presence in the interior only began to make itself widely felt in the early nineteenth century.

26. Particularly of Marxist theories of imperialism. For a sympathetic account of these theories see, e.g., Kemp (1967); for a much more critical one, Brewer (1990). Among the huge number of texts on the topic, those by Etherington (1984), Nederveen Pieterse (1989), Semmel (1993), and Cain and Hopkins (1993) stand out for the clarity and/or the insight with which they discuss the historical connections among imperialism, colonialism, and capitalism.

27. For the opposite view, see Kaviraj (1994:25f.), who claims that the state was the "controlling structure" at the epicenter of the colonial world. This, we believe, is belied by much African history.

28. Gluckman, Mitchell, and Barnes (1949:passim) used the term to refer to headmen in Central Africa. The "intercalary" position of these men, caught between the British administration and their own followers, derived from the fact that they were made, *de facto*, into colonial functionaries.

29. Gallagher and Robinson (1953, repr.1982) had it that, beyond the visible purview of the "formal" British empire, lay a huge "informal empire"; the limited horizons of the first being attributed to the reluctance of politicians to expand it further. While not ruled by governors or other personnel of state, this second empire fell under invisible forms of economic, cultural, and social influence emanating from London. For a brief but informative discussion of the argument, and its intellectual genealogy, see Cain and Hopkins (1993:7ff.); also Nederveen Pieterse (1989:12f.).

30. Although it did not take Great Britain long to annex the diamond fields, the grip of the colonial state on this "possession" was tenuous and uneven for many years (see, e.g., Turrell 1982:52f.). Not only did prisons remain in private hands, but much migrant labor came from beyond colonial borders. Even when it intervened in the recruitment of workers, the state often ran into difficulties; see chapter 4.

31. See, e.g., Marks (1990:115), who argues that daily life in Britain, "from diet to industrial discipline, from sexual mores to notions of governance," was "permeated by experiences of empire"; also Dirks (1992:21f.) and Stoler (1995:15). Stoler treats this as part of a move in nineteenth-century Europe toward viewing colonies more as "laboratories of modernity" than as "sites of exploitation."

32. But not always. Trotter (1990:4f.) claims that, some postcolonial writers notwithstanding, there were white colonizers who deliberately sought transformative experiences in the remote reaches of empire.

33. Orwell's (1962:108–9) comment is interesting: "[T]he attraction of India (more recently Kenya, Nigeria, etc.) for the lower-upper-middle-class . . . [is that] it was so easy [there] to play at being a gentleman. . . . Most clergymen and schoolmasters, for

instance, nearly all Anglo-Indian officials, a sprinkling of soldiers and sailors, and a fair number of professional men and artists, fall into this category. But the real importance of this class is that *they are the shock-absorbers of the bourgeoisie*" (italics added). This is reminiscent of our own characterization, in volume 1, of the colonial evangelists in South Africa.

34. For general discussion of "tensions of empire"—i.e., of patterns of conflict among colonizers—see Cooper and Stoler's (1989:609–21) introduction to a special number of the *American Ethnologist*, 16(4) on the topic (cf. also Cooper and Stoler 1997). The essay by J. L. Comaroff (1989:661–85) in that number lays out our own views.

35. For a notable instance, see Molema (1966:307–17). The term "non-civilized" is his; he also uses others of a similar sort to describe "the large mass" of "low grade . . . Bantu."

36. Again, for just one vivid case, see Brian Willan's (1984) biography of Sol Plaatje, which captures well the relations between African intellectuals and the English Christian liberals to whom they became close; also Plaatje (1996, 1973, n.d.).

37. See above, the fourth proposition. This, famously, was central to Said's *Orientalism* (1978), arguably the *fons et origo* of much postcolonial writing. But the point was also made in earlier texts, a few of which have also become part of the postcolonial canon(?), and some of which we have quoted—among them, Fanon (1963, 1967), Memmi (1965), and Sartre (1965).

38. Not always successfully, argues Thomas (1994:40ff.), who accuses Bhabha (1984) of reifying and reproducing the structure of colonial dominance rather than "pluralizing" or "disarticulating" it.

39. Coplan (1994:142) observes that we have been among those said to sustain "a dualistic view" of South African economy and society, and to depict rural blacks as people "of two worlds." It is true: we *have* been accused of just this, arising largely out of our essay, "The Madman and the Migrant" (1987, repr. 1992). Nowhere, however, have we ever argued for such a "dualistic view," let alone for the existence of "two worlds." Just the opposite; see, e.g., J. L. Comaroff (1980, 1982), Comaroff and Comaroff (1992:chaps. 4, 5). Our claim in "The Madman . . ." was that, in the late 1960s, older Tshidi-Rolong men (note the specificity) drew upon an *imaginative* opposition between *setswana* and *sekgoa* to come to terms with South Africa as they saw it, a society whose populations had long been part of a *single* material and social order; that they deployed this emic opposition in different ways—at times stressing continuities between the contexts of home and wage labor, at times asserting their disconnection—to make sense of their lives. How this is reducible to "a dualistic view" of economy and society is beyond us. The human beings of whom we wrote, it is true, made meaningful distinctions. These we accounted for by locating their voices and gestures (again, plural) in a complex poetics addressed to living conditions within an ever more complex, tightly integrated political economy—only to have our analysis caricatured in a variety of ways.

40. There is another side to the problem of stereotypy to which we return below; it was also mentioned in volume 1 (p. 126). It flows from the long-standing tendency to hold that non-Western cultures, being "cold" (Lévi-Strauss 1966:233f.) or "closed" (Horton 1967), do not actively seek out new forms of knowledge; or, when confronted

with them, either turn them aside or absorb them into existing, self-reproducing systems of signs and practices. (The use here of the ethnographic present captures the tenor of the claim.) The opposite was true of the world with which we are concerned in this study.

41. We repeat, lest our earlier qualification be forgotten, that we are speaking specifically of *modern* colonialism, the "new" European expansion of the nineteenth century (see *RRI*:8). Nor do we suggest that it—or the imperialism of which it was part—was a simple effect of the rise of industrial capitalism; hence our careful choice of words.

42. This point, and several others touched on here, are dealt with by Jean Lave (n.d.) in a discussion of the "epistemological everyday"; see her forthcoming book, *On Changing Practice*, a draft of which she kindly made available to us.

43. Interestingly, it is precisely the distance of the "everyday" from visible public institutions and practices—especially those which mark a particular epoch—that makes it an important site for historians who seek to trace continuity and change over the long run (see, e.g., Braudel 1981).

44. Arendt (1958:67) argues that Marx was not alone in seeing privacy, "in every sense," as a hindrance to the development of social capital; nor in believing that private ownership ought to be overruled in favor of the common weal. The idea ran to the core of modern society itself. The latter, she says, was born of the expropriation of church, monastic, and peasant holdings; it has always put collective interest above personal property.

45. In speaking of the "colonization of consciousness" in volume 1, we took care to show that Southern Tswana being-in-the-world was *not* simply eclipsed under the impact of colonialism (see also below, chapter 4, n. 114, for comment on Gable's 1995 elementary misreading of our argument in this respect). Hence (i) our treatment of the encounter between Africa and Europe as a complex, ambiguous process of mutual "challenge and riposte"; (ii) our insistence that it was a confrontation—between people possessed of the will and capacity to act upon one another—which, over time, transformed all concerned; (iii) our analysis of the failure of the Nonconformist effort to gain converts; (iv) our discussion of the difference between hegemony and ideology. Nonetheless, Southern Tswana and others like them *did* become subjects of empire, which, as many postcolonial scholars attest, had profoundly invasive effects.

46. A striking feature of the reviews of volume 1 is the consistency with which criticisms from one quarter are countered by others. For example, we are taken to task for mannered writing and for the use of jargon (e.g., Elphick 1992:184) and yet praised for the absence of the latter, indeed, for the clarity of our narrative (e. g. Fincham 1994:141) and the "grace" of our prose (de Kock 1992: 260); derided for our "fashionable" theorizing (I. Smith 1991:21) and commended on its promise (e.g., Elphick 1992:184–85; de Kock 1992: 260f.); censured for overinterpreting mission texts, thus eclipsing or misrepresenting the concerns of the evangelists themselves, and for not deconstructing them enough, thus allowing their perspective to invade our vision of the colonial past (Hexham 1993:500f.; du Bruyn 1994; Peel 1995); adjudged to have been too ambitious in our scope (Etherington 1992:213f.), and yet to have gained significant advantage by focusing in depth on a single case that cast a broad comparative shadow

(e.g., Kennedy 1992:395f.); had it said that we used too little archival or ethnographic material (by Crais 1994: 278, who asserts, breathtakingly, that we "have engaged in neither substantial archival research nor in any fieldwork") and that we used it not only in abundance but in a carefully principled, theoretically sophisticated fashion (e.g., de Kock 1994; Ranger n.d.[b]). On such things there seems very little point in commenting, just as, despite the temptation to do so, it is impossible to answer every criticism.

47. That social universe, patently, was very different from the one inhabited by contemporary Southern Tswana, although they did share some features. In our treatment of the two worlds, we did not pretend to give account of parallel or analogous practices, conventions, or institutions; neither did we do so in identical descriptive terms (which at least one reviewer seems to think we should have done; Etherington 1992:214). This would have been absurd, forcing similarities and equivalences where they did not exist. In each case we focused on what was experientially important to those concerned—in the terms that made the best sense of them.

48. Landau's book came out in Britain after we had completed all but the introduction to this volume, and had sent the manuscript off to press. We could not, therefore, take account of it in the chapters to follow. In general, we find the study illuminating, despite its criticisms of our own work. At the same time, we would have preferred to see it situated more firmly in comparison to other social histories of Bechuanaland; had Landau done this, we feel, he would have been compelled to modulate his broad claims about Tswana historical agency. In addition, some of his analyses (e.g., of nineteenth-century Tswana medical techniques and other cultural practices) are less than satisfying to the specialist. His narrative descriptions are rather thin for anthropological tastes; to wit, his reliance on interview data limits his ability to plumb the depths, the internal logic, of Tswana cultural understanding and religious experience. All this said, *The Realm of the Word* is the work of a talented historian, to whose further writings we greatly look forward.

49. For instance, its cover copy asserts, both grandly and inaccurately, that *The Realm of the Word* is "the first study of mission Christianity in colonial southern Africa to treat religion and society as a coherent whole." This is, of course, precisely the claim that structural functionalist monographs in anthropology were fond of making. There are many other examples of the internalization of anthropological idiom; so much so that it is hard to avoid a sense of *déjà vu*—especially when we come to a description of writing history that draws on the metaphor, used by Douglas and Leach long ago, of attempting to pin out butterflies (Landau 1995:219).

50. Despite the frequent appearance of colonial agents in the evidence he cites, Landau's treatment of their historical role is sparing. Also inadequate in this respect is the way in which he discusses the location of Ngwato in the wider political and economic world of the Tswana. At one point (1995:141) he says, tellingly, that, going through "the kingship's correspondence"—most of which dealt with finance and trade—was like "dropping in on a conversation already in progress," a conversation which he often found hard to understand. Yet without a comprehensive reading of precisely such transactions, many of them extending far beyond the Ngwato polity, it is impossible to situate local processes in context. Or even to interpret the full import of the religious events of the period.

51. See, e.g., the book feature on *Of Revelation and Revolution*, I and *Ethnography and the Historical Imagination* in the *South African Historical Journal*, 31(1994):273–309. Nor has this been the only context in which the two volumes have been at the center of debates on the present and future of history in (South) Africa (see, e.g., Ranger n.d.[b]:7f.)—a matter of surprise and discomfort to us, as they were not written with that in mind.

52. For thoughtful discussion of the topic, see de Kock (1994) and Vaughan (1994; but cf. Bunn 1994:24ff.). For a somewhat odd one, see Crais (1994:278), who accuses us of being postmodernists and structuralists at the same time. He also argues that, because *Of Revelation and Revolution* discusses the cultural commodification of Africa in the nineteenth century, it may itself be placed in the "tradition of tourism and the commodification of the sign." Here is criticism at its most creative, most postmodern.

53. Where Vansina (1993) got the idea that this was meant as a textbook, with which he begins and ends the review, is unclear. It is a curious statement, as elsewhere he says that the volume is an "anthology of [already published] articles" (p. 417). We find it hard to credit that such a senior scholar does not know the difference between the two genres.

54. We count at least eight: (i) that *Ethnography and the Historical Imagination* was intended as a textbook (see n. 53 above); (ii) that all the essays, except the introduction, were published before (see p. xiii); (iii) that all save the first are, in substance, about the Tshidi-Rolong (see chapters 2, 7, 8, 10); (iv) that we "saw" the madman of whom we wrote in chapter 6 at a railway station (we spent many hours with him in a mental hospital in 1970; see p. 155); (v) that we did not ask him what his clothes meant (we explain that he was deliberately mute; p. 155); (vi) that we did not ask other Tshidi about them (we did; see p. 173); (vii) that Bernard Cohn and Marshall Sahlins founded "the postmodern (or 'neomodern') group of 'historical anthropology' at Chicago in the late 1970s. The group now contains sociologists such as Wendy Griswold." (As we point out in the text below, there is no such group; it was not founded by Cohn or by Sahlins, who is a famously articulate *opponent* of postmodernism; there are no sociologists associated with historical anthropology at Chicago; and so on.) It is difficult to believe that such (mis)-statements do not conceal another agenda. Either that, or Vansina is a truly careless scholar—and a venal one, since he uses some of these very "facts" to accuse us of poor research and irresponsible work. Readers may draw their own conclusions, but see Werbner (n.d.[b]) for an insightful set of reflections salient to this point.

55. It becomes patent, toward the end of the review, that Vansina has a deep antipathy to *all* theory, and a slender grasp of the anthropological discourse that he is so quick to dismiss. Among other things, he says, our book is "riddled with allusions to a cocktail of every major sociological and anthropological theory propounded since the days of functionalism." Were we only so erudite! What he did not grasp, willfully it seems, is that we set out in pursuit of a principled theoretical synthesis. Perhaps we failed (for thoughtful comment, see, e.g., Elbourne n.d.:5ff.). But to the enterprise itself he gives no consideration. Not a single word. And then he accuses us, *ex nihilo*, of being "dogmatic" and "arrogant."

56. In the review (1993, n. 3), our pp. xi and 45 are noted, in parentheses, apparently in support of his statement about the existence of the group. No other evidence is offered. The first (p. xi) mentions the Anthropology Department, the African Studies Workshop, and the Committee on Critical Practice. None of these could possibly be confused with a "historical anthropology group." The second (p. 45) also contains nothing relevant; it simply has a throwaway comment to the effect that "historical anthropology . . . is more than a Chicago-cult." In sum, there is not even a hint in these passages of what Vansina suggests. Note that he accuses us of "innocence" of historiographic conventions because we do not follow received methods of annotation. And he admonishes us for acting as if historians have not dealt with questions of evidence. At least we, who stand indicted of hubris and disrespect for facts, try to ensure that the sources we quote actually exist—and may be found where we say they are. That requires no special technique. Just care. And honesty.

57. Vansina goes on at length about what we ought to have cited, what we "ignored," and so on; and he repeatedly pronounces, *ex cathedra*, on what we have and have not read. What he fails to realize is that our intention was not to "take on" his discipline, to consider the nature of evidence *sui generis*, or to write a review essay on postmodern historical anthropology. It was to draw eclectically, but always respectfully, from cultural history in order to arrive at a principled theoretical position for our own very different purposes (above, n. 55).

58. We mention the same study, in another connection, in n. 39 above.

59. The same question is raised by Elphick (1992:186), Gray (1993: 197), and Weir (1993:130f.)—but, interestingly, *not* in the (unexpectedly enthusiastic) notices that appeared in journals of religion (e.g., Baum 1993:154; Gorringe 1992; Petersen 1992:21).

60. In responding to Peel and Ranger together, we do not mean to suggest that their views on African religion, or on African history, are identical. They are not. However, in addressing our work, they cite each other extensively and evince no differences. Hence we feel that it is fair to answer them as one.

61. Ranger's account raises a number of independently important issues about the comparative relationship between indigenous narrative genres and historical consciousness, especially under the impact of colonialism. To this, alas, we cannot do justice here.

62. In this regard, Peel (1995:586) accuses us, cavalierly, of inattention to "the most universal and primary forms of narrative," stories told by people "from personal memory and experience." It is unclear to us how, precisely, Professor Peel presumes to know what we sought or did not seek to collect. As it happens, we did quite the opposite: we pursued such stories in every shape and form—down to eliciting school essays and recording texts on a wide range of topics. But they often did not yield historical narratives, *sensu stricto*, other than those told in a modernist genre or in response to our prompting.

63. We have excised another leading question posed by Peel (1995:587) here: "Could . . . Tswana chiefs have made their fine and complex judgements about how to respond to the dangers and opportunities presented by European encroachment except on the basis of historical assessments which must have taken a largely narrative form?" In our view, yes. Why, indeed, should these people have needed *narrative*, in the sense we have specified it, to assess the probable costs and benefits of an alien presence? If Peel

simply wants us to agree that the Africans were capable of telling themselves stories about the coming of whites, without any attention to the form and content of these stories, of course he is correct. But this, again, would be to use "narrative" to denote any form of telling—and hence no form in particular. Oddly, he adds citations, presumably to support the tacit proposition contained in the question, to Schapera (1970) and Gulbrandsen (1993); oddly, that is, as *neither* alludes to the existence of precolonial narrative forms.

64. One is noteworthy. It comes from George Thompson (1967,1), a merchant who visited Tswana communities in the 1820s. (We cite him several times below.) Quoting other Europeans in support of his own impressions, Thompson says that "Bechuanas are great story-tellers" (p. 83). But he stresses that their stories, even their retelling of "news," tended to be in the mode of the marvelous rather than the realist (p. 103); they were composed of an admixture of rumor and reportage related without attention to linearity or facticity. One such story put it about that the Colony had been attacked by "an army composed of myriads of pigmies, whose stature did not exceed six inches." Most whites took these tales as proof of the "native" propensity to lie and fabricate, to circulate "absurdities" and "false reports" (pp. 79, 83, 95, 103). In fact, it is more likely that they were part of a genre of magical realism, whose semantic and practical purpose was lost on the Europeans.

65. Molema (1951:181ff.), who says similar things in some of his other writings (e.g., 1920), takes a much more extreme position than do we on Southern Tswana "narrativity," although he would not have used the term. Ironically, his views on the matter are much closer to the ones which Peel and Ranger attribute to us than they are to our own.

66. Plaatje's first literary endeavor, his Boer War diary (1973), was written largely to gain skills in a European narrative form. Among his later work are writings in and on *setswana*. But, significantly, they are confined largely to orthographic and grammatical texts and to *lists* of proverbs and other usages.

67. This comment was made in the course of a discussion on the Nuafrica mailing list (nuafrica@listserv.acns.nwu.edu) in June 1996. Landau's posting was on 6/6/96 (11:44:47).

68. This is the same discussion on the Nuafrica mailing list alluded to in n. 67. Lowe's posting was on 6/3/96 (16:41:16).

69. This is a point Ranger (1995:x) himself makes in saying how singular was his opportunity to work on the Samkange family papers.

70. One is reminded here of the celebrated case of the Baining in New Britain, who, according to "their" ethnographers—Gregory Bateson among them—seem actively to have avoided most forms of linear narrative (see Fajans n.d.); also of various accounts from the Amazon, most recently that of Descola (1996).

71. This quote is also from the Nuafrica discussion alluded to in n. 67 above. Atwell's posting was on 6/4/96 (09:06:51). In it he also noted, as we did above, the convergence between Ranger's appeal for a "return to narrative" and postmodernism.

72. We should also like to note here that several of the chapters were first composed as many as eight years ago—some of them when we worked on volume 1. As a result,

they have circulated, in manuscript, for quite a while. A number have been presented as conference papers or lectures; passages from a few others, in various combinations and versions, have appeared in print. All of this may reinforce the impression of repetition, which we regret. But we took the risk knowingly—and always with a specific scholarly purpose in mind.

73. A word here about this metaphor: in speaking of "the long conversation" between Tswana and Europeans, we mean to include *not* only verbal interactions but also bodily gestures, exchanges of objects, and various other communicative acts. In the present volume, in fact, direct speech appears less often than it did in the first. We are concerned as much here with unspoken and partially vocalized forms of practice.

74. Because of the dissimilar nature of their subject matter, the precise proportions vary among the chapters. The earlier ones, which lay the ground for what follows, include more "thin" narratives of the long run, describing material and social processes as they unfold; some of the later ones focus in greater ethnographic depth on intersecting cultural practices. But these are tendencies. Both kinds of descriptive analysis appear side by side throughout.

T W O

1. This was implicit in the stress on original sin that accompanied the call for universal salvation by such influential evangelists as Whitefield and Wesley (Davies 1961:151f.). In his first sermon on the subject, Whitefield said: "We must first shew the people they are condemned, and then shew them how they must be saved" (also p. 151f.).

2. Note that both Wesley and Whitefield stressed the importance of extemporary preaching (Davies 1961:160).

3. Those who left the service of the missions did so for reasons ranging from ill-health and accident to personal conflict and ideological incompatibility with their brethren. None appear to have resigned because of doctrinal doubt or a loss of spiritual faith.

4. We stress this because Etherington (1992:215) has suggested that we pay insufficient attention to the impact of the "great theological controversies" of the age on the Nonconformist mission to South Africa—and too much to developments in literature, science, and other things.

5. R. Moffat, Cape Town, 28 June 1817 [CWM, LMS Incoming Letters (South Africa), 7–2-A].

6. R. Hamilton, New Lattakoo, 19 June 1818 [CWM, LMS Incoming Letters (South Africa), 7–4-D].

7. This conviction was not confined to the Bechuana mission; it had much deeper roots in the doctrine of universal salvation. Proclaimed Dr. Chalmers (1837:414), in a general lecture on teaching theology published in the *Evangelical Magazine,* "Every man has been visited by some imagination of a God."

8. S. Broadbent, Matlwasse, 8 June 1823 [WMMS, South Africa Correspondence, 300]; see also Baillie (1832).

9. As Davies (1961:201) notes, hymns were a crucial pedagogic vehicle in evangelical worship. They were also a source of emotional richness and communal feeling. We have seen (*RRI*:240f.) that the Nonconformists set great store by capacity of song to "charm the savage ear" (R. Moffat 1842:601) and to write the truths of salvation "imperceptibly" on Tswana minds. We shall return again to this topic in respect of African Christianity.

10. J. Read, Lattakoo, 15 March 1817 [CWM, LMS Incoming Letters (South Africa), 7–1-C]. Read compared the Tswana aversion to the gospel to that of "the Jews."

11. S. Broadbent, Matlwasse, 31 March 1824 [WMMS, South Africa Correspondence, 300]

12. R. Hamilton, New Lattakoo, 12 April 1824 [CWM, LMS Incoming Letters (South Africa), 9–1-A].

13. A number of early tickets, drawn from various parts of South Africa, are to be found in the Grey Collection at the South African Library. Their issue, possession, and display were still important to Rolong Methodists in the 1960s. On the usefulness of encouraging mottoes in teaching "[those who] in a religious point of view" were children, see Moffat and Moffat (1951:129).

14. James Archbell, for instance, used Genesis 27.2 ("I know not the day of my death") for an early funeral address; J. Archbell, Platberg, 20 March 1832 [WMMS, South Africa Correspondence, 303]. He chose Amos 4.12 ("Prepare to Meet Thy God, O Israel!") for a sermon given before Chief Moroka and an unusually large crowd of Seleka-Rolong in 1830 (Broadbent 1865:179).

15. Acts 16.9; R. Hamilton, New Lattakoo, 12 April 1824 [CWM, LMS Incoming Letters (South Africa), 9–1-A].

16. John Mackenzie (1871:479f.); on the teaching of the Gospel according to John, see also W. C. Willoughby , 22 September 1894 [CWM, LMS Incoming Letters (South Africa), 51–2-B].

17. It would be interesting to know what Tswana made of this in light of their own elaborate "first fruits" ritual. In Lesotho, a Christianized equivalent, *dilopotsiya*, an offering to the church of part of the early harvest, was developed under the tutelage of the Paris Evangelical Mission Society (Setiloane 1976:197f.).

18. See, e.g., J. Archbell, Platberg, 20 March 1832 [WMMS, South Africa Correspondence, 303]; Broadbent (1865:179); J. Mackenzie (1871:468f.).

19. John Mackenzie (1871:466) provides an illustration of the shift in his epigraph to the concluding chapter of *Ten Years North of the Orange River,* which deals with the progress of the mission. It was taken from Max Müller's *Comparative Mythology:*

Where the Greek saw barbarians, we see brethren; where the Greek saw heroes and demi-gods, we see our parents and ancestors; where the Greek saw nations . . . we see mankind, toiling and suffering . . . yet evermore tending, under a divine control, towards the fulfillment of that inscrutable purpose for which the world was created, and man placed in it, bearing the image of God.

20. J. S. Moffat, Kuruman, Annual Report for 1869 [CWM, LMS South Africa Reports, 1–2].

21. John Moffat, a Setswana speaker from birth, claimed that the understanding of the language among the evangelists was so poor that their preaching often made almost no sense. "The natives," he wrote, "have with docile gravity been listening to a vast amount of unmeaning sounds . . . interspersed with bits of sentences of the most astounding character"; J. Moffat, Kuruman, 20 December 1869 [CWM, LMS South Africa Reports, 1–1]. There is collateral evidence for Moffat's complaints. It was claimed, for instance, that Roger Price read his first sermon in Setswana after only two months in the field (E. Smith 1957:51).

22. The mission archives bear frequent testimony to the struggle over polygyny. In 1840, for instance, Cameron wrote from the Methodist field that it was "the grand remaining barrier behind which the prince of darkness entrenches himself"; J. Cameron, Mpukane, 24 July 1840 [WMMS, South Africa Correspondence, 315]. Like sending children to participate in initiation rites, "taking back concubines" was a frequent reason for members being "cut off" from the LMS church at Kuruman during the nineteenth century [see Records of the Congregational Church; Chapel of the LMS, Seoding-Kuruman]. Perhaps the best documented case of all was that of Sechele. The Kwena chief was eventually prevailed upon by Livingstone, who expressed some compassion for the "poor women" involved, to return all but one of his wives back to their natal families. He later "relapsed" (Livingstone 1857:19f.). Wrote Livingstone (1959,2:41f.): "The blame must not be put on Satan; he had done it of his own free will; . . . he had of his own free will forsaken the laws of Christ."

23. The source of this report was James Chapman; it is quoted in Chirenje (1977:68).

24. Kgosi Montshiwa, in *Mahoko a Becwana*, February 1891, 73(9); see also E. Lloyd, Kanye, 14 June 1893 [CWM, LMS Incoming Letters (South Africa), 50-2-A].

25. The Bechuana, he wrote, knew nothing of its origin or meaning, but chose to perform it at "Ishmael's age"; S. Broadbent, Matlwasse, 8 June 1823 [WMMS, South Africa Correspondence, 300].

26. J. Archbell, Platberg, 27 May 1833 [WMMS, South Africa Correspondence (Albany), 303]; see also *RRI*:260.

27. Thus, for example, as late as 1933, A. E. Jennings wrote a propaganda pamphlet attacking Tswana marriage practices. Similar attacks on the "wickedness" of initiation rites and other customary practices appeared regularly in the mission media throughout the nineteenth century. For example, when he introduced the first periodical in Setswana in 1856, Ludorf declared that one of his main aims was to counter the shameful customs that lingered in the Tswana heart, among which were the "shocking secrets" of circumcision; see *Molekoli Oa Bechuana*, 1(6), October 1856, WMMS Press, Thaba 'Nchu [Grey Collection (South African Library), Mission Presses].

28. A delightful early example is provided by Mrs. Hamilton, who wrote of one listener's response to the Rev. Read's preaching: "A young boy said he did not know what sort of heart others had, but he was sure he had a very bad one, [and] he wished . . . that God would make his word a Broom to sweep all the filth out of his heart"; Mrs. Hamilton, New Lattakoo, 16 February 1818 [CWM, LMS Incoming Correspondence (South Africa), 7-3-A].

29. Setiloane (1976:103) suggests that French Protestant missionaries were also less censorious of polygyny. Our reading in the Paris Evangelical Mission Society archives confirms this view.

30. Our qualification here—that Livingstone "*seems* to have thought"—is due to the somewhat ambiguous wording of his statement (1857:166f.) on the necessity for a united missionary stance on initiation.

31. Notwithstanding some later opinions to the contrary (see J. Mackenzie 1871:394f.; E. Smith 1925, 1950), Moffat's conviction that the Tswana lacked any idea of God seems already to have been fixed by the early 1820s (see Moffat and Moffat 1951:49, 56). Livingstone (1974:100) claimed that he had been influenced by the Rev. William Robey, who recruited Moffat to the LMS, and whose views on the lack of divine authority in "natural religion" are cited in *Missionary Labours and Scenes* (R. Moffat 1842:275).

32. As Setiloane (1976:77) and others have pointed out (cf. J. Comaroff 1974), Moffat had identified certain key attributes of the Tswana conception of *Modimo*—although he drew the wrong conclusions from them. *Modimo*, qua supreme being, is indeed an impersonal noun, of the same class as others denoting intangible forces and elements (like *mosi*, "smoke"; or *moya*, "wind/breath/spirit"), most of which have no plural form. And, as Setiloane notes (1976:82), *Modimo* does seem to have been associated, as were the ancestors, with the earth; also with the limits of tangible space and time, if not with "heaven" in the Christian sense (Willoughby 1928:67; *RRI*:155). *Badimo*, by contrast, was a personal noun that, as Mackenzie (1871:395) explained, had no accepted singular form. Both terms seem to have shared the sense of superhuman force (possibly derived from the verb *dima*, "searching, penetrating insight"; Brown [1931] 1987:56). For early Methodist understandings of these concepts, see S. Broadbent, Matlwasse, 8 June 1823 [WMMS, South Africa Correspondence, 300]; T. Hodgson, Platberg, 19 March 1828 [WMMS, South Africa Correspondence, 302].

33. In a letter to his brother, Livingstone (1959,1:192) acknowledged that this was a question "rather difficult of solution," especially after thirty years of mission influence. He also claimed that Moffat had "placed a veto" on further efforts to dispute his (Moffat's) views on the subject. (For Moffat's response to his son-in-law's criticism, see Livingstone 1974:110.)

34. Livingstone was to make much of this—and of available evidence of the existence of an indigenous moral conscience—to argue that Africans should be given responsibility for propagating the gospel; see below.

35. Drawing on Moffat's image of the stream run dry—and on the symbolic legacy of "irrigation and iconicity" (*RRI*:206f.)—Livingstone's choice of terms served to reiterate the idea that Tswana religion was a degenerate, vestigial form of an earlier God-given faith. The "remaining fragments" of a "defective tradition" had been handed down by forebears who had chosen "darkness rather than light" (R. Moffat 1842:275; Stuart 1993:384). A related metaphor, that of "excavation" (Livingstone 1961:149), stresses the possibility of spiritual recuperation and retrieval.

36. A. Sharp, Vryburg, 12 November 1886 [WMMS, South Africa Correspondence (Transvaal), 328].

37. For just one example of how this tension was expressed in Protestant mission fields elsewhere, see Langmore (1989:89) on the Papuan case.

38. "Let bronze be brought from Egypt, let Ethiopia hasten to stretch out her hands to God" (Psalms 68.31).

39. T. Hodgson and S. Broadbent, Matlwasse, 1 January 1824 [WMMS, South Africa Correspondence, 300]; LMS (1830:85); Livingstone (1961:14); R. Giddy, Thaba 'Nchu, 20 June 1843 [WMMS, South Africa Correspondence (Bechuana), 315].

40. Nokaneng was close to Dithakong, capital of Chief Mothibi of the Tlhaping between 1806 and 1817. Dithakong was also the site of the first LMS station in the region.

41. This move from lesser to greater regulation on the part of the Nonconformists makes it necessary to qualify Elbourne's (n.d.:22) interesting observation that, by 1816, "Christianity was out of missionary control and was being spread by people with many long range contacts." The moment of which she speaks was not indicative of a process of weakening control, but one in which oversight was not yet as firm as it would become. Our reading of the evidence would also lead us to temper her claim that the "many people of mixed race and Khoisan descent" who had already become Christians by this time "had a tremendous influence on the white missionary relationships with the Tswana" (Elbourne n.d.:22). That their mediation was crucial in the early years is beyond doubt; its longer-term impact is much less clear (see below). From the 1820s onward, the influence of these intermediaries was subject to stringent supervision and devaluation by the evangelists, who tended to force an increasingly "black and white" model on their sphere of operations—and to draw their African assistants from populations peripheral *within* the Tswana world (like the Bakgalagadi and the Tlharo; see, e.g., R. Moffat 1842:589f.; Livingstone 1959,1:90; 1961:81, 143).

42. There is some evidence of one earlier conversion: in 1820, before Moffat's arrival among the Tlhaping, a young blind woman entered the Christian fold (Setiloane 1976:141). On early Wesleyan conversions, see T. Hodgson, Boetsap, 18 August 1829 [WMMS, South Africa Correspondence, 302]; J. Archbell, Platberg, 28 August 1831 [WMMS, South Africa Correspondence, 303].

43. J. Archbell, Platberg, 28 August 1831 [WMMS, South Africa Correspondence, 303]; R. Giddy, Thaba 'Nchu, 20 June 1843 [WMMS, South Africa Correspondence (Bechuana), 315]; LMS 1837a:201. While the evangelists were wont, in English, to speak of African "teachers," they tended to use the term *bathusi* ("assistant"; sing., *mothusi*) in Setswana. *Moruti,* vernacular for "teacher" became the conventional usage for "missionary" or "minister" (*RRI*:233).

44. In 1969, when we began our first field work, this form of mimetic translation was still the norm in multilingual churches of mission origin throughout the Mafeking District.

45. A. Wookey, Kuruman, 24 December 1873 [CWM, LMS South Africa Reports, 1–1]; J. Moffat, Kuruman, 20 December 1869 [CWM, LMS South Africa Reports, 1–1].

46. This choice of words underlines again (i) the pragmatic approach of the mission to religious truth and (ii) its vision of evangelism as conversation. Elsewhere, Robert

Moffat (Moffat and Moffat 1951:64) wrote: "[W]e cannot, we dare not, leave them, till we have . . . conversed with them mouth to mouth on the things of God." Mouth-to-mouth resuscitation indeed!

47. The first two, his own converts, were already in the employ of the LMS by 1834. One, Arend Joseph, was an ex-slave from the Colony who had bought his freedom with money made from trading ivory (R. Moffat 1842:496; Moffat and Moffat 1951:106, n. 7). The other, Paul, was a Motshwene; like many of Moffat's early recruits, he came from a community of vassals who served the Tlhaping (Livingstone 1961:81, 148). Paul, described as "the oldest deacon of the church at Kuruman," later worked as an evangelist among Tswana to the north (see below). Both men are listed among the first group of converts—they entered the church on 5 July 1829—in the LMS Roll of Members at Kuruman [Records of the Congregational Church, Chapel of the LMS, Seoding/Kuruman, and the Outstations thereto Belonging].

48. R. Giddy, Thaba 'Nchu, 19 September 1839 [WMMS, South Africa Correspondence (Bechuana), 315].

49. Wesleyan Methodist Missionary Society (1842:115); J. Cameron, Platberg, 23 July 1840 [WMMS, South Africa Correspondence (Bechuana), 315]; R. Giddy, Thaba 'Nchu, 20 June 1843 [WMMS, South Africa Correspondence (Bechuana), 315]; Whiteside (1906:335).

50. J. Scott, Thaba 'Nchu, 11 September 1868 [WMMS, South Africa Correspondence (Bechuana), 316]; Balia (1991:29f.).

51. Livingstone's clearest statement on African agency and the "Native church" was published in the *British Quarterly Review* of August 1851. Its immediate context was a debate over the proposed withdrawal of the LMS from the "Colonial and Griqua" missions, said by many to be capable now of supporting their own pastors. This move, which Livingstone (1974:96f.) backed strongly, would have enabled the Society to concentrate its resources on the "really heathen" lands to the north.

52. See Livingstone (1974:111), who also noted (1961:xxii) his father-in-law's disagreement that Christianity would flourish independently once seeded in the African heart. Indeed, Moffat wrote to the director of the LMS complaining that Livingstone had abandoned Chief Sechele "at the very time he required most the watchful eye & encouraging voice of his Missionary." Sechele, of course, was baptized and then relapsed—although he continued to promote biblical teaching and Christian ritual (J. Mackenzie 1871:105f.; see below).

53. See, e.g., J. S. Moffat and W. Ashton, Kuruman, 20 January 1869 [CWM, LMS Incoming Letters (South Africa), 35-2-C]. This document gives an account of "native agents" in the various Southern Tswana districts. It lists eighteen men, seven of them paid. Nine were deemed "inattentive" to their duties and "inefficient"; six, zealous but not "good" or knowledgeable. The three singled out for praise—among them Paul (see n. 47) and Sebobe (Livingstone 1961:143)—labored as unpaid preachers at some distance from white oversight. For Wesleyan views of African agency, which were strikingly similar at this time, see J. Scott, Thaba 'Nchu, 11 September 1868 [WMMS, South Africa Correspondence (Bechuana), 316].

54. See, for example, J. Cameron, Platberg, 23 July 1840 [WMMS, South Africa Correspondence (Bechuana), 315]; Livingstone (1961:221). A case described by Livingstone (p. 59f.) also suggests that the wives of the men on both sides were sometimes drawn into these disputes.

55. Those opposed to the mission often made its African agents into targets for their disapproval. See R. Giddy, Thaba 'Nchu, 20 June 1843 [WMMS, South African Correspondence (Bechuana), 315]; Molema (1966:54); John Mackenzie (1871:82). Others seem to have rejected black teachers as inadequate substitutes for white benefactors and "protectors" (E. Smith 1957:309).

56. J. Brown, Kuruman, 5 January 1899 [CWM, LMS South Africa Reports, 3–1].

57. Including two African scholars of religion, one Tswana (Setiloane 1976) and the other Shona (Chirenje 1987); also "native" social scientists (e.g., Matthews n.d.) and commentators (e.g., Molema 1920, n.d.[a], n.d.[b]).

58. The source of the rumor was itself an object of bitter conflict. Peter Wright, from Griquatown, accused the "Bechuana church members of Kuruman," especially Chief Mahura (Mothibi's younger brother); others, notably Prosper Lemue of the PEMS, blamed leaders in Wright's own congregation. (Lemue, in fact, wrote to the LMS, calling for the culprits' excommunication. He was obviously upset that Moffat had been "in some measure obliged to undertake a voyage to Europe to plead his own innocency before his Directors"; see P. Wright, Griqua Town, 25 September 1840 [CWM, LMS Philip Papers, 3–1–C], also P. Lemue, Motito, 2 July 1840 [CWM, LMS Philip Papers, 3–1–C]). In the meanwhile, Edwards appears to have been involved in a dispute with "some Griquas"—there was debate as to whether they were "teachers"—from the outstation at Danielskuil (between Kuruman and Chief Mothibi's seat). He was alleged by Wright to have declared these men unworthy of church privileges, and to have evoked a rude response by calling them offensive names. Edwards would subsequently leave Kuruman to join Livingstone at Mabotsa, although they later fell out as well. The letter below regarding the Griqua leaders at "Mothibi's place" must be read in light of all of this.

59. R. Hamilton and R. Edwards, Kuruman, 1 April 1840 [CWM, LMS Philip Papers, 3–1–C].

60. P. Lemue, Motito, 2 July 1840 [CWM, LMS Philip Papers, 3–1–C].

61. Within missionary circles, stories of Sechele's biblical knowledge took on almost mythical proportions. Less so outside, however. While John Mackenzie (1871:105) claimed that "no native in Bechuana-land [was] better acquainted with the Bible than Sechele," Holub (1881,1:324) was more skeptical. "The King," he wrote, who "still practise[s] rain-magic," has "become familiar with some passages of Scripture."

62. J. Archbell, Platberg, 27 May 1833 [WMMS, South Africa Correspondence (Albany), 303]; J. Ludorf, Thaba 'Nchu, 8 February 1853 [WMMS, South Africa Correspondence (Bechuana), 315]; J. Mackenzie (1871:229f.).

63. E. Lloyd, Kanye, 14 June 1893 [CWM, LMS Incoming Letters (South Africa), 50–2–A].

64. This is reminiscent of the way in which Chief Khama is said to have established the "Plough Service" among Ngwato in the late nineteenth century, which is ironic,

since Khama was perhaps the most strictly orthodox of all the Christian rulers, and struggled with a number of missionaries as he tried to exercise close control over the church from within. When he became chief, Chirgwin (1932:47) says, he was approached to arrange the annual rainmaking rites. While he agreed that these rites might be held, he organized a Christian prayer meeting in the royal *kgotla*. Adds Chirgwin, tellingly: "Without any disruption . . . an old custom had been changed; a pagan rite had been filled with a Christian content." Of course, for many Ngwato, exactly the reverse might be said to have occurred. Again, what seems significant—in both this case and in that of Montshiwa's public worship—is not the overtaking of one spiritual order by another, but their fusion.

65. E. Lloyd, Kanye, 14 June 1893 [CWM, LMS Incoming Letters (South Africa), 50–2-A].

66. Montshiwa persuaded the WMMS to support him strongly in his disputes with settlers, the colonial state, and British servicemen; see *RRI*:352, n. 138; below, chapter 7, n. 36.

67. Gulbrandsen (1993:60) argues that northern Tswana chiefs resisted Christianity less than did their southern counterparts, largely because their colonial context was less divisive. It is important to bear in mind, in this respect, that there was also variation in the way that southern leaders reacted to the church. The two Tlhaping polities closest to the colonial border are a case in point. Mothibi converted in 1841 as an old man, and his son, Jantje, came to be seen as a "model Christian chief" (Shillington 1985:63). But his heathen brother, Mahura (and Mahura's successor, Mankurwane) continued to hold rain and initiation rites in the more centralized polity at Taung. While Mahura did consent to accept a missionary in 1844, relations between church and *kgotla* remained tense (*RRI*:262). Yet, in the unrest that followed the annexation of Griqualand West, it was Jantje and his sons who opposed the whites (including the evangelists)—and Mankurwane who tried, for his own reasons, to stay neutral (Shillington 1985:80). Later, though, he fell into conflict again with the LMS (see below).

68. This seems also to have been an indigenous perception. In an account of a "native history of the planting of Christianity" among the Matebele, John Mackenzie (1871:xiv, 319) says that his informant included Chief Sechele on his list of evangelists.

69. R. Giddy, Thaba 'Nchu, 20 June 1843 [WMMS, South Africa Correspondence (Bechuana), 315].

70. In fact, Joseph Ludorf worked among Tshidi-Rolong in the Molopo region, but only for a couple of years; he left them in the early 1850s when they went into exile at Moshaneng. Thereafter, except for occasional visits from LMS and WMMS emissaries, Molema never had a missionary at his side.

71. Again, we told parts of it in volume 1, albeit for different purposes (pp. 263f.). Here we reprise only its bare outlines.

72. The Rev. Owen Watkins visited Mafikeng in 1883, after the Rolong Mission had been transferred to the Transvaal and Swaziland District of the WMMS (Molema n.d.[b]:9). He noted that Molema had died, and that his son, Joshua, was firmly in control of the thriving church. Having witnessed several services, Watkins declared himself

satisfied with the way in which they were being conducted—though, knowing no Setswana, he could have understood little of the proceedings. Obviously relieved that the Mafikeng Christians expressed no opposition to his presence, he reported that they "almost wept for joy" at the sight of a white missionary. For his part, Montshiwa, hard pressed by the Boers at Stellaland, was especially anxious that a permanent evangelist be sent as soon as possible.

73. While the use of surnames became quite common among Tswana in the late nineteenth century, the evangelists tended to refer to African converts (indeed, to Africans in general) by their first names (*RRI*:219). By and large, we do not. There are three exceptions, however: Shomolekae Sebolai, Khukhwi Mogodi, and Mothowagae Motlogelwa (discussed below) are all known in the documentary record and in scholarly works by their Setswana first names alone; to avoid confusion we do the same thing.

74. J. T. Brown (1925:28f.) says that Sebolai had some rudimentary education at Kuruman as a child. But the missionaries regarded him as an unpromising candidate for further theological instruction. He was finally permitted to enter the Bible School of the Moffat Institution in 1883, when he was over forty.

75. This remark was contained in a letter to Dr. David Chamberlin of the LMS from Willoughby, then in Hartford, Connecticut. (Written on 8 February 1926, it is presently affixed to the copy of *The Apostle of the Marshes* in the LMS archives.) Although the reports of these African evangelists were rarely forwarded to London, occasionally one was. Wookey, for example, sent a letter (with translation) in which Mogodi acknowledged the receipt of medicines and thanked the "servants of God" for their patience with His "weakest lambs"; Khukhwi Mogodi in A. J. Wookey, Lake Ngami, 13 July 1893 [CWM, LMS Incoming Letters (South Africa), 50-2-A].

76. See, for example, "*Likoalo tse li koalecoeñ Morulaganyi*," *Mahoko a Becwana*, 56(6), September 1889; Jones (1972:119).

77. *Mahoko a Becwana* 1(1), 1883; J. D. Jones (1972:115, 119). In comparison with the moralistic writing of many of his European colleagues, Mogodi's texts were relatively free of subjective evaluation or overt disparagement—especially when recounting such things as graphic cruelty toward serfs or the customary killing of one of a pair of twins.

78. The two evangelists appear *en passant* in the correspondence of their white mentors. From time to time they alerted the missionaries to problems brewing among their congregants; see, e.g., E. Lloyd, Kanye, 14 June 1893 [CWM, LMS Incoming Letters (South Africa), 50–2–A].

79. E. Lloyd, Shoshong, Annual Report for 1908 [CWM, LMS South Africa Reports, 4–2].

80. As we shall see, the secessions in the Taung district occurred soon after John Brown returned to take charge of the mission there. For some years before, this station had been left in the charge of an African "teacher"—who became a leader of the breakaway church.

81. The program prepared by the NICC for its centenary celebration at Manthe in 1985 provides the following capsule history:

The Native Independent Congregational Church is a breakaway from the former LMS. During 1885 a small number of members of the LMS in Manthe Stad decided to organise a denomination which they named the Native Independent Congregational Church. They invited a certain Rev. James Puti of the Union Congregational Church who was stationed in Kimberley. They consulted with Kgosi Kgantlapane Motlhabane who was the ruler of the Bagamaidi Tribe then and was recognized by all as the founder of the Native Independent Congregational Church.

In his own version of this history, related to us in 1995, the NICC President's son, himself soon to become an ordained minister, added further detail. In the 1880s, he said, the people of Manthe had "suffered" the lack of a pastor, and were forced to walk miles to Taung for ministerial services. Kgantlapane tried to secure a clergyman from the LMS for his community, even journeying to Kimberley to do so. But he failed. The congregation then left the Society and obtained Rev. Puti from the UCC. This account is much like that given to Pauw (1960:53) in the 1950s; neither mentions the factional politics that underlay the split.

82. H. Williams, Taung, Annual Report for 1887 [CWM, LMS South Africa Reports, 2–2]; J. Brown, Taung, Annual Report for 1889 [CWM, LMS South Africa Reports, 2–2].

83. J. Brown, Taung, Annual Report for 1889; J. Brown, Taung, Annual Report for 1890 [CWM, LMS South Africa Reports, 2–2].

84. H. Williams, Taung, Annual Report for 1887 [CWM, LMS South Africa Reports, 2–2]; see also J. Brown, Taung, Annual Report for 1885/6 [CWM, LMS South Africa Reports, 2–1].

85. H. Williams, Taung, Annual Report for 1887; J. Brown, Taung, Annual Report and Ten Years Review of the Mission, 1890 [CWM, LMS South Africa Reports, 2–2].

86. J. Brown, Taung, Annual Report and Ten Years Review of the Mission, 1890 [CWM, LMS South Africa Reports, 2–2].

87. Pauw (1960:53f.) notes that, in 1922, the NICC split into two major factions. The one centered at Manthe traced its roots to the secession of 1885. The other, at Schmidtsdrift, refused to accept the first as the official center of the church; it claimed, in its own reading of a shared history, to have been founded in 1893. At the time Pauw did his field research, the second branch seemed preeminent. But, by the 1990s, especially with the political prominence of Rev. Kgaladi, the reverse appeared true. All evidence suggests that, at present, Manthe is the headquarters of a strong and united national organization. The elaborate centenary celebrations in 1985, which were attended by President Lucas Mangope of Bophuthatswana, authorized its version of NICC history—according to which the church has been joined, over the past hundred years, by five denominations and has suffered two secessions.

88. One outcome of the *Report of the Native Churches Commission* (South Africa 1925a) was to formalize the conditions for "recognizing" African Independent churches, thus to exert some control over them (Sundkler 1961:74f.). Recognition carried with it the promise of being granted school and church sites in black areas, and of ministers both serving as marriage officers and receiving railway concessions. Apart from demonstrating acceptable age and size, churches had to show that their clergy were properly trained,

and of appropriate ethical standing. By 1945, says Sundkler (1961:77), only 1 percent of the hundreds of applications had been successful.

89. The term *moperofeti* (sing.) had come into common Setswana usage by the turn of this century (J. T. Brown 1987:213), and is still widely applied to Zionist and Pentecostalist visionaries among Tshidi-Rolong (J. Comaroff 1974:232). While Setiloane (1976:207) claims that *bonoge* connoted the vernacular understanding of "prophecy," this seems to have been a Sotho word; Casalis (1861:284) reported that *noga* meant "to divine supernaturally" (cf. Willoughby 1928:113). We have found no real evidence of its use among Southern Tswana, past or present.

90. Willoughby (1928:126f.), for one, went to great lengths to account for the phenomenon of African "prophets." While he did not discount religious emotion entirely, his explanations focused on a wide range of temporal factors, from racial neurosis to chicanery. Sharing Wesley's distrust of "visions and voices," he told approvingly of a fellow missionary who treated the visions of two African teachers by giving each a dose of salts and sending them to bed.

91. W. McGee, Taung, Annual Report for 1909 [CWM, LMS South Africa Reports, 4–2].

92. For another case of the flogging of a prophet's followers, see H. Williams, Kanye, Annual Report for 1908 [CWM, LMS South Africa Reports, 4–2]. African rulers appear to have cooperated with alacrity in curbing the challenge of charismatics. In 1901, Chirenje (1977:206) notes, Chief Khama apprehended five "prophets" who claimed the power to solve the various "social and political" ills of the Ngwato. His court found them guilty of "false pretenses," and ordered the razing of their houses.

93. H. Williams, Kanye, Annual Report for 1908 [CWM, LMS South Africa Reports, 4–2].

94. W. McGee, Taung, Annual Report for 1909 [CWM, LMS South Africa Reports, 4–2].

95. See J. Cameron, Platberg, 28 February 1843 [WMMS, South Africa Correspondence (Bechuana), 315]. This prophetess, we are told, "pretend[ed] to have the power to procure rain."

96. H. Williams, Kanye, Annual Report for 1908 [CWM, LMS South Africa Reports, 4–2].

97. R. H. Lewis, Molepolole, Annual Report for 1908 [CWM, LMS South Africa Reports, 4–2].

98. See Willoughby (1928:115). This tendency to spurn European commodities sometimes caused traders among Southern Tswana to urge colonial authorities to apprehend prophets.

99. H. Williams, Kanye, Annual Report for 1908 [CWM, LMS South Africa Reports, 4–2].

100. As W. McGee noted, "both men and women claim to be 'sons' of God and tell people what to do and not to do"; W. McGee, Taung, Annual Report for 1909 [CWM, LMS South Africa Reports, 4–2].

101. Fires featured prominently in precolonial Tswana ritual, epitomizing heat in both its creative and destructive aspects. The hearth at the chiefly *kgotla* was kept perpetually alight; like its domestic counterpart in the family homestead, it only went out once a year, when it was ceremonially extinguished and rekindled during the annual first fruit ceremony of *go loma thôtse* (J. Comaroff 1985:66–67). This act of renewal was deemed necessary for the regeneration of the agricultural cycle and for the rainfall on which it depended. If the rains were alarmingly late, *dingaka* would douse and relight all fires in the community (Conder 1887:84).

102. In some English versions of the Bible, the verse is given as "Let bronze be brought from Egypt; let Ethiopia hasten to stretch out her hands to God." This more declamatory phrasing, with its call for urgent action, gives even greater force to the charter.

103. *The Cape Times,* 31 July 1893, p. 3; see also Chirenje (1987:24). The discussion focused specifically on the Thembu National Church, founded by the Rev. Nehemiah Tile in a secession from the Methodist Church in the Transkei in 1884.

104. J. Good, Kanye, 11 November 1898 [CWM, LMS Incoming Letters (South Africa), 55–2-D]; J. Brown, Kuruman, Report for 1898 [CWM, LMS South Africa Reports, 3–1].

105. H. Williams, Kanye, Annual Report for 1908 [CWM, LMS South Africa Reports, 4–2].

106. J. Brown, Kuruman, Report for 1898 [CWM, LMS South Africa Reports, 3–1].

107. J. Good, Kanye, 11 November 1898 [CWM, LMS Incoming Letters (South Africa), 55–2-D].

108. Minutes of the Bechuanaland District Committee meeting, Vryburg, 2–8 March 1899, submitted by J. Tom Brown, Kuruman, 24 March 1899 [CWM, LMS Incoming Letters (South Africa), 56–1-B]; J. Brown and W. C. Willoughby, Report of a Visit to Kanye, 2 March 1903 [CWM, LMS Incoming Letters (South Africa), 62–1].

109. In 1903, Chief Bathoen wrote that Mothowagae was regarded by his flock as their "missionary," although the term *moruti* also means "minister/teacher"; B. Gaseitsiwe, Kanye, 21 May 1903 [CWM, LMS Incoming Letters (South Africa), 62–2].

110. J. Brown and W. C. Willoughby, Report of a Visit to Kanye, 2 March 1903 [CWM, LMS Incoming Letters (South Africa), 62–1]. In a personal addendum, Willoughby wrote that he had thought it a mistake to "ride such a high horse" in respect of Mothowagae—but had felt it necessary to defer to the more "pedantic" views of his senior colleague.

111. E. Lloyd, Kanye, 14 June 1893 [CWM, LMS Incoming Letters (South Africa), 50–2-A]; Chirenje (1977:208); Schapera (1942:21).

112. Members of the Church, Kanye, 16 December 1902 [CWM, LMS Incoming Letters (South Africa), 62–1].

113. See the addendum by Willoughby to J. Brown and W. C. Willoughby, Report of a Visit to Kanye, 2 March 1903 [CWM, LMS Incoming Letters (South Africa) 62–1].

114. On this point, see H. Williams, Kanye, Annual Report for 1909 [CWM, LMS South Africa Reports, 4–2].

115. See, once again, the addendum by Willoughby to J. Brown and W. C. Willoughby, Report of a Visit to Kanye, 2 March 1903 [CWM, LMS Incoming Letters (Bechuana) 62–1].

116. E. Lloyd, Kanye, 23 September 1903 [CWM, LMS Incoming Letters (South Africa), 62–3].

117. Chidester (1992:122) points out that, while the early leadership of the SANNC was drawn primarily from mission churches, several prominent positions were held by (male and female) Ethiopians. The opening prayer at the founding of the Congress was delivered by an Ethiopian minister.

118. Reports from Bechuanaland around the turn of the century mention outstations where the "whole town has gone over to the Ethiopians"; see A. J. Wookey, Kuruman, 20 October 1903 [CWM, LMS Incoming Letters (South Africa), 62–4]; H. Williams, Kanye, Annual Report for 1907 [CWM, LMS South Africa Reports, 4-1]. In 1890, Brown reported from Taung that his congregants had complained of being stopped on the way to services and "made to go" to the Ethiopian Church; J. Brown, Taung, Annual Report for 1898 [CWM, LMS South Africa Reports, 3–1].

119. Chirenje (1977:220f.) argues that the Ethiopian presence also effected "a marked change" in missionary attitudes toward Tswana, especially in respect of education. It is true that the Nonconformists rethought many aspects of their policy and their practice at the turn of the century, not least in the sphere of pedagogy. But there were major forces at work in this process other than Ethiopianism. A thoughtful discussion of the various social factors impinging on the work of the mission, and laying it open to increasingly "impatient" critique, is to be found in H. Williams, Kanye, Annual Report for 1909 [CWM, LMS South Africa Reports, 4–2].

120. The leaders of the Ethiopian Church sought affiliation with the AME in 1896. But the formal connection only lasted a few years (Chidester 1992:117f.).

121. A number of statements to this effect are captured in the film *Heal the Whole Man* (Chigfield Films, London, 1973), based on our research in the Mafikeng District in the late 1960s. The title itself comes from one of them. Uttered by the Rev. O. Seodi, a local Methodist minister, it was intended to underscore what the mission churches had failed to do—and what they could and should have learned from other African Christianities.

122. Whiteside (1906:341f.) suggests that, in doing this, the Anglicans declared an "unfriendly rivalry" against the WMMS. But, as Molema (1951:129) points out, they were in fact invited in by Samuel, son of the Chief Moroka, for political reasons of his own. Relations between missionaries of the two denominations, Watson (1980:359) notes, were hostile.

123. Rev. Brown, especially, was put out by their presence. He complained bitterly about the "Anglican idea of Christianity," which, as a "creed apart from life," encouraged inferior standards of moral conduct; J. Tom Brown, Kuruman, Annual Report for 1907 [CWM, LMS South Africa Reports, 4–1].

124. The policy of making privileges for black "separatist" churches attendant on official recognition led to the submission of hundreds of applications to the Native Affairs Department from the early 1900s onward; see n. 88. A constitution, sometimes prepared with legal assistance, was typically included in these applications. Most constitutions, as we saw from official files in Pretoria and Mafikeng, dwelt on details of church government and rules and responsibilities of membership. Statements of doctrine, if provided at all, were brief—and often copied from the literature of the parent churches (J. Comaroff 1974:262).

125. See J. Comaroff (1974, 1985). Interestingly, one of the few Tswana theologians to provide a scholarly account of this historical process, Setiloane (1976:185f.), does so by describing a series of rites and dispositions that, he argues, compose an identifiable form of Sotho-Tswana Christian practice.

126. We heard many such stories about Sarwa in Mafikeng in 1969–70, several of them about a character named Qoba Gusha. Most memorable were those told to us by Victor Mapanye, a prominent figure at the *kgotla* of Chief Kebalepile, in the presence of, among others, the late Dr. David Tsatsi, a physician. Their telling led to lengthy discussions about the extraordinary ritual powers of Sarwa, then still widely seen as the social inferiors of Tswana.

127. The phrases quoted in this paragraph, and the statements of which they were part, are captured on film in *Heal the Whole Man* (see n. 121).

128. In Setswana, *Modimo* is gender-neutral. But translation at the hands of the missionaries fixed "God" as male (and upper case) in both reference and address. We therefore refer to Him accordingly.

129. The Southern Tswana evidence suggests that ideas of the trinity varied a great deal; see J. Comaroff (1974:282).

130. Setiloane (1976:219) cites Paul's statement to the Galatians (6.17) in this connection: "I bear on my body the marks of the dying of Christ."

131. John Mackenzie (1871:468) adds that this "keen" observation was not always undeserved. Interestingly, J. Tom Brown (1925:29) suggested that the verb *bòkòlela* (the cry of a dying animal or beaten person) might have been derived from *bòka* (to praise), a possibility which led him to speculate that the term could refer to the "dying shouts of oxen slaughtered to the god [ancestor], the bellowings being accepted as praises uttered." The verb *bòka*, however, is more generally taken to connote ritual praising, as performed by a praise poet or an indigenous doctor (Matumo 1993:583)—so the usage might have been less cynical than the missionaries assumed.

132. We ask the reader's indulgence in doing so, but we have been misread by a few historians and anthropologists of religion on this count.

133. Take, for example, Sol Plaatje (1996), a strongly identifying alumnus of the Lutheran mission, a moral leader of the new Christian elite, and an outspoken public figure. When pressed by the South African Native Affairs Commission (1905) to give his views of Ethiopianism, whose religious practices could not have been further from his own, he replied that, while he disapproved of some of its clergy, he had no differences with the church itself. [Note: in quoting from Plaatje's *Selected Writings* (1996), here and

below, we do not give page numbers. This is because the manuscript, kindly made available to us by Brian Willan, is only just going to press.]

134. Once more, our data here come from ethnohistories of Christianity collected in the late 1960s among elderly church members and senior Tswana clergy; these were "read" through our own participant observation in the mainstream denominations. All of our informants reported a striking continuity in the practices of which we speak here. In some cases, again, their comments were documented in *Heal the Whole Man* (see n. 121).

135. J. Tom Brown, Kuruman, Annual Report for 1909 [CWM, LMS South Africa Reports, 4–2]; see *RRI*:242, 339, n. 55.

T H R E E

1. These words are excerpted from Robert Moffat's journal for March–November 1825; they are most accessibly reproduced and annotated in Moffat and Moffat (1951:188).

2. As we noted in chapter 2, some Nonconformists were quite open about the limited evangelical efficacy of their performances in the pulpit. Said John Mackenzie (1871:71), fifty years after the mission to the Tswana commenced in earnest, "[S]ometimes the missionary in South Bechuana-land would as soon give some of his people a dinner as a sermon."

3. See, for an example from the LMS, Livingstone (1940:115) on the "daily labours" of an evangelist, circa 1848; and, for one from the WMMS, Edwards (1886:93).

4. Said Moffat (Moffat and Moffat 1951:116), in 1824, to Burder, Secretary of the LMS in London: "They could not view the wonders of science and art, and the advantages it confers on almost every member of society, without contrasting these with their own puerile advances in every part of domestic economy."

5. This view of Tswana was sustained throughout the century by many of the missionaries (and other whites in South Africa). As late as the 1920s, Willoughby (1923:255) wrote that "Bantu . . . are impressionable, imitative, adaptable."

6. For just one explicit example, see John Philip's (1828,1:204f.) discussion of the impact of shops, and the desire to consume goods, on the African impulse to industry.

7. See, for just one extended example among very many, Mark 4.3–32.

8. We shall encounter many examples as we proceed. However, one early one appears in a long quotation from John Philip included in a "Sketch of the Bechuana Mission" (LMS 1828, no pagination). In it, the "effect of the Gospel on the moral world" is likened to "the fertilizing effects" of irrigation on arid lands like Judea and South Africa. Elsewhere, Philip (1828,1:241) tells of the evangelical methods of (the much admired) Charles Pacalt, who taught Khoi to cultivate by laboring with them—while giving religious instruction at the same time.

9. In his remarkable *The Great War and Modern Memory* (1975:231f.), Fussell discusses the long-standing centrality of rural imaginings—the pastoral, the agri- and horti-

cultural, the floral—in "the British model world" after the industrial revolution (see also *RRI*:chap. 2).

10. For further details, see chapter 6, n. 2.

11. The evangelists read the accounts of these early visitors quite avidly—and, as we note elsewhere (chapter 6, n. 36), sometimes commented on them in their own writings.

12. For evidence to this effect, see the annotations to chapter 4 of volume 1, where we discuss the significance of cattle in the early nineteenth-century Southern Tswana world; indeed, that account relied in large measure on the (scattered but voluminous) notes made by missionaries on the subject.

13. Spenser wrote *A Veue of the Present State of Ireland* in 1595–96, but it was only published in 1633. Of course, Spenser was not alone, nor the first, to hold such views of the "wild Irish." For a history of early English writings on the topic, see Ong (1942).

14. Ironically, by 1815—says Halévy (1961:208)—Irish cattle keepers, now the occupants of "grazing farms," were very much wealthier than those who tenanted "tillage farms." But the graziers were despised, both by their compatriots and by Halévy, for their uncouth ways: among other things, they allowed animals to run free in the kitchens of their "absurdly luxurious" houses.

15. For discussion of some of the historical connections among the concepts of culture, cultivation, civilization, and evolution (or, more precisely, development and progress) see Williams (1976:76–82).

16. This may be traced back, in British anthropology, to Forde's *Habitat, Economy and Society* (1934). Although not an explicitly evolutionist work, its seminal division of the world into hunter-gatherers, pastoral nomads, and cultivators prefigured many later taxonomies, most of them either implicitly or explicitly evolutionary in conception. It also found its way into textbook "knowledge," a genre that reflects less the cutting edge of any discipline than its received wisdom. Some anthropologists (e.g., Nash 1966:37 and Meillassoux 1981:9f.) have argued cogently that economic systems are not reducible to, or distinguishable by, modes of *activity*. But this has had little impact on the continuing tendency to link cultivation to evolution.

17. An obvious case, of relevance here, is the role widely attributed to agriculture in catalyzing the British industrial revolution. For a brief (but usefully critical) overview of this difficult question, see Braudel (1984:558–64).

18. Note, for example, that the undertitle to Wallerstein's *The Modern World-System,* I (1974) is *Capitalist Agriculture and the Origins of the European World-Economy in the Sixteenth Century.* The significance of agrarian transformation in the rise of the modern world system, an undeniably complicated issue, has long been discussed in the literature of historical sociology.

19. It is not only in early modern England, or in its colonial domain, that nomadism was synonymous with barbarism, sedentarization with civilization. Take, for example, the world represented in Carlos Fuentes's novel, *The Campaign:* in 1810, in what was to become the Argentine, Fuentes's protagonist, Baltasar Bustos, speaks of the gauchos of the pampa as "savage." They "offended [his] sensibility . . . because they were

nomads who would never take root anywhere, mobile negations of the sedentary life he identified with civilization" (1992:36).

20. Some missionaries did speak of the enslavement of Tswana by Boers (e.g., Livingstone 1857:35); and most decried their treatment at the hands of white settlers (see J. L. Comaroff 1989:passim). But it was never suggested that these peoples suffered bondage in the same sense as had those much further to the north and to the south. It would simply not have been plausible.

21. In volume 1 (pp. 167f.), where we discussed both the historiography of *difaqane* and its variable impact on Southern Tswana, we cited other missionary accounts of the upheavals of the period (e.g., Broadbent 1865:74f.). These further confirm the point we seek to make here.

22. At least one version of the picture has a palm tree in the background, which suggests that the artist had never seen inland South Africa. Clearly these pictures were less illustrations of the "dark continent" than popular imaginings of the civilizing mission.

23. For a comment on the connection between consumer goods and ideological signs, with special reference to bread as a religious symbol in the Christian sacrament of communion, see Volosinov (1973:10).

24. J. Read, Lattakoo, 15 March 1817 [CWM, LMS Incoming Letters (South Africa), 7–1–C].

25. Thus was a refined European diet sacralized—and, with it, a particular agrarian mode of production. Bread, the product of "civilized" farming, contrasted with African sorghum ("kafir-corn") and, more significantly, with the staples of a pastoral economy.

26. This exchange, which occurred in Cape Town in 1823, was reported by the businessman George Thompson (1967:166). The Tlhaping counselor, an elderly man named Teysho, was one of two Tswana whom Moffat brought with him on a visit to the Colony. The evangelist and a "Hottentot" interpreter acted as translators. Thompson later visited Kuruman; we quote below from the report he wrote of his sojourn there.

27. This is noted in a biographical sketch of George Thompson by Vernon Forbes, editor of the Van Riebeeck Society re-issue of his *Travels and Adventures;* see Thompson (1967:xiii).

28. The point was sometimes made directly. But it was also made obliquely, by reference to the limited, fragile properties of beads, the "only circulating medium in the interior of South Africa" (Campbell 1822,1:246; cf. J. Philip 1828,2:131); we shall return to this in the next chapter.

29. We have added the emphasis, and inserted "[still]" into the quotation, less to make our own point than to capture the original spirit of Willoughby's text.

30. For a similar statement, see Hodgson's (1977:117) remark on Tswana gluttony in his diary entry of 20 January 1823. A century later, S. M. Molema (1920:119), himself a Motswana of course, also commented on the capacity of "the Bantu people to "consume surprisingly large quantities."

31. This is a corollary of the general point made in volume 1 (p. 200f.) about the aesthetics of cultural imperialism; namely, that Western colonizers everywhere tended to impose the square and the rectangle, favored shapes of European civilization, upon the "primitive" circle and the arc. Of the latter, it is said, Tswana were inordinately fond; see also chapter 6.

32. Livingstone (1857:46) added that the Kwena "[had] a curious inability to make or put things square."

33. John Philip (1828,2:122) did add, backhandedly perhaps, that the layout and state of the town did "nothing to offend any of the senses."

34. Nevertheless, said John Mackenzie (1871:92), a "fair beginning" had been made; these gardens were a "welcome sight" by comparison to what had been there before the arrival of the mission.

35. J. Brown, Taung, 1900, Report for 1900: Ten Years Review [CWM, LMS South Africa Reports, 3–1].

36. An example that captures all these aspects of the royal effort to sustain material and ritual control over the agricultural cycle may be found in the struggle between Chief Montshiwa and the first Tshidi-Rolong converts. The story, which dates to the early 1860s, is told in many mission texts (e.g., J. Mackenzie 1871, 1883), travel tales (e.g., Holub 1881), and local histories (e.g., Molema 1966); for an accessible summary, see John Mackenzie (1975:100f.).

37. It was not only evangelists who paid attention to the agrarian ministrations of "native doctors," to fertility rites, and to taboos regulating the agricultural cycle. For one account, including a description of the ceremonial digging of a "rain-field" (*tsimo ya pula*) among Ngwato, see Holub (1881,1:337).

38. See, e.g., Robert Moffat (1842:279). The analogy between biblical Judea and Africa raised once more the issue of the fall of the "dark continent" from grace. How had the hallowed agrarian practices of the former become the barbarisms of the latter? "Like shells without the kernel," we are told by Moffat and others, they had been emptied of their original content—by either (i) satanic intervention, or (ii) a more humdrum process whereby ancient forms, bereft of divine inspiration, had "[merged] into the ordinary habits of savage life." (Note, again, the iconography of emptiness and absence.)

39. Somerville (1979:130), for example, noted of *both* men and women that "their disposition to industry is a prominent part of their character," even if the "distribution of employments" by gender here was "very different from that which prevails in Europe." Similarly, Lichtenstein (1973:66): "Even when there is hardly anything to be done they are industrious and active."

40. Several early (non-missionary) observers noted the skill of Tlhaping smiths (see Stow 1905:419). Lichtenstein (1973:81) was most enthusiastic: "they are so much advanced," he said, "that they astonished the colonists who accompanied us by repairing our waggons and fixing up some of our iron tools." Somerville (1979:128) remarked on the range of implements manufactured by these smiths, but compared their quality unfavorably with their European counterparts. Only Burchell (1824,2:340) dissented: in 1812, he claimed, there was but one smith among Tlhaping, and he had recently acquired his craft "from the north-eastern nations."

41. The use of the term "scratching" to describe African hoe agriculture—with all its faunal resonances—was not uncommon in contemporary European writings; hence the title of Pratt's (1985) essay, "Scratches on the Face of the Country." As far as we are aware, it appears for the first time, in connection with the South African interior, in Somerville's (1979:139) diary entry for 1 December 1801.

42. Said Lichtenstein (1973:77), who voiced great admiration for Tswana women, and who expressed concern for their position: "They are quite happy to hoe, dig and build without ever showing any bad mood."

43. A. J. Wookey, Kuruman, 24 September 1873 [CWM, LMS South Africa Reports, 1–3].

44. To take just three examples: (i) Borcherds (1979:233), a member of the Trüter-Somerville expedition of 1799–1802, wrote that "the fields [of the Tlhaping] are planted in a way which is admirable when one considers the vastness of them." (ii) Somerville (1979:139) went as far as to say that Tswana agriculture "is little if at all inferior" to that of "the Dutch boors"; his account (pp. 122–23) also makes it clear that the range of crops planted was wider than the missionaries intimated. (iii) Stow (1905:440) noted that Dithakong was "surrounded by several large tracts of land, laid out and cultivated like so many gardens"; he also spoke of "the great agricultural settlements or towns" of these people. (p. 419).

45. For a summary statement of the Nonconformist vision of agrarian transformation in Africa, written with a century of hindsight, see Willoughby (1923:181). Although part of an essay on "native education," this passage captures succinctly the missionary perspective on material improvement among "a race whose feet are on the lower rungs of the ladder of progress."

46. Lord Ernle was the baronial title of Rowland Edmund Prothero. Although he is often referred to in the scholarly literature by his title, Prothero published the book under his birth name; we list it thus in our bibliography.

47. Even those, like Eric Jones (1968), who deny that the post-1815 years were disastrous, confirm that much public alarm was expressed at the time over the state of agriculture. Few could have been optimistic about its prospects in England—and this includes the circles whence came the early African missionaries.

48. The poem from which these lines are drawn was part of the romantic reaction to the early impact of the "age of revolution" on rural England (see *RRI*:chap. 2). Nonetheless, Goldsmith's observation—albeit excised from its broader poetic context—is applicable to a later epoch in British agrarian history as well.

49. A great deal has been written on the symbolic centrality of the domesticated landscape in nineteenth-century European self-imaginings; although, as Darian-Smith (1995:397; after W. J. Mitchell 1994 and others) reminds us, "the garden"—for all its salience in the construction of (i) generic Englishness, (ii) the idea of civilization, even (iii) the modernist British nation-state—"is a complex concept with a constantly changing meaning," one that defies "stable figural representation." Our concerns here, however, are not so much with its conceptual archaeology "at home" as with its transposition to, and evocation in, Africa.

50. For published accounts of the early development of mission gardens, see especially Robert Moffat's letters in Moffat and Moffat (1951) and Broadbent (1865:104f.).

51. J. Archbell, Platberg, 2 September 1833 [WMMS, South Africa Correspondence (Albany), 303]. For examples of the leases signed between the Wesleyans and African rulers, see Mears (1970:36–44).

52. Early on, the fearfulness of the evangelists for themselves, their families, and their mission was owed to the turbulence in the region; at times it was exacerbated by their reception at the hands of Tswana. They were also to feel threatened later, as they became embroiled in clashes between the Africans and white settlers. For particularly vivid expressions of the near panic felt by the Christians, see, e.g., Moffat and Moffat (1951:161, 175). We stress the point here again since a reviewer of volume 1 suggests that we made too little of it there. Such, however, was not our intention.

53. See, e.g., Livingstone (1857:21). Many of the evangelists feared the prospect of being forced, at the momentary whim of a local ruler, to give up everything they had built. In fact, as the century passed, efforts by the LMS and WMMS to buy their land had less and less to do with exemplary teaching and more and more to do with territorial possession and security; this, as we shall see, gave rise to bad feelings—even outright resistance—on the part of some local populations. (In at least one instance, mission land ownership also became embroiled in competition between Christian denominations; see Wales 1985:258).

54. Weir (1993:130), in response to volume 1, suggests that early missionaries evinced differing degrees of enthusiasm for making gardens and teaching cultivation; that, for example, Livingstone was readier to undertake this task than was Moffat; that it is mistaken, therefore, to imply that all the evangelists engaged alike in such activities. Perhaps. The evidence, however, shows that, whatever they might have felt about it, every one of the first generation planted crops and implored Tswana to follow their techniques. We are not sure how Weir has decided that Moffat was less given to agrarian enterprises than was Livingstone; the documentary record indicates otherwise. In any case, it was LMS policy that all mission stations make themselves as viable as possible through agriculture and craft production.

55. See, e.g., J. Archbell, Cradock, 23 May 1831 [WMMS, South Africa Correspondence (Albany), 303]; or, again, the reminiscences of John Moffat (R. U. Moffat 1921:14 et passim).

56. The evangelists had "Indian" corn, wheat, vegetables (beans, pumpkins, etc.), and fruit particularly in mind.

57. Would-be converts were urged "to do their work in quietness and to earn their own living" (*Thessalonians* 3.12).

58. Cf., on Jamaica, Holt (n.d.:15f.).

59. T. Hodgson, Matlwasse, 12 January 1824 [WMMS, South Africa Correspondence, 300].

60. "Pilfering and stealing" by Tswana was a favorite topic of early dispatches from the mission field. *Apprenticeship at Kuruman,* for example, is filled with references to it (Moffat and Moffat 1951:52, also p. 71 et passim).

61. Mahutu was not herself of Tlhaping origin. She was the daughter of a Khoi leader, and apparently the vehicle of a dynastic alliance. As Maingard (1933:599f.) notes, there is much evidence of such intermarriage from the mid eighteenth century onward; he insists, nonetheless, that there was little sign of Khoi influence on Tlhaping language and cultural practice.

62. The quickness of Tswana to "perceive the advantage of . . . [the] art" of irrigation, and their eagerness to experiment with it and with other agrarian techniques, was noted admiringly by George Thompson (1967:164–65) in 1823.

63. Lichtenstein was reporting here on the years *before* Moffat et al. had set up their station among the Tlhaping. The missionary of whom he speaks, Kok, was one of the very first to enter the region; as we have noted (*RRI*:190), he failed to establish a permanent evangelical presence among Southern Tswana.

64. In their *Report* for the following year, 1830, the directors of the LMS (LMS 1830:86) noted that the station had indeed prospered, its gardens having yielded "an abundance of different kinds of vegetables, &c."

65. For another example, circa 1823, see George Thompson (1967:164f.).

66. J. Cameron, Platberg, 26 September 1842 [WMMS, South Africa Correspondence (Bechuana), 315–121]; J. Allison, Lishuani, 1 August 1843 [WMMS, South Africa Correspondence (Bechuana), 315–123].

67. The directors of the LMS seem to have realized how restricted and fragile was that sphere of influence. In their *Report* for 1841 (LMS 1841:91), they noted that, once the interior had settled down after *difaqane*, numbers of people had "begun to wander . . . about the country and to reside at a greater distance from the station. In so doing, many of them believe that their cattle will increase more abundantly, and not a few are influenced by a desire to escape from the effects of the Gospel." If they were correct, Tswana had found a simultaneously temporal and spiritual motive for flight from the mission; we return to the point in passing below.

68. These were invariably translated by, or at the behest of, the evangelists (see, e.g., G. Thompson 1967:166).

69. Shillington (1985:16) stresses the impact of firearms, a large number of which fell into Tswana hands from the 1850s. This, he argues, led to animals being hunted to extinction in the old game fields—which made cultivation at once more necessary and also easier than before, when wild beasts threatened those working in the agricultural zones around settlements.

70. In cases of protracted drought or cattle disease, women sometimes returned to cultivating on a very small scale with hoes and digging sticks. But this became increasingly rare with the passage of time.

71. Neil Parsons (1977:123) points out that, in the arid climate and on the sandy soils of Bechuanaland, the plough also extended the time when cultivation was possible—an extremely important consideration in all Tswana agriculture.

72. David Livingstone (1974:78) was to invoke this in the 1850s as evidence of the relative unproductivity of Boer agriculture.

73. This statement was made to a Land Commission in 1885, and referred to a period nineteen years before.

74. This pattern was to prevail. Holub (1881,1:339) reported, in the 1870s, that women continued to do most of the hard work of cultivation. Where the plough was in use, it was driven by oxen—and hence led by men, as the old animal taboos remained intact. But all other agrarian labor still fell to females. Even Christian wives, added Holub, had not seen the "severity of their tasks" lightened.

75. John Mackenzie (1887,2:168), citing a trader who had lived in Taung since 1860, says that crops raised under irrigation in "several places" now included maize, wheat, millet, pumpkins, onions, potatoes, and various fruits.

76. See A. Wookey, Kuruman, 23 May 1884 [CWM, LMS Incoming Letters (South Africa), 42-3-C]; J. Mackenzie (1871:70). Shillington (1985:66) notes that a prominent trader in the Harts region claimed to have sold six hundred ploughs to Tlhaping between 1874 and 1877.

77. John Mackenzie (1871:70), among others, notes specifically that mission land was only given to a man if he was the "husband of one wife." The allotment of these well-watered plots, he says, was "not the most pleasant" of evangelical duties—presumably because it determined who would be rich and who would be poor.

78. J. Mackenzie, Kuruman, 17 February 1882 [CWM, LMS South Africa Reports, 2–1] details how farmers unable to irrigate were displaced by the "wealthy" who could. See n. 86 below for another, slightly later account—this one in an official state document—of land expropriation by the wealthiest members of Southern Tswana communities.

79. Cf. Krige and Krige (1943:320) on the Lovedu case.

80. The best source of Tswana narratives of events leading up to the annexation of Griqualand—especially of the expropriation of Rolong and Tlhaping land and labor—is to found in the evidence presented to the Bloemhof commission of 1871. (The commission, as we explained in volume 1 and will mention again later, was set up to investigate the claims of the various parties to ownership of the diamond fields.) Since the document has no author, and was not a publication of the colonial state, we list it in our bibliography as Bloemhof (1871).

81. Fifty years earlier, John Philip (1828,1:241) had remarked that, having been taught to toil for themselves, converts "did not feel the same objections as formerly, to work for [white] farmers."

82. This account does not make it clear whether Hurutshe actually sold tobacco, although it implies as much. Elsewhere, Holub (1881,2:424) says that, at the time, the Kwena at Molepolole were the only Tswana who cultivated it "as an article of commerce."

83. The troubled political history of southern Bechuanaland in the 1880s and 1890s—in particular, the struggles among Tswana, the British, and the Boers over land and sovereignty—have been well documented elsewhere (see, e.g., Sillery 1952, 1971; Maylam 1980; Shillington 1985; also *RRI*:chap. 7). Here we are concerned specifically with agrarian transformations and, hence, take as read the more general processes of

which they were part. What is more, we do not even try to detail the turbulent economic and political processes unfolding at Thaba 'Nchu during this period. They are far too complex to treat in a brief overview—and, in any case, are the subject of at least one comprehensive scholarly monograph (Murray 1992) and several briefer treatments (e.g., Watson 1980).

84. See also J. Brown, Taung, 1900, Report for 1900, Ten Years Review [CWM, LMS South Africa Reports, 3–1], who noted that the move of men into ploughing had made women "increasingly dependent upon husbands."

85. The various means by which this was done have been documented by a number of scholars; see, for just a few examples, J. Mackenzie (1887), Molema (1966), and Shillington (1985).

86. In the late 1880s, the annual reports for British Bechuanaland began to document specific cases of the concentration of "native" land in the hands of the most powerful members of Tswana communities; for an example from Kuruman see Great Britain (1889:50).

87. Echoes here of a remark made in *Howards End* by Henry Wilcox, businessman, about farming in Edwardian England: "The days for small farms are over. It doesn't pay—except with intensive cultivation. . . . Take it as a rule that nothing pays on a small scale" (Forster 1992:205). And this in a much less arid environment.

88. The Civil Commissioner at Mafeking tried, in the late 1880s, to arrange a "native agricultural show" to induce small farmers to grow "something besides Kafir corn, mealies, and pumpkins" (Great Britain 1889:51); this sixty years after the evangelists set about doing the same thing. But, in the unpromising circumstances that now prevailed, his efforts met with little success.

89. This is a general point to which we shall return in chapter 4. For one example, however, see A. J. Gould, Kuruman, 16 February 1891 [CWM, LMS Incoming Letters (South Africa), 48-1-B]; Gould wrote that, as a direct result of the pressure on grazing and garden land, he was telling Southern Tswana to "turn their hands to some industry."

90. J. Tom Brown, Kuruman, 28 May 1898 [CWM, LMS Incoming Letters (South Africa), 55-1-C]; see also E. Smith (1957:318).

91. A letter to the *Diamond Fields Advertiser,* 23 February 1897, p. 2, signed by "Bechuanaland Observers," objected to the government regulations.

92. See J. Brown, Kuruman, 5 January 1899, Report for 1898, Kuruman [CWM, LMS South Africa Reports, 3–1]. By this time, of course, there was little game, other than small animals, left to shoot.

93. Neil Parsons (1977:125) includes a remarkable passage in which Khama himself described agrarian change among his people; remarkable, that is, since its idyllic picture could as well have been written by a European missionary. It appeared in *Christian World* in September 1895, before the rinderpest struck: "It is a sure sign of advance when you see the men use the ploughs which have come to us from Sweden and America. . . . This generation of women . . . cut out dresses and sew for themselves, and sew for their husbands as well."

94. J. Brown, Taung, 1900, Report for 1900, Ten Years Review [CWM, LMS South Africa Reports, 3–1].

95. For a full report, see the *Diamond Fields Advertiser,* 1 November 1878, p. 3.

96. In the case of Southern Tswana, most notably Silas Modiri Molema, Zachariah Keodirelang Matthews (see n. 99), and Solomon Tshekisho Plaatje, all of whom we have quoted and will continue to quote as we proceed. In particular, Plaatje's extraordinary political and social commentaries, many of which have been recuperated and (re)published as a result of the outstanding scholarly work of Brian Willan, anticipated recent revisionist histories in interesting ways. Plaatje (1919, repr.1996), for example, makes it clear why—given existing material conditions, legislation, and labor recruitment arrangements—black migrant workers had either to move to urban areas under restrictive, unremunerative contracts or to take work in towns on absurdly exploitative terms. He also demonstrates why these conditions, contracts, and terms made it impossible for blacks to subsist either from their wages or from farming in the countryside.

97. Lest there be any misunderstanding, we do not, for our own part, believe that taxation (or any other blunt instrument of material dependency) was the sole, or even prime, cause of proletarianization—or, for that matter, of migrant labor (cf. Wylie 1990:58, on the Bechuanaland Protectorate). As should be clear from chapter 4 and from volume 1, we see the determinations of black South African history to be far more complex than a simple narrative of economic domination would allow. However, this is not to say that there was no connection between taxation, agricultural prices, land seizure, and the need for cash.

98. See, e.g., A. J. Wookey, Kuruman, 23 May 1884 [CWM, LMS Incoming Letters (South Africa), 42-3-C]; we return to this document in chapter 4.

99. Z. K. Matthews, as South African readers will know, was a black scholar and political figure of great stature. The author of *Freedom for My People* (1981), he did field work among the Rolong—under the informal supervision of Schapera and the aegis of the International African Institute—in the late 1930s. His notes, which we also drew on in volume 1, are housed in the Botswana National Archives. In his "First Quarterly Report on Field-Work among the Barolong of British Bechuanaland (December 1935–February 1936)," Matthews identified himself as a Mongwato, adding that his mother "belong[ed] to one of the leading kxotlas of the Tshidi section of the Barolong" (p. 1).

100. "Second Field Work Report" (November 1937–February 1938), pp. 1–2.

101. The data for this paragraph are drawn largely from handwritten field notes entitled "Agriculture." In these notes, which seem to have been based on information supplied by an agricultural demonstrator, Matthews wrote that the average yield of sorghum and maize "by native methods" was two to four bags per acre; by European methods it was seven to ten (weights not given).

102. This division of labor, as Matthews's "First Quarterly Report" shows (p. 7), followed long-received patterns—except for the mission-inspired innovation of ploughing being done by men.

103. Matthews, "Third Field Report (November 1938–February 1939)."

104. See Plaatje, "In Bechuanaland Today: Some Recent Travel Notes," *Diamond Fields Advertiser,* 17 April 1928 (repr. 1996).

105. The six-page narrative, written in longhand, is entitled "Life at the Cattle-Post." In the photocopied version made available to us, it is appended to Matthews's field notes on "Agriculture" (see n. 101).

106. These details about Leteane's church affiliation and descendants are our own addition; his grandson, Joseph Leteane, served as our research assistant and Setswana teacher in 1969–70.

107. Matthews, writing at a time when ethnic categories were more readily assumed to be primordial than is the case today, spoke of these servants as being "of [foreign, e.g.] Kgalagadi *origin*" (p. 2). However, as we (e.g., 1992:49ff.) and others have pointed out, the ethnicization ("othering") of people in servitude has been fairly common in Africa. This is not to deny the existence elsewhere of discrete political communities whose citizenry referred to themselves—and were referred to by others—as Kgalagadi; such communities certainly existed (see, e.g., Schapera and Comaroff 1991:8; A. Kuper 1970a, 1970b). It is, rather, to make the point that, *within* the Rolong world, "Kgalagadi" marked a particular social status by appeal to the terms of cultural difference.

108. Matthews suggests (p. 3) that, in such circumstances, the status of former servants—"whatever their economic position"—remained unaltered. Here we must disagree. Our own field notes include several cases of families which, once in servitude, had succeeded in raising their social position quite remarkably over the years.

109. According to our own family histories, taken in 1969, Leteane is remembered by his descendants to have been a progressive farmer. We were told that he introduced advanced agricultural techniques and implements wherever he could, and built up a large herd through painstaking management.

110. This is the master narrative on which Shillington (1985) bases his detailed, informative account of the colonization of the Southern Tswana, 1870–1900; it parallels Colin Bundy's work closely in its overall theoretical orientation.

111. A similar process of transformation—also evocative of Lenin's account of the Russian peasantry—was to occur some decades later on the so-called "Barolong Farms" (or "Barolong"), a Tshidi political community in southern Botswana. We have documented this case, and its theoretical implications, elsewhere (see J. L. Comaroff 1977, 1980, 1982, 1983).

112. We are aware, of course, of all the old debates surrounding the use of the term "peasant" in Africa—and, more broadly, surrounding the conceptualization of peasantries *sui generis* (see, e.g., Kearney 1996). While it would be easy enough to avoid the word altogether, we deploy it here, rather loosely, to label a population whose internal fractions we go on to typify in more precise terms. We do this for two reasons. First, it draws attention to the parallel with processes of rural class formation elsewhere. And, second, the term itself was used, in a nonpejorative manner, by both liberal missionaries and black South African literati to describe the land-based "native" population of the countryside. See, e.g., Plaatje, "A Happy New Year" [Editorial], *Tsala ea Batho*, 3 January 1914 (repr. Plaatje 1996); elsewhere, Plaatje (n.d.:380) describes blacks who had been removed from their lands as "the native proletariat."

113. A small portion of the seed was doctored and then mixed with the rest, "to which it import[ed] its qualities" (p. 11). Matthews does not say whether the doctoring

was done by a ritual specialist. But he suggests that, in the past, it had been undertaken communally, under the direction of the chief, an arrangement that made for less suspicion, competition, and conflict.

114. This is Matthews's rendering. We did not encounter it ourselves in the late 1960s, although we did come across other medicines for the treatment of cattle. We also observed the doctoring of fields—less so of seeds—by Tshidi-Rolong in the early 1970s.

115. Not all chiefs and headmen became members of the upper peasantry, however. Some fell into poverty, others joined the ranks of the middle peasantry. There was also a political factor involved: when the Cape Colony annexed Griqualand West in 1880, and imposed itself on the two Tlhaping polities in the territory, their ruling cadres were reduced to vassalage and penury (Shillington 1985:90ff.). Further north, in British Bechuanaland and the Bechuanaland Protectorate, overrule did not have the same drastic effect—British settler interests were not quite as pressing—but some local sovereigns did suffer hardship as a result.

116. The data for the following paragraphs are composited from Matthews's notes, our own agrarian histories and ethnohistories collected in the Mafikeng District (1969–70) and Barolong (1974–75 and 1976–77), and the various sources already quoted in this chapter. Shillington (1985:95f, 20f. et passim) also gives some account of wealthy peasants in both Griqualand West and British Bechuanaland.

117. For example, it was they who first purchased metal ploughs—initially single- and then double-furrow models—to replace earlier wooden ones (cf. Schapera 1933:638, on the Kgatla).

118. In 1975, while in southern Botswana, we were told a number of elaborate stories, dating back a long time, of nefarious land dealings by prominent people. For obvious reasons we have never published these, although we have documented struggles over arable land in more recent times (J. L. Comaroff 1977, 1980).

119. See, e.g., Shillington (1985:20, 30, n. 62) for the case of Piet Boromelo, a wealthy Motlhaping.

120. Although, as Matthews wrote in his field notes on agriculture (see n. 101), Southern Tswana at large were less quick to adopt new techniques in this sphere than they were in respect of cultivation (pp. 9f.). This is borne out by records in the Tshidi-Rolong Community Offices at Mafikeng: in 1969–70, the secretary to the chief, Stephen Phetlhu, showed us files on cattle culling, vaccination, dipping, feed supplements, and other innovations which were widely resisted even by some affluent stock owners.

121. In an address read on his behalf by W. E. B. Dubois to the Pan-African Congress in Paris (1921), Plaatje (1996) tells of a wealthy farmer who had invested $4,500—a great deal of money then—in agricultural machinery. Elsewhere he mentioned the purchase by Silas and Israel Molema of a steam threshing machine (see n. 123). Ironically, under the Machinery Act of 1912, which reserved skilled work in South Africa for whites, these men were technically forbidden to operate their machines—although it is unlikely that the terms of the Act were ever implemented in "native" areas.

122. In Barolong in 1974–75, we found that owners of mechanized means of production always demanded cash in advance for the rental of their machines and services

(J. L. Comaroff 1977). As a result, their income was guaranteed, irrespective of rainfall and other climatic factors; ecological risk was borne entirely by clients. We were told that this arrangement had prevailed as far back as anyone could remember—which, in the case of elderly farmers, was early in the century. Indeed, it was one of the reasons often given for the maintenance of wealth differences between the rich and the poor.

123. The Molema-Plaatje Papers include (i) copies of a number of leases in terms of which Silas Molema granted land to white farmers, some of it in the Mafeking Reserve (see, e.g., Aa 3.5.8; below, chapter 8); (ii) the Memorandum of Agreement covering his purchase of *Koranta ea Becoana* from George Nathanial Whales (Aa 3.6.1.1); and (iii) invoices covering the goods he bought from white importers to retail in Mafikeng (Aa 3.2). For an annotated catalogue of these papers, see Jacobson (1978). See also Silas Molema's obituary, by Plaatje, in the *Cape Times*, 13 September 1927 (repr. 1996).

124. See, for instance, Molema's (1966:201–9) account of the "heathen" chief Montshiwa in this respect.

125. Sebopiwa J. Molema, Kanye, 26 April 1918 [Molema-Plaatje Papers, Ac 1]. The Molema family correspondence provides an ample record of the life circumstances and the ideological orientations of the emerging elite. This correspondence also gives a sense of how the new bourgeoisie tended its private economic interests; for just one example, see another letter from Sebopiwa Molema to his uncle, quoted in chapter 4, n. 110.

126. It is not the case, as received stereotypes might suggest, that devout commoner Christians always advocated modernist innovation while royals, more invested in "tradition" and less in the church, showed themselves wary of the new. There were times in Tshidi-Rolong history, for instance, when the opposite occurred.

127. See *RRI*:chap. 4 for a discussion of these practices. Note also that identifying Christians engaged in them as avidly as did nominal and non-Christian royals; the headship of many wards and sections among Rolong, Tlhaping, and Tlharo were held by well-known church members. The latter also entered into the power struggles surrounding the various chiefships. Not only did Molema, the first Tshidi-Rolong Methodist, once try to relieve Montshiwa of his office (*RRI*:263), but his descendants continued to take an active part in palace politics well into this century. Even when he held an executive position in the ANC, Dr. S. M. Molema involved himself in the affairs of the *kgotla* at Mafikeng.

128. We discuss this further in chapter 6.

129. This occurred more among Tlhaping than among Rolong. After the 1850s, when the Tlhaping polity fragmented even further than it had before, some people dispersed "to form new, smaller settlements, where they could place greater emphasis upon cultivation" (Shillington 1985:20; see below). But, even then, wealthy men retained homes at the capital (Shillington 1985:20).

130. There is a major exception to this characterization, although it comes not from Bechuanaland but from the heartlands of the Orange Free State and the Transvaal. Among the black South Africans displaced by the Natives Land Act of 1913 were affluent families who had left their natal communities to purchase farms while it remained legal

to do so. (Also among them were middle peasants who leased arable acreages and pasturage from whites; see below.) After 1913, however, these freeholders were gradually dispossessed of their property, which they could neither sell nor bequeath to other blacks. While many of them were Sotho, some were also Tswana.

131. See, e.g., John Mackenzie (1887,1:76), who says that, although severely weakened by events on the frontier, Southern Tswana chiefs "tried to rally their people . . . for the old life in the large native town." In fact, these rulers were not all as impotent as he made out; some *did* sustain the centralization of their polities. Mackenzie's stress on the erosion of the chiefship, and on the dispersal of the population, was part wishful thinking, part rhetorical strategy: he was campaigning at the time for the decentralization of chiefdoms, so that Tswana might live as an independent peasantry, unencumbered by traditional authorities, on scattered farmsteads. We return to this topic again below.

132. We stress their lack of choice in the matter. As we have said before, wages paid to black men were kept at levels which ensured a continuing reliance on female agriculture at home. For an articulate account (by a black South African) of the regulation of "native" incomes by the state, see Plaatje's address to the Pan-African Congress (above, n. 121).

133. Statutes regulating "native" labor and movement at the time made it very difficult, even impossible, for wives to live with their husbands in towns. (So, too, of course, did migrant labor contracts.) Some municipalities disallowed it outright; others permitted women to stay with their menfolk, but charged them a fee and/or subjected them to a bewildering array of rules.

134. The civil commissioner at Mafeking said virtually the same thing in his report for that year (Cape of Good Hope 1907:30): "There is no progress in agricultural undertakings. . . . [O]nly the top of the soil is scratched here and there."

135. Later there would emerge other forms of pooling and communal exchange arrangements, even voluntary associations; (see chapter 8).

136. As we shall see in chapters 5 and 6, vernacular and bilingual newspapers—owned and produced by members of the local bourgeoisie—constantly urged Tswana to buy both "modern" implements and the consumer items required for a "respectable" lifestyle.

137. For those living in the western reaches of British Bechuanaland, where the ecology made cultivation impossible, this second consideration was of less importance. Even for these people, however, being able to tend their herds was much easier when they lived at their cattle posts.

138. See Matthews, "Second Field Work Report," p. 2.

139. We base this statement on two sources: (i) the detailed minutes of "tribal" meetings kept, from early this century, at the Tshidi-Rolong Community Offices (again, shown to us by Stephen Phetlhu; see n. 120); and (ii) the oral accounts of older informants, which we sought in response to the reports of missionaries (e.g., Campbell 1822,2:156f.; J. Philip 1828,2:133) about the remarkably open nature of Tlhaping and Rolong public assemblies. Both indicated that, while freedom of speech has always been highly valued among Tswana, not everyone participated equally; that the lowly seldom

expressed their views. Some of our informants added that these people were more likely to sit mute beside their headmen, announcing their tacit support, than to speak for themselves. We found that, with a few exceptions, much the same thing obtained in 1969–70 (J. L. Comaroff 1975).

140. The evidentiary basis for our portrayal of this class-in-formation is once again composited from several sources—among them, Plaatje's writings (e.g., 1996; n.d.), especially on the effects of the Natives Land Act (see n. 130); Matthews's field notes; missionary records; and our own agrarian histories.

141. The Setiloanes were clearly of the middle peasantry (in the specific sense we mean it here) from early on. Not of royal extraction, they converted to Methodism even before the WMMS moved to Thaba 'Nchu and adopted the agricultural methods taught by the mission (Setiloane 1976:168). But their economic fortunes fluctuated, especially as overrule eroded the material lives of Southern Tswana. They had to move often in search of employment and entered into sharecropping arrangements with Boer farmers more than once. At the same time, they regularly filled leading lay positions in the church, and in due course attained high levels of education.

142. Cf. Shillington (1985:96f.), who shows that, among the Tlhaping of Griqualand, settler incursion led to an acute shortage of pasture in the 1880s. As a result, many stock owners had to rent grazing land from whites. Most of them, it seems, were middle peasants. Shillington's data (e.g., p. 95) suggests (i) that the wealthiest local farmers had gained a huge disproportion of the range available in the "native locations" and (ii) that one or two of them had purchased freeholdings. They did not, therefore, need to rent.

143. Both Mhengwa Lecholo (a powerful section headman in Mafikeng who died, in his nineties, in 1992) and Chief Kebalepile (the Tshidi ruler who died, in his forties, in 1973) told us of cases in which this had happened among Rolong. By dating the creation of new wards and subwards, and correlating them with biographical information about their founding heads, we can confirm it to have been true.

144. For further analysis of these transformations—of their social, economic, and political dynamics; of the various ways in which they worked themselves out; of their gendered dimensions; of their long-term implications—see, e.g., J. L. Comaroff and J. Comaroff (1992:95–125); J. L. Comaroff (1976:71–75; 1987).

145. As Shillington (1985:19) notes, Helmore tried to dam the Harts River at Dikgatlhong, then a Tlhaping town under the authority of the Christian chief Jantje. This dam was destroyed by floods and not rebuilt. But other, less ambitious ones were successfully constructed.

146. "Khama's Disputes" [Willoughby Papers, 14]. This file, which is not numbered, contains two letters from W. C. Willoughby to R. W. Thompson in London; they are dated 12 February 1896 and 21 April 1896. It is from these documents that we quote here.

147. See Great Britain (1933:143f., especially #209). Having had difficulty in obtaining a copy of this document—known as the Pim Report—in the U.S.A., we worked from a typescript version made by Matthews and kept among his papers in the Botswana National Archives. Schapera (1943b:268f.) also discusses it *in extenso*.

148. For just one example, see Sol Plaatje's essay, "Segregation: Idea Ridiculed," written in 1910 and originally published in *Tsala ea Becoana*, 18 January 1911. It is republished, with other pieces of the same ilk and an explanatory comment, by Brian Willan in Plaatje (1996).

F O U R

1. As this implies, we are not concerned here with the vexed Weberian question of the Puritan impact on the rise of capitalism. Nor do we pursue the "elective affinity" in the other direction, as does Wearmouth (1937:13), who argues that movements like Methodism would not have been possible without the industrial revolution. While the connection is not unimportant, we think it ill-advised to attribute the growth of these religious movements to social and economic forces at the expense of their own internal dynamism (cf. Hempton 1984:16).

2. A similar synecdoche is apparent in Adam Smith's (1976:14) phrase, "the general business of society."

3. Evangelical attitudes to money would also have been influenced by prevailing material conditions. As Hart (1986:643) points out, English economics was born amidst the crisis of confidence in the coin of the realm that followed the triumph of Parliament over absolutism. The first banks were established in the late seventeenth century, when commercial expansion and industrial growth created a demand for capital. But it was only after 1750 that a national banking system emerged (Anderson and Cottrell 1974: 150f.). Banking developments—like the deposit and note system—enhanced the growth of capital resources, with provincial bankers issuing their own notes. The latter, together with drafts and bills, made up for shortages of mint coins and the irregular circulation of the Bank of England note (Anderson and Cottrell 1974:152). London would become the "money capital" of the world by the early nineteenth century (Jenks 1927:5), although popular experience of, and confidence in, currency and banking at the time was probably uneven. The widening socioeconomic divisions in Britain in the early 1900s positioned classes very differently in relation to the means of production and access to coin. Nonconformist missionaries, many of whom were from upwardly mobile, lower-middle-class backgrounds (*RRI*:80f.), seemed especially willing to put their trust into the liberal promise of money and trade (cf. Helmstadter 1992; Norman 1976:42).

4. The parallels between Wesley's theology and the liberal economics espoused by, among others, Adam Smith seem close here, so close that it is easy to see how they might be read as evidence that Methodism boosted capitalist expansion. As Shapiro (1993:13) writes, "Smith was fixated on the encouragement of trade and primarily concerned with extracting the idea of money from old notions of hoarding and accumulation so that it could circulate in an uninhibited way." Nonetheless, his political economy *was* widely taken to endorse the accumulation of wealth. Wesley certainly read it in this way and, Outler (1985:264f.) says, tried ever more strenuously to counter its effects on his followers.

5. As is often pointed out, Wesley's attitudes toward accumulation were conservative even in his time. He opposed depositing money in the Bank of England, for instance,

declaring that one might as well "bury [one's talent] in the earth" (1985:276; cf. Rack 1989:367). This underlines the significance, for him, of visible, "above ground" investment in established forms of manufacture and commerce.

6. In his extraordinary novel about the eighteenth-century English slave trade, Unsworth notes that how the Protestant ethic—later to serve abolitionists as an endorsement of free labor—was invoked by slavers to justify their commerce. He puts the following statement in the mouth of a boatswain on a ship carrying its human cargo across the Atlantic (1992:242):"[It] was all writ in the Bible long years ago. . . . Him that has got something already must always try to get hold of more. . . . An' the more he gets, the more will be given to him. That is in the Gospels. . . . [I]t is everyone's bounden duty to try to get more than they have got already."

7. See, e.g., Stuart's (1993:381) account of the popular radical evangelist Edward Irving, whose preaching attracted some leading political and intellectual figures in London in the 1820s. Irving, who claimed Coleridge among his mentors, lamented that "heroism and patriotism and virtue and other forms of disinterestedness, having no exchangeable value in the market place, must keep at home in books, or be shown only in family circles, like the antiquated dresses of our grandfather[s] and grandmothers, with whom the things so named were in fashion." But faith would overthrow "the idol of expediency." It is telling that Irving used the image of fashion to convey a sense of temporal and spatial displacement (see chapter 5).

8. Of six modern Hurutshe poems about cattle collected by van der Merwe (1941:309–11, transl., 321–24), four include this phrase. One of them also speaks of "God with the long straight nose."

9. So abundant were the cattle of some early nineteenth-century chiefs that they were rumored to have access to "a large deep hole" from which they could call forth stock (Campbell 1822,1:316–17). Note that, unlike most European morality myths about the "unnatural" production of wealth (Schneider 1989; Newborn 1994), this story does not imply that fabulous riches were obtained at the cost of the ability of others to prosper and reproduce.

10. Lichtenstein (1973:81) tells us that Tswana "bought" their pack oxen from the Kora, who specialized in breeding and training them.

11. Burchell (1824,2:538) recounts the effort of Molehabangwe, Mothibi's predecessor as Tlhaping chief, to prevent missionaries Kok and Edwards (*RRI*:190) from making contact with more northerly Rolong. The whites had hoped that peoples further in the interior might part with ivory at a better rate of exchange. As it turned out, the Rolong leaders proved to be familiar with prevailing terms of trade. What is more, they demanded payment in sheep, not beads, because the latter were available in abundance from the Tlhaping, who were short of small stock. The animals most prized were of the fat-tailed sort, used to make the "greasy" cosmetic that so displeased the evangelists (see below).

12. Lichtenstein (1930,2:388) added that his party could not obtain cattle except "at very high prices"; Tlhaping would only accept bar iron, nails, silk, or European clothes for them. Less valuable objects, including ivory, were exchanged for roll tobacco.

13. According to Beck (1989:220), beads were first introduced into southern Africa by the Portuguese, and continued to find their way into the interior in small quantities after the establishment of the Cape Colony (Saunders 1966:65). It was not until the early nineteenth century, however, that sizeable mass-produced stocks arrived from abroad (Somerville 1979:140). Metal rings and beads, especially of brass and copper, seem to have predated glass imports in long-distance trade (Stow 1905:489).

14. Campbell (quoted in Beck 1989:217) went on to suggest that trade was forced upon evangelists in the interior by the African "hunger for beads." The "natives," he claimed, would be "grossly disappointed" if denied such supplies.

15. It is not clear (i) how much these observations actually applied to Southern Tswana; or (ii) the extent to which the alleged capriciousness of African demand was a matter of European ignorance. We find little record of rapidly shifting tastes among Tlhaping. A very early document (see Saunders 1966:65) suggests that they traded in blue beads. In 1801, Somerville (1979:140) noted that they would only accept black and white ones; but blue reappears time and again in their preferences. In 1812, Burchell (1824,2:569) confirmed that light blue, as well as black and white, were their favorites. In the 1820s, Campbell (LMS 1824) found that blue was still greatly desired, although by then darker shades tended to be chosen (see chapter 5). Twenty-five years later, Livingstone (1959,1:151) observed that the Kwena preference—which, he implies, *was* a matter of changing "fashion"—was for solid, bright shades of red, blue, or white (see also Chapman 1971,1:127 on the Tawana). By then, however, the bottom had fallen out of the bead market to the south (see below).

16. What seems significant in the use of the coin, jewel, bead, or shell as personal adornment is that it be regarded as *intrinsically* valuable; not, like notes or credit cards, as tokens of value that resides elsewhere. Yet the distinction between "real" worth and its representation is often difficult to sustain. In South Africa, as Breckenridge (1995) demonstrates, perceptions of the worth of money in its various concrete forms have been volatile; they have changed, over the years, in relation to shifting patterns of value production. In many West African contexts, paper currency is used decoratively to "spray" (i.e., anoint appreciatively) the bodies of dancers and musicians.

17. Earlier discrepancies—and the fact that they could mass-produce trinket cash—had, of course, been advantageous to the Europeans. In 1802, LMS clergy in the eastern Cape actually contemplated setting up a button factory to assist their purchase of such things as stock (Beck 1989:214).

18. I.e., beads. As Smith suggests, only domestic consumables—probably offered for sale by women and poor retainers—were still obtainable by means of the devalued currency. (The worth of firewood and other provisions would rise dramatically with the development of the diamond mines around Kimberley in the 1870s; Shillington 1985:67f. But that is another story.)

19. These words were part of a message sent by the Kwena chief to Robert Moffat via his son John (E. Smith 1957:171). Sechele was engaged in an effort to have the LMS send a successor to David Livingstone.

20. There is much evidence, some of it already presented, to show that Tswana (and especially Tlhaping) rulers tried to control transactions between the colony and

peoples to the north. This supports the view that trade monopolies underpinned a Southern Tswana "confederation" in the eighteenth century (Legassick 1969; see Shillington 1985:11f.; *RRI*:161).

21. Beck (1989:211) implies that Livingstone was somewhat unusual in elevating commerce to a "matter of principle," and in stressing the role of trade in promoting the Gospel. His own account, however, shows that other evangelists had a similar sense of the civilizing effects of exchange.

22. Livingstone (1857:39) was not opposed to missionary trading on moral grounds: "[N]othing would be more fair and apostolical too," he wrote, "than that the man who devotes his time to the spiritual welfare of a people should derive temporal advantage from upright commerce." Rather, business was not an expedient use of the evangelist's time. (Interestingly, Willoughby copied out this passage from Livingstone, and included it among his papers, preparatory to writing one of his own books which voiced a similar view; see W. C. Willoughby, "Payment of Missionaries" [Willoughby Papers, General File: Church, 14].) Elsewhere, however, Livingstone (1959,1:113) did express concern about the "degrading" effect that Roger Edwards's trading activities might have on the image of the LMS (cf. Schapera in Livingstone 1959,1:12).

23. Livingstone's remarks about Edwards (see n. 22) belie this. In a "letter" to the *S.A. Commercial Advertiser* of 7 April 1852 (1974:116), he notes, more precisely, that it was "the nearly invariable practice of missionaries" in the interior to leave trade to the merchants.

24. Allegations went back and forth between the evangelists and their opponents over commerce with Africans. Some Boers complained in the newspapers about "missionary trading," to which Livingstone (1974:78) replied that "predicants' trading" was rife in their own camp. Tswana were aware of Nonconformist sensitivities in this respect; they played on the shifting lines between trade and other, less fraught forms of exchange, especially with regard to controversial goods. Livingstone (1959:1,113) recounts a revealing story: "[A man] came to me & asked if I should give him a cow for a large tusk. I replied, 'No, I am not a trader.' He said, 'Yes, I know you are not a trader, but Edwards helped me with a gun & I helped him with a tusk.'"

25. Between 1824 and 1830, the government at the Cape tried to regulate trade beyond its borders by means of regular markets held "a little way without" the colony (Moffat and Moffat 1951: 235; cf. Beck 1989:218f. on the eastern Cape). Here indigenous peoples could meet with merchants, who were forbidden access to the territories beyond. Moffat (Moffat and Moffat 1951:235) felt that little was gained by anyone from these markets. But, he added, "that traders are prohibited from entering a lawless country is perfectly consonant to our wishes." At least it was at the time. Later the LMS would introduce its own shopkeepers. The matter of missionaries providing Africans with guns remained contentious, as we have seen (*RRI*:274).

26. S. Broadbent, Matlwasse, 8 June 1823 [WMMS, South Africa Correspondence, 300].

27. Such accusations continued to be made against Moffat and other evangelists from time to time. They were dismissed as calumnies manufactured by opponents of the mission in the colony (see J. Moffat 1886:135).

28. S. Broadbent, Matlwasse, 8 June 1823 [WMMS, South Africa Correspondence, 300]; T. Hodgson and S. Broadbent, Matlwasse, 1 January 1824 [WMMS, South Africa Correspondence, 300].

29. Mrs. Hamilton, New Lattakoo, 16 February 1818 [CWM, LMS Incoming Letters (South Africa), 7-3-A].

30. Begging—i.e., requesting as gift that which should be given unsolicited or earned—had strongly negative connotations for nineteenth-century Protestants. However, the missionaries often used the term loosely to refer to what were deemed inappropriate efforts to engage them in exchange. Moffat (Moffat and Moffat 1951:129) wrote of a visit in 1824 to the capital of the Tshidi-Rolong chief, Tawana: "To-day we have been, *as usual*, surrounded with the Barolongs with a variety of articles for sale. . . . Their perpetual begging renders their company terribly annoying" (original italics).

31. S. Broadbent, Matlwasse, 8 June 1823 [WMMS, South Africa Correspondence, 300].

32. S. Broadbent, Matlwasse, 8 June 1823 [WMMS, South Africa Correspondence, 300].

33. The fact that Tswana tested the conventions of acceptable behavior when faced with novel temptations is illustrated by a case reported by Hodgson. A woman accused in the chief's court of stealing meat from the mission house, he wrote, claimed that "God had appointed her to do so"; T. Hodgson, Matlwasse, 12 January 1824 [WMMS, South Africa Correspondence, 300].

34. In his fine account of the effort by the Livingstonia Mission to restructure local economies in northern Malawi between 1875–1940, McCracken (1977:42f.) describes a similar ambivalence among church authorities toward business. This project was the most elaborate application of Livingstone's vision of the uses of commerce to counter slavery. It spawned the African Lakes Company, which aimed at procuring ivory, stimulating cash crop production, and breaking the monopoly of Arab merchant networks centered on the east coast. As McCracken and others have shown, however, the company failed to achieve its goals. Worse yet, it seems to have contributed—if indirectly—to conditions that expanded the slave trade in the region.

35. J. Archbell, Platberg, 15 July 1831 [WMMS, South Africa Correspondence, 303]; Platberg, 17 September 1833 [WMMS, South Africa Correspondence, 303].

36. J. Archbell, Platberg, 15 July 1831 [WMMS, South Africa Correspondence, 303]. It is perhaps a measure of the enduring ambivalence with which trade was viewed that this last phrase had been crossed out on receipt of the letter at the WMMS headquarters, presumably in preparation for re-presentation in some more public form.

37. Livingstone's (1974:114f.) "letter" concerning the conduct of "smouses" in the interior drew him into a sharp exchange with one local trader over the extent to which missionaries actually did business—and provided guns—to African peoples.

38. Andrew Smith (1939,1:232) gives some insight into margins of profit at the time. He notes that an iron pot, costing two and a half rixdollars in the colony, was sold in Tswana areas for ten; i.e., at four times the price.

39. Shillington (1985:24) adds that, in the latter half of the century, Southern Tswana hunters acquired guns by supplying ivory, skins, and ostrich feathers to colonial arms merchants with bases in Kuruman.

40. Mary Moffat (1967:19) noted that Africans with "property" tended to be "sparing" in using it to buy commodities. She went on to explain how the missionaries were trying to encourage greater expenditure on things like clothes (see chapter 5).

41. Wookey's views on alcohol were echoed at one time or another by all the evangelists. To take just one example, Alfred Sharp suggested, in 1886, that "[t]he white man's curse is in a deeper sense if possible the native's curse—drink. It makes him worse than a beast"; A. Sharp, Vryburg, 12 November 1886 [WMMS, South Africa Correspondence (Transvaal), 328]. Sharp went on say that Europeans were guilty of selling brandy to Tswana, despite laws to the contrary—and their strident denials. (For an illustration of the bitter conflict over this question between the missions and the white residents of frontier towns, see the minutes of a public meeting held in Mafeking just two months later; they are appended to O. Watkins, Pretoria, 22 February 1887 [WMMS, South Africa Correspondence (Transvaal), 328].

42. W. C. Willoughby, "Children, Education and Puberty" [Willoughby Papers, 14]. See also Schapera (1953:19).

43. Willoughby, who seemed more concerned with the moral than the medical implications of drink, remarked that, on this matter, "the conscience of the people in many centres appears to be imperfectly developed." He also remarked that the smell of beer "is often painfully obtrusive in the church, [e]specially on Sunday afternoons." W. C. Willoughby, "Children, Education and Puberty" [Willoughby Papers, 14].

44. Bathoen I was accompanied by Chiefs Khama III of the Ngwato and Sebele I of the Kwena. Willoughby, then working among Khama's people, served as secretary and interpreter (Schapera 1970:41; Sillery 1971:170).

45. Montsioa, Chief of Barolon (*sic*), Mafikeng, undated [1895], [Molema-Plaatje Papers, Ba16].

46. In 1909, for example, a report in the *Northern News* noted that traders were charging almost double for produce they had bought earlier from the people to whom they were now selling it; Native Affairs, *Northern News,* 25 May 1909, p. 3. (This report was itself based on information in the *Blue Book on Native Affairs, 1908* [Cape of Good Hope 1909:31–32]. We cite it again below.) While in the field in 1935, Z. K. Matthews observed that Rolong in the Mafeking District, having sold their grain to merchants at five shillings per bag ("to get supplementary commodities"), had to repurchase for fifteen; Matthews, "Agriculture" (see chapter 3, n. 101). The rates of markup we encountered between 1969 and 1976 varied between 50 percent and 150 percent.

47. While this phrase is widely used, its invocation here derives most directly from Simmel (1978:75).

48. There is evidence from elsewhere in South Africa that some African traders sold cattle in order to use the currency they received to buy more stock at lower prices (Beck 1989:214; Peires 1981:100).

49. A wry example of what Marx (1967,1:107) termed the enduring "love" between commodities and money, these fake notes appear to have born in the text of an advertise-

ment put out by a local dealer in imported goods. Dated 27 September 1883 and valued at five pounds, they were signed by "M. Spring, 120 Main Street" under the motto "New Goods always arriving" (Matthews 1887:196).

50. H. Alexander Parsons (1927:199) stressed this point in explaining why he referred to these pieces as "coins" rather than "tokens." The currency was obviously meant as "a national issue of money not only for Griqualand but also for the tribes round about."

51. A wry variation of this theme was recorded by Josiah Matthews (1887:196); he reported that crooked dealers at the diamond fields passed illiterate Africans fake sovereigns inscribed "Gone to Hanover."

52. The Griqualand coins were not dated, implying that the dies were intended to be deployed indefinitely. Evidence suggests that they were only used for two years, however (H. A. Parsons 1927:199).

53. Early travelers reported that Tswana made use of "decimal arithmetic" (Somerville 1979:128), their numbers ending at ten. Later, the missionary linguist Sandilands (1953:110) would describe their numeration as "logical . . . but clumsy," especially above twenty (see volume 3). It is clear, though, that exact tallies were kept of stock, however many (Burchell 1824,2:560). The decimal system was deployed in combination with the qualitative features of individual animals to effect an overall count. As this shows, quantity and quality often complement each other in practical systems of evaluation.

54. Some powerful northerly chiefs did manage for a time to control the terms of trade in their realms; Neil Parsons (1977:122) reports that, in 1888, Khama III banned merchants from giving credit to Ngwato on pain of expulsion, fixed the prices of such things as goats and sheep, and issued semi-franchises to particular trading companies.

55. *Diamond Fields Advertiser,* 1 November 1878, p. 3.

56. J. Mackenzie, Kuruman, 17 February 1882, Report for 1881 [CWM, LMS South Africa Reports, 2–1].

57. J. Mackenzie, Kuruman, 17 February 1882, Report for 1881 [CWM, LMS South Africa Reports, 2–1]; R. Price, Kuruman, 29 April 1885 [CWM, LMS Incoming Letters (South Africa), 43-1-B]; J. Mackenzie (1871:521; 1975:42f.); Wookey (1884:304f.).

58. This poem, composed by Klaas Segogwane for Chief Molefi (installed in 1929), was first recited at a public assembly in 1931. Recorded the same year by Hendrik Molefi, it is published with extensive annotations in Schapera (1965:112ff.; see p. 117).

59. A. Sharp, Vryburg, 12 November 1886 [WMMS, South Africa Correspondence (Transvaal), 328].

60. Interestingly, the first female secondary school to be established among Southern Tswana, in 1881, would be situated in the then-abandoned Moffat mission house at Kuruman (see volume 3).

61. The salary of a married evangelist in the LMS, Livingstone (1940:92) wrote, was only one hundred pounds, paid annually in cash. It was a sum that left him little option but to do a good deal of manual work himself.

62. See, for example, WMMS (1823–25:200); T. Hodgson, Platberg, 3 September 1827 [WMMS, South Africa Correspondence (Cape), 302]; Broadbent (1865:196).

63. Schapera (1947:25) notes that Kwena men were indeed being made to work on Dutch farms from as early as 1844. They—and, subsequently, Kgatla, Malete, and Tlôkwa—would seek to evade settler coercion by migrating westward into Bechuanaland.

64. The letter, signed "P.S.," was dated 27 July 1854, and was written in response to a parliamentary debate on the scarcity of labor at the Cape. It was republished as a pamphlet without author or further publication details; South African Library Pamphlets, 110.

65. J. Moffat, Kuruman, Report for 1874 [CWM, LMS South Africa Reports, 1–4].

66. Turrell (1982:52f.) notes that Africans were unwilling to toil in dangerous mine claims, or where finds and conditions were poor. They were also wary of rough treatment at the hands of white employers eager to get as much as they could from their work force.

67. J. Moffat, Kuruman, Report for 1874 [CWM, LMS South Africa Reports, 1–4].

68. See, for example, Town Talk, *Diamond Fields Advertiser*, 30 December 1878.

69. The Labour Difficulties, *Bechuanaland News*, 6 February 1892, p. 4. In the Cape Colony, a clutch of pass and vagrancy laws had been enacted to secure and regulate black labor.

70. The *Diamond Fields Advertiser*, 28 March 1879, reports a debate in the Kimberley Town Council of a bill proposing to prohibit the sale of liquor to Africans. Those in favor argued that, if blacks could buy alcohol, they would have no money left for guns to take as "tribute" to their chiefs. Under such conditions, it was claimed, the rulers would stop the flow of labor to the mines. Turrell (1982:50) confirms that the major component of African migrant purchases was guns, and that by 1875 the "streets [of Kimberley] were almost lined with stands of arms."

71. Plaatje (1996) noted, in 1903, that chiefs in Bechuanaland had "considerable difficulty in the collection of the annual hut-tax," their people grumbling about the scarcity of money, and the absence of any return in the form of roads or other amenities; see also Cape of Good Hope (1897a:71; 1899:62f.). A report of conditions in Kuruman and Vryburg in the drought-stricken year of 1908 records a large backlog of tax arrears in that year too; see Native Affairs, *Northern News*, 25 May 1909, p. 3.

72. Under the Glen Grey Act, tax was levied only on men judged fit for labor; in any year during which they were employed beyond the borders of their district for at least three months, however, they were exempted from paying. The Act applied, in whole or in part, to various Cape districts with large African populations—among them, Griqualand West (Macdonell 1901:370; Shillington 1985:110f.). It did not extend to the former British Bechuanaland.

73. This independent committee had been formed to "investigate dispassionately the social and economic condition of the natives." It included clergy of all denomina-

tions; among them, Wardlaw Thompson, W. C. Willoughby, J. S. Moffat, and Dr. James Stewart of Lovedale.

74. Not only industrialists, of course. See Fripp (1897:519) for an especially offensive example from an "independent" British observer, and Cape of Good Hope (1907:30) for one written by a state functionary, the Civil Commissioner at Mafeking.

75. Macdonell (1901:372–73) defended "high wages" as a "practical education" open to none of the "objections usually brought against the mission school." He also went on to warn of the dangers of a rapidly created, large "proletariat," cut off from its communal lands and "primitive social structures."

76. J. Brown, Kuruman, Report for 1898 [CWM, LMS South Africa Reports, 3–1].

77. M. Partridge, Molepolole, 27 November 1896 [CWM, LMS Incoming Letters (South Africa), 53-3-C].

78. A. J. Gould, Kuruman, 16 February 1891 [CWM, LMS Incoming Letters (South Africa), 48-1-B].

79. Compare this with a comment made ten years earlier, in 1888, by the Resident Magistrate at Mafeking. The local population, he said, was "not in any want." Those who worked "appear[ed] to do so with the object of procuring some article of clothing" (Great Britain 1889:45).

80. The Commission stated, rather disingenuously, that it was the duty of employers to deal with the danger by caring for "the character of female servants" (1905:83). Also, it said, "Societies" should be formed to secure suitable work for black women, and to provide them with "refuges" while they waited to take up jobs.

81. White South African policy makers took it for granted that black families were, or ought to be, composed of a husband, one wife, and dependent children; i.e., in the same manner as the conventional European "nuclear" unit.

82. On the basis of its inquiries into black living conditions in 1901 and 1908, the South African Natives Races Committee foresaw that the migrant labor system would persist. Its second report noted the difficulties of this system, acknowledging that Africans retained intense attachments to their "life on the tribal lands" and were hence not "genuine" miners. But, it said (1908:5), somewhat shamelessly, "[I]nconvenient and uneconomical as the system is, it has many advantages for employers. It provides them with a vast supply of cheap labour; it burdens them with no pauper class; it gives rise to no labour organizations; it leaves unskilled labour with little or no representation in South African politics."

83. Shula Marks has pointed out to us that recent historical research shows how, outside the Orange Free State, the Land Act was often obeyed more in the breach than the observance; that too many whites had an interest in selling and hiring land to Africans, as well as in sharecropping relations, for the Act to be given immediate force in the Transvaal or Natal. At the same time, the Act undeniably altered the balance of power between whites and blacks over the long run. All this ought to be borne in mind when reading Plaatje's eyewitness account, below, of conditions in the Orange Free State.

84. The vigorous battle to monopolize the movement of Africans by bus had a long and bitter history in the "old" South Africa, exacerbated by the arcane engineering of apartheid (Lelyveld 1987:119f.). More recently, a spate of mafia-style "taxi wars," fought by rival "tycoons" over the control of lucrative routes, has left trails of bodies—and established the masters of transport as supreme power brokers in urban black communities. Buses and trains have also been privileged sites of guerilla warfare and theater (cf. McClintock 1987).

85. See, e.g., *Supplementary Petition presented to the Right Honourable Joseph Chamberlain P.C. by the Paramount Chief, Headman and Councillors of the Barolong Nation*, Mafikeng, January 1903 [Papers of Chief Wessels; Molema-Plaatje Papers, Bb3].

86. See, e.g., the statistics of the Witwatersrand Native Labour Association, cited by the South African Native Races Committee (1908:29).

87. We are indebted here to a collegial exchange among members of the Nuafrica Network on the internet concerning snakes and mines in South Africa. Instigated by Keith Breckenridge, it was brought to our attention by Mark Auslander. This exchange suggests that, among black miners, there is a widespread association of snakes with dangers, accidents, and violent deaths; although the reptiles at issue appear often to have been fiery serpents rather than the water snakes we encountered. More generally, southern Africa abounds with rich iconographies in which reptiles have an ambivalent role in enabling dangerous interconnections and potent transformations—between spirits and humans, above ground and below, male and female, hot and cold, and so on.

88. Schapera (1971:36) writes that, in the Kgatla Reserve, a large rain snake was said to live in a pool on top of an isolated hill at Modipe, along the southern border of the territory. Rolong in the Mafikeng District told us, in the late 1960s, that a similar creature inhabited a small lake at Bodibe, near Lichtenburg (cf. Breutz 1956:77).

89. Livingstone's perceptions in this respect appear to have been infused with the iconography of the Fall—which probably found its way into African symbolic discourses as well. (This point was also made by contributors to the Nuafrica forum on the internet; see n. 87). Most Tshidi English-speakers referred to *dinenebu* as "serpents" rather than "snakes"; as our case of the prophet and the puff adder shows (chapter 2), they responded to them with heightened emotion, at times breaking the taboo on killing them. Interestingly, John Philip (1828,2:117) noted that large water snakes were commonly found, in the 1820s, in the "fountains" of the interior, and were regarded as guardians of their waters. There was thus great concern when the missionaries once attempted to catch one at the Kuruman "eye."

90. For just one example, see the newspaper report cited above; *Northern News*, 25 May 1909, p. 3.

91. See, once again, Native Affairs, *Northern News*, 25 May 1909, p. 3.

92. One qualification here. The Rolong to the north managed—through strong leadership, greater productive viability, and geographical situation—to remain freer of the labor market than their southerly neighbors. But, by the late 1800s, they too were forced increasingly to seek work, mostly on mines in the Transvaal. They were highly ambivalent about doing so, however, even in the late 1960s (Comaroff and Comaroff 1992:155f.).

93. Barclays Bank, a subsidiary of the British company, was one of the oldest financial houses in South Africa. (It no longer exists under its original name, or in its original form.) For much of this century it had branches in virtually every city and small town—as it once did throughout the empire. For black South Africans, it was a powerful symbol of established wealth. Mhengwa Lecholo (see also chapter 3, n. 143) was a senior adviser and ritual consultant to Chief Kebalepile of the Tshidi-Rolong; he was also head of a major section at Mafikeng. His words were occasioned by a discussion of the response of Tshidi to changing political and economic conditions in the countryside under apartheid.

94. Bathoen, Kgosi ea Bangwaketse, Kanye, 18 March 1909 [Molema-Plaatje Papers, Aa 2.28].

95. W. C. Willoughby, Palapye, 21 April 1896 [CWM, LMS Incoming Letters (South Africa), 53-1-D].

96. J. Mackenzie, Kuruman, Report for 1881 [CWM, LMS South Africa Reports, 2–1].

97. Shillington (1985:101) notes that these officials did nothing practical to combat this. They were colonists themselves, and accepted the laws protecting private land from "trespass."

98. John Mackenzie (1887,1:234f.); see also W. Ashton, Barkly West, 26 January 1887 [CWM, LMS Incoming Letters (South Africa), 44-5-A].

99. H. Williams, Molepolole, Report for 1897 [CWM, LMS South Africa Reports, 3–1].

100. M. Partridge, Molepolole, 27 November 1896 [CWM, LMS Incoming Letters (South Africa), 53-3-C].

101. R. Price, Kuruman, 12 December 1896, Report for 1896 [CWM, LMS South Africa Reports, 2–4].

102. W. C. Willoughby, Palapye, 21 April 1896 [CWM, LMS Incoming Letters (South Africa), 53-1-D].

103. J. Brown, Taung, Taungs Report 1896 [CWM, LMS South Africa Reports, 2–4]. This document contains an extensive, and particularly vivid eyewitness account of the ravages of rinderpest. See also J. Brown, Kuruman, 5 January 1899, Report for 1898 [CWM, LMS South Africa Reports, 3–1].

104. H. Williams, Molepolole, Report for 1896 [CWM, LMS South Africa Reports, 2–4]; see also Cape of Good Hope (1897a:69).

105. Annual reports published by the Department of Native Affairs in the Cape Colony at this time stress the high incidence of cattle theft around Kuruman and Vryburg (e.g., Cape of Good Hope 1899:60, 62).

106. J. Brown, Taung, Report for 1896 [CWM, LMS South Africa Reports, 2–4]; see also Cape of Good Hope (1897a:71f.) A letter in the *Diamond Fields Advertiser,* 23 February 1897, p. 2, inquired why "natives from the Taungs reserve" bound for Kimberley should be taken off the train en route and given "a fumigation bath." Seeing that there was no longer any rinderpest in the Taung District, the measure was unnecessary,

as was the ban on any poultry or firewood from Bechuanaland crossing the Vaal River. The writers, who signed themselves "Bechuanaland Observers," pointed out that this cessation of trade was causing additional hardship to an already stricken population.

107. This curious mission, under Dr. J. F. Soga, a government veterinarian, was officially mandated to ensure that the "natives . . . thoroughly understood the ravages caused by Rinderpest, and the regulation for preventing its spread" (Cape of Good Hope 1897b:1). Its report indicates, however, that the venture was also an attempt to investigate whether "uncredited" knowledge of cattle disease might provide a cheap and effective cure. Beasts were requisitioned from the depleted Taung herds for the team to experiment on, which seems to have exacerbated local suspicions of government intent. Clearly, no love was lost on either side. The report, which treated the Tlhaping as the personification of the scourge, described them as "a mean, degenerate race of conglomerate heredity believed to include the offscourings of the inferior races of this continent" (p. 3f.).

108. Cape of Good Hope (1897a:75f.). C. R. Chalmers, the Assistant Magistrate at Taung, believed that the rebellion at Phokwane was triggered by the cattle culling. But he also said that the local chief, Galeshewe, was an "ex-convict" and "a thorn-in-the-side" of any official stationed in the area. Chiefs Molala at Taung and Kgantlapane at Manthe, on the other hand, were pronounced loyal and worthy of recognition "in a substantial manner" by the government.

109. H. Williams, Kanye, Report for 1908 [CWM, LMS South Africa Reports, 4–2].

110. See, e.g., a letter from Sebopiwa J. Molema in Kanye (where he was serving as Interpreter to the Magistrate) to Silas, his father's younger brother, suggesting that he might buy cattle there on the latter's behalf; S. J. Molema, Kanye, 2 September 1916, also S. J. Molema, Mafikeng, 15 September 1918 [Molema-Plaatje Papers, Ac 1].

111. The term is Basil Sansom's (1976:145); see also Comaroff and Comaroff (1992:149f.).

112. It follows from what we said in chapter 3 that the very poor had little or no stock, or any other disposable resources. They depended on wage work, and whatever else came to hand, to eke out an existence for themselves and their families.

113. "Ralinki's Speedy P98 000 Win," *Gaming Gazette,* August 1995, 5(8):2. We do not include this in our bibliography as it is an advertising medium published and circulated within the corporate ambit of Sun Hotels and their clientele.

114. This *pace* Gable (1995), who misunderstands our argument, and, having taken our catchphrase purely at face value, offers an impassioned critique of a chimera.

F I V E

*The subheading of this chapter is an allusion to the title, if not the content, of Ariel Dorfman's *The Empire's Old Clothes* (1983).

1. Report of the Kuruman District, 1914. Unsigned (presumably J. T. Brown), Kuruman, 1914 [CWM, LMS South Africa Reports, 5–1].

2. Nunokawa (1991:149) makes a similar point in an insightful analysis of Charles Dickens's *Dombey and Son*. Speaking of Elizabeth Dombey, he notes that her beauty, her defining feature, is portrayed as "a costume *attached* to her figure," a "badge or livery" put on the surfaces of her body-as-mannikin (original italics). Clearly, Dickens's representation of fashion and identity in this novel was very much the cultural creature of its age.

3. *Sartor Resartus* (the "Tailor Patched") is a complex and passionate jest. It is cast as a dialogue between a plainspoken, practical British editor and a Kantian pedant, one Herr Teufelsdröckh, Professor of Things in General at the University of Nobody-knows-where (see LaValley 1968:69f.). Ironically, its attempt to reveal the meaning-lessness of external trivia is likely to strike the late twentieth-century reader as evidence for the significance of the everyday.

4. This foreshadowed what behavioral scientists would later characterize as the "conative aspect" of dress, its capacity to "channel strong emotions" and "move men [*sic*] to act in prescribed ways" (Schwarz 1979:28). In chapter 6, where the same point is made about the architecture of domestic life, we note that the evangelists also anticipated some of the tenets of modern practice theory.

5. Interestingly, a palpable thread joins the missionary view of clothes—of their capacity to mediate between the interiors of the self and the surfaces of the body—to some recent theoretical writings on contemporary fashion. Ash and Wilson (1992:xi), for example, write that "[f]ashion has dualities in its formation, a reputation for snob-bery and sin. . . . It is obsessive about outward appearances, yet speaks the unconscious and our deepest desires." We became aware of this comment from an epigraph in Hen-drickson (1996).

6. Speaking of a different context, nineteenth-century Paris, Auslander (1990:12) notes the contrast between "veneer" styles and those, such as sculpture, that "trans-formed the essence of the form and wood itself." She adds that the first, associated with dress and "make-up," was seen as female. This will be relevant to our discussion, later, of the feminization of clothing as a sign vehicle in colonial situations.

7. See n. 1.

8. In a reading of an earlier version of this analysis, Brad Weiss commented, per-ceptively, that the missionary vision here seems to have been that the Tswana were in fact "*clothed* in nakedness," rather than being unclad or scantily dressed; that this was important, at the time, to their construction of Africans as degenerate savages rather than "poor" innocents.

9. As McCormick notes (in Lessing 1984:132, n. 4), *The Connoisseur* ran for 140 numbers, and was published in four volumes in 1761. The article on the so-called "Hot-tentots" alluded to by Lessing was "ascribed to Lord Chesterfield" (under whose name we annotate it here)—although, in the original edition, it appeared without heading or byline.

10. We should like to thank Tom Cummins for alerting us to this example.

11. See, e.g., Dickens's (1853:337, repr. 1908b:229) essay on the "noble savage." In it, he describes the "savage" treatment of "his" body: "[He] paints one cheek red and the other blue, or tattoos himself or oils himself, or rubs his body with fat."

12. We are grateful, once more, to Brad Weiss for emphasizing this point to us; see also J. Comaroff (1985:110).

13. Burchell (1824,2:553) was not the only one to find the greasing of African skins perfectly understandable—and unobjectionable. Lichtenstein (1973:65) spoke approvingly of their "velvet-like sheen." And George Thompson (1967:87), who regarded Tswana as "fine-looking," described them as having a "glittering appearance," due partly to the mixing of mineral powder into their bodily ointments (see also A. Anderson 1888:83).

14. We have encountered this preoccupation with the erotic before (see, e.g., *RRI*:104f., 193f.) and will do so again below (see chapter 7).

15. According to Justine Cordwell (1979:64), interestingly, "Red ocher, and other ferrous oxide colors, such as orange and yellow, probably are the most widely used red cosmetic pigments in the history of mankind."

16. The theme of nakedness in Genesis—its association first with innocence (2.24); then with self-discovery, shame (3.7), and fear (3.10); and finally with divine wrath (3.11), followed by expulsion from Eden—provided a powerful narrative for the early missionaries in southern Africa. So, too, did Luke 8.35; see below.

17. Beidelman (1968:115) draws here on Clark's (1956) distinction between nudity and nakedness. But, in his analysis of the Nuer, he is careful *not* to suggest that this distinction features explicitly in their thought—or that his analytic categories themselves correspond to indigenous ones. While he agrees with Fischer (1966:68–70) that bodily shame is an innate, universal human sensibility, he stresses that the more salient question is why that sensibility varies in content and context from one society to the next.

18. A particularly interesting case from Namibia is reported by Hendrickson in the draft of an essay (n.d.), subsequently published (1994) but with the relevant passage omitted. It concerns Emma Hahn, an English woman, who, in the 1850s, sewed leather trousers, skin and wool caps, and a tanned hide blouse for her Rhenish missionary husband, Carl Hugo Hahn.

19. The source of John Mopharing's text is difficult to pin down. A copy of it was made available to us in 1969 by the late Stephen Phetlhu, then Tribal Secretary at the Tshidi-Rolong capital, Mafikeng. As a result, we do not know where it was filed. The description of "traditional" clothing itself is part (pp. 4–5) of a typescript archive, in English, entitled "Minor details about the Barolong and their activities in the Kalahari." It is numbered, variously, K32/11 and 7/11, and is dated 3 January 1939; it appears to have been collected and translated by one A. Leeuw of the Roman Catholic School, Koopmansfontein, Barkley West District, South Africa. We know little more about the document or its author, save that Mopharing appears to have been an old Tlhaping man. Given the difficulty of reference in dealing with this archive, we simply refer back to this note when citing it. Other confirmatory indigenous sources for this account—roughly contemporary or earlier than Mopharing's—come from Molema (n.d.[a]) and Matthews (n.d.).

20. See also W. C. Willoughby, "Clothes" [Willoughby Papers, 14].

21. Elsewhere, Lichtenstein (1930,2:389) added that, next to cattle, "there was nothing on which they set so high a value as their larger objects of clothing." It cost him two oxen and a great deal of difficulty to acquire a cloak in a complicated exchange. Eighty years later, Conder (1887:90) told the Royal Anthropological Institute that the manufacture of karosses continued to be a highly valued indigenous industry. "These skins," he reported, were "retailed at high profit by traders in the Kimberley market."

22. The plural prefix "*ba-*" refers to people, *kobò* to the cloak; *telele*, adj., denotes "long" or "tall."

23. Lichtenstein (1973:68) suggests that long, "sewn-together" coats were unaffordable to "poorer Beetjuanas" because they cost "between one or two oxen." Instead, those of lesser means made their shorter capes from the tanned skins of "hartebeest or other large antilopes."

24. Only Lichtenstein (1973:67f.) adds this explicitly, although Somerville's (1979:119) account gives much the same impression. Burchell (1824,2:563), who was not unappreciative of Tswana female beauty, commented that women "of the shorter size, resemble a mere bundle of skins."

25. Mopharing (see n. 19) seems, at first glance, to suggest that "ornaments," not clothing, were changed for "feast days." Elsewhere in his text, however, it becomes clear that the former are not distinguished from garments.

26. John Philip (1828,2:127), like Andrew Smith (1939,1:225), notes that both men and women also wore metal earrings.

27. Kurreechane (or Kurrechane) was Campbell's rendering of Kaditshwene, the Hurutshe capital (see Schapera in Moffat and Moffat 1951:74, n. 49). In order to avoid confusion, we retain the missionary's spelling where appropriate.

28. We render the proverb exactly as in the original, leaving its early twentieth-century orthography unchanged. Note that the translation given is said, by Plaatje himself, to be "literal."

29. See, e.g., J. Philip, Cape Town, 29 July 1820 [CWM, LMS Incoming Letters (South Africa), 8-2-B].

30. The color blue was associated with Nonconformism in many parts of the world, and continued to be in much of Africa until the age of independence. For just one example, that of Methodism in Ghana, see Bartels (1965:204, 313).

31. See below for an especially dramatic case recorded among the Ngwato in 1885.

32. Some linen goods, including Indian calico, found their way to Tswana peoples from the east coast of Africa in the late eighteenth and early nineteenth centuries, perhaps through Portuguese slavers and Arab traders (see Somerville 1979:141; also Campbell 1813:255; R. Moffat 1825b:64).

33. The term "cutting capers" appears in Moffat's (1825a:29) first description of the event; the illustration, in *Missionary Labours* (1842:348), is entitled "The Bechuana Parliament."

34. Striking, also, were local eyewitness accounts of the "Mantatee" [Tlokwa] armies which caused havoc among Southern Tswana in the 1820s (*RRI*:167f.): "[They

were] people of various complexions; the majority black and almost naked, others of a yellow or Hottentot colour, and some perfectly white, with long hair and beards, and dressed in European clothing" (G. Thompson 1967:80). The role of intermediary peoples in the spread of European fashions to the interiors of southern Africa is also discussed by Hendrickson (1994:46f.). She argues that the adoption of Western dress by Ovaherero was due to the fact that their rivals, the Orlams, had it.

35. One fascinating account in the documentary record concerns the dress of the Khoi bride of the Rev. James Read. According to the latter, the marriage occurred in 1803, causing outrage among white colonists and the evangelists of the London Missionary Society. Read wrote that, while he had wished her to don a kaross for the wedding, she had worn a "petticoat (as is, and was then still worn as a custom) on her shoulders"; J. Read, April 1819 [CWM, LMS Incoming Letters (South Africa), 8-1-B]. This incident was brought to our notice by Doug Stewart, who was himself alerted to it by Elizabeth Elbourne.

36. In some places, like Namibia, Western clothing became so valuable as to excite plunder (Hendrickson 1994:50f.). Among Southern Tswana, the seizure of European garments seems to have been confined to specific moments and acts of resistance later in the century. We have no evidence that it was a common practice at other times in Bechuanaland.

37. The "queen" (Mahutu) and the other women (her two daughters) seem to have been given these dresses by Jonathan Gleig and Captain Warren, recent European visitors to Dithakong (J. Philip 1828,2:104). Not much is known of these two men; Philip says little, save that one was from the East Indies and the other from Grahamstown (in the eastern Cape Colony).

38. Over fifty years later, Holub (1881,1:119) was to report—from Likatlong, then capital of the southernmost Tlhaping chiefdom—that many men wore just such a mix of European and Tswana attire.

39. Luke was a favorite text among the Nonconformists in South Africa and was among the first to be translated into Setswana.

40. According to Drewal (1979:190), following Bascom (1951), Yoruba associate nakedness with "different types of insanity." This is almost certainly true elsewhere in Africa as well. There is no evidence, however, that the evangelists believed it to be the case among nineteenth-century Tswana. Nor is there any hint that the connection they drew between clothing and "right-mindedness" was meant to evoke indigenous resonances. They seem only to have had Biblical symbolism in mind.

41. S. Broadbent, Matlwasse, August/September 1823 [WMMS, South Africa Correspondence, 300].

42. The injunction in this instance, added Tudur Jones (1962:194), was specifically connected to levels of employment in the garment industry: "[A]usterity in dress amongst [wealthy women] will mean unemployment amongst cloth-workers," were the precise words of the *Evangelical Magazine*. On the general point, interestingly, John Wesley (1986:250) had argued that, while the scriptures "manifestly forbid ordinary Christians" from wearing "costly" raiments, nothing in the Bible taught "that there ought to

be no difference at all" in the apparel of "persons of different stations." Indeed, his famous sermon "On Dress" might have served as a manifesto for the clothing campaign of the mission. It went to great lengths (i) to argue that bodily adornment was far from an "insignificant trifle" for God and man alike, (ii) to explain the difference between inner and outer verities, (iii) to rail against ostentation in all forms, and (iv) to link distinctions in attire to social standing.

43. J. Hepburn, Shoshong, 1887 [CWM, LMS South Africa Reports, 2–1]. The "servants" were from Tswapong, and were retainers of local non-Christian elites. While Shoshong is not a Southern Tswana town, this example casts light on the attitude of an evangelist whose major frame of reference was the mission centered in southern Bechuanaland.

44. W. C. Willoughby, "Clothes." Willoughby's comments are contained on a typed sheet of unpublished notes.

45. J. Moffat, Kuruman, 1 January 1867 [CWM, LMS South Africa Reports, 1–1].

46. An example is to be found in "Lispeth," a story by Kipling ([1888] 1994) about a "native girl" adopted and then destroyed by evangelists in India: "[H]ad she not been dressed in the abominable print-cloths affected by the Missions," she would have struck one as very beautiful (p. 2).

47. A. J. Wookey, Molepolole, 1888 [CWM, LMS South Africa Reports, 2–2].

48. An overcoat, especially of frock-coat shape.

49. Although, as we have seen, the evangelists did comment extensively about the "abuse" by Africans of such intimate apparel as petticoats and chemises. While it is difficult to obtain hard evidence, it seems that male and female underwear, probably both new and used, was in circulation from the earliest days on the Bechuanaland frontier.

50. W. C. Willoughby, "Clothes." (See also n. 20 and n. 44 above.)

51. "Boboyan" appears to have been the nickname of a Motswana of Willoughby's acquaintance; "bobbejaan," in Afrikaans, is a baboon.

52. Since this passage is from Willoughby's notes, it contains many spelling and typing errors; for example, "trousers big" is rendered "trosuers bigg." Rather than mark each of these errors—by [*sic*]—in the text, we have simply corrected them.

53. We infer that this was the year. On p. 459, John Mackenzie (1871) says that he started to build the church "early in 1867"; on p. 461, he gives the date of its opening only as "7 January." In light of the work involved, which is described in detail, we conclude that the building must have taken almost twelve months to complete.

54. This evokes two points made by Elizabeth Wilson (1985:5, 10–15), both of them suggestively debatable, in a study that is otherwise theoretically limited and anthropologically ill-informed: first, that determined efforts to avoid contemporary styles "represent a reaction against what *is* in fashion" (original italics), not necessarily an escape from the discourse *tout court;* and, second, that fashion—as a mode of expression, not as a specific vogue—often parodies itself, allowing anything and everything to become play. Indeed, she says, "fashion is modernist irony" (p. 15). If this is true, it was Tswana bricoleurs, not the missionaries, who were the vehicles of both fashion and modernity on the frontier!

55. J. Hepburn, Shoshong, 1 January 1885 [CWM, LMS Incoming Letters (South Africa), 43–1–A].

56. On occasion, John Mackenzie (1871:105) says, he also wore "an immense Mackintosh overcoat with huge water-boots."

57. It is difficult, for obvious reasons, to ascertain how long these chiefs dressed in such a manner. Photographs taken in the late 1880s and early 1890s suggest that they had moderated their garb by then, but we cannot be sure. We do know, however, that their heirs outfitted themselves in a quieter European style.

58. We reiterate the point not because we wish to labor it, but because casual misreadings of volume 1 have led some to accuse us of saying the opposite.

59. Beck (1989:passim; see above) makes this point as well in respect of the early trade in beads: the diversity, intensity, and evanescence of indigenous tastes across South Africa led to a stream of requests back to England for the rapid supply of objects that might satisfy local wants. The impact on the metropole of "native demand" for clothing was less straightforward, of course, since the missions and other colonizers tried so hard to condition it. In some measure, as this chapter shows, they succeeded. But black South Africans could and did affect manufacturers and markets. By refusing to buy garments of a certain color or cut, or by exercising subtle preferences among those on offer, they had a major impact on the economic fortunes of colonial producers.

60. George Thompson (1967:80) says that Moffat, with whom he spent time in 1823 (see text), had a "black bushy beard, about eight inches long." He added that "this Jewish fashion" was not surprising to him, since beards "are objects of no small respect" among the "natives." See Schapera's annotation in Moffat and Moffat (1951:56, n. 6), which first alerted us to Thompson's text; we return to it again below.

61. The italicization of "loincloth" here is intended to signal irony. As is demonstrated above, Tswana men's apparel was more complex and elaborate than was typically allowed by contemporary European accounts; indeed, the term itself—"loincloth," that is—was part of the stereotypic imputation of savagery.

62. In the original, the quote to follow was rendered in the present tense. For obvious reasons of sense, we have had to transpose it into the past. However, instead of making this transposition by inserting several hard brackets into the text—a highly distracting convention—we simply effect the change and note it here.

63. Schapera's choice of terms—about which he is always careful—implies a similar perspective to our own in two crucial respects: first, that the (variable) wearing of European clothes by Tswana was closely related to distinctions of wealth and class, a point made above and one to which we shall return; and second, that, while most people (save for the very poor) put on at least some of these clothes, the way that they *costumed* themselves differed widely in the degree to which it conformed to Western norms.

64. In the 1970s and 1980s, so-called "revisionist" historians took pains to demonstrate that black labor migration in South Africa had long been a product of the coercive workings of colonial capital, facilitated by a cooperative state. It is to be noted, however, that some liberal social scientists writing in the 1930s—Schapera and his colleagues among them—seem to have held similar, if not identical, views on this particular point;

see, e.g., Hutt (1934:212f., 227f.) and, to a lesser extent, Rheinallt-Jones (1934:161f.), both in Schapera (1934). All three take care to distinguish the material conditions underlying rural-urban migration from the attitudes of—as well as the effects upon—individual workers.

65. According to Hutt (1934:214), purchases from rural stores also came to have a "definite fashion element." But, during this period, both supply and demand in the countryside seem to have taken their lead from urban markets.

66. We first came across this term, used in a rather different connection, in Bartels (1965:250). There it referred to the bar against non-clergymen acceding to high positions in religious institutions (such as Wesley College in Ghana).

67. We shall return to Willoughby's photographs of domestic architecture in chapter 6.

68. A few—although not, by any means, most—chiefs had by now become part of the Protestant elite. While others had also joined churches, their membership was nominal rather than enthusiastic. In these instances, they did not see themselves, nor were they seen by others, as part of the Christian "party." (This term was often used in Bechuanaland in the nineteenth century to describe church groups that took active stands in local politics.) Still, for reasons noted in the text, their dress tended to converge with that of the petite bourgeoisie centered on the mission denominations.

69. This point comes through strongly in Willoughby's notes. See W. C. Willoughby, "Clothes"; n. 20.

70. See, for example, "*Go botlhe ba ba eang go Nyala*," *Tsala ea Becoana*, 30 December 1911, p. 1.

71. See "Wedding," *Tsala ea Becoana*, 5 August 1911, p. 2.

72. Clearly, "Eurocentric" is used generically (and loosely) here to make a point. In the twentieth century, it has to be understood to include the U.S.A. and U.S.S.R.; hence the tendency to describe modern neocolonialism (inaccurately) in terms of north-south domination. It is also the case, of course, that peripheralized, ethnicized populations are to be found within European nation-states.

73. See, for just a few good examples, Obeyesekere (1979); Hendrickson (1986); Franquemont (1986); Nag (1991); Tolen (n.d.).

74. This comes through strikingly, for example, in the essays on West Africa—and especially on the Yoruba—in Cordwell and Schwarz (1979), especially those by Houlberg, Drewal, Wass, and Ottenberg.

75. We are grateful to Carola Lentz for alerting us to this fact; see, also, e.g., Drewal (1979:191ff.).

76. Two qualifications here: (i) In South Africa, domestic service tended to be female (but cf. Hansen 1989 on Central Africa), as did some forms of agricultural labor. In a few places, moreover, women were also employed to do certain house-building tasks. (ii) While male labor was usually the first object of British colonial extraction, female workers were sometimes found to be cheaper and more desirable even for the most physically arduous toil; on Indian plantations, for example, "tribal" women came to be portrayed as "nimble-fingered tea pluckers" (Chatterjee n.d.).

77. For a relatively recent overview of anthropological studies of migration, see Kearney (1986). The South African literature on the topic is by now both very extensive and well-known; there is no reason to annotate it here. For an older but comprehensive account of the Tswana case, see Schapera (1947).

78. This, as has been pointed out many times (see, again, Kearney 1986), is also a major reason for the widespread preference among colonizers for contract labor—and, therefore, for patterns of oscillating migration—over a permanent, sedentarized work force.

79. Here, again, West Africa was different: a long history of female trade ensured that women participated in urban markets from the earliest colonial times, if often on their margins; see Bastian (1992). There is evidence—which seems to support the general lines of our argument here—that some West African females were more open to stylistic innovation than were males, and were more adventurous in seeking out the potential offered by colonial institutions. Ikem Stanley Okoye (personal communication) has suggested that, in designing local buildings (such as *Obu* hearths/shrines), Igbo women showed greater daring in incorporating European forms and elements than did men—who expressed concern that these women were "getting out of hand" (cf. Bastian 1985; Apter 1993).

80. While missionary sewing schools had given rise to a considerable amount of dress manufacture in Tswana communities by this time, most of it was still being done by hand. The evidence suggests that few sewing machines had found their way into the interior, at least into private hands. (Tigerkloof was to build a tailor's shop, but it was to be used by an emergent petite bourgeoisie, mainly destined for the urban areas; see volume 3). As late as 1932, merchant records from Bechuanaland note that these machines were never sold locally (Schapera 1947:229, 232), although they were occasionally sent home by men working on the mines.

81. The circumstances in which Duggan-Cronin took the photographs are unclear, despite his efforts to contrive for many of them an image of ethnographic naturalism. (He is said, among other things, to have carried "a leopard-skin in his kit, and lend it to chiefs whom he wished to photograph but who did not have one of their own" [Schapera, personal communication; Wylie 1990, opp. p. 146, has reproduced a chiefly portrait by Duggan-Cronin which is interesting for its juxtaposition of the ruler's Western suit of clothes with the animal skin on which he sits].) Nonetheless, as all our collateral evidence suggests, these portraits do appear to capture prevailing patterns of dress among Tswana women.

82. For example, Schapera's (1947:228f.) stock lists show that, in the 1940s, indigo prints were being replaced by a wider selection of dark patterned fabrics. And, in the 1960s, as we have already mentioned, mass-produced garments and used European clothes had gained some purchase in the Mafikeng District. After the establishment in South Africa of the "ethnic homeland" of Bophuthatswana, with its transplanted elites and its incentives for marketing, the practices described here began to undergo considerable transformation.

83. Alinah Segobye (personal communication) confirms that these fabrics continue to be worn in rural Botswana. She adds, intriguingly, that women who return from the

city must wear them if they wish to take part in funerals and other rituals. Even where stylistic variation is now tolerated—in particular among younger women—it appears that the dress materials themselves remain standard and unchanged.

84. See J. Tom Brown ([1875] 1987:375, 454); Matumo (1993:487, 547). Unlike the Swazi (H. Kuper 1973:356), who always used foreign words for imported clothing (even when a SiSwati equivalent existed for a garment with parallel function), Tswana linguistic usages were more mixed. Some Western items (e.g., shirt, *hempe;* jacket, *baki* [*baatje*]), became known by Dutch/Afrikaans terms; others (e.g., skirt, *mosese*) acquired a Setswana label that bore no hint of their alien origin. This echoed the major lines of difference between the way in which Swazi and Tswana, respectively, adopted Western dress (see n. 86 below): the latter created a synthetic bricolage with it, the former alternated between it and a distinctive vernacular costume.

85. The more Eurocentric dress of "school" people (i.e., converts) resembled that of rural Tswana women (see Mayer 1961:24f.)—with the notable exception that the costumes of the latter included blankets, whether or not they were Christians.

86. Both differed from the pattern described by Kuper (1973:357f.) for Swaziland, where rulers did not convert to Christianity and where secular schools were also established. Here European dress was not a requisite of high position and aristocrats "alternate[d] between Swazi and Western-style clothing," depending on the situation. Only Christian commoners, it seems, wore exclusively European garb.

87. A. J. Wookey, Molepolole, 1888 [CWM, LMS South Africa Reports, 2–2].

88. Leloba Molema informs us that the Botswana women's group *Emang Basadi* ("Women Arise") has drawn attention to this in a critique of the colonialist origins of female "tradition" in the country. It has even considered a return to skin costume as a more appropriate ethnic marker.

S I X

1. Some sections of this chapter were anticipated in an essay, entitled "Homemade Hegemony," published in Comaroff and Comaroff (1992) and, in abridged form, in Hansen (1992). They have, however, been substantially amended.

2. This passage comes from John Mackenzie's statement at his public ordination in Edinburgh, 19 April 1858, at which he was posed four questions. The most accessible accounts of his answers are to be found in W. D. Mackenzie (1902:37f.) and J. Mackenzie (1975:71f.).

3. An extraordinary example of this is provided by J. Baldwin Brown in a piece published by the *Evangelical Magazine* of 1868 (excerpted in Briggs and Sellers 1973:22–24). Brown ascribed the absence of revolution in England to its "holy and happy home-life." But he expressed concern that the "domestic character" of the nation was under threat—from "undomestic . . . continental peoples" and "the Americanization of . . . domestic life." The bulwark against its erosion, however, was "the great middle class" where proper family life still reigned. For discussion of the stress on domesticity in nineteenth-century Nonconformism, see, e.g., C. Hall 1990:60f. (The contemporary ob-

session with the family was not confined to Nonconformists, of course. In a well-known description of the "typical parochial clergyman" before 1825, Dean R. W. Church ([1891] 1966:3) offered that the "beauty of the [established] English Church in this time was its family life of purity and simplicity.")

4. Cited, incorrectly, in Crosby (1991:4) and Levine (1986:82).

5. Cf. on the Pacific Jolly and Macintyre (1989); especially the Introduction and chapters by Langmore, Macintyre, and Jolly.

6. In a review of Arnold Harvey (1994) and Michael Mason (1994), Porter (1994:5) notes the "tidal wave of prudery" that swept England in about 1800. Echoing Mason, he claims that this was not because the Victorians "hated or feared sex," but because they held it so dear; to the extent that they turned it from the hedonistic into the holy, making of it "a sacrament, an expression of all that was noble and ethical." Whether or not this is a fair historical summary, it captures well the view of the Nonconformist missionaries. It also illuminates the connections they drew between domesticity, the refined femininity of home, and marital intimacy.

7. These attributes also set the bourgeois home off from the "dangerously amoral" public world outside; the world into which men, as social actors, had to venture—and from which they returned for sustenance (C. Hall 1990:74 et passim). By now there is a large, well-known literature on the contrast between the private and public spheres, on its history, and on its political salience in cross-cultural perspective; see, e.g., Collier and Yanagisako (1984). We simply take this literature as read here.

8. This is confirmed by many of the so-called "condition of England novels" written at roughly the same time; among them, Gaskell's *Mary Barton* (1848), Disraeli's *Sybil* ([1845]1980), and Dickens's *Hard Times* ([1854]1985); for insightful commentary on these works, see Raymond Williams (1961:99–119).

9. There is, of course, a large literature to this effect. See, for just a few examples, Davidoff and Hall (1987); C. Hall (1985); Morgan (1985); Hausen (1981); and Darrow (1979).

10. Stone (1979:416f.), as is well-known, has argued strongly against the view— especially as formulated by Engels and "accepted [as] dogma" in "Parsonian functionalist sociology"—that the modern family was "a product of industrial capitalism"; he sees its origin in the upper bourgeoisie and the rural squirearchy of eighteenth-century Britain. We do not seek here to enter the deep waters of European family history. Our point is merely that, as an ideology and a social construct, the modernist idea of domesticity came to maturity during the age of revolution.

11. In both country and city, among both working and middle classes, domestic arrangements were undergoing palpable transformations at the time. Thus, for example, Rowbotham (1976:23f.) shows how the architecture of prosperous farmhouses was changing: among other things, large communal eating-kitchens were giving way to small functional spaces staffed by servants (cf. Fussell and Fussell 1953:172f.). As Webb (1981:19) remarks, such changes were themselves part of an ongoing history of social differentiation in rural England; the "yeoman" England, that is, whence came much of the imagery exported by Nonconformist evangelists to Africa.

12. See Gallagher (1985:122–23) for examples.

13. Literary theorists have made a similar observation with reference to "classic" Victorian literature. Take one example: in *Jane Eyre,* says Susan Meyer (1991:passim), the creation of clean, healthy bourgeois homes in England appears as a counterpoint to the "dark" threat of unruly savagery in the colonies; cleanliness, colonialism, and domestic civility were all of a piece.

14. Rodman (1985:269) makes much the same point about missionaries in the Pacific. In Longana, Vanuatu, she says, they sought to "persuade islanders of the attractions of the nuclear family home partly by redesigning the house itself."

15. It will be recalled, from volume 1 (pp. 100f.), that the "dependence of an organism upon external sensations" was taken, in contemporary scientific discourses, to reflect an absence of reason and self-control—itself a criterion of lowly position on early nineteenth-century bioevolutionary scales.

16. Carter (1989:9, 17, 27–28, 32), writing of Captain Cook's voyages of discovery along the Australian coast, stresses that it was his act of naming that made space into place. Not so in the South African interior, where early white visitors tended to use indigenous names. Here it was the European presence itself—in the double sense of "being there" and "of the present time"—that brought "undiscovered" terrain into historical existence.

17. For further amplification of this point, see our discussion of the politics of space in volume 1 (pp. 200f.). Many early evangelists of both the LMS and WMMS tried to have chiefs move their capitals to new sites; sites chosen, ostensibly, because they were more healthful or fertile or defensible. For the Europeans, this gesture had several layers of significance. It set in motion the history of previously "prehistoric" peoples on (what was taken to be) empty terrain, thus marking spatially a radical departure from "traditional" times past. Of course, the imaginative investment of the landscape was, simultaneously, a political one: as new capitals (re)placed old ones, they acquired two centers, the chiefly court and the church.

18. For another example, see Barrow's (1801–4,1) influential *Account of Travels,* which also portrayed the interior as a vacant moral terrain (*RRI*:95f.).

19. J. Campbell, Klaarwater, 26 July 1813 [CWM, LMS Incoming Letters (South Africa), 5-2-D]; this passage is quoted in full in the previous volume (*RRI*:178).

20. Recall, from chapter 5, n. 27, that Kurreechane was John Campbell's rendering of Kaditshwene, the Hurutshe capital.

21. This passage is from a letter written by Cameron at Platberg on 27 August 1841. It is reproduced in Broadbent (1865:189f.).

22. Cameron's disappointment at the absence of "splendid fanes, or spires" is ironic. British Methodist buildings, prior to the 1840s, were not known for *their* elevated design. To the contrary: despite having some defenders, Wesleyan meetinghouses were widely excoriated as "crudely utilitarian" (see Davies 1962:47)—even, as we remarked earlier, "hideous" (Halévy 1924:428–29; see *RR* I:65). Later, Davies (1962:48) notes, Dissenting religious architecture would undergo Gothicization. In part, he argues (after Peter Taylor Forsyth, a distinguished nineteenth-century divine), this was because the

upward-soaring lines of the Gothic suggested aspiration and inspiration—in contrast to horizontal classicism, which "reflected sober and decorous rationality."

23. The Rev. William Shaw, General Superintendent of the WMMS Kaffrarian and Bechuana Missions, made the comment after a visit to Thaba 'Nchu in 1848; see Broadbent (1865:199).

24. A. J. Wookey, Kuruman, 23 May 1884 [CWM, LMS Incoming Letters (South Africa), 42–3-C], also published in Wookey (1884:259–64).

25. This comment (Livingstone 1960:272) came in a private journal entry (26 October 1853) after a statement to the effect that he had "not yet met with a beautiful woman among the black people." Earlier in the same journal (13 October), he had urged that "missionaries . . . cultivate a taste for the beautiful"—although it is not clear whether he meant in themselves or in Africans.

26. See chapter 3. This refers to the stated position of the Principal Medical Officer of the Bechuanaland Protectorate. It is documented in Great Britain (1933).

27. Cf. Macintyre (1989:159): in Tubetube, Polynesia, "straight paths . . . [are] the legacy of the mission."

28. The trope of "making the crooked straight" also arose in evangelists' accounts of religious conversations—and did so in such a way as to underscore the iconic connection between the aesthetics of civilization and a Christian moral sensibility. For example, John Mackenzie (1871:408) wrote of an exchange, quoted earlier (p. 45), between himself and the Ngwato chief in which the latter is said to have declared: "God made us with a crooked heart. . . . [W]hen a black man tells a story, he goes round and round. . . . [B]ut when you open your mouth your tale proceeds like a straight line."

29. A brief but illuminating discussion of this topic is contained in a pamphlet—describing a research initiative—entitled *Urbanity and Aesthetics,* distributed by the Research Programme of Urbanity and Aesthetics, Department of Art History, Comparative Literature and Theatre Studies, University of Copenhagen (under whose authorship we list it in our bibliography); see, in particular, "Specifications" (pp. 2–15) prepared by Martin Zerlang. Cf. also Kostof (1991) and Crook (1992).

30. We cannot here repeat, or even summarize, our account of the workings of the contemporary Southern Tswana social world. We have, perforce, to take our description in volume 1 as read.

31. For three examples—one early and from the south, another later and from the heart of the region, and the third still later and from the north—see Campbell (1813:187f., 255f.; 1822,1:222f., 2:152f.); Livingstone (1857:17); J. Mackenzie (1871:367–69).

32. Isaac Schapera has reminded us of two important points about the early history of Tswana settlement, both brought to mind by the differences among contemporary accounts. First, that broader "streets" were necessitated by wagons: as more of them made their way into the interior, such thoroughfares became more common. And second, that, as long as Tswana moved about often, their habitations tended to be simple and modest; they became gradually more elaborate as towns became more permanent.

Of course, the censure of the missionaries was not confined to older, rudimentary settlements. It was also addressed to some of the most elaborate, longest-standing capitals.

33. This view was to be echoed, a hundred and seventy years later, by some archaeologists. McGuire and Schiffer (1983), for example, argue that, because round dwellings involve low construction (but high maintenance) costs, they are found in societies with mobile populations (and brief use expectancies); rectangular buildings, more expensive to erect but cheaper to keep up, tend to predominate in more complex, sedentary, wealth-accumulating societies. This thesis is questionable, however. Not only does it make broad evolutionary and functionalist assumptions, but it cannot be easily sustained in empirical terms.

34. Both Burchell (1824,2) and Lichtenstein (1973) also provide detailed descriptions of household architecture, including the proportions and measurements of internal space, roofs, walls, doors, and so on. These need not detain us here, however.

35. As Rodman (1985:271) reminds us, there are many cultures in which houses "may be only a part of a domestic space that extends out of doors." This was true of Southern Tswana dwellings, a fact which many of the missionaries understood well.

36. Robert Moffat (1842:223f.) commented on some of these accounts. Of Burchell's he approved; Lichtenstein's he found "tolerably accurate" (but see p. 253).

37. Europeans often spoke in this vein of African architecture at the time (*RRI*:96f.; cf. Ranger 1987). As we shall see, the habitations of the urban poor in Britain were also likened to nests.

38. A few evangelists, especially in the early years, also remarked on the cleanliness and orderliness of Tswana homes (e.g., J. Philip 1828,2:122). The discrepancies between such statements and the more conventional, pejorative descriptions are patent. No mission text, to our knowledge, ever sought to reconcile them.

39. Burchell (1824,2:521) continues: "Nothing can exceed their *neatness;* and by *cleanness* I mean to say, the great carefulness which they show to remove all rubbish and every thing unsightly . . .; nothing lies out of its place" (original emphasis). George Thompson (1967:85) says almost exactly the same thing about Tswana towns. We do not exaggerate the degree to which secular observers were struck by Tswana orderliness—or the difference between their accounts and those of many of the evangelists.

40. Some missionaries told of the fierce loyalties that bound sons to their mothers and matrikin (e.g., J. Mackenzie 1871:410f.). Others, however, merely dismissed this as evidence of the workings of "the selfish principle" (e.g., Hodgson 1977:157; above, chapter 3); even Mackenzie (1871:410f.) translated it into the coin of political interest. Fortes's (1969:219f.) "axiom of amity" was a principle, clearly, that did not strike the evangelists.

41. Cf., for a similar view from further south, A. J. Wookey, Kuruman, 23 May 1884 [CWM, LMS Incoming Letters (South Africa), 42–3–C], also in Wookey (1884:259–64). The great attention paid by the evangelists to polygyny had its roots in their religious beliefs, of course. But their preoccupation with it may also have been due to the fact that they spent so much time with royals and headmen; i.e., those most likely

to marry in this manner. Not that their concern was *culturally* inappropriate: as we have said, polygamy lay at the core of the conceptual world of Southern Tswana (*RRI*:132f.).

42. It is instructive to compare the texts of the evangelists with those of other Europeans on this topic. All agree that females played "a very inferior part in the life of the tribe" (Lichtenstein [1807] 1973:77). In his own narrative, Lichtenstein (1973) sought an explanation for their "servitude" in demographic and economic factors—not simply in the "tyranny" of Tswana men. The early missionaries, by contrast, tended to pay no attention to such factors. They preferred to blame the laziness and moral turpitude of the males for existing arrangements (e.g., LMS 1824).

43. This was an indigenously coined usage (Edwards 1886:90). Its connotations and associations are unclear.

44. By the 1870s, as sketch plans in the LMS archives show, most mission premises were yet more elaborate. One had ten rooms: two bedrooms, a nursery, sitting and dining rooms, a study, a pantry, kitchen, and two stores. We found these plans—and a watercolor of the mission house at Molepolole—attached in the CWM archives to a letter from Charles Williams; C. Williams, Molepolole, 25 September 1876 [CWM, LMS Incoming Letters (South Africa), 38–3-C]. We return to them below.

45. Sometimes house walls were constructed with the aid of skilled artisans, either itinerant Europeans or men temporarily hired by the mission; a few evangelists learned brick making and laying from them (Moffat and Moffat 1951:190; J. Mackenzie 1871:411).

46. When, for example, the LMS delayed funding a new mission house, Willoughby wrote: "[I]t needs the utmost care to protect our children in this country from influences of a terribly degrading order. It is very much more difficult when the home has but two bedrooms in it." W. C. Willoughby, Palapye, 22 September 1894 [CWM, LMS Incoming Letters (South Africa), 51–2-B].

47. Livingstone (1961:162) later lost his appetite for building and began to cast doubt on its importance (1959,1:164). This appears to have occurred as he became less enamored of mission work and more drawn to exploration—although, even earlier, he did sometimes speak of his manual labors as an "amusement."

48. The evangelists seem implicitly to have shared, with some modern theorists in geography, the idea that the spatial and the social division of labor emerge and exist interdependently (see Pred 1985:342)—although they would not, of course, have put the matter in quite this way.

49. For a detailed description of early LMS efforts to have Africans learn skills and trades, see J. Philip (1828,1:206–23).

50. Perhaps the most extreme case of an evangelist using construction to teach a European sense of the value of labor was that of Charles Pacalt, missionary among Khoi, whom we encountered earlier; on his activities, see J. Philip (1828,1:240f.).

51. This presupposes that missionaries were married. Most LMS and WMMS evangelists were. Not so, however, those of the PEMS in South Africa. (Early nineteenth-century archives in Paris indicate that the Directorate of the Society believed marriage to be an excessive burden on the time of their agents.) This led to some interest-

ing exchanges in mission circles, exchanges that underscore our point. For example, Samuel Rolland, who was influenced by Moffat et al., wrote to Paris pleading to be allowed to wed; in this he had been encouraged by Philip. He "needed a woman," he said, not for his pleasure, but to socialize, domesticate, and inculcate morality into young Tswana females. This woman would also be able to start an infant school. Stations with European wives, he concluded, were doing much better than those without—precisely because of the kind of Christian work a family man could do. See S. Rolland, Kuruman, 19 November 1830 [SMEP/DEFAP, Correspondance des champs de mission, Afrique australe (H-2100), vol. 1831–32, #7; although dated 1830, the letter is included in the microfiche volume of a year later].

52. For an exemplary account in a "serious" mission text, if one that enjoyed a very large readership, see Livingstone (1857:47).

53. More than a century later—and in a very different context—Mathias Guenther (1977:457) described mission stations in Botswana as "condensed replicas . . . of the society which they represent."

54. The same LMS source tells us that the church at Kuruman was built by Moffat with the aid of "friends in the colony." No further details are given, however.

55. For other accounts of large-scale church building, albeit later and further north, see Lloyd (1889:162f.) and J. Mackenzie (1871:459f.); cf. also Broadbent (1865:201), who says that the chapel at Thaba 'Nchu was built for fifteen hundred people. The similarity between such accounts and Moffat's earlier one is striking. It confirms the impression that Kuruman was both a model for and the epicenter of the Protestant presence in the South African interior for much of the nineteenth century.

56. W. C. Willoughby, Palapye, 22 September 1894 [CWM, LMS Incoming Letters (South Africa), 51–2-B].

57. A. Sharp, Vryburg, 12 November 1886 [WMMS, South Africa Correspondence (Transvaal), 328].

58. Although some evangelists were discouraged by it, and gave less energy to building as time went by (see n. 47).

59. "Comfort," as we said in chapter 5, was itself a construct of particular vintage, coming in eighteenth-century English to connote a certain level of domestic order, civility, and amenity (cf. Rybczynski 1986:21–22).

60. For examples, see *Tsala ea Becoana*. On p. 4 of almost every edition in 1911–12, there appeared illustrated advertisements for beds, organs, and pianos—as well (without illustration) as soap and other household commodities.

61. In his address to the University of the Witwatersrand in 1933, the Kgatla ruler, Isang, commented that "[c]ivilization held out a great attraction to a good many of my people in the shape of double beds." He referred to the latter, with a heavy touch of irony, as "this symbol of civilization"—and made it clear that he would rather have had Kgatla buy double furrow ploughs (Schapera 1980:53).

62. This occurred at the PEMS station at Motito as well. According to Lemue, a man—(re)named Dante, in striking contrast to the biblical "Johns" and "Pauls" conferred on British converts—began to build a school in his village after having been

church member for some years. Unfortunately, no further details are given; see P. Lemue, Motito, 25 February 1840 [SMEP/DEFAP, Correspondance des champs de mission, Afrique australe (H-2100), vol. 1840, #55].

63. R. Moffat, Kuruman, 14 July 1845 [CWM, LMS Incoming Letters (South Africa), 3-1-D]. See also Livingstone (in LMS 1843:58); Broadbent (1865:187, 195); W. C. Willoughby, Palapye, 22 September 1894 [CWM, LMS Incoming Letters (South Africa), 51-2-B].

64. Cf. Langmore (1989:85–86) on the Pacific, where a "major feature of the missionary wife's routine was the training of Papuan women and girls in domestic accomplishments. Girls were brought into the house to work—with the dual intention of their providing cheap labour for the missionaries' family, while learning the refinements of 'civilized' living."

65. For a sensitive account of similar practices among evangelists of the Baptist Missionary Society based at Yakusu in the Belgian Congo early this century, see Hunt (1992:143ff.).

66. Even in boarding schools, pupils were long to be left to feed themselves (see volume 3). Later, black South Africans would also be taught culinary and other domestic skills by white employers on farms and in towns—who expected to be served according to their own tastes.

67. In volume 3 we discuss further the important, at times controversial, role of vocational training and domestic science in late nineteenth- and early twentieth-century mission schools.

68. There are many accounts, by evangelists, of the sabbath at Tswana stations. Perhaps the most lyrical is by John Mackenzie (1871:467f.); it describes a Sunday at Shoshong in the 1860s.

69. B. Shaw, Lily Fountain, 9 December 1823 [WMMS, South Africa Correspondence, 300].

70. In this respect, cf. Larsson and Larsson (1984:13) on the persistence of "traditional" architecture in Botswana. (As our account should make clear, we do not ourselves subscribe to the concept of the "traditional." We see it as an ideologically freighted way of flattening out the past, of devaluing its historical dynamics, and of legitimating a dualist vision of the world. We reiterate this—even though the point is now a tired one—since some commentators have, despite all our efforts to demonstrate the contrary, characterized us as "dualists," "world systems theorists," "structuralists," and various other things that misconstrue our project.)

71. The parallel here between Southern Tswana blankets and buildings, both of which remained versatile in form and function, is striking.

72. J. Cameron, Platberg, 26 September 1842 [WMMS, South Africa Correspondence, 315–121]. It is not clear whether these people were actually Tswana or Sotho; but this made no difference to the way in which the settlement was taken as a sign of progress.

73. Cf. Krige and Krige (1943:318) on the Lovedu.

74. Shaw was not alone in noting the walls at Thaba 'Nchu. His successor, William Impey, who visited in 1862, found "the aggregate amount" of stone wall "astonishing" (Broadbent 1865:201).

75. A. J. Wookey, Kuruman, 23 May 1884 [CWM, LMS Incoming Letters (South Africa), 42–3–C]; also (1884:263).

76. Christian converts among the Zulu, for example, were said to have been "spat out" by their communities (Guy 1979:19); see Hutchinson (1957) on the effect of different indigenous settlement patterns for the success of the missions.

77. A few stations were established or sustained in small villages and scattered settlements. Typically this occurred (i) when the first missionaries to an area arrived during a time of population upheaval (caused by political conflict, warfare, or ecological reverse) and stayed on at the site; (ii) when a small outpost was created to give access to a wider hinterland for an itinerant evangelist; or, most often, (iii) when patterns of settlement changed as a result of the internal dynamics inherent in the organization of Tswana chiefdoms (see *RRI*:126–60; also J. L. Comaroff 1982; Comaroff and Comaroff 1992:95–125.)

78. This example comes from further north and later in the century. However, we include it here since it is one of most illuminating of its kind in the nineteenth-century documentary record.

79. We were struck, in this respect, by a letter to the PEMS written for Chief Moshweshwe by his son. In it, the Sotho ruler protested the threatened removal of "his" missionaries. Speaking of Eugene Casalis, he noted, with approval, how the evangelist had "built" his city; "Translation of a letter written by the son of Chief Moshesh [Moshweshwe] at the instruction of his father," Thaba Bossiou, 18 September 1855 [SMEP/DEFAP, Correspondance des champs de mission, Afrique australe (H-2100), vol. 1855, #160].

80. His model, added Campbell (1822,2:82), came from the houses of the missionaries "that he had seen at Lattakoo [Dithakong]." No further details of the construction are given.

81. Missionary accounts of such places—like that of Wookey (see n. 75)—were corroborated by other Europeans. Holub (1881), for one, whom we cite in the text below, gave account of several.

82. Holub visited Likatlong in 1873. Interestingly, after passing through the village in 1859, Mackenzie (1871:91–92) had written in less positive terms. He complained that the water furrow was not straight and that "the gardens and arable land are laid out in a manner which offends the eye of a European."

83. A fairly typical example of the mix of circular and rectangular houses in a Southern Tswana settlement, circa 1938, may be read off a diagram drawn by Schapera (1943b, opp. p. 77) of the Tsopye ward in Kanye, the Ngwaketse capital. Of the total of 16 homestead compounds, 11 had only round structures; 5 had a combination of round and square ones. Of the 38 buildings in those 16 compounds, 10 were used for storage (8 round, 2 square). The remaining 28 were residential, 22 being circular and 6 square; as far as can be discerned, 5 of the 6 of *sekgoa* design were among the largest houses in

the ward. Professor Schapera has also made available to us his field notes on housing arrangements in select Kgatla, Tlokwa, and Kwena wards in 1940. These evince very similar distributions—save that, in each case, there are one or two compounds with only rectangular dwellings. In sum, this material confirms exactly the pattern we have been describing in the text (as do our own maps of five wards in Mafikeng drawn some thirty years later). Note, also, the dates: 1938, 1940, 1970. They reinforce our point that this mixed pattern was to be an enduring one.

84. This was the case among the more northerly Ngwato. In Palapye, wrote Fripp (1897:520), an artist and adventurer, "Khama lives in an iron-roofed brick building of the same character as the better dwellings and stores of the Europeans."

85. These were not the only Southern Tswana royals to live in *setswana* abodes while adopting European dress. Others did too, some of them until well into this century. A striking case is that of the Tshidi Methodist leader Molema, who persisted "in adhering to the native style of architecture" until the 1870s. And this in spite of the fact that his son and other residents of Mafikeng, the Christian town of which he was head, had built in *sekgoa* mode (Holub 1881,2:13). We shall return to Mafikeng below.

86. As a counterpoint to Willoughby's statement, Schapera has stressed to us—based on his work in the 1930s—that there were certainly improvements in building during the early twentieth century; that these went together with a new division of labor and the training of artisans; that, as a result, erecting houses became more costly. For details, see Schapera (1943b:93–94).

87. This qualification is ours, not Willoughby's. It is based on such pictorial sources as Burton's *Cape Colony Today* (n.d.), published in Cape Town circa 1907.

88. The houses in plates 6.4 and 6.6, both of which we have seen (albeit in somewhat reconstructed form), still exist in the Ngwaketse capital, Kanye.

89. This was the pattern we encountered among Tshidi and other Southern Tswana in visits to the field between 1969 and 1995. We were also told repeatedly—when doing a household survey in 1970—that it had been the case as long as anyone could remember.

90. Holub (1881,1:320f.) tells how Sechele—a self-styled cultural Christian, if not an accepted member of the church—served him tea from a silver service on a handsome, white-clothed dining table. "The tea," said the Austrian physician, "was good, and the cakes unexceptional." The chief's house, a "trim-looking edifice," was built entirely in European style. Its "drawing room" was furnished with walnut chairs and couches covered in velvet.

91. Evidence of this is to be found in Schapera's (1943b:94f.) account of the household composition of the Tsopye ward (Kanye, 1938), whose domestic architecture is discussed in n. 83. (See also his classic paper, "The Social Structure of the Tswana Ward" [1935]). Our own census, genealogies, and household histories—collected in 1969–70 from 387 households in Mafikeng and Mareetsane—confirm a picture of growing diversity over the past three generations (i.e., as far back as our data appears reliable).

92. Converts too poor to erect even small *sekgoa* cottages also lived in synthetic homes of this kind, including in them as many things European as their means allowed.

One such case appears to be the subject of a photograph taken by Willoughby (n.d.[a]:48); we reproduced it, for different purposes, to illustrate a point in chapter 5 (plate 5.5). Captioned "Cottar's Saturday Night, Secwana Version"—a "cottar" is a Scottish cottager—it shows a family, dressed in church garb, sitting in formal Christian sociality before its house. The latter is round and made from local materials, but it has a stout wooden door of English design and a straight, high fence. Unfortunately, we cannot see anything more of the dwelling.

93. The return of Montshiwa from exile, and the establishment of his capital at Mafikeng, are recounted—from a Tshidi-Rolong royal perspective—by Molema (1966:118 et passim).

94. As we explained in our notes to chapter 3, Z. K. Matthews, distinguished Rolong scholar, worked in Mafikeng in the 1930s. Among his field reports is a document dated 6/21/37 and headed "The Barolong Town or Stad." The second paragraph reads: "The expression 'town' must not give the impression that the Barolong town is anything like a European town. It has no well laid-out streets, no sanitary conveniences, etc. The first impression one gets in walking around it is one of complete lack of order or system in its structure. Like Topsy it seems to have just "growed" haphazardly, and it is only after a more intimate acquaintance with Barolong society that any semblance of order can be discerned in the whole town."

95. Our own rough census, conducted in 1969–70, indicated that the population was then somewhere in the region of twenty-five thousand people.

96. Our most recent visits to Mafikeng were in the (U.S.) summers of 1992, 1995, and 1996.

97. This is evident from a wide range of missionary communications. For just two examples—separated, for emphasis, by seventy years and hundreds of miles—see W. C. Willoughby, Palapye, 22 September 1894 [CWM, LMS Incoming Letters (South Africa), 51-2-B)] and S. Broadbent, Matlwasse, 23 August 1823 [WMMS, South Africa Correspondence, 300].

98. Northcott (1961:82–83) excerpts a letter in which Mary Moffat describes how she and Mrs. Helm smeared their floors regularly with cow dung. Quoting this letter, de Kock (1993:82–83) offers an insightful analysis of private confessions, by missionaries and their wives, of the adoption of African domestic practices.

99. Mary Moffat also grew to like soured "Bechuana milk," despite its preparation in "dirty vessels"; what was described early on as a heathen refreshment was said later to be "quite delightful" (quoted in Northcott 1961:82–83). The Moffats' private correspondence (1951:passim) shows that some of their diet was of indigenous provenance and was consumed in ways little different from those of the Tswana. See also Livingstone (1974:125, 77), who often purchased foodstuffs from Tswana, and Elizabeth Price (1956:443), who recalled how much her family enjoyed "Sechwana porridge."

100. W. C. Willoughby, Palapye, 22 September 1894 [CWM, LMS Incoming Letters (South Africa), 51-2-B].

101. The term *rondavel* (or *rondoval;* "suites-in-the-round") traveled to other British colonial outposts as well. It has recently turned up in advertisements for luxurious

holiday accommodations in the English-speaking Caribbean. See, e.g., the British *Observer,* Life magazine section, 29 January 1995, p. 39.

102. This capsule description is based on notes made during a visit to Lobatse in August, 1995, although we first came to know St. Marks in 1970. Outside the serene, shaded church grounds, exuberant street noises assaulted the ear. Sidewalk stalls sold everything from cowbells to Chicago Bulls caps, worn Bob Marley cassettes to gaudy posters of the Crucifixion, quietly melting chocolate bars to highly colored cosmetics. All of which served to frame St. Marks with particular clarity, underscoring the ironic history of its social and physical architecture.

103. Kitson Clark (1962:150) claims that anyone "not blind and deaf" was aware of "the large areas of *heathendom*" in contemporary Britain. He goes on (p. 163) to quote Bishop Selwyn, who, reflecting on a recent religious census, spoke in 1854 of the enormous problems raised by "*the dark masses* of our uninstructed people" (italics added; they are the source of the words in quotation marks in our text).

104. It is hardly necessary to underscore the point—made in both this and the previous volume, and much better by such social historians as Edward Thompson (1963) and Gareth Stedman Jones (1971)—that "the poor" (like "the working class") did not compose an undifferentiated, steady-state sociological reality.

105. Some of these are well described in Victorian novels, a notable case being the home of the Bartons, carefully sketched by Elizabeth Gaskell in the second chapter of *Mary Barton.* True, these are fictional accounts. But, notes Kitson Clark (1962:120), himself a hard-nosed empirical historian, the likes of Dickens (and, we would add, Gaskell) were fine social observers with first-hand experience of the worlds of which they wrote.

106. For primary sources, see chapters 5 and 7. Lichtenstein's (1973:67) report that Tswana wore "broad ugly caps of jackal or cat fur sewn together" is strikingly reminiscent of later descriptions of costermonger headwear.

107. The term "realistic," used by many contemporary writers of "factual" accounts, did more than merely connote "objective" or "scientific." It disclaimed sectional political interests and moral agendas—in the name of which many documentary treatises were also published. See, for just one example, Booth (1891:7).

108. Hebdige (1988:21) makes a similar point, but does not annotate it.

109. Mayhew (1851:1) cites the work of Andrew Smith as the model for his own study. In every society, he says, wanderers are distinct from settlers, vagabonds from citizens, nomads from civilized people; in every society, elements of each "race" are to be found. According to this Africa-derived scheme, London laborers had a "savage and wandering mode of life" (p. 2)—like "bushmen" living beside more settled ("Hottentot") peoples.

110. The most persuasive body of "hard" evidence would come from large-scale socioeconomic surveys; among them, those done in London in 1886–88 and reported in Charles Booth's various volumes. Writing on "the classes," Booth (1891:3–171) indicates—in dry, scientific tones—that the predicament of the poor was as bad as that described by Engels ([1844] 1968) some forty years before. Housing stock (p. 30f.) was shown to be dismal at best, dreadful at worst. Here, clearly, was strong evidence for the descriptions of underclass domesticity in the London novels of the period.

111. The old would suffer a similar fate, underlining the role of Africans and other ethnicized peoples as markers of bourgeois margins. Spandrell, a character in Huxley's *Point Counter Point* (1994:134) remarks: "You speak of the old as though they were Kaffirs or Eskimos."

112. As Stedman Jones (1971:part 3) notes, late nineteenth-century writings on the predicament of the casual poor in London underwent several transformations—largely as a product of rapidly changing social and economic conditions. For present purposes, however, these transformations are not directly significant. The bourgeois ideology of domesticity did not change much over the period; nor did the efforts of middle-class reformers and missionaries to reconstruct the home life of the poor.

113. According to Perkin (1969:149–50), Engels took "most of his notions of the development of the family" from this widely read text by P. Gaskell (1836). In it, Gaskell argues (p. 89) that "a [poor] household . . . in which all the decencies and moral observances of domestic life are constantly violated, reduces its inmates to a condition little elevated above that of the savage. Recklessness, improvidence, and unnecessary poverty, starvation, drunkenness, parental cruelty and carelessness, filial disobedience, neglect of conjugal rights, absence of maternal love, destruction of brotherly and sisterly affection, are too often its constituents."

114. It also appeared in the narratives of French missionaries. Arbousset, for example, translated a Christian song sung by Tswana women to evangelists as they left the interior. Its first line reads: *Nous sommes étrangers dans ce val de misère*, "We are strangers in this vale of misery"; T. Arbousset, Ville du Cap (Cape Town), 26 February 1845 [SMEP/DEFAP, Correspondance des champs de mission, Afrique australe (H-2100), v.1835, #86].

115. The evocation of Africa as a constructive model appeared in other popular genres as well, most notably in children's literature. Church educators seem to have regarded the young as a major target for stories of savage improvement. For a striking example, see Georgina Gollock's *Aunt Africa* (1909), published by the Church Missionary Society. We discuss the infantilization of Africa, and its relegation to the nursery, in volume 1 (p. 117).

S E V E N

1. We would like to thank Peter Pels, in particular, for insisting that we underline these unique features of the healing mission. Some of the material dealt with in this chapter is also included in an earlier essay, "Medicine, Colonialism, and the Black Body," by Jean Comaroff (in Comaroff and Comaroff 1992; see also J. Comaroff 1993).

2. S. Broadbent, Matlwasse, August/September 1823 [WMMS, South Africa Correspondence, 300–31]; on efforts at early sickbed conversions by WMMS evangelists, see, e.g., T. Hodgson, Bootchnaap, 18 August 1829 [WMMS, South Africa Correspondence, 302]. Writing from the small PEMS station at Motito, situated along the margins of Southern Tswana territory, French missionaries also gave examples of baptisms occasioned by illness. One involved a woman from an influential family who, it was hoped, might draw others into the church; see P. Lemue, Motito, 1 July 1838 [SMEP/DEFAP, Correspondance des champs de mission, Afrique australe (H-2100), v.1838, #40].

3. A partial exception to this was Joseph Ludorf of the WMMS, who, Whiteside (1906:339–40) suggests, was a qualified doctor. While Ludorf certainly did treat both Tswana and white settlers, and gives matter-of-fact account of his ministrations, he did not style himself as a medical missionary.

4. Bradford (n.d.) has recently pointed out, interestingly, that—notwithstanding its professionalization and growing authority in Britain—medicine was actually less secure, less influential in early twentieth-century colonial South Africa than it was at the metropole. In the years following the Anglo-Boer War, she shows, Afrikaners regarded it as a foreign, imperialist pursuit.

5. We are grateful to Isaac Schapera for pointing out to us that, in anonymous publications in *The British Banner* of 1849, Livingstone signed himself "A Surgeon" (see Livingstone 1959,2:78, n.5). Today he would be thought of as a physician; surgery, in the strict sense of the term, comprised a relatively small proportion of his practice. But he was trained at Edinburgh rather than Oxford or Cambridge. In any case, as historians have noted, in early modern England "the public did not overtly distinguish the disorders that surgeons treated from the treatments offered by physicians, apothecaries, barbers, wise women and quacks" (Wilson 1992:43).

6. Read's copy of this volume is in the South African Library, Cape Town.

7. In the late 1830s, the publications of the LMS and other societies were to carry lengthy appeals for "well-qualified medical men, of decided piety . . . to labour as Missionaries in China" (LMS 1837b:272f.).

8. For Africans, that is. In the settler colonies, like South Africa, secular biomedicine, provided both by the state and by private physicians, was directed largely at whites (cf. MacLeod 1988:8f.). In the twentieth century, black populations became the object of biomedical concern primarily at the workplace.

9. See Packard (1989:22f.; also below). It seems clear, on the basis of available evidence, that death from tuberculosis owed much less to indigenous living arrangements throughout South Africa than to the effects of an exploitative colonial economy.

10. A. J. Wookey, Molepolole, 30 October 1888 [CWM, LMS Incoming Letters (South Africa), 45–3-E]. According to Wookey, "over fifty boys"—including children of church members who were "stolen and carried away"—died as a result of initiation rites and an "epidemic" that broke out among participants. He goes on to claim that the flesh of two or three of the early victims was "cut up and mixed with the food of the other boys and given them to eat."

11. The term was used by David Livingstone (1961:293) in 1855. He seems to have intended it, broadly, to mean "human and natural ecology."

12. Moffat (Moffat and Moffat 1951:263) once remarked that, if he "were to keep a diary of every minutiae, lice would be a daily topic." Even in Namaqualand, before he began his work among Tlhaping, he showed himself to be concerned about lice and cleanliness. On one occasion, he wrote to his supervisors in London:

> Cleanliness is a lesson hard to teach [Africans].. . . [P]unishments are . . . necessary to drive the younger to this important duty. . . . Neither, say they, are [they] troubled with so many lice. Formerly, the most of their attention in church was

taken with slaughtering these their fat companions and I always got my share of these restless inhabitants while preaching.

See R. Moffat, Vreedeberg (Groot Namaqualand), 22 June 1818 [CWM, LMS Incoming Letters (South Africa), 7-4-D].

13. A. Sharp, Vryburg, 12 November 1886 [WMMS, South Africa Correspondence (Transvaal), 328].

14. The exception was Roger Price who, in 1880, built a "hospital" composed of wagons at Molepolole, among the more northerly Kwena (Seeley 1973:81–82). Here patients could remain under the treatment of the missionary and his wife, although they brought their own food and paid for their medicines. Price's colleagues regarded the enterprise with ambivalence. They frequently found cause to mention his numerous cattle, which grazed on land purchased privately—albeit with approval of the colonial Land Commission—from the local chief.; see, e.g., J. Brown, Taung, 9 July 1894 [CWM, LMS Incoming Letters (South Africa), 51-1-D]. Another partial exception, later and further north, was Willoughby, who held a daily clinic and charged small sums for preparations. He reported on his medical activities in, among other correspondence, W. C. Willoughby, Palapye, 21 July 1894 [CWM, LMS Incoming Letters (South Africa), 51-1-D]; Palapye, 20 March 1895 [CWM, LMS South Africa Reports, 2-4]. As Gaitskell (1992:183) notes, the establishment of African mission hospitals really came later, well into the twentieth century.

15. So were the French Protestants at their one station among Southern Tswana; see, e.g., J. Lauga, Motito, 13 July 1840 [SMEP/ DEFAP, Correspondance des champs de mission, Afrique australe (H-2100), v.1840, #55]. Given their similar ideology and their cordial relations with the British Nonconformists—some PEMS emissaries actually received training at Kuruman (Zorn 1993:369), and visited LMS and WMMS centers regularly—it is not surprising that the early history of their medical activities ran a close parallel to that of their English-speaking counterparts. A further comparative note here: Etherington (1978:52–53), in an insightful comment on missionary curing among Nguni-speaking peoples, notes several of the things we have mentioned here: the constant appeals made to evangelists for medications and "magical services" (often accompanied by explicit statements of disinterest in conversion); a tendency to see God's Word itself as "medicine"; the great popularity of Europeans with professional training as doctors, as well as a willingness to travel long distances to consult them; a recognition by some clerics that healing did more than anything to attract black South Africans "to the house of God"; and the ambivalence among the clergymen about using health as a material means to their spiritual ends. See also his informative essay on mission doctors and indigenous healers (Etherington 1987).

16. Somerville (1979:149) claims that it was he who, in 1801, first told a Tlhaping chief about inoculation against smallpox. (Edward Jenner had used the technique successfully in England in 1796.) According to Somerville's diary, he furnished the ruler with a lancet, and taught him and some of his followers how to vaccinate with it; the Africans, worried about the virulence of the disease, are said to have been impressed with the procedure and were eager to try it out. This account of the origin of indigenous vaccination, if true, gives yet further evidence for our assertion that Southern Tswana

were remarkably open to the cultural ways and means of others—and willing to experiment with even radically different forms of expertise.

17. Other missionaries also operated on Tswana, but few seem to have done so with much confidence. Even Willoughby, who reported that he did regular surgical work, confessed to knowing "little . . . about medicine or surgery"; W. C. Willoughby, Palapye, 21 July 1894 [CWM, LMS Incoming Letters (South Africa), 51–1-D].

18. Livingstone received, among other journals, the *British and Foreign Medical Review* and *Lancet* (Schapera in Livingstone 1959,1:102, n. 6; 172, n. 6). Seeley (1973:80) provides the following list of instruments in his possession in Africa: "thermometer, tourniquet, trephines, probes, forceps, lion forceps, dental forceps, tooth extractor, umbilical scissors, surgical scissors, scalpels, artery forceps, spatula, surgical needles, knives, bone saws, ligature silk, tissue forceps, curettes, catheters, and catheter introducers." This list was compiled from collections of objects in the hands of the LMS, the Livingstone Museum (Zambia), and the Blantyre Memorial Museum (Scotland). Seeley notes, however, that the equipment used by Livingstone during the early years of his work was destroyed in the Boer attack on Kolobeng in 1852.

19. See, e.g., W. C. Willoughby, Palapye, 21 July 1894 [CWM, LMS Incoming Letters (South Africa), 51–1-D].

20. By the time these shipments reached the African interior, however, they had sometimes been "lightened of their contents" (Gelfand 1984:38; Livingstone 1961:110).

21. See J. Brown, Taung, 9 July 1894 [CWM, LMS Incoming Letters (South Africa), 51–1-D]; W. C. Willoughby, Palapye, 21 July 1894 [CWM, LMS Incoming Letters (South Africa), 51–1-D]. The issue of payment for mission healing (by both blacks and whites), and the question of what should be done with the income, became the subject of anguished correspondence in the last decades of the century; especially since the Foreign Secretary of the LMS "endorsed the principle that even natives, when able, should pay for medical treatment" (J. Brown, in the 9 July 1894 letter cited above). These two letters are just samples of a longer set of exchanges.

22. From early on, as we intimated in chapter 4, the missionaries expected those Tswana who joined the church to pay subscriptions. Some of these were offered in cash, others in produce (LMS 1838:42).

23. Livingstone (1857:145) nonetheless intervened often enough to make some interesting observations, most notably about the comparative character of childbirth (see below). He also remarked that Tswana took pride in their ability to bear pain without wincing (see also John Mackenzie 1871:379–80).

24. See, for two instances among many, J. Brown, Taung, 9 July 1894 [CWM, LMS Incoming Letters (South Africa), 51–1-D]; W. C. Willoughby, Palapye, 21 July 1894 [CWM, LMS Incoming Letters (South Africa), 51–1-D]. Willoughby's letter contains one of the many appeals to the LMS, made by himself and others, for qualified Christian healers (see above; also W. Ashton, Kuruman, 20 November 1861 [CWM, LMS Incoming Letters (South Africa), 32–3-B]); although he liked treating the sick, he obviously felt torn by having to do so. The terms on which untrained evangelists gave medical aid to both whites and blacks were to change, of course, after the colonial state restricted all nonprofessional curing.

25. For example, Livingstone's (1961:36) successful treatment of Sechele's son seems to have piqued the interest of the chief in the Christian message. But he was to prove a notoriously inconstant convert.

26. In Setswana, *"ngaka"* was to become the functional equivalent of the English "doctor," which it remains today. While a qualifier is sometimes added to denote indigenous healers (*dingaka tsa setswana*), the sense of the term—whether, that is, it refers to allopathic or "traditional" practice—usually derives from its immediate context of use.

27. S. Broadbent, Matlwasse, 23 August 1823 [WMMS, South Africa Correspondence, 300].

28. Sechele had previously purchased a preparation to make himself invulnerable to musket balls; but it is not clear from Livingstone's account (1857:280) whether the chief thought this medicine to be of European provenance.

29. Recall that, especially in the early years, the firearms used along the frontier were often as dangerous to their users as to their targets (see *RRI*:275–76).

30. Mission rhetoric, especially in the early nineteenth century, located sentience and reason in the heart. Since the latter was the site of feeling as well, physical perception and thought were united in it. As we have noted, the poetics of conversion also centered upon this organ ("melting their flinty hearts"; "God's word . . . work[ing] in their hearts" [*RRI*:239, 214]). In this, Christian rhetoric readily translated into Setswana, which today has a wealth of epithets denoting personal disposition by means of qualities of the heart (e.g., *peloethata*, "hard-hearted," from *pelo* [heart] and *thata* [hard, strong]; *pelonamagadi*, "tenderhearted," from *pelo* and *namagadi* [female]; *pelotelele*, "long-suffering," from *pelo* and *telele* [long]). These compound adjectives are probably linguistic calques—i.e., translations into the vernacular of English idiomatic usages—produced in the speech field created by the mission encounter (Debra Spitulnik, personal communication). There have long been terms in Setswana for embodied perceptions and qualities, however—among them, *utlwa* ("understand," "hear") or *bona* ("realize," "see"); interestingly, in the early 1820s, Broadbent (1865:117) was asked by a Seleka-Rolong chief whether an evangelist about to join the local WMMS station "was a man of a 'little or great heart;' meaning, was he a timid or a courageous man?" (For another, later, example see Mackenzie 1871:380). The word for liver (*seriti*) also connoted "personal presence" and "dignity" (J. Comaroff 1980:643). But it shows no sign of the semantic elaboration that has attached to the "heart." It is worth noting that Western usage—technical usage, in particular—has tended increasingly to segregate emotion from cognition, heart from mind; this has culminated in recent legal and ethical debates over, among other things, whether the heart or the brain should be the "official" site of death.

31. The encounter between endogenous and exogenous agents of infection in Africa has a complex history. Historians (e.g., Curtin 1964) have taken care to document morbidity and mortality among European visitors to the continent. But the impact of colonialism on the health of local populations has received less systematic treatment. As Livingstone (1857:694) noted, inhabitants of the southern African coastline had long been prey to diseases brought by ships (see Laidler and Gelfand 1971:267, 40). Then, with the permanent settlement of whites at the Cape, they suffered a series of epidemics. These, which were exacerbated by shifting patterns of contact, included measles, ty-

phoid, diphtheria, and smallpox—the last thought to have been brought in 1713 by an East India vessel.

32. Note that the *partial* adoption of European clothing had long been blamed for illness among non-European populations. In South Africa, for example, the Native Affairs Commission, 1903–5, asserted that Western dress was a cause of disease among "natives" who "adopted our style" with an "imperfect understanding of the laws of health"; these "natives," the Commission report went on, failed to realize that civilized attire required "more frequent cleansing" than did "ancestral garb" (South Africa 1905:51; see also chapter 5). There is also a foreshadowing of this view in, of all things, the 1874 edition of *Notes and Queries on Anthropology*. In part 3, no. XCV ("Contact With Civilized Races"), pp. 139–41, visitors to "aboriginal" peoples are advised to ask: "What effect, in causing disease, has a partial change of diet and dress?" This entry was written by Sir T. Gore Browne, and is listed in our bibliography accordingly.

33. While many scholars have addressed the connections between rural privation and urban conditions in determining the health of black South Africans—see, for just a few examples, Schapera (1934:58); Laidler and Gelfand (1971:427f.); Packard (1989:passim); van Onselen (1982:44f.)—others have denied or downplayed them. Rheinallt Jones (1934:182–86), for one, saw life in mining compounds as a potential panacea for the physical state of impoverished migrants from the reserves. So did a report published earlier by the South African Native Races Committee (1908:26–28)—despite giving evidence of startlingly high mortality rates on the mines. Unlike Schapera (1934), neither Rheinallt Jones nor the SANRC grasped the fact that prevailing urban conditions ensured the export of pathologies to the countryside.

34. As Andrew Smith (1939,1:241, 269, 275 et passim) observed in 1834–35, Southern Tswana also suffered from "bloodzichte" ("bloedsiekte" or anthrax) as a result of eating the meat of diseased livestock. Although he gives graphic descriptions of its symptoms, comments on its seasonality, mentions that Europeans were also afflicted by it, and says that it could be fatal in pregnant women, it is difficult to decide how common a condition it really was at the time.

35. Lichtenstein ([1807] 1973:70–71) does temper his account, however, by noting that smallpox epidemics occurred often, and that many Tswana died from them. (The disease, he adds, came not from the Cape, but from Central Africa.) Burchell (1824,2:580; also Campbell 1822,1:307) confirms that there had been outbreaks, but says that they had only occurred "once or twice"; Smith (1939,1:391–92), writing a decade later, in 1835, says "thrice," most recently in about 1831.

36. See, e.g., Cape of Good Hope (1907:28f.). Shula Marks has suggested to us, with her usual perspicacity, that the British military could also have spread venereal disease among Southern Tswana. Although we have not ourselves investigated this question, her hypothesis is highly plausible. In the wake of the discovery of diamonds, and the extended conflict that followed, imperial soldiers certainly made their presence felt in the region, culminating in the arrival of the Warren Commission in the mid-1880s. Syphilis may well have been endemic among these troops—as it was among others in South Africa—many of whom cohabited with Tswana women. As we note in volume 1 (p. 352, n.138), Chief Montshiwa of the Tshidi-Rolong was gravely concerned about the

behavior of members of the Bechuanaland Border Police, in particular about their sexual exploits. So much so that he persuaded the WMMS to complain to the Secretary of State for the Colonies on his behalf—an act which led to bitter conflict with whites in Mafeking after the matter was reported in the *Times* Weekly Edition in London. (For an account of a very fractious public meeting held in Mafeking to discuss this and other allegations, see the minutes and press cuttings attached to O. Watkins, Pretoria, 22 February 1887 [WMMS, South Africa Correspondence (Transvaal), 328].) The formal complaint was later published in London (WMMS 1887).

37. It is impossible to establish the epidemiology of disease among Southern Tswana during this period. Nor is there any basis on which to ascertain whether rates of illnesses varied according to social rank and class, gender or age. However, from the indigenous perspective—which is what we are most concerned with here—the spread of affliction appeared to be a *general* phenomenon; or so local leaders said in making their complaints. The colonial state, which was also becoming alarmed at the prevalence of syphilis, if for more cynical reasons, did eventually respond. By 1908, it paid "selected headmen" a bounty of sixpence for each case brought in for treatment (Cape of Good Hope 1909:31). During the early years of this century, the annual *Blue Books on Native Affairs,* mentioned before, carried numerous reports of the spread of the disease.

38. On contemporary white South African perceptions of the "unhealthy" presence of blacks in their midst, see, e.g., Great Britain (1891–92); Swanson (1977:387f.); Comaroff and Comaroff (1992:226). For a striking example of these perceptions, as expressed among those who lived close by Southern Tswana, see "The Servant Question" in the *Northern News,* 2 June 1911, p. 2. This editorial—directed at "European" readers in the towns of Vryburg, Taung, and Kuruman—argued that all domestic servants ought to be required to produce a "medical certificate of health" before being employed. It added that, if such a requirement were made into law, given the state of cleanliness and contagion among blacks, a "very large population of [white] homes would be without any servants at all." The final sentence concludes with the assertion that such "ordinary health precautions . . . [would] do a great deal to improve the health of the servants themselves" (see also Cape of Good Hope 1907:34). Two decades earlier, the medical officer in Mafeking had voiced a similar concern (Comaroff and Comaroff 1992:229).

39. It appears in *The Secret Agent,* published in 1907 but set in 1886. Verloc, the agent of the title, uses the term in the course of a bitter soliloquy: "Protection," he complains, "is the first necessity of opulence and luxury. . . . [T]he source of their wealth had to be protected in the heart of the city and the heart of the country; the whole social order favourable to their hygienic idleness had to be protected against the shallow enviousness of unhygienic labour" (1994:20).

40. As we know from our own childhoods in postwar South Africa, even late into the twentieth century many whites believed that the dry, clear atmosphere of the interior had healing properties.

41. According to both Curtin (1964:179; see also 1961) and Killam (1968:2), citing Fyfe's *History of Sierra Leone* (1962:151), the coast of West Africa—Sierra Leone in particular—came to be dubbed "the white man's grave" in the early 1820s; at just the time, in other words, that the LMS and WMMS missions in the Bechuana interior were establishing themselves.

42. For another dramatic example, see P. Lemue, Motito, 25 February 1840 [SMEP/DEFAP, Correspondance des champs de mission, Afrique australe (H-2100), v.1840, #55]. At one point in his *Missionary Travels*, Livingstone (1857:146) asserts blandly that "the health and longevity of the missionaries have always been fair." This statement, perhaps made with an eye to continued public support for the evangelists in Britain, is flatly contradicted by the evidence. Many Nonconformists of the first generation in the South African interior wrote of suffering serious illness; some withdrew from their stations because of it. (See citations in the text below. For two examples of an ongoing litany of physical distress, see Broadbent 1865:7f., 64, 72, 76, 105, 119f.; J. Lauga, Motito, 12 October 1840 [SMEP/DEFAP, Correspondance des champs de mission, Afrique australe (H-2100), v.1840, #55]).

43. This was true also of the correspondence of the small band of French missionaries who worked among Sotho and Tswana from the early 1830s onward. For example, in writing from Platberg [Plaat Berg] to his sister in London in 1831, Prosper Lemue complained of being so ill—from chronic inflammation of the stomach—that he thought he might well die; P. Lemue, Platberg, 30 August 1831 [SMEP/DEFAP, Correspondance des champs de mission, Afrique australe (H-2100), v.1831–32, #6].

44. Livingstone (1961:194), in fact, confessed himself so concerned about the effect of his wife's pregnancies on her health that he encouraged her return to England for an extended rest. As an interesting aside, which we once again owe to Isaac Schapera, Livingstone gives some sense in this passage of his views on birth control. "A residence in England of two or three years would prevent the frequent confinements which, notwithstanding the preaching of Dr. Malthus & Miss Martineau, periodically prevail." Only absence and abstinence, it seems, was an effective prophylactic. It is noteworthy that those missionary wives who did not suffer sustained ill-health in South Africa proved gynecologically sturdy: Elizabeth (Moffat) Price, who was born in Bechuanaland, for example, bore fourteen children.

45. See, e.g., J. Lauga, Motito, 12 October 1840 [SMEP/DEFAP, Correspondance des champs de mission, Afrique australe (H-2100), v. 1840, #55]; F. Taylor, Thaba 'Nchu, 26 February 1844 [WMMS, South Africa Correspondence (Bechuana), 315]; also Moffat and Moffat (1951:68, 246, 248), and Broadbent (1865), who, despite commenting that the local climate was not "insalubrious" (p. 119), blamed a debilitating outbreak of ophthalmia among WMMS mission families on "some peculiarity in the atmosphere" (p. 111).

46. Tiryakian (1993:212f.), in an excellent essay on "white women in darkest Africa," points out that the image of the continent as, above all else, a "white woman's grave" developed over the course of the nineteenth century, buttressed by the biological myth of the "weaker sex." As he goes on to show (e.g., pp. 230f.), the empirical foundations of this image were contested in the writings of several women who traveled extensively in Africa (cf. also Mills 1991).

47. Thus, for instance, James Cameron, Platberg, 6 July 1844 [WMMS, South Africa Correspondence (Bechuana), 315]: "My dear wife having suffered much for some years past, indeed ever since we came to the Bechuana country, has gone to Cape Town in quest of health." For more examples, see Moffat and Moffat (1951:114); J. Lauga,

Motito, 12 October 1840 [SMEP/DEFAP, Correspondance des champs de mission, Afrique australe (H-2100), v.1840, #55].

48. J. Mackenzie, Kuruman, 1 March 1859 [CWM, LMS Incoming Letters (South Africa), 31-3-A]; also Mackenzie (1975:76). In his published account, Mackenzie (1871:34) also took pains to defend the missionaries' decision to proceed with the expedition despite his misgivings—partly because the British press had criticized them for putting their families at risk.

49. Several other missionaries also claimed to have advised Price and Helmore not to take women and children with them on the expedition; see, e.g., W. Ashton, Kuruman, 16 April 1861 [CWM, LMS Incoming Letters (South Africa), 32-3-A].

50. Mackenzie persisted in blaming European fatality on "African" conditions for a long time even though, as he well knew, the climate varied greatly across southern Africa; even across Bechuanaland. In recording the deaths of two missionary wives (1871:36), in fact, he went so far as to express his "satisfaction" that "neither . . . was . . . caused by anything connected with the climate of Africa"—thereby reinforcing the impression that the opposite was usually true.

51. This is evident from, among other things, a paper read to the LMS Founders' Week Convention by the Rev. Lloyd (1895:168) in the closing years of the century—*long* after "African" fevers, beasts, and the like were an acute threat to evangelists among the Tswana. "Think of the perils to your missionaries!" he declaimed. "You think of perils from wild beasts; of perils from fever, dysentery, and other African diseases; of perils from wild and savage tribes among whom we go; and these perils are often present." As Killam (1968:2) notes, although prophylactics and vaccines for fever became available in the 1880s, Africa's reputation for unhealthfulness increased rather than abated.

52. See, e.g., R. Moffat, Cape Town, 20 July 1824 [CWM, LMS Incoming Letters (South Africa), 9-1-A] on the scandal surrounding Mrs. Hamilton's "abandon[ment of] her husband." Moffat described her conduct as "universally detested."

53. J. Cameron, Platberg, 6 July 1844 [WMMS, South Africa Correspondence (Bechuana), 315].

54. Sometimes the evangelists wrote quite intimate details about the physical condition of their wives, especially after childbirth. Robert Moffat, for example, told a missionary colleague, James Kitchingman, about the soreness of Mary Moffat's breasts—in an otherwise business-like communication about the movements of John Philip. The letter, dated 24 September 1825, is published among the Kitchingman papers (Kitchingman 1976:81).

55. Although Livingstone (1960:24) noted that Tswana women secluded themselves while menstruating, he said nothing of the disposal of their menstrual discharge. Elsewhere (1861; also in Gelfand 1957:297–98), however, he offered an explanation for the way in which polluting effluvia was spread by riverain means. During the dry months, he wrote, there collected around every African village large amounts of human waste—which was later swept into rivers by the heavy rains of the wet season. (We shall return to this explanation, in another connection, below.) The imaginative connection between pollution and fever was further underscored by Livingstone's (1861) treatment

for malaria, which he described in excruciating detail. It began with the administration of a strong purgative to encourage the extrusion of whatever foreign substances had been ingested. This produced "an enormous discharge of black bile." The patient, he added, "frequently calls it blood."

56. Gilman (1985) also notes that some nineteenth-century medical men believed that syphilis had been long been present in Africa, and was brought thence to Europe in the middle ages.

57. A pointed example is to be found in Wilkie Collins's *The Moonstone;* in particular, in the wretched character of Ezra Jennings, a medical practitioner born in "one of our colonies" (1966:420). As drawn by Collins, whose authorial intentions were sympathetic, Jennings is a physically deformed social outcast—his predicament the result of his racially mixed parentage. And this notwithstanding his fine, even heroic disposition, his cultivated tastes, and his extensive scientific knowledge.

58. As Schapera has reminded us, Livingstone (1963:218; also 155, 189) showed a further interest, as he traveled across East Africa: learning Portuguese techniques for treating malaria.

59. See Gelfand (1957:47–48, 65). The pill was composed of quinine, calomel, rhubarb, resin of jalap, and a little spirit. Of these, the first was the vital ingredient; Livingstone (1963:206) believed that, in its pure form, quinine was an "effectual remedy" on its own—although he did find an indigenous tree in Mozambique whose bark had the same medical properties (p. 469). For one example of his own treatment of the condition (circa 1854), which included the use of leeches, see Livingstone (1963:186f.).

60. See Kipling (1994:124); the short story, "A Germ-Destroyer," was first published in 1888. There is a striking continuity between these nineteenth-century images of African etiology and contemporary Western discourses on AIDS. As Watney (1990) and others have shown, both popular representations and government policies now focus on the idea that the virus is airborne; that it is carried across the world from Africa, in the era of mass jet transport, by infected travelers and workers.

61. See also J. Cameron, Platberg, 28 February 1843 [WMMS, South Africa Correspondence (Bechuana), 315]; above, chapter 2.

62. Nor, in this century, was it to be a replica of the forms of biomedicine to which the Nonconformist healing ministry gave way.

63. See "Return of a Young Native Doctor," *Tsala ea Batho,* 21 June 1913, p. 3; also Molema (1951:196).

64. See, e.g., "Natives and Liquor. Conditions in Bechuanaland." *Tsala ea Batho,* 3 July 1915, p. 4; "The Native and Drink." *Tsala ea Batho,* 24 July 1915, p. 4.

65. "Notes and Comments: Those Patent Medicines!" *Tsala ea Batho,* 14 March 1914, p. 4. Such preparations were both South African and European in origin. Orsmond's remedies, for example, were produced in Kingwilliamstown. Among their regular advertisements was the one reproduced in plate 7.3. Invoking Livingstone and Stanley, it extolled an "extract" that was said to cure conditions ranging from "the universal weaknesses of children" through African fevers to "Cape complications." It also promised to "insure" the "health of the crown and constitution." The marketing of patent

preparations for blacks would flourish as the century progressed; see *Heal the Whole Man* (chapter 2, n. 121).

66. This was said in his address to the Pan-African Congress, from which we quoted in chapter 3 (repr. 1996).

67. See, e.g., "Native Health Society Notes." *Tsala ea Becoana*, 30 September 1911, p. 2; "'Health.' To the Members of the Native Health Society." *Tsala ea Batho*, 16 May 1914, p. 2. Neither of these pieces were published under a byline.

68. "Emergencies. What to Do While Awaiting the Doctor." *Tsala ea Batho*, 16 May 1914, p. 2.

69. "'Health.' To the Members of the Native Health Society." *Tsala ea Batho*, 16 May 1914, p. 2. All the quotes through the following paragraph are from this article.

70. Even the most enthusiastic Tswana apologists for the civilizing mission, such as S. M. Molema (1920:chap. 25), were quick to point out the contradictions of life for blacks in colonial South Africa; Molema himself stressed, in particular, the difficulties faced by uneducated or "semi-civilized" blacks.

71. "Lost Tribes, Lost Knowledge," *Time* [International], 23 September 1991, no. 38:40–48.

72. All the statements made in the following paragraphs come from data we collected ourselves while doing fieldwork in the Mafikeng District, South Africa, during the late 1960s and early 1970s.

73. South African readers are likely to have seen these announcements; they appear regularly in such magazines and newspapers as *Huisgenoot* and the *Sunday Times*. For just one example, see *You*, 4 June 1992. There is, on p. 68, an illustrated advertisement under the headline "SANGOMA SAYS." The text reads: "Hear me throw the bones and tell you everything about your future."

E I G H T

1. Some sections of this chapter are included, in amended form, in J. L. Comaroff (1995). The quoted passage is from a letter, dated 12 March 1886, sent by Montshiwa to John Mackenzie (Mackenzie 1975:186).

2. We place "it" in quotation marks to note the fact that several disparate things are often lumped together under the term "law" in the anthropology of colonialism (cf. Snyder 1981:6): among them, (European) legal institutions and sensibilities; a variety of constitutional and administrative processes; dispute management of diverse kinds; and the workings of "customary" law.

3. See, for example, Mann and Roberts (1991), who introduce their volume with a comprehensive overview of recent scholarship on law and colonialism in Africa; they also include a large bibliography. For two other review essays on law, colonialism, power, and resistance—both thoughtful and cogently argued—see Merry (1991) and Hirsch and Lazarus-Black (1994).

4. Chanock's (1991:62) own citation of Bentham's statement is not to the original (*Principles of the Civil Code*, chapter 8, "Of Property"), but to the excerpted version in Macpherson (1978:52).

5. While this is not Chanock's choice of term, it captures his point nicely. We are, of course, aware of its complex provenance in the history of Western ideas (see, e.g., Macpherson 1962), not to mention the debates sparked by it (see Shapiro 1986:274f.). Nonetheless, we use it, in connection with Chanock's very thoughtful writings on colonialism and law, to evoke the multifaceted construction of the self that arose with what Taylor (1989:285f.) glosses as the "the culture of modernity." See below.

6. See, for example, the essays in the *American Ethnologist* 16:609–65 (1989) under the title "Tensions of Empire."

7. The phrase is from Romans (3.31): "Do we then make void the law through faith? God forbid! Yea, we establish the law." This Epistle of St. Paul was central to the debate. In declaring that the "righteousness of God has been manifested apart from the law" (3.21), and that "man is justified by faith apart from works of law" (3.28), it appeared to support an antinomian view. Wesley (1985:10) argued the opposite in his Sermons on Law, however. He insisted that God had given his creatures an inborn moral sense so that they might recognize the law as a "transcript of the divine nature." The "properties" of that law were to convict, convert, and sustain the believer "in and after justification"; i.e., during and after coming to Christ (Wesley 1985:15–16). The law itself was Christological, Outler (1985:2) points out, "as if Torah and Christ are in some sense to be equated."

8. For a pertinent example of the recasting of sin and divine justice in the idiom of contemporary criminal procedure, see Davies's (1962:228f.) description of the sermons of the Congregationalist Thomas Binney; also Wesley, "The Great Assize" (1984:355).

9. For discussion, from a Marxist perspective, of the relationship between the modern "legal" subject and bourgeois ideology, see Snyder (1981:8ff.).

10. There is, of course, much more to the archaeology of "modern" personhood and subjectivity than these summary sentences suggest. This, however, is not the context in which to address the issue. Our concern is limited to the tropes born by the civilizing mission to southern Africa.

11. We are grateful to Martin Chanock for drawing our attention to this inquiry. He discusses it in his forthcoming study (n.d.) of law and the state in early twentieth-century South Africa. For the full text of the report, see South Africa (1925b); the quoted passages are to be found on p. 119.

12. Compare, for instance, John Philip's (1828,2:118) account of the success of "rational ideas" and modes of reasoning introduced by the missionaries in inducing Tswana to depart from the "customs of their ancestors"; also above, chapter 3.

13. For an insightful comment on the relegation of custom to a "peripheral, contained and decadent category" in the British legal imagination, see Fitzpatrick (1990:92 et passim).

14. The evangelists took the task of implanting this form of personhood to be a sacred one from the first. Said John Philip (1828,2:361), quoting an unnamed source:

"Religious institutions are the channels . . . by which the ideas of order, of duty, of humanity, and of justice, flow through the different ranks of the [human] community."

15. The phrase in question occurs in Wesley's sermon (no. 34) on "The Original Nature, Properties, and Use of the Law." It refers to the role of the law in convicting the sinner and bringing him to God (1985:16): "'Tis true, in performing both these offices it acts the part of a severe schoolmaster. It drives us by force, rather than draws us by love."

16. We are told, for example, that, by 1842, "numerous gardens . . . [had] been walled in" at Platberg; J. Cameron, Platberg, 26 September 1842 [WMMS, South Africa Correspondence, 315–121]. Similarly, at Lishuani, "sixty large gardens [had] been enclosed"; J. Allison, Lishuani, 1 August 1843 [WMMS, South Africa Correspondence, 315–123].

17. We refer here to Wordsworth's (1948:54) "perfect Republic of Shepherds and agriculturalists" described in his sketch of the Lake District and mentioned in volume 1 (pp. 71–72).

18. The pioneer evangelists wrote often of having addressed congregations on the subject of church discipline, which they appear to have approached in highly legalistic terms. *Vide,* for instance, Moffat (Moffat and Moffat 1951:20): "Sabbath. This evening I preached on the nature and order of a Christian church. This I did to prepare the minds of the members for the exercising [of] church discipline."

19. Our use of terms such as "lesson" and "teaching" is intended to capture the rhetoric of the evangelists. In John Mackenzie's account of the conversations excerpted here, he refers (1887,1:79) to his interlocutors, chiefs among them, as "my students."

20. The classic work on the subject is, of course, Schapera's *Handbook of Tswana Law and Custom* (1938), although he has also written several important essays that deal with aspects of *mekgwa le melao.* Some years ago, Comaroff and Roberts (1981) took issue with the *Handbook* on the character of this body of norms: on its internal composition, on the nature of the "laws" and "customs" that are said to compose it, on their capacity to decide the outcome of disputes, and so on. Schapera (1985), in turn, responded vigorously; others have since joined in the lively but constructive debate. The matter is not finally settled, nor is there any reason that it can or should be. There *is* agreement over a number of important things, however: that *mekgwa le melao* have a long history and are not a recently invented tradition, although there is evidence that they have been increasingly rationalized (see Roberts 1985; *RRI*:129); that they mutate over time, partly as a result of chiefly legislation and partly as a product of changing patterns of social practice (see, e.g., Schapera 1985, 1943c; Comaroff and Roberts 1977; Molokomme 1991); that they are not a *corpus juris* in the Western sense of the term.

21. As we were careful to annotate our discussion of Southern Tswana personhood in volume 1—and as we have also discussed the topic in detail elsewhere (e.g., Comaroff and Comaroff 1992; Comaroff and Roberts 1981; J. Comaroff 1985)—we do not do so again. This and the next paragraph are summary statements, the evidentiary basis for which may be recalled as necessary (*RRI*:142f.).

22. One qualification to this, discussed before (*RRI*:143): persons were sometimes invaded by malign human or spiritual forces. This condition, known as *sefifi* (also *sehihi*), caused the visible eclipse of the self in otherwise sentient beings.

23. Citizenship in a Tswana polity was, above all, a matter of allegiance to its chiefship. It might be acquired by birth, immigration, or conquest—although, as Schapera (1938:118f.) notes, a clear distinction was made between members and visitors or other "aliens." While all citizens were protected by *mekgwa le melao*, not all had the same access to the courts; adult women, for example, had to be represented by senior male kin. Furthermore, not everyone in a community counted as citizens: those held to be of inferior stock (Sarwa, Kgalagadi, and so on) were treated as serfs (*RRI*:129) and enjoyed only very limited rights.

24. The *mekgwa le melao* regulating land tenure, and their changes over time, have been thoroughly documented by Schapera (especially 1938:195ff., 1943b:passim, 1970:96f.). Since we are only concerned to make a few summary points here, we do not annotate them in detail; rather, we take as given the evidence provided in these major works.

25. In chapter 3 (n. 123) we noted that the Molema-Plaatje Papers [Aa 3.5—Aa 3.5.15] contained copies of a substantial number of land and property leases granted by Silas Molema, in his private capacity, to white farmers. Among these papers are also memoranda of agreement and land leases by other members of the Molema family [e.g., Ab 3] and the Tshidi chief, Lekoko [Bd 2.1—Bd 2.3].

26. Of the leases mentioned in n. 25, many involved land in the "Mafeking Native Reserve." Under both prevailing state law and *mekgwa le melao*, this could have been neither freehold nor leasehold; it must have been held under "traditional" tenure. Among the files which we read in 1969–70 in the Tshidi-Rolong Community Offices in Mafikeng, one was marked "Land Agreements." In it was a letter written to an attorney in 1901 by Chief Besele which attested that Silas Molema had the right, under "tribal law," to rent a specified piece of land *in the Reserve*. Given the prevailing tenurial arrangements, this simply could not have been so; it suggests that the ambiguities surrounding land rights at the time were being thoroughly exploited by those in a position to do so.

27. Private landholding in the Bechuanaland Protectorate was not debarred by the state. But it appears never to have occurred on a large scale either until much later (Schapera 1947:55f.).

28. The renting of land *within* the reserves (see above, n. 26) continued for a very long time, however.

29. J. Brown, Taung, Annual Report and Ten Years Review of the Mission, 1900 [CWM, LMS South Africa Reports, 3–1].

30. This refers to military action during the early part of the Anglo-Boer War (1899–1902), when Boer commandoes attacked and invested English settlements in British Bechuanaland—most notably, of course, Mafeking/Mafikeng.

31. This article appeared on 14 February 1903. In it, Plaatje noted that the tax was not levied in the Cape Colony. He called on the clergy of the various denominations— hitherto unmoved in this matter—to bring the inequity to the attention of the High Commissioner and to urge for the repeal of the "impediment."

32. The Molema-Plaatje Papers contain many examples of such materials [see, e.g., Aa 3.5; Be 4]. For a dispute spanning three generations, see *re The Application Concerning*

the Estates of the Late Badirile Montshioa and John Bakolopang Montshioa, S. B. Kitchin, Kimberley, 3 June 1926 [Molema-Plaatje Papers, Be 4].

33. See also chapter 2. In the early years, marriage by civil ceremony was infrequent. Later, especially with the rise of independent denominations whose leaders were not recognized marriage officers, most weddings were performed by Bantu Affairs Commissioners. These were often consecrated afterwards in church (cf. Pauw 1960:153).

34. Matthews noted that, in the 1930s among Rolong, "quite well educated couples" still practiced *go ralala,* the bride remaining at her natal home until the birth of one or two children. He also remarked on the continuing salience of the mother's brother in everyday life, and of a preference for endogamous marriage; "First Quarterly Report on Field-work among the Barolong of British Bechuanaland (December 1935–February 1936)."

35. This passage was contained in an essay written as a homework assignment by (the equivalent of) a sophomore for a regular English class taught by a Tshidi-Rolong instructor. We were assisting as volunteer teachers in the school at the time.

36. Our statements here are based on marital histories collected from 357 Tshidi-Rolong households in 1969. These histories traced unions—both genealogically and through oral accounts—as far back as reportage was possible (typically, the early years of the century).

37. Those disenfranchised in this way often joined the independent churches. But, because the leaders of these churches were not recognized marriage officers, their marginalization in this respect was perpetuated.

38. Maingard (1933:597) claimed that the Kora "called and still call the Bechuana *brikwa,*" a name derived from the word for goat, because they first acquired these animals from them.

39. For just a few examples, see Campbell (1822,2:193f.); J. Philip (1828,2:107–43); R. Moffat (1842:chaps. 1, 15, 17); Solomon (1855:41f.); Livingstone (1857:9f., 122f.; J. Mackenzie 1871:483ff., 1887,1:21f.). Harries's (1988) excellent analysis of the relationship between the politics of language and the formation of ethnic groups in northeastern South Africa documents similar processes.

40. As this implies, we do not see ethnicity, *sui generis,* purely as a product of colonialism; it may arise, and often has arisen, in other circumstances as well. A further qualification is to be added here: elsewhere (1992:chap. 2) we differentiate ethnic consciousness (which has its roots in relations of inequality and structural opposition) from totemic consciousness (a form of marking among structurally similar political groupings implicated in broadly symmetrical relations). Prior to the arrival of the Europeans, when local (Tswana) polities were known by the eponymous names of their ruling lines—before they were labeled, collectively, as Bechuana—this form of totemic consciousness seems to have prevailed among their citizenry. (This was in sharp contrast to the treatment of peoples like the Sarwa and Kgalagadi, who had been reduced to servitude, ethnicized, and were seen as a different species of [semi]social being.) Every *morafe* (nation) included, in addition to members of its core group, (often a majority of) persons of other totemic affiliations (see Schapera 1952). This pattern continued well into the present century. Its traces are still found in many places today.

41. See Native Conference of the South African District Circuit of 1907; W. C. Willoughby, "Children, Education and Puberty" [Willoughby Papers, 14].

42. Each independent chief had his own advisers and a council of headmen; each also called meetings of various kinds. There was, as we have said, no larger "Bechuana" confederation with its own ruler, councils, or assemblies.

43. This is a topic which we covered extensively in volume 1; here we are merely concerned with the general point. For just one example of this view, culled from the mission archive, see J. Freeman, Mabotsa, 25 December 1849 [CWM, LMS Home Odds (Freeman Deputation 1849–50), 2-4-D]; also, for further discussion, Comaroff and Comaroff (1992:181ff.).

44. In the Bechuanaland Protectorate, indigenous invocations of "Bechuana" identity became more frequent after overrule in 1885, and often had an undisguised political character. For example, Chirenje (1978:27–28; quoted by Ramsay 1991:189) tells how Chief Sebele of the Kwena tried to persuade another local ruler "to adopt a pan-Tswana and anti-British attitude . . . to colonial rule."

45. See Chirenje (1987:26f.) and J. D. Jones (1972). Both deal with the LMS publications *Mokaedi oa Becwana* (1857–59) and *Mahoko a Becwana* (1883–96), but neither mentions that the first such paper, *Molekoli oa Bechuana*, was a Methodist monthly. It was published at Thaba 'Nchu between 1856 and 1858 by Ludorf (Switzer and Switzer 1979:258–59), who had also established an earlier, short-lived periodical in Sesotho, *Lenqosana la Lesuto* (1850). Almost complete runs of these publications are held in the Grey Collection of the South African Library.

46. It was known in English as the *Bechuana Gazette*. Founded by George Whales (the owner of the *Mafeking Mail*), *Koranta* was a weekly paper. It was bought by Silas Molema in 1901 and edited by Sol Plaatje. Financial straits forced it to publish less frequently from 1906 to 1908, when it closed (Switzer and Switzer 1979:48–49; Plaatje 1916:6).

47. [Draft] Treaty between Paramount Chief Montsioa, his Sons and Councillors and the Imperial Government, Mafikeng, 22 May 1884 [Molema-Plaatje Papers, Ba 9].

48. Chief Montshiwa's Letter Book, S. M. Molema Papers; School of Oriental and African Studies, University of London.

49. Supplementary Petition presented to the Rt. Honourable Joseph Chamberlain P. C. by the Paramount Chief, Headmen and Councillors of the Baralong Nation, Mafikeng, January 1903 [Molema-Plaatje Papers, Bb 3].

50. Barolong National Council, Johannesburg, 18 April 1918 [Molema-Plaatje Papers, Cc 4.1].

51. In the years prior to the independence of Botswana, Seretse Khama, heir to the Ngwato chiefship—the most powerful of all "traditional" Tswana offices—emerged as leader of the Botswana Democratic Party. He became the president of the new republic in 1966. Within the country itself, his prominence was widely attributed to his place in the cartography of customary politics. But that is too simple: the rise of Khama, a modernist politician in every way, was fostered by processes and forces characteristic of late colonialism.

52. In the Bechuanaland Protectorate, chiefs (and other notables) formed an African Advisory Council from 1920 onward; in South Africa, a few Tswana rulers found their way onto a Natives' Representative Council (1936–51). See Schapera (1953:49–50); Schapera and Comaroff (1991:44). These councils were ostensibly created to allow for "native leadership" to influence policy. But, official rhetoric aside, it is clear that they had little impact. The Bechuanaland diaries of Sir Charles Rey (1988) give revealing glimpses of the manner in which Tswana chiefs were regarded; although Rey's writings are not an especially reliable historical source, his often unguarded comments provide fascinating material for an ethnographer of the archives.

53. This is from the closing paragraph of a letter written to the Governor of Quilimane in protest against the Portuguese involvement in land disputes on the side of the Transvaal. It is included with the evidence presented to the Bloemhof Commission (Bloemhof 1871:165). Montshiwa signed the letter as the Tshidi-Rolong sovereign, the other two as Maebu-Rolong chiefs.

54. For the rest of this chapter our discussion is confined primarily to the Union (and then Republic) of South Africa. As we have already implied, the Bechuanaland Protectorate was a very different kind of colonial society; as a result, struggles over rights there did not take the same form. We concentrate on the first, however, because that is where the vast majority of Southern Tswana live[d].

55. See Great Britain (1886a; 1886b; 1886c); and, especially, Schapera ([1943a] 1983:16) for a summary and analysis of the relevant official materials. John Mackenzie (1887,2:336f.), who became directly involved himself, wrote a commentary as well. Our own account is composited, synoptically, from these sources; consequently we do not annotate it point by point.

56. For an excellent analysis of the impact of government inquiries and official discourse on the (re)construction of indigenous populations, see Ashforth (1990). Although based in South Africa, this study has important comparative implications.

57. We refer here to Mill's (1965,2:274) famous popularization of Arthur Young's (1794,1:50) statement: "The magic of property turns sand into gold. . . . Give a man the secure possession of a bleak rock, and he will turn it into a garden."

58. This is underlined by the fact that, less than ten years before but in different political circumstances, Sir Gordon Sprigg, Prime Minister at the Cape, took the exact opposite line. He declared that, in order to "teach [blacks] to work," it made sense to give "every head of family a . . . piece of land for which he should have a title." This was said in a speech, which we have quoted before, delivered by Sprigg on his tour of the colony; *Diamond Fields Advertiser,* 1 November 1878, p. 3.

59. Great Britain (1886a:53ff.); J. Brown, Taung, 9 March 1886 [CWM, LMS Incoming Letters (South Africa), 44-1-A]. According to John Mackenzie (1887,2:340–41), the original land grant given by Chief Mothibi to the LMS and ratified by his successors had given "uninterrupted use." But there were no documents asked or given "as such a procedure was unknown to the natives, who were then entirely ignorant of the use of books, letters, or title-deeds." After some thirty years, a survey was made of the station, garden lots, and village site, and a title deed was drawn up by Moffat, to which "the names of such chiefs and headmen were appended as their missionary deemed neces-

sary." When the land at Kuruman and use of the stream were granted by Mothibi, Mackenzie continued, a "quantity of European goods, representing a large amount of money in that country at that time," were paid to him by Hamilton and Moffat on behalf of the LMS. The commission found the deed filed in support of this claim "irregular," but still gave the Society the whole of the ground on certain conditions; because of its expenditure on improving the site, moreover, it was granted saleable title (cf. E. Smith 1957:314f.).

60. This commission, which we have quoted from frequently above, was set up before the establishment of the Union of South Africa to prepare the way for a future "native administration" (South Africa 1905:5). While recommending that most blacks continue to live under "the communal system," it suggested that individual leasehold of "arable plots" should be permitted in very limited circumstances and under highly restricted conditions (p. 28).

61. The implicit evocation here of W. E. B. Du Bois, and of the African American experience, is, of course, deliberate.

62. Among the differences were (i) an engagement in armed struggle (after a long period of commitment to nonviolence); and (ii) talk, between the time of the Freedom Charter of the 1950s and the negotiations leading up to the first free elections in 1994, of the nationalization of some public resources and utilities.

63. Although, as is well recognized in South Africa, the IFP does not, by any means, enjoy the backing of all Zulus. On the other hand, it also has a block of non-Zulu electoral support.

N I N E

1. During August 1996, while teaching at the University of the North West and writing the final version of this Conclusion, we met regularly with a group of some ten B.A.(Honours) students. On several occasions, discussion turned to the Southern Tswana past and its representation.

2. Most insightfully by Shula Marks (personal communication).

3. The quoted phrases are from Elbourne (n.d.:24), whom we cite, again, because she has been one of our most thoughtful and constructive critics.

BIBLIOGRAPHY

Adam, Ian, and Helen Tiffin, eds.

1991   *Past the Last Post: Theorizing Post-Colonialism and Post-Modernism.* New York: Harvester Wheatsheaf.

Adams, Annmarie

1991   *Corpus Sanum in Domo Sano: The Architecture of the Domestic Sanitation Movement, 1870–1914.* Montreal: Canadian Center for Architecture.

Adams, Henry Gardiner

1870   *The Life and Adventures of Dr. Livingston: In the Interior of South Africa; Comprising a Description of the Regions which he Traversed; An Account of Missionary Pioneers; and Chapters on Cotton Cultivation, Slavery, Wild Animals, etc., etc.* New York: G.P. Putnam & Sons.

Adams, Ian H.

1968   The Land Surveyor and His Influence on the Scottish Rural Landscape. *Scottish Geographical Magazine,* 84:248–55.

1980   The Agents of Agricultural Change. In *The Making of the Scottish Countryside,* eds. M. L. Parry and T. R. Slater. London: Croom Helm.

Alloula, Malek

1986   *The Colonial Harem.* Translated by M. and W. Godzich. Minneapolis: University of Minnesota Press.

Alverson, Hoyt

1978   *Mind in the Heart of Darkness: Value and Self-Identity among the Tswana of Southern Africa.* New Haven and London: Yale University Press.

Ames, Kenneth L.

1978   Meaning in Artifacts: Hall Furnishings in Victorian America. *Journal of Interdisciplinary History,* 9:19–46.

Amin, Samir

1974   *Neo-Colonialism in West Africa.* Translated by F. McDonagh. New York: Monthly Review Press.

Anderson, Andrew A.

1888   *Twenty-five Years in a Waggon: Sport and Travel in South Africa.* London: Chapman & Hall. Reprinted, 1964; Cape Town: Struik.

Anderson, Benedict

1983   *Imagined Communities: Reflections on the Origin and Spread of Nationalism.* London: Verso.

Anderson, Bruce Louis, and Philip Leonard Cottrell
1974   *Money and Banking in England: The Development of the Banking System, 1694–1914.* Newton Abbot, London, and Vancouver: David & Charles.

Appadurai, Arjun
1990   Disjuncture and Difference in the Global Economy. *Public Culture,* 2(2):1–24.
1993   Consumption, Duration, and History. *Stanford Literary Review,* 10(1–2):11–33.

Apter, Andrew
1993   Atinga Revisited: Yoruba Witchcraft and the Cocoa Economy, 1950–1951. In *Modernity and its Malcontents: Ritual and Power in Post-Colonial Africa,* eds. J. and J. L. Comaroff. Chicago: University of Chicago Press.

Archer, Thomas
1865   *The Pauper, the Thief, and the Convict; Sketches of Some of their Homes, Haunts, and Habits.* London: Groombridge.

Arendt, Hannah
1958   *The Human Condition.* Chicago: University of Chicago Press.

Arndt, Ernst Heinrich Daniel
1928   *Banking and Currency Development in South Africa, 1652–1927.* Cape Town: Juta.

Ash, Juliet, and Elizabeth Wilson
1992   Introduction. In *Chic Thrills: A Fashion Reader,* eds. J. Ash and E. Wilson. Berkeley: University of California Press.

Ashforth, Adam
1990   *The Politics of Official Discourse in Twentieth-Century South Africa.* Oxford: Clarendon Press.

Atkins, Keletso E.
1993   *The Moon Is Dead! Give Us Our Money! The Cultural Origins of an African Work Ethic, Natal, South Africa, 1843–1900.* London: James Currey.

Auslander, Leora
1990   Rethinking Class Formation: Production and Consumption among the Parisian Petite Bourgeoisie. *Wilder House Working Papers,* no. 3.
1996   *Taste and Power: Furnishing Modern France.* Berkeley: University of California Press.

Auslander, Mark
1993   "Open the Wombs!": The Symbolic Politics of Modern Ngoni Witch-finding. In *Modernity and Its Malcontents: Ritual and Power in Postcolonial Africa,* eds. J. Comaroff and J. L. Comaroff. Chicago: University of Chicago Press.
1997   *Fertilizer Has Brought Poison: Crises and Reproduction in Ngoni Society and History.* Ph.D. diss., University of Chicago.

Baillie, John
 1832   Extracts from the Journal of Rev. John Baillie, New Lattakoo, 30 September
    1830. *Transactions of the Missionary Society*, April 1832; contained in *Quarterly
    Chronicle of Transactions of The London Missionary Society, in the Years 1829, 1830,
    1831, and 1832*, 4:442–48.

Bain, Andrew G.
 1949   *Journals of Andrew Geddes Bain*. Edited by M. H. Lister. Cape Town:
    Van Riebeeck Society.

Balia, Daryl M.
 1991   *Black Methodists and White Supremacy in South Africa*. Durban: Madiba Publi-
    cations for the Institute for Black Research.

Barker, Diana L.
 1978   Regulation of Marriage. In *Power and the State*, eds. G. Littlejohn et al.
    New York: St. Martin's Press.

Barker, Francis
 1984   *The Tremulous Private Body: Essays on Subjection*. London: Methuen.

Barrett, David B.
 1968   *Schism and Renewal in Africa: An Analysis of Six Thousand Contemporary
    Religious Movements*. Nairobi: Oxford University Press.

Barrow, John
 1801–4   *An Account of Travels into the Interior of Southern Africa in the Years 1797 and
    1798*. 2 vols. London: T. Cadell & W. Davies.
 1806   *A Voyage to Cochinchina, in the Years 1792 and 1793 . . . To Which is Annexed an
    Account of a Journey, Made in the Years 1801 and 1802, to the Residence of the Chief of
    the Booshuana Nation. . . .* London: T. Cadell & W. Davies. Reprinted, 1978;
    Kuala Lumpur: Oxford University Press.

Bartels, Francis Ludowic
 1965   *The Roots of Ghana Methodism*. Cambridge: Cambridge University Press in
    association with the Methodist Book Depot Ltd., Ghana.

Barthes, Roland
 1967   *Système de la Mode*. Paris: Éditions du Seuil.
 1973   *Mythologies*. Translated by A. Lavers. St. Albans: Paladin.

Bascom, William R.
 1951   Social Status, Wealth, and Individual Differences among the Yoruba.
    American Anthropologist, 53:490–505.

Bastian, Misty
 1985   *Useful Women and the Good of the Land: The Igbo Women's War of 1929*. M.A.
    thesis, Department of Anthropology, University of Chicago.
 1992   *The World as Marketplace: Historical, Cosmological, and Popular Constructions of
    the Onitsha Market System*. Ph.D. diss., University of Chicago.

Baudrillard, Jean
 1970   *La Société de Consommation: Ses Mythes Ses Structures*. Paris: S.G.P.P.

1973   *The Mirror of Production.* St. Louis: Telos Press.

1988   *Jean Baudrillard: Selected Writings.* Edited by M. Poster. Cambridge: Polity Press in association with Blackwell.

Baum, Robert M.
1993   Review of *Of Revelation and Revolution,* vol. 1. *Journal of Religion,* 73:154.

Beames, Thomas
1852   *The Rookeries of London: Past, Present, Prospective.* London: Thomas Bosworth.

Beck, Roger B.
1989   Bibles and Beads: Missionaries as Traders in Southern Africa in the Early Nineteenth Century. *Journal of African History,* 30:211–25.

Beidelman, Thomas O.
1968   Some Nuer Notions of Nakedness, Nudity, and Sexuality. *Africa,* 38:113–32.
1982   *Colonial Evangelism: A Socio-Historical Study of an East African Mission at the Grassroots.* Bloomington: Indiana University Press.

Bell, Quentin
1949   *On Human Finery.* New York: A. A. Wyn.

Bentham, Jeremy
1838   *Principles of the Civil Code.* Edinburgh: W. Tait. First French edition, 1802.

Berman, Edward H.
1975   Christian Missions in Africa. In *African Reactions to Missionary Education,* ed. E. H. Berman. New York: Teachers College Press.

Bhabha, Homi K.
1984   Of Mimicry and Man: The Ambivalence of Colonial Discourse. *October,* 28:125–33.
1994   *The Location of Culture.* New York: Routledge.

Blake, William
1975   *The Marriage of Heaven and Hell.* With an Introduction and Commentary by Sir Geoffrey Keynes. London: Oxford University Press.

Blauner, Robert
1969   Internal Colonialism and Ghetto Revolt. *Social Problems,* 16:393–408.

Bloemhof
1871   *Evidence Taken at Bloemhof before the Commission Appointed to Investigate the Claims of the South Africa Republic, Captain N. Waterboer, Chief of West Griqualand, and Certain Other Native Chiefs, to Portions of the Territory on the Vaal River Now Known as the Diamond-Fields.* Cape Town: Saul Solomon.

Bohannan, Paul
1964   *Africa and Africans.* New York: The Natural History Press.

Booth, Charles, ed.
1891   *Labour and Life of the People,* vol. 1: *East London.* Third edition. London: Williams & Norgate.

Borcherds, Petrus Borchardus
1979   Letter Written by Petrus Borchardus Borcherds to His Father Rev. Meent Borcherds (Undated [circa 1802]). Published as Appendix I in *William Somerville's Narrative of His Journeys to the Eastern Cape Frontier and to Lattakoe 1799–1802.* Edited by E. and F. Bradlow. Cape Town: Van Riebeeck Society.

Bosanquet, Charles B. P.
1868   *London: Some Account of Its Growth, Charitable Agencies, and Wants.* London: Hatchard.

Bourdieu, Pierre
1977   *Outline of a Theory of Practice.* Translated by R. Nice. Cambridge: Cambridge University Press.
1979   *Algeria 1960.* Translated by R. Nice. Cambridge: Cambridge University Press.
1984   *Distinction: A Social Critique of the Judgement of Taste.* Translated by R. Nice. Cambridge: Cambridge University Press.

Bowlby, Rachel
1985   Modes of Shopping: Mallarmé at the Bon Marché. In *The Ideology of Conduct: Essays in Literature and the History of Sexuality,* eds. N. Armstrong and L. Tennenhouse. New York: Methuen.

Bradford, Helen
n.d.   Creating a Crime: Doctors, Abortion and Contraception in South Africa, c. 1870–1918. Paper read to a seminar of the Program on International Cooperation in Africa, Northwestern University, 25 February 1993.

Braudel, Fernand
1981   *Civilization and Capitalism, 15th–18th Century,* vol. 1: *The Structures of Everyday Life: The Limits of the Possible.* Revised translation by S. Reynolds. New York: Harper & Row.
1984   *Civilization and Capitalism, 15th–18th Century,* vol. 3: *The Perspective of the World.* Translated by S. Reynolds. New York: Harper & Row.

Brecht, Bertolt
1980   Against Georg Lukács. Translated by S. Hood. In *Aesthetics and Politics,* E. Bloch, G. Lukács, B. Brecht, W. Benjamin, T. Adorno; translation ed. R. Taylor. London: Verso.

Breckenridge, Keith
1995   "Money with Dignity": Migrants, Minelords and the Cultural Politics of the South African Gold Standard Crisis, 1920–1933. *Journal of African History,* 36:271–304.

Breutz, Paul-Lenert
1956   *The Tribes of Mafeking District.* Union of South Africa, Department of Native Affairs, Ethnological Publication no. 32. Pretoria: Department of Native Affairs.

Brewer, Anthony
1990   *Marxist Theories of Imperialism: A Critical Survey.* Second edition. London: Routledge.

Briggs, Asa
1979   *Iron Bridge to Crystal Palace: Impact and Images of the Industrial Revolution.*
        London: Thames & Hudson.

Briggs, John, and Ian Sellars, eds.
1973   *Victorian Noncomformity.* London: Edward Arnold.

British Medical Journal
1913   David Livingstone. *British Medical Journal,* 1913(1):564–66.

Broadbent, Samuel
1865   *A Narrative of the First Introduction of Christianity amongst the Barolong Tribe of
        Bechuanas, South Africa.* London: Wesleyan Mission House.

Brontë, Charlotte
1969   *Jane Eyre.* Edited by J. Jack and M. Smith. London: Oxford University
        Press. First edition, under the pseudonym Currer Bell, 1847.

Brown, J. Baldwin
1868   The Domestic Character of Englishmen. *The Evangelical Magazine and Mis-
        sionary Chronicle,* 10(N.S.):584–86. Excerpted, under the title "Domesticity," in
        Victorian Nonconformity, eds. J. Briggs and I. Sellers. London: Edward Arnold,
        1973.

Brown, J. Tom
1921   Circumcision Rites of the Becwana Tribes. *Journal of the Royal Anthropologi-
        cal Institute,* 51:419–27.
1925   *The Apostle of the Marshes: The Story of Shomolekae.* London: The Religious
        Tract Society.
1926   *Among the Bantu Nomads: A Record of Forty Years Spent among the Bechuana*
        . . . London: Seeley Service.
1987   *Setswana-English Dictionary.* Gaborone: Pula Press. First edition, c. 1875;
        third edition, 1925, revised and enlarged, 1931.

Browne, (Sir) T. Gore
1874   Contact with Civilized Races. In *Notes and Queries on Anthropology for the Use
        of Travellers and Residents in Uncivilized Lands,* part 3, no. XCV. Published by the
        British Association for the Advancement of Science. London: Edward Stanford.

Bruce, John Collingwood
1851   *The Roman Wall: A Historical, Topographical and Descriptive Account of the Bar-
        rier of the Lower Isthmus, Extending from the Tyne to the Solway, Deduced from Numer-
        ous Personal Surveys.* London: J. R. Smith.

Bundy, Colin
1972   The Emergence and Decline of a South African Peasantry. *African Affairs,*
        71(285):369–88.
1979   *The Rise and Fall of the South African Peasantry.* London: Heinemann.

Bunn, David
1994   The Insistence of Theory: Three Questions for Megan Vaughan. *Social Dy-
        namics,* 20:24–34.

Burchell, William J.
1822–24   *Travels in the Interior of Southern Africa.* 2 vols. London: Longman, Hurst, Rees, Orme, Brown & Green. Reprinted, 1967; Cape Town: Struik.

Burke, Timothy
1996   *Lifebuoy Men, Lux Women: Commodification, Consumption, and Cleanliness in Modern Zimbabwe.* Durham: Duke University Press.

Burrow, John
1971   *Travels in the Wilds of Africa: Being the Diary of a Young Scientific Assistant who Accompanied Sir Andrew Smith in the Expedition of 1834–1836.* Edited by P. R. Kirby. Cape Town: A. A. Balkema.

Burton, A. R. E.
n.d.   *Cape Colony Today* [Illustrated]. Cape Town: No publisher given.

Cain, Peter J., and Anthony Gerald Hopkins
1993   *British Imperialism: Innovation and Expansion 1688–1914.* London: Longman.

Caird, James
1849   *High Farming, under Liberal Covenants, the Best Substitute for Protection.* Fourth edition. Edinburgh and London: Wiiliam (*sic*) Blackwood & Sons.

Caird, James B.
1980   The Reshaped Agricultural Landscape. In *The Making of the Scottish Country-side,* eds. M. L. Parry and T. R. Slater. London: Croom Helm.

Campbell, John
1813   *Travels in South Africa.* London: Black, Parry. Reprinted, 1974; Cape Town: Struik.
1822   *Travels in South Africa . . . Being a Narrative of a Second Journey . . .* 2 vols. London: Westley. Reprinted, 1967; New York and London: Johnson Reprint Corporation.

Camporesi, Piero
1989   *Bread of Dreams: Food and Fantasy in Early Modern Europe.* Translated by D. Gentilcore. Chicago: University of Chicago Press.

Cape of Good Hope
1897a   *Blue Book of Native Affairs, 1897* [G19-'97]. Cape Town: Cape Times Ltd., Government Printer.
1897b   *Rinderpest: Report of Visit of Native Representatives to Bechuanaland* [G78-'97]. Cape Town: Cape Times Ltd., Government Printer.
1898   *Blue Book on Native Affairs* [G42-'98]. Cape Town: Cape Times Ltd., Government Printer.
1899   *Blue Book on Native Affairs* [G31-'99]. Cape Town: Cape Times Ltd., Government Printer.
1905   *Blue Book on Native Affairs, 1904* [G12-1905]. Cape Town: Cape Times Ltd., Government Printer.
1907   *Blue Book on Native Affairs, 1906* [G36-1907]. Cape Town: Cape Times Ltd., Government Printer.

1908   *Blue Book on Native Affairs, 1907* [G24–1908]. Cape Town: Cape Times Ltd., Government Printer.
1909   *Blue Book on Native Affairs, 1908* [G19–1909]. Cape Town: Cape Times Ltd., Government Printer.

Carlson, Dennis G.
1984   *African Fever: A Study of British Science, Technology, and Politics in West Africa, 1787–1864.* New York: Science History Publications.

Carlyle, James Edward
1878   *South Africa and Its Mission Fields.* London: James Nisbet.

Carlyle, Thomas
1920   *Sartor Resartus* [and *On Heroes, Hero-Worship and the Heroic in History*]. London: Macmillan. First edition, 1834, reprinted from *Fraser's Magazine;* London: J. Fraser.

Carter, Paul
1989   *The Road to Botany Bay: An Exploration of Landscape and History.* Chicago: University of Chicago Press.

Cary, Joyce
1953   *The African Witch.* London: Michael Joseph.

Casalis, Eugene Arnaud
1861   *The Basutos; or, Twenty-Three Years in South Africa.* London: James Nisbet.

Chadwick, Owen
1966   *The Victorian Church*, part 1. London: Adam & Charles Black.

Chalmers, [Dr.] Thomas
1837   Proper Mode of Studying Theology. *Evangelical Magazine and Missionary Chronicle,* 15:413–15.

Chanock, Martin
1985   *Law, Custom, and Social Order: The Colonial Experience in Malawi and Zambia.* Cambridge: Cambridge University Press.
1991   Paradigms, Policies, and Property: A Review of the Customary Law of Land Tenure. In *Law in Colonial Africa,* eds. K. Mann and R. Roberts. London: James Currey.
n.d.   *Fear, Favour and Defection: Law, State and Society in South Africa, 1902–1936.* [In preparation.]

Chapman, James
1971   *Travels in the Interior of South Africa, 1849–1863: Hunting and Trading Journeys from Natal to Walvis Bay & Visits to Lake Ngami & Victoria Falls,* part 1. Cape Town: Balkema. First edition, 1868.

Chatterjee, Piya
n.d.   Tea Times: Gender, Labour and Politics on an Indian Plantation. Doctoral Research Proposal, Department of Anthropology, University of Chicago, 1991.

Chesterfield, Lord (?)
1761   Tquassouw and Knonmquaiha. *The Connoisseur,* 1(21):161–170.

Chidester, David
1992   *Religions in South Africa.* London: Routledge.

Chirenje, J. Mutero
1977   *A History of Northern Botswana 1850–1910.* London: Associated University Presses.
1978   *Chief Kgama and His Times c. 1835–1923: The Story of a Southern African Ruler.* London: Rex Collings.
1987   *Ethiopianism and Afro-Americans in Southern Africa, 1883–1916.* Baton Rouge and London: Louisiana State University Press.

Chirgwin, Arthur Mitchell
1932   *An African Pilgrimage.* London: Student Christian Movement Press.

Church, Richard William
1966   *The Oxford Movement: Twelve Years 1835–45.* London: Macmillan. First edition, 1891.

Clark, (Sir) Kenneth Mackenzie
1956   *The Nude: A Study of Ideal Art.* London: John Murray.

Clifford, James
1988   *The Predicament of Culture: Twentieth-Century Ethnography, Literature, and Art.* Cambridge: Harvard University Press.

Cobbett, William
1930   *Rural Rides in the Southern, Western and Eastern Counties of England, Together with Tours in Scotland and in the Northern and Midland Counties of England, and Letters from Ireland.* 3 vols. Edited by G. D. H. Cole and M. Cole. London: Peter Davies. First edition, 1830.

Cobbing, Julian
1988   The Mfecane as Alibi: Thoughts on Dithakong and Mbolompo. *Journal of African History,* 29:487–519.

Cock, Jacklyn
1980   *Maids and Madams: A Study of the Politics of Exploitation.* Johannesburg: Ravan Press.

Coetzee, John M.
1988   *White Writing: On the Culture of Letters in South Africa.* New Haven: Yale University Press.
1994   *The Master of Petersburg.* London: Secker & Warburg.

Cohn, Bernard S.
1989   Cloth, Clothes, and Colonialism: India in the Nineteenth Century. In *Cloth and Human Experience,* eds. A. Weiner and J. Schneider. Washington: Smithsonian Institution Press.

Cohn, Norman Rufus Colin
1957   *The Pursuit of the Millennium: Revolutionary Millenarians and Mystical Anarchists of the Middle Ages.* London: Secker and Warburg.

Collier, Jane F., and Sylvia J. Yanagisako, eds.
1987   *Gender and Kinship: Toward a Unified Analysis.* Stanford: Stanford University Press.

Collins, Wilkie
1966   *The Moonstone.* Edited by J. I. M. Stewart. Harmondsworth: Penguin Books. First edition, 1868.

Comaroff, Jean
1974   *Barolong Cosmology: A Study of Religious Pluralism in a Tswana Town.* Ph.D. diss., University of London.
1980   Healing and the Cultural Order: The Case of the Barolong-boo-Ratshidi of Southern Africa. *American Ethnologist,* 7:637–57.
1981   Healing and Cultural Transformation: The Case of the Tswana of Southern Africa. *Social Science and Medicine,* 15B:367–78.
1985   *Body of Power, Spirit of Resistance: The Culture and History of a South African People.* Chicago: University of Chicago Press.
1993   The Diseased Heart of Africa: Medicine, Colonialism and the Black Body. In *Knowledge, Power, and Practice: The Anthropology of Medicine and Everyday Life,* eds. M. Lock and S. Lindenbaum. Berkeley: University of California Press.

Comaroff, Jean, and John L. Comaroff
1986   Christianity and Colonialism in South Africa. *American Ethnologist,* 13:1–20.
1989   The Colonization of Consciousness in South Africa. *Economy and Society,* 12:267–95.
1991   *Of Revelation and Revolution: Christianity, Colonialism, and Consciousness in South Africa,* vol. 1. Chicago: University of Chicago Press.
1992   Home-Made Hegemony: Domesticity, Modernity, and Colonialism in South Africa. In *African Encounters with Domesticity,* ed. K. T. Hansen. New Brunswick: Rutgers University Press.
1993   *Modernity and Its Malcontents: Ritual and Power in Postcolonial Africa.* Chicago: University of Chicago Press

Comaroff, John L.
1973   *Competition for Office and Political Processes among the Barolong boo Ratshidi of the South Africa–Botswana Borderland.* Ph.D. diss., University of London.
1975   Talking Politics: Oratory and Authority in an African Chiefdom. In *Political Language and Oratory in Traditional Societies,* ed. M. Bloch. London: Academic Press.
1976   Tswana Transformations, 1953–1975. Supplementary chapter in *The Tswana,* I. Schapera [revised edition]. London: Kegan Paul International in association with the International African Institute.
1977   *The Structure of Agricultural Transformation in Barolong.* Gaborone: Botswana Government Printer.

Bibliography

1978   Rules and Rulers: Political Processes in a Tswana Chiefdom. *Man,*
        13(1):1–20.
1980   Class and Culture in a Peasant Economy: The Transformation of Land Ten-
        ure in Barolong. *Journal of African Law,* 24:85–113. Republished in *Land Reform
        in the Making,* ed. R. P. Werbner, 1982; London: Rex Collings.
1982   Dialectical Systems, History and Anthropology: Units of Study and Ques-
        tions of Theory. *Journal of Southern African Studies,* 8:143–72.
1983   Barolong Agriculture Revisited: Gross Statistics and Subtle Explanations.
        In *Barolong Agriculture Reconsidered,* P. Ntseane, D. Narayan-Parker, P. Heisey
        and J. L. Comaroff. Madison: University of Wisconsin Land Tenure Center;
        Gaborone: Republic of Botswana, Agricultural Research Unit.
1987   *Sui Genderis:* Feminism, Kinship Theory, and Structural "Domains." In *Gen-
        der and Kinship: Essays toward a Unified Theory,* eds. J. Collier and S. Yanagisako.
        Stanford: Stanford University Press.
1989   Images of Empire, Contests of Conscience: Models of Colonial Domination
        in South Africa. *American Ethnologist,* 16:661–85.
1994   Etnicidad, Violencia y Política de Identidad: Temas Teóricos, Escenas Suda-
        fricanas [Ethnicity, Violence, and the Politics of Identity: Theoretical Themes,
        South African Scenes]. In *Etnicidad y Violencia,* ed. J. Antonio Fernández de
        Rota. La Coruña: Universidade da Coruña.
1995   The Discourse of Rights in Colonial South Africa: Subjectivity, Sovereignty,
        Modernity. In *Identity, Politics, and Rights,* eds. A. Sarat and T. Kearns. Ann
        Arbor: University of Michigan Press.
1996   Ethnicity, Nationalism, and the Politics of Difference in an Age of Revolu-
        tion. In *The Politics of Difference: Ethnic Premises in a World of Power,* eds. E. Wilm-
        sen and P. MacAllister. Chicago: University of Chicago Press.

Comaroff, John L., and Jean Comaroff
1987   The Madman and the Migrant: Work and Labor in the Historical Con-
        sciousness of a South African People. *American Ethnologist,* 14:191–209.
1992   *Ethnography and the Historical Imagination.* Boulder: Westview Press.

Comaroff, John L., and Simon A. Roberts
1977   Marriage and Extramarital Sexuality: The Dialectics of Legal Change
        amongst the Kgatla. *Journal of African Law,* 21:97–123.
1981   *Rules and Processes: The Cultural Logic of Dispute in an African Context.* Chicago:
        University of Chicago Press.

Conder, (Captain) C. R.
1887   The Present Condition of the Native Tribes in Bechuanaland. *Journal of the
        Royal Anthropological Institute,* 16:76–96.

Conrad, Joseph
1994   *The Secret Agent: A Simple Tale.* London: Penguin Books. First edition, 1907.

Cooper, Frederick, and Ann L. Stoler
1989   Introduction to Special Issue on "Tensions of Empire: Colonial Control and
        Visions of Rule." *American Ethnologist,* 16:609–21.

1997   Between Metropole and Colony: Rethinking a Research Agenda. In *Tensions of Empire: Colonial Cultures in a Bourgeois World,* eds. F. Cooper and A. Stoler. Berkeley: University of California Press.

Coplan, David B.
1994   *In the Time of Cannibals: The Word Music of South Africa's Basotho Migrants.* Chicago: University of Chicago Press.

Cordwell, Justine M.
1979   The Very Human Arts of Transformation. In *The Fabrics of Culture: The Anthropology of Clothing and Adornment,* eds. J. M. Cordwell and R. A. Schwarz. The Hague: Mouton.

Cordwell, Justine M., and Ronald A. Schwarz, eds.
1979   *The Fabrics of Culture: The Anthropology of Clothing and Adornment.* The Hague: Mouton.

Corrigan, Philip, and Derek Sayer
1985   *The Great Arch: English State Formation as Cultural Revolution.* Oxford: Blackwell.

Crais, Clifton C.
1994   South Africa and the Pitfalls of Postmodern. *South African Historical Journal,* 31:274–79.

Crisp, William
1896   *The Bechuana of South Africa.* London: SPCK.
1905   *Notes towards a Secoana Grammar.* Fourth edition. London: SPCG.

Crook, Joseph Mordaunt
1992   We Are Where We Live. *New York Times Book Review,* January 5:21.

Crosby, Christina
1991   *The Ends of History: Victorians and "the Woman Question."* New York and London: Routledge.

Curtin, Philip D.
1961   "The White Man's Grave": Image and Reality. *Journal of British Studies,* 1:94–110.
1964   *The Image of Africa: British Ideas and Action, 1780–1850.* Madison: University of Wisconsin Press.

Dachs, Anthony J.
1972   Missionary Imperialism: The Case of Bechuanaland. *Journal of African History,* 13:647–58.

Darian-Smith, Eve
1995   Legal Imagery in the "Garden of England." *Indiana Journal of Global Legal Studies,* 2:395–411.

Darrow, Margaret H.
1979   French Noblewomen and the New Domesticity 1750–1850. *Feminist Studies,* 5:41–65.

Davidoff, Leonore, and Catherine Hall
1987   *Family Fortunes: Men and Women of the English Middle Class, 1780–1850.* Chicago: University of Chicago Press.

Davies, Horton
1961   *Worship and Theology in England: From Watts and Wesley to Maurice, 1690–1850.* Princeton: Princeton University Press.
1962   *Worship and Theology in England from Newman to Martineau, 1850–1900.* Princeton: Princeton University Press.

de Certeau, Michel
1984   *The Practice of Everyday Life.* Translated by S. Rendall. Berkeley: University of California Press.

de Gruchy, John W.
1979   *The Church Struggle in South Africa.* Cape Town: David Philip.

de Kock, Leon
1992   Review of *Of Revelation and Revolution,* vol. 1. *South African Historical Journal,* 26:260–63.
1993   *'Civilising Barbarians': Missionary Narrative and African Textual Response in Nineteenth-Century South Africa.* Ph.D. diss., University of South Africa.
1994   For and against the Comaroffs: Postmodernist Puffery and Competing Conceptions of the 'Archive'. *South African Historical Journal,* 31:280–89.

Delavignette, Robert
1964   *Christianity and Colonialism.* London: Burns & Oates.

Delius, Peter
1984   *The Conversion: Death Cell Conversations of 'Rooizak' and the Missionaries, Lydenburg 1875.* Johannesburg: Ravan Press.

Départment Evangélique Français d'Action Apostolique, Paris
1987   *Guide to the Microform Collection, Paris Evangelical Missionary Society Archives 1822–1935.* Leiden: IDC Microform Publishers.

Derby, Lauren
1994   Haitians, Magic, and Money: *Raza* and Society in the Haitian-Dominican Borderlands, 1900 to 1937. *Comparative Studies in Society and History,* 36:488–526.

Descola, Philippe
1996   *The Spears of Twilight: Life and Death with the Last Free Tribe of the Amazon.* Translated by J. Lloyd. New York: New Press; distributed by W. W. Norton. First French edition, 1993.

Dickens, Charles
1853   *Bleak House.* London: Bradbury & Evans.
1908a   The Niger Expedition. In *The Works of Charles Dickens* [National Edition], vol. 35: *Miscellaneous Papers, Plays and Poems,* I. London: Chapman & Hall. First published in the *Examiner,* 19 August 1848.

1908b   The Noble Savage. In *The Works of Charles Dickens* [National Edition], vol. 34: *Reprinted Pieces*. London: Chapman & Hall.
1972   *American Notes for General Circulation.* Edited by J. S. Whitley and A. Gold-man. Harmondsworth: Penguin Books. First edition, 1842.
1985   *Hard Times. For These Times.* Edited by D. Craig. London: Penguin Books. First edition, 1854.

Dirks, Nicholas B.
1992   Introduction: Colonialism and Culture. In *Colonialism and Culture,* ed. N. Dirks. Ann Arbor: University of Michigan Press.

Disraeli, Benjamin
1980   *Sybil; or, The Two Nations.* Harmondsworth: Penguin Books. First edition, 1845.

Dorfman, Ariel
1983   *The Empire's Old Clothes: What the Lone Ranger, Babar, and Other Innocent Heroes Do to Our Minds.* New York: Pantheon.

Douglas, Mary
1966   *Purity and Danger: An Analysis of Concepts of Pollution and Taboo.* London: Routledge & Kegan Paul.

Drewal, Henry John
1979   Pageantry and Power in Yoruba Costuming. In *The Fabrics of Culture: The Anthropology of Clothing and Adornment,* eds. J. M. Cordwell and R. A. Schwarz. The Hague: Mouton.

Dreyer, Frederick
1983   Faith and Experience in the Thought of John Wesley. *American Historical Review,* 88:12–30.

du Bruyn, Johannes
1994   Of Muffled Southern Tswana and Overwhelming Missionaries: The Comaroffs and the Colonial Encounter. *South African Historical Journal,* 31:294–309.

Duggan-Cronin, Alfred Martin
1929   *The Bantu Tribes of South Africa: Reproductions of Photographic Studies,* vol. 2, sect. 1: *The Suto-Chuana Tribes.* Cambridge: Deighton, Bell; Kimberley: Alexander McGregor Memorial Museum.

Durham, Deborah L.
1993   *Images of Culture: Being Herero in a Liberal Democracy.* Ph.D. diss., University of Chicago.

During, Simon
1987   Postmodernism or Post-Colonialism Today. *Textual Practice,* 1:32–47.
1991   Waiting for the Post: Some Relations between Modernity, Colonization, and Writing. In *Past the Last Post: Theorizing Post-Colonialism and Post-Modernism,* eds. I. Adam and H. Tiffin. New York: Harvester Wheatsheaf.

Durkheim, Emile
1947   *The Elementary Forms of the Religious Life: A Study in Religious Sociology.* Translated by J. W. Swain. Glencoe: Free Press.

Edwards, John
1886   *Reminiscences of the Early Life and Missionary Labours of the Rev. John Edwards.* Edited by W. C. Holden. Grahamstown: T. H. Grocott.

Elbourne, Elizabeth
n.d.   Colonialism, Conversion and Cultural Change: Shifting Paradigms of Religious Interaction in South African History. Paper read to the *Journal of Southern African Studies* Twentieth Anniversary Conference, University of York, September 1994.

Eliade, Mircea
1964   *Shamanism: Archaic Techniques of Ecstasy.* Translated by W. R. Trask. New York: Pantheon for the Bollingen Foundation.

Elias, Norbert
1982   *The Civilizing Process,* vol. 1: *The History of Manners.* Translated by E. Jephcott. New York: Pantheon. First German edition, 1939.

Elphick, Richard
1992   South African Christianity and the Historian's Vision. *South African Historical Journal,* 26:182–90.

Engels, Friedrich
1968   *The Condition of the Working Class in England.* Translated and edited from the 1844 edition by W. Henderson and W. Chaloner. Stanford: Stanford University Press.

Etherington, Norman
1978   *Preachers, Peasants, and Politics in Southeast Africa, 1835–1880: African Christian Communities in Natal, Pondoland, and Zululand.* London: Royal Historical Society.
1984   *Theories of Imperialism: War, Conquest and Capital.* London and Canberra: Croom Helm.
1987   Missionary Doctors and African Healers in Mid-Victorian South Africa. *South African Historical Journal,* 19:77–91.
1992   Review of *Of Revelation and Revolution,* vol. 1. *International Journal of African Historical Studies,* 25(1):213–16.
n.d.   Recent Trends in the Historiography of Missions in Southern Africa: Quantitative Survey and Key Issues. Paper read to the *Journal of Southern African Studies* Twentieth Anniversary Conference, University of York, September 1994.

Evans-Pritchard, Edward E.
1940   *The Nuer: A Description of the Modes of Livelihood and Political Institutions of a Nilotic People.* Oxford: Clarendon Press.

Fajans, Jane
n.d.   *They Make Themselves: Work and Play among the Baining of Papua New Guinea.* Chicago: University of Chicago Press. [Forthcoming, May 1997.]

Fanon, Frantz
1963   *The Wretched of the Earth.* Translated by C. Farrington. New York: Grove Press.
1967   *Black Skin, White Masks.* Translated by C. L. Markmann. New York: Grove Press.

Faurschou, Gail
1990   Obsolescence and Desire: Fashion and the Commodity. In *Postmodernism in Philosophy and Art,* ed. H. Silverman. London: Routledge.

Febvre, Lucien
1973   *Frontière:* The Word and the Concept. In *A New Kind of History: From the Writings of [Lucien] Febvre,* ed. P. Burke. New York: Harper & Row.

Ferguson, D. Frances
1976   Rural/Urban Relations and Peasant Radicalism: A Preliminary Statement. *Comparative Studies in Society and History,* 18:106–18.

Ferguson, James
1985   The Bovine Mystique: Power, Property and Livestock in Rural Lesotho. *Man* (NS), 20:647–74.

Fieldhouse, David Kenneth
1981   *Colonialism 1870–1945: An Introduction.* London: Weidenfeld & Nicolson.
1982   *The Colonial Empires: A Comparative Survey from the Eighteenth Century.* London: Macmillan.

Fields, Karen E.
1985   *Revival and Rebellion in Colonial Central Africa.* Princeton: Princeton University Press.

Fincham, Gail
1994   Contested Frontiers: Colonialism, Christianity and the Construction of Ethnicity. *Current Writing,* 5(2):141–46.

Fischer, H. Th.
1966   The Clothes of the Naked Nuer. *International Archives of Ethnography,* 50:60–71.

Fitzpatrick, Peter
1990   'The Desperate Vacuum': Imperialism and Law in the Experience of Enlightenment. In *Post-Modern Law: Enlightenment, Revolution and the Death of Man,* ed. A. Carter. Edinburgh: Edinburgh University Press.

Forbes, Derek
1995   *'Re A O Phethola Mmuso wa Mangope': The End of Mangope Regime.* Mmabatho: Department of Communication, University of the North West.

Forde, C. Daryll
1934   *Habitat, Economy and Society: A Geographical Introduction to Ethnology.* London: Methuen.

Forster, Edward Morgan
1992 *Howards End.* Edited by O. Stallybrass. London: Penguin Books. Reset and reprinted from the Abinger Edition, 1975. First edition, 1910.

Fortes, Meyer
1969 *Kinship and the Social Order: The Legacy of Lewis Henry Morgan.* Chicago: Aldine.

Foucault, Michel
1975 *The Birth of the Clinic: An Archaeology of Medical Perception.* Translated by A. M. Sheridan Smith. New York: Vintage Books.
1976 *La Volonté de savoir.* Paris: Gallimard.
1978 *The History of Sexuality.* Translated by R. Hurley. New York: Pantheon.
1979 *Discipline and Punish: The Birth of the Prison.* Translated by A. Sheridan. New York: Vintage Books.

Francis, Mark, and John Morrow
1994 *A History of English Political Thought in the Nineteenth Century.* New York: St. Martin's Press.

Franquemont, Edward M.
1986 Threads of Time: Andean Cloth and Costume. In *Costume as Communication: Ethnographic Costumes and Textiles from Middle America and the Central Andes of South America . . .,* ed. M. B. Schevill. Studies in Anthropology and Material Culture, vol. 4. Bristol, R.I.: Haffenreffer Museum of Anthropology, Brown University; Seattle: University of Washington Press.

Fraser, Nancy
1989 *Unruly Practices: Power, Discourse, and Gender in Contemporary Social Theory.* Minneapolis: University of Minnesota Press.

Freeman, Joseph John
1851 *A Tour in South Africa, with Notices of Natal, Mauritius, Madagascar, Ceylon, Egypt, and Palestine.* London: John Snow.

Fripp, C. E.
1897 Recent Travels in Rhodesia and British Bechuanaland. *Journal of the Society of Arts,* 45 (no. 2318, 23 April):515–31.

Frow, John
1991 What Was Post-Modernism? In *Past the Last Post: Theorizing Post-Colonialism and Post-Modernism,* eds. I. Adam and H. Tiffin. New York: Harvester Wheatsheaf.

Fuentes, Carlos
1992 *The Campaign.* Translated by A. M. Adam. New York: Harper Collins. First English edition, 1991.
1994 *The Orange Tree.* Translated by A. M. Adam. New York: Farrar, Straus & Giroux.

Fussell, George E., and K. R. Fussell
1953   *The English Countrywoman. A Farmhouse Social History: The Internal Aspect of Rural Life A.D. 1500–1900.* London: Andrew Melrose.

Fussell, Paul
1975   *The Great War and Modern Memory.* London and New York: Oxford University Press.

Fyfe, Christopher
1962   *A History of Sierra Leone.* London: Oxford University Press.

Gable, Eric
1995   The Decolonization of Consciousness: Local Skeptics and the 'Will to be Modern' in a West African Village. *American Ethnologist,* 22:242–57.

Gaitskell, Deborah
1983   Housewives, Maids or Mothers: Some Contradictions of Domesticity for Christian Women in Johannesburg, 1903–1939. *Journal of African History,* 24:241–56.
1990   Devout Domesticity? A Century of African Women's Christianity in South Africa. In *Women and Gender in Southern Africa to 1945,* ed. C. Walker. London: James Currey.
1992   'Getting Close to the Hearts of Mothers': Medical Missionaries among African Women and Children in Johannesburg between the Wars. In *Women and Children First: International Maternal and Infant Welfare 1870–1945,* eds. V. Fildes, L. Marks, and H. Marland. London: Routledge.
n.d.   Girls' Education in South Africa: Domesticity or Domestic Service? Paper read to the annual meeting of the African Studies Association (UK), Canterbury, 1986.

Gallagher, Catherine
1985   *The Industrial Reformation of English Fiction: Social Discourse and Narrative Form, 1832–1867.* Chicago: University of Chicago Press.

Gallagher, John, and Ronald Edward Robinson
1953   The Imperialism of Free Trade. *Economic History Review,* 2nd ser., 6:1–15. Reprinted in *The Decline, Revival and Fall of the British Empire,* J. Gallagher. Edited by A. Seal. Cambridge: Cambridge University Press, 1982.

Gann, Lewis H., and Peter Duignan
1967   *Burden of Empire: An Appraisal of Western Colonialism in Africa South of the Sahara.* New York: Praeger.

Garlick, Phyllis L.
1943   *The Wholeness of Man: A Study in the History of Healing.* The James Long Lectures, 1943. London: The Highway Press.

Garwood, John
1853   *The Million-Peopled City.* [*The Rise of Urban Britain.*] London: Wertheim & Macintosh.

Gaskell, Elizabeth Cleghorn
1848   *Mary Barton. A Tale of Manchester Life.* London: Chapman & Hall. First edition published anonymously; subtitle omitted from later editions.

Gaskell, P.
1836   *Artisans and Machinery: The Moral and Physical Condition of the Manufacturing Population.* London: J. W. Parker.

Geertz, Clifford
1963   The Integrative Revolution: Primordial Sentiments and Civil Politics in the New States. In *Old Societies and New States,* ed. C. Geertz. New York: Free Press.

Gelfand, Michael
1957   *Livingstone the Doctor, His Life and Travels: A Study in Medical History.* Oxford: Blackwell.
1984   *Christian Doctor and Nurse: The History of Medical Missions in South Africa from 1799–1976.* Limited edition published by the Aitken family and friends, 93 East Avenue, Atholl, Sandton 2196, Republic of South Africa; printed at Marianhill Press.

Gellner, Ernest
1983   *Nations and Nationalism.* Ithaca: Cornell University Press.
1987   *Culture, Identity, and Politics.* New York: Cambridge University Press.

Genovese, Eugene D.
1974   *Roll, Jordan, Roll: The World the Slaves Made.* New York: Pantheon.

Giddens, Anthony
1985   Time, Space and Regionalisation. In *Social Relations and Spatial Structures,* eds. D. Gregory and J. Urry. London: Macmillan.

Gilman, Sander
1985   Black Bodies, White Bodies: Toward an Iconography of Female Sexuality in Late Nineteenth-Century Art, Medicine, and Literature. *Critical Inquiry,* 12:204–42.

Gluckman, Max
1968   *Analysis of a Social Situation in Modern Zululand.* Manchester: Manchester University Press.

Gluckman, Max, J. Clyde Mitchell, and John A. Barnes
1949   The Village Headman in British Central Africa. *Africa,* 19:89–106.

Godelier, Maurice
1977   *Perspectives in Marxist Anthropology.* Translated by R. Brain. Cambridge: Cambridge University Press.

Goffman, Erving
1959   *The Presentation of Self in Everyday Life.* Garden City, N.Y.: Doubleday.

Goldsmith, Oliver
1857   *The Deserted Village.* New York: D. Appleton. First edition, 1770.

Gollock, Georgina Anne
1909   *Aunt Africa: A Family Affair.* London: Church Missionary Society.

Gorringe, Timothy J.
1992   Review of *Of Revelation and Revolution,* vol. 1. *Theological Book Review,* 5(1):53.

Graeber, David
1996   Beads and Money: Notes toward a Theory of Wealth and Money. *American Ethnologist,* 23:4–24.

Gray, Richard
1993   Review of *Of Revelation and Revolution,* vol. 1. *Bulletin of the School of Oriental and African Studies, University of London,* 56:196–98.

Gray, Stephen
1993   The Importance of Solomon T. Plaatje's *Mhudi* in South African Literature. Solomon Tshekisho Plaatje Memorial Lecture, 9 September 1981. In *Solomon Tshekisho Plaatje Memorial Lectures, 1981–1992.* Mmabatho: Institute of African Studies, University of Bophuthatswana.

Great Britain
1886a *Report of the Commissioners Appointed to Determine Land Claims . . . in British Bechuanaland* [C.4889]. London: H.M.S.O.
1886b *Further Correspondence re Affairs of Transvaal and Adjacent Territories* [C.4839]. London: H.M.S.O.
1886c *Further Correspondence re Affairs of Transvaal and Adjacent Territories* [C.4890]. London: H.M.S.O.
1889   *British Bechuanaland: Report of the Acting Administrator for the Year Ended 30th September 1888* [C.5620]. Papers Relating to Her Majesty's Colonial Possessions, No. 44. London: H.M.S.O.
1891–92 *Bechuanaland Protectorate: Annual Report.* London: Colonial Office.
1933   *Financial and Economic Position of the Bechuanaland Protectorate* [Cmd.4368]. Report of the Commission Appointed by the Secretary of State for Dominion Affairs, March 1933. London: H.M.S.O.

Greenblatt, Stephen Jay
1980   *Renaissance Self-Fashioning: From More to Shakespeare.* Chicago: University of Chicago Press.

Greene, Graham
1963   *A Burnt-Out Case.* London: Penguin Books. First English edition, 1961.

Greenwood, James
1869   *The Seven Curses of London.* London: S. Rivers.
1874   *The Wilds of London.* London: Chatto & Windus.

Grove, Richard
1989   Scottish Missionaries, Evangelical Discourses and the Origin of Conservation Thinking in Southern Africa 1820–1900. *Journal of Southern African Studies,* 15:163–87.

Guenther, Mathias Georg
1977   The Mission Station as "Sample Community": A Contemporary Case from Botswana. *Missiology, An International Review,* 5:457–65.

Gulbrandsen, Ornulf
1993   Missionaries and Northern Tswana Rulers: Who Used Whom? *Journal of Religion in Africa,* 23:44–83.

Guy, Jeff
1979   *The Destruction of the Zulu Kingdom: The Civil War in Zululand, 1879–1884.* London: Longman.

Haas, Ernst
1986   What Is Nationalism and Why Should We Study It? *International Organization,* 40:707–44.

Halévy, Elie
1924   *A History of the English People,* vol. 1: *In 1815.* Translated by E. I. Watkin and D. A. Barker. New York: Harcourt, Brace.
1961   *England in 1815.* Translated by E. Watkin and D. Barker. New York: Barnes & Noble.

Hall, Catherine
1985   Private Persons versus Public Someones: Class, Gender and Politics in England, 1780–1850. In *Language, Gender and Childhood,* eds. C. Steedman, C. Urwin, and V. Walkerdine. London: Routledge & Kegan Paul.
1990   The Sweet Delights of Home. In *A History of Private Life,* vol. 4: *From the Fires of the French Revolution to the Great War,* ed. M. Perrot. Cambridge: The Belknap Press, Harvard University Press.

Hall, Kenneth O.
1975   Humanitarianism and Racial Subordination: John Mackenzie and the Transformation of Tswana Society. *International Journal of African Historical Studies,* 8:97–110.

Hansen, Karen Tranberg
1989   *Distant Companions: Servants and Employers in Zambia, 1900–1985.* Ithaca: Cornell University Press.
n.d.   Second-hand Clothing in Zambia. Paper read at an international conference on *Symbols of Change in Southern Africa,* Freie Universität, Berlin, January 1992.

Hardy, Thomas
1963   *The Return of the Native.* London: Macmillan. First edition, 3 vols., 1878.

Harries, Patrick
1988   The Roots of Ethnicity: Discourse and the Politics of Language Construction in South-East Africa. *African Affairs,* 87 (no. 346):25–52.

Hart, Keith
1986   Heads or Tails? Two Sides of the Coin. *Man* (NS), 21:637–56.

Hartwig, Gerald W., and K. David Paterson, eds.
1978   *Disease in African History: An Introductory Survey and Case Studies.* Durham: Duke University Press.

Harvey, Arnold D.
1994   *Sex in Georgian England: Attitudes and Prejudices from the 1720s to the 1820s.* New York: St. Martin's Press.

Harvey, David
1989   *The Condition of Postmodernity: An Enquiry into the Origins of Cultural Change.* Oxford: Blackwell.

Hattersley, Alan F.
1952   The Missionary in South African History. *Theoria,* 4:86–88.

Hausen, Karin
1981   Family and Role-division: the Polarisation of Sexual Stereotypes in the Nineteenth Century. In *The German Family,* eds. R. Evans and W. Lee. London: Croom Helm; Totowa: Barnes & Noble.

Hay, Douglas
1975   Property, Authority and the Criminal Law. In *Albion's Fatal Tree: Crime and Society in Eighteenth-Century England,* D. Hay et al. New York: Pantheon.

Hay, John
n.d.   Representation of the Body in Traditional China. Paper presented at the Triangle East Asia Colloquium, Raleigh, N.C., February 29, 1989.

Headrick, Rita
1987   *The Impact of Colonialism on Health in French Equatorial Africa, 1880–1934.* 3 vols. Ph.D. diss., University of Chicago.

Hebdige, Dick
1979   *Subculture: The Meaning of Style.* New York: Methuen.
1988   *Hiding in the Light: On Images and Things.* New York: Routledge.

Hechter, Michael
1975   *Internal Colonialism: The Celtic Fringe in British National Development, 1536–1966.* Berkeley: University of California Press.

Heller, Agnes
1984   *Everyday Life.* Translated by G. L. Campbell. London: Routledge.

Helmstadter, Richard J.
1992   The Reverend Andrew Reed (1787–1862): Evangelical Pastor as Entrepreneur. In *Religion and Irreligion in Victorian Society: Essays in Honor of R. K. Webb,* eds. R. W. Davis and R. J. Helmstadter. New York: Routledge.

Hempton, David
1984   *Methodism and Politics in British Society, 1750–1850.* London: Hutchinson.

Hendrickson, Carol E.
1986   *Handmade and Thought-woven: The Construction of Dress and Social Identity in Tecpán Guatemala.* Ph.D. diss., University of Chicago.

Hendrickson, Hildi
1994   The 'Long' Dress and the Construction of Herero Identities in Southern Africa. *African Studies*, 53(2):25–54.
1996   Introduction: African Dress and Postmodern Politics. In *Embodying Identities in Colonial and Post-Colonial Africa*, ed. H. Hendrickson. Durham: Duke University Press.
n.d.   A Symbolic History of the "Traditional" Herero Dress in Namibia and Botswana. [Manuscript.]

Hepburn, James Davidson
1895   *Twenty Years in Khama's Country*. Edited by C. H. Lyall. London: Hodder & Stoughton.

Hexham, Irving
1993   Review of *Of Revelation and Revolution*, vol. 1. *Canadian Journal of African Studies*, 27:499–503.

Hill, A. Wesley
1960   Introduction. In *Primitive Physic*, John Wesley. London: Epworth Press.

Hirsch, Susan F., and Mindie Lazarus-Black
1994   Introduction. In *Contested States: Law, Hegemony, and Resistance*, eds. M. Lazarus-Black and S. F. Hirsch. New York: Routledge.

Hobsbawm, Eric J.
1992   Ethnicity and Nationalism in Europe Today. *Anthropology Today*, 8:3–8.

Hodgson, Thomas L.
1977   *The Journals of the Rev. T. L. Hodgson: Missionary to the Seleka-Rolong and the Griquas, 1821–1831*. Edited by R. L. Cope. Johannesburg: Witwatersrand University Press for the African Studies Institute.

Hollingshead, John
1861   *Ragged London in 1861*. London: Smith, Elder.

Holmberg, Ake
1966   *African Tribes and European Agencies: Colonialism and Humanitarianism in British South and East Africa, 1870–1895*. Göteborg: Scandinavian University Books.

Holt, Thomas C.
1992   *The Problem of Freedom: Race, Labor, and Politics in Jamaica and Britain, 1832–1938*. Baltimore: Johns Hopkins University Press.
n.d.   The Essence of the Contract: The Articulation of Race, Gender, and Political Economy in British Emancipation Policy, 1838–1866. Paper read to a seminar on *Racism and Race Relations in the Countries of the African Diaspora*, Rio de Janiero, April 1992.

Holub, Emil
1881   *Seven Years in South Africa: Travels, Researches, and Hunting Adventures, between the Diamond-Fields and the Zambesi* (1872–79). 2 vols. Translated by E. E. Frewer. Boston: Houghton Mifflin.

Horton, Robin
1967 African Traditional Thought and Western Science. *Africa*, 31(1):50–71; (2): 155–87.

Horvath, Ronald, J.
1972 A Definition of Colonialism. *Current Anthropology*, 13(1):45–51.

Houlberg, Marilyn Hammersley
1979 Social Hair: Tradition and Change in Yoruba Hairstyles in Southwestern Nigeria. In *The Fabrics of Culture: The Anthropology of Clothing and Adornment*, eds. J. M. Cordwell and R. A. Schwarz. The Hague: Mouton.

Hughes, Isaac
1841 Missionary Labours among the Batlapi. *The Evangelical Magazine and Missionary Chronicle*, 19:522–23.

Hunt, Nancy R.
1990a Domesticity and Colonialism in Belgian Africa: Usumbura's *Foyer Social*, 1946–1960. *Signs*, 15:447–74.
1990b 'Single Ladies on the Congo:' Protestant Missionary Tensions and Voices. *Women's Studies International Forum*, 13:395–403.
1992 Colonial Fairy Tales and the Knife and Fork Doctrine in the Heart of Africa. In *African Encounters with Domesticity*, ed. K. T. Hansen. New Brunswick: Rutgers University Press.

Hutcheon, Linda
1991 "Circling the Downspout of Empire." In *Past the Last Post: Theorizing Post-Colonialism and Post-Modernism*, eds. I. Adam and H. Tiffin. New York: Harvester Wheatsheaf.

Hutchinson, Bertram
1957 Some Social Consequences of 19th Century Mission Activity among the South African Bantu. *Africa*, 27:160–77.

Hutt, W. H.
1934 The Economic Position of the Bantu in South African. In *Western Civilization and the Natives of South Africa: Studies in Culture Contact*, ed. I. Schapera. London: Routledge & Kegan Paul.

Huxley, Aldous
1994 *Point Counter Point*. London: Flamingo [HarperCollins]. First edition, 1928.

Jacobson, Marcelle (comp.)
1978 The Silas Molema and Solomon T. Plaatje Papers. Historical and Literary Papers: Inventories of Collections. Johannesburg: University of the Witwatersrand Library.

Jacyna, Stephen
1992 'Mr Scott's Case': A View of London Medicine in 1825. In *The Popularization of Medicine, 1650–1850*, ed. R. Porter. London: Routledge.

Jameson, Fredric
1984   Postmodernism, or the Cultural Logic of Late Capitalism. *New Left Review,*
146 (July–August):53–92.
1990   Modernism and Imperialism. In *Nationalism, Colonialism, and Literature,*
T. Eagleton, F. Jameson, and E. W. Said. Minneapolis: University of Minnesota
Press.

Jenks, Leland Hamilton
1927   *The Migration of British Capital to 1875.* New York and London: Alfred
A. Knopf.

Jennings, Alfred E.
1933   *Bogadi: A Study of the Marriage Laws and Customs of the Bechuana Tribes of
South Africa.* Pamphlet. Tiger Kloof: London Missionary Society.

Jephson, Henry
1907   *The Sanitary Evolution of London.* New York: A. Wessels.

Jolly, Margaret
1989   Sacred Spaces: Churches, Men's Houses and Households in South Pentecost, Vanuatu. In *Family and Gender in the Pacific: Domestic Contradictions and the
Colonial Impact,* eds. M. Jolly and M. Macintyre. Cambridge: Cambridge University Press.

Jolly, Margaret, and Martha Macintyre
1989   Introduction. In *Family and Gender in the Pacific: Domestic Contradictions and
the Colonial Impact,* eds. M. Jolly and M. Macintyre. Cambridge: Cambridge University Press.

Jones, Coby P.
1988   *Leeches on Society: Bloodletting and Economies of Blood in British Heroic Medical
Practice.* M.A. thesis, Department of Anthropology, University of Chicago.

Jones, Eric Lionel
1968   *The Development of English Agriculture, 1815–1873.* London: Macmillan.

Jones, J. Derek
1972   "Mahoko a Becwana:" the Second seTswana Newspaper. *Botswana Notes and
Records,* 4:111–120.

Jordanova, Ludmilla J.
1989   *Sexual Visions: Images of Gender in Science and Medicine between the Eighteenth
and Twentieth Centuries.* Madison: University of Wisconsin Press.

Kaviraj, Sudipta
1994   On the Construction of Colonial Power: Structure, Discourse, Hegemony.
In *Contesting Colonial Hegemony: State and Society in Africa and India,* eds. D. Engels and S. Marks. London: British Academic Press.

Kay, Stephen
1834   *Travels and Researches in Caffraria.* 2 vols. New York: Harper & Brothers.

Kearney, Michael
1986   From the Invisible Hand to Visible Feet: Anthropological Studies of Migration and Development. *Annual Review of Anthropology*, 15:331–61.
1996   *Reconceptualizing the Peasantry: Anthropology in Global Perspective.* Boulder: Westview Press.

Kemp, Tom
1967   *Theories of Imperialism.* London: Dennis Dobson.

Kennedy, Dane
1992   Review of *Of Revelation and Revolution*, vol. 1. *Journal of the History of the Behavioral Sciences*, 28(40):395–97.

Killam, G. D.
1968   *Africa in English Fiction 1874–1939.* Ibadan: Ibadan University Press.

Kinsman, Margaret
1983   'Beasts of Burden': The Subordination of Southern Tswana Women, ca. 1800–1840. *Journal of Southern African Studies*, 10:39–54.

Kipling, Rudyard
1994   *Plain Tales from the Hills.* London: Penguin Books. First edition, 1888.

Kitchingman, James
1976   *The Kitchingman Papers: Missionary Letters and Journals, 1817 to 1848 from the Brenthurst Collection Johannesburg.* Edited by B. le Cordeur and C. Saunders. Johannesburg: Brenthurst Press.

Kitson Clark, George Sidney Roberts
1962   *The Making of Victorian England.* Being the Ford Lectures Delivered before the University of Oxford. Cambridge: Harvard University Press.
1973   *Churchmen and the Condition of England 1832–1885: A Study in the Development of Social Ideas and Practice from the Old Regime to the Modern State.* London: Methuen.

Kostof, Spiro
1991   *The City Shaped: Urban Patterns and Meanings through History.* Boston: Little, Brown & Company.

Krige, Eileen J., and Jacob D. Krige
1943   *The Realm of a Rain-Queen: A Study of the Pattern of Lovedu Society.* London: Oxford University Press for the International African Institute.

Kuper, Adam
1970a   The Kgaladadi in the Nineteenth Century. *Botswana Notes and Records*, 2:45–51.
1970b   *Kalahari Village Politics: An African Democracy.* Cambridge: Cambridge University Press.
1975   The Social Structure of the Sotho-Speaking Peoples of Southern Africa. *Africa*, 45(1):67–81; (2):139–49.

Kuper, Hilda
1973   Costume and Identity. *Comparative Studies in Society and History*, 15:348–67.

Kuper, Leo
1971   African Nationalism in South Africa, 1910–1964. *The Oxford History of South Africa*, vol. 2, eds. M. Wilson and L. M. Thompson. London: Oxford University Press.

Laidler, Percy W., and Michael Gelfand
1971   *South Africa: Its Medical History, 1652–1898*. Cape Town: Struik.

Landau, Paul Stuart
1995   *The Realm of the Word: Language, Gender, and Christianity in a Southern African Kingdom*. London: James Currey.

Langmore, Diane
1989   The Object Lesson of a Civilized, Christian Home. In *Family and Gender in the Pacific: Domestic Contradictions and the Colonial Impact*, eds. M. Jolly and M. Macintyre. Cambridge: Cambridge University Press.

Larsson, Anita, and Viera Larsson
1984   *Traditional Tswana Housing: A Study in Four Villages in Eastern Botswana*. Stockholm: Swedish Council for Building Research.

LaValley, Albert J.
1968   *Carlyle and the Idea of the Modern: Studies in Carlyle's Prophetic Literature and Its Relation to Blake, Nietzsche, Marx, and Others*. New Haven and London: Yale University Press.

Lave, Jean
n.d.   *On Changing Practice: The Anthropology of Apprenticeship and the Social Ontology of Learning*. [Ms in preparation.]

Lawrence, Denise L., and Setha M. Low
1990   The Built Environment and Spatial Form. *Annual Review of Anthropology*, 19:453–505.

Lawrence, Michael, and Andrew Manson
1994   The 'Dog of the Boers': The Rise and Fall of Mangope in Bophuthatswana. *Journal of Southern African Studies*, 20:447–61.

Leach, Edmund R.
1954   *Political Systems of Highland Burma*. London: Bell.

Lefebvre, Henri
1971   *Everyday Life in the Modern World*. Translated by S. Rabinovitch. New York: Harper & Row. First French edition, 1968.
1991   *The Production of Space*. Translated by D. Nicholson-Smith. Oxford: Blackwell. First French edition, 1974.

Legassick, Martin C.
1969   *The Griqua, the Sotho-Tswana and the Missionaries, 1700–1840: The Politics of a Frontier Zone*. Ph.D. diss., University of California, Los Angeles.

Le Goff, Jacques
1980   *Time, Work and Culture in the Middle Ages*. Translated by A. Goldhammer. Chicago: University of Chicago Press.

Lelyveld, Joseph
1987   *Move Your Shadow: South Africa, Black and White.* London: Abacus.

Lenin, Vladimir Illich
1971   Selections from *The Development of Capitalism in Russia.* In *Essential Works of Lenin,* ed. H. M. Christman. New York: Bantam.

Lessing, Gotthold Ephraim
1984   *Laocoön: An Essay on the Limits of Painting and Poetry.* Translated by E. A. McCormick. Baltimore: Johns Hokpins University Press. First edition, 1766.

Levine, Philippa
1986   *The Amateur and the Professional: Antiquarians, Historians and Archaeologists in Victorian England, 1838–1886.* Cambridge: Cambridge University Press.

Lévi-Strauss, Claude
1966   *The Savage Mind.* London: Weidenfeld & Nicolson.
1972   *Tristes Tropiques.* Translated by J. Russell. New York: Atheneum.

Leys, Colin
1974   *Underdevelopment in Kenya: The Political Economy of Neo-Colonialism, 1967–1971.* Berkeley: University of California Press.

Lichtenstein, Henry (M.H.C.)
1928–30   *Travels in Southern Africa in the Years 1803, 1804, 1805 and 1806.* 2 vols. Translated from the 1812–15 edition by A. Plumptre. Cape Town: Van Riebeeck Society.
1973   *Foundation of the Cape* (1811) [and] *About the Bechuanas* (1807). Translated and edited by O. H. Spohr. Cape Town: A.A. Balkema.

Liebmann, James A.
1901   Briton, Boer, and Black in South Africa. In *British Africa,* British Empire Series, vol. 2. London: Kegan Paul, Trench, Trubner. First edition, 1899.

Lienhardt, Godfrey
1961   *Divinity and Experience: The Religion of the Dinka.* Oxford: Clarendon Press.

Livingstone, David
1857   *Missionary Travels and Researches in South Africa,* etc. London: J. Murray.
1861   On Fever in the Zambesi. A Note from Dr. Livingstone to Dr. M'William. Transmitted by Captain Washington, R.N., F.R.S., Hydrographer to the Admiralty. *Lancet,* 2 (24 August):184–87.
1940   *Some Letters from Livingstone 1840–1872.* Edited by D. Chamberlin. London: Oxford University Press.
1959   *David Livingstone: Family Letters 1841–1856.* 2 vols. Edited by I. Schapera. London: Chatto & Windus.
1960   *Livingstone's Private Journals 1851–1853.* Edited by I. Schapera. Berkeley: University of California Press.
1961   *Livingstone's Missionary Correspondence 1841–56.* Edited by I. Schapera. London: Chatto & Windus.
1963   *Livingstone's African Journal 1853–1856.* 2 vols. Edited by I. Schapera. London: Chatto & Windus.

1974   *David Livingstone: South African Papers, 1849–1853.* Edited by I. Schapera. Cape Town: Van Riebeeck Society.

Lloyd, Edwin
1895   The Work in Bechwanaland and at Lake Ngami. *Proceedings of the Founders' Week Convention* (September 1895). London: London Missionary Society.
1889   The New Phaleng Church, Mangwato. *Chronicle of the London Missionary Society*, (May):162–66.

London Missionary Society
1819   *Observations on the Means of Preserving Health in Hot Climates for the Use of the Missionaries of the London Missionary Society.* London: London Missionary Society.
1824   Kurreechane. *Missionary Sketches* (April), no. XXV. [South African Library, Cape Town: South African Bound Pamphlets, no. 54.]
1828   Sketch of the Bechuana Mission. *Missionary Sketches* (October), no. XL111. [South African Library, Cape Town: South African Bound Pamphlets, no. 54.]
1830   *Report of the Directors of the London Missionary Society, May 1830.* London: Westly & Davis.
1837a   The Tribe of the Batlapi in South Africa. *Evangelical Magazine and Missionary Chronicle*, 15:200–201.
1837b   Important Notice to Pious Medical Men. *Evangelical Magazine and Missionary Chronicle*, 15:272–73
1838   Lattakoo Mission, in South Africa. *Evangelical Magazine and Missionary Chronicle*, 16:40–42.
1840   South Africa.—Lattakoo Mission. *Evangelical Magazine and Missionary Chronicle*, 18:142–43.
1841   *The Report of the Directors of the Forty-Seventh General Meeting of the Missionary Society (Usually called the London Missionary Society).* London: William Tylor.
1843   State and Progress of the Kuruman Mission. *Evangelical Magazine and Missionary Chronicle*, 21:201–2.
1886   Ladies' Meeting. *Chronicle of the London Missionary Society* (June):254–59.
1895   *Proceedings of the Founders' Week Convention* (September 1895). London: London Missionary Society.
1918   Advertisement for Tabloid Medical Outfits. *Chronicle of the London Missionary Society*, (NS) 26 [Old Series, 83], back cover.
n.d.   Some Account of the Bechuana Mission, Extracted from a Paper Drawn up by the Rev. Dr. Philip. *Transactions of the Missionary Society*, July 1826; contained in *Quarterly Chronicle of Transactions of The London Missionary Society, in the Years 1824, 1825, 1826, 1827, and 1828*, 3:221–24.

Lovell, Reginald I.
1934   *The Struggle for South Africa, 1875–1899: A Study in Economic Imperialism.* New York: Macmillan.

Lowe, John
n.d.   *Medical Missions: Their Place and Power.* New York and Chicago: Fleming H. Revell Company. Second edition, 1887.

Lukacs, John
1970   The Bourgeois Interior. *American Scholar,* 39 (Autumn):616–30.

Lüdtke, Alf
1982   The Historiography of Everyday Life: The Personal and the Political. In *Culture, Ideology and Politics: Essays for Eric Hobsbawm,* eds. R. Samuel and G. Stedman Jones. History Workshop Series. London: Routledge & Kegan Paul.

1995   Introduction: What Is the History of Everyday Life and Who Are Its Practitioners? In *The History of Everyday Life: Reconstructing Historical Experiences and Ways of Life,* ed. A. Lüdtke. Translated by W. Templer. Princeton: Princeton University Press.

Lüthy, Herbert
1964   Colonization and the Making of Mankind. In *Imperialism and Colonialism,* eds. G. H. Nadel and P. Curtis. New York: Macmillan. First published in 1961 in *Journal of Economic History,* Supplement [The Tasks of Economic History], 21(4):483–95.

MacDonald, Margaret
1949   Natural Rights. *Proceedings of the Aristotelian Society 1947–48,* 35–55. Reprinted in *Theories of Rights,* ed. J. Waldron. Oxford: Oxford University Press, 1984.

Macdonell, John
1901   The Question of the Native Races in South Africa. *The Nineteenth Century,* (February):367–76.

Macfarlane, Alan
1987   *The Culture of Capitalism.* Oxford: Blackwell.

Macintyre, Martha
1989   Better Homes and Gardens. In *Family and Gender in the Pacific: Domestic Contradictions and the Colonial Impact,* eds. M. Jolly and M. Macintyre. Cambridge: Cambridge University Press.

Mackenzie, John
1871   *Ten Years North of the Orange River: A Story of Everyday Life and Work among the South African Tribes.* Edinburgh: Edmonston & Douglas.

1883   *Day Dawn in Dark Places: A Story of Wanderings and Work in Bechwanaland.* London: Cassell. Reprinted, 1969; New York: Negro Universities Press.

1887   *Austral Africa: Losing It or Ruling It.* 2 vols. London: Sampson Low, Marston, Searle & Rivington.

1975   *Papers of John Mackenzie.* Edited by A. J. Dachs. Johannesburg: Witwatersrand University Press.

Mackenzie, William D.
1902   *John Mackenzie: South African Missionary and Statesman.* New York: A. C. Armstrong & Son.

MacLeod, Roy
1988   Introduction. In *Disease, Medicine, and Empire: Perspectives on Western Medicine and the Experience of European Expansion*, eds. R. MacLeod and M. Lewis. London: Routledge.

Macmillan, William M.
1929   *Bantu, Boer, and Briton: The Making of the South African Native Problem*. London: Faber & Gwyer.

MacNair, James I.
1976   *Livingstone the Liberator: A Study of a Dynamic Personality*. Glasgow: The David Livingstone Trust. First edition, 1940.

Macpherson, Crawford Brough
1962   *The Political Theory of Possessive Individualism: Hobbes to Locke*. Oxford: Oxford University Press.

Macpherson, Crawford Brough, ed.
1978   *Property: Mainstream and Critical Positions*. Oxford: Blackwell.

Mafela, Lily
1994   Domesticity: The Basis for Missionary Education of Batswana Women to the End of the 19th Century. *Botswana Notes and Records*, 26:87–93.

Magdoff, Harry
1978   *Imperialism: From the Colonial Age to the Present*. New York: Monthly Review Press.

Maine, (Sir) Henry Sumner
1986   *Ancient Law. Its Connection with the Early History of Society, and Its Relation to Modern Ideas*. Tucson: University of Arizona Press. First edition, 1861.

Maingard, Louis Fernand
1933   The Brikwa and the Ethnic Origins of the Batlhaping. *South African Journal of Science*, 30:597–602.

Mandel, Ernest
1978   *Late Capitalism*. Translated by J. De Bres. London: Verso.

Mann, Kristin, and Richard Roberts, eds.
1991   *Law in Colonial Africa*. London: James Currey.

Marks, Shula
1990   History, the Nation and Empire: Sniping from the Periphery. *History Workshop Journal*, 29:111–19.

Marks, Shula, and Richard Rathbone, eds.
1982   *Industrialization and Social Change in South Africa: African Class Formation, Culture, and Consciousness, 1870–1930*. London: Longman.

Marx, Karl
1967   *Capital: A Critique of Political Economy*. 3 vols. New York: International Publishers.

Marx, Karl, and Frederick Engels
1970   *The German Ideology,* part 1. Edited by C. J. Arthur. New York: International
       Publishers.

Mason, Michael
1994   *The Making of Victorian Sexual Attitudes.* London: Oxford University Press.

Matthews, Josiah Wright
1887   *Incwadi Yami, or Twenty Years' Personal Experience in South Africa.* New York:
       Rogers & Sherwood. Reprinted, 1976; Johannesburg: Africana Book Society.

Matthews, Zachariah Keodirelang
1945   A Short History of the Tshidi Barolong. *Fort Hare Papers,* 1:9–28.
1981   *Freedom for My People: The Autobiography of Z. K. Matthews, Southern Africa
       1901 to 1968.* London: R. Collings; Cape Town: David Philip.
n.d.   Fieldwork Reports. Botswana National Archives.

Matumo, Z. I.
1993   *Setswana-English-Setswana Dictionary.* Gaborone: Macmillan Botswana and
       Botswana Book Centre. First edition, circa 1875.

Mauss, Marcel
1954   *The Gift: Forms and Functions of Exchange in Archaic Societies.* Translated by
       I. Cunnison. London: Cohen & West.

Mayer, Philip
1961   *Townsmen or Tribesmen: Conservatism and the Process of Urbanization in a South
       African City.* Cape Town: Oxford University Press.

Mayhew, Henry
1851   *London Labour and the London Poor: A Cyclopaedia of the Condition of Those
       That Will Work, Those That Cannot Work, and Those That Will Not Work,* vol. 1.
       London: G. Woodfall.

Maylam, Paul R.
1980   *Rhodes, the Tswana, and the British: Colonialism, Collaboration, and Conflict in
       the Bechuanaland Protectorate, 1885–1899.* Westport and London: Greenwood
       Press.

Mbembe, Achille
1992   The Banality of Power and the Aesthetics of Vulgarity in the Postcolony.
       Public Culture, 4(2):1–30.

McClintock, Anne
1987   'Azikwelwa' (We Will Not Ride): Politics and Value in Black South African
       Poetry. In *Politics and Poetic Value,* ed. R. von Hallberg. Chicago: University of
       Chicago Press. Also published in *Critical Inquiry,* 13:159–78.

McCracken, John
1977   *Politics and Christianity in Malawi 1875–1940: The Impact of the Livingstonia
       Mission in the Northern Province.* Cambridge: Cambridge University Press.

McGuire, Randall H., and Michael B. Schiffer
1983   A Theory of Architectural Design. *Journal of Anthropological Archaeology,*
       2:227–303.

Mears, W. Gordon A.
1934   The Educated Native in Bantu Communal Life. In *Western Civilization and
       the Natives of South Africa,* ed. I. Schapera. London: George Routledge & Sons.
1970   *Wesleyan Baralong Mission in Trans-Orangia 1821–1884.* Cape Town: Struik.
n.d.   The Bechuana Mission or the Advance of Christianity into the Transvaal and
       the Orange Free State. *Methodist Missionaries,* no. 4. Rondebosch, Cape Town:
       The Methodist Missionary Department.

Meillassoux, Claude
1981   *Maidens, Meal and Money: Capitalism and the Domestic Community.* Cambridge:
       Cambridge University Press.

Memmi, Albert
1965   *The Colonizer and the Colonized.* Translated by H. Greenfeld. New York:
       The Orion Press. First French edition, 1957.

Merry, Sally Engel
1991   Law and Colonialism: Review Essay. *Law and Society Review,* 25:889–922.

Meyer, Susan
1991   Colonialism and the Figurative Strategy of *Jane Eyre.* In *Macropolitics of Nine-
       teenth-Century Literature: Nationalism, Exoticism, Imperialism,* eds. J. Arac and H.
       Ritvo. Philadelphia: University of Pennsylvania Press.

Mill, John Stuart
1965   *Collected Works of John Stuart Mill,* general editor, F. E. L. Priestley. Vols. 2
       and 3: *Principles of Political Economy with Some of Their Applications to Social Philoso-
       phy,* textual editor, J. M. Robson. Toronto: University of Toronto Press; Lon-
       don: Routledge & Kegan Paul.

Miller, Elmer S.
1973   The Christian Missionary: Agent of Secularization. *Missiology: An Interna-
       tional Review,* 1:99–107.

Mills, Sara
1991   *Discourses of Difference: An Analysis of Women's Travel Writing and Colonialism.*
       London: Routledge.

Mintz, Sidney Wilfred
1985   *Sweetness and Power: The Place of Sugar in Modern History.* New York: Viking.

Mitchell, Timothy
1991   *Colonising Egypt.* Berkeley: University of California Press. First edition,
       1988.

Mitchell, W. J. Thomas
1986   *Iconology: Image, Text, Ideology.* Chicago: University of Chicago Press.
1994   Introduction. In *Landscape and Power,* ed. W. J. T. Mitchell. Chicago:
       University of Chicago Press.

Moffat, John S.
    1886   *The Lives of Robert and Mary Moffat.* New York: A. C. Armstrong & Son.

Moffat, Mary
    1967   Letter to a Well-Wisher. *Quarterly Bulletin of the South African Library,* 22:16–19.

Moffat, Robert
    1825a   Extracts from the Journal of Mr. Robert Moffat. *Transactions of the Missionary Society,* 33:27–29.
    1825b   Extracts from the Journal of Mr. Robert Moffat. *Transactions of the Missionary Society,* 34:61–64.
    1834   Extracts from a Letter from Rev. R. Moffat dated Kuruman (or Lattakoo), January 10th 1833. *Evangelical Magazine and Missionary Chronicle,* 12:123–25.
    1842   *Missionary Labours and Scenes in Southern Africa.* London: John Snow. Reprinted, 1969; New York: Johnson Reprint Corporation.
    1845   Kuruman. [Copy of a letter to the Rev. Arundel, Home Secretary, Kuruman, 6 August 1844]. *Evangelical Magazine and Missionary Chronicle,* 23:219–20.

Moffat, Robert, and Mary Moffat
    1951   *Apprenticeship at Kuruman: Being the Journals and Letters of Robert and Mary Moffat, 1820–1828.* Edited by I. Schapera. London: Chatto & Windus.

Moffat, Robert U.
    1921   *John Smith Moffat C.M.G, Missionary: A Memoir.* London: J. Murray.

Molema, Silas Modiri
    1920   *The Bantu, Past and Present.* Edinburgh: W. Green & Son.
    1951   *Chief Moroka: His Life, His Times, His Country and His People.* Cape Town: Methodist Publishing House.
    1966   *Montshiwa, 1815–1896: Barolong Chief and Patriot.* Cape Town: Struik.
    n.d.[a]   Research Notes and Personal Papers. Held by the Molema family and the University of the Witwatersrand, Johannesburg.
    n.d.[b]   *Methodism Marches into the Midlands.* Pamphlet written for the Rolong celebrations of the one hundred and fiftieth anniversary of Methodism in South Africa.

Molokomme, Athaliah L.
    1991   *'Children of the Fence': The Maintenance of Extra-Marital Children under Law and Practice in Botswana.* Leiden: African Studies Center, University of Leiden.

Monro, John
    1837   Pretences of a Bechuana Woman to Immediate Communion with the Divine Being. *Evangelical Magazine and Missionary Chronicle,* 15:396–97.

Monthly Review, The
    1790   Review of *Proceedings of the Association for Promoting the Discovery of the Interior Parts of Africa,* 2:60–68.

Moore, Sally Falk
1986   *Social Facts and Fabrications: 'Customary' Law on Kilimanjaro.* Cambridge: Cambridge University Press.

Morgan, David H. J.
1985   *The Family, Politics and Social Theory.* London: Routledge & Kegan Paul.

Mphahlele, Es'kia [Ezekiel]
1962   *The African Image.* London: Faber & Faber.

Muldoon, James
1975   The Indian as Irishman. *Essex Institute Historical Collections,* 3:267–89.

Munn, Nancy D.
1974   Symbolism in a Ritual Context: Aspects of Symbolic Action. In *Handbook of Social and Cultural Anthropology,* ed. J. J. Honigmann. New York: Rand McNally.
1977   The Spaciotemporal Transformation of Gawa Canoes. *Journal de la Société des Océnistes,* 33:39–53.
1986   *The Fame of Gawa: A Symbolic Study of Value Transformation in a Massim (Papua New Guinea) Society.* Cambridge and New York: Cambridge University Press.

Murphree, Marshall W.
1969   *Christianity and the Shona.* London: The Athlone Press.

Murray, Colin
1992   *Black Mountain: Land, Class and Power in the Eastern Orange Free State, 1880s to 1980s.* Washington, D.C.: Smithsonian Institution Press.

Mutwa, Vusamazulu Credo
1966   *Indaba, My Children.* London: Kahn & Averill.

Nadel, George H., and Perry Curtis
1964   Introduction. In *Imperialism and Colonialism,* eds. G. H. Nadel and P. Curtis. New York: Macmillan.

Nag, Dulali
1991   Fashion, Gender, and the Bengali Middle Class. *Public Culture,* 3:93–112.

Nash, Manning
1966   *Primitive and Peasant Economic Systems.* San Francisco: Chandler.

Ndebele, Njabulo S.
1991   *Rediscovery of the Ordinary: Essays on South African Literature and Culture.* Johannesburg: Congress of South African Writers.

Nederveen Pieterse, Jan P.
1989   *Empire and Emancipation: Power and Liberation on a World Scale.* London: Pluto Press.

Newborn, Jud
1994   *Work Makes Free: The Hidden Cultural Meaning of the Holocast.* Ph.D. diss., University of Chicago.

Nielsen, Ruth
1979   The History and Development of Wax-Printed Textiles Intended for West Africa and Zaire. In *The Fabrics of Culture: The Anthropology of Clothing and Adornment*, eds. J. M. Cordwell and R. A. Schwarz. The Hague: Mouton.

Norman, Edward R.
1976   *Church and Society in England 1770–1970: A Historical Study.* Oxford: Clarendon Press.

Northcott, William C.
1945   *Glorious Company: One Hundred and Fifty Years Life and Work of the London Missionary Society 1795–1945.* London: Livingstone Press (LMS).
1961   *Robert Moffat: Pioneer in Africa, 1817–1870.* London: Lutterworth Press.

Nunokawa, Jeff
1991   For Your Eyes Only: Private Property and the Oriental Body in *Dombey and Son.* In *Macropolitics of Nineteenth-Century Literature: Nationalism, Exoticism, Imperialism*, eds. J. Arac and H. Ritvo. Philadelphia: University of Pennsylvania Press.

Oakley, Ann
1974   *Woman's Work: The Housewife, Past and Present.* New York: Pantheon.

Obelkevich, James
1976   *Religion and Rural Society: South Lindsey, 1825–1875.* Oxford: Clarendon Press.

Obeyesekere, Gananath
1979   The Vicissitudes of the Sinhala-Buddhist Identity through Time and Change. In *Collective Identities, Nationalisms and Protest in Modern Sri Lanka*, ed. M. Roberts. Colombo: Marga Institute.

Oliver, Roland A.
1952   *The Missionary Factor in East Africa.* London: Longmans.

Ong, Walter J.
1942   Spenser's *View* and the Tradition of the "Wild" Irish. *Modern Language Quarterly*, 3:561–71.

Oosthuizen, Gerhardus Cornelius
1968   *Post Christianity in Africa: A Theological and Anthropological Study.* London: Hurst.

Orwell, George
1962   *The Road to Wigan Pier.* Harmondsworth: Penguin Books. First edition, 1937.

Ottenberg, Simon
1979   Analysis of an African Masked Parade. In *The Fabrics of Culture: The Anthropology of Clothing and Adornment*, eds. J. M. Cordwell and R. A. Schwarz. The Hague: Mouton.

Outler, Albert C.
1985   An Introductory Comment on Sermons 34–36. *The Works of John Wesley,* vol. 2 (Sermons 34–70), ed. A. C. Outler. Nashville: Abingdon Press.

Owen, David Edward
1964   *English Philanthropy, 1660–1960.* Cambridge: Belknap Press of Harvard University Press.

Oxford University Press
1983   *The Oxford Paperback Dictionary.* Compiled by J. M. Hawkins. Second edition. Oxford: Oxford University Press.

Packard, Randall M.
1989   The 'Healthy Reserve' and the 'Dressed Native': Discourses on Black Health and the Language of Legitimation in South Africa. *American Ethnologist,* 16:686–703.

Pader, Ellen-J.
1993   Spatiality and Social Change: Domestic Space Use in Mexico and the United States. *American Ethnologist,* 20:114–37.

Palmer, Robin H., and Neil Q. Parsons, eds.
1977   *The Roots of Rural Poverty in Central and Southern Africa.* Berkeley: University of California Press.

Park, Mungo
1799   *Travels in the Interior Districts of Africa . . . in the Years 1795, 1796, and 1797.* London: W. Bulmer.

Parry, Benita
1987   Problems in Current Theories of Colonial Discourse. *Oxford Literary Review,* 9(1–2):27–58.

Parry, Jonathan, and Maurice Bloch, eds.
1989   *Money and the Morality of Exchange.* Cambridge: Cambridge University Press.

Parson, Jack
1984   *Botswana: Liberal Democracy and the Labor Reserve in Southern Africa.* Boulder: Westview Press.

Parsons, H. Alexander
1927   The Coinage of Griqualand. *Spink & Son's Numismatic Circular,* 4 (April):197–201.

Parsons, Neil Q.
1977   The Economic History of Khama's Country in Botswana, 1844–1930. In *The Roots of Rural Poverty in Central and Southern Africa,* eds. R. Palmer and N. Q. Parsons. Berkeley: University of California Press

Patton, Cindy
1988   Inventing African AIDS. Review of *Aids, Africa and Racism* by R. C. and R. J.

Chirimuuta and *Blaming Others*, eds. R. Sabatier et al. *City Limits*, no. 363 (September 15–22):85.

1990   *Inventing AIDS*. New York: Routledge.

Pauw, Berthold A.

1960   *Religion in a Tswana Chiefdom*. London: Oxford University Press for the International African Institute.

Pawley, Martin

1971   *Architecture Versus Housing*. New York: Praeger.

Paz, Octavio

1976   Foreword: The Flight of Quetzalcóatl and the Quest for Legitimacy. In *Quetzalcóatl and Guadalupe: The Formation of Mexican National Consciousness 1531–1813*, Jacques Lafaye. Chicago: University of Chicago Press. First French edition, 1974.

Peel, John D. Y.

1992   The Colonization of Consciousness. Review of *Of Revelation and Revolution*, vol. 1. *Journal of African History*, 33:328–29.

1995   For Who Hath Despised the Day of Small Things? Missionary Narratives and Historical Anthropology. *Comparative Studies in Society and History*, 37(3):581–607.

Peires, Jeffrey B.

1981   *The House of Phalo: A History of the Xhosa People in the Days of Their Independence*. Johannesburg: Ravan Press.

Penguin Books

1991   *The Penguin Concise English Dictionary*. Compiled by G. N. Garmonsway with J. Simpson. Revised edition (1969). London: Bloomsbury Books.

Perkin, Harold James

1969   *The Origins of Modern English Society 1780–1880*. London: Routledge & Kegan Paul; Toronto: University of Toronto Press.

Perniola, Mario

1989   Between Clothing and Nudity. In *Fragments for a History of the Human Body*, vol. 2, eds. M. Feher, with R. Naddaff and N. Tazi. New York: Zone (distributed by the M.I.T. Press).

Perrot, Michelle

1990a   Roles and Characters. In *A History of Private Life*, vol. 4: *From the Fires of the French Revolution to the Great War*, ed. M. Perrot. Cambridge: The Belknap Press, Harvard University Press.

1990b   The Family Triumphant. In *A History of Private Life*, vol. 4: *From the Fires of the French Revolution to the Great War*, ed. M. Perrot. Cambridge: The Belknap Press, Harvard University Press.

Petersen, Robin M.

1992   Review of *Of Revelation and Revolution*, vol. 1. *The Christian Century*, 109 (January):21.

1995   *Time, Resistance and Reconstruction: Rethinking* Kairos *Theology.* Ph.D. diss., University of Chicago.

Philip, John
1828   *Researches in South Africa; Illustrating the Civil, Moral, and Religious Condition of the Native Tribes.* 2 vols. London: James Duncan. Reprinted, 1969; New York: Negro Universities Press.
1842   Report of the State and Progress of the Missions beyond the North Frontier. *Evangelical Magazine and Missionary Chronicle,* 20:183–86.

Philip, Robert
1841   *The Life, Times, and Missionary Enterprises of the Rev. John Campbell.* London: John Snow.

Phillips, Anne
1989   *The Enigma of Colonialism: British Policy in West Africa.* London: James Currey.

Plaatje, Solomon Tshekisho
1916   *Sechuana Proverbs with Literal Translations and Their European Equivalents.* London: Kegan Paul, Trench, Trubner & Co.
1919   *Some of the Legal Disabilities Suffered by the Native Population of the Union of South Africa and Imperial Responsibility.* Pamphlet. London: by the author. Reprinted in *Selected Writings,* ed. Brian Willam. Johannesburg: Witswatersrand University Press, 1996.
1921   *The Mote and the Beam: An Epic on Sex-Relationship 'Twixt White and Black in British South Africa.* Pamphlet. New York: by the author. Reprinted in *Selected Writings,* ed. Brian Willan. (Johannesburg: Witswatersrand University Press, 1996.)
1957   *Mhudi: An Epic of South African Native Life a Hundred Years Ago.* Alice: Lovedale Press. First edition, 1930.
1973   *The Diary of Sol T. Plaatje: An African at Mafeking.* Edited by J. L. Comaroff. London: Macmillan.
1996   *Selected Writings.* Edited by Brian Willan. Johannesburg: Witwatersrand University Press.
n.d.   *Native Life in South Africa.* New York: The Crisis.

Porter, Roy
1992a   Introduction. In *The Popularization of Medicine, 1650–1850,* ed. R. Porter. London: Routledge.
1992b   Spreading Medical Enlightenment: The Popularization of Medicine in Georgian England, and Its Paradoxes. In *The Popularization of Medicine 1650–1850,* ed. R. Porter. London: Routledge.
1994   Between the Sheets. *The Sunday Times,* Books (sect. 7), 16 October:5.

Pratt, Mary Louise
1985   Scratches on the Face of the Country; or, What Mr. Barrow Saw in the Land of the Bushmen. *Critical Inquiry,* 12:119–43.

Pred, Allan
1985   The Social Becomes the Spatial, the Spatial Becomes the Social: Enclosures, Social Change and the Becoming of Places in the Swedish Provice of Skåne. In

Social Relations and Spatial Structures, eds. D. Gregory and J. Urry. London: Macmillan.

Price, Elizabeth Lees
1956   *The Journals of Elizabeth Lees Price written in Bechuanaland, Southern Africa 1854–1883 with an Epilogue: 1889 and 1900.* Edited by U. Long. London: Edward Arnold.

Prothero, Rowland Edmund [Lord Ernle]
1912   *English Farming Past and Present.* London: Longmans, Green.

Pugh, Simon
1988   *Garden, Nature, Landscape.* Manchester: Manchester University Press.

Rack, Henry D.
1989   *Reasonable Enthusiast: John Wesley and the Rise of Methodism.* Philadelphia: Trinity Press International.

Radcliffe-Brown, Alfred Reginald
1950   Introduction. In *African Systems of Kinship and Marriage*, eds. A. R. Radcliffe-Brown and D. Forde. London: Oxford University Press for the International African Institute.

Ramsay, Federick J.
1991   *The Rise and Fall of the Bakwena Dynasty of South-Central Botswana, 1820–1940.* 2 vols. Ph.D. diss., Boston University.

Ranger, Terence O.
1982a   Race and Tribe in Southern Africa: European Ideas and African Acceptance. In *Racism and Colonialism*, ed. R. Ross. The Hague: Martinus Nijhoff for the Leiden University Press.
1982b   Medical Science and the Pentecost: The Dilemma of Anglicanism in Africa. In *The Church and Healing: Papers Read at the Twentieth Summer Meeting and Twenty-First Winter Meeting of the Ecclesiastical History Society*, ed. W. J. Sheils. Oxford: Blackwell for the Ecclesiastical History Society.
1987   Taking Hold of the Land: Holy Places and Pilgrimages in Twentieth Century Zimbabwe. *Past and Present*, 117:158–94.
1995   *Are We Not Also Men?: The Samkange Family and African Politics in Zimbabwe, 1920–64.* Harare: Baobab; Portsmouth, NH: Heinemann.
n.d.[a]   No Missionary: No Exchange: No Story? Narrative in Southern Africa. Paper read at All Souls College, Oxford University, June 1992. [Manuscript.]
n.d.[b]   Africa in the Age of Extremes: The Irrelevance of African History. Paper read at the Center of African Studies, University of Edinburgh, May 1996. [Manuscript.]

Read, James
1850   Report on the Bechuana Mission. *Evangelical Magazine and Missionary Chronicle*, 28:445–47.

Reader, William Joseph
1966 *Professional Men: The Rise of the Professional Classes in Nineteenth-Century England.* London: Weidenfeld & Nicolson.

Religious Tract Society, The
n.d. *Rivers of Water in a Dry Place: An Account of the Introduction of Christianity into South Africa, and of Mr. Moffat's Missionary Labours, Designed for the Young.* London: The Religious Tract Society.

Renan, Ernest
1990 What Is a Nation? Translated by M. Thom. In *Nation and Narration,* ed. H. K. Bhabha. London: Routledge. [Original lecture, in French, 1882.]

Rey, Charles F.
1988 *Monarch of All I Survey: Bechuanaland Diaries, 1929–1937,* eds. N. Parsons and M. Crowder. London: James Currey.

Reyburn, Hugh Adam
1933 The Missionary as Rain Maker. *The Critic,* 1:146–53.

Rheinallt Jones, John David
1934 Social and Economic Condition of the Urban Native. In *Western Civilization and the Natives of South Africa: Studies in Culture Contact,* ed. I. Schapera. London: Routledge & Kegan Paul.

Roberts, Simon A.
1985 The Tswana Polity and 'Tswana Law and Custom' Reconsidered. *Journal of Southern African Studies,* 12:75–87.

Rodman, Margaret
1985 Contemporary Custom: Redefining Domestic Space in Longana, Vanuatu. *Ethnology,* 24:269–79.

Rowbotham, Sheila
1976 *Hidden from History: Rediscovering Women in History from the 17th Century to the Present.* New York: Vintage Books.

Rushdie, Salman
1981 *Midnight's Children: A Novel.* New York: Alfred Knopf.

Rybczynski, Witold
1986 *Home: A Short History of an Idea.* New York: Viking Penguin.

Rymer, James M.
1844 *The White Slave: A Romance for the Nineteenth Century.* London: E. Lloyd.

Sahlins, Marshall D.
1981 *Historical Metaphors and Mythical Realities: Structure in the Early History of the Sandwich Islands Kingdom.* Ann Arbor: University of Michigan Press.
1985 *Islands of History.* Chicago: University of Chicago Press.
1989 Cosmologies of Capitalism: The Trans-Pacific Sector of the World System. *Proceedings of the British Academy for 1988,* 1–51.

Said, Edward W.
1978   *Orientalism.* New York: Pantheon.

Sandilands, Alexander
1953   *Introduction to Tswana.* Tiger Kloof: London Missionary Society.

Sanneh, Lamin
1993   *Encountering the West: Christianity and the Global Cultural Process: The African Dimension.* Maryknoll, N.Y.: Orbis Books.

Sansom, Basil
1976   A Signal Transaction and Its Currency. In *Transaction and Meaning: Directions in the Anthropology of Exchange and Symbolic Behaviour,* ed. B. Kapferer. Philadalephia: Institute for the Study of Human Issues.

Saro-Wiwa, Ken
1995   *A Month and a Day: A Detention Diary.* London: Penguin Books.

Sartre, Jean-Paul
1955   *Literary and Philosophical Essays.* Translated by A. Michelson. New York: Criterion Books.
1965   Introduction. In *The Colonizer and the Colonized,* A. Memmi. New York: The Orion Press.

Saunders, Christopher Charles
1966   Early Knowledge of the Sotho: Seventeenth and Eighteenth Century Accounts of the Tswana. *Quarterly Bulletin of the South African Library,* 20:60–70.

Schapera, Isaac
1933   Economic Conditions in a Bechuanaland Native Reserve. *South African Journal of Science,* 30:633–55.
1934   Present-Day Life in the Native Reserves. In *Western Civilization and the Natives of South Africa: Studies in Culture Contact,* ed. I. Schapera. London: Routledge & Kegan Paul.
1935   The Social Structure of the Tswana Ward. *Bantu Studies,* 9:203–24.
1936   The Contributions of Western Civilisation to Modern Kxatla Culture. *Transactions of the Royal Society of South Africa,* 24:221–52.
1938   *A Handbook of Tswana Law and Custom.* London: Oxford University Press for the International African Institute. Second edition, 1955.
1940a   *Married Life in an African Tribe.* London: Faber & Faber.
1940b   The Political Organization of the Ngwato in Bechuanaland Protectorate. In *African Political Systems,* eds. M. Fortes and E. E. Evans-Pritchard. London: Oxford University Press for the International African Institute.
1942   A Short History of the Bangwaketse, *African Studies,* 1:1–26.
1943a   *Report on the System of Land-Tenure on the Barolong Farms in the Bechuanaland Protectorate.* Report submitted to the Bechuanaland Protectorate Government. Unpublished ms., held by the Botswana National Archives, Gaborone.
1943b   *Native Land Tenure in the Bechuanaland Protectorate.* Alice: Lovedale Press.

1943c   *Tribal Legislation among the Tswana of the Bechuanaland Protectorate.* London: London School of Economics.
1947   *Migrant Labour and Tribal Life: A Study of Conditions in the Bechuanaland Protectorate.* London: Oxford University Press.
1951   Introduction. In *Apprenticeship at Kuruman: Being the Journals and Letters of Robert and Mary Moffat, 1820–1828,* ed. I. Schapera. London: Chatto & Windus.
1952   *The Ethnic Composition of Tswana Tribes.* London: London School of Economics and Political Science.
1953   *The Tswana.* London: International African Institute. Revised edition, I. Schapera and J. L. Comaroff, 1991.
1958   Christianity and the Tswana. *Journal of the Royal Anthropological Institute,* 88:1–9.
1961   Introduction. In *Livingstone's Missionary Correspondence 1841–56,* ed. I. Schapera. London: Chatto & Windus.
1962   Cultural Changes in Tribal Life. In *The Bantu-Speaking Tribes of South Africa: An Ethnographic Survey,* ed. I. Schapera. London: Routledge & Kegan Paul. First edition, 1937.
1965   *Praise-Poems of Tswana Chiefs.* Oxford: Clarendon Press.
1970   *Tribal Innovators: Tswana Chiefs and Social Change, 1795–1940.* London: Athlone Press.
1971   *Rainmaking Rites of Tswana Tribes.* Leiden: Afrika-Studiecentrum.
1980   *A History of the BaKgatla-bagaKgafêla.* Mochudi: Phuthadikobo Museum. First edition, 1942; Cape Town: University of Cape Town, School of African Studies, *Communications* (NS), no. 3.
1983   Report on the System of Land-Tenure on the Barolong Farms in the Bechuanaland Protectorate [1943]. Abridged. *Botswana Notes and Records,* 15:15–38.
1985   Tswana Concepts of Custom and Law. *Journal of African Law,* 27:141–49.

Schapera, Isaac, and John L. Comaroff
1991   *The Tswana.* Revised edition. London: Kegan Paul International.

Schapera, Isaac, and Astley John Hilary Goodwin
1937   Work and Wealth. In *The Bantu-Speaking Tribes of South Africa: An Ethnographical Survey,* ed. I. Schapera. London: Routledge.

Schlereth, Thomas J.
1991   *Victorian America: Transformations in Everyday Life, 1876–1915.* New York: HarperCollins.

Schneider, Jane
1989   Rumpelstiltskin's Bargain: Folklore and the Merchant Capitalist Intensification of Linen Manufacture in Early Modern Europe. In *Cloth and Human Experience,* eds. A. Weiner and J. Schneider. Washington: Smithsonian Institution Press.

Schwarz, Ronald A.
1979   Uncovering the Secret Vice: Toward an Anthropology of Clothing and Adornment. In *The Fabrics of Culture: The Anthropology of Clothing and Adornment,* eds. J. M. Cordwell and R. A. Schwarz. The Hague: Mouton.

Seed, Patricia
1991   Colonial and Postcolonial Discourse. *Latin American Research Review,*
       26:181–200.

Seeley, Caroline F.
1973   *The Reaction of Batswana to the Practice of Western Medicine.* M. Phil. thesis, De-
       partment of Anthropology, London School of Economics, University of
       London.

Seif, Jennifer
1995   *Engendering Christian Life in Natal: The Zulu Mission of the American Board,*
       1835–1900. M.A. thesis, Department of Anthropology, University of Chicago.

Semmel, Bernard
1974   *The Methodist Revolution.* London: Heinemann.
1993   *The Liberal Ideal and the Demons of Empire: Theories of Imperialism from Adam*
       Smith to Lenin. Baltimore: Johns Hopkins University Press.

Setiloane, Gabriel M.
1976   *The Image of God among the Sotho-Tswana.* Rotterdam: A. A. Balkema.

Seton-Watson, Hugh
1977   *Nations and States: An Enquiry into the Origins of Nations and the Politics of Na-*
       tionalism. Boulder: Westview Press.

Shapiro, Ian
1986   *The Evolution of Rights in Liberal Theory.* Cambridge: Cambridge University
       Press.

Shapiro, Michael J.
1993   *Reading 'Adam Smith': Desire, History and Value.* London: Sage Publications.

Shaw, Margaret
1974   Material Culture. In *The Bantu-speaking Peoples of Southern Africa,* ed. W. D.
       Hammond-Tooke. London: Routledge & Kegan Paul.

Shepherd, Peter M.
1947   *Molepolole: A Missionary Record.* Glasgow: The Youth and Overseas Commit-
       tees of the United Free Church of Scotland.

Shillington, Kevin
1982   The Impact of the Diamond Discoveries on the Kimberley Hinterland:
       Class Formation, Colonialism and Resistance among the Tlhaping of Griqua-
       land West in the 1870s. In *Industrialisation and Social Change in South Africa: Afri-*
       can Class Formation, Culture, and Consciousness, 1870–1930, eds. S. Marks and R.
       Rathbone. London: Longman.
1985   *The Colonisation of the Southern Tswana, 1870–1900.* Johannesburg: Ravan
       Press.

Shrewsbury, Charles John Chetwynd Talbot [Viscount Ingestre], ed.
1852   *Meliora: or, Better Times to Come; Being the Contribution of Many Men Touching*
       the Present State and Prospects of Society. London: Parker.

Sillery, Anthony
1952 *The Bechuanaland Protectorate.* Cape Town and New York: Oxford University Press.
1971 *John Mackenzie of Bechuanaland, 1835–1899: A Study in Humanitarian Imperialism.* Cape Town: A. A. Balkema.

Simmel, Georg
1904 Fashion. *International Quarterly,* 10. Reprinted, 1971, in G. Simmel, *On Individuality and Social Forms: Selected Writings,* ed. D. N. Levine. Chicago: University of Chicago Press.
1978 *The Philosophy of Money.* Edited by D. Frisby; translated from the second enlarged edition [1907] by T. Bottomore and D. Frisby. London: Routledge & Kegan Paul.

Sinclair, Andrew
1977 *The Savage: A History of Misunderstanding.* London: Weidenfeld & Nicolson.

Slemon, Stephen
1991 Modernism's Last Post. In *Past the Last Post: Theorizing Post-Colonialism and Post-Modernism,* eds. I. Adam and H. Tiffin. New York: Harvester Wheatsheaf.

Smith, Adam
1976 *An Inquiry into the Nature and Causes of the Wealth of Nations,* vol. 1. Edited by R. H. Campbell and A. S. Skinner. Oxford: Clarendon Press. First edition, 1776.

Smith, Andrew
1939–40 *The Diary of Dr. Andrew Smith, 1834–1836.* 2 vols. Edited by P. R. Kirby. Cape Town: Van Riebeeck Society.

Smith, Iain
1991 Pale Proselytisers. Review of *Of Revelation and Revolution,* vol. 1. *Times Higher Education Supplement,* December 20, no. 998:21.

Smith, Edwin W.
1925 *Robert Moffat, One of God's Gardeners.* London: Church Missionary Society.
1950 The Idea of God among South African Tribes. In *African Ideas of God: A Symposium,* ed. E. W. Smith. London: Edinburgh House Press.
1957 *Great Lion of Bechuanaland: The Life and Times of Roger Price, Missionary.* London: Independent Press Ltd. for the London Missionary Society.

Snyder, Francis G.
1981 *Capitalism and Legal Change: An African Transformation.* London: Academic Press.
1982 Colonialism and Legal Form: The Creation of 'Customary Law' in Senegal. In *Crime, Justice and Underdevelopment,* ed. C. Sumner. London: Heinemann.

Soja, Edward W.
1985 The Spatiality of Social Life: Towards a Transformative Retheorization. In *Social Relations and Spatial Structures,* eds. D. Gregory and J. Urry. London: Macmillan.

Solomon, Edward S.
1855   *Two Lectures on the Native Tribes of the Interior.* Cape Town: Saul Solomon.

Somerville, William
1979   *William Somerville's Narrative of His Journeys to the Eastern Cape Frontier and to Lattakoe 1799–1802.* Edited by E. and F. Bradlow. Cape Town: Van Riebeeck Society.

South Africa, British Crown Colony of
1905   *Report of the South African Native Affairs Commission, 1903–5.* Cape Town: Cape Times Ltd., Government Printer.

South Africa, Union of
1925a   *Report of the Native Churches Commission* [UG 39–25]. Cape Town: Cape Times Ltd., Government Printer.
1925b   *Report of the Select Committee on Subject-Matter of Masters and Servants Law (Transvaal) Amendment Bill* [SC 12–25]. Cape Town: Cape Times Ltd., Government Printer.

South African Native Races Committee, ed.
1908   *The South African Natives: Their Progress and Present Condition.* London: J. Murray. Reprinted, 1969; New York: Negro Universities Press.

Spenser, Edmund
1882–84   *A Veue of the Present State of Ireland* (1596). Reprinted in *The Complete Works in Verse and Prose of Edmund Spenser,* vol. 9. Edited by A. B. Grosart. London: Printed by Hazell, Watson, and Viney for private circulation.

Spyer, Patricia
1996   Serial Conversion/Conversion to Seriality: Religion, State, and Number in Aru, Eastern Indonesia. In *Conversion to Modernity: The Globalization of Christianity,* ed. P. van der Veer. London: Routledge.

Stamp, Patricia
1991   Burying Otieno: The Politics of Gender and Ethnicity in Kenya. *Signs,* 16:808–45.

Stedman Jones, Gareth
1971   *Outcast London: A Study of the Relationship between the Classes in Victorian Society.* Oxford: Clarendon Press.

Steedman, Andrew
1835   *Wanderings and Adventures in the Interior of Southern Africa.* 2 vols. London: Longman.

Stoler, Ann Laura
1989   Rethinking Colonial Categories: European Communities and the Boundaries of Rule. *Comparative Studies in Society and History,* 31:134–61.
1995   *Race and the Education of Desire: Foucault's* History of Sexuality *and the Colonial Order of Things.* Durham: Duke University Press.

Stone, Lawrence
1979   *The Family, Sex and Marriage in England 1500–1800.* Abridged version. Harmondsworth: Penguin Books.

Stow, George W.
1905   *The Native Races of South Africa.* London: Swan Sonnenschein.

Stuart, Doug
1993   'For England and For Christ': The Gospel of Liberation and Subordination in Early Nineteenth Century Southern Africa. *Journal of Historical Sociology,* 6:377–95.

Sundkler, Bengt G. M.
1961   *Bantu Prophets in South Africa.* Second Edition. London: Oxford University Press for the International African Institute.
1965   *The World of the Mission.* London: Lutterworth Press.

Swanson, Maynard W.
1977   The Sanitation Syndrome: Bubonic Plague and Urban Native Policy in the Cape Colony, 1900–1909. *Journal of African History,* 18:387–410.

Sweet, C. Louise
1982   Inventing Crime: British Colonial Land Policy in Tanganyika. In *Crime, Justice and Underdevelopment,* ed. C. Sumner. London: Heinemann.

Switzer, Les, and Donna Switzer
1979   *The Black Press in South Africa and Lesotho: A Descriptive Bibliographic Guide to African, Coloured and Indian Newspapers, Newsletters and Magazines 1836–1976.* Boston: G. K. Hall.

Taussig, Michael
1987   *Shamanism, Colonialism, and the Wild Man: A Study in Terror and Healing.* Chicago: University of Chicago Press.

Taylor, Charles
1989   *Sources of the Self: The Making of Modern Identity.* Cambridge: Harvard University Press.

Theal, George McCall
1910   *The Yellow and Dark-Skinned People of Africa South of the Zambesi: A Description of the Bushmen, the Hottentots, and Particularly the Bantu. . . .* London: Swan Sonnenschein. Reprinted, 1969; New York: Negro Universities Press.

Thema, Benjamin C.
1939   The Trend of Setswana Poetry. *Tiger Kloof Magazine,* 21 (December):43–45.

Thomas, Nicholas J.
1990   Sanitation and Seeing: The Creation of State Power in Early Colonial Fiji. *Comparative Studies in Society and History,* 32:149–70.
1994   *Colonialism's Culture: Anthropology, Travel and Government.* Cambridge: Polity Press in association with Blackwell.

Thompson, Edward P.
1963   *The Making of the English Working Class.* London: Gollancz.
1993   *Customs in Common.* London: Penguin Books.

Thompson, George
1967   *Travels and Adventures in Southern Africa,* vol. 1. Edited by V.S. Forbes. Cape Town: Van Riebeeck Society. First edition, 1827.

Thompson, Humphrey C.
1976   *Distant Horizons: An Autobiography of One Man's Forty Years of Missionary Service In and Around Kuruman, South Africa.* Privately published in limited edition. Kimberley: Northern Cape Printers.

Thomson, W. Burns
1854   *Medical Missions: A Prize Essay.* Edinburgh: Johnstone & Hunter.

Thoreau, Henry D.
1908   *Walden, or Life in the Woods.* London and Toronto: J. M. Dent & Sons. First edition, 1854.

Tilby, A. Wyatt
1914   Some Missionary Pioneers in South Africa. In *United Empire: The Royal Colonial Institute Journal* (NS), 4:190–95, ed. A. R. Colquhoun. London: Sir Isaac Pitman & Sons.

Tiryakian, Edward A.
1993   White Women in Darkest Africa: Marginals as Observers in No-Woman's Land. In *Melanges Pierre Salmon,* vol. 2: *Histoire et ethnologie africaines,* special issue of *Civilisations* (Brussels), 41 (no. 1–2).

Tolen, Rebecca
n.d.   The Production of Cloth and the Construction of Persons. Doctoral Research Proposal, Department of Anthropology, University of Chicago, 1988.

Tomlinson, John
1991   *Cultural Imperialism: A Critical Introduction.* London: Pinter.

Tonna, Charlotte Elizabeth
1844   *The Wrongs of Woman.* New York: J. S. Taylor.

Tristan, Flora
1980   *Flora Tristan's London Journal.* Translated by D. Palmer and G. Pincetl. Boston: Charles River Books. First published as *Promenades dans Londres,* 1840.

Trollope, Anthony
1878   *South Africa.* 2 vols. London: Chapman & Hall.

Trotter, David
1990   Colonial Subjects. *Critical Quarterly,* 32(3):3–20.

Tudur Jones, R.
1962   *Congregationalism in England 1662–1962.* London: Independent Press.

Turner, Ernest Sackville
1959   *Call the Doctor: A Social History of Medical Men.* New York: St. Martin's Press.

Turner, Terence S.
1980   The Social Skin. In *Not Work Alone,* eds. J. Cherfas and R. Lewin. London: Temple Smith.
n.d.   The Social Skin. Unabridged manuscript.

Turrell, Rob
1982   Kimberley: Labour and Compounds, 1871–1888. In *Industrialisation and Social Change in South Africa: African Class Formation, Culture, and Consciousness, 1870–1930,* eds. S. Marks and R. Rathbone. London: Longman.

Tyrrell, Barbara H.
1968   *Tribal Peoples of Southern Africa.* Cape Town: Books of Africa.

University of Copenhagen, Research Programme of Urbanity and Aesthetics
n.d.   *Urbanity and Aesthetics.* Translated by L. Wilkinson and U. L. Poulsen. Copenhagen: Department of Art History, Comparative Literature and Theatre Studies, University of Copenhagen.

Unsworth, Barry
1992   *Sacred Hunger.* New York and London: W. W. Norton.

Untersteiner, Mario
1954   *The Sophists.* Translated by K. Freeman. New York: Philosophical Society.

van Binsbergen, Wim
1995   Four-Tablet Divination as Trans-Regional Medical Technology in Southern Africa: Mechanics, Origin, Spread and Contemporary Significance. *Journal of Religion in Africa,* 25(2):114–40.

van der Merwe, D.F.
1941   Hurutshe Poems. *Bantu Studies,* 15:307–37.

van Erp-Houtepen, Anne
1986   The Etymological Origin of the Garden. *Journal of Garden History,* 6(3):227–31.

van Onselen, Charles
1972   Reactions to Rinderpest in Southern Africa, 1896–97. *Journal of African History,* 13:473–88.
1982   *Studies in the Social and Economic History of the Witwatersrand, 1886–1914.* 2 vols. Johannesburg: Ravan Press; New York: Longman.

Vansina, Jan
1993   Review of *Ethnography and the Historical Imagination,* J. L. and J. Comaroff, 1992. *International Journal of African Historical Studies,* 26(2):417–20.
1994   *Living with Africa.* Madison: University of Wisconsin Press.

Vaughan, Megan
1991   *Curing Their Ills: Colonial Power and African Illness.* Cambridge: Cambridge University Press.

1994   Colonial Discourse Theory and African History, Or Has Postmodernism Passed Us By? *Social Dynamics,* 20:1–23.

Veblen, Thorstein
1934   *The Theory of the Leisure Class: An Economic Study of Institutions.* New York: Modern Library. First edition, 1899.

Verne, Jules
1876   *The Adventures of Three Englishmen and Three Russians in South Africa.* Third edition. Translated by E. E. Frewer. London: Sampson Low, Marston, Searle, & Rivington.

Villa-Vicencio, Charles
1988   *Trapped in Apartheid: A Socio-Theological History of the English-Speaking Churches.* Maryknoll, N.Y.: Orbis Books.

Volosinov, Valentin Nikolaevic
1973   *Marxism and the Philosophy of Language.* Translated by L. Matejka and I. R. Titunik. New York: Seminar Press.

W.E., of Wimbledon (anon.)
1834   The Missionary's Farewell Song. *Evangelical Magazine and Missionary Chronicle,* 12:278.

Wales, J. M.
1985   *The Relationship between the Orange Free State and the Rolong of Thaba 'Nchu during the Presidency of J. H. Brandt, 1864–1888.* M.A. thesis, Department of History, University of Rhodes, 1979; published in *Archives Year Book for South African History, 1985, I.* Pretoria: The Government Printer.

Wallerstein, Immanuel
1974   *The Modern World-System,* vol. 1: *Capitalist Agriculture and the Origins of the European World-Economy in the Sixteenth Century.* New York: Academic Press.

Waltzer, Michael
1985   *Exodus and Revolution.* New York: Basic Books.

Warner, Wellman J.
1930   *The Wesleyan Movement in the Industrial Revolution.* London and New York: Longmans, Green.

Warren, Max
1967   *Social History and Christian Mission.* London: SCM Press.

Wass, Betty M.
1979   Yoruba Dress in Five Generations of a Lagos Family. In *The Fabrics of Culture: The Anthropology of Clothing and Adornment,* eds. J. M. Cordwell and R. A. Schwarz. The Hague: Mouton.

Waterman, Anthony Michael C.
1991   *Revolution, Economics and Religion: Christian Political Economy, 1798–1833.* Cambridge: Cambridge University Press.

Watney, Simon
1990   Missionary Positions: AIDS, 'Africa,' and Race. In *Out There: Marginaliza-tion and Contemporary Cultures*, eds. R. Ferguson et al. New York: New Museum of Contemporary Art; Cambridge: M.I.T. Press.

Watson, R. L.
1980   The Subjection of a South African State: Thaba Nchu, 1880–1884. *Journal of African History*, 21:357–73.

Wear, Andrew
1992   The Popularization of Medicine in Early Modern England. In *The Populari-zation of Medicine, 1650–1850*, ed. R. Porter. London: Routledge.

Wearmouth, Robert F.
1937   *Methodism and the Working-Class Movements of England, 1800–1850*. London: The Epworth Press.

Webb, Igor
1981   *From Custom to Capital: The English Novel and the Industrial Revolution*. Ithaca and London: Cornell University Press.

Weber, Max
1958   *The Protestant Ethic and the Spirit of Capitalism*. Translated by T. Parsons. New York: C. Scribner's.

Weiner, Annette B., and Jane Schneider, eds,
1989   *Cloth and Human Experience*. Washington: Smithsonian Institution Press.

Weir, Christine
1993   Review of *Of Revelation and Revolution*, vol. 1. *Canberra Anthropology*, 16(2):129–31.

Weiss, Brad
n.d.   Northwest Tanzania on a Single Shilling: Sociality, Embodiment, Valuation. Paper presented at the Sattherthwaite Colloquium on African Ritual and Reli-gion, April 1995.

Werbner, Richard P.
1973   The Superabundance of Understanding: Kalanga Rhetoric and Domestic Divination. *American Anthropologist*, 75:414–40.
n.d.[a] Sacrifice and the Suffering Body: Allegory in Christian Encounters. Paper read to the *Journal of Southern African Studies* Twentieth Anniversary Confer-ence, University of York, September 1994.
n.d.[b] African Past, American Present: An Anglicised American Reads and Amer-icanised Belgian. Review of *Living with Africa*, J. Vansina, 1994. *Cultural Dynam-ics*. [In press.]

Wesley, John
1833   *The Works of the Reverend John Wesley, A.M.* 2 vols. New York: B. Waugh & T. Mason for the Methodist Episcopal Church.

1960   *Primitive Physic: or An Easy and Natural Method of Curing Most Diseases.* London: Epworth Press. First edition, 1791.

1984   *The Works of John Wesley,* vol. 1, ed. A. C. Outler. Nashville: Abingdon Press.

1985   *The Works of John Wesley,* vol. 2, ed. A. C. Outler. Nashville: Abingdon Press.

1986   *The Works of John Wesley,* vol. 3, ed. A. C. Outler. Nashville: Abingdon Press.

Wesleyan Methodist Missionary Society

1823–25   Missions in South Africa. *Missionary Notices Relating Principally to the Foreign Missions. . .,* 4 (no. 97):199–201.

1829–31   Boschuana Country: Extract of a Letter from Mr. Hodgson, dated Bootchnaap, November 24th, 1828. *Missionary Notices Relating Principally to the Foreign Missions. . .,* 6 (no. 164):120.

1842   Letter from the Bechuana Mission. *Wesleyan Missionary Notices* (NS), 2:115–16.

1887   *Affairs of Bechuanaland: A Letter to the Right Honourable The Secretary of State for the Colonies, from the Wesleyan Missionary Committee Concerning the Complaints of Chief Montsioa, of Mafeking.* Pamphlet. London: Wesleyan Mission House.

n.d.   *Methodist Missionaries,* no. 4. Cape Town: The Methodist Missionary Department.

Whiteside, J.

1906   *History of the Wesleyan Methodist Church of South Africa.* London: Elliot Stock.

Wiener, Martin J.

1981   *English Culture and the Decline of the Industrial Spirit, 1850–1980.* Cambridge: Cambridge University Press.

Willan, Brian

1984   *Sol Plaatje: South African Nationalist, 1876–1932.* Berkeley and Los Angeles: University of California Press.

Williams, Howard

1887   First Experiences in the Kuruman District. *Chronicle of the London Missionary Society* (March):110–17.

Williams, Raymond

1961   *Culture and Society 1780–1950.* Harmondsworth: Penguin Books.

1976   *Keywords: A Vocabulary of Culture and Society.* New York: Oxford University Press.

Williamson, Janice

1992   I-less and Gaga in the West Edmonton Mall: Towards a Pedestrian Feminist Reading. In *The Anatomy of Gender: Women's Struggle for the Body,* eds. D. H. Currie and V. Raoul. Ottawa: Carleton University Press.

Williamson, J. Rutter

1899   *The Healing of the Nations: A Treatise on Medical Missions, Statement and Appeal.* New York: Student Volunteer Movement for Foreign Missions.

Willoughby, William C.
1899   Our People: What they Are Like and How They Live. *News from Afar: LMS Magazine for Young People* (NS), 15(6):84–86.
1905   Notes on the Totemism of the Becwana. *Journal of the Royal Anthropological Institute*, 35:295–314.
1911   *A Paper Read before the South African Council of the London Missionary Society at Tiger Kloof, March, 1911.* Pamphlet. Tiger Kloof: Tiger Kloof Native Institution.
1923   *Race Problems in the New Africa: A Study of the Relation of Bantu and Britons in Those Parts of Bantu Africa Which Are under British Control.* Oxford: Clarendon Press.
1928   *The Soul of the Bantu: A Sympathetic Study of the Magico-religious Practices and Beliefs of the Bantu Tribes of Africa.* New York: Doubleday.
1932   *Nature-Worship and Taboo: Further Studies in 'The Soul of the Bantu.'* Hartford: Hartford Seminary Press.
n.d.[a]   *Native Life on the Transvaal Border.* London: Simpkin, Marshall, Hamilton, Kent. [Published in 1899.]
n.d.[b]   *Letter from Africa.* Pamphlet. London: London Missionary Society for the Manchester and Salford Young Men's Missionary Band.

Wilson, Elizabeth
1985   *Adorned in Dreams: Fashion and Modernity.* London: Virago Press.

Wilson, Monica
1971   The Growth of Peasant Communities. In *The Oxford History of South Africa,* vol. 2, eds. M. Wilson and L. Thompson. New York and London: Oxford University Press.

Wilson, Philip K.
1992   Acquiring Surgical Know-How: Occupational and Lay Instruction in Early Eighteenth-Century London. In *The Popularization of Medicine, 1650–1850,* ed. R. Porter. London: Routledge.

Wookey, Alfred J.
1884   South Bechuanaland, Some Changes Which Have Taken Place. *Chronicle of the London Missionary Society* (September):303–7.
1902   Literature for the Bechuana: Its Preparation and Influence. *Chronicle of the London Missionary Society* (NS), 11(123):56–58.
1904   *Secwana and English Phrases, with Short Introduction to Grammar and a Vocabulary.* Third Edition. Cape Town: Townshend & Son. First edition, 1900.

Wordsworth, William
1948   *A Guide through the District of the Lakes in the North of England, with a Description of the Scenery, &c. for the Use of Tourists and Residents.* Malvern: Tantivy Press. Facsimile of the fifth edition, 1835.

Wright, Gwendolyn
1991   *The Politics of Design in French Colonial Urbanism.* Chicago: University of Chicago Press.

Wright, Peter, and Isaac Hughes
1842 The Value of Native Agency. *Evangelical Magazine and Missionary Chronicle,*
20:42.

Wylie, Diana
1990 *A Little God: The Twilight of Patriarchy in a Southern African Chiefdom.* Hanover and London: University Press of New England/Wesleyan University Press.

Young, Allan A.
1978 Modes of Production of Medical Knowledge. *Medical Anthropology,*
2:97–122.

Young, Arthur
1794 *Travels in France during the Years 1787, 1788, & 1789; undertaken more particularly with a view of ascertaining the cultivation, wealth, resources, and national prosperity of the Kingdom of France.* 2 vols. Second edition. London: Richardson.

Zahar, Renate
1974 *Frantz Fanon: Colonialism and Alienation. Concerning Frantz Fanon's Political
Theory.* Translated by W. F. Feuser. New York: Monthly Review Press. First German edition, 1969.

Zorn, Jean-François
1993 *Le Grand Siècle d'une Mission Protestante: La Mission de Paris de 1822 à 1914.*
Paris: Karthala-Les Bergers et les Mages.

INDEX

4822